The
ENGLISH PEOPLE
and the
ENGLISH REVOLUTION

This book is published with the aid of the Bookmarks Publishing Cooperative. Many socialists have some savings put aside, probably in a bank or savings bank. While there, this money is being loaned out by the bank to some business or other to further the capitalist search for profit. We believe it is better loaned to a socialist venture to further the struggle for socialism. That's how the cooperative works: in return for a loan, repayable at a month's notice, members receive free copies of books published by Bookmarks. At the time this book was published, the cooperative had 430 members, from as far apart as London and Malaysia, Canada and Norway. Since 1980, the cooperative has helped publish more than fifty books.

Like to know more?

Write to the Bookmarks Publishing Cooperative, 265 Seven Sisters Road, Finsbury Park, London N4 2DE, England.

The

ENGLISH PEOPLE
and the

ENGLISH REVOLUTION

BRIAN MANNING
with a new introduction

BOOKMARKS

The English People and the English Revolution / *Brian Manning*
Second edition published by Bookmarks July 1991.
Bookmarks, 265 Seven Sisters Road, London N4 2DE, England.
Bookmarks, PO Box 16085, Chicago, IL 60616, USA.
Bookmarks, GPO Box 1473N, Melbourne 3001, Australia.

First published by Heinemann Educational Books 1976.
Copyright © Brian Manning 1976 and 1991.

ISBN 0 906224 62 4 paperback
ISBN 0 906224 66 7 hardback

Printed by Cox and Wyman Limited, Reading, England.
Editorial production and design by
Ersy Contogouris, Ian Goodyer, Peter Marsden and Steve Wright.

Bookmarks is linked to an international grouping of socialist
organisations:
Australia: *International Socialist Organisation*, GPO Box 1473N,
    Melbourne 3001
Belgium: *Socialisme International,* rue Lovinfosse 60, 4030 Grivegnée
Britain: *Socialist Workers Party,* PO Box 82, London E3 3LH
Canada: *International Socialists,* PO Box 339, Station E, Toronto,
    Ontario M6H 4E3
Denmark: *Internationale Socialister,* Ryesgade 8, 3, 8000 Århus C
France: *Socialisme International,* BP 189, 75926 Paris Cedex 19
Germany: *Sozialistische Arbeitergruppe,* Wolfsgangstrasse 81,
    W-6000 Frankfurt 1
Greece: *Organosi Sosialistiki Epanastasi,* PO Box 8161,
    10010 Omonia, Athens.
Holland: *Groep Internationale Socialisten,* PO Box 9720,
    3506 GR Utrecht.
Ireland: *Socialist Workers Movement,* PO Box 1648, Dublin 8
Norway: *Internasjonale Sosialister,* Postboks 5370, Majorstua,
    0304 Oslo 3
Poland: *Solidarnosc Socjalistyczna,* PO Box 12, 01-900 Warszawa 118.
United States: *International Socialist Organization,* PO Box 16085,
    Chicago, IL 60616

CONTENTS

Author

Brian Manning has been professor of history at the University of Ulster since 1980. He was editor of the book **Politics, Religion and the English Civil War,** to which he contributed the chapter on 'The artistocracy and the downfall of Charles I '. His other writings include 'The Levellers and Religion', in **Radical Religion and the English Revolution** (edited by J F McGregor and B Reay), 'Class and revolution in seventeenth-century England', in **International Socialism** number 2:38, and the chapter on the English Revolution in the fifth volume of *La Storia: I grandi problemi dal Medioevo all'Età Contemporanea,* published in Italy in 1986.

INTRODUCTION TO THE SECOND EDITION

THE 'MIDDLE SORT' OF PEOPLE
AND THE ENGLISH REVOLUTION

The primary purpose of this book, when it appeared first in 1976, was to revise the common view that the English civil war was no more than a conflict within the ruling class.[1] Few historians would hold that view now. 'The Marxist model... is useful', writes David Underdown, 'in that it reminds us that the English Revolution was not simply a collision between groups of peers and gentry operating in a social vacuum.'[2] John Morrill says that historians must question the old assumption 'that it is the gentry alone who determined the political alignment of a county in the civil war': 'Interpretations of allegiance which rest content with analysis of gentry activity are thus inadequate'.[3] Derek Hirst concludes that the civil war was 'clearly not merely a division within the élite.'[4] And Keith Wrightson comments that 'the English Revolution of the 1640s was not an affair confined to the aristocracy, the greater gentry and their retainers, but involved the aspirations and willing participation of thousands of their immediate social inferiors among the minor "parochial" gentry and the "middling sort" of town and country.'[5]

The thesis of this book is that some of the 'middling sort' played a crucial role in the revolution. They ranged from the larger farmers (called 'yeomen') and the substantial tradesmen to the mass of land-holding peasants (called 'husbandmen') and self-employed craftsmen. 'Typically the peasant was a small farmer, who worked his land with his own labour and that of his family, did not employ outside wage-labour and produced for his own subsistence rather than for the market'; while the bigger farmers produced primarily for the market and made their profits from the employment of wage-labour. 'Typically the craftsman was a small master, who purchased his own raw materials, worked in his own home, owned his own tools and instruments of production, sold his own goods either direct to the public or to a merchant for retail or export, and though he might have an apprentice or servant living in his household, he did not generally depend for his profits on the employment of wage-labour'. But some of the tradesmen and merchants purchased the raw materials, put them out to craftsmen or artisans to work up with their own tools in their own homes and paid them for their product, organised the various stages of production and marketed the finished goods; thus they took their profits from the employment of craftsmen and artisans, but the latter were not formally wage-workers, for they still sold the product of their labour and not their labour-power itself. Smallholding peasants who combined farming with working as agricultural labourers, or as artisans under the putting-out system, retained a degree of independence from landlords and employers that they defended fiercely.[6]

The range in wealth and social standing is very large between prosperous yeomen or tradesmen and the poor small-holding workers in agriculture or manufacture, and the whole social constellation only gains some coherence by demarcation from the gentry above them and the landless wage-labourers and paupers below them, and this demarcation is very important for the thesis of this book. Barry Reay estimates that the 'middling sort', who lived above and sometimes well above the level of subsistence, comprised 30-40 per cent of the population below the level of the gentry, and the wage-labourers and paupers (the 'poor' or 'poorer sort') who lived at or below the level of subsistence, formed 50-60 per cent.[7]

Tim Harris refers to the 'rediscovery of the "middling sort" ' by historians,[8] and Barry Reay says: 'In many respects the seventeenth century is the century of the "middling sort". They took advantage of the socially selective "educational revolution", and improved their literacy. They made up the expanded electorate... They joined the sects and the radical movements of the 1640s and 1650s. They petitioned, demonstrated and agitated in London in 1640-2, forcing the pace of the English Revolution.'[9] But many historians would question the radicalism, influence and historical importance of the 'middling sort'.

In a survey of the debate on the English Revolution, published in 1985, F D Dow observes that 'for at least a decade the thrust of much new research has been to impose a conservative interpretation on events.' Many historians 'leave out of account some important pressures and influences which were working on the governing classes and which on closer examination give a different dimension to the conflict. Brian Manning, for example, has forcefully argued that economic discontent and popular unrest were important elements in producing an atmosphere of crisis before and after 1640'; 'that this eruption of the lower and middling orders into the political arena crucially affected the alignment of political groupings within the élite'; that 'there is a stark and fundamental contrast between the willingness of the parliamentarians to harness "the people" to their cause and the desire of the royalists to repress them'; and that 'parliament's appeal to "the middle sort of people" was in turn to release one of the most dynamic forces of the decade and substantially promote the cause of popular radicalism.' However, says Dow, few historians 'would go so far as Manning in according to the "governed" a truly formative role in the crisis, but he is not alone in pointing to the existence of social unrest and political interest outside the ranks of the élite.'[10]

John Morrill judges that this work 'makes it obvious that the "middling sort" were capable of independent action and that many did not wait upon the gentry's decisions'; but he questions whether their role was decisive and concludes that 'in most counties they played, and were content to play, a secondary role.'[11] While they were involved in political debate, petitioning campaigns and popular demonstrations, Anthony Fletcher says that they did not seize the initiative: 'it was always gentry who took the lead.'[12] Thus the 'middling sort' are no longer ignored, but interpretation has shifted only from a conflict between gentry to one in which the gentry take the lead. And Dow concludes: 'Overall, then, the conservative case is secure when it maintains that radical demands and popular agitation were not the causes of the civil war'.[13]

In this new introduction I will explore further the role of the 'middle sort' of people in the English Revolution in the light of relevant studies that have appeared since the publication of **The English People and the English Revolution** in 1976. Since my sources are often pamphlets written for propagandist purposes, the question of whether I have taken sufficiently into account the biases of such sources, is triable in the extent to which my interpretations have stood the test of subsequent research and critical scrutiny by other scholars.

My suggestion in Chapter Six that the 'middle sort' of people were antagonised by the regime of Charles I has gained additional support regarding taxation and religion. Unlike ordinary taxation ('the subsidy'), which was voted by parliament and which did not touch the bulk of the population, the levy of shipmoney by royal prerogative 'hit the pockets of a very extensive group'. 'In Essex, for example, where only 3,200 names occur in the 1640 subsidy roll, 14,500 families were assessed for shipmoney.' In the case of Chichester numerous tradesmen and craftsmen who did not pay the subsidy were taxed for shipmoney and others who did pay the subsidy found themselves charged two or three times more for shipmoney, while a wealthy Sussex landowner such as Sir Thomas Pelham paid no more for shipmoney than he did for the subsidy. 'It is probable that the weight of the increased tax burden fell on the middle ranks of society.' Sir Roger Twysden noted that shipmoney increased the prejudice of 'the common people' against the king's government. Opposition to this tax appeared first among the 'middling sort' rather than the gentry. 'In many places such opposition as existed on 1634-8 came not from the county leadership but from the yeomanry and tenant farmers. In Lancashire, only three gentlemen can be found who were actively opposed to shipmoney... Only one Yorkshire gentleman appeared in opposition before 1638... Sir Francis Astley, sheriff of Norfolk, listing defaulters in May 1638, could name no one more prominent than four head constables, two attorneys and a clergyman. In 1636, a report from Dorset claimed that "the

greatest part of the arrears falls among the poorer sort"... and...
the escheator of Worcester wrote that the gentry were not to
blame for the remissness of the county. Some reports do
mention gentry leadership, but they were a minority until
1639.' Anthony Fletcher concludes that 'parish gentry and
wealthy yeomen, rather than the great magnates, bore the
brunt of the Stuart fiscal projects.'[14]

The richer farmers and tradesmen, who were coming to
dominate the villages, were concerned to control, discipline and
inure the poor to labour, and they resented the policies of
Archbishop Laud that impeded this, for example when the
church courts encouraged idleness by punishing men for
working on saints' days, and when the **Book of Sports** (1633)
undermined their conception of the sabbath by animating
people to engage on Sundays in the traditional village
pastimes, which they regarded as pagan, 'popish', and causes
of disorder, drunkenness and sexual licence. Christopher Hill
thinks that the policies of Laud were directed 'against the
growing control of local affairs by the "middling sort" ' or rather
by the élite of the 'middling sort'.[15]

The changes which Laud and his bishops imposed on the
church in the 1630s, notably the removal of the communion
table from the nave and putting it behind rails in the chancel,
enraged some of the 'middle sort' of people and some of the
poorer sort as well, who saw them as the re-introduction of
'popish' practices, although others accepted or supported the
changes. 'Godly Essex villagers had a very precise idea of what
they did and did not want in matters of religion, and the
"innovations" of the 1630s...were categorically among the
things they did not want.' In some Cambridgeshire villages
yeomen, husbandmen, even labourers 'were already convinced
by 1640 that they wanted a total reform in church government'
and petitioned parliament for the abolition of episcopacy. 'Their
radical ideas were not planted in their heads' by their social
superiors or dissident clergy but arose among themselves.[16]

Derek Hirst shows that with the expansion of the
electorate to embrace perhaps about one-third of the adult male
population (or much of the 'middling sort'), MPs had to take
account of the opinions of their constituents. By the time of the
two general elections in 1640 'the common people were

certainly actively involved in national political affairs' and had an impact on the results. Electors made their own decisions, 'not just because they had been pressured by their superiors, bribed or made drunk', but because they had their own views on national issues: the gentry and the oligarchic governing bodies of towns were no longer the sole forces in politics. 'The majority of the "property" grievances, patents and monopolies, forest laws, the law courts in general, distraint of knighthood, those which affected primarily the more substantial of the population, were agitated rarely at elections... The most common complaints against candidates all relate to what might be called the most "popular" grievances'—shipmoney, the levying of men and money for the king's war against the Scots in 1640, and above all religion: 'These were the matters affecting the widest range of people.'[17]

From the assembling of the Long Parliament in November 1640 to the outbreak of civil war in the autumn of 1642 popular agitation against the bishops and 'popery' became widespread. 'Anti-catholicism was the one genuine religio-political conviction of ordinary people in the early seventeenth century... It was a real and not just a manufactured issue.'[18] Peter Lake discerns that attacks on everything 'popish', by which was understood all that was flat opposite to protestant, expressed through the negative the positive beliefs and values of protestants. 'The popular violence and iconoclasm which accompanied some of these panics, as they have been described by Professor Manning and Dr Hunt, were scarcely the products of indiscriminate hooliganism. Rather, they were directed at what were taken to be ritually impure or threatening objects— either the possessions of known papists or the altar rails and images introduced into parish churches under Laudian rule and commonly associated with popery.' They were not the result of 'an irrational panic or knee-jerk response to a non-existent popish threat'. 'Certainly anti-popery appealed to people's emotions. It did so because it incorporated deeply held beliefs and values and it helped to dramatise and exorcise the fears and anxieties produced when those values came under threat. But that, surely, is what political ideologies do, and it is from their capacity to do it that they derive their ability to motivate and mobilise large numbers of people.'[19] Fear of 'popish plots' to destroy protestants and protestantism in England, in which the king, bishops, courtiers and aristocrats were suspected or believed to be involved, did much to form the crisis which led to civil war.[20] Behind this lay anti-popery, a popular ideology, which caused people to demand that parliament protect them against papists and root out popery and dangers from papists in their own communities and the nation. It must be noted, however, that there was also popular hostility towards the more radical religious reformers, and anti-popery does not make people religious radicals.

Chapters One to Five of this book deal with the demonstrations in London. Keith Lindley describes the growing inability of the king and his allies in the city government to prevent or to suppress these demonstrations.[21] He also gives an impressionistic account of the composition of the crowds, indicating its social breadth and changeability. 'The royalist tendency to dismiss the demonstrators and petitioners of 1640-2 as "the meaner sort of people", dredged up out of the city and its suburbs, distorted reality... Men of substance and social standing, joined by craftsmen, tradesmen and others of the middle rank, clearly played a prominent role in some demonstrations. Yet the social composition and character of demonstrations could change markedly... when the leading issues were bishops, popery or economic hardship lower social elements were more likely to be in the forefront'.[22]

I am concerned with the impact of the demonstrations on political alignments in the Long Parliament between 1640 and 1642, and this is re-examined in the detailed narratives of Robert Ashton and Anthony Fletcher.[23] Ashton says that in 1640 'the London mob had burst into frightening prominence' and become 'a formidable instrument in the hands of the radical group in the House of Commons.' According to this interpretation, Pym and his associates used popular demonstrations 'to further their own political ends', and as a means 'of bringing pressure to bear on parliament' and 'of intimidating their opponents.'[24] This raises questions about who led the demonstrations, how far they were independent of political leaders in parliament, and to what extent they were spontaneous. The royalists became convinced that Pym and his allies orchestrated and encouraged popular interventions in parliamentary affairs. 'Although the full conspiracy theory of popular pressure cunningly engineered by parliamentary leaders... is non-proven and improbable,' writes Keith Lindley, 'the timing of many of the protests, and the pressures they exerted, were certainly not unwelcome to such leaders.' They countenanced or encouraged many petitions and demonstrations, they defended the right of the people to petition parliament, and they signalled their consent to mass lobbying of parliament. Lindley judges that 'there neither was nor could be any one influence moulding and directing street politics in London. Petitions and demonstrations could be alternately more radical or more conservative than parliamentary leaders like Pym would have wished.'[25]

William Hunt rejects the notion of some historians that the rank and file of the London crowds 'were merely passive tools in the hands of the opposition leadership... It is best to think of a constant interplay between the action of the opposition at Westminster and a relatively autonomous (and heterogeneous) popular movement'.[26] Lindley draws attention to 'the fortuitous or spontaneous element in some demonstrations',[27] and Fletcher writes: 'It is not in fact fanciful to see a good deal of spontaneity about the demonstrations.' He doubts that there was a sustained leadership by religious radicals and feels that lack of leadership characterised the tumults. 'Clearly there were religious radicals who urged their friends to join them down the road to Westminster. There may have been something more formal, such as notices in shops and alehouses, but the only specific evidence we have of drumming up support is the paper thrust into the hands of the minister of Christ Church for him to read to the congregation on 29 December: "Sir be pleased to direct your prayers to God and move the congregation of saints here met to join with you that he would be pleased to assist the apprentices and others with strength and power and to bless their undertakings, which are speedily to root out superstitions out of this and all other Churches and to extirpate all innovations of the bishops and clergy".[28] In the absence of other evidence, however, this points to the militant activity of religious radicals in the popular politics of London; and evidence from later demonstrations would suggest that if one minister received such a paper it is likely that other congregations were being canvassed similarly.

'In the December days of 1641, which Brian Manning has described so vividly,' writes Fletcher, 'the crowds that came down to Westminster from the city of London had a crucial impact on the political process. But this is not to say that they seized the initiative or that Pym went into alliance with them. The demonstrations frightened him almost as much as they frightened the king.'[29] My argument, however, is that Pym and his associates feared that the king intended to resort to force against the parliament, and they condoned popular demonstrations as the only counter they had against such a royal coup. The point is that Pym was more frightened of the king than of the mob, for he would be bound to fall victim to such a royal coup, while others now feared the mob more than the king. The failure of Pym and his associates to agree to action to prevent demonstrations at Westminster seemed to the king proof that they were conspiring with the mob and this led him to attempt a coup by trying to arrest Pym and others for treason. Clearly both Pym and the king were reacting to the demonstrations which were setting the pace and shape of events.

Historians now dwell on the popular disorders in many parts of the country that ushered in the civil war. John Morrill lists 'attacks on Laudian ornaments in the churches (altar rails and stained glass windows were prime targets); disruption of religious services... Enclosure riots spread across the country, particularly in the midlands and north; in some cases not only the fences but the houses of the gentry were attacked. I have found evidence of enclosure rioting in twenty-six English counties in the years 1640-4. Apprentices, affected by the dislocation of the cloth trade, rioted in many towns, and these riots often extended to attacks on the homes of respectable catholics; there was widespread opposition to the payment of tithes, with tithebarns and manorial records being burned'. 'A wave of rumours about popish plots, and about the intention of the Irish rebels to carry their campaign into England, also led to fresh rioting.'[30] Anthony Fletcher notes enclosure rioting in a number of districts at one time or another in 1642 and anti-catholic rioting in Essex and Suffolk.[31] 'It is unclear whether rioting and violence were more extensive than hitherto,' comments Morrill, 'but most gentlemen certainly believed that they were', and they were 'profoundly shocked'.[32]

Nor do these historians ignore the appearance of an element of class conflict. 'Fear of disorder and social disintegration, which was certainly present but must have varied greatly in its intensity from place to place, rested on a mosaic of impressions and incidents', writes Fletcher: 'The main ingredients of this fear were economic dislocation, plunder and rapine, enclosure riots, anti-catholic riots and evidence of class hostility.'[33] 'Disruption, often with an overt class basis, was certainly widespread', concludes Morrill.[34]

My argument is widely accepted that the popular demonstrations and disorders in London and the provinces were a major factor in provoking the formation of a royalist party amongst the peers and gentry. This comes close to according to 'the people' the decisive role in precipitating the civil war, for, as Morrill says: 'There could be no civil war before 1642 because there was no royalist party.'[35] 'The association of the parliamentary opposition with lower-class violence', writes William Hunt, 'helped to drive conservative gentlemen over to the side of the king, a process that has been described in great detail by Brian Manning.'[36] Robert Ashton stresses the impact on moderate members of parliament, who were very alarmed by the popular tumults at Westminster and demanded that 'some exemplary punishment may be inflicted upon the principal fomenters of them' as well as on the demonstrators themselves. 'There can be little doubt' that the resistance of Pym and his associates to this demand provoked 'some moderate reformers into the royalist camp'.[37] Ann Hughes finds 'convincing' my view that 'the royalist party of 1642 was a "party of order" terrified by popular demonstrations in support of parliament, particularly by the artisans and small merchants of London.'[38] 'Brian Manning has argued compellingly', writes Barry Reay, 'that popular agitation forced the pace of the English Revolution (much in the manner of the French Revolution) and that this pressure from below, combined with the emergence of radical forms of religion, terrified many of the nobility and gentry, welding together a royalist party—"the party of order", a party which stood for stability and the preservation of hierarchy in both church and state.'[39] 'The unrest of the early 1640s, particularly in London and in the fens, played a large part in attracting gentry support to the king and to his emphasis on order, obedience and hierarchy.'[40]

Writing of the fens, Keith Lindley observes that the riots were 'at the forefront of a growing wave of rural protest principally directed against the enclosure of common land which, combined with increasing disorder in the capital, convinced a section of the ruling élite that their future lay with the king, as a symbol of order and orthodoxy, rather than with a parliament which appeared too tolerant of, or was believed to be blatantly encouraging, social and economic protest and heterodoxy.'[41] 'The support for parliament and puritanism apparent amongst middling and lower ranks in some industrial and wood-pasture regions encouraged the greater gentry of those areas into support for the king as the guarantor of social and political order. This process—a "Manning model"—can be seen in north Warwickshire, in Derbyshire, and in the West Riding of Yorkshire'.[42] Morrill records that in Staffordshire the popular rising of the Moorlanders for parliament 'appears to have driven many gentlemen finally into the royalist camp'.[43]

Clive Holmes adds that this factor also had contradictory effects, for the riots in Essex and Suffolk not only propelled some of the gentry into the king's party but also others into the parliament's party, because in the eastern counties many gentry saw parliament as more likely than the king to be able to restore order, so they collaborated with parliament's militia ordinance, not so much to defend themselves against the king's forces as against lower-class revolts.[44] But this situation came about, as Hunt notes, because potential royalist gentry were terrorised into submission to parliament and would-be neutralist gentry were intimidated into co-operation with parliament by popular uprisings against royalists, and therefore in this region parliament was the only authority and power that could hope to control the popular tumults.[45]

I describe in Chapter Seven the riots against royalist nobles and gentlemen and the popular resistance in parts of the country to their attempts to raise forces for the king. I write that these were 'fundamentally spontaneous popular movements, which were up to a point provoked or condoned by some parliamentarian gentry and urban magistrates.' More controversially, I argue that the 'popular attacks on the royalist nobility and gentry veered out of control of the parliamentarian nobility and gentry, and revealed an underlying rebelliousness against the ruling order' and 'a measure of popular hostility towards the ruling class'. Despite the support of some peers and gentry for parliament, 'nobles and gentlemen were sufficiently numerous and prominent on the king's side to give the impression that the royalist party was the party of the nobility and gentry... and in popular eyes the ruling class was identified with the king's party.'[46] This last point is also made by David Underdown: 'It was a common assumption that the king's side was that of the gentry... This idea was widely accepted by parliamentarians as well as royalists.'[47] In relation to the attacks on catholics, Robin Clifton observes that the strength of catholicism amongst 'courtiers, aristocracy, gentry', and its weakness amongst the common people except where protected by local catholic landowners, created the impression that 'catholicism was a religion of the gentry.'[48]

There are two arguments opposing the suggestion that the riots against royalist or recusant gentry expressed hostility towards the ruling class. One is that the rioters were selective in their targets and attacked only cavaliers or catholics, and were set on by parliamentarian gentry or believed that they were obeying parliament's orders; and the other is that anger against the ruling class did surface but was soon channelled into support for parliament. Ann Hughes endorses the first argument: 'There is little evidence... of any developed general attack on landowners as such; rather specific attacks on leading royalists and catholics were sanctioned or even initiated by the parliamentary leaders... Plunder was confined mainly to "papists and malignants".'[49] And Hunt says that 'popular violence was directed exclusively against royalists and recusants': 'The rioters were very selective. They attacked not clergy and aristocrats as such but Laudians, royalists, and especially catholics. The victims of enclosure riots were all "malignant". Even the numerous poachers... confined their activities to the parks of royalists and recusants... Many of the rioters were puritan only in their animosities. If they burned altar rails and terrorised catholics, they also got drunk and stole silverware, poached deer, and levelled enclosures.' He also suggests that 'the more radical puritan preachers' managed 'to channel hostility that might have been directed against the rich in general toward that section of the upper class that clung to the old religion or displayed obtrusive loyalty to the crown'.[50]

That leads on to the second argument, which does not deny the existence of class feeling. Fletcher and Underdown agree that 'a bitter vein of class hostility' towards the gentry did emerge during the riots in Essex and Suffolk. But Fletcher goes on to say with regard to Suffolk: 'In September the countrymen of the Stour valley, by their unbridled enthusiasm for the cause, at last forced the parliamentarian clique led by Sir Nathaniel Barnardiston to come into the open and implement the militia ordinance. This enthusiasm, which was mixed with anti-papist hysteria and political panic, threatened to turn itself against the gentry as a whole if those who were able to give a lead failed to do so. By acting swiftly the parliamentarian gentry quelled the anti-catholic rioting and channelled popular energy into the mundane business of mustering and organising arms. Incipient social tension was quickly brought under control.' And Underdown says that outside Essex and Suffolk 'there were few signs of hostility to gentry as a class, or of anything beyond a desire to resist the imagined catholic-cavalier conspiracy', and 'embryonic class feeling was kept under élite control and channelled into support for parliament.'[51]

All of this is consistent with my view that royalist and recusant gentry symbolised the ruling class, that latent class conflict surfaced in some places in 1642 and flowed into the parliamentarian party, where it continued as a potential threat to the parliamentarian gentry.

According to Ann Hughes: 'Manning found in the attitude of parliament's popular support evidence of class hostility towards landowners in general'.[52] But I do not speak of landowners in general but of royalist landowners, and what in fact I say is that parliamentarian peasants or craftsmen 'took up arms against royalist squires because they were squires as well as for political or religious reasons.'[53]

The question I pose is about the social context of the riots against royalist gentry or, for example, whether the people of Colchester and surrounding area, to whom I devote some attention, rose against Sir John Lucas because he was a royalist or because he was an unpopular landlord. Lucas 'was a kind of provincial Strafford, loyal, arrogant, and unpopular. He was a high churchman by upbringing... Sir John had already been involved in bitter litigation with his neighbours in Colchester. He had attempted to suppress windmills that competed with a water mill in his possession; he had torn up the town's water pipes that ran through his property.' As sheriff he had been zealous in collecting shipmoney. In 1641 his enclosures at Rovers Tye were levelled and his brick kilns destroyed by the weavers of Colchester. They were led by Roger Roberts, a strong opponent of episcopacy, who took the title of 'Bishop Blaze' (St Blaze was the patron saint of weavers). 'There were strong grounds for suspicion that the town chamberlains had encouraged the weavers to attack him. John Langley, the puritan captain of the trained band, had already tangled with him in a dispute over the collection of saltpetre.' During the riot in August 1642 his 'house was thoroughly rifled, its walls and gardens defaced, the deer slaughtered, the cattle driven out, and the Lucas ancestral tombs desecrated. The corpses were dismembered, and the rioters paraded through the town with the hair of the dead in their caps.' William Hunt describes the latter as a symbolic act of 'social resentment' and 'a crude affirmation of human equality in the face of death, the Great Leveller, as well as an act of retroactive vengeance.'[54]

Clearly Sir John Lucas had made many enemies and there was a mixture of motives for attacking him, but it is difficult to resist the impression that his attempt to join the king with horses and arms provided the occasion and the means to punish him for his actions as a landowner at least as much as a royalist. In other words, royalist or recusant gentry were not selected for attack just because they were royalists or recusants.

My argument relates to popular resistance to royalist nobles and gentlemen; nevertheless I give full weight to the leadership of parliamentarian peers and gentry. I write that the popular uprising provoked by the attempt of the Marquis of Hertford to raise forces for the king in Somerset 'was evoked and led throughout by the parliamentarian gentry... It involved rejection of the political leadership of royalist landlords, repudiation of most of the old-established heads of the community and a decision to follow the minority party in the ruling class. It achieved the immediate objective of the parliamentarian gentry and went no further.' [55] Now it is in reference to this that John Morrill writes: 'This book will make us question whether the middling sort meekly followed the lead of the gentry in 1640-3. It does not convince when it goes to the other extreme. Thus: "what was happening was the people were choosing between one set of rulers and another... and this meant that power lay with the people". By looking at those of the middling sort who supported the parliamentarians, he misrepresents what happened. Since in every county the middle sort divided amongst themselves, that power, if it existed, was dissipated.' Morrill omits in this quotation from my book the qualification at the end of the sentence—'power lay with the people... at least for the moment.' [56] But his comment is beside the point, which is not about the 'middling sort', whether royalist or parliamentarian or neutral, but about the undeniable fact of the small amount of popular support which the Marquis of Hertford and the royalist gentry mustered in Somerset in 1642, and the massive popular uprising which drove them out of the county.[57] David Underdown does grasp the point: 'Such local magnates as the Horners and Pophams, Bayntuns and Hungerfords played their part in harnessing the enthusiasm of the clothing districts for parliament, and the rising of August 1642 was preceded by gatherings of neighbours and tenants at Mells, Hunstrete, and other gentlemen's houses. Yet there were also plenty of influential royalist gentry in the region. The inhabitants could have followed Hopton, Sir Francis Dodington, and Thomas Smyth into the royalist camp' but they did not, and that was decisive.[58]

William Hunt points out that the king had no army in Essex 'in large part because more men chose to obey the militia ordinance than the crown's proclamation. This was one of those occasions when the beliefs and prejudices of ordinary people really made a difference. Charles had aristocratic supporters everywhere in England, but his writ ran only where his agents could exact compliance' or there was sufficient popular support for the king's cause.[59] Although Clive Holmes considers that the influence of the parliamentarian earl of Warwick was decisive in securing Essex for parliament, he asks the question: 'Did the inhabitants of the county observe the militia ordinance, contribute upon the propositions, and march to the defence of the city because of their "zeal to the parliament"— their ideological commitment to the cause? Or were their actions more a function of their "love to the earl of Warwick", whose dynamic leadership they followed with minimal consideration of the substantive issues involved, because his local prestige was great, and his authority familiar?' He answers that 'the behaviour of some of the Essex men suggests that... the influential leadership provided by a great peer was the dominant consideration informing their actions in 1642', and gives evidence 'that loyalty to Warwick predominated over affection to the parliamentary cause for many of the Essex men', but he also shows that the earl's power in Essex declined when it did not coincide with the views of Essex men.[60]

Underdown's conclusion is well-judged: 'Where the sympathies of the gentry coincided with those of the population —as in parliamentarian Suffolk and wealden Sussex, or in royalist west Somerset and downland Dorset—élite leadership was little impaired by the civil war. But where a landlord was seriously out of step with the general opinion of the neighbourhood war conditions might make it impossible to impose his authority', as both royalist and parliamentarian landlords found out to their cost.[61] It was not gentry opinion but popular opinion that was decisive.

While in Essex, Somerset, Devon, Gloucestershire, Warwickshire, Lancashire and the West Riding of Yorkshire, popular support enabled parliament to counter the royalists, popular disorders continued in the forests of the west country and the fens of the eastern counties to a considerable degree independently of the conflict between king and parliament.[62] Buchanan Sharp has studied the disorders in the forests and Keith Lindley the disorders in the fens. 'Hostility to the crown's policy of disafforestation between 1626 and 1632', writes Sharp, 'did not politicise the ordinary forest dwellers and drive them into the hands of parliament in its struggle with the king.' 'There is no real evidence', says Lindley, 'that the generality of fenmen had been politically educated by their experiences in the 1630s'. 'The inhabitants of these forests took advantage of political turmoil and the breakdown of regular enforcement of the law' 'to strike with near-impunity at the objects of popular animosity.' 'So far as most fenmen were concerned' the chief significance of the political crisis and the civil war 'was the opportunity it afforded them to level enclosures, and regain common lands'. 'When the civil war came, the inhabitants of forests rioted against those who held and profited from the enclosed lands. It did not matter that the earl of Elgin was a parliamentarian, that George Kirke and Sir John Wintour were royalists, or that lord Broghill was a royalist turned parliamentarian: political alignments were incidental to the hated reality of enclosure.' 'As far as the vast majority of fenland commoners were concerned, their main pre-occupation... probably extended no further than the desire to rectify wrongs sustained at the hands of the undertakers'.

Sharp thinks that the people of the western forests were probably indifferent to 'the great issues—political, social, and religious—raised by the civil war and its aftermath.' Lindley maintains that 'the vast majority of fenland commoners' were oblivious or indifferent to 'the great issues debated at Westminster in the months leading up to the outbreak of the civil war.' 'The struggle to regain former commons,' Lindley says of the fens, 'and resist undertaker pretensions, continued into the civil war from the 1630s, mirroring the situation in many forests, and indeed for most fenmen their war was with enclosures, loss of common rights and enforced change, rather than with king or parliament.' However, he does show that many fen commoners ostensibly supported parliament in the civil war. 'In fact,' concludes Sharp, 'it can be argued that the division in the forests in the 1630s was not between the crown and its projectors as proto-royalists and the gentry as proto-parliamentarians, but between the propertied and powerful, whether future royalists or parliamentarians, and the poor and powerless.'[63]

The conclusions of Sharp and Lindley are not inconsistent with my argument, in which I say that 'while London and its suburbs were disturbed by political and religious demonstrations... the countryside was troubled by riots which were... only indirectly connected with politics and religion.' 'The enclosures of forests and wastes, marshes and fens, provoked violent conflicts between lords and tenants', which 'did not mean that the aggrieved peasants necessarily supported parliament; far from it, in many cases.' I also say that the attacks on deerparks were 'only loosely connected with the challenge of parliament to the king: the rioters often had little sympathy with parliament or interest in the disputes between the king and the two houses.' [64] The consequence that I suggest follows from this is that these conflicts undermined the deference and loyalty of many peasants to the king and their lords, and this had a more damaging effect on the royalist party, which relied more than the parliamentarian party on the loyalties of peasants to their lords: 'the erosion or disappearance of that loyalty in parts of the countryside restricted the amount of support and resources the king and the royalist nobility and gentry could command'. [65]

'There is little solid evidence', Sharp asserts, 'that the widespread outbreaks of popular disorder in 1641 and 1642 were in any sense motivated by pro-parliament political sympathies or viewed with anything but suspicion by prominent parliamentarians. The evidence gathered... by B Manning... especially chapters 6 and 7, does not seem to me to demonstrate widespread popular support for parliament. It indicates, rather, on the part of the poorer sort—many of whom were artisans by Manning's own reckoning—a deep-felt hostility to men of property, status, and wealth, especially landlords. The fact that many of the people towards whose persons and properties the populace directed their animosities happened to be royalists was quite incidental. Certainly the riots which broke out in the new-drapery areas of Suffolk and Essex in 1642 owed much more to the chronic problems of poverty and unemployment among the workers than they did to any deep-rooted political sympathies for parliament. Furthermore, the local parliamentary gentry were horrified at this potentially dangerous manifestation of real social conflict'. [66]

It is, of course, an integral part of my argument that 'prominent parliamentarians' did view with 'suspicion' the outbreaks of popular disorder and that 'local parliamentary gentry were horrified' by the riots in Essex and Suffolk. In his interpretation of those riots Sharp follows Holmes, whose explanation in terms of 'a subsistence crisis' fails to give sufficient weight to the strength of popular feeling against 'popery' and in favour of parliament. While I agree that there was 'real social conflict' and that some of 'the poorer sort' exhibited 'a deep-felt hostility to men of property, status, and wealth, especially landlords', in so far as riotous crowds were selective in their targets it cannot have been 'quite incidental' that they chose to attack the royalists.

Sharp goes against all the evidence when he denies that there was 'widespread popular support for parliament' and he fails to notice the crucial distinction in my argument between the 'poorer sort' and the 'middling sort'. Popular disorders in 1640-42 were heterogeneous in causes and aims, sometimes they united the 'middling sort' with the 'poorer sort', sometimes they involved only the 'poorer sort'. These disorders ushered in the civil war because they influenced many nobles and gentlemen to rally to the king's cause. But the popular support which enabled parliament to fight and win the civil war came mainly from amongst the 'middling sort'.

The actions of the 'poorer sort' over their grievances, which were intensified by their sufferings at the hands of both sides during the war, increasingly separated from the conflict between king and parliament. What Sharp does make clear is that not all social or class conflict was channelled into the struggle between royalists and parliamentarians, or between different sorts of parliamentarians, but that other social or class conflicts continued and developed with some intensity separately from the war between the king and parliament, between the 'poorer sort' and the gentry, and sometimes between the 'poorer sort' and the 'middle sort'. This is 'the revolution within the revolution' which I will be examining in a forthcoming book continuing this present study.

Sharp's work deals with poor rural artisans who were not engaged in the civil war between king and parliament but were engaged in a class war. They had little or no land and depended on wages in the cloth, metal and mining industries, and probably they belonged to the 'poorer sort'. Sharp says that they expressed 'a deep hatred of the people possessed of the power, social standing, and landed wealth denied to them.' Their 'intense hatred of their social superiors, especially the gentry' approached 'class hatred'. 'The wrath of the poor was directed at the rich, mainly the gentry, but also including prosperous yeomen', and Sharp considers that the popular uprisings in the forests of the west country 'fit within a long tradition of anti-aristocratic and anti-gentry popular rebellion in England; this type of disorder was the result of social and economic grievances of such intensity that they took expression in violent outbreaks of what can only be called class hatred for the wealthy.'[67]

I attach critical importance to the evidence that in some of the popular tumults that ushered in the civil war some of the 'middle sort' of people joined and led some of the demonstrations and riots: 'there was one significant element in the popular disturbances of the late summer and autumn of 1642 that made them of a rather different character from other mutinies of the common people... The readiness of the "middle rank of men" to join with the "rabble" gave to the riots a greater social and political significance. The "rabble" was expected to be disorderly whenever it got the chance, and was as likely to favour the king as parliament, or neither, but the rebelliousness of the middle sort of men was far more a political act and orientated towards support of parliament: it converted riot into revolution.' Thereafter the actions of the 'middle sort' increasingly diverged from the social and economic disorders of the lower orders.

My hypothesis is that 'the parliamentarian party derived crucial support from the middle rank of people, which sustained and stiffened it, gave the direction to the cause, and effective leadership below the level of the gentry... The middle sort of people who supported parliament did not generally do so merely out of respect for their social superiors or at the behest of the parliamentarian gentry and clergy, but for their own political and religious ideals, and they injected into the parliamentarian cause an emphasis on godly reformation and a growing note of social rebellion' against the aristocracy and the greater gentry. 'On the whole it would seem to have been from amongst the more independent sections of the peasantry that parliament got support: some of the richer farmers, commonly called yeomen, and some of the smaller farmers who gained their independence by combining manufacture with agriculture.' I stress especially the parliamentarism of some of the manufacturing districts, where it may have extended lower down the social scale: 'In the West Riding of Yorkshire, south-east Lancashire, the Birmingham area and elsewhere the smallholding handicraftsmen were the firmest and most radical supporters of parliament. They were part-farmers and part-manufacturers, not wholly dependent on the gentry, nor wholly dependent on the merchants or larger manufacturers; men not rich, nor yet impoverished, independent in their economic life and in their opinions. The clothiers of Halifax and Bradford, the weavers of the Manchester area, the metal-workers of the Birmingham district, exhibited a close resemblance in their attitudes and actions during the civil war. Their motives were many: fear of attacks by papists, royalists, and plundering soldiers; distress at the disruption of their livelihoods by economic depression and war; hope that parliament would redress their grievances and give them a more secure future; they were yet sustained by ideals of religious reformation and political democracy as cures for all their problems and ills, and they were fearful and suspicious of the intentions of all superiors, whether royalist or parliamentarian or what.' [68]

John Morrill has repeatedly questioned my interpretation on the grounds that many of the 'middle sort' of people were royalists or neutrals in the civil war. 'There is no evidence that the middling sort were more parliamentarian than royalist'; 'it needs to be shown why local studies have failed to find numerically significant differences in the number of yeomen and other freeholders among the known activists on each side'; 'it seems likely that the "middling sort" were as divided as were the gentry' and 'that in most counties, the proportion of royalists, neutrals and parliamentarians amongst the "middling sorts" is broadly similar to the proportion amongst the gentry.' Morrill stresses especially neutralism among the 'middle sort': 'it needs to be shown why before, and even more during, the war so much of the neutralism arose from precisely these middling sort'; 'there is plenty of evidence that these very social groups contained some of the most committed neutral and anti-war sentiment'; 'both in 1642 and again in 1645 many of them took the initiative in demanding a halt to the war, or at least the neutralisation of their area. Clubmen risings, led by, indeed initiated by the middling sort were more numerous and far more imposing than any provincial Leveller organisations'; 'the Clubmen risings in 1645... were the creation of the middling sort.'[69]

In fact I point out that there were 'numerous royalists among the trading and industrial classes'.[70] But B G Blackwood's study of the parties in Lancashire reinforces my scepticism about how numerous they were in reality: 'In the royalist composition papers eighty-nine yeomen and seventy husbandmen are named as having supported the king. In a list of just over 1,000 suspected Lancashire royalists drawn up by major-general Charles Worsley in 1655 208 yeomen and 343 husbandmen are recorded. Even allowing for underestimates, these figures... are not impressive, especially as there must have been, at the very least, 8,000 peasant families in Lancashire in 1642. Indeed, it can be calculated that probably barely 7 per cent of the peasant population of Lancashire was royalist'.[71] Nevertheless, I continue, 'it is true that there were many yeomen and handicraftsmen in the king's ranks, as the parliament's records of delinquents amply demonstrate. But the king's party was essentially the party of gentlemen, who dominated its whole ethos. It was the more deferential and the less independent of the middle and poorer sort that followed the king, accepting the lead of their social superiors and contributing little to the royalist cause except perhaps a more virulent hostility towards puritans and puritanism.'[72]

There cannot be any dispute about the domination of the royalist party by big landowners. In the north and west, writes Morrill, it seems likely that 'the committed royalists' were 'powerful groups of leading gentry, including dominant elements within the ruling élite, bound together by a fear of social revolution from below and the need to preserve hierarchy in church and state'. He counts in the six northern counties 793 royalist gentry to 489 parliamentarian gentry, and 'the royalists are particularly strong amongst those with the highest income, largest estates and the largest share of county offices.'[73] Ann Hughes finds that in Warwickshire, out of a total of 288 gentry, 48 are known to have supported parliament, 90 gave some support to the king, and 110 may have been neutral, and the proportion of royalists is even greater amongst the JPs and the wealthiest and most influential gentry.[74]

Anthony Fletcher observes that initially the king's forces were raised by royalist gentry from amongst their tenants, and the parliament's forces relied heavily on volunteers from London: 'In a broad sense the armies that met at Edgehill were a citizen army led by puritan gentry and an army of tenantry led by conservative squires.'[75] 'All over England forces were raised, especially for the king, by men who could expect their tenants to follow them.'[76] I explain that where royalists were successful in recruiting popular support it was based on 'traditional ties of loyalty and habits of deference' which 'were rooted in the self-interest of tenants whose landlords could do them so much good or so much harm', plus 'fear and force'.[77]

David Underdown implies that I make too much of 'deference' and 'fear'. He says that the royalist gentry were most successful in raising forces in areas where 'paternalist social relations' best survived, and he adds: 'Tenant deference always contained elements of fear and self-interest, but if the royalists had relied on fear alone it is unlikely that they would have found many to follow them for long.' He has extracted and analysed statistics on royalist support in Wiltshire, Dorset and Somerset which reveal few labourers or paupers but numbers of 'people of some economic independence'—husbandmen, tradesmen and craftsmen. His researches 'confirm the existence of a widespread popular royalism (stronger... in some places than in others), which cannot be dismissed as the mere product of deferential obedience to the élite.' Husbandmen may have been 'vulnerable to pressures from the gentry' but it is unlikely that 'all the butchers, bakers, and chandlers, the blacksmiths, carpenters, weavers, and the hundred and one other trades that abound in the lists, can have been royalists simply because they were told to be by their employers or patrons... The royalists, no less than parliamentarians, had their following among the middling and industrious sorts of people.'[78]

While I do not disagree with 'the conservative argument that there was no innate or necessary connection between radicalism and the people in the 1640s',[79] I may have underestimated the autonomy and ideological content of popular royalism. Keith Lindley notes the popular hostility in

London of some citizens of 'middle social rank', along with some of the apprentices and some of the lower orders, towards the religious radicals.[80] And John Morrill stresses the strength of popular support for the traditional services and festivals of the Church of England, which 'had achieved not only an intellectual self-confidence but a rhythm of worship, piety, practice, that had earthed itself into the Englishman's consciousness and had sunk deep roots in popular culture.' He argues that it is possible that the strength of Anglicanism throughout the revolution 'was not gentry-led but frequently owed its strength to the very middling sort who we are often told were the bedrock of puritanism.'[81] This fits comfortably into the pattern of the 'church and king' riots which figure amongst popular movements in early modern, pre-industrial Europe.[82] As the defender of the Church of England, Charles I probably won some popular support, but this should not be exaggerated, for Morrill also shows that support for Anglicanism was strong amongst neutrals, and as a factor it may have been more significant in deterring people from parliamentarism than in winning them to royalism.[83]

I do, of course, note that most of the people were neutral in the civil war,[84] but I should have elaborated and analysed this further. David Underdown expresses surprise that I ignore 'popular neutralist outbreaks', particularly the revolts of country people in 1645 against the plundering by soldiers and the demands of garrisons, expressing a desire for a speedy end to the war, the so-called risings of the clubmen, which he describes as 'the most widespread popular protest movement of the entire revolutionary period.'[85] Much work has been done on these since I gave considerable attention to them in my unpublished thesis of 1959.[86] They should have been comprehended within the present book to the extent of noting that the risings occurred mostly in royalist areas and damaged the royalist cause much more than the parliamentarian cause, that they showed the capacity of peasants to act independently of their social superiors, and that in so far as they were conservative and traditionalist in their views of the issues involved in the civil war, they illustrated the failure of the gentry-led royalist party to harness to the king's cause much of the popular dislike of change, thus rendering conservatism and traditionalism less capable of preventing a parliamentarian victory. Mark Gould comments: 'There is nearly unanimous agreement that the most general attitude assumed by the English populace was the desire to remain neutral in the face of conflict... This was especially important for the parliamentarians, as it resulted in reluctance on the part of most people to take up arms on behalf of the king or to provide any material assistance to him'. 'Widespread neutrality allowed the revolution to occur' and provided room for it to grow and develop: neutrality was 'the ocean within which the revolutionary fish could swim'.[87]

My view on the importance for parliament of popular support, within which the 'middle sort' formed the crucial element, has received much support from historians of the period. Anthony Fletcher says that on the outbreak of the civil war 'the initiative and vigour of the people becomes indisputable.' 'At the start of the war popular support was crucial to the parliamentarians' strength. In a county like Sussex the entrenched puritan oligarchy could surely not have fought parliament's battles without the spontaneous enthusiasm of the yeomen families of the weald and the eastern rapes, an enthusiasm that was nourished by decades of household piety and yearning for a godly commonwealth. If men like Sir William Brereton, Herbert Morley and John Pyne offered the necessary leadership, men like the tradesman Nehemiah Wallington of London, the Yorkshire clothier Samuel Priestley and the fervent townsman John Coulton of Rye sustained the parliamentarian cause in the field.'[88]

William Hunt judges that without the alliance of 'disaffected members of the middle and lower classes' with some aristocrats and gentry 'it is doubtful that a county like Essex could have been secured for parliament or that a civil war could have been waged, let alone have been won, by the rebels.'[89] 'Popular support in 1642', writes Derek Hirst, 'helped win for parliament the pastoral and industrial areas of Somerset, parts of the textile-working north, and the wooded north of Warwickshire; most importantly, eager recruits rallied from the city and its suburbs.' 'Visible proof of the importance of the middling and meaner sort came in the dark days of 1642-3 when royalist cavalry threatened to carry the country.' [90] 'Nor can it be disputed', writes F D Dow, 'that among the parliamentary armies the puritan "middle sort" were to play an important role.' [91] 'The puritan middling sort', concludes Underdown, 'provided much of both the popular support and the manpower which enabled parliament to win the civil war.' [92]

John Morrill's call for more local studies to test my conclusion that the most important element in the support for parliament came from the 'middle sort' has been answered and has generally passed the test. Roger Howell, however, questions its longer-term impact in a number of provincial towns: 'Whatever the aspirations and loyalties of the "middling sort" in provincial towns were, they do not appear to have had much in the way of sustained success in ousting the entrenched élite. To assert... that "the rebelliousness of the middle sort... converted riot into revolution" may have some validity with respect to the choosing of sides in the conflict, but at a fundamental level it is not an adequate description of what actually transpired during the course of the revolution in most provincial towns. The level in question is that of control of the political machinery of the towns. Traditional oligarchs, though threatened and shaken, obstinately retained their privileged positions.' [93] But the immediate issue is the choosing of sides.

If the struggle of the people in the fens to recover their commons lost to the drainage undertakers led them to parliamentarianism when the undertakers were royalists or to royalism when the undertakers were parliamentarians, and if many of them supported parliament, not from love of its cause, but only so far as they could hope it would redress their grievances, nevertheless the parliamentarianism that Lindley describes in this region must sometimes have contained a positive element, otherwise they would have been more inclined towards the neutralism which Sharp believes was the response of the people fighting against enclosures of forest commons in the west of England. In the Lindsey Level and the East and West Fens most of the undertakers 'were staunchly royalist while the commoners were equally ardent parliamentarians.' 'Areas like Boston and its surrounding countryside, the scene of earlier anti-undertaker uprisings, provided a fertile recruiting ground for parliament.' Commoners in the Isle of

Axholme raised and maintained throughout the war two companies of foot for parliament. Their leader, Daniel Noddel, was a strong parliamentarian and lieutenant in captain Dyneley's company. He acted as attorney and solicitor for the Epworth commoners from 1646 to 1662 and was an associate of John Lilburne, the Leveller leader. 'The behaviour of the Isle of Ely commoners at Sutton does lend support to the commoner-parliamentarian equation' although clearly that is only one side of the story of the allegiance of the fenmen in the civil war.[94] Clive Holmes points out that there were few gentry resident in the fens and that the villages were dominated by 'middling-rich yeomen'. It was 'the middling sort'—'minor gentry, yeomen, richer husbandmen, some tradesmen'—who led the resistance of the commoners to the drainage of the fens and the enclosure of the commons, and it may be assumed that in those places which supported parliament such people continued to provide the leadership.[95]

Ian Roy describes the country near Bristol and Gloucester as fertile farming vales producing butter and cheese and engaged in clothmaking. Here, he says, 'manorial control was absent: there was less gentry dominance than in most areas of England', and the people showed an independent outlook in politics and religion. 'The dairymen, graziers, part-time farmers and workers in industry in this region constituted a fairly representative sample of what contemporaries described as the "middling sort"... The politics of the dairy farmers were largely parliamentarian, their religion puritan.'[96]

Underdown describes how in Somerset 'the clothworkers and yeomen of the villages to the north and east' of the county rallied to parliament against most of the chief gentry.[97] Warwickshire was another county where the wealthiest and most influential gentry supported the king, yet it was won for parliament and remained a parliamentarian stronghold throughout the war because, according to Ann Hughes, the support which the parliamentarian leader, lord Brooke, received, 'mainly from the ranks below the gentry, was more powerful than the overwhelming advantage' which the royalist leader, the earl of Northampton had amongst the gentry. 'In Warwickshire, the majority of the gentry were irrelevant in 1642: most of them... were either royalist or neutral'. 'Brian

Manning has emphasised the importance for parliament of the support of the "middling sort" of people, and north Warwickshire is one of the examples he uses', writes Ann Hughes: 'My own research supports what Manning says about the parliamentarianism of significant sections of the "people" of north Warwickshire, and about the important part this support played in parliament's success.' 'The north of the country, the old forest area with its abundance of enterprising small landholders and industrial craftsmen, was typical of those areas where parliament obtained support in 1642... areas where gentry control was weak and where there were few resident magnates... In such areas smaller men had, relatively speaking, more control over their own lives and were more susceptible to the call from parliament to come to the defence of liberty, property and true religion, against arbitrary government and popery. In addition, many of the towns of north Warwickshire had puritan ministers' who probably 'played an important part in rallying support to parliament's side.' [98]

I place emphasis on the parliamentarianism of Birmingham,[99] and Ann Hughes provides additional information on the background to this: 'The major developments took place in the north of the county where the necessary raw materials—coal and wood—were available; and the more open society encouraged immigration and gave room for enterprise to flourish. By the early seventeenth century Birmingham was already the thriving marketing and credit centre of the Black Country covering southern Staffordshire, northern Worcestershire and north-western Warwickshire. This was one of the most prosperous iron smelting areas of the country'. Birmingham's population grew from 1500 in the early sixteenth century to about 5000 in the mid-seventeenth century, of which over 60 per cent was involved in trade, mainly in metal-working industries. 'Nailmaking and cutlery were the main Birmingham trades, the work being done under the putting-out system, often on a part-time basis, but the organisation of the trades was coming increasingly into the hands of commercial capitalists who dominated marketing, and the great ironmongers who controlled the production of raw materials.'

Technological innovations in the late sixteenth and early

seventeenth century had increased capital investment, the number of large concerns and productivity in the nailmaking industry. 'The Birmingham area thus underwent a great transformation in this period: new industrial methods and a greatly increased and mobile population produced a society very different from the more traditional rural areas. The local gentry, apart from leasing their land for mills, were not greatly involved in the iron industry; more typical were men who had made their own way in the world like John Jennens, the greatest of the Birmingham ironmongers, and his brother Ambrose who marketed his product in London. Birmingham had no resident lord of the manor from 1530 on, and in this relatively free society enterprising men found opportunities to make their fortunes in new ways and social relationships became increasingly based on commercial ties rather than deference and paternalism. This area, to contemporaries, was one where traditional loyalties seemed weaker'. 'In 1642 the royalist William Dugdale described the inhabitants as "sectaries and schismatics" and saw their actions as vital in securing the county for parliament.'[100]

Derek Hirst says that 'anti-Marxist scholars have yet to explain the parliamentarianism found in textile areas in the west country and in Yorkshire.'[101] 'Throughout the war parliament had most success in recruiting its forces from the middling sort of the clothing districts', writes David Underdown, who provides statistical confirmation for the parliamentarianism of west country clothing districts.[102] Hirst explains this, and the parliamentarianism of the lead-mining district of the Somerset Mendips and the metal-working area of the west midlands, by the prevalence of independent small producers rather than of large capitalist enterprises such as in coal-mining with a more dependent labour force. 'There does seem some correlation between industrial organisation and popular alignment'.[103]

Nevertheless the contrast should not be made too sharp, for these were areas where capitalism was growing, as Ann Hughes's description of the Birmingham area shows, and a dependent labour force was increasing and the independence of the small producers was threatened, as likewise in William Hunt's account of the cloth industry in Essex. He estimates that weavers and other textile workers probably formed at least 15 per cent of the adult male population of Essex and most of them were poor. A great economic gulf separated these from the capitalist clothiers who bought wool from the chapmen and fellmongers, put it out to the combers, spinners, weavers, and fullers, and then sold the finished product to London merchants for export. One clothier of Colchester employed '400 households of spinners, 52 of weavers, and 33 of others' in the 1630s and another of Coggeshall left an estate of £100,000 at his death in 1653, though most clothiers operated on a much smaller scale.[104]

Similarly in another parliamentarian area, the lead industry in Derbyshire had expanded greatly from the sixteenth century onwards and by 1642 it was said to employ 20,000 men, women and children, of whom less than 2,000 were independent miners and the rest hired labourers or workmen in associated trades. A few miners grew wealthy: Anthony Coates, a miner of Wirksworth, employed 300 labourers in his lead works by 1640. The richer miners became lead-smelters and their wealth carried them up into the gentry, but 'such men were in a minority... the majority of miners probably stayed poor men.' The leaders of the miners were 'wealthy and sufficient freeholders'. 'Despite the undoubted complexity of motives for division within Derbyshire's ruling minority,' writes Jill Dias, 'the distribution of political allegiances in general suggests a correlation between regional economic and social differences and the choice of sides. Thus the more fertile iron and coal belt along the eastern and southern edges of the shire seems to have contained few or no obvious adherents of parliament, the several large landowners in this region being staunchly royalist and able to exert a strong influence over the loyalties of their tenants. It was among the more numerous independent and prosperous freeholders of the Duchy hundreds, in the lead-mining and sheep-rearing districts of the north, west and centre of the county, that parliament found most support'. Most of the parliamentarian gentry and yeomen lived in this part of the shire, where there was mass support for parliament. Religion was also a factor, for before the civil war 'religious radicalism' was propagated 'by "godly preachers" who were especially active among the populous lead-mining communities of High Peak and Wirksworth, where their sermons were drawing large crowds by the 1630s.' 'Most of the prominent parliamentarians in the county held radical, if not puritan, religious views, and fear of catholic conspiracy played a crucial part in their initial swiftness of action.'[105]

There is an argument that religion was the decisive factor in drawing people in industrial districts to the parliamentarian party. David Underdown finds an exception to the parliament-arianism of cloth-making districts in the royalism of the clothing town of Shepton Mallet in Somerset, where two-thirds of the royalists were clothworkers of one sort or another, and he draws the conclusion that this is 'a salutary reminder that there is no automatic causal connection between cloth-working and support for parliament.' He explains this exception by contrasting the presence of puritanism in the parliamentarian cloth-making districts with the absence of puritanism in royalist Shepton Mallet.[106]

The overall impression from these researches is that they confirm the importance of the 'middle sort' in the parliament-arian party, that parliamentarianism was strongest amongst the independent small producers in agriculture and industry in areas where aristocratic and gentry control was weak, in industrial areas where capitalism was developing but only beginning to lead to concentrations of landless, poor, and dependent wage-labourers in larger enterprises, and in agricultural and industrial areas where puritanism or religious radicalism was a powerful force.

In fact, it is central to my argument is that religion was the dynamic force in the parliamentarian party and this provides further confirmation that the "middle sort" of people were the driving force in the parliamentarian party, for the sections of the 'middle sort' that supported parliament were those which were motivated by zeal for godly reformation. It was they who shifted the emphasis of the parliamentarian cause to radical reform of the church, and it was they who were the religious radicals that spearheaded the revolution.[107] John Morrill acknowledges that the 'yeomanry, clothworkers and urban craftsmen certainly included some highly motivated and committed radicals (particularly on religious questions)'. 'Those parliamentarians committed to a vision of a godly reformation and uncorrupt commonwealth were probably the most highly motivated men on either side, and may well have been drawn heavily from the middling sort, but they were a tiny minority'.[108] Underdown says that 'the goal of puritan reformation certainly inspired many of the middling sort.'[109] Blackwood concludes that religion was 'the most important single issue in the civil war in Lancashire', but it had a social context, for 'puritanism... was apparently strongest among the "middle sort", and less than 15 per cent of gentry heads of families supported it.'[110]

In London, 'the court records of the separatists list glovers, cobblers, bakers, haberdashers, leather dressers, gunmakers, last makers, cord-wainers, weavers, tailors, feltmakers, clothmakers, and an occasional merchant.' They were not 'the disorderly rabble depicted in the anti-sectarian literature of the period.' They were established in trades though 'most of them must have been relatively poor', but a few were well-to-do manufacturers and merchants.[111]

The main strength of the Baptists was in the south, the west and the midlands. Particular and General Baptists flourished in London and the midlands, while General Baptists were also strong in the Weald of Kent, the Lincolnshire fens, and the Chiltern Hills of Buckinghamshire. 'Small craftsmen and tradesmen predominate: weavers, shoemakers, tailors, ironmongers, bakers, glovers, and button makers... There is no doubt, however, that the surviving evidence underestimates the number of rank and file Baptists wholly or partly engaged in agriculture. While the movement had its first strength in the metropolis' it became well established in the countryside. 'The leadership may have been predominantly tradesmen and artisans' but there were also husbandmen in the movement. 'There were prosperous merchants and manufacturers among the Baptists' and a small number of minor gentry, but the mass of followers 'consisted of the middling sort'.[112]

From the milieu of the radical sects in the 1640s sprang the Levellers and Diggers, and in the 1650s the Fifth Monarchists and the Quakers. The Fifth Monarchists attracted 'persons of most of the "mechanic" occupations, both small producers and retailers, but there were no big producers and only three "merchants"... The clothing industry and trade was dominant, involving about a third of the total': urban artisans predominate but there were also numbers of apprentices and journeymen.[113] The Quaker movement 'mainly drew its membership from what were known as the "middling sort of people": wholesale and retail traders, artisans, yeomen, husbandmen... Few belonged to the gentry élite, few to the labouring poor.' 'Though there were substantial numbers of the poorer sort in the movement, most belonged to the relatively comfortable middle section of the community'. 'A significant number of the early Quakers were yeomen... There were also a substantial number of Quaker wholesale traders and large producers, often, as with the yeomen, men of some means: merchants, clothiers, millers, maltsters'. Husbandmen, retailers and artisans (blacksmiths, shoemakers, tailors, butchers, weavers, carpenters) were quite numerous in the early movement, but 'the number of Quaker servants and labourers was minimal.' A large percentage of Quakers was involved in agriculture: 'Quakerism was predominantly a rural movement.' 'Quakerism was essential an affair of the middling sort.'[114]

Barry Reay sums up that the general political and economic outlook of the various brands of radicalism in the English Revolution 'seems to have reflected their social support: in the towns, independent craftsmen and small traders; in the country, the same groups plus husbandmen and yeomen. The ideologists and leaders of the radicals and sectaries were quite often men (or women) of substance'—merchants, lesser gentry, yeomen—'but the rank and file was firmly of the "middle sort of people". '[115]

I contend that 'puritanism taught the middle sort of people to think for themselves and to assert their independence against king, lords and bishops. Godliness gave them status and the ability to express their identity as a separate class; and it enabled them to formulate and dignify their hostility towards the ruling class.' (In this revised edition I qualify this generalisation by limiting it to 'some of the middle sort of people').[116] Here I move into the most controversial area, though my arguments are more tentative and modest than some of my critics care to admit.[117] I say that those of the 'middle sort' who supported parliament injected into that cause 'a growing note of social rebellion', and that amongst the rank and file of the parliamentarian party there was an 'undercurrent' of 'hostility towards the nobility and gentry, from which parliamentarian nobles and gentlemen were only partially and for a time exempt.' In conclusion I write that 'class conflict... was always present but latent before 1640; it came close to the surface in 1641-2 and propelled parliament to challenge the king and the king to resist parliament; it drove parliament to victory, and became explicit in the aftermath of economic hardship and disillusionment with the result of victory': 'between 1646 and 1649, the revolution became an open class conflict' with the emergence of the Levellers, that is in the sense of a fully conscious class conflict.[118]

The applicability of the concept of class to seventeenth-century English society is questioned by most historians of the period. 'A major ingredient in class formation', writes Derek Hirst, 'must be class consciousness, and while the rhetoric of the Levellers of the 1640s—the first genuine popular political movement in history—did display a strain of class hostility, the 1640s were extraordinary times. When both agriculture and industrial production were firmly rooted in the family, workers were more likely to identify with a family in whose household they might live, rather than with workers elsewhere. Poor communications and localised horizons made the latter identification still less likely. Probably most thought of themselves primarily as residents of a particular village or town, or as weavers, blacksmiths, or whatever, than as members of the "commons".'[119] Keith Wrightson says that 'it was not a society dominated by class affiliation; for however strong the awareness of status within a specific local context, broader class consciousness was inhibited for those below the level of the gentry by their lack of alternative conceptions of the social order, their envelopment in relationships of communality and deference, by the localism which gave those ties force and meaning and by a lack of institutions which might organise and express a horizontal group consciousness of a broader kind.'[120] And David Underdown writes: 'Class is a concept that can be applied to seventeenth-century English society only with the greatest possible caution. We can identify "horizontal" social divisions existing across the boundaries of village, town, and region—between landowners, tenant farmers, artisans, and labourers. We can identify certain interests shared by members of each group. But it is not easy to detect the element of consciousness necessary to transform a status or occupational group into a class. Most people still thought of themselves in "vertical", local terms: as members of communities. Within those communities they were very conscious of their status and their roles as masters or servants, but were much less conscious of possessing an identity of interests with other masters or servants throughout the land.'[121] Wrightson continues that 'it was perhaps a society which possessed an incipient class dimension in its distribution of wealth, productive relations and market situation, and in which antagonisms between social strata undoubtedly existed. But these were too limited to a specific social situation and too temporary an element in cognitive experience to allow us to speak of class as a dominant principle in social relations.'[122]

It is not necessary, however, to assume that solidarities are always either 'vertical' or 'horizontal' in a society, nor to deny the possibility of localised class conflict and class consciousness. Robin Briggs in his analysis of revolts in seventeenth-century France argues that 'both kinds of solidarity operate with variable force according to circumstances.' The local community 'was the scene of intense exploitation of the poor by their richer neighbours' but the logic of certain situations, such as external pressure or demands uniting various strata of the local community in resistance, would have the effect of making 'vertical solidarities seem stronger, so that they might mask the horizontal divisions which would nevertheless persist, and eventually tend to reassert themselves.' 'Even within a revolt lasting only a few days it is often possible to observe quite sharp shifts of position by the various groups involved.' 'If vertical solidarities were crucial in starting many revolts, horizontal divisions generally' took over later.[123]

Most historians reject the idea that the civil war was a class conflict. Roger Howell writes: 'A considerable volume of contemporary comment would seem to lend strong support to the observation that the king's cause was favoured by the social extremes of the town, while parliament and godly religion drew their support from the solid "middling" sort... But the situation is by no means so firmly established as its reiteration in the pamphlet literature of the time might seem to indicate... There was, of course, a marked tendency for the grandest of the oligarchs, especially those with a hand in a monopoly like the Newcastle coal-trade, to identify with the royalist side, but this should not be taken to indicate that those who opposed them were necessarily of a significantly different socio-economic level or that their opposition was the product of national issues. In a number of cases, the division into parties represents more a struggle of élites than it does a genuine class conflict.'[124]

But, says Blackwood, 'it does look as though there were social differences between the parties in Lancashire, though we must beware of exaggeration. If we exclude the possibly large neutral population, it would seem that the royalists were supported by all three peers, by a clear majority of the gentry, probably by a large minority of the towns and possibly by a minority of the peasantry. By contrast, the parliamentarians were sustained by no peers, by a minority of the gentry, probably a small majority of the towns and possibly a majority of the peasantry. Does this therefore mean that the civil war in Lancashire was a class conflict? No. There were class differences but no class antagonisms between the royalists and the parliamentarians; or if there were class antagonisms and social issues, they were of limited importance.'[125]

Nevertheless, evidence of class hostility has proved impossible to ignore completely. 'In a few areas,' Hirst notes, 'where there had been a particularly aggressive landlord—like Charles himself in the fens—there is something to be said for the Marxists who see rural and urban middling sort lining up against oppressive (although scarcely "feudal") superiors. But such an argument has its limits, for... the economic profiles of the leaders of both sides were broadly similar.'[126]

While Lindley finds that there was an 'absence of expressions of hatred for men of property in the fens' because 'the generality of fenmen had no immediate reason to feel hatred for the gentry as such because individual gentry associated themselves with the fenmen's cause and thereby afforded some counterbalance for those who allied with the drainers', he records the exception of Sutton in the Isle of Ely where the commoners 'apparently saw their own struggle against rich oppressors as part of a generalised struggle between rich and poor. They had "found by woeful experience, the proverb is true, wealth maketh many friends, but the poor is separate from his neighbour" and therefore looked to the House of Commons "as being the instrument of God, to be the deliverers of the poor, out of the hand of his rich neighbour, that was stronger than he". Moved by millenarian enthusiasm, the poor of Sutton eagerly awaited the day "when in this nation the poor do enjoy their own".'[127]

Ann Hughes discovers 'little evidence... of any developed general attack on landowners as such', although she has 'no reason to doubt' that in the assaults on deer parks by parliamentarian soldiers 'social antagonisms played a part', and she also records a parliamentarian pamphlet from Warwickshire that 'does add a socially radical tinge to the usual mixture of fighting for God and the liberties of England against papist conspiracy: "The enemies thou art to fight withal, are Court Parasites, Papists, both Gentry and Laic, Prelates, and their adherents, the Courts, and Ministers of the Law, who have abused the Law, selling Justice to the adversary, and the poor innocent to ruin and destruction; Projectors and Monopolizers, who for private gain have robbed thee of thy liberty; so that between the Prelate and the Projector, thou enjoyedest but the tythe to whom the whole did belong".'[128] This adds something to my argument that after the civil war the Levellers systematically articulated what at least some parliamentarians believed they had been fighting against.

In Derbyshire, before the civil war, several greater land-owners had sought to cash in on the profits of the growing lead industry. The resistance of the miners was led by 'wealthy and sufficient freeholders' and entrepreneurs. 'More than a few' of the miners, suggests Jill Dias, perhaps supported parliament in the civil war in the hope of 'emancipation from the long-term economic and political pressures imposed on them by greater landowners like the Cavendishes or Leeks.'[129] 'The burgeoning industrial areas', Hirst acknowledges, 'could also generate something close to class anger when the political controls fractured in the midst of a deep depression', for example in 'the anti-catholic rioting and looting in 1642 in the East Anglian coast clothing villages of the Stour valley..., the fierceness of the rebuff to the earl of Derby's attempt to raise Manchester for the king, and the marquis of Hertford's bid for the clothing towns of Somerset'.[130]

'A process of social differentiation was under way, more noticeably in some places than in others, and where this was happening wartime allegiances sometimes reflected a rudimentary sense of class identity.' Underdown finds my evidence for this 'impressive' and concludes that 'it is impossible to doubt the existence of a rudimentary sort of class consciousness' in some 'semi-industrial communities'. 'Dr Manning has argued persuasively' that 'embryonic class feeling... provided a significant motivation for clothworkers—smallholders of the West Riding of Yorkshire and of south Lancashire, and for the metal workers of the Birmingham area'. 'Even in these areas, though, its extent should not be exaggerated'. 'Partially realised class feeling' 'may help to explain the solidarity' of these districts for parliament but it is not in itself 'a sufficient explanation'. 'The analysis is most valid for places in which industrial or commercial development had produced something resembling a class society'. 'It is less easily applied to the wider world of rural England' where 'the vertical ties of community still determined the behaviour of ordinary Englishmen far more compellingly than any hypothetical sense of class.'[131] There is not an enormous gap between some of what Hirst and Underdown say and most of what I say.

Ann Hughes holds that 'on Manning's view it is hard to explain why any member of the social élite sided with parliament'.[132] In fact I explain the parliamentarianism of that small number of aristocrats and gentry in terms of the 'godliness' that they shared with the 'middle sort' of people, and their willingness to take or accept the leadership of a popular movement.[133] It may be that I should have said more about the parliamentarian peers and gentlemen. William Hunt argues that religion broke the unity of the ruling class and created a solidarity across class boundaries between the 'godly' aristocrats and gentry and the 'godly' 'middle sort' of people.[134] I think that Ann Hughes' account of lord Brooke's leadership of the parliamentarian party in Warwickshire fills a gap in my relation. 'His political practice is marked... by support for broad participation and like Cromwell he chose his allies for their zeal to the cause, not for their social status. Locally, his influence was as a leader of the godly not as a major landowner who was a focus for the county élite... Brooke relied on godly clerics and middle-ranking or lesser gentry who shared his views'. His success in gaining control of Warwickshire for parliament was due most importantly to the popular support that he received 'particularly in Coventry and amongst the lesser gentry, independent freeholders and metal workers in the Arden region'. Brooke was a skilled popular leader and he portrayed the war as a religious struggle for the cause of God. He prayed 'that God almighty will arise and maintain his own cause, scattering and confounding the devices of his enemies, not suffering the ungodly to prevail over his poor innocent flock. Lord we are but a handful in consideration of Thine and our enemies, therefore O Lord fight Thou our battles, go out as Thou didst in the time of King David before the hosts of the servants, and strengthen and give us hearts that we show ourselves men for the defence of Thy true religion and our own and the Kingdom's safety.' 'Ideological and social change had produced a situation where aristocratic leadership could not be based on landed power alone', writes Ann Hughes. 'In fact Brooke's appeal was best supported not near his own estates... but in the industrial and urban areas of north Warwickshire where men of middling wealth had a greater degree of independence and control over their own lives.'[135]

Hughes says that 'there is no reason to doubt the genuineness and spontaneity of the popular support for parliament' but she believes that it was 'under control of their aristocratic and gentry leaders' on whom it was 'very dependent' and without whom it was 'not effective'.[136] But it would make a more balanced judgement to add that the aristocratic and gentry leaders were 'very dependent' on the 'middle sort' of people and 'not effective' without them, as her account of lord Brooke's leadership implies. J H Elliott's dictum applies here: 'In early modern Europe a revolt stood some chance of success only if it could count on the active participation of at least a section of the traditional governing class, and on the neutrality, if not the goodwill, of the greater part of the political nation.'[137] But as the war progressed, and in its aftermath, the alliance across class lines was broken and hostility towards the aristocrats and greater gentry reasserted itself and they lost control of the parliamentary party, which passed to some middling gentry, some minor gentry, and some of the 'middle sort' of people.[138]

The causes and outcome of the revolution were determined by fundamental changes taking place in English society. Underdown writes that 'demographic and economic forces were widening the gap between the few, the parish élites of wealthy yeomen and clothiers, and the many, the small landholders and landless poor.' 'There was within seventeenth-century England a process of growing social differentiation', observe Morrill and Walter: 'At one extreme this saw the growth in poverty that so alarmed contemporaries... But the corollary of this was the consolidation of the smaller but more significant growth of the "middling sort", the yeomen and richer husbandmen in the countryside.' Generally, says Underdown, the pattern was 'the consolidation of the yeomen oligarchies that decisively changed the realities of village life': 'By the early seventeenth century, therefore, the orderly, vertically integrated society assumed by Tudor theorists was seriously diverging from reality. Rural society was dividing, with a minority of middling property-owners acquiring a sense of identity which detached them from the previously relatively homogeneous village community, and led them to devise new mechanisms for imposing their own conception of order on those below them.' 'There was a subtle shifting of alliances in the countryside which predated the revolution', argue Morrill and Walter: the village oligarchies of the 'middling sort' turned to an alliance with the gentry. 'This was an alliance eased by an identity of economic interests in service of the market, facilitated by the trend towards enclosure by agreement and cemented where there occurred a shared religion and literate culture.'[139] But it was partial and incomplete and in the 1630s the king, bishops. and groups of aristocrats and gentry counter-attacked against the village élites.[140] The latter's demands in 1640-42 for political and religious reforms were resisted by the king, bishops, and many peers and gentlemen; therefore, in alliance with as many gentry as were responsive to their concerns, they turned to popular support to overthrow the old order and replace it with a 'godly' one. But they desired this, as Morrill and Walter maintain 'not least to strengthen their position over their poorer neighbours. But they did not seek the radical social and economic reforms that the poorer sort might have sought. To challenge the drift of agrarian capitalism would have been to bite the hand that fed them their profits.'[141]

Here the ambiguities of the 'middle sort' became clearer and the divergence became sharper between those who were benefiting from the development of capitalism and those who were threatened with being reduced from independent small producers to dependent wage-workers.[142] The Levellers wished to push reforms further but this could be done only with the support of a broad popular movement and by offering protection to the independent small producers. The élite of the middle sort became more alarmed and more concerned to discipline the poor, extend and intensify the exploitation of wage-labour, and increase production, rather than to end the rule of the aristocracy and gentry.

This determined the outcome of the revolution. 'There was a gradual pushing apart of the clusters of social groups which constituted the established social hierarchy', concludes Wrightson. 'The "middling sort" moved closer to their immediate superiors among the gentry and urban élite in both interests and life-style.' 'This process of transition was essentially completed by 1660, following the marked furtherance of its national penetration which resulted from the social and religious policies of the Interregnum.' For the most part the 'middling sort' played 'a crucial role' by entering into 'a closer alliance with the "improving" gentry. They were readier to agree to schemes of enclosure and improvement... save where their personal interests were directly at risk.'[143] The cleavage between this élite of the 'middling sort', or emerging capitalist class, and the 'ever-growing army of landless labourers' deepened, and in the words of Alan Everitt: 'the civil war and Interregnum dealt a death-blow to the age-old conception of society as a hierarchy of interdependent orders, and went far to replace it by the notion of society as a series of independent and necessarily antagonistic classes.'[144]

Brian Manning
22 March 1991

1

THE PEOPLE AND THE LONG PARLIAMENT

THERE was great rejoicing when Charles I bowed to the opposition that his rule had aroused and summoned parliament to meet on 3 November 1640. 'We are all mad with joy here that his majesty calls his parliament', reported Edmund Rossingham. 'All men's hopes and prayers are upon the parliament', Thomas Gower told the earl of Rutland. 'A strong expectation of much ensuing good has possessed every man', wrote Francis Read. All men expected 'such a medicament to each private malady, that not any humour in the body politic, or itch in the breech of the kingdom' but would be cured by this parliament.[1]

Normally people accept the world as they find it: they grumble and complain, but they can see no hope of altering it. Then something happens to interrupt the normal course of things and the feeling grows that change is possible, that grievances can be redressed, that oppressions can be brought to an end, and that the system can be altered. The rousing of hopes and the raising of expectations is the first step towards revolution, as the disappointment when these hopes are not quickly realised and those expectations are not speedily satisfied is the second. That is why the meeting of the Long Parliament created a revolutionary situation.

There was an increased amount of interest in the elections to this parliament. Traditionally the lords and leading gentry decided who should sit in parliament, and on the day of the election their nominees were returned unopposed: contests were rare. But from the 1620s contests had been becoming more common and in the elections to the Long Parliament there was an unprecedented number of contests, and 'in at least 70, probably more, of the 259 original constituencies' the electorate went to the poll to choose between rival candidates.[2] This was symptomatic of divisions amongst the gentry, but it also reflected the growing involvement of the people in politics. Traditionally the gentlemen ruled and the people obeyed, and politics concerned only the upper classes. But in the earlier seventeenth century the electorate had expanded and by the time of the elections to the Long Parliament it included not only the gentry and rich merchants but also the yeomen and poorer peasants in the counties and the shopkeepers and craftsmen and some of the poor in many towns. This enlarged electorate was less easy for the gentry to control and more capable of asserting its own opinions.[3]

In the election at Great Marlow in Buckinghamshire Whitelock was told by a local lawyer—'a country fellow in plain and mean habit'—that lord Paget had recommended Gabriel Hippesley for one of the seats 'and thought to have carried it because he is lord of the town: but that will not do in these times, blessed be god'. And Whitelock was elected by the votes of 'the bargemen of the town' and 'generally the ordinary sort of townsmen'.[4] At Wigan in Lancashire there were six candidates and 'some inferior persons, inhabitants, labourers, and handicraftsmen, being free only to trade with Wigan, and not enrolled or sworn burgesses of the corporation, had combined and confederated and plotted together to disannul and annihilate the election of Bridgeman and Rigby by the burgesses of the corporation'.[5] Political and religious questions became issues in the contests partly because of the intervention of the lower classes. At Salisbury in Wiltshire there was a dispute whether the franchise was restricted to the oligarchy that ruled the town or extended to the citizens at large, and this dispute was connected with political and religious divisions, because one of the candidates nominated by the oligarchy was opposed on the grounds that he had promoted the collection of shipmoney, suppressed preaching, and discouraged the education of poor children.[6] Clearly the nobility and gentry would not be left to settle things in the Long Parliament without taking into account the demands and expectations of the people.

One of the first acts of the Long Parliament was to release Prynne, Burton and Bastwick from the prisons to which they had been sent by the court of Star Chamber in 1637. In popular eyes they were the victims of a persecuting regime and religious martyrs. On 28 November 1640 Prynne and Burton were met at Brentford and escorted into London by more than a hundred coaches and thousands of men and women, on horse and on foot, carrying branches of rosemary, 'for remembrance', and laurel, 'in token of joy and triumph'. In the city, crowds lined the streets to see them pass, 'the common people strewing flowers and herbs in the ways as they passed, making great noise and expressions of joy for their deliverance and return'. 'It was a kind of triumph, the people flocking together to behold them, and receiving them with acclamations, and almost adoration, as if they had been let down from heaven'.[7] A few days later Bastwick was met at Blackheath by another large crowd and escorted into London with similar demonstrations of joy.[8]

Clarendon thought that the crowds consisted of 'multitudes of people of several conditions', including 'many citizens of good estates'.[9] Heylyn attributed the demonstrations to 'the puritan faction out of London and Southwark';[10] and the acclamations of the crowds were said to be mingled with 'loud and virulent exclamations against the bishops, "who had so cruelly prosecuted such godly men"'.[11] Two puritans who were present testified to the religious enthusiasm which inspired the demonstrations. Nehemiah Wallington, a turner, who lived in Little Eastcheap in the City, rejoiced at the return of 'those worthy and dear servants of god';[12] and Robert Woodford, steward of the puritan town of Northampton, wrote in his diary: 'Oh, blessed be the Lord for this day! This day those living holy martyrs Mr Burton and Mr Prynne came to town, and the Lord's Providence brought me out of the temple to see them. My heart rejoiceth in the Lord for this day; it's even like the return of the captivity from Babylon'.[13] 'God is making here a new world', exclaimed Robert Baillie, a presbyterian minister newly arrived in London as a representative of the successful rebellion in Scotland against episcopacy and the Laudian prayer-book.[14]

Clarendon's description of this peaceful and orderly demonstration as an 'insurrection (for it was no better) and frenzy of the people'[15] seems grotesquely exaggerated, until it is remembered that it was an unusual and even unprecedented event, and the first instance of popular intervention in the affairs of the Long Parliament. It was generally assumed to be a demonstration against the courts of Star Chamber and High Commission: an 'intolerable affront to the Courts of Justice, and his majesty's government';[16] and, indeed, it was 'generally esteemed the greatest affront that ever was given to the Courts of Justice in England'.[17] Thomas May thought that the purpose was to 'work good effects in the king's mind, and to make him sensible how his people stood disaffected to the rigour of such proceedings', and to bring about 'the ruin of those two courts, the High Commission and Star Chamber'.[18] And Clarendon suggested that the intention was also to put pressure on the parliament: 'to try and publish the temper of the people; and to satisfy themselves in the activity and interests of their tribunes, to whom that province of showing the people was committed'.[19] No doubt some MPs sympathised with the sufferings of Prynne, Burton and Bastwick, and others hoped for the abolition of the courts of Star Chamber and High Commission for a variety of reasons unconnected with the treatment of these men, and a few welcomed the demonstration as a sign of the unpopularity of the bishops.[20] But the significant result was the appearance of the first signs of the division that was in the end to split the ruling class irretrievably. 'The king takes a great disgust'; 'some, both of the clergy, of the Court, and other gentlemen besides, did not conceal their dislike of it, affirming that it was a bold and tumultuous affront to courts of justice and the king's authority'; and some members of parliament were reported to have advocated the punishment of the 'giddy zealots' responsible.[21] Their reaction is reflected in Heylyn's criticism of the king for 'conniving at the insolency or not daring to punish it';[22] and Clarendon's complaint: 'Nor had any minister of justice or the State itself courage enough to examine or prosecute in justice any persons who were part of that riotous assembly... so low the reputation of the government was fallen, and so heedless all who should have supported it': 'Whilst the ministers of the State, and judges of the law, like men in an ecstasy, surprised and amazed with several apparitions, had no speech or motion... Whereas, without doubt, if either the Privy Council, or the judges and the king's learned counsel, had assumed the courage to have questioned... the seditious riots upon the triumph of these three scandalous men... it had been no hard matter to have destroyed those seeds and pulled up those plants, which, neglected, grew up and prospered to a full harvest of rebellion and treason.'[23] May probably reflected the attitude of moderate MPs in questioning whether 'actions of that nature, where the people, of their own accords, in a seeming tumultuous manner, do express their liking or dislike of matters in government' would not make the king less likely to consent to reform.[24] At all events, Clarendon did not think that the demonstration was organised by the leaders of the opposition in parliament, where it received 'no visible countenance or approbation', whatever secret machinations some of the leaders may have been engaged in with their friends in the City.[25]

The religious radicals, with considerable popular support in London, wanted more sweeping and revolutionary changes in the church than the leaders of parliament, and most of its members, contemplated. This difference soon became apparent. Early in November 1640 a petition for the abolition of episcopacy, 'root and branch', was drawn up in London and signed by 15,000 citizens. But it was not welcome to the leaders of parliament at this time, and 'friends in both Houses' advised the promoters of the petition to delay its presentation until they had completed the charge against the earl of Strafford (Lord-Deputy of Ireland), impeached the archbishop of Canterbury, and removed all the rest of the bishops from their places in the House of Lords by a charge of *praemunire* for the 'illegal canons' of May 1640. But the petitioners became impatient and would not wait very long.[26] On 11 December the petition was carried to the House of Commons by 'a world of honest citizens, in their best apparel', to the number of 1,200-1,500, who behaved 'in a very modest way', and were led by two aldermen. Some 300-400 of the 'better sort' crowded into Westminster Hall, and the petition was presented to the House of Commons by Isaac Pennington, one of the four MPs for the City.[27] Pennington, an alderman of London, was a substantial merchant trading in cloth through the Levant Company, and a prominent puritan of a more radical sort.[28] It was claimed that the petition was delivered without tumult or disorder, and that at a word from the House, the petitioners departed quietly to their homes, 'though many in number'.[29] But Sir Henry Vane the elder, Treasurer of the King's Household and Secretary of State, the chief government spokesman in the House of Commons, expressed himself 'scandalized that such a great number of the City came into Westminster Hall with the same petition', and he advised the House not to receive it because it 'struck at the alteration of those ecclesiastical matters which were established by parliament'.[30] There was a long debate and at length it was decided to receive the petition but to put off consideration of its demands.[31] On 16 December the canons of May 1640 were voted illegal, and on 18 December archbishop Laud was impeached; but still the House postponed consideration of the 'Root and Branch' petition, which was not discussed until 8 February 1641.[32]

Many members of parliament were critical of the bishops, but only a few advocated a change in the form of church government, and most wanted to retain episcopacy on a reformed basis, with some limitation of the powers of the bishops over the church and, more especially, with the removal of the bishops from political power and influence, by excluding them from the House of Lords and all secular offices.[33] At this time, in the early months of 1641, the earl of Bedford, the chief leader of the opposition to the Court, and his ally in the House of Commons, John Pym, were negotiating with the king for a settlement on the basis of the reform, rather than the abolition, of episcopacy. Apart from viscount Saye and lord Brooke in the Lords, and Nathaniel Fiennes (Saye's son) and Sir Henry Vane the younger in the Commons, the chief leaders of the opposition (the earls of Bedford, Essex and Warwick in the Lords, and John Pym, Denzil Holles and John Hampden in the Commons) were not at this time in favour of a change in the form of church government.[34] 'My lord Digby, the viscount Falkland, Sir Benjamin Rudyerd... did declaim most acutely, as we would have wished, against the corruptions of bishops', wrote Baillie, the Scots presbyterian minister; 'but their conclusion was, the keeping in of a limited episcopacy. Learned Selden, and a great faction in the House ran all their way'.[35] But some members did favour the abolition of episcopacy, and it was a divisive issue. The leaders of the opposition wished to evade it so as to maintain the unity of the broad alliance against Strafford, most members being more concerned to get on with his trial than to bring down the bishops.

The differences within parliament over church government, that were brought out into the open by the London 'Root and Branch' petition, were not as yet very serious because the leadership adopted the moderate line of reform, not abolition. But lord Digby focused attention on another issue that was beginning to divide the opposition to the crown, and to drive him and other critics of the government towards reconciliation with the king: that was the question of intervention by the people in the affairs of parliament, and pressure from the people upon parliament to adopt more radical policies. Digby thought that 'the manner of the delivery' of the 'Root and Branch' petition was 'a thing of the highest consequence'; 'I am confident, there is no man of judgement, that will think it fit for a parliament, under a monarchy, to give countenance to irregular, and tumultuous assemblies of people, be it for never so good an end: besides, there is no man of the least insight into nature, or history, but knows the danger, when either true or pretended stimulation, of conscience, hath once given a multitude agitation... For the bold part of this petition, Sir, what can there be of greater presumption, than for petitioners, not only to prescribe to a parliament, what, and how it shall do; but for a multitude to teach a parliament, what, and what is not, the government, according to God's Word.' He urged the House 'not to be led on by passion to popular and vulgar errors: it is natural... to the multitude to fly unto extremes, that seems ever the best to them, that is most opposite to the presentest object of their hate.' He claimed that he was 'as unbiased by popularity, as by any Court respects': 'had my fortune placed me near a king, I could not have flattered a king. And I do not intend now to flatter a multitude.' [36] Digby and others regarded 'the manner of bringing' the petition to parliament, accompanied by a crowd of people, as in itself sufficient grounds for rejecting it. Nathaniel Fiennes replied that the number of signatories to the petition and the number that came with it to Westminster, were not grounds for rejecting the petition, but rather for giving it serious consideration. 'For the first, it is alleged that the long tail of this blazing star, is ominous, and that such a number of petitioners, and such a number that brought the petition to the House, was irregular. Hereunto I answer, that the fault was either in the multitude of the petitioners, or in their carriages, and demeanours: if a multitude find themselves aggrieved, why it should be a fault in them to express their grievances more than in one, or a few, I cannot see; nay, to me it seems rather a reason that their petitions should be committed, and taken into serious consideration, for thereby they may receive satisfaction, though all be not granted that they desire. But if we shall throw their petition behind the door, and refuse to consider it, that it may seem an act of will in us. And whether an act of will in us, may not produce an act of will in the people, I leave it to your consideration. Sure I am, acts of will are more dangerous there than here, because usually they are more tumultuous. All laws are made, principally for the quiet and peace of a kingdom; and a law may be of such indifferent nature many times, that it is a good reason to alter it, only because a great number desires it, if there were nothing else in it, and therefore I do not see the number of petitioners is any good reason, why it should not be committed, but rather the contrary.'[37]

Obviously, Fiennes defended the petitioners because he agreed with their petition; but his speech showed that there were leaders in the parliament who were willing to encourage popular pressure on the Houses in support of their policies. It also became clear that there were some men of wealth and authority who were willing to associate themselves with popular movements. Alderman Pennington defended the petitioners against the allegation that they were 'mean rebellious' people, and insisted that they were 'men of worth and known integrity': 'If there were any mean men's hands to it, yet if they were honest men, there was no reason but these hands should be received... There was no course used to rake up hands, for... he might boldly say, if that course had been taken, instead of 15,000 hands they might have had fifteen times 15,000.' He defended the 'carriages and demeanours' of the petitioners: the petition was delivered 'without tumult, and then upon a word... they... departed quietly'.[38]

The debate on the 'Root and Branch' petition lasted from eight in the morning on 8 February until six at night, when it was adjourned to the next day. 'All that night our party', wrote one of the Scots, 'solicited as hard as they could.' The next day 'some thousands of citizens, but in a very peaceable way, went down to Westminster Hall to countenance their petition'. At length it was resolved to send the petition to the committee on church affairs, to which six members were added, including two opponents of episcopacy (after a vote with a majority of thirty-five in favour); but the committee was barred from considering the question whether episcopacy should be abolished or retained.[39] The committee reported in favour of the removal of the bishops from the House of Lords, and the exclusion of the clergy from secular offices; and on 10-11 March these proposals were approved by the House of Commons.[40] The leaders of parliament were anxious to divert the question of church government until the trial of Strafford had been carried through to a successful conclusion, and they hoped to appease the agitation against bishops with the bill to exclude them from the House of Lords.[41]

Strafford may have been more an object of hatred to his own class than to the common people;[42] and there are grounds for thinking that Laud was far more the target of popular hatred. The archbishop was taken to the Tower on 1 March 1641. Until then he had been in the custody of Black Rod, who tried to smuggle him unnoticed through the city in his coach, at noon when the citizens were at dinner: 'All was well, till I passed through Newgate shamble, and entered into Cheapside', related Laud: 'There some one prentice first hallooed out; more and [more] followed the coach, (the number still increasing as they went,) till by that time I came to the Exchange, the shouting was exceeding great. And so they followed me with clamour and revilings, even beyond barbarity itself; not giving over, till the coach was entered in at the Tower gate.'[43] The whipping up of hatred for Strafford rather than Laud in the following weeks was a diversion from the religious issues that stirred the mob, to the constitutional issues that interested the nobility and gentry.

Popular discontent, however, did come to focus upon the

trial of Strafford. Everything seemed to hang upon the outcome of the trial—hopes of all sorts of reforms, desires for a settlement of constitutional and ecclesiastical questions, and an end to the continuing state of crisis, so that life and business could run on normally again. The delays in bringing the earl to trial were highly frustrating. On 8 March the Venetian ambassador reported that the dispatch of the trial was 'impatiently demanded by the universal voice'. But the king was working hard on behalf of Strafford, who had many supporters in the House of Lords; there was doubt whether a conviction would be obtained and fear that if he were not found guilty 'the most serious disorders may occur'.[44] The trial began on 22 March but went badly for the prosecution. 'The Lords (excepting some few) are supposed to be his sure friends', wrote Sir John Coke the younger, a member of parliament: 'In the House of Commons he hath not any party considerable, some think about a hundred. To balance the Lords there is a petition preparing in the City with 20,000 or 30,000 hands subscribed... to demand justice against the earl of Strafford.'[45] This petition declared: 'At the first sitting of this parliament we hoped we should soon have our grievances removed and the incendiaries of the kingdom and oppressors of our liberties speedily condignly punished...; yet after five months sitting of the parliament we see none condignly punished, no man's estate confiscate, the earl of Strafford himself used with unusual favour, though charged by all three kingdoms, and whose life and our safety are, we conceive, incompatible, which cannot be but a great encouragement to the rest of the great incendiaries and other highly guilty offenders.'

This petition was evidently the work of the puritans of the capital, for they were angry not only at the failure to bring Strafford to speedy punishment, but also at the failure to carry through speedy reform of the church, complaining of 'the great affairs of the church sticking in debate and not yet determined'. Since they were told that religious reformation, and the redress of other grievances, had to wait until Strafford had been dealt with, they became desperate for a quick condemnation and execution of the earl. They feared that their enemies, the 'papists', were working to prevent reform of the church. They were alarmed that the laws against Roman Catholics were not put into vigorous execution, and 'papists still armed, some of the most active still resident at Court; the Irish popish army not yet disbanded... And we fear there are practices to put off all agitations that tend to reformation by them that desire to confound all things.' These, together with the delays in Strafford's trial and the allowing other guilty ministers to escape abroad, 'make us fear we now lie under a deeper and more dangerous plot than we can yet discover'.[46] On 10 April the king ordered the lord mayor of London to put a stop to this petition,[47] but on the same day the House of Commons responded to the mounting pressure from London by deciding to abandon the proceeding by impeachment, in which the Commons were the prosecutors and the Lords the judges, and to resort to the more drastic process of attainder, by which the earl would simply be declared guilty of treason and condemned to death by an Act of Parliament. Sir John Coke the younger, very conscious of the agitation in London, heard rumours that the Scots were collecting ships at Newcastle and proposing 'to transport their forces to London, where they have a very strong party amongst the discontented citizens; so that unless this earl be sacrificed to the public discontentment I see not what hopes we have of peace'.[48] The king was unable to stop the petition of the Londoners for the execution of justice against Strafford, and on 21 April it 'was brought down to the Commons by a great multitude of citizens, ten thousand it was said, led by three City captains in the trained bands, one of whom was the radical John Venn, soon to succeed Matthew Cradock as a Member for the city'.[49]

The commons were divided over the bill of attainder, and the leadership was split: lord Digby, who was already disturbed by the popular pressure on parliament for the abolition of episcopacy, and that some members were ready to use this pressure in support of their own minority views, was still more alarmed by the popular agitation for the execution of Strafford, and that many members seemed unwilling to resist popular demands. He opposed the bill at its third reading: 'Away with all flatteries to the people in being the sharper against him, because he is odious to them; away with all fears, lest in the sparing his blood they may be incensed'.[50] But, on the same day that the Londoners presented their petition, the bill passed the Commons by a majority of 204 to 59. 'Hereby you will perceive', Sir John Coke the younger wrote to his father, 'that near 200 were absent, a symptom of no great satisfaction';[51] which was no doubt not unconnected with an unwillingness to risk the unpopularity of voting for Strafford. Arthur Capel, MP for Hertfordshire and one of the wealthiest landowners in England, later regretted giving his vote against Strafford, and confessed 'that he had done it out of a base fear... of a prevailing party': 'truly it was unworthy cowardice, not to resist so great a torrent, as carried that business at that time'.[52] At the Exchange, and 'in many places in London and Westminster', including at the doors of parliament itself, placards were posted up bearing the legend 'Enemies of Justice, and Straffordians', containing a list of the names of the MPs who had voted against the attainder, 'who to save a traitor would betray their country', and concluding with the demand: 'That these and all other enemies of the Commonwealth should perish with Strafford.' 'And withal... some insolent painter did (seditiously) draw the pictures of the chief of them that were for saving the Lord Deputy, and calling them the Straffordians... hanged them with their heels upwards on the Exchange.' These members were subjected to abuse in the streets.[53] The list of the names was obtained from a puritan member of parliament, William Wheeler, a Londoner, though he represented a Wiltshire constituency.[54]

The bill of attainder was now sent to the House of Lords, together with the Londoners' petition for the execution of justice on the earl. 'Much depends upon the bill of attainder, which will hardly pass with the Lords, who are much divided thereupon... Things are near to a crisis I fear.'[55] On 1 May the king informed the Lords that his conscience would not permit him to consent to the death of the earl, but he would be willing to exclude him permanently from all offices. Reports of the king's intervention brought feeling in London to the point of explosion.[56] The next day, being a Sunday, 'from some pulpits it was preached to the people the necessity of justice upon some great delinquents now to be acted'.[57] Rumours flooded through the City: the leaders of the parliament knew that there had been talk at Court with some of the officers of the army about the possibility of the military marching on London to suppress the London mob and overawe the parliament; something of this had seeped through to the citizens, who heard it said that the king was going to the north to join the army 'and that the queen is to repair unto Portsmouth where Colonel Goring hath been fortifying these two months'.[58] It was known that the Commons were investigating reports of a plot to rescue Strafford from the Tower, and on Sunday night came the news that that morning Captain Billingsley had presented himself at the Tower with an order from the king to the Lieutenant of the Tower, Sir William Balfour, to admit him with a hundred soldiers, but Balfour refused; and Sir John Suckling, the courtier and poet, who was nearby at a tavern in Bread Street with sixty armed men, dismissed them with instructions to return the next evening.[59] This set in motion the demonstrations of the following two days.

Early on Monday morning, 3 May, crowds gathered at Westminster: they were estimated to number five, six, or seven thousand;[60] but Sir William Uvedale guessed ten thousand—'I speak within compass';[61] and Nehemiah Wallington wrote: 'it is to be thought that there were about fifteen thousand people, and I myself was there, and surely I never did see so many together in all my life'.[62] They made a lane through which the peers had to pass to get to their House and 'cried to every lord as they went out and in, in a loud and hideous voice, for justice against Strafford, and all traitors'. The cries for justice mingled with shouts of 'Execution', and the whole crowd took up the slogan 'Justice and Execution': 'they sent forth such hideous cries, as were enough to create amazement in persons of the greatest constancy'.[63] When the earl of Arundel, who as Lord Steward presided over the trial, approached in his coach, the shouting reached a crescendo and about a thousand people blocked his way. He called to them that 'they should have justice, if they would have patience'. They replied 'No, they had already had too much patience, longer we will not stay; and before you part from us, we will have a promise of execution.' Arundel said that 'he was going to the House for that purpose, and that he would endeavour to content them'. Some of the crowd cried 'We will take his word for once' and the rest fell back and let him pass.[64] The House of Lords sent to know the reason for this assembly of the people and were told that they wanted a reply to their petition of 21 April for the execution of justice on Strafford. The Lords immediately read the petition and called in six or ten of the citizens, led by Captain Venn, who 'spake for the rest', and told them that the peers were 'resolved to do in it that which shall be honourable and just; and that with all expedition', and desired them 'to depart to their own habitations'. But the crowds did not disperse and the king, 'who purposed to be at the House that morning, (his barge waiting at the privy-stairs to that end;) but by reason of the tumult did not come', sent a message to the Lords about 'the great tumult and concourse of people that do assemble together in these parts', desiring them to 'take into their consideration some speedy course to settle peace and prevent these tumults'. The Lords requested a conference with the Commons and then decided to adjourn.[65] Most of the lords went home by water, to avoid the crowds, but when the earl of Pembroke (the Lord Chamberlain), the earl of Holland and the earl of Bristol 'came out to take coach, they redoubled their cry, and coming up to the earl of Bristol's coach, some of them told him: "For you my lord of Bristol, we know you are an apostate from the cause of Christ, and our mortal enemy, we do not therefore crave justice from you, but shall shortly crave justice upon you, and your false son the lord Digby." '[66] But the earl of Pembroke was greeted with a huge shout for 'Justice'. He 'went out of his coach (some other of the lords being with him) and with his hat in his hand, prayed them to be quiet, and what lay in his power should be done, and he would likewise move his majesty, that justice might be executed according to their requests; and accordingly the Lord Chamberlain [Pembroke], and some other lords went to the king... and acquainted him with the citizens' complaints and desires, moving his majesty therein. And upon their return certified the citizens that his majesty had promised they should have speedy execution of justice to their desires'. And the other lords giving them 'good words', 'they rested well satisfied and went home'.[67] Pembroke was a supporter of the bill of attainder and the king regarded his action as 'countenancing of those tumultuous people'; but Whitelock praised him for giving the mob 'good words' and endeavouring 'to pacify them', which was 'the best way in popular tumults'; and indeed Pembroke succeeded in restoring order, which was more than the king, the lord mayor of London and the House of Lords had managed to do.[68] John Lilburne was one of the leaders of the crowd that day. When a bystander asked him why the people had assembled in such numbers, he replied that they came for justice; that there were six or seven thousand of them today but tomorrow there would be forty or fifty thousand; and that they came unarmed today but tomorrow they would bring their swords. He was asked what would be the end of the business and was alleged to have answered: 'If we have not the Lieutenant's life, we will have the king's.'[69] As the crowds dispersed they did 'boldly deliver themselves that tomorrow they will send their servants if they do not expedite justice speedily', and 'further threatened that after Wednesday they will shut their shops, and never rest from petitioning, till not only the Lieutenant's matter, but also all things else that concern a Reformation, be fully perfected'.[70]

Whitelock described the crowds as 'rabble';[71] Nalson called them 'porters, carmen and other dissolute and rude fellows';[72] but Baillie spoke of them as 'citizens and prentices'.[73] The more careful accounts, however, were agreed that the crowds comprised 'for the most part men of good fashion'; 'many of them captains of the City and men of eminent rank'; 'many thousand of the most substantial of the citizens'; 'citizens of very good account, some worth £30,000, some £40,000'.[74] The most prominent leader was John Venn. The son of a Somerset yeoman, he was a merchant-tailor of London, with a silk shop in Bread Street and a substantial trade in wool and silk with the West of England and Ireland. He was a wealthy man, but not one of the wealthiest in the City, for in his ward there were at least twenty-eight citizens richer than he. He was a puritan and churchwarden of All Hallows, Bread Street, which was a parish noted for puritanism. He was a prominent member of the Common Council of London, and was a captain of the London Artillery Company. He was elected a member of parliament for the City in June 1641 on the death of Matthew Cradock.[75] Not much less prominent, but more radical, and already with a following amongst the apprentices, the youth and the lower classes of London, was John Lilburne, the son of a Durham gentleman, who had been apprenticed to a London cloth-merchant. He was a radical puritan and had been imprisoned in 1638 for distributing the books of Bastwick, until released by the Long Parliament.[76] He was arrested for his speech to the crowd during this demonstration and brought before the House of Lords. He denied that 'he spake any such words as were alleged against him, but only spake them as words which were generally spoken of the multitude of people which came out of London, and told them only as news, which he heard reported abroad'. And the witnesses 'differing and disagreeing in their informations' he was discharged.[77]

The next day crowds gathered again at Westminster, but the well-to-do demonstrators of the previous day seem to have carried out their threat and sent their servants; for they were of a lower social rank, many of them being described as ordinary 'mechanic folk' from Southwark, and they came armed with 'swords and staves'.[78] 'These people press upon the Lords in a way unknown in the English government, or in any settled government in Christendom';[79] 'with great rudeness and insolence pressing upon and thrusting those lords whom they suspected not to favour that bill; professing aloud that "they would be governed and disposed by the honourable House of Commons, and would defend their privileges".'[80] The House of Lords complained to the Commons that while they were drawing to a conclusion with the bill of attainder, they 'were so encompassed with multitudes of people' that they 'might be conceived not to be free'. They desired the Commons to consider how to prevent this concourse of the people, which was hindering their proceedings. The Commons sent Cornelius Burgess, the prominent puritan preacher, to read to the crowd the Protestation which the two Houses had taken the day before. This was a pledge to oppose and bring to justice all who practised against the person, honour and estate of the king, or the power and privileges of parliament, or the lawful rights and liberties of the subject.[81] This gave the crowd 'some satisfaction' and he asked them to return to their homes. The Lords also desired them 'to repair to their dwellings, and within few days they should have further satisfaction in their desires'.[82] 'After repeated promises that they should have their will', reported the Venetian ambassador, 'they departed upon the condition that inside this week the Lieutenant should be condemned to death, otherwise they promise the most violent action.'[83]

The demonstrators did not immediately return to Westminster, but the situation remained very tense. 'I assure you things are grown to a great height here', wrote Sir William Uvedale, 'and almost every day we expect a commotion. Truly these unsettled times do much trouble me.' [84] It was panic, more than anger at delays in executing Strafford and reforming the church, that now gripped London. On 5 May Pym revealed to the Commons what he knew of the conversations between army officers, courtiers and the king about the possibility of intervention by the army on the king's side. It was believed that the French king was sending an army to Portsmouth to help the queen, his sister; that the army which Strafford had built up in Ireland was about to invade; that the papists in England were about to rise and seize power. [85] The state of fear was well illustrated on 19 May when debate in the Commons was interrupted by a loud crack. Sir John Wray called out that 'he smelt gunpowder' and cried 'Treason!' 'The gentlemen in the gallery most of them ran away into the committee chamber, where they drew their swords... All the gentlemen under the gallery in an amaze leaped down, and some fell one upon another'. Sir Edward Rodney and Thomas Earle fell heavily, the latter breaking his shin. Other members ran out of the House, including lord Cranborne, scattering the people waiting in the lobby, who fled through Westminster Hall. 'Old Sir Robert Mansell drew his sword, and bade them stand like true Englishmen, no man being able to report the cause of their fright; but no man stayed with him. But he advanced alone out of the Hall towards the House of Commons, with his sword drawn... Mr John Hotham met some of our House running away, and asked the cause; but they not telling it, pursuing their flight', he assumed that there had been some division in the House over ecclesiastical questions. But the people running from Westminster were shrieking that 'the parliament-house was falling, and the members slain'. The news ran through London 'that the papists had set the Lower House on fire, and had beset it with arms: in a clap all the city is in alarum; shops closed; a world of people in arms runs down to Westminster'. 'I, and abundance more out of the city, and other parts', wrote Nehemiah Wallington, 'went up thither with swords and other weapons'. But when they came there they found that it was a false alarm, and a regiment of the trained bands, which had marched as far as Covent Garden, turned back. The cause of the bang which so frightened the House had been discovered: a fat member leaning over between the gallery and the window to pick up a piece of paper, 'with his weight broke a few laths, which made a sudden noise'. 'It is very true', commented Sir Simonds D'Ewes, 'that this had been a great pussillanimity and weakness in such a great and honourable assembly as the House of Commons was, to have been affrighted at so small and trivial an accident; but the truth is, the late great treacherous design of the papists being not yet fully discovered to the House... we may be a little excused in our too deep apprehensions of the accident.'[86] On second thoughts the incident must have been reassuring, for it demonstrated the readiness of the citizens to rush to the defence of the House of Commons. In fear that the army intended to march on London, most members of parliament must have been most unwilling to discourage citizens who brought petitions and demonstrated at Westminster, seeing them as 'the only balance' to the army.[87]

On Saturday 8 May the House of Lords passed the bill of attainder against Strafford. 'Many who had appeared much for him absented themselves'; 'the greatest part of his friends absented themselves upon pretence, (whether true or suppositious) that they feared the multitude'; 'the lords and judges were much affrighted, and the most of his friends in the Lords have forsaken him, all the popish lords did absent themselves, the lord of Holland, and Hertford, were absent, so was Bristol, and others '.[88] It was widely believed that fear of the reaction of the London mob if they had voted down the attainder persuaded the Lords to let the bill through.[89] The Venetian ambassador thought that the Lords were 'unwilling to resist the people';[90] and Clarendon asserted that 'many lords grew so really apprehensive of having their brains beaten out that they absented themselves from the House, and others, finding what seconds the House of Commons was like to have to compass whatever they desired, changed their minds' and voted for the attainder.[91] But C H Firth argued that 'the reduction of the number of peers voting... was not due to fear of mob violence... The tumults took place on the third and fourth of May, and were practically over before the bill was considered in committee, or read for the third time.' This, however, is beside the point because it was the disorders that would follow the rejection of the bill that the lords had to consider. But Firth conceded that a few of the peers may have been influenced by the fear of mob violence.[92] S R Gardiner thought that 'the Catholic peers were in dread of their lives, and were excluded by their refusal to take the Protestation. Many of the other peers absented themselves when the votes were taken. Some of them may have been too timid to appear', but 'it is by no means likely that the peers as a body changed their mind through craven fear of mob violence.'[93] 'The real explanation', according to Firth, 'is the change in the political situation during the last few days of the bill. The implacability of the Commons—their absolute refusal to accept any compromise—was a fact which events had made clearer than it had been when the trial began. In the second place, the king, by showing an inclination to appeal to force against the parliament instead of confining himself to legal ways, had created a feeling of alarm and distrust which weakened the middle party. The necessity for an agreement between the two Houses, even at the cost of Strafford's life, became clear. The acceptance by the Lords of the bill against the dissolution of the existing parliament without its own consent was a sign of this.'[94] And Gardiner also thought that the decisive influence on the Lords was the revelation of the so-called Army Plot.[95] It is true that fear of army intervention, foreign invasion and 'popish plots' influenced the Lords and undermined Strafford's party. These factors also agitated the mobs that demonstrated at Westminster. But the issue that faced the peers was exactly the same as the one that the king was about to face: rejection of the bill of attainder was not just a matter of personal courage and willingness to face mob violence; the issue was more practical than that, and was whether the means existed to suppress the disorders that would be bound to follow the failure of the attainder. The queen's confessor, Father Philips, protested that if the king 'had but an ordinary spirit' he 'might easily quash and suppress these people'.[96] But the only force available to do that was the army and some at Court might argue that the king should dissolve the parliament and withdraw 'from that seditious city and put himself in the head of his own army'. The crucial fact, though, was that the king 'had no ground to be very confident of his army'.[97] The soundings of the officers in April had not been encouraging and the idea of intervention by the army had been abandoned before Pym revealed the 'army plot' to the House of Commons.[98] Indeed, as D'Ewes observed, the uncovering of the evidence of the plot meant that fears became less because the plot was seen to have failed and the army to be not so menacing.[99] In any case the danger from the army was more remote, but the danger from the London mob was more immediate. 'The tumults of sectaries, corner-creepers, and debauched hang-bys, that beset the dutiful Lords and Commons with poniards and clubs, were worse than an army far off... There is no equal temperature, or counterpoise of power against the strong ingredient of a multitude.'[100] If the peers as a body made any sort of realistic appraisal of the situation on 8 May, they must have concluded that there was no alternative to passing the attainder, because in face of the hostility of the London mob, seconded by the majority of the House of Commons, they did not have the power to resist the demand for Strafford's death.

The bill of attainder now lay with the king. On Saturday 8 May rumours spread through the city that the king had concluded a treaty with France to bring in a French army, and the citizens 'girded their arms and prepared to march to the palace to secure the royal persons. These on hearing the news and full of terror, made up their minds to leave this City without more ado.' But the French minister persuaded them to stay and the leaders of the people were assured that the rumours were false, and that the king would give his answer to the bill of attainder at ten o'clock on Monday morning. 'God knows the king is much dejected'. He 'passed the night in great anguish, the City being full of confusion and entirely under arms'.[101] The next day it was urged upon the king 'that no other expedient could be found to appease the enraged people, and that the consequences of a furious multitude would be very terrible'.[102] 'All day long nothing sounded in the king's ears, but fears, terrors, and threatenings of worse and worse, the noise of drums, and trumpets were imagined to be heard of rebelling people from every corner of the kingdom, yea apprentices, cobblers, and fruiterers, presented themselves as already running into the king's bedchamber'.[103] 'The king was so laid at, and so frighted with these bugbears, that if justice were not done, and the bill passed for the earl of Strafford's execution, the multitude would come the next day, and pull down Whitehall, (and God knows what might become of the king himself)'.[104] In London, 'most of the City made account to go up again and would have all our shops shut up, and so all to go up to Westminster with weapons, for to have justice executed on this traitor, the earl of Strafford', but they were persuaded to wait at home until the king gave his answer. This is clear evidence that there was leadership and organisation, as well as a political strategy, directing the London mob. However, not all accepted this leadership, and some did go to Whitehall.[105] At nine o'clock in the night of Sunday 9 May the king, in tears, announced to his privy council: 'If my own person only were in danger, I would gladly venture it to save lord Strafford's life; but seeing my wife, children, and all my kingdom are concerned in it, I am forced to give way unto it'.[106] His nephew, the Elector Palatine, wrote: 'the people stood upon it with such violence, that he would have put himself and his, in a great danger by denying execution'.[107]

On 12 May Strafford was beheaded 'amid universal rejoicing'.[108] The degree of tension that had built up in London during the previous weeks was shown by the release which the execution gave. 'And to show, how mad this whole people were, especially in and about this then bloody and brutish City', wrote an MP who had voted against the attainder, 'in the evening of the day, wherein he was executed, the greatest demonstrations of joy, that possibly could be expressed, ran through the whole town and counties hereabouts; and many, that came up to town on purpose to see the execution, rode in triumph back, waving their hats, and with all expression of joy, through every town they went crying, "His head is off", his head is off !" and in many places committing insolencies upon, and breaking the windows of those persons, who would not solemnise this festival with a bonfire. So ignorant and brutish is a multitude.'[109]

The aftermath of this popular triumph was intensification of the split in parliament. Not the law, not the parliament, not the king, had decided this issue, but the mob: it seemed that power had passed to the rabble in the streets. Some lords and gentlemen believed that parliament had been overawed by the mob; this became a major count in the future royalist indictment of the parliamentarians; but it was successful propaganda, for these lords and gentlemen became royalists precisely because they believed this. They were shocked that many peers and MPs were prepared to condone or acquiesce in attempts to influence votes in parliament by popular tumults, and to accept that it was a sufficient justification for an act that the people wanted it: they feared the consequence of this must be the abdication of the nobility and gentry and the rule of democracy, or rather anarchy. Worse still was the suspicion that some chief men in parliament, and their allies in the city, in order to force their own policies upon the Houses and the king, were actively encouraging and directing the mob. 'And it is not unlikely that some of the parliament-men did encourage them to this, as thinking that some backward members would be quickened by popular applause... Those that connived at them were glad to see the people of their own mind in the main, and thought it would do much to facilitate their work, and hold the looser members to their cause.'[110] Some officers of the army were troubled when 'they heard of great tumults about London', 'which seemed to threaten the safety of the members of both Houses, at least of those who were known not to agree with the designs' of the leaders; and they proposed that the army petition the king and both Houses and offer to restore order in the capital, which they hoped 'might confirm those, who might be shaken with any fears of power or force by the tumults'. The king approved this, and the draft of the petition: 'may it please your excellent majesty, and this High Court of Parliament, to give us leave with grief and anguish of heart, to represent unto you, that we hear that there are certain persons stirring and practical, who... remain yet as unsatisfied and mutinous as ever; who... are daily forging new and unreasonable demands'. They would have no influence in parliament, 'but that which begets the trouble and disquiet of our loyal hearts at this present, is, that we hear those ill-affected persons are backed in their violence by the multitude, and the power of raising tumults, that thousands flock at their call, and beset the parliament (and Whitehall itself) not only to the prejudice of that freedom which is necessary to great councils and judicatories, but possibly to some personal danger of your sacred majesty and peers. The vast consequence of those persons' malignity, and of the licentiousness of those multitudes that follow them, considered... our humble petition is, that in your wisdoms, you would be pleased to remove such dangers, by punishing the ring-leaders of these tumults, that your Majesty, and the parliament may be secured from such insolencies hereafter: for the suppressing of which, in all humility we offer ourselves to wait upon you (if you please)'.[111] This petition did not gain much support in the army and was quickly suppressed by the senior officers; but the views it expressed were not confined to a few officers and courtiers. When 'the Londoners petitioned for justice: and too great number of apprentices and others... did too triumphantly and disorderly urge the parliament, crying Justice, Justice', 'and honoured those members who were for the punishment of delinquents, and dishonoured those that pleased the king, a breach began to be made amongst themselves: and the lord Digby, the lord Falkland, and divers others, from that time forward joined with the king'.[112]

It is not very likely that the leaders of parliament were involved in organising popular tumults; all the hints of their involvement point to their influence being thrown on the side of restraint, as in trying to delay the petition against episcopacy, and in discouraging demonstrations while the king was making up his mind about the bill of attainder. The leaders would have been aware that for every member that might be overawed by popular tumults, another would be antagonised. Indeed the demonstrations against Strafford stimulated the formation of a royalist party. The question of the best form of church government, and the question of the justice of the proceedings against Strafford, were both controversial and divided the parliament; but these two separate questions were fused together by the fact that popular pressure was involved in both; and they were transcended by the question whether crowds should be prevented from gathering at Westminster and the leaders of tumults punished. The genesis of the royalist party arose from dislike of popular tumults: it was less the party of episcopalians or Straffordians than the party of order.

2

FEAR OF POPISH PLOTS AND THE RISE OF RELIGIOUS RADICALISM

THE AGITATION in London against episcopacy and against Strafford were closely interrelated and both were organised by the puritans of the capital. But the appearance of angry mobs at Westminster on 3 and 4 May had at least as much, if not more, to do with fear of popish plots. The petition that the Londoners presented to parliament on 21 April for justice 'on notorious offenders' said more about papists than about Strafford. The questions of Strafford and of the church were related to each other by the belief that the influence of the papists was responsible for the delays in both the trial of the one and the reform of the other.

Hatred of papists flared up frequently in London and the people took into their own hands the suppression of the mass. On 29 April 'a great many apprentices, and loose people' threatened to kill the Spanish ambassador and pull down his house in Bishopsgate. The lord mayor persuaded them to disperse, explaining to the ambassador that they 'were of the base and inferior sort of people', but they 'were discontented because mass was publicly said in his house' and English papists 'were permitted to frequent his house at mass, which was contrary to law'. The lord mayor set a guard on the house to protect the ambassador, but also to prevent English papists attending mass.[1] The Queen-Mother's house was another place where mass was said and English papists resorted. On 11 May she sent a message to the House of Lords: 'That, in regard of tumults of people that are dispersed abroad, and the report that some of them will come shortly into St James's Fields, the Queen-Mother desires that she may have a guard about St James's, for safety.' The earl of Holland, as lord lieutenant of Middlesex, ordered a hundred musketeers of the trained bands to her house, but he reported: 'I find great unwillingness in some of them to go; they thought fitter to do other things, than guard any stranger'. The Lords proposed that the king issue a proclamation taking her into his protection, and declaring that she should have a guard of the trained bands; but the Commons recommended that she leave England, fearing that 'they shall not be able to protect her from the violence of the people'. The Queen-Mother left England in August.[2] At the end of August about a hundred people threw stones at the French ambassador's house in Lincoln's Inn Fields.[3] Soon after there was a riot at the Portuguese ambassador's house, also in Lincoln's Inn Fields, when 'a great and disorderly tumult of people gathered together... in time of divine service' and tried to arrest English papists arriving for mass.[4]

All fears and anxieties were channelled into, and expressed by, anti-popery. On 10 August the king set out for Scotland with the scarcely concealed intention of trying to win support there against his opponents in England. A committee of the Lords and Commons accompanied him with the no more concealed intention of keeping a watch on his activities. On 9 September parliament adjourned, leaving a committee to manage affairs during the recess, and more especially to keep an eye on Scotland. On 12 October the earl of Argyle, the marquis of Hamilton and his brother the earl of Lanark fled from Edinburgh, declaring that their lives were threatened. When parliament reassembled on 20 October Pym informed the Commons that lord Almond was to have seized the three noblemen on a charge of treason, and probably killed them on the spot, and that the earl of Crawford and the earl of Roxburgh had forces prepared to seize Edinburgh and arrest or kill General Leslie, lord Loudoun, and 'all such other worthy instruments either of the nobility, gentry or commons as stood for the good of the church or commonwealth'. There was indeed a plot of a section of the Scots nobility to break the power of Argyle and Hamilton, and Charles was a party to it, but Argyle and Hamilton had advance warning and the plot was frustrated. 'The Incident', as this affair was called, might have had no more effect in England than as a further warning that the king was not to be trusted, and that he would try to regain the power that he had lost, by intrigue and force. But it had a greater effect as it snowballed into a torrent of suspicion and distrust not only of the king, but also of his councillors, the bishops, the episcopalian clergy, the House of Lords and those members of the House of Commons who supported the king. Pym at once associated the plot in Scotland with the plot in England to employ the army to overawe the parliament, which had been renewed since the execution of Strafford as the so-called 'Second Army Plot'. 'He feared the conspiracy went round and that there was a complicity in this new design both in Scotland and England'; 'the same actors against Hamilton, Argyle and Lanark are conceived to have hand in the bringing up the late army... this design was spoken of here before this plot was acted in Scotland'. Although the army had now been disbanded and was no longer a threat, Pym further associated both the Incident and the Second Army Plot with a more general popish plot. 'One of the chiefest actors' in the plot of Scotland 'was the earl of Crawford, a popish recusant; and... there is a great probability that the actors in it have correspondency here, to work the same horrid and malicious attempts'. 'He had been advertised at several times for the space of about ten days last past that there was some great and dangerous design plotting again here at home wherein he did now believe that there was a correspondence with those conspirators of Scotland and he feared that the design in England was to be put in execution this night or tomorrow morning upon the first meeting of the parliament'. 'Secret forces were ready in some places and secret meetings had been in Hampshire, by sundry great recusants, which might justly give us occasion to conceive that some wicked design were still in hatching.' At the request of the two Houses the earl of Essex, as commander of all the forces south of Trent during the absence of the king, placed a constant guard of a hundred men from the trained bands to defend parliament.[5]

At this very moment, on 1 November, the privy council informed parliament that the papists in Ireland had risen in rebellion and that the English and Protestants there were in great danger. 'When the express that brought the news was read in the House, it produced a general silence for a time, all men being struck with horror. When it was told without doors it flew like flashes of lightning, and spread universal terror over the whole kingdom. Every day, and almost every hour, produced new messengers of misery, who brought further intelligence of the merciless cruelty of the papists towards the poor protestants'.[6] The ground had been well prepared for at once linking this news from Ireland with the plots in England and Scotland. Owen O'Conolly, who gave advance warning of the rising to the government in Dublin, added in his report that the rebels had friends in England, amongst the king's councillors, amongst the bishops and amongst the aldermen of London: 'That the same would be done in England and Scotland this week or the last or this week and the next, but he well remembered not which.' Elizabeth Harding, widow, gave evidence to the House of Commons that a Captain Robert Steward that lodged with her in her house in St Martin's-le-Grand under the name of Robert Roberts 'said upon hearing of the Irish rebellion that the worst of the plot was not yet discovered there, and that the protestants' heels would go up apace'; and her testimony was confirmed by Mary Baker, widow. The Commons resolved 'that the persons of papists of quality, in the several counties of this kingdom where they reside, may be secured', and that the government of the Isle of Wight be taken from the earl of Portland, whose 'father, mother, and wife, were and are recusants; and... a sister of his married a recusant'. Recusants were disarmed in Hampshire and 'arms for about 300 horse and 1200 foot' were taken from the marquis of Winchester.[7] On 11 November a goldsmith named Baggstarre gave information to Sir Walter Earle that there were forty Irishmen in London apparently under the command of a Colonel FitzWilliams and being paid 12d a day, and it was feared that there was altogether 'a body of 1000 men in several places and might occasion us much danger'.[8] On 12 November the mayor and JPs of Colchester reported that a Mrs Payne, a papist dwelling in that town, was sending letters to Ireland and had arms in her house: the Commons ordered them to search the house, seize the arms and intercept her letters.[9]

The same day, Sir William Acton, an alderman of London, brought John Davis, servant of an inn at Ross in Herefordshire, to the House of Commons to relate the story that he had first told to the alderman's coachman. Davis was 'a plain country-fellow, and not able so fully to express himself', but the tale he told was that he had acted as guide to several gentlemen who had come to his inn and wanted to get to Raglan Castle, the seat of the earl of Worcester, a Roman Catholic. There a groom took Davis's horse to a stable where there were about sixty horses. Then the groom showed him a vault underground where he told him there were another forty horses, and another place underground where furniture for about 100 or 120 horses was kept, 'with great store of match and powder, and other ammunition belonging to war', enough 'for about 2000 men'. 'He told me', continued Davis, 'that his master the earl of Worcester, gave notice privately, that any man would be entertained, should have thirteen pence a day, good pay for him, in case they would be true to him... He told me that his master had at this time 700 men under pay.' Davis's story was published as a pamphlet, which ended with the query: 'Whether we have not as just cause to fear the papists in England, as they had in Ireland and Wales, and if they should once take a head, and be not prevented, what evil consequences may ensue thereof ?'[10]

On 15 November a young man named Thomas Beale came to the door of the House of Commons 'and sent in word that he had matters of a high nature to reveal'. He was a tailor and was probably out of work and in some sort of trouble with the law. Being without lodgings he had decided to spend the night in a ditch on Moor Fields, an open space to the north of the city which was a popular place for recreation. There, so he told the House of Commons, he overheard two gentlemen talking about a plot. 'There was 108 men appointed to kill 108 persons of the parliament, every one his man; some were lords, and the others were to be members of the House of Commons, all puritans'; 'those that were to kill the lords were brave gallants, in their scarlet-coats, and had received every man £10 a-piece'; those that were to kill the members of the House of Commons had 40s each, and 'Dick Jones was appointed to kill that rascally puritan Pym; and that four tradesmen, citizens, were to kill the puritan citizens that were parliament-men'. (It must have been some comfort to the parliament that the social hierarchy and the proprieties were preserved even in popish plots.) The assassinations were to take place during the night of 18 November, as the members were 'coming downstairs, or taking their coaches, or entering into their lodgings, or any other way as they should see opportunity'; and while London was in tumult, the papists were to rise in Buckinghamshire, Warwickshire, Worcestershire and Lancashire, and two 'other places he remembers not'. The object was to prevent the sending of forces from England against the Catholics in Ireland, 'because, if they prevailed there, they should not have cause to fear here'.[11]

The Commons 'then fell into debate touching the securing of the persons of some of the popish lords and other papists of eminency in the kingdom'. Members named the chief papists in Buckinghamshire, Warwickshire, Worcestershire, Lancashire and some other counties where papists were numerous, and who, it was said, 'do meet in some numbers and hold consultations'. Most of the Catholic peers were named and a list was drawn up of sixty-five papists that the Commons thought ought to be secured.[12] 'Dick Jones', a papist priest, was said to be in the earl of Worcester's house in London; another priest mentioned by Beale was said to frequent Sir Basil Brooke's house; and there were said to be 'very dangerous persons in the lord Petre's house in Aldersgate street'. These houses were searched but no priests or jesuits were found.[13] Lord Wharton reported a letter from lord Strange in Lancashire: 'That his lordship was upon his guard; that some in that county were stronger than he', and 'that if ever need was to look to Lancashire in our time, it is now'.[14] Sir Walter Earle had information that 'there were great fears conceived at Portsmouth: by reason a Frenchman of the Romish religion brought in there to be a surgeon to the garrison, and that a post went between Oatlands where the queen lay and Portsmouth several times weekly: that new fortifications were raised there next the land side especially, which did already command almost the whole town, and that brass ordnance was brought out of the ships to man the said fortifications: whilst in the meantime the works next the sea, which were to serve for defence against a foreign enemy were neglected and suffered to decay. That the papists and jovial clergymen thereabouts were merrier than ever, which made them fear that there was some new design in hand.'[15] A report was heard that the French had 30,000 men in Picardy and that 300 fishing boats were at hand that could transport 20,000 men.[16]

At Guildford in Surrey three separate fires started mysteriously in different parts of the town simultaneously, 'and it is thought it were papists did it, and had it not been for a good watch it had been set on fire again the next night'.[17] On 17 November there was 'a great uproar in Norwich concerning the papists arising there, they being intended to burn the whole city...two being appointed privily for the same purpose, one to begin at one end of the city, and the second at the other end, the one was discovered being about to set fire to a thatched house, the other he set the house on fire joining to High Bridge Street, which was burnt to the ground, to the great astonishment of the whole city, but now there is strong watching and warding in every corner of the city to prevent further danger'.[18] At Fingest in Buckinghamshire the watch seized 'a suspicious person... armed with pistols and divers knives'. He tore up some letters that he was carrying and confessed that he was a Roman Catholic and that he had been in Staffordshire, Warwickshire, Cheshire and Lancashire, but he insisted 'that he knew of no meetings of papists, nor of any conspiracy or designs against the king, state or parliament', and the torn papers when pieced together revealed nothing incriminating. Nevertheless he was lodged in Aylesbury gaol.[19]

On 17 November Pym told the Commons 'that some six papists were this night come out of Lancashire armed with pistols and swords and were all together in one house in London'. The next day, according to Beale's information, was to be the day of the assassinations and risings: that night, by order of parliament, the guards and watches were doubled in London and a great search was made in all places for 'papists' and 'suspected persons'.[20] 'We were in great fears here in the city among us of plots and treacheries, with papists and superstitious wretches', wrote Nehemiah Wallington, 'so that there were double watching and warding here among us; for there were many plots and designs discovered in the kingdoms.'

[21] Foreigners from Roman Catholic countries were the object of fear and hatred: French merchants in London found themselves 'being dragged along the streets to the justices of the peace, others having their houses broken open at midnight under pretence of searching for arms and gunpowder, and divers other insolencies they have endured, for no other reason but for being papists'. To the complaints of the French government, the English agent at Paris replied that 'these were the acts of the meaner sort of people, neither commanded nor avowed by any magistracy, and that in the distemper of these times it was scarce possible to prevent such disorders'.[22]

'The alarm of popish plots amuse and fright the people here, more than anything', Edward Nicholas, the acting Secretary of State, reported to the king.[23] 'There was nothing that with the people wrought so much, as the Irish massacre and rebellion... This filled all England with a fear both of the Irish, and of the papists at home... Insomuch, that when the rumour of a plot was occasioned at London, the poor people, all the counties over, were ready either to run to arms, or hide themselves, thinking that the papists were ready to rise and cut their throats.'[24] Sir Robert Harley, a member of the House of Commons, warned his wife at Brampton Bryan in Hereford-shire of the danger of a rising of the papists and told her to put the house in a state of defence. He also wrote to John Aston at Ludlow to 'look well to your town, for the papists are discovered to have a bloody design, in general, as well against this kingdom as elsewhere'. On the night of 19 November rumours spread through Herefordshire, Worcestershire and Shropshire that the papists had risen. 'At Brampton Bryan they were all in arms upon the top of Sir Robert's castle, and took up provisions thither with them, and in great fear'. It would seem that the panic spread from Brampton Bryan, which is in the northernmost parts of Herefordshire on the border with Shrop-shire, along the main road to the east as far as Kidderminster, on the way gripping Ludlow and then Bewdley, where it 'caused them all in the town to be up in arms, with watch all night in very great fear'. And so to Kidderminster; then it sped north to Bridgnorth, where the bailiffs and townsmen made a great fire in the high street, near the market cross, and kept watch all night, fortifying their courage with beer and mulled sack. In one night a rumour had been carried fifty-five miles. The next day, the fact that the rumour had proved to be false did little to reassure lady Harley, who reported to her husband: 'I have, according to your directions caused a good provision of bullets to be made and the pieces charged. There are no men in the house except Samuel and another. I do not propose this out of fear, but out of care for the children, whether you think it would be best for me and the children with no more servants than necessary to take a house in some town. I think Shrewsbury is the best to go to. If the papists should rise or there be any commotion, to me apprehension a town is safest... If we should be put to it, I do not believe we at Brampton should be able to stand siege'.[25]

When news of the rebellion in Ireland came to the West Riding of Yorkshire, followed by reports of the massacre of the protestants there, 'great fear came upon the protestants in England, these villains giving it out, that what they had done there was by the king's commission, and that in a little time the English protestants (or heretics as they called them) should drink of the same cup; and it was verily believed by many, it would be so'. One fast day when the puritans from Bradford were at Pudsey chapel hearing Elkana Wales preach, at about three o'clock in the afternoon, 'a certain man that I remember well (his name was John Sugden), came and stood up in the chapel door, and cried out with a lamentable voice, "Friends", said he, "we are all as good as dead men, for the Irish rebels are coming; they are come as far as Rochdale, and Littlebrough, and the Batings, and will be at Halifax and Bradford shortly"... And having given this alarm, away he ran towards Bradford again, where the same report was spread about. Upon which the congregation was all in confusion, some ran out, others wept, others fell to talking to friends... The Rev Mr Wales desired the congregation to compose themselves as well as they could, while he put himself and them into the hands of Almighty God by prayer, and so he did, and so dismissed us. But O what a sad and sorrowful going home had we that evening, for we must needs go to Bradford, and knew not but Incarnate Devils and Death would be there before us, and meet us there. What sad and strange conjectures, or rather conclusions, will surprise and fear make! Methinks I shall never forget this time. Well we got home, and found friends and neighbours in our case, and expecting the cut-throats coming. But at last some few horsemen were prevailed with to go to Halifax, to know how the case stood. They went with a great deal of fear, but found matters better when they came there, it proving only to be some protestants that were escaping out of Ireland for their lives into England; and this news we received with great joy, and spent the residue of that night in praises and thanksgivings to God.'[26]

Generally the upper classes were more sceptical about popish plots than the masses.[27] Sir Simonds D'Ewes doubted the truthfulness of Thomas Beale's revelations.[28] Lady Harley found that her son Edward did not share her fears and was 'so far from thinking of a place of safety that he does not think the papists have any strength, in which I think he is mistaken'.[29] Edward Nicholas thought that the people were easily frightened by reports of 'popish plots' 'and therefore that is the drum that is so frequently beaten upon all occasions' to excite prejudice against the king, and the government of church and state.[30] 'We charge the prelatical clergy with popery to make them odious, though we know they are guilty of no such thing', said John Selden;[31] and the same could be said of sticking the label 'papist' upon the king's lay advisers. Nevertheless, Nicholas' and Selden's suspicions were based upon the assumption that the people were hostile to papists and ready to believe that the bishops and the king's advisers were secret papists. The significance of the panic fear of popish plots was that it immediately increased the hostility towards the existing government in church and state. 'The noise of an intention to introduce popery', Nicholas told the king, 'was that which first brought into dislike with the people the government both of the church and commonwealth': 'I am confident that your majesty doth by this time clearly perceive, how it is here insinuated upon all occasions that popery (which is generally exceeding distasteful to your subjects of this kingdom) is too much favoured by your clergy here, and in your own Court, and that this opinion... hath and doth (more than anything) prejudice your majesty in the esteem and affection of your people'.[32] The puritan clothiers of the West Riding of Yorkshire went in fear of 'desperate, bloody' papists, and turned violently against the king when they heard that such men 'were put into offices and places of trust' about the king: 'King Charles the first... to say nothing of his own wicked disposition, did by the constant solicitation of the bloody queen, together with the swarms of jesuits and evil-affected councillors, bishops, and men of great estate, place, and trust, all put their heads together to destroy Christ's interest in the nation, and betray their trust every way to the utter ruin and overthrow of religion, and to cut off the lives of the protestants, and so have enslaved this land to Rome, the mother of harlots; whose kingdom is established by blood. These things being so plain to be seen, that he must be blind that did not see it'.[33] 'I confess I would not have the papists so powerful', wrote the countess of Sussex; 'the most of them I believe would be glad to see the protestants of England in as miserable a condition as they are in Ireland, if it was in their power to make them so.'[34] Even Sir Simonds D'Ewes, though more critical of rumours and tales of plots, declared that a large part of the clergy of the Church of England was engaged in a conspiracy to change the religion of England from protestant-ism to popery: 'let us but examine the true root and spring whence all these conspiracies do arise', he said of the Army Plots in England and the Incident in Scotland: 'and that is certainly from those wicked Linsey-Woolsey clergymen amongst us: they devour the fat and wealth of the church, correspond with the Romanists and discover the secrets of our state to foreign parts. These and the papists, falsely conceiving that to be truth which is not, desire to subvert the true religion professed amongst us, and this makes them venture their lives, estates, fortunes and all. The logicians say that the final cause is the first in intention though it be the last in execution: and so here let us but look to the ultimate end of all those conspiracies and we shall find them to be to subvert the truth which I am confident the papists would never have hope of were they not assured of a party they have in our church'.[35]

The fear of papists did not arise from the existence of known recusants but from the belief in the existence of unknown numbers of secret catholics and sympathizers with catholicism. More than that, all who resisted the demands for reform of the church and religion in a more protestant direction were suspected of being papists. Since there was so much resistance to these demands from the king and his advisers, and amongst courtiers, bishops and the chief clergy, peers and the leading gentry, and prominent merchants, it followed that the papists must have influence and a secret party at Court, amongst the king's councillors and the heads of the church, in the House of Lords, even in the House of Commons and amongst the chief officers of towns and cities. Since it was these same people and groups who also opposed the demand for new advisers and councillors to be imposed on the king, it further followed that the opponents of this political demand were also suspected of being papists or under papist influence. So, what made popular prejudice against papists stronger, politically more effective and socially more dangerous, was its association and fusion with prejudice against the king's government in church and state, against the men in power, and against large sections of the governing class itself—'men of great estate, place, and trust'.

The puritans and radical protestants were animated by hatred of popery and fear of papists, and the fact that they were regarded as the firmest opponents of popery and the scourge of papists, meant that the intensification of popular fear of popery and papists led to a flow of popular sympathy and support towards the puritans, and favoured especially the spread of the most radical protestantism, which was the most fiercely anti-papist.

With the meeting of the Long Parliament puritans and radical protestants came out into the open: puritans were able to preach publicly again, to gain adherents, and to organise pressure for the reform of the church; the more radical protestants no longer had to meet in secret, but held their assemblies openly, propagated their doctrines and won converts to a more fundamental reformation of religion. Nehemiah Wallington, the puritan turner of Little Eastcheap in London, called 1641 'a great praying year'.[36] 'The godly here', reported Robert Baillie from London on 29 January 1641, 'in great numbers, meets oft in private houses, for in public they dare not, fasts and prays, and hear sermons, for whole days, sundry times in the week.'[37] But increasingly the puritans openly met in private houses for days of fasting and prayer without fear of being prosecuted for holding conventicles. 'I think most days of this parliament time there have been private meetings in fasting and prayer and thanksgiving, for I have been at many places, and at some places there have been hundreds and some persons of no small account, for there have been coaches at the door of them. On Whitsun Tuesday, being the 14th of May, I heard of four or five great meetings of God's people in humiliation, and fasting, and prayer. And many youths and apprentices did meet at Dyers' Hall in fasting and prayer on that day. And, as some do think, there were five hundred of them, and six able ministers with them to go through the day in the performance of duties with them. And some of them did continue till ten o'clock at night.' [38]

Puritans and radical protestants looked to parliament for the reform of religion, and so they necessarily became involved with politics and political questions, and concerned about the divisions in parliament which delayed decisions on religion and about threats to the continued existence of parliament. The puritans and radical protestants, in both London and the provinces, followed the proceedings of parliament closely, and the debates on ecclesiastical questions were marked by prayer-meetings in private houses to seek god's guidance for parliament. 'We at Brampton keep the day to show to our God for his direction of the parliament', wrote lady Harley from Herefordshire in January 1641 when she heard that the Commons were to debate about bishops: 'I believe that hierarchy must down, and I hope now.' [39] At Bradford in Yorkshire the puritan clothiers held prayer-meetings in their houses to seek god's help in persuading parliament to reform the church. Joseph Lister was a boy at the time but later he remembered those meetings at his mother's house during the critical days of the Long Parliament: 'O what fasting and praying, publicly and privately, what wrestling with God was there day and night. Many of those weeping, praying, and wrestling seasons, both day and night, were kept in my dear mother's house, and the fasts were kept with great strictness and severity; not any of us, old or young, eating so much as a morsel of bread for twenty-four hours together; which was a great weariness to me, and went much against my carnal heart, (fool and wretch that I was) with shame and grief would I think of it.' [40] Oliver Heywood similarly remembered the meetings for prayer, fasting and conference held at this time by his father, a clothier of Bolton in Lancashire, and other puritans: 'I remember a whole night wherein he, Dr Bradsha, Adam Ferniside, Thomas Crompton and several more excellent men did pray all night in a parlour at Ralph Whittels, as I remember upon occasion of King Charles I demanding the five members of the House of Commons, such a night of prayers, tears, groans as I was never present at in all my life: the case was extraordinary, and the work was extraordinary.'[41]

Clarendon noted that the puritans 'were not at all satisfied' with the leaders of the parliament 'for their want of zeal in the matters of religion'.[42] They became increasingly impatient with the failure of their moderate leaders in parliament and in the church to secure reforms, and tended to turn towards the more radical protestants. Most of the puritans continued to attend their parish churches, hoping that parliament would eventually remove the practices to which they objected, but increasingly some got tired of waiting and joined the more radical protestants in taking direct action against the things which offended them. At St Margaret's, Westminster, on the day of the public fast, proclaimed by parliament, 'the minister officiating the second service at the Communion Table, according to the ancient custom, was unexpectedly interrupted by the naming and singing of a psalm'.[43] Baillie reported that 'in divers churches, the people raised psalms to sing out the service'.[44] 'And in many churches have some members of their private authority forbid the priests to read divine service, others in contempt thereof put on their hats during the reading of prayers, which gave such encouragement to the rabble rout of that faction in the City, that in divers churches unheard of violences were offered to ministers officiating in full congregations by a few sectaries, yet scarce durst any man either rescue the minister, or defend their own religion; and it's too well known how a few... young fellows with their wenches rushing into any church in London could have set up a psalm, and thereby sing a whole parish out of their religion... into such a lukewarmness were most men grown towards God's service'.[45] At a City church 'a good number' of godly people 'in time of divine service came into the church, and did tear the book of Common Prayer, and [committed] some misdemeanours against the minister'.[46] At Halstead, one of the puritan cloth-manufacturing towns in Essex, during divine service in the parish church, as the curate was about to baptise a child, a group of men and women struck the prayer-book from his hand and kicked it about the church, saying that it was a 'popish book'. They forced the clerk to give them the surplice and hood, which they 'rent in pieces'. The constable of the town arrested the ring-leaders but they 'were immediately rescued by a multitude of people', and it required the intervention of the lords lieutenant of the county to secure the eight chief offenders, who were brought before the House of Lords and admonished to behave in future and to make submission in the church.[47] At Chelmsford, also in Essex, 'a young clothier with others' at the end of divine service tried to tear the surplice from the back of the minister.[48] On Sunday 8 May at St Olave's church in the Old Jewry, London, the lord mayor and some members of parliament being in the congregation, as the bishop went up into the pulpit 'in his lawn sleeves and other vestments suitable to a prelate', a hundred 'rude rascals' began to shout 'A Pope, a Pope, a Pope'. They were thrust out of the church by the lord mayor's officers, and in the street they shouted that the people in the church were at mass and the lord mayor was a papist, and they broke the windows of the church.[49] The king complained to parliament that divine service was being 'irreverently interrupted',[50] and an MP, William Pleydell, raised the matter of 'irreverence in churches' and 'profanation of God's service' in a speech to the House of Commons.[51] On 16 January 1641 the House of Lords made an Order: 'That the Divine Service be performed as it is appointed by the Acts of Parliament of this realm; and that all such as shall disturb that wholesome order shall be severely punished, according to law; and that the parsons, vicars, and curates, in several parishes, shall forbear to introduce any rites or ceremonies that may give offence, otherwise than those which are established by the laws of the land.'[52] This Order was renewed in April when the Lords received reports of disorders in several churches in Cheshire and disturbance of divine service.[53]

On 29 January 1641 Baillie reported that in some churches the people 'pulled down the rails before the altars'.[54]

And on 1 March the Lords ordered that the communion table should stand in the position it had been for the past sixty years, before the recent innovations,[55] which did not settle the question whether it should be railed around. In June the rails were violently pulled down from about the altar at St Saviour's church in Southwark. Those responsible were brought before the Lords and condemned to make public acknowledgement of their fault in the church on Sunday, to pay for the erection of new rails, and to be imprisoned during the pleasure of the House. On 19 July they were released from prison and on the plea of poverty they were relieved from paying for new rails.[56]

The churchwardens of St Olave's church in Southwark, anticipating similar trouble there, because hundreds of the parishioners refused to come to the communion because of the rails round the altar; and being unable to persuade the minister to agree to their removal, they took the matter into their own hands, took down and sold the rails, putting the proceeds into the parish funds. The minister and his supporters in the parish initiated a prosecution against the churchwardens. Then, when the curate was administering the communion to the people kneeling, there was a violent uproar from another section of the congregation, demanding to receive the communion sitting, and threatening to drag the curate about the church by his ears if he did not comply. Four of the offenders were brought before the Lords, who sent them to prison for six months, fined them £20, and ordered them to make public acknowledgement of their fault. But on 22 July the Lords released two of them, who petitioned that they were poor watermen: they had made public acknowledgement of their fault on the high stool in Cheapside and Southwark on market day, served six weeks of their sentence, but could not afford to pay the fine and would be ruined if they remained in prison.[57]

On 11 June at the church of St Thomas the Apostle, in Vintry ward of the City of London, John Blackwell, the king's grocer, and 'some youths' pulled down the rails round the communion table and burnt them outside the church. They struck the churchwardens who tried to interfere, and threatened that if the minister came to read the service in his surplice, they would burn his surplice with him in it. The minister, churchwardens and some of the parishioners complained to the House of Lords; but Blackwell, one churchwarden and another group of the parishioners petitioned the House of Commons, saying that the rails had been set up only three years before and had caused great offence. The Lords sent for Blackwell and his companions but they refused to appear on the grounds that the case was under the cognisance of the House of Commons. The Lords then asked lord Seymour to mediate between the two factions in the congregation, and he succeeded in composing the differences, though on what terms does not appear.[58] The disparity between the treatment of the poor watermen of Southwark and the king's grocer is marked.

In September the Commons ordered churchwardens to remove the communion table from the east end of the church and take away the rails, to remove all crucifixes, all pictures of any of the persons of the Trinity, all images of the Virgin Mary, and all tapers, candlesticks, basins from the communion table. They also ordered that bowing at the name of Jesus be forborne, and that the Lord's Day be observed and all sports and dancing banned on that day.[59] The Lords agreed that rails round the communion table should be taken away, but did not agree that the table must be removed from the east end of the church; they agreed that crucifixes, pictures of any member of the Trinity and the Virgin Mary, should be removed, but they did not agree that bowing at the name of Jesus should be prohibited. The Commons therefore issued the orders on their own authority, and the Lords repeated their order of January 'that the divine service be performed as it is appointed by the Acts of Parliament of this realm: and that all such as shall disturb that wholesome order shall be severely punished'. The Commons would not agree to this order, on the grounds that it was 'unseasonable, at this time, to urge the severe execution of the said laws', and so the Lords issued the order on their own authority. The Commons in reply issued a declaration that they had received many complaints of excessive pressing of matters concerning religion 'which are, in their own nature, indifferent, by pretext or colour of the laws now in force; and by the unlawful enforcing other things, without colour of law'. 'A full reformation cannot be made in this strait of time' and they desired the people 'in the meantime' to 'quietly attend the reformation intended, without any tumultuous disturbance of the worship of God and peace of the kingdom'.[60] The two Houses were not only divided from each other, but each House was split within itself, over these questions: their disagreements reflected the differences in the country at large.

At St George's in Southwark one of the churchwardens and some of the parishioners opposed the taking down of the rails round the communion table and set them up again, and the other faction in the parish took them down again. At St Giles in the Fields the minister resisted the removal of the rails and the transference of the communion table from the east end. At St Giles Cripplegate the minister, curate, one of the churchwardens and a party of the parishioners opposed the pulling down of the rails and the setting up of a puritan lectureship.[61] Sir Robert Harley complained to the churchwardens of Leominster that there was still a crucifix on the stone cross in the churchyard, another over the church porch, two in the glass of the great west window, as well as pictures of persons of the Trinity and another crucifix in the glass of the great east window: 'all which I do require you to abolish, according to the order of the House of Commons'.[62] In the church near John Hutchinson's house in Nottinghamshire there was a crucifix in the window over the altar, a picture of the Virgin Mary, 'and sundry other superstitious paintings... drawn upon the walls'. The minister took down only the heads of the images 'and laid them carefully up in his closet, and would have had the church officers to have certified that the thing was done according to order; whereupon they came to Mr Hutchinson, and desired him that he would take pains to come and view their church, which he did, and upon discourse with the parson, persuaded him to blot out all the superstitious paintings, and break the images in the glass'.[63]

At Kidderminster the judgement of the minister, Richard Baxter, 'was for obeying of this order, thinking it came from just authority; but I meddled not in it, but left the churchwarden to do what he thought good'. The churchwarden went to take down a crucifix on the cross in the churchyard, but 'a crew of the drunken riotous party of the town (poor journeymen and servants)...run altogether with weapons to defend the crucifix, and the church images... The report was among them, that I was the actor, and it was me they sought; but I was walking about a mile out of town... When they missed me and the churchwarden both, they went raving about the streets to seek us... When they had foamed about half an hour, and met with none of us, and were newly housed, I came in from my walk... hearing the people cursing me in their doors'.[64]

But where the puritans were strong, the order of the Commons loosed an outburst of iconoclasm during the autumn of 1641, which provided the militants with a release from the burden of the past and an assurance that they were about to enter a new era. But although they had the authority of the House of Commons for what they did, and the support of some squires, some ministers, and some men of substance in the congregations, the rest of the population was shocked at the destruction of familiar and revered symbols. Thomas Wiseman wrote to Sir John Pennington on 7 October deploring the 'havoc in our churches by pulling down ancient monuments, glass windows, and rails'.[65] 'On the beginning of October, 1641, at Leonard's Eastcheap, being our church', wrote Wallington, 'the idol in the wall was cut down, and the superstitious pictures in the glass was broken in pieces, and the superstitious things and prayers for the dead in brass picked up, and broken, and the pictures of the Virgin Mary on the branches of candlesticks was broken.'[66] One of the churchwardens of Woolchurch in London was reprimanded by the Commons for exceeding their orders in taking up brass inscriptions and breaking statues on tombs.[67] At Chelmsford in Essex the churchwardens removed pictures of the Virgin and Child from the east window, but on 1 November 'in the evening, all the sectaries assemble together, and in a riotous manner with long poles and stones beat down and deface the whole window', which showed the history of Christ from conception to ascension, and also contained 'the escutcheons and arms of the ancient nobility and gentry, who had contributed to the building and beautifying' the church.[68] Wallington carefully kept some of the broken glass from his church 'for a remembrance to show to the generation to come what God hath done for us, to give us such a reformation that our forefathers never saw the like'.[69]

Puritan members of parliament and puritan ministers were under pressure from their more militant followers. 'The headiness and rashness of the younger unexperienced sort of religious people, made many parliament men and ministers overgo themselves, to keep pace with those hotspurs'.[70] The pace was set by the most radical protestants—the separatists—who utterly rejected the established church. When the Long Parliament first met the number of separatists was small. 'The remnant of the old Separatists and Anabaptists in London was then very small, and scarce considerable', wrote a puritan minister, 'but they were enough to stir up the younger and unexperienced sort of religious people, to speak too vehemently and intemperately against the bishops and the church and ceremonies, and to jeer and deride at the Common Prayer, and all that was against their minds'. 'No doubt but much indiscretion appeared... and much sin was committed... in the uncivil language against the bishops and liturgy of the church: but these things came principally from the sectarian separating spirit, which blew the coals among foolish apprentices... I have myself been in London, when they have on the Lord's Day stood at the church doors while the Common Prayer was reading, saying, "We must stay till he is out of his pottage." And such unchristian scorns and jests did please inconsiderate wits'.[71]

The radical protestants withdrew from the services in their parish churches and attended conventicles in private houses, because 'the liturgy, discipline, government, rites, and ceremonies of the Church of England, are all of them so many branches of popery'. In the first place, the prayer-book of the Church of England was merely 'translated out of the Romish Latin Liturgy', and was 'a service of men's devising' not god's. In the second place, there was no proper discipline in the Church of England: the 'ignorant and profane' were not excluded from the sacrament of the Lord's Supper, and people were not submitted to an examination of their lives and knowledge before being deemed worthy to receive the communion: 'if God's ordinances be profaned (as they are by profane and ignorant persons coming to the Lord's Table) then others also that communicate with them are guilty of the same profanation of them': 'To communicate with known evil doers... is to partake of their evil deeds.' And in the third place, the Church of England was governed by 'archbishops, bishops, archdeacons, deans, commissaries, officials, and the rest of that fraternity: if this be not popery, yea and a top-branch of it, I know not what is. Sure we are, not one of all this rabble is found to be in the Scripture; and therefore of divine institution this government is not'.[72] Many radical puritans would return to their parish churches when the services were purged of popish survivals, episcopacy abolished, ignorant and profane persons excluded from the Lord's Supper, and a proper test of worthiness to receive the sacrament imposed. But besides these, there were complete separatists who believed that the godly should separate themselves entirely from the ungodly, that the true church consisted only of the saints, and that a national church, whether episcopalian or presbyterian, that included the whole population, could not be a true church because it was bound to contain the ignorant and profane as well as the informed and holy. It was impossible, in the opinion of the separatists, to constitute a national church agreeable 'to a true and visible Congregation of Christ. For a particular church or congregation rightly collected and constituted, consists of none, but such as are visible living Members of Christ the head, and visible Saints under him, the one and only King of Saints: but so it is not with a National Church, all the members thereof are not visible Saints, or visible living Members, wherein the greatest part of a nation commonly is found to consist of persons either ignorant or profane'. In the separate church 'none are admitted members of the congregation, but such as are approved of by the whole assembly, for their profession and conversation, as against which there is no just exception'; and 'none are admitted members thereof but such as are both willing and desirous, and do freely enter into Covenant to observe all the conditions and orders thereof according to God's Word'.[73]

So long as the Church of England remained unreformed godly puritans were under great pressure and temptation to reject the national church with all its 'popish' ways entirely and join a separatist congregation; that is why reform became a matter of such desperate urgency to the orthodox puritan leaders who wished to preserve a national and parochial church system, for with every delay their followers drifted towards separation. To the intensely religious the idea of dissociating wholly from the wicked was attractive and drew them towards the separating sects.

During 1641 the separatists increased dramatically in numbers and influence. At Bristol in 1640 a small group of puritans—including a farmer, a butcher and a farrier—decided to separate from the Church of England. Soon their number grew to 160, and by August 1641 there were several separatist congregations in the city.[74] 'Conventicles every night in Norwich', reported Thomas Knyvett on 17 January 1641, 'as publicly known as the sermons in the daytime, and they say much more frequented.'[75] It was related that at Chelmsford in Essex (a parish of 2,000 communicants) since the meeting of the parliament, 'this town... is so filled with sectaries, especially Brownists and Anabaptists' that one-third of the congregation refused to communicate 'in the Church-Liturgy', and half refused to receive the sacrament kneeling.[76] 'The Brownists are very busy in meetings', Thomas Harley wrote from Herefordshire on 29 January 1641;[77] and Katharine Wilkinson explained to Edward Harley: 'I know you have been told of the meeting that was accounted a conventicle; if there had been a let some would have found it so by the punishment that would have been inflicted. But yet nothing is done to any of them, but some great ones advise their friends to take heed that they venture no more to such kind of meetings.'[78]

A separatist congregation, which had led a secret existence in Southwark since 1621 and had a cobbler, Samuel Howe, as its minister until his death in 1640, came out into the open in January 1641. On a Sunday afternoon, at the time of divine service, the constables and churchwardens of St Saviour's parish in Southwark entered the house where they were meeting and found more than sixty persons who 'said they met to teach and edify one another in Christ'. They were taken before Sir John Lenthall, who asked them why they would not go to their parish church as required by the law of *35 Eliz.* They replied 'that the law of *35 Eliz* was not a true law, for it was made by the bishops; and that they would not obey it'; 'that they would not go to their parish churches: that those churches were not true churches; and that there was no true church but where the faithful met'. The king referred this matter to the House of Lords, which examined the separatists and ordered them to attend their parish churches in future; but they did not obey and continued to maintain their separate church without concealment.[79] There were other established congregations of separatists in London and its suburbs, that until this time had met secretly. They were mostly offshoots of the separate church that Henry Jacob had set up in London in 1616. One of these was meeting in the house of a Mr Porter in Goat Alley off Whitecross Street, and Richard Rogers, a glover, was preaching, in August 1641, when they were raided and the chief of them apprehended and committed to prison. But after their release they continued to meet as before.[80] Hostility came not only from the authorities. Praise-God Barebone, a leather-seller in Fleet Street, led a well-established separatist congregation. On 19 December he was preaching in his house to a hundred or a hundred and fifty people, 'as many women as men', when a hostile crowd gathered outside and began to break the windows. A constable came and arrested some of the separatists, but order was not fully restored until the lord mayor and sheriffs arrived.[81] A tract listed seventeen separatist congregations in London and its suburbs in 1641, and there were certainly others.[82] Bishop Hall told the House of Lords that there were eighty congregations of separatists in the capital and its environs.[83] It was essentially a movement of urban artisans.

The manner of the separatists' meetings was described as follows: they came in twos and threes; one man kept the door to warn the others if any came against them; the man appointed to teach stood in the middle of the room, while the congregation gathered around him; he prayed for half-an-hour and then preached for about an hour. Their preachers said 'that the Book of Common Prayer had its first original from the Mass'; 'that the bishops' function is an Antichristian calling... none of these bishops... but hath a Pope in their bellies, yea they are Papists in grain'; that they have separated from a profane church where idols are worshipped and copes and surplices are worn; that wherever they meet is the church of God, and not the parish churches where 'good and bad come both hither'; and that it is not lawful 'to have any society with the wicked'.[84] These separatists did not believe in an ordained priesthood but chose a gifted layman to lead them, who was maintained partly by the voluntary contributions of his flock and partly by continuing to work at his secular occupation. 'An orthodox and lawfully called, and allowed minister is not minded amongst them; for they hold it as lawful for artificers, and laymen, to preach in public, and those that are most inferior, as cobblers, weavers, leather-sellers, box-makers, ironmongers, felt-makers, and such mechanic fellows.' [85] Bishop Hall complained to the House of Lords of preaching by cobblers, tailors, felt-makers 'and such like trash'.[86] Denzil Holles complained to the House of Commons of certain 'mechanical men' who were preaching in London, 'as if, instead of suppressing popery', the Houses 'intend to bring in atheism and confusion'.

In June 1641 the Commons sent for a number of these lay preachers and when three of them appeared 'Mr Speaker gave them a sharp reprehension, and a general distaste of this House, of their proceedings, and that, if they should offend at any time in the like again, this House would take care they should be severely punished'.[87] Chief among them were 'the two Arch-Separatists, Greene and Spencer, both which are accounted as Demi-Gods' by their many followers. John Greene was a hatmaker or feltmaker by trade, and John Spencer was a coachman or horseman, 'having been a servingman, a porter, a groom to a stable, a chandler, a weaver, yea more, of as many trades almost as religions'. Other lay preachers were Nathaniel Robinson, a clerk in the customs-house; Adam Bankes, 'lately a seller of stockings, and now a shopkeeper near the Old Exchange'; 'Quartermine the brewer's clerk'; 'Marler, a button-maker'; Jonas Hawkins, a fisherman; as well as Richard Rogers the glover and Praise-God Barebone the leather-seller.[88] 'It is not the custom', protested a critic of the separatists, 'of any well settled church in Europe to ordain such as you, I mean hat-makers, cobblers, tailors, horsekeepers, upon one and the same day to be plank and the pulpit, in the forenoon making a hat, or rubbing a horse, in the afternoon preaching a sermon.' 'God... doth furnish our church plentifully with learned men' and does not need 'such as you to preach the Gospel'. 'I tell you I am angry with you, my very purse feels it, it is your enticing to conventicles and private meetings that makes men and women to neglect their callings and trades two or three days a week to follow your heels; and though they do not follow you so oft, yet they spend away that precious time that they should work for themselves and families... to prate your doctrines, and to set other upon admiring what strange gifts and abilities you have given to God.'[89] Even more shocking, there were women preachers—two in London (one the wife of a bricklayer), two in Kent, one in Cambridgeshire and one in Wiltshire.[90]

> *When Women Preach, and Cobblers Pray*
> *The Fiends in Hell, make holiday*[91]

Despite the occasional arrests, persecution of the separatists virtually ceased in 1641. It was recorded of the congregation in Southwark that until then they 'were much harassed... by their enemies, and were forced to meet together in fields and woods to avoid them', but in 1641 'their case was altered for the better, and they who used to be avoided, and who were hardly reckoned among men, but looked on as a kind of wild creatures, and greatly persecuted, met with some respite of peace'; and after their arrest and appearance before the Lords in January 1641, they had no further interruption given to them.[92] Increasingly the separatists shed their secrecy and preached and worshipped openly, gaining many converts. Greene and Spencer were said to have 'called an assembly upon Tuesday being the 28 of September in Houndsditch'.[93] On 12 December a great assembly of separatists in Southwark listened to a sermon by a cobbler.[94] A petition from Huntingdonshire complained of 'the great increase of late of schismatics and sectaries, and of persons not only separating and sequestering themselves from the public assembly at Common Prayers and Divine Service, but also opposing, and tumultuously interrupting others in the performance thereof in the public congregation; the frequent and many conventicles held amongst them, and their often meetings at all public conventions of assizes, sessions, fairs, markets, and other public assemblies, their earnest labouring to solicit and draw people to them, and the general correspondence held amongst them to advance their ends herein'.[95]

The disorders in the churches were attributed to the separatists: 'hence come those violent outrages, and sacrilegious disorders committed in the church, even in the time of divine service, and hubbubs and strange tumults raised, where nothing but reverent silence ought to be used, by laying violent hands upon the minister, rending his Master of Arts hood from his neck, and tearing the surplice to tatters upon his back, he hardly escaping from being torn piecemeal in his own person, and this even when the psalm was singing, and the preacher ready to go up to deliver his sermon, as likewise rending the rails from before the communion table, and then chopping them in pieces, and burning them in the churchyard, and this to be riotously done without authority, commission, or order'.[96] 'The Brownists and other sectaries', complained Thomas Wiseman, 'make such havoc in our churches by pulling down ancient monuments, glass windows, and rails, that their madness is intolerable.'[97] It was held that the separatists 'stirred up the apprentices to join them in petitions, and to go in great numbers to Westminster to present them', and to demonstrate against bishops.[98]

The liberty and *de facto* toleration that the separatists had gained since the meeting of the Long Parliament, their public preaching of their doctrines and their growing following, had become a major political issue by the autumn of 1641. On 24 June 1641 Thomas Wiseman told Sir John Pennington that there could be no conclusion of the political crisis 'till the government of the church which is so distracted be again settled, and all these separatists and sectaries be brought to a good conformity'. And he wrote again on 4 November: 'were it not for these separatists, we should hope all would quickly go well with us in the City; but they do so disturb the peace of it, that if parliament take not speedy order with them, I know not what will become of us'.[99] 'I hope the parliament', wrote a pamphleteer, 'will take into their wise and grave consideration and pious care, the peace of the church, and not suffer it to be clouded or eclipsed by these mists and errors of darkness and ignorance; my prayer is... that these Egyptian locusts, that swarm in every corner of this City and kingdom, may be expelled'. He called on 'well-affected Christians, to complain of them' to parliament, 'for unless they be prevented and suppressed, it is to be feared, that this kingdom will never be free from divisions, disturbances, and distractions'.[100] On 20 November Sir Edward Dering, an erstwhile reformer turned conservative by the growing radicalism on the left of the reforming party, complained in the House of Commons: 'there is at present, such an all-daring liberty, such a lewd licentiousness, for all men's venting of their several senses (senseless senses) in matter of religion, as never was in any age, in any nation, until this parliament was met together'; and he drew attention to the 'frequent schismatical conventicles' and protested 'that tailors, shoemakers, braziers, feltmakers do climb our public pulpits'.[101] A petition from Kent demanded 'that some speedy and good provision may be made... against the odious and abominable scandal of schismatical and seditious sermons and pamphlets, and some severe law made against laymen, for daring to arrogate to themselves, and to execute the holy function of the ministry'.[102]

Moderate puritans were as disturbed as conservative churchmen. A puritan minister wrote to a puritan MP: 'there are rumours on both sides, that I trust your wisdom will remove. On the one side papists that erect their Babel amongst us; and on the other side, Brownists that discourage your Reformation of our Zion, whilst they contend for their independent government, their sires and ancestors the Anabaptists did hinder the Reformation in the days of Luther, and brought boors to war against the protestant princes, till at length by strict laws and Luther's vehement writing and preaching against them they were taken out of the way. It were good—methinks—that your honourable House should timely meet with this anarchy and confusion'.[103] Cornelius Burgess, the spokesman of moderate puritan ministers, warned the House of Commons on 5 November 1641: 'Matters of religion lie a bleeding; all government and discipline of the church is laid in her grave, and all putridinous vermin of bold schismatics and frantic sectaries glory in her ashes, making her fall their own rising to mount our pulpits, to offer strange fire, to expel the gravest, ablest, and most eminent ministers in the kingdom, (if not out of their pulpits, yet) out of the hearts of their people as a company of weak men, formalists, time-servers, no ministers of Christ, but limbs of Antichrist, having no calling except from the Devil; and so forsake our assemblies as Babylonish and Antichristian, so as in short time they will not leave us the face of a church. And yet, no course is taken to suppress their fury, and to reduce them to order'.[104]

The ruling and richer classes feared the separatists more for social than religious reasons. Bishop Hall warned the House of Lords about the increase of sectaries and mechanic preachers: 'My lords, if these men may, with impunity and freedom, thus bear down ecclesiastical authority, it is to be feared they will not rest there, but will be ready to affront civil power too. Your lordships know, that the Jack Straws, and Cades, and Wat Tylers of former times, did not more cry down learning than nobility; and those of your lordships that have read the History of the Anabaptistical Tumults at Munster, will need no other item; let it be enough to say, that many of these sectaries are of the same profession.'[105] For those who had not read history, the pamphleteers soon reminded them of the events at Munster, and one drew these lessons: 'I am afraid that Anabaptism is very rife in England, though not perhaps in one entire body, but... here one tenet of Anabaptism, and there another; yet not so scattered but they meet in one head, which is hatred of all rule:... what rule soever our wise and pious parliament shall think fit, it will not set bounds to the unquiet spirit of a lawless generation, which is now crying, let Christ rule, because they would have no rule: it is not so much the misrule of episcopacy, that they strike at, they have a quarrel at all rules.'

They were governed by prophecies and believed that the temporal kingdom of Christ was imminent: 'This fancy is most dangerous for all states, for to promote that kingdom of Christ, they teach that all the ungodly must be killed, that the wicked have no propriety in their estates, and that now the promise must be fulfilled, that the meek shall inherit the earth. This doctrine filleth the simple people with a furious and unnatural zeal', which 'maketh them look upon their countrymen with such an eye as the Anabaptists cast upon Munster, when they came first into it, a malignant and covetous eye, already designing their prey, and marking the rich to ruin and destruction. God save us from a reformation wrought by a multitude misled with a frantic zeal, and giddy revelations, for then, God help them that have plate, or coin in their houses, they shall be sure to be taken for limbs of the Antichrist'. 'The seditious pamphlets, the tumultuous risings of rude multitudes threatening blood and destruction; the preaching of the cobblers, feltmakers, tailors, grooms, and women, the choosing of any place for God's service but the church... These things if they be not looked into, will bring us in time to community of wives, community of goods, and destruction of all.'[106] Lurid propaganda such as this no doubt generated some alarm in the governing and wealthier classes, but it was a caricature of the opinions of the great body of separatists. Although the social and economic grievances of the lower classes could gain expression through radical religious agitations,[107] the separatists generally had no thoughts of exterminating the nobility and gentry or abolishing private property.

But what did frighten the ruling and richer classes was just the fact that separatism was a movement of the lower classes, and generally under lower-class leadership. The act of separating and following a mechanic preacher, whether recognised or not by those who did it, was an assertion of independence from their superiors in church, state and society, and an act of class defiance.[108] The author of a pamphlet in reply to Henry Burton, who was the most authoritative and influential leader of separatism, showed more insight than the historians of the Anabaptists into the direction in which separatism might draw the lower classes: 'the dross, the off-scourings of the multitude are yours; these, and these only, you are able to induce by promises, or deceive by pretences: tell them, as you do, that they are the people of God, set apart for the great work, and shall not this ambition blow up the unconstant vulgar? Show them they may change their fortunes, and at last share in the public government, you may draw them along with you to the slaughter'.[109] Separatism led 'the middle and poorer sort of people' to conceive that they should have a voice and a share in the government of their country as they had in the government of their own congregations.

Separatism involved the sectaries in politics because they had to demand and secure from the state liberty to have their own independent congregations outside the authority of the established national church, and toleration of their religious opinions and practices. They saw the bishops as the main opponents of such liberty and toleration, and so they were in the forefront of the campaign to abolish bishops. They had gained under parliament a *de facto* liberty and toleration and therefore they were among the first to come to the defence of parliament when it was feared that the king meant to dissolve it by force. The agitations of the religious radicals and separatists pushed the puritans into a more militant stance, and split the original broad alliance of reformers by bringing the social issue to the fore, so hiving off the socially conservative towards the emerging 'party of order'. The drift of the nobility and gentry towards support of the king and the bishops was in reaction to the growth of sects and separatism, and the demand for the suppression of sects and separatism was a main plank of the royalist platform. 'Many gentlemen who forsook the parliament, were very bitter against it for the proceedings in religion, in countenancing, or not suppressing, the rudeness of people in churches'. They 'were not bad men', wrote the Long Parliament's historian, but they were troubled by the licence of the common people in disturbing services, tearing prayer-books and rending surplices: on the parliament's side it was argued that they would lose the support of a great party if they proceeded against these people, on the other side it was said that they would lose a more considerable party of gentlemen if they did not.[110]

3

THE POPULAR PARTY AND
THE PARTY OF ORDER

THE LEADERS of the parliamentary opposition to the king
had intended to make their main demand in the second session
of the Long Parliament that in future the two Houses of
Parliament should approve those persons chosen by the king
to be his officers and councillors (a claim, not to nominate, but
to have a veto over the king's nominations); and they seized
upon the fears generated by the Army Plots, the Incident in
Scotland, and the Rebellion in Ireland, to press this demand.
A large number of members of the House of Commons defended
the king's prerogative to choose his own ministers and advisers,
but the House passed by 151 votes to 110 a representation to
the king: 'That we cannot without much grief remember the
great miseries, burdens, and distempers, which have, for divers
years, afflicted all his kingdoms and dominions, and brought
them to the last point of ruin and destruction; all which have
issued from the cunning, false, and malicious practices of some
of those who have been admitted into very near places of
counsel and authority about him, who have been favourers of
popery, superstition, and innovation, subverters of religion,
honour, and justice, factors for promoting the designs of foreign
princes and states... authors of false scandals and jealousies
betwixt his majesty and his loyal subjects, enemies to the peace,
union, and confidence, betwixt him and his parliament... That
we have just cause of belief, that those conspiracies and
commotions in Ireland are but the effects of the same counsels;

and, if persons of such aims and conditions shall continue in credit, authority, and employment, the great aids which we shall be enforced to draw from his people, for subduing the rebellion in Ireland, will be applied to fomenting and cherishing of it there, and encouraging some such like attempts by the papists and ill-affected subjects in England; and, in the end, to the subversion of religion, and destruction of his loyal subjects in both kingdoms; and do therefore most humbly beseech his majesty to change those counsels...and that he will be graciously pleased to employ such councillors and ministers as shall be approved by his parliament'. Pym asked the House of Lords to approve this representation on the grounds 'that there have been lately, and still are, ill counsels here in this kingdom, and about the king... That these ill counsels have proceeded from a spirit and inclination to popery, and have had a dependence in popery, and all of them tend unto it... That, unless these ill counsels be changed, as long as they continue it is impossible that any assistance, aid, or advice, that the parliament can take to reform, will be effectual'. 'There hath been common counsel at Rome and in Spain, to reduce us to popery'; 'great provision is made' abroad and our neighbours 'have such great fleets at sea as will open a way to sudden ruin and destruction before we can be prepared'.[1] But the House of Lords refused to join with the Commons in this representation to the king.

The bishops and the 'papist lords' were considered responsible for the obstructiveness of the House of Lords. The peers were willing to exclude the clergy from secular functions, but they were not prepared to remove the bishops from parliament. A bill for the abolition of episcopacy was introduced in the House of Commons, and carried at its second reading by 139 votes to 108, but it was designed merely to frighten the Lords into agreeing to the exclusion of the bishops from the Upper House, as a lesser evil than the abolition of bishops altogether. The mover of the bill, Sir Edward Dering, revealed that 'the chief end then was to expedite the progress of another bill against the secular jurisdiction of the bishops (at that time) labouring in the House of Lords'. 'I did not dream', he confessed, 'at that time of extirpation and abolition of any more than his archiepiscopacy: our professed rooters themselves (many of them) at that hour had, I persuade myself, more moderate hopes than since are entertained.'[2] The majority of the Commons still favoured the reform rather than the abolition of episcopacy; but the failure of the bishops to show real evidence of readiness to reform themselves, and consent to a reduction of their powers, privileges and profits',[3] and their appearance as an obstacle to reform not only of the church but also of the state, meant that there could be no further progress in ecclesiastical and secular reforms until they were removed from the House of Lords. The Upper House, however, finally rejected the bill to exclude the bishops from the Lords and the clergy from secular offices. 'This bred much murmuring in the City; the discourse of all men is they must now strike at root and branch and not slip this occasion.'[4] 'The business of the bishops will be of dangerous consequence', wrote Sidney Bere, 'they being violent and passionate in their own defence, and having engaged, as it were, the Lords by their late votes in their favour, to the maintenance of their cause; ...it may justly be feared the City will prove as turbulent as in Strafford's cause.'[5]

The Commons seemed to be intent on pushing ahead with the bill for the abolition of episcopacy, and discussed alternative forms of church government; but then they let the matter drop and instead impeached thirteen bishops for their part in making canons for the church in May 1640 without the consent of parliament, and introduced another bill 'for disabling all persons in holy orders to exercise any temporal jurisdiction or authority', which was designed to remove the bishops from the House of Lords as well as all clergymen from secular offices. The king declared: 'I am constant for the doctrine and discipline of the Church of England as it was established by Queen Elizabeth and my father, and resolve, by the grace of God, to live and die in the maintenance of it';[6] and underlined this by filling five vacant bishoprics. In the Commons Sir Walter Earle 'moved that some course might be taken for the stop of the making of these five new bishops now to be installed'. He was supported by Cromwell and D'Ewes, the latter arguing that 'if at this time when there is a general reformation expected, before anything be amended in church matters, these new bishops shall be created, I know into what desperation people may be drawn and what tumults may arise'.[7] The Commons were under pressure from London, and needed the help of the richer citizens to finance an expedition to suppress the Irish rebellion. They asked the City for a loan of £50,000. The lord mayor and aldermen called a meeting of the Common Council, which approved of such a loan, but the view was expressed at the meeting and reported to the House of Commons 'that in respect of the tyrannical and bloody dealing of the Irish people and the conspiracies at home, that the persons of all the great lords of the popish religion and of other papists of quality might be secured as there might no possible danger arise from them'; 'that there were divers laws, and good motions, sent up to the Lords, for the good of this church and commonwealth; and that the great impediment, which did arise there, that they passed not, was from the bishops; and did conceive, so long as their votes was in parliament, it would be a hindrance to the progress of all good laws and motions; and therefore desired a further endeavour to take away their votes'.[8] These were not conditions for making the loan but indications that it would not be easy to raise the money if the citizens were not satisfied in these matters. The cooperation of the city was necessary for the suppression of the rebellion in Ireland; the support of the citizens was needed to force reforms through parliament. MPs who favoured further reforms were obliged to look for popular support to overcome the opposition of a large part of the House of Commons and a substantial majority of the House of Lords. In order to win that support, especially of the more organised and forceful groups of Londoners, they had to advance towards more radical demands, especially in religion.

At this point the Grand Remonstrance was introduced into the House of Commons. It was a narrative and recapitulation of grievances against the government of Charles I in church and state since the beginning of his reign, and a declaration of the reforms that parliament had so far achieved and of the changes that were still needed. It announced the intention of petitioning the king 'to employ such councillors, ambassadors and other ministers, in managing his business at home and abroad as the parliament may have cause to confide in'; 'and that, as far as the church was concerned, the bishops should be removed from the House of Lords, their power over the clergy limited, 'needless and superstitious ceremonies', 'innovations', and 'monuments of idolatory' taken away, and a synod of protestant divines summoned to advise parliament on the reform of the doctrine and discipline of the church.[9] It did not propose the abolition of episcopacy, and it put forward what was essentially a moderate programme, but it was carried on 22 November by only 159 votes to 148. 'If you set Pym, Holles and Hampden aside, the best of the House voted against it,' reported Sir John Coke the younger, 'as Sir John Colepeper, lord Falkland, Mr Crew, Sir Robert Pye, Sir John Strangways, all the best of the lawyers, Alderman Soame, Sir Edward Dering, Mr Waller, Sir Ralph Hopton, etc'.

This opposition was aroused chiefly by the fact that the Remonstrance was in form and in intention an appeal to the people against the Lords and the king. 'They desire not the concurrence of the Lords, neither is it addressed to the king as all remonstrances of grievances have ever been, but to the people. Other remonstrances have been complaints of the people to the king. Some say this is a complaint of the king to the people.' Sir John Colepeper objected: 'That this not sent to the Lords. Against the form of it. This a remonstrance to the people. Remonstrances ought to be to the king for redress... We not sent to please the people': 'Our writ doth not warrant us to send any declarations to the people, but to treat with the king and Lords; neither was it ever done by any parliament heretofore. Dangerous for the public peace.' Edward Hyde 'spake very vehemently against it': 'this seemed to be an instrument to the people, in the nature of an appeal to them, which had never been practised, and might prove of very dangerous consequence... it would probably infuse into the people a dislike of the settled form of government'; it would 'lessen in many particulars the reverence due to his majesty' and to the House of Peers, when they should be 'presented to the people as the obstructors of the public justice and enemies to a reformation'. 'When I first heard of a Remonstrance', protested Sir Edward Dering, 'I did not dream that we should remonstrate downward, tell stories to the people, and talk of the king as of a third person. The use and end of such Remonstrance I understand not: at least, I hope, I do not.' 'I neither look for cure of our complaints from the common people, nor do desire to be cured by them'.

On the other side Pym argued that 'this declaration will bind the people's hearts to us', and John Glyn declared: 'The people trust us, *ergo*, no dishonour to strive to satisfy them.'[10] It was this act of appeal to the people that produced the deepest difference of opinion that had occurred so far in the Long Parliament, as shown by the fact that the most violent opposition appeared after the Remonstrance had been carried, when George Peard moved that it be printed and so focused the issue wholly upon the appeal to the people. Colepeper and Hyde desired to record protests against it being printed, but they were told that they could not do so without the consent of the House, and the matter seemed to be laid aside for future debate, when Geoffrey Palmer repeatedly demanded 'that a protestation might be entered in the name of himself and all the rest, upon which divers cried *"All! All!"*, and some waved their hats over their heads, and others took their swords in their scabbards out of their belts and held them by the pommels in their hands setting the lower part on the ground'. 'I thought, we had all sat in the valley of the shadow of death', recorded Sir Philip Warwick; 'for we, like Joab's and Abner's young men, had catched at each other's locks, and sheathed our swords in each other's bowels, had not the sagacity and great calmness of Mr Hampden by a short speech prevented it'. The proposal for printing was laid aside for the moment and tempers cooled.[11] In the excitement it was easy to overlook that the appeal to the people was on a moderate rather than a radical programme—a programme to which many who voted against the Remonstrance had few serious objections—and that it could be regarded as an appeal to the more moderate popular opinion against the more radical, revolutionary elements in London and the provinces.

On 24 November it was moved in the Commons that Palmer be charged with inflaming the temper of the House to a point at which violence was only narrowly averted, and this was carried by 190 votes to 142.[12] While the debate was going on that evening, Mrs Venn, the wife of John Venn, an MP for the City, received a message from her husband, brought by 'a very good Christian', and she at once sent one of her servants to the shop of Lavender, a grocer in Bread Street, to tell him 'that in the House of Commons they were together by the ears, that the worser party was like to get the better of the good party, therefore he was desired from Captain Venn to come to Westminster with his arms to help the good party'. Lavender was not at his shop and the servant sought him out at Farlow's house in Wood Street, where he was 'taking tobacco with some others there'; he told him that 'there was an uproar in the parliament house, and swords drawn', that 'the well-affected party was like to be overborne by the others', and that Captain Venn desired him to come quickly to Westminster 'with his company and arms'. Lavender hurried away, taking his sword and a pistol, and went to Mrs Venn's shop, where he found her 'crying and wringing her hands for her husband whom she feared would be killed'. Lavender 'bade her be of good comfort, he and many more would go to Westminster'.

Similar messages had gone to others. Mr Mansfield, a haberdasher of Distaffe Lane, who was a constable, gave his apprentice, Cole, 'a lusty young man', a sword and told him to go to Westminster: some parliament-men sent for them because 'some division was like to be amongst the members of the Lower House, and... the best-affected party were likely to be overborne by the others' and needed their assistance. The masters of other apprentices did the same. Soon three hundred were at Westminster, and more kept on coming until there were a thousand when the Houses rose. But they found no uproar and 'that they had agreed well enough together' and they returned home peacefully. Between nine and ten o'clock that night Cole went to look for his uncle, who had come up from Chelmsford, and found him at the lodgings of Dr John Michaelson, the minister of Chelmsford. He burst in excitedly, boasting that 'he was newly come from Westminster palace yard, where he had been with a thousand more, and that himself and the rest of that number were there armed with swords'.[13]

This story comes from sources hostile to radical demonstrations at Westminster, but it has the ring of truth and, though no doubt the details have been embroidered, it throws light on the means by which crowds were brought together at Westminster in political crises. After the scene on 22 November, Venn and other radicals may well have feared an outbreak of violence in the House, directed chiefly against themselves, and have sent for some of the trained bands to maintain order or to protect them if there were disorder. Venn was evidently using his position as an officer in the trained bands to bring his own men to Westminster, and this position was a main part of his means of organising a popular demonstration. The shopkeeper who was also a constable was a man of some influence and authority in his neighbourhood; he was accustomed to calling upon his neighbours to assist him in maintaining law and order, and he employed the same power to raise a force of political demonstrators. At the same time the story illuminates the manner by which the apprentices came to be involved: they were encouraged to demonstrate by their employers, but probably this was not just a matter of servants blindly obeying their masters in this as in other things, for they also acquired political and religious ideas from their masters.[14]

The next day, 25 November, the king made a ceremonial entry into London on his return from Scotland. He was given a magnificent reception by the municipality, and greeted with popular applause. Charles was impressed, and said in reply to the speech of welcome from the recorder: 'now I see, that all those former tumults, and disorders, have only risen from the meaner sort of people, and that the affections of the better sort and main part of the City have ever been loyal and affectionate to my person and government'. But the committee which had organised the festivity knew better the fear and discontent that lay not far beneath the jollity induced by free beer and wine: 'And, because some seditious libels were at that time dispersed, which bred a panic fear in some, order was likewise taken, that there should be two companies of the City's trained bands, placed in several parts of the City upon that day; as also, that at every door a man should be placed, sufficiently appointed, to be ready upon all occasions, to appease any disorders.'[15]

At the king's return the earl of Essex's commission as Captain-General of the forces south of Trent lapsed, and Charles's first act was to remove the guard which Essex had placed to protect the two Houses against 'popish plots'. The Commons asked the Lords to join them in a petition to the king that this guard should be continued. The Lords, by a majority, refused. Then the Commons asked the peers to send some of their own number to request the king to continue the guard. The Lords, by a majority, agreed, and sent the earl of Warwick and lord Digby to the king, who accordingly commanded the earl of Dorset to guard the two Houses with some men from the trained bands.'[16] On Sunday, 28 November, 'the factious citizens begin to come again to the House with their swords by their sides, hundreds in companies: their pretence is only against episcopacy'.[17] There was a hubbub in Westminster Hall and shouts of 'Down with the Bishops—Down with Antichrist'. Four men were brought before the Lords for making this disturbance 'and saying, if they could not be heard, they would have a far greater number the next day to back them'. They denied that these were their words and they were dismissed with a sharp rebuke for flocking about parliament.

The next day 'many hundred citizens', armed with swords and staves, gathered about parliament, calling on the members as they passed to suppress bishops: they 'never cease yawling and crying *"No bishops! No bishops!"*,' calling them 'the limbs of Antichrist'. They also cried out against the prayer-book. 'There is scarce passage between the two Houses, the Court of Requests is so thronged with them'. Sir John Strangways was hemmed in by some two hundred people demanding 'his vote for the putting down of the bishops'. 'I saw old Sir John Strangways in the Court of Requests', wrote a witness, 'so crowded up into a corner by a multitude of people, and so clamoured with this noise, that I truly thought him in danger.' Sir John told the crowd 'that they must desire in a legal way what they would have legally done; and so drew himself from them and in his departure he could hear them say: "Do you know who you spoke to?" it was answered "No". "Why it was Sir John Strangways one of the greatest enemies we have."'[18] The House of Lords 'was informed that great company of men are in the Court of Requests with swords and clubs crying down with the papist lords and bishops'. The Lords sent orders for them to depart, but they remained, and 'some were called into the Lords' House and examined and charged to depart'. But still the crowd did not disperse, 'and some of them with great rudeness pressing to the door of the House of Peers', their lordships directed the earl of Dorset to call up the guard and remove them. Dorset asked the crowd to leave: 'I saw and heard my lord of Dorset entreat them with his hat in his hand, and yet the scoundrels would not move.' The guards tried without success to push them back, and 'the citizens blustered at them'. Dorset lost his temper and ordered the guards 'to give fire upon them': 'whereupon the rabble, frightened, left the place, and hasted away'. It does not appear that any shots were actually fired, and in any case it seems that the muskets were loaded only with powder, merely to scare the people with the bang.[19]

Captain Robert Slyngesbie described the demonstrators as 'the ruder sort of people'.[20] Some of the chief men of the City happened to be 'at Westminster, attending other occasions, when those people met there, and took a heedful view of them', and, though they 'had lived in the City above forty years together' and 'knew the City and the better sort of citizens', they recognised 'not the face of one man among them'.[21] Sidney Bere called them 'sectaries and others ill-affected', and hostile observers assumed that the crowd was composed of 'Brownists or Separatists'.[22] The slogans shouted by the demonstrators bore testimony to the presence of religious radicals; and they were not demonstrating in support of the House of Commons and the programme of the Grand Remonstrance, for they went beyond the demand for the removal of the bishops from the House of Lords, and called for the abolition of episcopacy and the prayer-book. But the crowd was also influenced by the king discharging the guard which the earl of Essex had given the Houses to protect them, and by fears of papists and plots against parliament. Some of the crowd had come to offer themselves to guard the Houses.[23] Jeremy Baines, Griffith Marshall and other inhabitants of London and the suburbs said that 'they heard that the guard was discharged, so in a peaceable manner they came down here to see what was done and to know what became of their petitions that depend here'.[24] 'If we shall but thoroughly inquire into the cause of the citizens first coming down', Sir Simonds D'Ewes told the Commons, 'it was for the security of the parliament when they first heard on Monday last past that our guard was taken from us and when they heard afterwards which was much worse that a guard was imposed upon us against our wills'.[25] That many of the crowd came because they feared a popish plot against the parliament, or simply to hear the news or to see what was going on, is shown by the answers of the demonstrators examined by the House of Lords: 'B— Waller of Coleman Street, tallow chandler, with a sword. That he came to his customs in the Strand. That he afraid in regard of papists and others ill-affected. Jo Broome in Bread Street. That he came to Westminster to hear news. That he heard some say down with the bishops and the papists lords.'[26] The next day citizens came again to Westminster shouting against bishops, 'but being entreated to forbear, and depart home to their houses, the tumult ceased for that time'.[27]

When the tumult first began the Lords had a conference with the Commons 'touching the tumultuous people that are assembled in the Court of Requests and the Hall': 'the Lords did conceive this confluence of citizens in great numbers, many of them being armed with swords, to be of dangerous consequence: they desired' the Commons 'therefore to join with them in a declaration to inhibit and restrain their said coming and that especially for two reasons. 1. Because else it might give a wound to those good laws we had made and should make; to have the validity of them hereafter questioned as if we had been compelled to make them. 2. Because it would be a great scandal to the parliament to suffer such unruly assemblies and disorderly multitudes so near them, without taking some timely care for prevention thereof.'[28] This condemnation of the demonstrations was not confined to the House of Lords. On 3 December a deputation from the City government, consisting of six aldermen, eight common council-men, the recorder and the two sheriffs, waited on the king at Hampton Court and expressed regret that 'there had been some late disorders about Westminster, among some people that met there'. They asked the king that he 'would not impute this, to the body of the City, or to the better sort of citizens'.[29] William Montagu wrote to his father, lord Montagu of Boughton: 'I begin to be of your lordship's mind, that we are running to ruin... Sects in the body and factions in the head are dangerous diseases, and do desperately threaten the dissolution of a well-governed estate'; and he added, referring to the tumults at Westminster, 'I think this would provoke authority to the height of rigour'.[30]

In the House of Commons Sir John Strangways complained about the way in which he had been surrounded by the citizens and pressed to give his vote against bishops: 'Mr

Hyde and others insisted upon the citizens coming down being armed with swords and staves, and surrounding Sir John Strangways and pressing him to give his vote against bishops, would scarce permit him to go away quietly... and therefore it was desired that we would advise upon some course to inhibit the confluence of the citizens for the future. Sir John Strangways pressed the matter further and said that the privilege of parliament was utterly broken if men might not come in safety to give their votes freely.' Edmund Waller 'much inveighed against the Londoners in coming down after so tumultuous a manner, and crying openly "No Bishop No Bishop" '; and Sir John Colepeper 'said that for his part he conceived the late assembling of the citizens to have been a very great tumult'. Alarm was expressed by moderate reformers such as Sir John Holland, MP for Castle Rising and a wealthy landowner in Norfolk, who declared: 'It hath ever been observed, in every well governed state as a thing of dangerous consequence to suffer the people to assemble and arm at their own wills and pleasures, and though I am as confident as any man can, of the fair and clear intention of the citizens that have resorted in such numbers in such manner to our doors, that it is rather for the preservation of our peace and safety than of disturbance; yet truly I conceive it cannot stand with the wisdom of this House to permit it, in respect of the danger in the possible consequence thereof... Sir, though the intention of these citizens be peace, yet God only knows what the issue may be; possibly such, as may endanger the reputation of all the proceedings in this parliament, which I hope I shall never live to see; this reason was touched by a worthy gentleman last day. It then stuck and still doth with me. I am confident it is understood and in that confidence, shall humbly move that we may join with the Lords in the prevention of the like assembly here for the time to come.' [31]

Moderate MPs, as well as the Court's outright supporters, were concerned that the king or his successors or future parliaments might seek to revoke the legislation of the Long Parliament on the grounds that it had been forced through by mob violence. But they were also worried that the popular pressure would result in some MPs acquiescing in more radical measures than they would otherwise have supported. It was this that alarmed Thomas Warmstry, a moderate reforming minister who wanted to retain episcopacy.[32] He warned the people that their impatience might force the parliament to go too fast and too far: 'Beseech you in the name of God, and for the mercies of Christ Jesus, that you would not by any unseasonable pressures, or tumultuous solicitations of the business in hand, attempt the disturbance of this happy conjuncture, but that it may be permitted to glide on smoothly and calmly and peaceably, as is most correspondent unto those peaceable ends, which they drive at, not interrupting that great assembly, either by any uncivil or distempered concourses, or by any rude or immodest clamours'.[33]

But behind this lay distaste at the common people attempting to influence political decisions, for that was an attack on the established social order, in which it was for the gentlemen to rule and the plebeians to be ruled. William Thomason told the people that it was true that every man in his place should endeavour a reformation, but not by means of tumultuous and seditious meetings. What private men could do was to inform parliament of public grievances in a peaceable way by means of petitions; but for them to forget their station and seek to say how those grievances should be redressed, and to lay down what measures should be taken, this was to involve themselves in the mysteries of government which were no business of theirs, and to be 'reformers' whereas their place was to be only 'informers'.[34] 'It is not fit for you to trouble yourselves and them in this kind, because of your different constitution, and various interest you have in the business... Your constitution is different from theirs... It is well if you have enough wisdom to steer you right in your private and mechanical affairs, which is your proper station or calling, and you may do well to consider, whether you do well to neglect that business God hath set you about, to meddle with that you have no calling unto. But they are stars of a greater magnitude, and therefore may move in a higher sphere, and you may be content to receive their influences. I hope, it is not in you all to challenge so much light unto yourselves, as to judge of laws being made, much less to determine and set down magisterially unto them, what constitutions they are to frame.' The parliament's place is to do the work, the people's place is to receive the benefit.

'Let it be your study to live uprightly and honestly in your trades and callings, and to keep yourselves within your limits, and to the conscionable exercise of your proper employments, and not to intrude into what you understand not: if you will needs be active in reformation, let it be in the reformation of yourselves.'[35] 'Let discreet knowing judgements meddle with their markets, and not with state matters, let them talk and think with reverence of the king and his great council the parliament, ever praying for the prosperity of both, and the tranquility and peace of the kingdom.'[36] All this said in the confident tone that the people only had to be told it to accept it; and indeed that was generally the case, except where religious radicalism was teaching the humble plebeian to form his own opinions, that a godly poor man's opinions were better than an ungodly gentleman's opinions, and that he did not need any rank or qualification or authority other than godliness to get up and express them in public.

But when the people told parliament what to do, the next step would be for them to do it themselves without parliament. 'The Roman Story tells us', Edmund Waller warned the House of Commons, 'that when the people began to flock about the Senate, and were more curious to direct and know what was done, than to obey, that commonwealth soon came to ruin. Their *legum rogare* grew quickly to be a *legem ferre*, and after, when their legions had found that they could make a dictator, they never suffered the Senate to have a voice any more in such election'.[37] Already some of the people were taking the law into their own hands and carrying through a reformation by direct action. Dr John Michaelson, minister of Chelmsford in Essex, where 'sectaries, especially Brownists and Anabaptists', had been active and growing in strength since the beginning of the parliament, preached a sermon early in November 1641 'against popular tumultuous reformations, though to the better: as being vitiated, first, by the defect of lawful authority, which cannot reside in the people; secondly, in the intemperancy of the prosecution, who commonly cast out one devil by another; abolishing superstition with sedition'.[38] Many members of both the House of Lords and the House of Commons, as well as the wealthy gentry that governed the counties and the merchant-oligarchies that ruled the towns, were shocked by the doctrine propounded by some leaders of the opposition and radical MPs, that parliament should do what the people wanted. 'I see some are moved with a number of hands against the bishops, which I confess', said Edmund Waller, 'rather inclines me to their defence, for I look upon episcopacy, as a counterscarp, or outwork, which if it be taken by this assault of the people, and withal this mystery once revealed, that we must deny them nothing when they ask it thus in troops, we may in the next place, have as hard a task to defend our property, as we have lately had to recover it from the prerogative.' Waller, a very wealthy landowner in Buckinghamshire, was one of those MPs who recognized with great clarity that fundamentally the interests of the people and of a parliament dominated by great landowners, were antagonistic; and that was why it was dangerous to propagate the notion that parliament should follow the will of the people or to permit the people to think they could make parliament do what they wanted. He feared that 'if by multiplying hands, and petitions, they prevail for an equality in things ecclesiastical, this next demand perhaps may be *Lex graria*, the like equality in things temporal.' It was alleged that the existing form of government in the church was contrary to Scripture, but he was 'confident that whenever an equal division of lands and goods shall be desired, there will be as many places in Scripture found out, which seem to favour that, as there are now alleged against the prelacy or preferment in the church'. The bishops were accused of abuses: 'And as for abuses where you are now in the Remonstrance told, what this and that poor man hath suffered by the bishops, you may be presented with a thousand instances of poor men, that have received hard measure from their landlords'.[39] If abuses of power were deemed sufficient grounds for abolishing the power itself, then landlords would go the same way as bishops; and if Scripture was to be the test of arrangements in this world, then communism would replace private property. If the landlords allowed the bishops to be dispossessed of their power and possessions at the behest of popular agitators, the rest of the ruling class would invite the same fate upon themselves.

A party of order had now emerged in parliament, with allies amongst the clergy and the ruling groups in town and country. They did not rely on words alone, and were planning a concerted and strenuous effort to re-establish order and put the people in their place. They were alienated from the opposition and drawn towards the king by the unwillingness of the leaders of the opposition to take action against popular demonstrations at Westminster, and believed that there must therefore be links between the parliamentary leaders and the mobs in the streets. Now they set out to establish that there were in fact such links, and that there was a conspiracy to force the votes in parliament; thinking that if they could verify this, they would be able to discredit the existing leadership and then rally the moderates to support measures to restore order. Sir John Strangways, a great landowner in Dorset and Somerset and old friend of the earl of Bristol and lord Digby, told the Commons 'that he received information of a plot or conspiracy for the destruction of some of the members of this House which he conceived to be little less than treason and said that he was informed that some of the members of this House were either contrivers or consenters to it'. This information was a deposition from Dr John Michaelson, the minister of Chelmsford who had recently voiced a strong condemnation of popular tumults, reporting the statement of Cole the apprentice that he had gone with others armed to Westminster to help 'the best affected party'. It was passed on to Strangways by another divine Dr Daniel Eastcourt. Edward Kirton, a Somerset gentleman who represented Milborne Port in parliament, a dependent and agent of the marquis of Hertford and the Seymours, was at hand with further information and a sheaf of depositions from Mr Bradshaw ('a gentleman of Gray's Inn'), Mr Lawrence Rudyerd, Mr Farlow of Wood Street, and Mr Farlow of Cambridge, testifying that Captain Venn sent a message to his wife telling her to send the citizens to Westminster with their weapons.

Strangways demanded a select committee of five to inquire into this business, and proceeded to nominate lord Falkland and Sir John Colepeper to be on the committee.[40] William Chillingworth, the divine, and old friend of Falkland and Hyde, was with Strangways when Dr Eastcourt brought his information. Chillingworth then went to see an attorney in Clements Inn and after talking of Palmer's case, he told what he had just heard at Strangways' lodgings, adding 'that some

of the other party who were against Mr Palmer should be
questioned for as great a treason as the earl of Strafford'.[41]
There can be little doubt that Chillingworth said something of
this sort, reflecting the talk in the circles he frequented, and it
fits well with the allegation of treason with which Strangways
introduced Michaelson's evidence to the House. Strangways
and Kirton were avowedly acting in concert, and they produced
their revelations in association with the fierce attacks by Hyde,
Colepeper and Waller on the tumultuous behaviour of the
Londoners. It seems likely that Strangways, Kirton, Falkland,
Hyde, Colepeper and Waller were operating as a group: they
had strong aristocratic and Court connections and were already
working together in the king's interest in defence of his
prerogatives, and with a group of divines in defence of
episcopacy. Clearly they had formed a plan to accuse leaders of
the radical party of treason for conspiring with the mob to
overawe parliament—a thought which had been in the minds
of the king and some courtiers ever since the riots against
Strafford, and no doubt Charles approved of the plan. But the
weakness of their position was that they had evidence only
against one radical, Venn. An even greater weakness was
Chillingworth's indiscretion. Pym seized upon this to divert the
House from the Strangways-Kirton revelations: he jumped in
to announce 'that he was informed that there was a conspiracy
by some members of this House to accuse other members of the
same of treason'.[42] Chillingworth made a disastrous
impression when he was examined by the House and was sent
to the Tower 'to keep Mr Palmer company'.[43] The depositions
submitted by Strangways and Kirton were ignored and their
witnesses waited many days 'but, notwithstanding all the
importunity that could be used, were never admitted to be
heard'.[44]

Whatever alarm may have been produced by the tumults
of the mob, and whatever suspicion there may have been that
there was probably something in the Strangways-Kirton
revelations, were outweighed by the greater fears of the king's
intentions. Strangways and his friends were distrusted
because they had become too obviously linked with the king
and the Court. The king's removal of the guard on parliament
commanded by Essex, and his substitution of a guard

commanded by the earl of Dorset, represented a greater and more immediate threat of force being used against the parliament than the London mob. The Commons ordered the withdrawal of the earl of Dorset and his guard and asked the Lords to join them in a petition to the king for a guard 'that shall be commanded and appointed by one that shall be nominated by the parliament'. The guard departed on 30 November and two MPs who were JPs in Westminster were instructed to set a strong watch on parliament.[45] There were growing rumours that the king intended some coup against the parliament, and the only security against this, and the only counterweight to the king and his allies in parliament and the City government, was the London mob. So those reforming MPs who feared the king more than the mob, defended the Londoners. 'I do not conceive', declared Sir Simonds D'Ewes, 'that this act of the Londoners can be properly styled a tumultuous coming hither... they came hither in a peaceable manner to know what issue their former petitions had received here; and that is not only lawful for them to do but all others also who have like petitions depending before us; and if a thousand persons should come from several counties to that end I know no crime they should commit therein... And though some of them came armed with swords yet that might well be excused also because they came in the evening. But it is further objected against them as a great crime that they cried, No Bishops. I cannot tell but that desire of theirs might relate to their sitting and having votes in the Lords' House; against which there is a bill passed this House and sent up to the Lords'. The special pleading that is so evident in this speech reflects that defence of the mob did not come naturally or easily to D'Ewes and he had to cast around rather desperately for arguments to justify it.

But it was the behaviour of the earl of Dorset that presented the defenders of the citizens with their most effective argument. This was 'a matter of an high nature and of dangerous consequence'; 'for there must be great caution had to avoid the spilling of innocent blood: and for him to bid the musketeers discharge upon so many citizens and the pikemen to run them through, we may well consider how dangerous effects it might have produced not only of much slaughter between the guard and the citizens, but of danger to the members of both Houses also'. 'For any person how great soever to command loyal citizens to be slaughtered and so to execute martial law without all colour of authority at the very parliament door this was to bring confusion itself to a great height'. The citizens came for the security of the parliament 'and therefore if we suffer these men for their affection and faithfulness to us to have their lives thus endangered we shall justly deserve hereafter to be deserted by them'. 'Besides we have been formerly and now lately beholding to the City for the loan of great sums, and we are still likely to need their assistance in the same kind, and therefore this was of all times the most unseasonable to provoke them.' Strode spoke, probably with more effect, in defence of the citizens, and 'the sense of the House did incline very strongly... that the citizens had not come down in any unlawful or tumultuous manner', and that Dorset had been rash and provocative. The House decided that it would not join with the Lords in a declaration forbidding the people to come to parliament.[46] No doubt moderate MPs were fearful that actions like that of Dorset would provoke more serious popular disorders than had yet occurred, and were influenced by the argument that they needed to be on good terms with the citizens.

There was a petition for the removal of bishops and papists from the House of Lords preparing in London. It expressed fear of papist plots and declared 'the great terrors, fears, etc, distractions they lay under of a sudden surprise by their bloody hands; by means whereof the trading of the City and kingdom is much more of late decayed than it hath been for many years past, no man following his trade cheerfully, whiles the lives of himself and family, and the public safety of the kingdom are in danger, and while he knoweth not how soon they may feel the like cruelty and inhumanity from the papists, and their adherents, as those in Ireland have done'. They have prepared the way for this, said the petition, by dividing king and parliament, raising disrespects in the hearts of the people against parliament, and misconstruing the City's welcome for the king on his return from Scotland as if the citizens had deserted the parliament. Evidently the purpose of this petition was to rally the radicals of London and to challenge the right of the City government, which so clearly sided with the king, to speak for the citizens. The petition demanded that considerable forces be sent forthwith to Ireland to subdue the rebellion; that the City and the kingdom be put into a posture of defence 'for prevention of the like mischief'; that the bishops and Roman Catholic peers be removed from the House of Lords; so that the petitioners may be 'freed from their fears, encouraged in their trades'.[47]

This petition was opposed by the lord mayor, recorder, sheriffs and a number of the aldermen of the City, but it was organized by some men of substance, whose leader was John Fowke. He was 'a merchant dwelling in Marke Lane', 'of very good fortune', who traded in the Levant and East India companies. He had been imprisoned once for refusing to pay tonnage and poundage in 1627, and a second time for refusing to pay the imposition on currants, and he 'was one of the crown's most persistent opponents amongst the merchants of the city'. He was a radical and not a member of the city's governing élite, but he was shortly to be elected to the Common Council on that tide of radical opinion that he was doing so much to promote.[48] On this occasion it is possible to gain a glimpse of how petitions and agitations were organized by the puritans in the City. It seems that they were conducted by ward committees that sat in taverns and 'in divers private houses in London' such as 'Browne's house, a grocer, near Cheapside Cross; also a draper's house in Watling Street'. And it is possible that the puritans had striven to obtain the minor offices of authority in the wards and parishes: 'not an office in the city, though chargeable, and troublesome; yet how ambitious were the faction of those places, even to a constableship'.[49] It was said that William Hobson, a mercer in Ave Maria Lane, sent a constable to summon parishioners to his house between nine and ten o'clock at night and there exhorted them to sign the petition, saying that anyone who refused was neither a good christian, nor an honest man, nor well-affected to the commonwealth. Taylor of Paternoster Row, a deputy alderman, also sent for parishioners to come to his house and there urged them to sign the petition. Thus a group of men of some status and authority in their wards and parishes held small meetings in their houses to expound the petition and used their influence to obtain the signatures of their neighbours. Clearly the leadership of the agitation and the immediate challenge to the City government came from men on the fringes, but nevertheless outside of the governing élite, whose power would fall to them in an upheaval. Canvassers for signatures to the petition also went round shops and houses. John Greensmith, a tobacconist, went to the shop of Edward Curle, a drugster, and asked him to sign the petition, but Curle replied that he would not subscribe against bishops, and Greensmith retorted 'then you are like to have your throat cut'.[50] Now, it is evident that the petition expressed, and even exploited, the fear of papists; and Greensmith no doubt meant that the papists would be doing the throat cutting; still, the pressure to sign must have been great, for refusal could mark a man as a secret papist or papist sympathizer. These scraps of evidence reveal that the local organizers and supporters of the petition thought of it as much a petition against papists and for security against popish plots as for the removal of bishops from the House of Lords, and that fear of popery was an organizing principle of the agitation. The examination of the petitioners by the lord mayor did not obtain any admissions that pressure had been used on the signatories, 'and none seemed to regret being among the signers: a certain Hugh Ratcliffe even boldly asserted that "if it were to do again he would do it" '.[51]

Energetic and concerted efforts were made by the Court, the City government and the local authorities responsible for the suburbs, to put a stop to this petition, probably acting in close alliance with the party of order in parliament. The lord mayor, three aldermen, the recorder and sheriffs of the City examined several of the citizens who had signed the petition and obtained the names of the Common Council-men and others who were collecting the signatures. It was alleged 'that the lord mayor said, they were either ignorant or idle people, that did subscribe it;... that it tended to mutiny'. The recorder was alleged to have said that 'they deserved to be disfranchised: that they did not know into what danger they had run themselves. And, reading of the petition, when they came to that part of it declared the Common Council, the representative body of the City, did desire the removal of bishops and papists lords from the Lords' House; Mr Recorder swore by etc, that it was a lie: and said further, that this petition did tend to sedition, and to set men together by the ears: and, being told it was for peace: No, said he, it is for blood, and cutting of throats; and if it come to cutting of throats, thank yourselves; and your blood be upon your own heads; and this petition would rather confirm episcopacy, than otherwise; and that he hated a papist, and detested this petition.'[52] The fierce reaction of the recorder, Sir Thomas Gardiner, probably sprang from the fears he expressed on other occasions that there was a movement abroad amongst the common people to throw off the rule of their social superiors: 'The gentry (say they) have been our masters a long time and now we may chance to master them'.[53] While it may be true, not altogether surprisingly, that the minutes of the examination of the petitioners 'contain no record of threatening language used by the lord mayor or the recorder', yet 'it is evident that the examiners showed their resentment towards the petitioners'. 'Mr Deputy Taylor' was required by the sheriff, Sir George Clarke, 'to answer whether or not from henceforth he would disavow any further proceedings upon that petition'. Taylor must have been overawed and browbeaten for he replied 'that he would desire to have some time to consider of it'.[54] Obviously the intention was to try to put a stop to the collection of signatures. But it was not just the petition that was objectionable. The real fear was that the presentation of such a petition would be the occasion for big popular demonstrations at Westminster against the House of Lords. The Court and its allies in the two Houses, the City government and the local authorities that controlled the suburbs, were intent upon heading off such pressure on the Lords, breaking the alliance between the dominant faction in the Commons and the London mob, and crushing the growing popular agitations in the capital.

In the absence of cooperation from the majority party in the Commons, the Lords had decided to act on their own initiative against popular tumults. They asked the judges to consider what course should be taken to prevent riots and unlawful assemblies, and the judges replied that the best way was to issue writs under the statute *2 Henry V cap viii*. The Lords instructed the lord keeper to issue such writs to the sheriffs and JPs of London, Middlesex and Surrey, and to the JPs of Westminster.[55] It was believed that the petition would be presented on 10 December. On 9 December the king sent a writ under the Great Seal to the JPs and sheriffs of London: 'Whereas our sovereign lord the king having received information that many riots and unlawful assemblies are daily made at the City of Westminster and within the City of London', he ordered them to put into execution the statute against such riots and unlawful assemblies. The lord mayor gave instructions for this order to be communicated by 'Common Council-men, constables or other discreet persons unto every householder within your ward, charging every of them at their uttermost peril from henceforth not to permit any of their apprentices or servants to have the liberty of going abroad to make any tumults or unlawful meetings and assemblies within this city or elsewhere upon any pretence whatsoever, and by themselves to the uttermost of their power and best endeavour to hinder and let the committing of any such offence... and further that you make known unto the masters and servants, that if they or any of them shall be found to offend in the premises, then they are to be proceeded with according to the laws in this case made'.[56] In a society in which trade and industry was organized in family units, and the apprentices and workmen lived and worked in the household of their employer as part of his family, control over the lower classes depended ultimately on the patriarchal authority of masters over their servants. The lord mayor further ordered all constables to raise their watches and to be ready in arms.[57]

Also on 9 December writs went from the lord keeper, acting on the authority of the House of Lords, to the JPs of Surrey, Middlesex and Westminster, ordering them to prevent or suppress unlawful assemblies and riots. George Long, a JP in Middlesex, held a meeting at his office in Lincoln's Inn early on the morning of the tenth with six other JPs and the under-sheriff. He said that he had information that the Londoners intended to come down in great multitudes that day to present a petition to parliament against bishops; that 'one Godwine' had come to him 'to get him to set his hand to a petition, and said that 10,000 persons would come down to the parliament house to present it'; and he concluded that they must take action to prevent tumults, as directed by the lord keeper and the House of Lords. So they sent warrants to the constables of Westminster to raise three hundred men and go to the Palace of Westminster to prevent 'tumults and assemblies of the people' and suppress 'riots and routs'. When the two Houses assembled they found themselves under the guard of two hundred men with halberds, under the command of the bailiff of the Liberty of the Duchy of Westminster and some constables.[58] Sir Simonds D'Ewes declared 'that it was against the privileges of this House, to set a guard upon us without our consent, be the pretences for doing it never so fair or specious... We know there was a late design to bring up the army to overawe the parliament, and to give a law to us; and for ought I know a thousand men may as well effect this as well as twenty thousand... For as it was pretended in the issuing out of the writs for shipmoney, that the kingdom was in imminent danger when it never enjoyed greater peace and security, so now if upon any feigned pretence a guard of 200 men may be set upon us, by the same reason a guard of a thousand or a greater number may be placed about us; by which means we shall neither be able to sit safely nor to speak freely; and so not only our privileges, but the liberty also of the whole commons of England whom we represent shall be all taken away at one blow. But it is said that these men are assembled to suppress riots and routs: certainly that must be intended of real dangers not of imaginary; and especially they ought not under this colour to bring armed men even to the parliament doors, where all things are in peace and quiet.' The Commons ordered the removal of the guards and Long was sent to the Tower.[59] There was no petition delivered that day and no demonstration.

The organisers of the petition were men of substance and local authority, and they did not want to provoke popular tumults and demonstrations. No doubt this was partly because such tumults and demonstrations antagonised moderate men in parliament and the City; but it was also because they were uneasy about the activities and intentions of their more radical supporters in the lower classes. Further, they were offended by the slur that the demand for the removal of bishops and popish lords from parliament was supported only by 'the meaner sort of people'. On Friday, 10 December, they gave out that the petition would be delivered on the following Monday, but secretly resolved to present it the next day, Saturday, informing only four men in each ward, 'so they avoided the coming down of multitudes'. The 'aldermen, aldermen's deputies, merchants, Common Council-men, and many others of great rank and fashion, to the number of 400, who were selected to deliver the petition', rode to Westminster in fifty coaches and 'accoutred in the best manner they could... to prevent the aspersion that they were of the basest sort of people only which were that way affected'. Alderman Pennington announced to the Commons that 'there were divers able and grave citizens of London attending without, to present this House with the formidable petition we had been told of that should be brought to us by 10,000 persons: but he said that a small number was come with it, and that in a peaceable and humble manner'. The House laid all other business aside and ten or twelve of the deputation were admitted. The petition was 'about three quarters of a yard in breadth and 24 yards in length' and was signed by 15,000 or 20,000 'aldermen, aldermen's deputies, merchants, Common Council-men, subsidy-men, and citizens of London, of rank and quality'. It was presented by Fowke, 'with a speech civil and discreet': he said 'that they had got many thousand hands more to it but that they found many obstructions and much opposition from the lord mayor and others'.[60] This was an impressive demonstration of power and wealth, immaculately organized, and a brilliant counter to the allegations of the Court and the conservatives in parliament and City: a truly bourgeois conception of how to run a revolution. It was followed up by a petition from the apprentices of London, said to be subscribed by 30,000 hands, demanding that bishops be removed from the House of Lords and their powers in the church limited; and complaining of 'the fearful dangers, perilous plots, and conspiracies which have, and are still pretended by the papists against us', as well as of economic grievances.[61]

The deeper significance, however, of the petition of 11 December and its manner of presentation, was that it revealed that there were two levels of agitation taking place in London. The one was being conducted by merchants and shopkeepers, men of substance, often holding minor positions of influence in their neighbourhoods, but not generally members of the power-élite of the City, rather on the fringes of power. They were associated with the leading puritan ministers and with the opposition leaders in the House of Commons, and their agitation was designed to give support to the demands and policies of the majority faction in the Lower House. But alongside this there was another agitation being conducted by religious radicals and separatists, amongst the apprentices and young men, the craftsmen and journeymen, and the lower classes generally. Its strength lay in the suburbs, where the industries were located and where the poorer people lived. It was designed not only to overcome the opposition of the Lords but also to pressure the Commons to go further than the limited demands for the removal of bishops and papists from parliament, and to abolish episcopacy altogether and the prayer-book. It could not look to the power of wealth and influence to back its demands but only to the power of the numbers it could muster in the streets. 'All the world was now run into one trade, and that was state-mending and church modelling, in which matters "the godly and well-affected" have ever in their own opinion such a peculiar gift, that every little blue- apron boy behind the counter undertakes as boldly, as if he had served an apprenticeship at the Council-board'.[62] 'These wicked sectaries and schismatics of our City undo us all', complained Thomas Wiseman, 'they will obey no government, neither is there any hope it can be better until religion be settled, which they have great hope will be to the extirpation of bishops and the abolishing of the Book of Common Prayer'.[63]

'The faction now began to be bold and daring, and... to affront the government in the most insolent manner, imaginable, and under the pretence of petitioning the Commons to gather together in such tumultuous routs and riots, as if they would bid open defiance to the king and the laws'.[64] 'All the factious and schismatical people about the City and suburbs assembled themselves together with great licence, and would frequently, as well in the night as the day, convene themselves, by the sound of a bell or other token, in the fields, or some convenient place, to consult and receive orders from those by whom they were to be disposed.'[65] There were several big meetings in Southwark. One was described as 'a great assembly of these Brownists gathered about St George's church in Southwark, and one of their preachers a cobbler by profession violently went up into the pulpit, and made a sermon about an hour long, whom they assisted, until all the constables thereabouts had raised aid to suppress these tumultuous outrages. After this he went from thence to St Olave's church near the bridge, with all his illiterate audience after him, thinking to make another sermon there also, but being prevented, and that they could not get into the church, this preaching cobbler stood up in the church porch, and made a sermon to them all.' It may have been this or another meeting that was convened to draw up and promote a petition against bishops. According to the petitioners a constable, who was 'a friend to bishops, came amongst them to cross them, and to hinder men from subscribing' the petition. According to opponents of the petition, 'the constable, being a sober man, and known to be an enemy to those acts of sedition, went amongst them to observe what they did: he was no sooner espied but he was reproached with disdainful words, beaten, and dragged in so barbarous a manner that he hardly escaped with his life'. This assembly, wrote Nalson, 'would in any other age have been reputed a plain rebellion, as in truth it was a prologue to it, and a kind of general muster of the strength and effective numbers which the several tribes of the schismatics were able upon occasion, at the beat of their pulpit or petition drums, to bring into the field against the king, the laws, and the established government'. Sir Thomas Grimes, Sir John Lenthall and other JPs of Surrey were informed by the constables of the assemblies and disorders in Southwark and they sent a warrant to the sheriff 'to empanel a jury to inquire of these riots and routs'. But complaint was made by the petitioners to the House of Commons, which ordered the sheriff and JPs to stay 'all further proceedings'.[66]

The petition was eventually presented to the House of Commons on 23 December, and was said to be signed by 30,000 apprentices and other young men (the latter being, presumably, servants who had completed their apprenticeships to their crafts, but were employed as wage-earning journeymen while hoping soon to set up as small masters with their own businesses). These petitioners demanded that popish lords and other eminent papists be secured, the laws against priests and jesuits be executed and prelacy be extirpated 'root and branch'. They complained that, despite the efforts of the House of Commons, popery was not yet subdued, nor bishops removed, and as a result the papists 'have taken great encouragement, desperately to plot against the peace and safety' of the king's dominions, hence the rebellion in Ireland. They identified the bishops with the papists, and declared: 'We stand solemnly engaged... with the utmost of our lives, power, and estates to defend your sacred majesty and royal issue, with the rights, and liberties of parliaments, and all your majesty's subjects, against papists and popish innovators, such as archbishops, bishops, and their dependents appear to be'.[67] While these petitioners talked conventionally of defending the king as well as the two Houses, they were preparing to counter an expected royal coup against the opposition to the crown in parliament: 'The 'prentices dare give out that they will be able if need be to overmatch a royal coup.'[68]

This petition was received by the House of Commons with markedly less enthusiasm and more controversy than the petition of the wealthier citizens on 11 December. Once again, though, it was alderman Pennington who informed the House that there were 'divers young men of this City of London' outside with a petition. They were admitted with their petition 'made up into a great roll of paper with about 30,000 hands to it'. They complained 'that they had had divers interruptions and hindrances from the lord mayor and recorder of London in their getting hands to the... petition and some of them had been therefore imprisoned'. Their petition was read, 'wherein they desired amongst other things that episcopacy might be rooted out of the Church of England. After the petitions were read there followed a general silence for a while. I first stood up and spake in effect following', wrote D'Ewes: 'That I desired the House to take notice in what an orderly and peaceable a way a few of them had come to present this petition: and that they might receive the approbation of this House for the same, neither did I doubt but that they had proceeded with the like order and discretion in getting hands to it, and that for the petition itself we would take it into consideration in due time being glad that the meanest of the people were sensible of the danger and safety of the king. Divers spake after me, some against the petition earnestly moving that it might be cast out of the House and yet many of them seconded the first part of my motion... Others spake as earnestly for the petition' and to give them redress against the lord mayor. The House agreed to express approval of the orderly manner in which the petition had been delivered; to take it into consideration 'as soon as the great affairs of the kingdom will permit'; and to inquire into the actions of the lord mayor.[69]

Popular movements in London had become increasingly vocal and organized, demanding radical changes in religion, and as the first step, the abolition of episcopacy. In reaction against these movements a party of order had come into existence in the ruling class, less concerned about constitutional issues like the king's prerogative to choose his ministers and ecclesiastical questions such as the precise form of church government or the details of the liturgy, than about the threat of popular demands and tumults to the domination of the political and social system by the nobility, gentry and richer classes, and very anxious for strong action to restore order and to put the people in their place. But there had also appeared in the ruling class a popular party, especially in the House of Commons, which saw in the emergence of the party of order the growing threat of a coup by the king and the Court to crush the opposition and get rid of the parliament. It was also conscious that the only defence against such a coup, and the only hope now of pushing through further moderate reforms, was popular support; but it was at the same time nervous of popular movements, and sought further moderate reforms as the means of diverting the people away from more radical demands, and would ally with the people with the aim of controlling and drawing the teeth of popular movements, so as to ensure the safety of the ruling class.

4

THE DECEMBER DAYS

THE POPULATION of London and its suburbs may have numbered as many as 450,000 at this time. It comprised 8 per cent of the population of the entire kingdom, and was by very far the largest urban area, no other town in the country having more than 25,000 inhabitants.[1] London contained the most massive concentration of poor people in the whole kingdom, and a very high proportion of its population consisted of recent immigrants from the provinces. Crowded together in the slums, the latter shed many of the traditions of authority and deference into which they had been born in their villages, and many of the assumptions and ideas in which they had been brought up in the rural areas. They were open to new impressions and to radical notions; and, removed from the more hierarchical and more patriarchal structures of rural society, they felt more of a sense of solidarity with others in their own condition and less of a sense of loyalty towards superiors, and out of this was born class-consciousness. London had grown too fast for its machinery of government, with the forces of repression at its disposal, to be able very easily to control its population and maintain order; but it had not grown too large for rumours and ideas to spread quickly over the whole area, and for popular movements to embrace the entire city.[2]

The Londoners and the members of the parliament had become more overwrought as the months passed. It was not only rumours and fears of popish plots but an unusual combination of stresses and anxieties that agitated the capital. Political and religious demonstrations were unsettling, but so were the outbreak of plague and the arrival of gangs of ex-soldiers disbanded from the army which the king had raised in 1640 to fight the Scots.[3] During the summer of 1641 plague and smallpox had increased and spread in London and Westminster, and this was always seen as a sign of god's growing displeasure, and it fired the zeal of the godly to rid England of popery and papists. MPs retired to the country and were reluctant to return for the second session of the parliament, causing a decline in attendance at crucial divisions, which probably favoured the radicals, who never absented themselves. Well-to-do citizens got out of the City, causing the poor, who had no choice but to remain and take their chance with death, to feel more bitter against the wealthier classes; and at the same time reducing the forces of the rich who normally controlled and ordered the people.[4]

Since the disbandment of the army its ex-officers had been hanging about London waiting for their arrears of pay and hoping for employment in the forthcoming expedition against the Irish rebels. 'These behaved with unusual insolence, and struck terror into the minds of the common people'; and Nehemiah Wallington described them as 'armies of men come out of the north parts, with fierce countenances, and with deadly weapons, that puts all us citizens in great fear that there is no good meant towards us'. And, it followed, that they were believed many of them to be papists.[5] These officers were professional soldiers—mercenaries willing to fight for any paymaster; they were generally younger sons of the gentry, with a reputation for drunkenness, swearing, quarrelling, and a readiness to draw their swords at any imagined affront. The citizens disliked and feared them—no doubt in part because they did not pay their bills—and the officers treated the citizens with snobbish contempt. These cavaliers, as they were called, who were soon to give their name to a party, paraded their gentility, regarding themselves as models of what gentlemen were like, and in so doing brought dislike upon the whole class they claimed to exemplify. They exhibited in their arrogance and stupidity all that the common people, especially in the middle ranks of the citizens, most disliked about the ruling class. And they posed indeed a serious threat: they were adventurers whose swords were for hire, ready to be employed, but in what service?

These officers had their own grievances against the House of Commons. When they were disbanded they were given half their arrears of pay and promised the rest by 10 November. But the money was not forthcoming and on 19 November they petitioned their late general, the earl of Holland, who persuaded the Lords to take up the matter with the Commons.[6] On 2 December the Commons told the officers that they could not pay them anything until the end of February, because 'of the great businesses of this kingdom, and the occasions late fallen out in Ireland'.[7] This made the officers very angry and they drew up a petition to the Commons, 'in which they showed their great necessity having neither money nor credit left; and therefore desired this House to take some speedy course for their pay'. They persuaded Hampden to present their petition and their case to the House. About £26,000 was due to the officers, and at first the Commons seemed prepared to vote them half of this, but at length, on 9 December, they voted them only £6,000. And two days later Sir William Lewis had to point out that the House had overlooked to say where this money was to come from or who was to pay it out; then the House ordered that it should come out of the subsidies and poll-money lodged in the Chamber of London and be paid out by Sir William Uvedale, the late treasurer of the army.[8] This would have given the officers about £25 each, whereas they were owed over £100 each, and in addition claimed that they ought to have been given a month's extra pay on disbandment, which, they said, was the practice of all other armies in all other nations. They protested in another petition to the Commons that the £25 each 'would no ways satisfy their necessities, they most of them standing engaged for most of that which was due to them, so as they daily feared arrests and imprisonments, and therefore they desired the House to make payment to them of the whole arrears'. Sir John Colepeper took up their cause on 18 December and some of the officers were called in and told by the Speaker 'that the House had taken into consideration their petition and had before this time given them satisfaction had they not been pressed with the unexpected necessities of the kingdom and that we did intend with all convenient speed to advise of some means to give them content'.[9] On 21 December, on Hampden's motion, the Commons voted to pay the officers £13,000 instead of £6,000, or half of what they were owed; and it seems that this was now actually paid.[10] After hanging about Westminster for weeks and lobbying MPs the officers had at last got half their money. They had no reason to be grateful to the House of Commons, and the prospect of getting the rest of what they were owed seemed remote. They hoped to be taken on for service in Ireland, and this was another reason why they were hanging about Westminster, for they were lobbying for commands in the army that was to be raised. The delay, as a result of the political crisis, in forming this army, was very frustrating to the officers, and no doubt they were inclined to blame the Commons. They were a disgruntled and discontented group: a pool of experienced swordsmen ready for violent actions, mostly lodged in and about Covent Garden, and with friends at Court, they were conveniently at hand to provide the king with the means of using force against the parliament.

On 15 December the Commons, after a fierce debate, resolved by 135 votes to 83 to print the Grand Remonstrance.[11] On 21 December the elections took place for the Common Council of London and went 'largely in favour of the puritan opposition'.[12] The puritan Nehemiah Wallington called this the 'putting out of those Common Council-men that were not well affected, and there were chosen in most wards very wise and sound Common Council-men, which was a great mercy of God'.[13] The City being distracted with 'fear and jealousies', wrote an opponent of the puritans, 'it was no difficult matter for this active faction to instil into their fellow-citizens how much it concerned them to make choice of godly men... and such as would oppose the popish party... They accuse the old Common council-men as men not zealous for religion, ready to comply with the Court for loans of monies', and as promoters of a petition in favour of episcopacy and the prayer-book. 'These objections... so prevailed with these silly men, (who thought all to be in danger unless the government were put into new hands,) that, in most wards, the old Common Council-men were turned out, and new chosen in, wholly devoted to the puritan faction'.[14] 'By the concurrence and number of the meaner people, all such who were moderate men and lovers of the present government' were rejected, 'and in their places men of the most active and pragmatical heads, (of how mean fortunes soever,)' were elected, who were ready to take their directions from the dominant faction in the House of Commons, 'and as forward to encroach upon their superiors, the mayor and aldermen, as the other upon the House of Peers'.[15] There was also an element of social as well as political and religious discontent in this democratic upsurge in London, for one objection to the old Common Council-men was that they had assessed taxes unfairly, so that they weighed unduly on the poor, who were then prosecuted if they did not pay.[16]

On his return from Scotland the king had banked on a shift of opinion in his favour both in parliament and in the City; but his party remained in a minority in the Commons, and his opponents amongst the citizens were advancing towards control of the government of London. In order to keep control of the capital and maintain order, the king looked to the Tower. On 21 December the Lieutenant of the Tower, Sir William Balfour, whose sympathies lay with the opposition, for which he had done signal service by frustrating attempts to procure Strafford's escape, was dismissed. The king intended, on the advice of lord Digby, to appoint Sir Lewis Dyves, 'but he being not at that time in town', and the king and Digby evidently having plans that did not allow of delay, Digby recommended Colonel Thomas Lunsford instead. On 23 December Lunsford was appointed Lieutenant of the Tower.[17] He was one of the ex-officers hanging about London at this time and there could not have been an appointment better calculated to provoke alarm amongst the citizens, and to confirm suspicions that the king was planning to use force against the opposition. The same day that the appointment was announced, some Common Council-men and other citizens, led by Randall Mainwaring and Maximilian Bond, two captains in the City's trained bands, brought a petition to the Commons against Lunsford.[18] The Commons heard that he was 'a man given to drinking, swearing and quarrelling, much in debt and very desperate', who 'may be tempted to undertake any ill design'. They even heard that he was 'not right in his religion', for 'when he was a commander in the north... he did not go to church'. This last allegation was later withdrawn, but the damage had been done. Such a man, it was agreed, would not have been appointed 'unless there were some dangerous design in hand against us'; and the Commons resolved that he was 'not fit, to be or continue Lieutenant of the Tower of London, as a person in whom the Commons of England cannot confide'.[19]

But the Lords would not agree to join with the Commons in the request to remove Lunsford and appoint Sir John Conyers in his stead. The Commons drew up a Declaration: 'We... being very sensible of the great and imminent danger of the kingdom, through the design of the papists and other persons disaffected to the public peace, and finding, by frequent and evident symptoms, that the same groweth very near to maturity, amongst which we reckon this not to be the least, that the Tower... should be put into the hands of a man so unworthy, and of so dangerous a disposition': the House of Lords refusing to join with the Commons in the request to the king to remove this man, the Commons 'do hereby declare, before God and the whole kingdom, that, from the beginnings of this parliament, we have done our uttermost to preserve the state from ruin', and though they have prevailed against so many plots, yet the rebellion in Ireland encourages the malignant party here', and so does the obstructiveness of the House of Lords, which is caused by the votes of bishops and papists; therefore the Commons do 'declare and protest, that we are innocent of the blood which is like to be spilt, and of the confusions which may overwhelm this state, if this person be continued in his charge'. The Commons announced that they were resolved to petition the king to remove Lunsford 'and if any of your lordships have the same apprehensions that we have, we hope they likewise will take some course to make the same known to his Majesty'. The Lords decided, by a majority, to put off consideration of the Commons' statement until Monday, but this crisis seriously split the Upper House and twenty-two of the peers in the minority registered their protests against the decision.[20] 'So as now all things hastened apace to confusion and calamity', lamented D'Ewes, 'from which I scarce saw any possibility in human reason for this poor church and kingdom to be delivered.'[21] The majority in the

Commons was not only appealing to the dissident peers, it was also appealing to the people, which meant in practice the London mob.

The next day was a Sunday, and no doubt many a puritan pulpit sounded the alarm. The news rapidly spread through London 'that wicked bloody Colonel Lunsford... was sworn Lieutenant of the Tower. I did hear', wrote Wallington, 'he was an outlawed man, and that he had killed two, and was put into Newgate, and that he broke forth of Newgate, and fled beyond sea. And now he was come to have the charge of the strength of our City, that upon the least occasion he might batter down our houses on our heads, insomuch that now all in the City and many other places were much displeased'.[22] There was uproar in London and twice the lord mayor hurried to the palace to tell the king that the apprentices and 'other inferior persons' were rising in tumults and threatening to storm the Tower if Lunsford were not removed at once, and that he could not control them. The king called a meeting of the privy council, at which it was decided to dismiss Lunsford and to issue a proclamation against unlawful assemblies in London and Westminster.[23]

It was the panic in London over Lunsford's appointment that precipitated the demonstrations and disturbances of the next few days, coupled with the belief that the Lords, or rather the bishops and papists in the Upper House, were putting the kingdom in peril, and the lives and properties of the citizens, by refusing to co-operate with the Commons, plus frustration at the lack of success so far in the campaign against episcopacy and the prayer-book. On Monday 27 December 'great companies' of Londoners marched to Westminster to know the answer to their petition against Lunsford, still unaware that he had been dismissed. When they heard the news, they did not disperse but remained to know the answer to their other petitions, against bishops and popish lords. They made a lane 'in both the Palace yards, and no man could pass but whom the rabble gave leave to, crying, "A good lord", or "A good man—let him pass".' Soon they set up the cry of *'No bishops! No bishops!';* and the bishops were 'assaulted as they went upstairs to the Lords' House, and their gowns torn'. As the archbishop of York (lately bishop of Lincoln), 'passed from the stairhead into the

entry that leads to the Lords' House', he was jostled and
assaulted and his gown torn: 'Had it not been for my lord of
Dover and my lord Fauconberg that rescued him, he had been
pulled in pieces, but he had no harm, only his tippet torn off.'
But accounts more sympathetic towards the crowd maintained
that the people did not go beyond verbal violence, and that the
archbishop himself provoked the trouble by seizing hold of a
youth who was crying 'No bishops'. The archbishop was
immediately surrounded by a hundred people who 'hemmed
him in that he could not stir; and then all of them with a loud
voice cried out *"No bishops! No bishops!"*; and presently after
let him go'.[24]

By a strange coincidence, Colonel Lunsford himself was in
Westminster Hall, together with a number of other officers, at
their usual stations lobbying for their arrears of pay and for
commands in Ireland. According to Lunsford and the officers,
the citizens shouted abuse at them, and, fearing assault, they
drew their swords. The crowd then began to throw stones, so
in self-defence they drove them off with their swords.[25] But,
according to the citizens, 'there came some sixteen or seventeen
gentlemen-like men, and in a kind of foolish way said they
would drive away all the citizens out of Westminster Hall, and
every man drew his sword and flourished up and down the Hall
as if were to invite combat, but struck no man'.[26] Then Captain
David Hyde 'began to bustle, and said he would cut the throats
of those roundheaded dogs that bawled against bishops (which
passionate expressions of his, as far as I could ever learn,
was the first minting of that term or compellation of
Roundheads...)'.[27] He shouted 'Who says no bishops?' and some
of the citizens replied 'We say no bishops': 'With that Captain
Hyde drew his sword, and Colonel Lunsford with six more of
that crew, drew their swords, and drived out of the hall the
citizens, and cut many of them very sore', chasing them about
the Hall.[28] Citizens fled into the Court of Wards, where Pym
was sitting with a committee of the House of Commons, and
into the Court of Requests, defending themselves by tearing
bricks and tiles from the walls and hurling them at the
officers.[29] The House of Lords had sent the Gentleman Usher
to tell the people to return to their homes on pain of being
proceeded against according to the law, but he came back to

report that the people said that they were afraid to go because Colonel Lunsford and other soldiers lay in wait for them in Westminster Hall, and some of them had been wounded already.[30] Sir Thomas Fanshawe told the Commons 'that in Westminster Hall there was a tumult of near upon 500 persons, and that divers swords were drawn'; and alderman Pennington brought in some citizens who gave evidence that they had been attacked by Lunsford and other gentlemen.[31] In the meantime, Lunsford and his companions had been driven back by the hail of missiles, and then John Lilburne, with 'about a hundred citizens, some six with swords, as many with cudgels', some sailors with truncheons, 'and the rest with stones, came against the gentlemen thus flourishing with their swords, and first with a volley of stones let fly at them, then came up close to them, half of the gentlemen running away. The rest, some eight of either side, maintain the fight until the gentlemen were all run away or beat down. Two or three only were hurt of the gentlemen, more of the citizens, who fought like enraged lions'. 'And this', according to the author of this account, 'was all that passed, myself being against my will, a beholder of the whole business'.[32]

The news of Lunsford's attack on the citizens travelled swiftly to London, and 'many hundreds of apprentices and others came down to the parliament, with swords and staves and other weapons; which caused a great uproar as well in the City as at Westminster'.[33] Some of the apprentices were arrested and held prisoner in the Mermaid Tavern. This angered their comrades, and Peter Scott, one of the constables of the parish of St Martin-in-the-Fields, sought to appease the crowd by saying that he would try to get the prisoners released. He went to the tavern, accompanied by another constable, but when he tried to enter a sword was thrust at him and he was cut on the leg. This enraged the apprentices, who stormed the tavern and freed their comrades.[34] The crowds still milling about parliament, the Lords sent the Gentleman Usher a second time to tell them 'that this House dislikes their coming in multitudes, and commands them to be gone'; and dispatched a message to the Commons 'concerning the multitudes of people gathered about the Houses of Parliament', asking the Lower House to join them in a petition to the king 'that the Houses of

Parliament may have a guard', and in a Declaration forbidding the people to assemble 'in such companies and disorders, about the Houses of Parliament'.[35]

The king issued the proclamation, which had been prepared at the meeting of the privy council the previous evening, commanding the people to disperse and return to their homes. 'His Majesty taking into his princely consideration the manifold inconveniences and mischiefs that may arise and happen by the riotous and tumultuous assemblies, in and about the cities of London and Westminster, not only to the violation of his majesty's peace, and scandal of government, but to the disturbance of his Houses of Parliament now assembled; doth straitly charge and command all the inhabitants of his cities of London and Westminster, and the liberties thereof... that upon no occasion they do assemble themselves in any tumultuous or riotous manner, in any part or place in or near the said cities or liberties, and that all persons now assembled in any numbers, (without his majesty's authority) do forthwith... dissolve their assemblies and companies, and repair to their dwellings or places of abode, upon their perils of being proceeded against as violators of the public peace of this his majesty's kingdom, and of being punished according to the severity of the laws and statutes of the same.'[36] The king commanded the trained bands of Westminster and Middlesex to be raised and sent to guard the Palace of Whitehall night and day.[37] The lord mayor and sheriffs of London rode about all evening trying 'to appease the tumults': they ordered the gates of the City to be shut and strong watches to be set in every place, 'as well men in arms as otherwise'. The king instructed the lord mayor to raise the trained bands of London to help him to restore order, by shooting to kill if the crowds resisted them or refused to disperse, 'for however we are unwilling and sorry to use such extremity against any our subjects, yet since we are by their disorder constrained, we have thought it better that so strict and severe a course be taken against some disorderly persons than that there should happen an inconvenience to our good people in general, which such insolencies do threaten'. The lord mayor accordingly summoned the trained bands to muster the next day for the safety of the city.[38]

In the House of Lords the bishops sat anxiously on their

bench listening to the roars of the crowds outside; and the bishop of Exeter recalled: 'It grew to be torch-light, one of the lords, the marquis of Hertford, came up to the bishops' form, told us we were in great danger, advised us to take some course for our safety, and being desired to tell us what he thought was the best way, counselled us to continue in the Parliament House all that night; for (saith he) these people vow they will watch you at your going out, and will search every coach for you with torches, so as you cannot escape.' But the earl of Manchester and some other lords 'undertook the protection of the archbishop of York, and his company (whose shelter I went under) to their lodgings; the rest, some of them by their long stay; others, by secret and far-fetched passages escaped home'.[39] As the peers and MPs left the Houses, the earl of Huntingdon described the scene that met them: 'ten thousand prentices were betwixt York House and Charing Cross with halberds, staves and some swords. They stood so thick that we had much ado to pass with our coaches, and though it were a dark night their innumerable number of links made it as light as day. They cried, "No bishops, no papist lords", looked in our coaches whether any bishops were therein, that we went in great danger.'[40]

Early next morning, Tuesday 28 December, 'the citizens and apprentices flocked... in greater numbers to the Houses than the day before, divers of them being armed with halberds, swords, and other offensive weapons'.[41] An Irish bishop reported 'mine eyes did see them, and mine ears did hear it said, "What bishop soever they met would be his death", and I thanked God they knew not me to be a bishop'.[42] 'The rout did not stick openly to profess that they would pull the bishops in pieces.'[43] As the bishop of Winchester was coming in by boat to land at the parliament-stairs, he saw 'a company of prentices and others standing on the shore, crying "No bishops"'. Onlookers 'cried out to his lordship, and advised him not to land there; and thereupon he caused the boat in which he was to turn off, and carry him to Lambeth'.[44] Whenever a bishop's boat appeared on the horizon the apprentices shouted 'a bishop, a bishop', 'and so with cries kept them from landing, they rowing up and down about an hour, and at last went back'.[45] Only one or two bishops succeeded in taking their seats in the

House of Lords this day, the rest saying 'that, by reason of the great concourse of people, and their menaces, they were afraid to come to the parliament'.[46]

The apprentices having successfully driven away the bishops, 'there was a buzz among them to take their way to Westminster Abbey' and throw down the organs, monuments and other relics of popery.[47] The archbishop of York, being also dean of Westminster, had advance warning of the coming attack, and he collected his own servants, the officers of the church and the servants of the canons, and barred the doors of the abbey. The crowd forced open one of the doors but were driven back by stones and missiles hurled from the roof of the abbey, and by some of the archbishop's gentlemen, who 'rushed out with swords drawn, and drove them before them like fearful hares'.[48] But according to accounts more sympathetic towards the people, the crowd did not go to smash the monuments. Some apprentices had been arrested while demonstrating before parliament and detained in the abbey to be examined by the archbishop. 'The rest of the apprentices hearing thereof, came in a great company to relieve those that were detained'. They were led by John Lilburne and Sir Richard Wiseman, who went to ask for the release of the youths, but as they approached 'there issued some thirty or forty gentlemen from the abbey church, and fell pell-mell, with swords and pistols upon them, and hurt many of them'. Lilburne and Wiseman were both injured, and Wiseman subsequently died of his wounds, to become 'the martyred hero of the apprentices', who collected money amongst themselves to pay for his funeral.[49] Angry crowds now really threatened the abbey and a guard of the trained bands was stationed in the church and kept watch there all night, while the officers of the church stood on the roof.[50]

The king commanded the courtiers to wear swords, and Captain Robert Slyngesbie wrote: 'I never saw the Court so full of gentlemen; everyone comes thither with his sword'.[51] 'The mechanic citizens, and apprentices... offering very uncivil affronts not only to the bishops' persons, but even to the king himself, as they passed by his house; this incensed many gentlemen, and especially the commanders and soldiers about the town'.[52] The officers, led by Lunsford, offered their services to the king, who promptly accepted and entertained them at the palace, to the number of one hundred and twenty. A court-of-guard was built at the entrance to Whitehall, which the officers manned with a company of the Middlesex trained bands.[53] The king turned for advice to the three men who seemed to be the strong ones in this crisis, bent on vigorous measures to crush the citizens—lord Digby, the archbishop of York and the lord mayor of London—who could be relied upon to support a counter-stroke against the opposition. The archbishop called the bishops to his house to discuss some form of protest at being kept from parliament by the violence of the mob. Here was the opportunity to discredit the leaders of the opposition, and to rally support for the stand of the Lords in defence of the bishops' historic right to seats in parliament, and of the king in defence of his ancient prerogative to choose his own ministers, by demonstrating that the opposition was trying to accomplish its ends by mob violence. In the Lords, Digby moved that in view of 'the rabble's coming and pressing about the parliament', 'this is no free parliament'. After 'much dispute' it was resolved, by a majority of only four votes, 'that this parliament is at present a free parliament'.[54] 'The jesuitical faction according to their wonted custom fomenting still jealousies between the king and the people, and the bishops continually concurring with the popish lords...their last plot has been their endeavour to make this parliament no parliament, and so overthrow all acts passed and to cause a dissolution of it for the present; which has been so strongly followed by the popish party that it was fain to be put to the vote'.[55] Ironically the absence of the bishops, which justified Digby's motion, ensured its defeat. The object had been to give the king the pretext to declare the parliament incapacitated from further proceedings, and so to circumvent the Act to which he had assented, at the time of the attainder of Strafford, prohibiting the dissolution of the parliament without its own consent. The failure of this manoeuvre swept Digby and the king further along the path to violence against the parliament. It is probable that the plan had already been formed of accusing some of the leaders of the Commons of treason for inciting the mobs to come to Westminster and overawe parliament.

Order could not be restored immediately in the capital because the Commons would not take any action and the demonstrators felt they had the support of the Lower House. The Commons 'debated long and earnestly of either side near upon two hours', whether to join the Lords in a Declaration forbidding assemblies of the people about parliament, 'and the greater part of the House thought it unseasonable to make any such declaration at this time to discontent the citizens of London our surest friends when so many designs and plots were consulted against our safety'. Pym was reported to have exclaimed: 'God forbid that the House of Commons should proceed in any way to dishearten people to obtain their just desires in such a way.' 'And so it was resolved upon the question that no question touching the said Declaration should at this time be put.' The Commons informed the Lords: 'That this House will do whatsoever is fit to suppress any tumults that shall be against the safety or privilege of parliament: that the Declaration is a matter of that consequence, that they cannot as yet agree upon it'; but that they would join in a petition to the king for a guard, providing that it was commanded by the earl of Essex.[56]

The leaders of the Commons were in a dilemma. Few or no MPs actually liked or welcomed the popular tumult, which Whitelock, a lawyer and moderate reformer, described as 'a dismal thing to all sober men, especially members of parliament, to see and hear'.[57] 'Here hath been the saddest and most tumultuous Christmas that in all my life I ever yet knew', wrote another lawyer and conservative MP, Thomas Coke.[58] A speech, probably by William Smith, another lawyer MP and client of the duke of Richmond, reflected the views of the king's supporters and the Court party in the Commons: 'The greatest stop in our proceedings, is the riotous, and tumultuous assembly of vain and idle persons, who presume to begirt our House, not only in an irregular manner to prefer their petitions, but with open clamour would prescribe us what laws to enact, and what not; and what persons to prosecute, and who not.' And he urged that a speedy course be taken to suppress these tumults by having a guard about the House with orders to fire if the people did not disperse. Further, petitions 'from abrupt and disordered persons without any matter that may deserve our consideration', should be rejected; for, appeasing and tolerating these people, merely encourages them.[59] But many members of the Commons were a little frightened by the mobs, and nervous of taking actions against them that might make the disorders more serious and turn the popular fury against themselves as well as against the bishops and popish lords. 'Their friends in their ragged rows were too many to be chidden; they were more afraid of them than of the ruin of a kingdom; as little children are more afraid of a wizard than of the fire; therefore they stroke them with fair words when they meet them.'[60] The leaders of the Commons, fearful that the king planned to seize them or dissolve the parliament by force, could not afford to antagonize demonstrators who represented their only means of countering such a coup. But if the majority of the Commons had accepted the advice of William Smith and joined in measures to restore order, it would either have had to call in the king and his armed guards, which would as likely be used against the leaders of the parliament and to force a dissolution as against the mob, or have had to rely upon the trained bands, constables and 'better sort' of citizens. But it could not rely upon the latter other than in support of its existing stand against the king and the Lords; and it could not throw its weight behind the lord mayor to restore order with the forces of the City because he was a supporter of the king and opponent of the demands of the Commons majority. More significant, indeed, than the attitude of the Commons was the fact that the traditional machinery of maintaining order was coming to pieces in the lord mayor's hands. The 'several precepts' that he issued, 'for a continual watch and ward day and night for prevention and suppression' of 'the tumultuous and riotous assemblies lately spread night and day in several parts of the city', were frequently ignored; and many members of the trained bands, 'in contempt of authority', failed to obey his orders to muster.[61] Many of the trained bands were in sympathy with the demonstrators;[62] and so were some of the constables.[63] The trained bands and the constables were drawn from the middle ranks of the citizens; and it was upon these middle ranks—the small employers of the capital—that the maintenance of order amongst the apprentices, journeymen and the lower classes generally, depended. But many of these small employers were in sympathy with the aims of the mobs; sometimes openly encouraged their apprentices and servants to take part in the demonstrations, and sometimes themselves joined the crowd to shout against bishops and papists.[64] If the majority of the Commons was unwilling to place itself at the mercy of forces commanded by the king and the lord mayor, it had no choice but to acquiesce in the tumults of the middling and poorer sorts of citizens of London.

On Wednesday 29 December the citizens and apprentices, armed with clubs and swords, again assembled early in the morning about the two Houses, and as the members arrived, roared out *'No bishops! No popish lords!'*[65] The House of Lords sent for the sheriffs of Middlesex and London, and some of the JPs of Westminster, and asked them why they did not stop the people coming down to parliament, and why they did not obey the king's writ to prevent and suppress routs and tumults. They replied that when they had obeyed that writ on 10 December and sent guards to parliament, they had been questioned by the Commons and their guards sent away. The Lords asked the Judges 'what is fit to be done for to disperse and prevent multitudes of people assembling hither'. They answered that the best way was to put into execution the statute *13 Henry IV cap vii*. Asked what was the usual practice in other courts for preventing tumults and routs, they replied 'that it is usual at assizes, for the sheriff of the county to attend all the while, with a competent number of men'. The Lords then ordered the sheriffs of Middlesex and London and the JPs of Westminster to do their duty according to the statute, 'at their own perils; and, if they doubted of anything, then they are to resort to this House for advice and directions therein'; and they instructed the under-sheriff of Middlesex and two of the JPs of Westminster to attend the House daily to receive directions 'for the preventing and suppressing of riots and tumults hereafter'. The Lords also decided that an order should be drafted to forbid any but members of parliament to wear swords or other weapons near the two Houses.[66] The king issued another proclamation commanding the citizens and apprentices to disperse and return to their homes, which was published by the sheriffs of London that afternoon.[67]

As the citizens and apprentices made their way to and from Westminster, they surged about Whitehall, keeping up their shouts of 'No bishops! No papist lords!' They pressed about the gates of the palace, 'and their tongues were so lavish, that they talked treason so loud, that the king and queen did hear them... Sometimes they called out for Religion, sometimes for Justice... Every tinker and tapster called for Justice'. 'They cried "They would have no Porter's Lodge, but would come to speak to the king themselves" '.[68] The gates were guarded by some of the officers, some of the gentlemen of the Court, 'and divers servingmen and footmen'. 'Some words of distaste' passed between the citizens and the gentlemen. 'There stand redcoats, a knot of papists!', shouted one of the crowd, and threw a clot of dirt. At this 'the gentlemen, with their swords drawn', leapt over the rails, calling the citizens 'ram-headed rogues', abusing them 'with base language, not only apprentices but men of good rank and quality... to the great disparaging and disheartening of them in their trades and callings'. 'Cavaliers', shrieked the citizens: 'Roundheads', replied the officers; and so the party labels were first established in this clash between citizens and gentlemen. They expressed a conflict of classes, for 'Cavalier' meant a gentleman and 'Roundhead' referred to the short hair of citizens, in contrast with the long locks of gentlemen. 'And so the affray began, many swords being drawn on either side, and those who would deliver their swords, the gentlemen gave them a kick, and bade them begone; others that resisted had some hurt.'[69] On the gentlemen's side it was claimed that they had shown great restraint: 'In all these skirmishes they have avoided thrusting because they would not kill them', reported Captain Robert Slyngesbie;[70] 'they are dealing cautiously with these last to avoid provoking more dangerous disturbances', wrote the Venetian ambassador.[71] But on the citizens' side it was said that 'many of the 'prentices were wounded', perhaps forty to fifty or sixty, others 'lost their hats and cloaks', and many were disarmed; 'much hurt hath ensued, very many wounded and hurt on both sides, some hands cut off, others arms, others sides of their faces cut off, very many wounded and hurt'.[72] Whether anyone was killed is uncertain: one of the citizens may have been, and after 1649 the legend grew up that he was killed on the spot where the king later lost his head.[73] Eight or nine apprentices were arrested by guards drawn together by the sheriffs of London and Middlesex and committed to the

Gatehouse Prison.[74]

The Commons took the side of the citizens and told the Lords: 'That the House of Commons have received information of great disorders committed between this and Charing Cross; that certain persons in the habits of gentlemen, who are reported to be officers in the late English army, and are now in Whitehall, or some places thereabouts, backed and countenanced by a guard of the trained bands attending about Whitehall, do issue out in numbers, and assault the king's subjects going and returning in the king's peace to and from the parliament, offering them (as they are credibly informed) no offence at all, and twenty or thirty of them are wounded. This the House of Commons conceive to be a true violation of the liberty of the subject, and an affront to the parliament, and will, in the end, strike an awe and terror into the parliament, if not prevented by the wisdom of your lordships and the House of Commons.'[75] The Commons also sent four of their members, including alderman Pennington, to discover why the apprentices had been imprisoned in the Gatehouse, and by whose authority. They went and secured their release.[76] The Commons were by now far more frightened by the armed men that the king was gathering at Whitehall than of the mob. And even more frightened when they heard that the archbishop of York was assembling soldiers in Westminster Abbey: 'if this is to be suffered, to have guards set about the parliament in this manner', they told the Lords, 'to the terror and affray of the people, the House of Commons submit it to your lordships' judgement; and therefore, to prevent all inconveniences', desire the Lords to join them in a petition to the king for a guard under the command of the earl of Essex, 'otherwise there will follow certain mischief in the end; which the House of Commons foreseeing, do give their lordships timely warning, that, if it happen, they may clear themselves to all the world; therefore, that we may still be a free parliament', ask the Upper House to concur with them. But, after a long debate, the Lords refused.[77] The Commons ordered the JPs and Bailiffs of Westminster to set a double watch and guard about the city of Westminster.[78]

The situation, however, was in danger of getting out of hand. The leaders of the Commons needed the support and protection of the people of London, but they did not directly control the mob, whose leaders tended to be more radical than themselves; and they did not want to provoke the king and the party of order into violent action if it could be avoided. Although they did not join publicly with the Lords in measures to restore order, their allies in the City leadership were at the same time engaged in calming rather than inciting the crowds. Two thousand apprentices 'with clubs, swords, halberds' gathered in the City to go to the rescue of some apprentices that they heard had been arrested and sent to prison by the lord mayor. Some cried 'To the White Lion' (a prison), 'and others cried out, to my lord mayor's; but by the providence of God, and the grave wisdom of Captain Venn, they were prevented'. Venn met them in Cheapside and spoke to them: 'Gentlemen. Let me entreat you to be at peace and quietness, and return everyone to his own habitation, and you shall find we will be as ready to do any favour for you, and relieve you in any of your just grievances, as you can or shall yourselves, and as you show your willingness to us, so shall we with our lives be willing and ready to help you: therefore pray depart every man to his own home in peace, that it may not be said of you, they are rude and tumultuous, but that you show yourselves to be discreet in all your affairs, to the advancing of the cause you have in hand; and refer the cause to us which will be ready to support you to our powers in all that shall be just. Then some cried out, "But what should they do for their brethren that were committed by my Lord Mayor, and at Westminster, before they shall suffer we will spend all our lives".' Venn replied that the House of Commons had already secured the release of those committed at Westminster: 'And if my lord mayor hath committed any, I will warrant you, if you will be quiet, and take my word, they shall be released every one. And as soon as I have refreshed myself, I will go to my lord mayor, and have them discharged; but do you by no means go, but return home: so they all cried, Home, Home, Home, with a mighty noise. Then the major party went away, but some of them remained there which would not be satisfied, but went down to the Counter in Wood Street, where they were withstood by the officers thereto belonging, with swords and half-pikes, but some rushed in upon them, and got away one of the halfpikes from one of them, and then went up to Cheapside again, but could not be satisfied, but down they went again, and the door being shut against them, they broke it, and broke the windows. After this, the keepers of the Counter let some of them come in, and search for them in every ward, and questioned the prisoners whether there was any' apprentices there or no, 'but they found none there, and therefore went away'.[79] Reformers and men of substance like Venn were in a dilemma: far from leading the tumults they were trying to bring them to an end; but they had to move cautiously, the reforms they desired could not be achieved, against the opposition of the king, Lords, bishops, and many rich and powerful men, without popular support, often in the shape of the rowdy apprentices and youths that Venn encountered; at the same time they were anxious to maintain law and order, and the security of property, and did not want to release radical forces that they could not control. They could up to a point control the crowd because they expressed sympathy with them and desire to obtain for them what they wanted, but their leadership was not unchallenged and a more radical section of the crowd defied Venn.

Led by the archbishop of York, twelve bishops protested that 'they have been at several times, violently menaced, affronted, and assaulted, by multitudes of people, in their coming to perform their service in that honourable House; and lately chased away, and put in danger of their lives, and can find no redress or protection, upon sundry complaints made to both Houses in these particulars... They dare not sit or vote in the House of Peers, until your majesty shall further secure them from all affronts, indignities, and dangers'. They declared that all laws, orders, votes and resolutions passed in their enforced absence since 27 December were null and void.[80] This was probably an attempt to reverse the vote that had been carried in the Lords in the absence of the bishops on 28 December that it was still 'a free parliament'; and a further attempt by the Court to find a pretext for an illegal dissolution of the parliament. The king sent the bishops' protest to the Lords, who passed it on to the Commons. The Commons promptly impeached the twelve bishops and the Lords sent them to prison on 30 December 1641. Bells in the City churches pealed joyfully and bonfires blazed in the streets as the citizens celebrated the news. The speed and eagerness with which both Houses seized on the political miscalculation and naivety of the bishops, were probably not unconnected with the recognition that this would give 'some satisfaction to the citizens' and allay the tumults, and with the feeling that the bishops were an obstacle to a settlement of the political crisis.[81]

The assemblies of the citizens at Westminster and Whitehall were not resumed on 30 December, partly because they were 'satisfied with the impeachment of the twelve bishops'.[82] But there were other reasons. The main object of their hatred being quite suddenly and unexpectedly gratified, and it not being easy to go on demonstrating continuously for more than three days on end, the marching and shouting and fighting on Monday, Tuesday and Wednesday had released many of the tensions and fears that had been building up for weeks in the City, exhausted the citizens and drained their emotions. At the same time, it is important not to under-estimate the opposition that the citizens had encountered: they had taken on the state and a large part of its ruling class and, even in Charles I's England, the state and its masters were a formidable enemy: the forces of order were still powerful and still undefeated. In the latter stages of the riots the demonstrators had been thrown on the defensive, increasingly concerned with protecting themselves against the onslaughts of the king's guards and with rescuing their comrades arrested by the lord mayor and sheriffs. 'The citizens being more tongue than soldier', had few weapons and less skill to pit against the professional soldiers ranged in Whitehall.[83] They were still nursing their wounds from the clashes, while still more formidable forces were rallying to the defence of established authority. The Court, in fact, expected greater attacks on Whitehall in revenge for the casualties the apprentices had suffered: the guards were increased and the defences strengthened, and this was a deterrent to further demonstrations.[84] A considerable addition of strength came to the Court on 30 December: some three to five hundred young gentlemen of the four Inns of Court, the academies of nobility and gentry, marched to the palace, vowed their love for the king, the queen and the royal family, whose persons they believed were in danger, and offered 'their service for the suppression of these tumultuous assemblies'.[85] In the opinion of Captain Robert Slyngesbie, the tumults died down, not only because the citizens were satisfied with the imprisonment of the bishops, but also because they were 'terrified by the multitudes of gentry and soldiers who flock to the Court, which I never saw so thronged as now it is, and the rough entertainment that was like to be given them if they came again'.[86]

The City government was also pulling itself together again and the wealthier citizens were rallying to the side of law and order against the defiance of authority and disorders of the lower classes. On 31 December the Common Council of London met and heard a message from the king, brought by lord Newburgh: 'There having been of late many tumultuary and riotous assemblies of people about our palaces of Whitehall and Westminster, to the great disturbance of us and our parliament: and we having received information, that some ill-affected persons do still endeavour to incite the like tumults again, we have thought fit to recommend to your especial care the preventing them, as far as in you lies, especially the ensuing holidays, at which the idleness of many may make them apter to such disorders. We have thought fit likewise to let you know, that we are so well assured of the good affections of our City of London, by the great expressions which it hath made unto us of them of late, that we can no wise understand it to have any share in the fault of these tumults and distempers, but that they proceed merely from the mean and unruly people of the suburbs.' The Common Council replied to the king that neither 'this court, nor any particular member thereof, hath had any hand in these tumultuous and riotous proceedings', which had been 'to the great trouble and affrightment of his majesty's good subjects' in the City, 'and that they, and every of them do disavow and disclaim the same'. They promised 'from henceforth their best endeavours to prevent and suppress in time to come (as far as in them lieth) all such, or the like tumultuous assemblies, and all mutinous and rebellious persons. And lastly... that all the delinquents and causers of these tumults, whatsoever they be, being apprehended, may be brought into examination, and receive condign punishment according to the law.' The Common Council then proceeded to reprimand the citizens for failing to obey the lord mayor's orders for keeping watch and ward and the trained bands for failing to obey the lord mayor's summons to muster during the tumults. They agreed 'that every member of this Common Council... shall in their several precincts, spread it abroad... that if any person, or persons, shall from henceforth neglect his duty and service to be performed... and shall not do his best endeavour to suppress, or prevent any tumults, or riotous assemblies, that shall hereafter be attempted within this City, or liberties thereof, that then he or they offending, shall receive condign punishment'. The Common Council authorized the lord mayor and aldermen to make all necessary orders for watch and ward and the safety of the City, and promised obedience to all such orders as they would make.[87] This, it should be noted, was not the old Common Council, but, contrary to custom, the newly elected and more radical Councilmen attended this meeting, and presumably approved these resolutions.[88] The printing and circulating of these resolutions indicated the efforts that were being made to restore order in the City, by the leading citizens, both conservatives and reformers. The new orders for watch and ward, issued by the lord mayor and aldermen on the authority of the Common Council, directed that watches be doubled at gates, posterns and landing places; that every householder keep his servants and apprentices within doors, and be answerable for any disorders committed by them.[89] The king again authorized the lord mayor to raise the trained bands if 'any great numbers of people' again assembled together 'in a tumultuous and disorderly manner within the City', and to disperse them, by shooting if necessary.[90]

Sir Edward Walker deemed that the king was able now 'with force' to have suppressed any tumults: 'he had not wanted power; for I know the then lord mayor, most of the aldermen and eighteen of the twenty-four companies of the City would have been at his devotion; and so all the nobler and wiser part of the gentry then about London'.[91] With some hundreds of armed men (courtiers, officers and other gentlemen) guarding him at Whitehall, some hundreds of young gentlemen of the Inns of Court ready to come at his summons, backed by the City government and the richer citizens, and with the Tower of London, though Lunsford had gone, still in the hands of his own nominee, Sir John Byron, who remained loyal, the king felt confident of being able to suppress any further popular disorders. As confidence came flooding back at Court, the time now seemed to be ripe to crush the small clique that the king believed retained its power in parliament only with the help of mob violence to scare the other members.

The composition of the crowds that had demonstrated for the three 'December Days' at Westminster was variously described according to the prejudices of the observer: the less sympathetic the observer the more he stressed the low social origins of the demonstrators; the more sympathetic the observer the more he stressed their respectability. 'Many thousand of the lower sort of citizens';[92] 'multitudes of the baser sort of people';[93] thousands of 'the mechanic citizens, and apprentices';[94] 'the prentices and baser sort of citizens, sailors, and watermen';[95] 'the basest and the refuse of all men, watermen, porters, and the worst of all the apprentices';[96] the 'meanest and poorest people of those our cities and suburbs';[97] 'great store of the scum of the people';[98] 'the scum of all the profanest rout, the vilest of all men, and the outcast of the people'.[99] The king thought that they were mostly 'mean and unruly people of the suburbs', 'desperate persons of the suburbs, and the neighbouring towns', rather than inhabitants of the City proper.[100] As their opponents assumed they were mean people, so they also assumed they were 'separatists and sectaries';[101] 'multitude of the zealous sectaries, and rabble of ignorant people';[102] 'Brownists, Anabaptists, and other sectaries' and all the 'desperate varlets in city and suburbs'.[103] Accounts more sympathetic towards the demonstrators claimed that the crowds included 'men of good rank and quality',[104] but generally did not set their social status very high. There were 'no aldermen, merchants or Common Councilmen' among them, but they 'were most of them men of mean or a middle quality themselves'. They were men of 'public spirits' 'in whose breasts the spirit of liberty had some place'; religious men, 'modest in their apparel' but not on this occasion in their language; sober men, though on this occasion 'they were even glad to vent out their sighs and sufferings in this rather tumultuous than civil manner'; 'in general they were very honest and well-meaning' and feared the dissolution of the parliament.[105] It was common for contemporaries to divide the population of London into three classes: at the top the merchants engaged in overseas trade, the wholesale dealers in inland trades, and the retail shopkeepers; in the middle, the handicraftsmen, who had served an apprenticeship and exercised arts that required skill as well as manual labour; and at the bottom the labourers, who sold their labour not their skill, and included the porters who loaded and unloaded goods at the docks, the carmen or carters who carried goods to and from the docks and about the City, and the watermen who ferried passengers on the Thames, which was the main traffic artery of London. But when the analysis was made by wealth rather than by occupations, most of the retail shopkeepers fell into the middle rank.[106] There can be little doubt, from all accounts, that apprentices played a very large part in the demonstrations;[107] and parliament itself described the crowd as 'a company of boys and 'prentices'.[108] And though apprentices were frequently lumped together with the lowest class, because they had no household of their own but were in service in the household of their master, they belonged by origins and vocation to the middle rank, where they certainly felt their own place to be.[109] But as a group they were unsettled by the difficulties they knew they would encounter on ending their service in mustering the resources to set up as masters of their crafts with their own shops, and by the knowledge that many of them would not succeed and would have to become wage-earning journeymen for the rest of their lives.[110] The sympathizers with the demonstrations admitted, however, that the crowds contained some less respectable elements: 'some particular fools or others perhaps now and then got in amongst them, greatly to the disadvantage of the more sober', wrote Lilly;[111] 'thieves, and boutefures intermingled themselves for rapine's sake', and the Commons were as anxious as the king to see that they were brought to justice.[112]

Lilly admitted that the demonstrators were 'set on by some of better quality';[113] and the Venetian ambassador thought that the apprentices took part 'with the connivance of their masters, puritans for the most part'.[114] But the big question was whether the demonstrations were being organized secretly by leading politicians in parliament and City: 'There was a kind of discipline in disorder, tumults being ready at command, upon a watch-word given.'[115] 'But how it came to pass that these multitudes should come down in such disorder, and yet be sent back and dissolved so easily at a word or beck of some men, let the world judge.'[116] When the king charged Lord Mandeville and five members of the Commons —Pym, Holles, Hampden, Haselrig and Strode—with treason, one of the counts of the indictment was that 'they have endeavoured (as far as in them lay) by force and terror to compel the parliament to join with them in their traitorous designs, and to that end have actually raised and countenanced tumults against the king and parliament'; their power was such 'with a multitude of Brownists, Anabaptists, and other sectaries about London', that they were ready to appear in a body at their command' and demonstrate violently at Westminster.[117] The less extravagant and more persuasive charge against the leaders of the House of Commons, however, was that they indirectly encouraged the tumults by obstructing efforts to suppress them.[118]

No evidence was ever produced of direct involvement by lord Mandeville and the Five Members in organizing the demonstrations, but it was claimed that they operated behind the scenes through some of the City's MPs, Common Council-men and puritan preachers, who did the actual organizing. The king accused Pennington and Venn, the two radical MPs for the City, of bringing down 'their myrmidons to assault and terrify the members of both Houses, whose faces or whose opinions they liked not, and by that army to awe the parliament'.[119] Fowke and Mainwaring, the two radical Common Council-men, were also accused of being contrivers of the tumults: 'who went from house to house and brought this Hydras Head to Westminster, and put in their mouths to cry out, "No Bishops, No Popish Lords", as they had formerly in the same tumultuous manner caused them to cry for justice against the earl of Strafford'.[120] Amongst the puritan clergy, Cornelius Burgess was singled out as the ringleader of the mobs, assisted by Downing, Calamy, Harding, Bridge and Marshall, and indeed, the manipulators of the lay leaders, in that they 'get Venn and Mainwaring, and others of the same sect, to gather together' the crowds.[121] Clearly Pennington, Venn, Fowke and Mainwaring were prominent in organizing petitions and active in protecting the radical citizens, but beyond that there was only some evidence produced against Venn for organizing tumults to overawe parliament. Yet Venn, like Burgess, was to be found calming the crowds and persuading them to disperse. If some puritan preachers did organize the mobs, it was not the leading puritan preachers, who condemned attempts of the people to achieve reforms by any tumultuous, disorderly, illegal way'.[122] 'If a multitude appear in a tumult', declared the influential puritan minister Herbert Palmer, their ends 'may after plead for a mitigation of punishment toward the whole number, except the chief ring-leaders; yet it both makes those that have authority and strength to suppress, put forth both, and more speedily and effectually; and afterwards to take the most exact care for the preventing of the like, even for the multitudes sake'.[123] The leaders of the Commons and the chief puritan ministers would go so far as to explain and excuse the mobs, but never so far as to endorse popular assemblies as a legitimate means of achieving religious or political ends. Palmer explained that the tumults were caused by the refusal of the Lords to agree with the Commons on the exclusion of bishops and popish lords from parliament, and on the relief of Ireland and the militia, but, he added, 'which tumults yet I approve not nor ever did'.[124] 'I must confess 'tis much to be wished there had been none', wrote Charles Herle, puritan minister and pamphleteer for parliament in the civil war.[125] The citizens, it was claimed, were provoked by the king's guards at Whitehall, but the 'tumults and disorders' were 'never in the least countenanced or connived at by both or either Houses of Parliament'.[126] If separatists were as prominent as alleged in the crowds, this would not have endeared the demonstrators to either the parliamentary or the puritan leadership.

Few leaders in the streets can be identified. Samuel Barnardiston, an apprentice in London, and a younger son of Sir Nathaniel Barnardiston, puritan MP for Suffolk and one of the wealthiest landowners in that county, led the demonstrators during the clashes in Whitehall on 29 December, and gave rise to yet another claim to have coined the name 'Roundhead'; for Queen Henrietta Maria, looking out of a window of the palace and noticing this tall young man with closely cropped hair, exclaimed 'What a handsome young round-head!'[127] He, indeed, serves as the nearest evidence to a link between the parliamentary and puritan leaders and the mob. But more prominent than Barnardiston were Sir Richard Wiseman—'the crazy broken-down Sir Richard Wiseman, who had been a Star Chamber victim'[128]—and John Lilburne:[129] Lilburne had also been prominent in the riots against Strafford; his influence over the apprentices and the middling and poorer citizens of London was one of the constant factors of the English Revolution; and there cannot be much doubt that he must have played a major organizational role. Later the royalists were to claim that one Boys, 'the distiller of hot waters', whom they executed as a spy during the civil war, confessed before he died that he was one of the leaders of the tumults in London: 'that he was one in all the tumults of London, *viz* in that seditious assembly of unruly people crying for justice, against the earl of Strafford, in that for the assistance of the Five Members against his majesty, and in many of those tumults, he had procured others to come down to Westminster'.[130] At least this points, like the presence of Lilburne, to a continuity of leadership of the London mob in the years 1641 to 1642. But this question of leadership is not very vital: the crowd was perfectly capable of throwing up its own leaders to serve the occasion.

By and large there can be little doubt that the mob was inspired by religious radicalism, with which went a large mixture of fear of papists and anti-clericalism. William Smith, who was anxious for the suppression of the tumults, told the Commons that fear of papists was one of the causes of the troubles, and that the apprehension of leading papists would do much to allay the tumults.[131] The lord mayor told the king that the tumults 'arose from the distraction and unsettled state in religion': they complained of 'the unsettled form in divine service' and the innovations which had been introduced, that they feared were leading to the reintroduction of 'the Romish Religion'; and they grumbled at 'the pride of the bishops' and that parliament 'had now sat above a whole year, yet nothing was concluded of, or enacted to the reformation of the abuses, with which the subject was much aggrieved'.[132] Lilly described the demonstrators as 'men of mean or a middle quality' who mostly 'lived a more religious life than the vulgar, and were usually called puritans, and had suffered under the tyranny of the bishops': 'they were even glad to vent out their sighs and sufferings in this rather tumultuous than civil manner; being assured, if ever this parliament had been dissolved, they must have been wrackt, whipt and stript by the snotty clergy and other extravagant courses'.[133]

The apparent success of the Court in repelling the mob, however, was causing attitudes to harden. The citizens were in a mood of non-cooperation and were planning what amounted to a strike. 'The citizens have debated and resolved, in case things take not issue suddenly, to shut up shops and desist trade, which if three or four hundred should do all will grow to confusion suddenly.'[134] Indeed, since the clashes in Whitehall, 'many tradesmen have shut up shops and given over their trades, because they are so abused: and the adverse party, papists and their adherents, greatly countenanced and encouraged'.[135] 'The citizens', it was confirmed, 'for the most part shut up their shops'.[136] The clashes, first in Westminster and then at the gates of Whitehall, between gentlemen and citizens, in which the terms 'Cavalier', meaning a gentleman, and 'Roundhead', meaning a citizen, became for the first time the battle-slogans of parties, introduced a note of class conflict which heightened the crisis. 'The present hatred of the citizens were such unto gentlemen especially courtiers, that few durst come into the city, or if they did, they were sure to receive affronts and be abused.'[137] In the lull following the riots the situation was in fact worsening rapidly, and armed conflict was expected shortly to break out. The king maintained that he and his family were in danger of violence from the citizens and therefore he was 'compelled at our great charges to entertain a guard for securing us from that danger'.[138] But his defensive preparations persuaded the citizens that he was about to attack them. Nehemiah Wallington heard that the king 'hath armies of men come out of the north parts, with fierce countenances, and with deadly weapons, that puts all us citizens in great fear that there is no good meant towards us'.[139] 'All gentlemen provide themselves with arms as in time of open hostility.'[140] The citizens also armed themselves. 'There is now nothing sought for so much as guns and trimming up of old ones'.[141] The king received information 'that several persons

of mean quality have of late taken into their houses the unusual
number of twenty to forty muskets with ammunition' and he
ordered the lord mayor to inquire and search.[142] 'We talk now
of nothing but drawing of swords, and a war between the
Protestants and Papists', wrote Thomas Smith to Sir John
Pennington on 29 December;[143] 'it is a wonder there is no more
blood yet spilt, seeing how earnest both sides are.'[144] If in the
aftermath of the tumults the king thought himself sufficiently
strong, and the citizens sufficiently cowed, for him to carry out
a coup, the exact opposite might equally well have been deemed
to have been the case, in the light of the mood and preparations
of the citizens of London. 'There is no doubt but if the king do
not comply with the Commons in all things they desire, a
sudden civil war must ensue, which every day we see approaches nearer.'[145]

On 3 January 1642 the king charged lord Mandeville,
Pym, Holles, Hampden, Haselrig and Strode with high treason.
That day 'there was a great confluence of armed men about
Whitehall'; and Sir William Killigrew and Sir William Fleming
went to the Inns of Court, made known the charges against lord
Mandeville and the Five Members, and desired the young
gentlemen 'to be in readiness... to attend at Whitehall, and to
be ready at an hour's warning to defend his Majesty's person'.
At ten o'clock that night 'between thirty and forty cannoneers'
went into the Tower.[146] This 'put the City to much trouble and
great fear... with knocking at the doors for men to stand up on
their guard'; 'the aldermen, and the sheriffs were up that night,
and the gates looked unto, and the chains pulled cross the
streets'; 'and it was much feared that that night would have
been a bloody night, but God of his mercy kept us, that it was
not so bad as we feared'.[147] It seems that the tumult in the City
died away after midnight and the messenger sent by the king
to the lord mayor reported back: 'I was till one o'clock about the
town, and found all places very well guarded and the
tumultuous rout dispersed.'[148] But the next morning all the
shops in the City remained shut, 'with every man his halberd
and weapons in readiness'.[149] In the afternoon of that day, 4
January 1642, the king came to the House of Commons to arrest
the Five Members, accompanied by an armed guard of eighty
to a hundred of the officers, including the notorious Captain

David Hyde. But notice of his intentions having preceded him, the Five Members had taken refuge in the City. By 170 votes to 86 the House decided to resolve itself into a committee and to adjourn for a week to Guildhall 'to consider and resolve of all things, that may concern the good and safety of the City and kingdom; and particularly, how our privileges may be vindicated, and our persons secured'.[150]

The leaders of the Commons had thrown themselves upon the mercy of the City of London: everything now turned upon the loyalty of the citizens. It was a decisive moment in history and the decision lay, not with the king, not with the parliament, not with the nobility and gentry, not with armed soldiers, not with the lord mayor, aldermen or Common Council, but with the mass of the ordinary people of London. In the City and Southwark there was now what amounted to a general strike: all the shops were shut and the citizens stood in the streets with their arms.[151] 'The shops of the city generally shut up, as if an enemy were at their gates ready to enter and to plunder; and the people in all places at a gaze, as if they looked only for directions, and were then disposed to any undertaking.'[152] 'We are daily in fear of uproars', reported Thomas Smith[153]; 'we are not free from fears of an insurrection', pronounced Thomas Wiseman;[154] 'every hour here threatens public insurrection and confusion', cried Thomas Coke.[155]

On 5 January the king went into the City to address a special meeting of the Common Council called at his request. He explained his reasons for going to parliament the previous day and admonished the City not to harbour or protect the five accused members. Fowke got up and spoke of 'fears and jealousies touching the members accused, the privileges of parliament, and that they might not be tried but in a parliamentary way'. The king replied that 'they should have a just trial, according to the laws of the land; adding, that they were dangerous men, and that neither he nor they could be in safety as long as these men were permitted to go on in their way'.[156] The meeting was divided and as the king left one party cried 'God bless the king' and the other party shouted 'Parliament! Privileges of Parliament!' But as the king went into 'the outer hall', which was filled with 'a multitude of the ruder people', no such division appeared and he was greeted with a unanimous 'great cry "The Privileges of Parliament!" '[157] The king left the Guildhall and went to dine with the sheriff, Sir George Garrett. All the shops were shut, the people 'standing at their doors, with swords and halberds'.[158] 'There was nothing echoed in his ears but "Privileges of Parliament! Privileges of Parliament!" Great is Diana of the Ephesians, was never roared louder'. While he was at dinner, Garrett's house 'was beset, and the streets leading unto it thronged with people, thousands of them flocking from all parts of the city; and the clamour still was, "Privileges of Parliament!"... This tumult swelled to that height, that the king, in his return, was in great danger'.[159] A 'rude multitude' followed his coach shouting 'Privileges of Parliament! Privileges of Parliament!';[160] 'in a most undutiful manner, pressing upon, looking into, and laying hold on his coach: nay, in defiance of his sacred person, and authority, that seditious pamphlet of Walker's, "To your tents, O Israel", was thrown either into, or very near his coach: insomuch, that those few friends which the king had in the City were heartily glad when they heard that the king was safely arrived at Whitehall'.[161]

This demonstration 'made an impression on his majesty', noted the Venetian ambassador.[162] 'The king had the worst day in London... that ever he had';[163] 'the good king was somewhat moved, and I believe was glad when he was at home'.[164] As the lord mayor, aldermen and recorder were returning from escorting the king to Temple Bar, they were met with cries of 'Remember the Protestation' and called 'half-protesters'. Near Ludgate they 'were set upon by some rude persons, my lord mayor being plucked off his horse, and some of the aldermen'. 'The citizens' wives fell upon the lord mayor, and pulled his chain from his neck, and called him traitor to the City, and to the liberties of it, and had like to have torn him and the recorder to pieces.' Escaping, they and some of the aldermen were forced to make their ways home on foot, abuse being shouted at them all the way.[165]

The night of 6 January saw a panic in the City which nevertheless demonstrated the massive defence that the Five Members could expect if the king tried to enter the City and take them by force. The alarm was raised 'that the king and cavaliers, with fifteen hundred horse, were coming to surprise the City' and fetch in the Five Members by force. Wallington never forgot the terror of that night. 'We heard (as we lay in our beds) a great cry in the streets that there were horse and foot coming against the City', and there was a tremendous banging on his door and shouts of 'Arm! Arm!' 'Fear and trembling entered on all'; some women being with child were so affrighted therewith as they miscarried', and the wife of an alderman (a neighbour of Wallington) died of fright. Within an hour thousands of men were in the streets in their full arms, and many thousands more with halberds, swords, clubs and such weapons as they could lay their hands on. The gates were shut, the portcullises lowered and the chains put across the streets to stop horses. Women brought stools, forms and tubs from their houses to build barricades, and boiled water 'to throw on the cavaliers'. But the lord mayor ascertained that there were no forces coming against the City and, reassured that they were safe for the moment, the citizens returned to their beds. The cause of the alarm was variously reported to have been the accidental discharge of a carbine in Covent Garden, where many of the officers of the king's guard had their lodgings, or some men from a troop of horse, which had been raised for service in Ireland, and billeted at Barnet, riding near London and being taken for 'the forerunners of five hundred horse that were that night to come into the City'.[166]

Offers of support to defend the Five Members poured into the committee sitting at Guildhall—from the apprentices of London; from the trained bands of Southwark; from over 1,000 mariners and seamen, including 'the masters and inferior officers as well of the king's own ships as of merchants'' (foreshadowing the revolt of the fleet from the king that was to contribute so much to his defeat in the civil war).[167] A crowd of several thousand assembled in Buckinghamshire and resolved to march to London to defend their member, John Hampden. This made some members of parliament nervous and they urged that they be ordered back, but the majority decided to take no action and let them come.[168] The leaders of the Commons were now confident of their strength and of their ability to control the crowds. Parliament was to reassemble at Westminster on 11 January and the trained bands of London were detailed to protect the accused members. The apprentices were asked 'to keep at home... for the guard of the City'; and the Southwark trained bands were asked to stay on their own side of the river and to guard the south bank.[169] The king fled from London on 10 January, going first to Hampton Court and then to Windsor. He said that he and his family could no longer feel safe from the mob if they remained at Whitehall.[170] 'They who wished the king best were not sorry that he then withdrew from Whitehall; for the insolence with which all that people were transported, and the animosity which was infused into the hearts of the people in general against the Court, and even against the person of the king, cannot be expressed.'[171] On 11 January the accused members returned in triumph to Westminster. As the crowds passed the deserted palace of Whitehall they jeered 'What was become of the king and his cavaliers?'[172] The City was now the parliament's—or rather, the parliament was now the City's.

5

ECONOMIC CRISIS AND POPULAR TRIUMPH

BEHIND the popular agitation that triumphed over the king and carried the leaders of the Commons to power lay the growing economic distress of the people. The English economy was not in a flourishing condition before the assembling of the Long Parliament. 'The stop of trade here, through men's unwillingness to venture these three or four years bygone, has made this people much poorer than ordinary', observed the Scots minister Baillie, when he came to England.[1] The west country cloth industry was in a depressed state in the 1630s due to the 'long-term contraction in the traditional markets for English broadcloth.'[2] Then in 1641 there was a decline of trade in London. London dominated the bulk of the export trade of England, in which textiles formed by far the biggest part, and it had a very large share in the internal trade of the country. 'The overwhelming importance of London for much internal trade and for those sectors of the economy which relied upon overseas commerce, meant that a cessation of economic activity in the capital might have drastic repercussions for outlying areas.' The broadcloth industry, being already in a gravely weakened condition, was plunged at once into a deeper depression.[3] In the spring of 1641 the clothiers of Wiltshire, Somerset, Gloucestershire, Worcestershire, Hampshire, Berkshire, Kent and Suffolk complained 'of the deadness of their trade in London and that the merchants would not take off their cloth, or part with monies owing to them'.[4] 'Cloth production and the price of wool fell as demand, exerted through London, declined'; and the depression spread through the whole of the textile industry and then to agriculture and the rest of the economy. Henry Robinson wrote, in 1641, that 'the decay of trade is in everybody's mouth from the sheepshearer to the merchant, and even a weak statist, without Galileo's prospective glass, may see both our wealth and safety therewith declining'. This depression was caused 'by political events'. As the constitutional crisis developed, especially as the conflict over Strafford's fate became more critical, the uncertainties of the situation led foreigners to withdraw their funds from London and Englishmen became anxious 'to hold money rather than credit instruments or goods'. 'Money was taken out of circulation', leading to the growing complaints of 'scarcity of money': 'The money market became excessively tight, and commodity dealings fell off '.[5]

The petition that the Londoners had presented to parliament on 21 April 1641 for justice against Strafford said more about papists than about Strafford, and far more about trade than about papists. 'Whereas there had been a great decay of trade in this kingdom, and great scarcity of money thereby, since the first motions in Scotland... this state being looked upon by foreign nations as unsettled, it has caused strangers who were wont to furnish great sums of money at interest to call in and remit those moneys by exchange into foreign parts, and such of our own nation as were lenders to call in their money and stand in expectation of the issue of things'. The seizure of the bullion in the mint by the king in July 1640 'has caused great scarcity of money, for now the merchants and strangers forbear to bring in bullion to the mint'. Moneys owing to Londoners from Scotland and Ireland were not paid. 'Commodities also brought in find no usual vent, but at great loss, which if it continue will hinder exportation, from the high exchange abroad, whereby there is as great loss as by goods imported.' 'And by our distractions the inland trade of the kingdom is so decayed that country tradesmen cannot pay their debts in London, and many have been ruined.' Since the causes of the depression were political and not economic, the remedies must be political. The Londoners had hoped that the redress of grievances and the punishment of incendiaries would have made 'all things so settled that a free and full trade might return as before'. But since grievances have not been redressed, notorious offenders not punished, papists not suppressed, the church not reformed, fears still increased; these were 'the true grounds of the decay of trade' and 'the scarcity of money'.[6]

Cries for 'Bread' were mingled with shouts for 'Justice' from the crowds that demonstrated against Strafford on 3 and 4 May 1641 at Westminster. They followed the lords 'calling upon them for justice against the earl of Strafford... complaining that they are undone... that trading was so decayed' because of the failure to execute justice on the earl, 'that they could scarce get bread to maintain their families'. They said that they could not pay subsidies or other taxes 'if justice had not its due course, whereby there might be a free and open way of trade as formerly'.[7] On 5 May the ports were temporarily closed in an attempt to prevent the escape of the army plotters: shipping was brought to a standstill for a time and the seamen thrown out of work. On the night of 10 May a thousand seamen gathered together and declaring 'ships were stopped, trading was dead, and they must not want', and carrying the flag of a ship they marched towards the Tower and 'pulled down two houses'. The trained bands, which were guarding the Tower, fired on them, killing two and wounding others, and dispersed the rest.[8]

When the king returned to London from Scotland on 25 November, anxious to win the City to his side, he declared in his speech of thanks for the welcome from the corporation: 'I shall study to re-establish that flourishing trade, which now is in some disorder amongst you, which I doubt not to effect, with the good assistance of the parliament.'[9] The deputation from the City that waited on the king at Hampton Court on 3 December urged him to reside at Whitehall, for that 'would give a good quickening to the retailing trade, and, by consequence, to the merchants'.[10] The difficulties of the economy were caused by the political crisis, which produced the lack of confidence that led merchants to hoard money and cease trading, and it was easy to blame the king and the House of Lords for the crisis; by obstructing the measures advanced by the House of Commons, they frustrated the hopes of a political and religious settlement, without which there would not be the security and confidence for trade to revive. Since the obstructions and disagreements were attributed to the machinations of the papists, the economic distress was blamed on them and intensified the hostility towards them. The petition of 11 December for the removal of bishops and papists from parliament, signed by 15,000 or 20,000 Londoners, declared: 'the great terrors, fears, etc, distractions they lay under of a sudden surprise by their bloody hands, by means whereof the trading of the City and kingdom is much more of late decayed than it hath been for many years past, no man following his trade cheerfully, whiles the lives of himself and family, and the public safety of the kingdom are in danger, and while he knoweth not how soon they may feel the like cruelty and inhumanity from the papists, and their adherents, as those in Ireland have done'. If their demands were granted they would be 'freed from their fears, encouraged in their trades'.[11]

It may almost have been in the nature of this economic crisis that in some ways the rich got richer and the poor got poorer; in that merchants could withdraw from trading and still live comfortably on the capital which they had for months been turning into ready cash, and were perhaps better off than when undertaking the risks of trade; whereas the small shopkeepers and the handicraftsmen had to sell their wares every week to live, and the labourers had to have work or starve. The well-to-do remained concerned primarily with political and religious issues, but amongst the lower classes bread-and-butter questions loomed larger. At the same time economic distress led more of the middling and poorer people to become involved in demonstrations and to become aware of political and religious questions. And when this happened, economic questions advanced from the rear to the front of the stage, and social conflicts and class antagonisms were added to political conflicts and religious antagonisms.

The petition of 23 December from 30,000 apprentices, demanding the arrest of eminent papists and the abolition of bishops, stated: 'Whereas we, though the lowest members of the City and kingdom... do by experience find both by our own and our masters' tradings, the beginning of great mischief coming upon us, to nip us in the bud, when we are first entering into the world; the cause of which we can attribute to no others, but the papists, and prelates, and that malignant party which adheres unto them', which obstructed the measures necessary for the security of the country and the restoration of the confidence needed for trade. They believed that if their demands were granted, so that 'the reformation may be prosperously carried on, our distracting fears removed', then 'the freedom of commerce and trade may pass once more cheerfully'.[12] Another petition, also said to be signed by 30,000 apprentices and others, making the more moderate demand for the removal of the bishops from the House of Lords, included, incongruously, an attack on competition from foreign workmen —a sure pointer to economic depression: the petitioners complained that they could not afford to buy shops or houses and set themselves up in business because prices were forced up by immigrants from France and the Netherlands.[13] These immigrants were protestants fleeing from persecution by papists, but economic facts are more strongly felt than the need for consistency of principles, and this points to the agitation being concerned as much with economic difficulties as with 'popery' or 'reformation'. It was more consistent with the stated ideals to beat up the French merchants in London, because they were papists, but perhaps these attacks were also expressions of anger at the decline of the Englishman's trade.[14]

One of the reasons for the violent reaction in the City against the appointment of Lunsford as Lieutenant of the Tower arose from the fact that the mint was located in the Tower. It was believed this would further damage trade because merchants, both foreign and native, would be frightened to deposit their bullion in the mint for fear that it would be seized, as it had been in July 1640. 'Trade by this means will be decayed if Colonel Lunsford continue Lieutenant, being a man that we cannot confide in. No coin will be coined in the Tower for nobody will bring it in.'[15] The scarcity of money would be increased. The prospect of a royal coup and further disturbances in the capital made merchants collect their debts and cease to trade. The riots of 27-29 December against bishops and popish lords sprang in some measure from the economic distress of the poorer citizens of London. William Smith, in his speech calling for strong action to suppress the tumults, nevertheless pointed out that one cause of the disorders was that trading was decayed and it was hard for many of these people to subsist.[16] The lord mayor of London also attributed the tumults partly to the depression of trade.[17] The king's attempt to arrest the Five Members and the fear of civil war brought trade almost to a standstill for a time. The crisis that followed the king's flight from London was dominated by the growing economic distress of the people.

The political issue was still whether the House of Lords could be persuaded to support the demands of the majority of the House of Commons for the removal of evil counsellors from about the king, for the expulsion of bishops and papists from the Upper House, and for putting the Tower of London, the forts and the militia of the kingdom into the hands of such persons as the two Houses could trust. Despite the imprisonment of twelve of the bishops, the majority of the peers still resisted the demands of the Commons. Petitions in support of the Commons came in a flood, but now they were accompanied by large crowds marching up from the provinces, in a blatant attempt to intimidate the Lords. The petitioners were influenced by fear of an insurrection of the papists and of an invasion by the Catholic powers, and they constantly demanded the disarming and securing of papists; but their main and most insistent theme was the decay of trade and industry. The leaders of the Commons and their allies amongst the gentry in the provinces were anxious for orderly demonstrations in support of their political aims, and the obvious implication for the Lords was that if they did not take account of these peaceful and disciplined demonstrations organised by gentry and ministers, more disorderly and radical elements would take over. The reforming gentry and ministers kept control because they threw in their lot with popular demonstrations and took more account of the needs of the people. The leaders of the Commons were conscious that the economic distress which was channelled into support for their political aims, could easily break out into popular insurrections that they could no longer control. But for the present the people were persuaded that if the king and Lords would consent to the measures proposed by the Commons, confidence would return, merchants would invest their money in trade again and the economy would revive. But if the people thought they needed control of the Tower of London, they also knew that they needed bread, and if the achievement of political ends did not also bring them economic relief, they would cease to follow the lead of the reforming gentry.

On 11 January 1642, the same day that the citizens of London escorted lord Mandeville and the Five Members in triumph back to Westminster, the men of Buckinghamshire marched into the capital. 'There was above three thousand on horseback, every man with his protestation in his hand, intimating that they had a petition to present to the honourable court; the others were on foot; but they reached in all from the Exchange to Newgate, three and four in a rank, coming to Westminster'. There was said to be as many as five or six thousand altogether.[18] The London mob was no longer on its own: the involvement of the provinces inaugurated a new and more revolutionary phase: 'So that from this day we may reasonably date the levying of war in England; whatsoever hath been since done being but the superstructure upon those foundations which were then laid', commented Clarendon on the arrival of the Buckinghamshire petitioners.[19] During the next six weeks Londoners regularly witnessed the arrival of columns of men from the provinces on foot and on horse coming to Westminster to protest at the refusal of the Lords to agree with the Commons. On 20 January six thousand came from Essex, and on 25 January three or four thousand from Hertfordshire.[20] On 8 February petitioners marched in from Kent: 'These Kentish men I did see myself come up Fish Street Hill', wrote Wallington, 'many hundred of them, on horseback, with their protestations sticking in their hats and girdles; they came in order, three in a rank, first the knights, and gentlemen, then about twenty ministers, then the other horse and footmen.'[21] On 10 February a petition was brought in from Northamptonshire, 'the best attended by gentlemen of quality of any petition that hath been yet delivered'.[22] 'Near a thousand' people arrived in London on 15 February with a petition from Leicestershire, and two days later between fifteen hundred and three thousand from Sussex, led by their sheriff, followed by knights, gentlemen, freeholders, 'on horseback, ranked in a decent manner'.[23] These demonstrations were well under control of the gentry. But the House of Commons became uneasy when it heard that sixteen or seventeen thousand people had assembled in the depressed clothing manufacturing districts of Essex and Suffolk, to march with their petition to London. Parliament asked them to send no more than a thousand and for the rest to disperse, and was profusely grateful when this request was obeyed.[24]

The mayor, aldermen and other inhabitants of Colchester complained to the House of Commons: 'We find the trade of clothing, and new drapery, upon which the livelihoods of many thousands, men, women and children in this town do depend, to be almost wholly decayed, and poverty abundantly to grow upon us.' The people of Essex told the two Houses: 'Our trading, especially of clothing and farming', which are 'the two trades of our county, whereby the multitudes of our people have lived', 'grow apace to so great a damp, as many thousand are like to come to sudden want', and 'we tremble to think, what may follow thereupon'.[25] The clothiers of Essex and Suffolk petitioned the king as well as the two Houses of Parliament that the merchants of London had ceased to buy cloth for export and 'our cloths for the most part, for the space of this eighteen months remain upon our hands, our stocks lying dead therein, and we can maintain our trading no longer: the cries for food of many thousands of poor, who depend on this trade, do continually press us, not without threats, and some beginnings of mutinies: so that, if some speedy relief do not intervene, we can expect no less than confusion'.[26] The people of Suffolk warned the House of Lords 'of the stop of trade, especially that of clothing, upon which the estates and livelihoods of many thousands do depend, who very lately, in regard of their wants, by their speeches and gestures, express sad intentions of disturbing our public peace if they be not speedily prevented'.[27] 'There is little doubt concerning the plight of the Essex textile industry', and the same may be said of the adjacent and related industry in Suffolk: 'Seemingly enduring long-term stagnation, it suffered particularly in this period. Its principal petition to the Commons was presented by Grimston, who spoke feelingly of "the exceeding great decay of their trade of clothing especially... occasioned by the present distractions and distempers of the state", and told a long tale of woe: of weavers leaving their occupations to take up other ways of livelihood, and of the dependent poor being "brought many of them to beg their bread, and the rest live upon the parish's charge".[28] The mayor, aldermen and common council of Exeter informed the Lords of petitions from their citizens 'wherein they present the great decay and deadness in the trades of the said city, especially in the manufacture of serges or perpetuanyet'; and declared 'that (unless God by some speedy and timely remedy do prevent it) this city and county are like greatly to be endangered, by reason of the decay of commerce (with its inseparable companion poverty), which will, as they justly fear, stir up many thousand persons to insolent and outrageous actions'.[29] These complaints were echoed by Gloucester and Marlborough.[30] It was not only the eastern and western cloth-manufacturing regions that were affected: Yorkshire complained 'of the manufacturing trades of our county daily decaying, which we visibly discern, not only tending much to the present impoverishing of a great number of families, whose maintenance and livelihood hath become hitherto wholly supported upon that foundation, which, being not prevented, may prove to be of dangerous consequence, but also to the weakening of the estates of farmers and others, (because the benefit of wools and other commodities of our county, do much depend upon the prospering of these foresaid trades of manufacture)'.[31] Hertfordshire spoke of 'the total decay of trade, and great scarcity of money, and thereby the impoverishing and unsettlement of the whole kingdom'; and Northamptonshire begged the House of Lords 'to take into consideration the distressed state of the poorer sort of people, who, for want of trade and employment, are brought to extremity, which (without timely prevention) may prove of dangerous consequence'.[32]

'The depression which settled on the economy in 1641-2 owed little to purely economic factors... By directly and indirectly reducing confidence' the constitutional crisis 'increased the liquidity preference of merchants, and this must have manifested itself as a shortage of cash, a restriction of credit, and a reduction in demand: "the tradesmen now hath not half the employment, nor is so readily and well paid for his commodities as in former times, there being little store of money".' [33] The paralysis of the economy had spread outwards from London, but the acuteness of the depression in the first three months of 1642 owed much to the strike of London merchants and tradesmen in protest against the king's actions. 'Amid these events', reported the Venetian ambassador on 14 February, 'the trade of this City and the kingdom is stopping altogether. The ordinary course of all trade has been interrupted'. And he added on 14 March that 'these continued disturbances... have reduced trade to the very smallest dimensions and, caused a loss this year to the London customs alone of 600,000 ducats'. 'And those who obtain their daily food by the work of their hands alone are reduced to the limits of despair.' [34] 'Here are millions of poor people reduced to the extremity of want by the decay of trade', Sidney Bere told Sir John Pennington. [35] 'Trade being stopped', wrote Henry Oxinden on 27 January, 'the poor of City are daily feared to rise, and also of other parts of the kingdom.' A little later he reported: 'The poor handicraftsmen are already driven to miserable want in all counties and especially in this City; it is said that they are risen in Essex, and it is feared that they will do so in all parts else. In London they have much ado to hold out any longer... they begin to inquire after the malignant lords, the obstructions of their welfare, and doubtless if there be not a speedy change in them and course taken with the poor, they will destroy them and their houses.' [36] The petitions blamed the depression on the refusal of the Lords to agree with the Commons, which was attributed to the influence of a 'popish' and disaffected party. 'These ignorant people', wrote the Venetian ambassador, are 'persuaded by those who profit from trouble, that these calamities proceed from the presence of the bishops and Catholic lords in parliament'. [37]

The lord mayor, aldermen and Common Council of the City of London petitioned the House of Lords on 25 January that 'they cannot but represent further to your lordships, that very many thousands of clothiers and handicraftsmen and their families, who have their dependence for their livelihood upon this city, do daily more and more make sad moans and lamentable cries that they are no way able any longer to subsist, because the petitioners and others do not buy off their wares as formerly they did; that the petitioners cannot do so till trade be quickened by the speedy relief of Ireland, till papists be fully disarmed, and the strength of the kingdom by land and sea put into the hands of such as the parliament may confide in, through want whereof the trade of the kingdom is fallen to so low an ebb, that the petitioners are not able longer to proceed therein as formerly; which necessitated forbearance of trade and scarcity of money, will (as they verily believe) in very short time cast innumerable multitudes of those poor men into such a depth of poverty and extremity, as will enforce them upon some dangerous and desperate attempts not fit to be expressed, much less justified'.[38] But by 40 votes to 32 the House of Lords refused to join with the Commons in a petition to the king to put the Tower, forts and militia of the kingdom 'into the hands of such persons as your parliament may confide in, and as shall be recommended unto your majesty by both Houses of Parliament'. The minority protested that this measure was 'absolutely necessary to the settling of the present distempers' and 'to the furtherance of trade, now much obstructed and decayed'.[39] At a conference Pym warned the Lords of the danger 'of tumults and insurrections of the meaner sort of people, by reason of their ill vent of cloth and other manufactures, whereby great multitudes are set on work, who live for the most part on their daily gettings, and will in a very short time be brought to great extremity, if not employed; nothing is more sharp and pressing than necessity and want; what they cannot buy, they will take; and from them the like necessity will quickly be derived to the farmers and husbandmen, and so grow higher, and involve all in an equality of misery and distress, if not prevented'.[40]

On 26 January apprentices and seamen of London petitioned the Lords that 'trading is extraordinarily decayed, and fears greatly multiplied... by reason of the exposedness of this kingdom unto dangers foreign and intestine'; they demanded the names of those who were obstructing the putting of the kingdom into a position to be able to defend itself against foreign invasion and internal insurrection, and the removal of 'the heavy pressures lying upon us, and growing insupportable by the delay of relief': 'your petitioners greatly fearing, that, if present remedy be not afforded, from the hands of this honourable parliament (as from wise physicians), multitudes will be ready to take hold upon that remedy which is next at hand; "Oppression" (as Solomon saith) "maketh wise men mad" '.[41] On 31 January hundreds of artificers and poor people gathered in Moor Fields and marched to the House of Commons with a petition. They 'seemed prepared for any exploit' and it was alleged that some members of parliament were 'assaulted and ill entreated by that rabble in their passage to the House'. In their petition they protested that they were 'utterly impoverished' by the great decay of trade, which was caused by the prevalency of the bishops, papists and a malignant faction in the House of Lords. They said that they had spent all their money and could not get bread to eat, 'so that unless some speedy remedy be taken for the removal of all such obstructions, which hinders the happy progress of your great endeavours, your petitioners shall not rest in quietness, but shall be enforced to lay hold on the next remedy which is to hand, to remove the disturbers of our peace, want and necessity breaking the bounds of modesty: and rather than your petitioners will suffer themselves and their families to perish through hunger and misery, (though hitherto patiently groaned under) they cannot leave any means unassayed for their relief '. They demanded the publication of the names of the hinderers of the happy proceedings of the parliament (such as the lords voting in the majority), 'and that noble worthies of the House of Peers, who concur with you in your happy votes, may be earnestly desired to join with this honourable House, and to sit and vote as one entire body, which we hope will remove from us our distracted fears, and prevent that which oppression will make the wisest and peaceablest men to put in execution'.

When the Speaker told them that the House was considering those things they complained of 'some of that rabble, (no doubt as they had been taught,) replied, "that they never doubted the House of Commons, but they heard all stuck in the Lords' House, and they desired to know the names of those peers who hindered the agreement between the good lords and the Commons": which', according to Clarendon, 'they pressed with unheard of rudeness and importunity, and with a seeming unwillingness withdrew whilst the House took the matter into further consultation'.[42] 'A petition of an extraordinary nature', exclaimed Sir John Coke the younger;[43] 'this horrible petition', shouted Clarendon;[44] 'that most tumultuous petition', moaned the king.[45] 'You may perceive', concluded Captain Robert Fox, 'what doings we have when the rude multitude shall dare to say more in a petition than armed men in a battle'.[46] The lords of the majority could not have been given a clearer threat of violence, which received some countenance from the dominant party in the Commons, who sent Denzil Holles to inform the Lords of this petition: 'He said, there were some things in the petition extraordinary, which at another time the parliament should be tender of; but now, considering the necessity of a multitude, the House of Commons thinks it not good to waken a sleepy lion; for it would pull on the mischief sooner.' 'They have not bread to put in their mouths', he told the Lords: 'relief they must have, which must be by setting them to work: that cannot be but by settling of trade, and restoring it: trade will not be settled till these fears and distractions be taken away: fears will not remove till we see a change, that the great affairs of our kingdom be carried on in another channel; that those evil counsellors be removed who have discomposed our frame of this commonwealth; that we may secure ourselves, and be in a posture of defence; whereas we are now exposed to dangers, and no man is sure of anything but what he carries about him: till this be, we cannot expect trade should run in such a way as that the poor may be set on work.'[47]

The same day there was a petition from women, complaining of 'their wants and necessities by reason of the great decay of trading' caused by the obstructions of the Lords. On 1 February the Houses were besieged by hundreds of women crying for bread. They handed their petition to the duke of Richmond, who exclaimed 'Away with these women, we were best to have a parliament of women.' They seized hold of his staff, which broke as he pulled it away, 'whereupon the said duke was enforced to send for another staff'.[48] The next day a petition was delivered to the Commons in the name of 15,000 'poor labouring men, known by the name of porters, and the lowest members of the city'. They said they were without employment and having sold or pawned what little they possessed, they were unable to pay the rents of their lodgings and were 'very nigh turning into the streets'. Soon they would be forced 'to extremities, not fit to be named, and to make good that saying, "That necessity hath no law"; it is true, that we have nothing to lose but our lives'.[49]

The Commons instructed Holles to give the Lords a message that 'if they will not join with this House now that things are brought to the last gasp, then to desire those Lords, that are of opinion with this House, to declare themselves with this House, that we may know them from the rest; and to protest ourselves innocent of whatever mischief or inconveniency may fall out; and to tell them plainly, they must not expect this House to come to them again in this business'.[50] Under this pressure the conservative majority in the Lords collapsed on 1-2 February and the peers joined with the Commons in a petition to the king 'to put the Tower of London, and all other forts, and the whole militia of the kingdom, into the hands of such persons as shall be recommended unto your majesty by both Houses of Parliament'.[51] On 5 February the Lords agreed to exclude the bishops from their House.[52]

'The crowds of petitioners who had been appearing during the last few days at Westminster were not without effect on the House of Lords.'[53] The king maintained that the Lords were frightened by the demand for 'the names of those lords who would not agree with the House of Commons', and for the minority peers to withdraw from the Upper House and sit with the Commons.[54] 'The rabble being at the door to execute whatever they were directed' by the leaders of the Commons,[55] the Lords gave way, 'influenced by fresh movements among the common people, who openly support the design of the most seditious'.[56] Further resistance would clearly result in far more serious and dangerous disturbances than had yet been seen, and the Lords were influenced by their experiences of past tumults and the 'danger of future tumults'.[57] The opponents of the popular party began to withdraw from parliament to their houses in the country;[58] since they had a majority in the Lords the only reason could be unwillingness to risk further confrontations with the mob. 'Some of those who with evident danger to themselves have hitherto vigorously held to the royal side, realising that they can no longer resist the violence of the other side, although they are less numerous, have withdrawn to their country houses, while others propose to cross the sea, sick at heart at seeing the government of their country under the control of the shameless cupidity of a few, supported by the passions of a licentious populace'.[59] 'Many of the popish and malignant party, as they call them', reported Thomas Smith to Sir John Pennington, 'begin now to leave the Houses, and retire to their houses in the country out of a panic fear of the multitude, who from all the counties come daily in thousands with petitions to the Houses.'[60]

On 4 February the earl of Bath asked the king for leave to absent himself from parliament, 'being utterly unable to do him service there by reason of the violation of the fundamental privilege of parliament, which is the free debating and voting with safety and indemnity, without which no man is capable to sit in any parliament'.[61] Later he explained that he had 'received many interruptions, by scorn, menaces, and affronts, from the people inhabiting about the City of London and Westminster'; and did not return because 'I do not yet see the minds of those people so settled and composed, that I may hope for better usage.'[62] Lord Mohun claimed that he felt unable to sit any longer in the House of Lords with safety to his person and honour because of the tumults 'that then swarmed about both Houses of Parliament' and did not see any prospect of being able to return with safety.[63] On 4 June nine peers issued a manifesto that they could not return to sit in the House of Lords until they had security 'to sit with the liberty and that condition that the peerage of England formerly have done, secured from all menaces, or demanding any account of our particular votes, and from tumultuary assemblies'.[64] 'So that many lords out of a just indignation to see their honours and their liberties sacrificed to the people by themselves, others out of real fear of being murdered if they should in that conjuncture of time insist on their former resolutions, withdrawing themselves, the major part of those who stayed concluded to join with the House of Commons in the desire of the militia.'[65]

The royalists always maintained that a majority of the peers, and many of the Commons, were driven away from the parliament in fear for their lives;[66] and that many of those that remained were overawed by the mob: 'the greatest part of both Houses, by means of popular menacings, tumults, posting up of names, branding men with the name of malignants... have been so overawed, that they have been forced to suppress their votes, or give them contrary to their judgements, to hide themselves, or to fly from the Houses'.[67] Though exaggerated, there was a considerable measure of truth in this; but even if there were not, the countenance that the majority of the Commons and a few of the peers gave to popular tumults, and their willingness to advance their political and religious aims in alliance with apprentices, handicraftsmen, porters and labourers, antagonised and frightened a large part of the nobility and gentry, and did more than anything else to weld them into a royalist party, which was essentially the party of order. The intervention of the people in the politics of the Long Parliament drove a wedge into the ruling class and divided it, and assured the triumph of the popular party. King, Lords and bishops were defeated: this was achieved not by the Commons, but by the mob.

6

THE MIDDLE AND POORER
SORT OF PEOPLE

THE PEASANTS*

While London and its suburbs were disturbed by political and religious demonstrations, which were fuelled by economic distress, the countryside was troubled by riots which were economic and social in their origins and aims, and only indirectly connected with politics and religion. The great majority of the English people lived in the countryside: some three quarters of the population dwelt in villages ranging from a few score to a few hundred inhabitants, and most of them were engaged wholly, or for part of the time, in farming.[1] There was a good deal of agrarian discontent in England before the civil war, its causes varying from region to region,[2] and it is necessary at this point to examine the state of the peasantry on the eve of the revolution.

In the sixteenth and early seventeenth centuries prices generally were rising, and the prices of agricultural produce were rising faster than the prices of industrial products.[3] In the earlier part of that period, farmers' rents and other payments to their landlords were fixed, or advanced more slowly than prices; most peasants had security of tenure as free-holders or copyholders; those who were leaseholders had long leases; and few peasants had to pay national taxes. From

---

*I am grateful to Dr C B Phillips of Manchester University for assistance with this section.

about the early or middle years of the reign of Queen Elizabeth I down to about 1620 the standard of living of many farmers was rising: they were better housed, their household goods and furniture increased and so did their farm equipment.[4] But it was the bigger farmers chiefly, and the medium farmers to a lesser degree, who benefited. Most of the peasants were subsistence farmers, with only occasional and marginal surpluses to sell on the market, and the smaller cultivators often had to buy grain in times of bad harvests. So the greater part of the profits from rising agricultural prices went to the bigger peasant farmers, who had large marketable surpluses for sale and produced primarily for the market.[5] At the end of the fifteenth century there were already larger and smaller peasant farmers, and the profit-inflation in agriculture in the sixteenth and early seventeenth centuries increased and accelerated this differentiation. More peasants became big farmers and big farmers generally became wealthier, forming the yeomanry of Tudor and Stuart England;[6] but at the same time the poorer peasants grew poorer, and the number increased of those with little or no land, who were obliged to work for wages as labourers on the farms of the richer peasantry and the gentry.[7]

Stability of rents and security of tenure in a time of rising prices produced a redistribution of wealth from the landlords to sections of the peasantry. The economic advance of the upper strata of farmers threatened to undermine the economic power of the nobility and greater gentry; and further, it threatened their monopoly of political power as well: the more substantial peasants undertook a more and more dominant role in the conduct of the affairs of their local communities, began to assert themselves in religion and politics, and to demand a greater degree of social esteem and a larger share in political power.[8] But the crushing of the popular revolts of the mid-sixteenth century and the establishment of a strong and stable central government under Elizabeth had strengthened the political position of the landlords; and by the second and third decades of the seventeenth century they had restored their economic position as well. By then the tide had turned against the peasants: landlords were prospering, but most peasant farmers were experiencing a decline in their fortunes, and fewer were continuing to advance.

The majority of peasants held their lands by copy of court roll according to the customs of the manor. These customs varied from manor to manor, but they were upheld and enforced by the manorial courts (composed of the tenants themselves) and by the king's courts. Where the custom was that the tenant had an estate of inheritance and his heir an automatic right of succession, the copyholder was in a more advantageous position than where the tenant had an estate for his life only or a period of years. Sometimes the custom was that the annual rents and the fines on every change of tenant were fixed by custom; but where the custom was that, though the rents were fixed, the fines were arbitrary (which meant that they were established by negotiation between the lord of the manor and the incoming tenant), the lord could periodically raise the fines on estates of inheritance as well as on those for life or years. If the lord could find any evidence that the fines in a particular manor had been variable at some time in the past, this was sufficient to establish that in law they were arbitrary still, even though for many years the fines had remained unchanged, the tenants had regarded them as fixed by custom and the steward of the manor had so recorded them. Landlords, including the monarch, widely asserted claims that fines, which appeared to be fixed and had been levied as such for some time, were in law arbitrary; but this was often accompanied by a readiness to compound with the tenants for ascertainment of their fines; that is, to sell them the right to fixed fines for the future. 'Copyholders were... made to pay dearly for ascertainments, sometimes as much as thirty or forty years' purchase of the customary rents, and it is understandable that some preferred arbitrary fines.'[9] James I claimed that, according to the strict legal position rather than the practice of recent years, fines were arbitrary in the crown's manors of the Honor of Clitheroe in Lancashire; but in 1618 he offered to make them certain on the payment of a sufficient composition. The tenants of Haslingden agreed to pay £469 15s 10d and the tenants of Accrington and Oswaldtwistle £324 1s 8d, the equivalent of forty years' customary rent, for confirmation that their fines would be fixed and certain in future. In all £6,906 17s 6d was levied on the tenants in the Honor. The money was to be paid in two instalments: the first was due immediately and was paid; the second was due after the passing of an Act of Parliament to confirm the agreement and the tenants' titles, but no such Act had been passed by the time of the civil war, and the tenants still felt insecure, as well as aggrieved at the thought of the large sum of money they would still have to find.[10]

Many tenants who thought that they were copyholders of inheritance, at customary rents and with fixed fines, and who had been treated as such for generations by the stewards of their manors, and who had documents to prove it, suddenly found that in the eyes of the law they had no such estates at all. The courts had decided that a copyhold estate was one that had existed from time immemorial, but that an estate which had been created out of the demesnes or the wastes of a manor obviously had not existed from time immemorial, and therefore was no more than a tenancy-at-will, liable to be terminated whenever the lord chose and re-let at a higher rent, even though the lord had granted it as a 'copyhold' and his steward had treated it for many years as an estate of inheritance, at customary rents and fixed fines.[11] On the king's manors in the Honor of Clitheroe many tenancies had been created out of the waste lands or forest and had evolved into copyholds of inheritance at customary rents, with fines fixed at one year's rent. For a hundred years these tenants 'continued in peaceful possession of their estates, with never a suspicion that their titles were less valid than those of the tenants of the older copyholds'. But in 1607 James I challenged their titles and insisted that they were tenants-at-will. The tenants found that the law was on the side of the crown and in the manors of Accrington, Colne and Ightenhill many were forced to pay twelve years' rent for confirmation of their estates as copyholds. In all a total of £3,763 was paid by these tenants.[12] But on the lands of other landlords in the north of England many 'copyholders' whose tenancies were of demesne or waste land were evicted. 'Many of the tenants-at-will, when the occasion arose, were treated strictly on their legal merits and displaced from their holdings at short notice. In law they could claim no more than the safe harvesting of the crops they had put in the ground.' 'Numerous demesne copyholds were swept away in the north of England, particularly in the north-eastern lowlands, and especially after the Rebellion of the Earls [1569]... Many hoped against hope, clung to worthless copies, and forced trials that could only go against them. Sometimes the lord leased the entire demesne at the old rent, without a fine, to a man willing to shoulder the burden of clearing the estate'.[13]

By the early seventeenth century, however, landlords were often trying to get rid of copyholds and replace them by leaseholds for terms of years at competitive rents, as the best protection against inflation and the best method of tapping the rising profits of farming.[14] Frequently the real purpose behind the challenges to the titles of copyholders, and the attempts to prove that their fines were arbitrary or their estates were but tenancies-at-will, was to 'persuade' them to exchange their copies for leases. The earl of Northumberland's tenants in Northumberland were unable to prove that their estates were of inheritance or their fines fixed, and rather than be subjected to insecurity and massive fines, they surrendered their copies and accepted leases.[15]

In Northumberland, south-west Durham, north Yorkshire, Cumberland, Westmorland and north-west Lancashire the peasants held by tenant-right. In effect this was generally a customary estate under which the heir of the tenant had a right of succession, paid a small annual rent and an entry fine of one year's rent, but was obliged to serve in the defence of the border with Scotland. In Elizabeth's reign landlords were seeking to abolish this form of tenure, claiming that their tenants were no other than tenants-at-will, and that their fines were arbitrary, in an effort to force them to take leases instead. They did not have much success until the accession of James I and the union of the crowns of England and Scotland gave them the pretext to assert that tenant-right was abolished because border-service was no longer required. The king himself led the attack and in 1618-19 filed a bill in Chancery against his tenants in the barony of Kendal claiming that tenant-right was no longer valid, and other lords of Westmorland manors followed suit. 'The lords of the private manors, who had been invited to follow the royal example, proceeded to eject their tenants, and, though they secured several decrees in the courts of Chancery and Exchequer in support of their action, the opposition was intensified rather than allayed.' The tenants held mass meetings, petitioned the king, pursued lawsuits and tried to get a bill through parliament. The king issued a proclamation declaring that tenant-right was extinguished and instructing judges and manorial courts to refuse all pleas of tenant-right. But in 1625 the judges decided that border-service was not a condition of tenure but an obligation of all freeholders, and that the ending of border-service could not therefore have altered forms of tenure. This thrust the issue back upon the customs of the manor: if the tenants could produce documentary evidence that in their manor the tenants had always possessed estates of inheritance at fixed rents and fines, their estates were secure and continued as before under tenant-right though not legally by that name; but often they could not produce legally watertight evidence.

In the barony of Kendal the crown confirmed its tenants in possession of estates of inheritance according to the ancient customs in return for the payment of £2,700, and the tenants of other landlords were able to prove that by the ancient customs of the manors they did possess estates of inheritance at fixed fines. But lord Howard de Walden's tenants in Wark and Harbottle in Northumberland could not produce sufficient documentary evidence to prove that they held estates of inheritance, and the court rolls of the manor were so badly kept that neither could they prove that their fines had always been fixed. They were miserably poor, they could not afford to hire competent legal advisers and they failed to cooperate with the tenants of other landlords who were in similar difficulties. They surrendered their copyholds: some took leases, some bought their estates, some lost one-third of their land.[16] In the Lonsdale Hundred of Lancashire on the eve of the civil war landlords were denying that their tenants had estates of inheritance or fixed fines, were insisting that they were tenants-at-will or that they were liable to arbitrary fines, and were demanding greatly increased fines.[17] The object was probably to persuade the tenants to accept leases for years at higher rents. Thus in the north of England, at the time of the outbreak of the civil war, many tenants were struggling against challenges to their security of tenure, demands for greater fines and pressure to make them give up their copyholds for leases at increased rents.

By the 1630s the lords of big estates were replacing long leases, with high entry fines and low annual rents, by shorter leases, with reduced entry fines but higher annual rents —'rack- rents'.[18] At the same time there was a 'revival of fiscal feudalism': landlords sought 'to enforce the payment of every obsolete and obsolescent feudal due for which a legal case could be extracted from medieval records'.[19] Between the 1570s or 1580s and the civil war 'rent rolls on estate after estate doubled, trebled, and quadrupled in a matter of decades', rising much faster than prices. There was 'a massive redistribution of income' in favour of the landlords, at the expense of tenant-farmers and wage-earners.[20] The agents in this redistribution were surveyors and lawyers, and the instruments were the courts of law and the legal system: peasants had good reason to distrust and hate all these as much if not more than landlords.

The middling and poorer strata of the peasantry suffered a reversal of their expectations in the 1620s and 1630s. Their ability to withstand the resurgence of the landlords was weakened by the growth in the size of the population, which increased by 75 to 100 per cent between the middle of the fifteenth and the middle of the seventeenth century.[21] There was greater pressure on the supply of land; holdings were sub-divided until they grew too small to support a family; pasture land was ploughed up to meet the growing demand for grain and a shortage of grazing developed, with more animals to support on less land;[22] peasants bid against each other for leases and so forced up rents to a level which only the richer peasants could afford to pay;[23] an increasing number of peasants were reduced to having little or no land and moved to places where they could obtain some land and a livelihood. This surplus population moved from the more overcrowded areas to the regions of fen and marsh, heath and forest, moor and mountain, where there were extensive commons still, on which a cottager with a little or no land could make a living from the rights of common, by which he could pasture some animals on the common and take fuel and building materials; where there were still unoccupied waste lands, on which the poor could squat in little cabins and carve out small farms for themselves;

and where there were industrial by-employments by which a cottager or small farmer could supplement his income. By this migration and from these resources of common rights, waste-lands and industry, the small peasant survived and many poor or landless peasants were saved from decline into wage-labourers or paupers.[24]

As the peasantry were adapting themselves with some success to the increase in the number of mouths to feed, however, they were struck by the depression that fell upon agriculture and industry in the 1620s and 1630s. A succession of good harvests, which reduced the prices of corn and the profits of arable farmers, was followed by a succession of bad harvests, which impoverished all who had to buy grain —the smaller cultivators, pasture farmers, agricultural labourers and industrial workers. Outbreaks of plague paralysed markets, and the cloth industry as a whole experienced a series of disastrous slumps, and the broadcloth manufacture in particular plunged into a persistent depression as a result of the long-term contraction of its traditional markets abroad, depriving many smaller peasants and cottagers of some or all of the part-time employment by which they made up their incomes to an adequate livelihood. It was the great host of medium and small peasants, especially in the pastoral and forest areas, who suffered most from this combination of increased population, bad harvests and industrial depression.[25] But to these factors must be added the actions and policies of the crown and the great landlords, which, at this very time of economic stress, contributed to the deterioration of the position of the bulk of the peasantry, and ensured that the weight of the depression fell upon peasants rather than landlords. It was at this very time that landlords in many parts of the country were appropriating a greater share of the peasants' income, by increasing rents and fines, and a greater share of the peasants' resources, by taking away some of their common pastures; and the crown was extracting more from the peasants by taxation.[26]

The landlords, led by the greatest of them—the king—set out to exploit the waste lands, the areas of woods and forest, marsh and fen, heath and moor. These were not really wastes, for they were already productive, providing extensive common pastures for the animals of old-established peasant communities as well as for newcomers: timber and stone for building, reeds and osiers for thatch and baskets, wood and turf for fuel, wild animals and birds, fish and fowl, as well as berries and nuts for food. These areas supported large numbers of small peasants by means of these common rights. And these areas received the poorer and landless peasants who migrated from the overcrowded open-field villages of the corn-growing districts. But at the same time these wastes and unimproved commons were 'the richest seams of untouched wealth that a landlord could hope to find on his estate in the seventeenth century', apart from minerals.[27] By clearing trees, draining marshes, fertilizing barren soils and enclosing the improved grounds and parcelling them out into large farms for lease at competitive rents, the lords of the manors could tap great new wealth. It would be a benefit not only to them but also to those who could afford to take the leases—some of the richer peasants and the gentry; but it would be at the expense of the landless peasants hoping to acquire smallholdings on the wastes, of the medium and smaller peasants who would be impoverished by the loss of some of their pasture and common rights, on which the viability of their farms so often depended, of the cottagers, labourers and industrial workers who would be deprived of the resources that kept them from being entirely dependent on wages or poor-relief. Thus there developed a head-on clash between the lords of manors and the main body of the peasantry in many parts of the country over their respective rights and shares in the unimproved commons and wastes. This conflict was to decide whether the landlords and big farmers or the mass of the peasantry were to control and develop the wastes and commons. This was the central agrarian issue of the 1630s and 1640s and of the English Revolution.[28]

The crown possessed forests which covered extensive tracts of country in many parts of England. Legally a royal forest was simply an area subject to the Forest Law: it did not consist merely of trees, it included agricultural land and villages, where the inhabitants possessed common rights in the woods proper and over the open ranges of grassland that lay between the trees—pasture for cattle, pannage for pigs, wood for fuel, timber for building.[29] In the Forest of Dean there were

13,611 people with rights of common, from which came a large part of their livelihoods.[30] Charles I adopted a policy of disafforestation—freeing a number of forests from the Forest Law, selling parts and dividing other parts into shares for those who had rights in the forest—lords of manors and commoners. The peasants lost much of their pastures and common rights, and the crown and lords of manors enclosed their parts and parcelled them into large farms for lease at economic rents. In the west country the disafforestation and enclosure of the royal forests of Frome Selwood and Neroche in Somerset, Gillingham in Dorset, and Braydon in Wiltshire, led to 'perhaps the largest single outbreak of popular discontent in the thirty-five years which preceded the start of the civil war'. The bulk of the land ended up in the hands of the nobility and gentry, and the small peasant farmers of the region did not think that the diminutive tracts which they were awarded compensated for the loss of the common rights which they had previously enjoyed to pasture their animals throughout the entire forest. In the period 1628 to 1631 large crowds attacked and broke down the enclosures and the region was for a time virtually in a state of rebellion. Concessions were made but the main grievances of the peasants remained and discontent was still great at the time of the civil war.[31]

The Forest of Dean was also involved in the riots of this period as a result of partial enclosure, but there the main conflict was not joined until 1639, when the machinery was set in motion for disafforestation. An agreement was reached with the 'lords, freeholders, and commoners' by which 17,000 to 18,000 acres of the forest were to be removed from common rights and enclosed for the king's use, and 4,000 acres were to be left open for the commoners' use. In 1640 the king sold his 17,000 to 18,000 acres to Sir John Wintour (a catholic and secretary to the queen) and confirmed the grant of the 4,000 acres to the commoners. Many of the commoners, however, disclaimed the agreement and 'there was much doubt as to how many freeholders and other commoners had "consented" to the agreement'. In 1641 the freeholders, inhabitants and commoners of the several parishes in the Forest of Dean protested at the loss of their ancient rights and privileges, and complained that the 4,000 acres allotted to them were too small a proportion and consisted of 'the basest and barrenest ground, apt to bear gorse, briars, and brambles, unapt to bear grass'.[32]

The crown asserted a claim to own all coastal land reclaimed from the sea. In Lincolnshire there was much saltmarsh which had been recovered from the sea and added piecemeal to the coastal parishes, where it provided much common grazing for the villagers' animals, enabling a large number of small peasants to gain an adequate, even comfortable, livelihood.[33] The commoners were given the option to buy their marshes from the king, but some villages refused and their marshes were granted to outsiders. The marshes of North and South Somercotes in Lincolnshire were granted to the courtier Endymion Porter in 1633-4, who allotted a quarter of the 2,000 acres to the commoners.[34] But the inhabitants of Lutton, Sutton, Sutton St James and Sutton St Edmunds, in the Parts of Holland, Lincolnshire, adjoining the Wash, numbering about 3,000 persons, reluctantly agreed to buy from the king for £758 6s 8d the marshes of Sutton and Lutton, which they had used as their common pasture 'from time out of mind' and which they regarded as their own property created by their own labour. They duly paid the money into the Exchequer, but the agreement was subject to confirmation by Act of Parliament, which did not take place, and the crown later granted the marshes to lord Herbert of Cardiff (son of the catholic earl of Worcester), viscount Grandison, lord Dacre and Sir Thomas Glemham, who tried to oust the inhabitants. Legal proceedings followed in which the commoners were at first successful, but a decree was obtained against them in the Court of the Duchy of Lancaster, and, faced with the prospect of a long series of expensive legal battles, the inhabitants agreed to a 'compromise', by which in return for being left with 3,200 acres they would give up their claim over all the rest. They were promised that this would be confirmed in the decree of the Duchy Court, but when the decree appeared it awarded them only 2,200 acres.

At this point, in 1633, the inhabitants persuaded one of the local gentry, Bevill Wymberley Esq of Pinchbeck, who was himself a freeholder and copyholder with rights of common in the marshes, to take up their case (and his own) with the king: his price was half of whatever more he could get for them.

Charles agreed that they should have 2,450 acres, and, in return for this small improvement, the inhabitants surrendered their claims over the whole of the marshes to the king, who, ignoring Herbert, Grandison, Dacre and Glemham, promptly granted the marshes to the duke of Lennox (later duke of Richmond). But the people only had the word of a king, and Lennox gave them not 2,450 acres but 2,200, and let all the rest of the marshes to big farmers, who enclosed the grounds, built houses and planted crops. There were now two sets of aggrieved parties: Herbert, Grandison, Dacre and Glemham, who had been outsmarted in their raid on the commons by the superior influence of Lennox, the king's close friend; and the commoners, who had been cheated of 250 acres, still thought themselves legally entitled to a further 750 acres, and in their hearts never gave up the belief that the whole of the marshes really belonged to them: but, of course, neither of these parties had any sympathy with the other. In 1641 Herbert and his friends petitioned the House of Lords for an inquiry into Lennox's title to the marshes, and the commoners followed with a petition of their grievances. As far as the latter were concerned the issue focused on the difference between the 2,200 acres Lennox had given them and the 3,200 acres to which they were entitled under the original 'compromise' agreement. The case remained pending before the House of Lords without decision, but discontent was rising in the villages.[35]

According to the law the lords of manors had the right to enclose the wastes of a manor, providing that they left sufficient open for the requirements of the tenants of the manor who had rights of common. But it was extremely difficult to decide what the legitimate requirements of the commoners were and how much waste was surplus to their needs: the lords wanted to take as much as possible, and the commoners wanted to keep as much as possible; indeed, faced with an increasing population and a growing shortage of pasture, the commoners needed more not less grazing on the wastes.[36] There were hundreds of thousands of acres of marsh and fen that brought no profit to the lords of the manors in which they lay, but provided common rights which supported a large population of small but thriving peasant farmers: they gave good grazing for their animals in summer, fish and fowl in winter, turves and

reeds for fuel and thatch.[37] Sedgemoor was a 'vast watery
wilderness' of 14,000 acres in Somerset, where 'the countryside
round about and neighbouring counties pastured their stock
and its own amphibious folk made a living by netting ducks
and fishing'. James I proposed to drain and enclose the area,
allowing 10,000 acres to the lords of the adjacent manors and
the commoners, and keeping 4,000 acres for himself. 'The small
tenants... had nothing to gain in the exchange of extensive
commons for minute parcels of fenced-in, seasonally
waterlogged sod. The small commoners recognized that the
lion's share of an enclosed Sedgemoor would go to the earls of
Pembroke and Northampton, Sir John Stowell, John Mallett,
and the other adjacent manor lords. So, they instituted an
obstructive campaign which buzzed continuously over fifteen
years. And in the end the buzzing sapped the vitality of the
whole programme.[38]

It was in the fens of Lincolnshire, however, that the
biggest drainage projects were carried out and the largest and
longest peasant rebellion of this period took place. The fenland
was a prosperous farming region that was able to support a
large population of small peasant farmers. These might not
have much land of their own but they could gain a decent
livelihood because they had rights of common in the fens, where
they pastured animals and geese, fished and fowled, dug turves
and cut reeds. But the king joined with some great landowners
to exploit the wealth of the fens under the guise of draining the
land. He adopted a scheme which minimized his expenses and
maximized his profits: the work of draining was financed in
part by a tax on the fenlanders and in part by wealthy
landowners and courtiers, who received one-third of the
drained grounds to recoup their outlay; another third went to
the lords of the manors in which the fens lay, amongst whom
the crown was foremost; and the remaining third was left to
the tenants of the manors in place of their common rights over
the whole. Beginning in 1626 and continuing through the
1630s, most of the fenland of Lincolnshire was drained after a
fashion and the drainage undertakers took their allotments,
enclosed them and parcelled them into large farms, which they
leased to tenants. The commoners lost two-thirds of their
grazing and their stocks of cattle consequently declined by

two-thirds or more: the small peasants, who had been comfortably off, were impoverished; the landless peasants, who had been able to subsist and maintain their independence only as a result of their common rights, were ruined. Some of the local gentry and some of the bigger peasant farmers supported the drainage undertakers throughout, and it was they who took the leases of the drained lands. But the drainage undertakers encountered opposition from powerful interests, including local landlords who lost their own common rights, or whose tenants were impoverished and rendered less able to pay their rents.

The mass of the peasants, however, were the chief losers as a result of the drainage operations and they provided the main opposition. They waged 'a fierce struggle against the crown' from the moment the drainage was first mooted. They showed a strong sense of communal loyalty and a powerful spirit of solidarity in defence of their rights and property; they set up a common purse, 'to which every villager contributed according to the size of his holding', to finance lawsuits in defence of their cause; they threw up scores of local leaders from amongst themselves, relying only occasionally on the assistance of sympathetic local gentry and lawyers; 'and threats and orders from outside, even though backed by wealth and political authority, failed to intimidate them'. At first they fought constitutionally by means of appeals for justice and their rights to the king and the courts, but the king was the leader of the drainage undertakers, and the courts were only slightly less obviously biased in favour of the undertakers. Then the peasants took to direct action, breaking down enclosures and smashing the drainage works. 'Disputes resulting from the drainage works first began to cause serious alarm in the 1630s', and by the time of the civil war the whole fenland was in a state of open rebellion.[39]

Thus in the reign of Charles I the livelihoods of all those small pasture-farming peasants who lived in or near royal forests, or who dwelt near fens or coastal saltmarshes, or who had grazing rights or holdings on the wastes of manors, came under attack from landlords, led and incited by the king and the court circle.[40] There was a direct and bitter conflict taking place between the great mass of the peasants in these areas and the aristocrats and courtiers, allied with wealthy local gentry and yeomen, who were the agents and beneficiaries of the crown's policies. Many landlords thus lost the respect and loyalty of the peasants; though some of the local gentry and yeomen sympathized with the cause of their poorer neighbours and thereby won great credit amongst the peasantry. The resistance of the peasants eroded the authority of manorial lords, local authorities, law-courts and the crown in the decade before the civil war. The last was the most significant because traditionally the peasantry had looked upon the monarch as a protector who would see that they had justice against the oppressions of local lords;[41] but now the faith of many of them in the justice, impartiality and benevolence of the king was undermined, and Charles I appeared as no different from any other oppressive and exploiting landlord, only more powerful and better able to get away with it. It was Charles I who adopted the policy of disafforestation and enclosure of the royal forests, and in the west country the 'resentment and hostility' of the forest commoners 'was directed mainly against the authority of the crown in the period immediately preceding the civil war'.[42] It was Charles I who maintained a close alliance with the drainers of the fens, tried to prevent the commoners from taking their cases to law, and in a paper delivered to the House of Lords in 1641 deplored the perversity of the fenlanders, objected to their many actions at common law, and expressed complete confidence in the benefits of drainage, which would produce 'as great profit to this commonwealth as the whole province of Holland and Zeeland in the Low Countries now do'.[43]

Between the assembling of the Long Parliament in 1640 and the outbreak of the civil war in 1642 there was a rising tide of protest and riot in the countryside. This was directed chiefly against the enclosures of commons, wastes and fens, and the invasions of common rights by the king, members of the royal family, courtiers, bishops and great aristocrats. The pales of an enclosure made by the king on Hounslow Heath in Middlesex were pulled down.[44] The enclosure of 100 acres of waste in the South Fen at Balderton in Nottinghamshire, which the queen had leased to Sir Gregory Fenner and Edward Wingfield Esq for draining, was thrown down in the summer of 1641. It was set up again, but in 1642 the farmers, with their servants, broke down the fences a second time, put in their cattle to pasture and refused to pay any rent.[45] In February 1641 people entered by night the enclosures that had been made from the wastes on the Prince of Wales' manors at Berkhamsted in Hertfordshire and Mere in Wiltshire, pulled down the hedges and fences and laid the grounds open again. When the hedges and fences were repaired, the people demolished them once more in 1642.[46] Six hundred acres of waste grounds had been enclosed on the Prince of Wales' lands in Norfolk. This was done with the 'agreement' of the commoners, and 100 acres were allotted to the poor; but the commoners must have regarded the agreement as imposed on them by force, for on 7 June 1641 a hundred people pulled down the enclosure and put in their cattle. They refused to obey the orders of the sheriff to withdraw; they ignored the command of the House of lords to restore the land to the prince, and although some of them were imprisoned, they remained in possession.[47]

In December 1641 the enclosures made by the courtier Endymion Porter on the saltmarshes of North and South Somercotes in Lincolnshire, which had been granted him by the king, were thrown down and the inhabitants took over the whole of the marshes as their common again.[48] In 1642 the fishermen of Burnham Norton, Burnham Deepdale and Burnham Overy in Norfolk cast down the enclosures made by the Dutchman to whom the king had granted their salt-marshes, complaining that he had stopped up their old havens so that they could not bring their boats up to their houses, deprived them of their common rights and impounded their cattle grazing in the marshes.[49] In 1641 the enclosures made by Sir John Wintour (the queen's secretary and a catholic) in the Forest of Dean in Gloucestershire were demolished, 'mostly at night', the people declaring 'that so often as the said enclosure shall be repaired, they will do the like, and turn in their cattle as they were wont to do before the said improvement'. They successfully reoccupied their common rights over most of the forest.[50]

At Buckden in Huntingdonshire the bishop of Lincoln had enclosed part of the demesne, and in exchange had granted the commons to the tenants of the manor. Evidently this was not regarded as a fair exchange, for on 18 June 1641 'some hundreds of women and boys, armed with daggers and javelins, in a very tumultuous and riotous manner, entered upon the grounds, threw open the gates, and broke down the quicksets of the said enclosure, and turned in great herds of cattle upon the premises'. The House of Lords ordered that the bishop should be left in quiet possession, but a JP who went to investigate the riot and enforce the order, found a crowd of about a hundred, mostly women and boys, in occupation of the land with their cattle, having done £10 of damage to fences and hedges. 'When he asked them with fair speeches, to drive out their cattle until the matter should be lawfully determined, they only answered him with contemptuous words, and refused to obey the order of the House, though read three times to them.' These rioters had a leader from the gentry, Orwell Shelley, who had a personal feud with the bishop: he was arrested and imprisoned by the Lords, as were others, including some of the women.[51] In March 1642 'great multitudes of people' assembled in several places in Durham 'to the number of three or four hundred in one company, in a warlike manner', and pulled down some enclosures made by the bishop of Durham and others. The sheriff and JPs tried to prevent them 'but have been beaten off'.[52]

An enclosure made by the earl of Hertford of 160 acres of Godney Moor in Somerset was broken down and cattle put in by people who 'give out threatening speeches, that they will use violence to any man that shall offer to oppose such their doings'.[53] The people of Stamford in Lincolnshire, led by a weaver, a carpenter, a wheelwright and his wife, a heelmaker, an alehouse-keeper and his wife, and a deserter from the army, all described as 'very poor men', on 30 December 1640 demolished the banks of a water-course and broke down a stone bridge in order to stop the flow of water to mills owned by the countess of Exeter. But they enjoyed the sympathy of the local authorities, for two JPs, one of them an alderman of Stamford, admitted that they took no action to stop the riot or to punish the offenders.[54] Fishermen in Essex claimed that, time out of mind, they had taken oysters in an arm of the sea called Burnham Water, but the earl of Sussex asserted that he had the sole right of fishing there, and he got a decision in his favour from the Court of Common Pleas. In April 1642 the fishermen made a plan to go with sixty or a hundred boats and collect the spat of the oysters and other fish in Burnham Water and take them to breeding places in rivers where the earl did not claim the fishing rights. They defied an order from the House of Lords and led by George Asser, a fisherman of Barking, and his servants, they carried out their plan, doing great damage, so the earl said, to his oyster beds.[55]

The most serious disturbances, however, occurred in the fens of Huntingdonshire, Cambridgeshire and Lincolnshire, as a result of drainage projects. The queen had enclosed the wastes of the manor of Somersham, lying on the eastern boundary of Huntingdonshire towards Cambridgeshire, which was part of the jointure she had received from the king on her marriage. Four hundred and sixty-five acres were taken out of Somersham Heath, 240 acres out of Somersham Fen, 205 acres out of Colne Fen, 260 acres out of Bluntisham Fen and 65 acres out of Earith Little Fen. These grounds were then leased for £400 a year to the earl of Manchester, who owned the nearby manor of Holywell-with-Needingworth, the intention being to drain them. In 1641 the inhabitants and commoners of Somersham petitioned the House of Commons that these enclosures had been made without the consent of the tenants of the manor, who had been deprived of their rights of common in these wastes, as had the tenants of Holywell-with-Needingworth and other manors. They complained of 'a great oppression carried upon them with a very high hand supported by power'. This petition was referred to the committee on the queen's jointure, which was examining a bill to confirm the grants that the king had made to his wife.[56] The people of Somersham and the neighbouring villages of Earith, Colne and Bluntisham were threatening to break down the enclosures and pasture their cattle on the wastes as they had been accustomed to do. On 2 April 1641 the House of Lords issued an order forbidding interference with the queen's possessions in Somersham, and soon after another order to the same effect covering the earl of Manchester's possessions in Holywell-with-Needingworth. The people took these orders as rejections of their claims. Drums were beaten, the people assembled, threw down the fences and filled in the ditches. The House of Lords sent messengers to arrest the leaders of the riot, but the messengers and their servants were driven off and barely escaped with their lives. The Lords ordered the sheriff and JPs to take the trained bands to restore order and apprehend the rioters.[57]

Not far to the east of Somersham, an enclosure of some fen grounds made about seven years before by Sir Robert Heath, a judge in the Court of King's Bench, in the manor of Soham in Cambridgeshire, was destroyed.[58] Also not far from Somersham, to the north-west, the earls of Bedford and Portland were grappling with serious peasant discontent. They were jointly lords of the manor of Whittlesey, in the Isle of Ely, Cambridgeshire. By agreement with the tenants of the manor, confirmed in the Court of Exchequer, about 20,000 acres of marsh, 'common and waste grounds', around Whittlesey and Thorney, were divided between the earls and their tenants. Later most of the tenants sold their shares to the earls, who invested large sums of money in enclosing, draining and 'improving' the grounds. But the inhabitants of Ramsey in Huntingdonshire complained that they had been deprived of their common rights in that part of the grounds lying within their parish. In 1641 they broke down fences and banks and put in their cattle. The House of Lords ordered that the two earls should not be disturbed in their possessions, but the commoners of Ramsey disobeyed the order and continued to keep their cattle on the disputed grounds by force. The Lords ordered the sheriff and JPs to take a party to restore order; and the bailiffs and servants of the earls impounded the Ramsey men's cattle. The Ramsey men replied by bringing actions for trespass and replevin. This conflict unsettled the tenants of the manor of Whittlesey, who began to dispute their agreement with the earls and to claim that their consent to the division of the commons and to the sales of their shares had been extracted by force. They too threw down the fences and enclosures on their old commons. The House of Lords made an order for the earls to remain in possession until the dispute was settled at law. The tenants agreed to leave the matter to the courts and withdrew from their occupation of the grounds. But the earls provocatively resumed their 'improvements' and sowed crops.[59]

The earl of Lindsey had undertaken the drainage of 35,000

acres of fens between South Kyme and Morton in Lincolnshire and received an allotment of 14,000 acres of the drained land for his pains.[60] Sir Anthony Thomas had undertaken the draining of the East and West Fens in Lincolnshire and he and his associates were rewarded with half of the East Fen and 5,000 out of the 17,000 acres of the West Fen.[61] In December 1640 the inhabitants and freeholders of Surfleet complained of the loss of common in the fens drained by Lindsey, and that they were under pressure to renounce their rights in the fens.[62] Also in December 1640 the inhabitants of East Holland and Sibsey complained to the House of Commons that the draining of the East and West Fens had deprived them of the greater part of their common rights which time out of mind they had enjoyed in those fens for pasture of their cattle and turbary. They alleged that Thomas had taken the best land for his share and that the poorer land left to them was still subject to flooding.[63]

In the spring of 1641 banks were demolished, ditches filled in and sluices, sewers and other drainage works damaged on the East and West Fens, and cattle put in. Thomas was dead but the House of Lords ordered that his widow be left in possession of the disputed grounds.[64] At about the same time fences and banks were broken down and cattle put on the fens drained by the earl of Lindsey. The House of Lords ordered that Lindsey be left in quiet possession, but this order was disobeyed and some of the offenders were brought before the Lords and sent to prison. The House declared that its orders had 'not only been disobeyed, but contemned and rudely despised by many of the inhabitants in these parts', and commanded the sheriff and JPs to gather 'such persons as they shall think fit' and go to the scenes of these disorders to protect the possessions of the earl, his assigns and tenants. But the sheriff and JPs failed to act, either because they sympathized with the people or because they were frightened of them; and the people continued to demolish banks, destroy crops and menace the houses of the earl's tenants.[65] The Lords' orders were no more effective in the East and West Fens and Sir Anthony Thomas's widow complained that they were contemptuously disregarded and that attempts to drive off the people's cattle were resisted by force.[66]

Thus in 1641 a large part of the fenlands was in a state of open rebellion, and the situation was bound to have repercussions in parliament. On 13 May the king made his position abundantly clear in a memorandum to the House of Lords, commending the draining of the fens as a great benefit to the commonwealth and urging the Lords to take notice of the riots and secure the possessions of the drainers. On 2 June a bill was read in the Commons to secure the earl of Lindsey in the possession of his 14,000 acres. But on 29 June a committee reported that the Lords' order of 6 April in Lindsey's favour was an attempt by the Upper House to appropriate sole jurisdiction over the matter, whereas the commoners had a petition depending in the House of Commons. The Commons voted the Lords' order of 6 April was a breach of their privileges and not binding. They also resolved to have a conference with the Lords and to inquire into the imprisonment of persons for disobeying the order. But on 10 July lord Falkland introduced a petition from the drainers, in which they said that they had sown a lot of corn and that all they asked was protection until the harvest. 'Many spoke against this petition, showing that the country first petitioned here in this House for redress, and after that, the cause depending here, the undertakers got out an order from the Lords to settle their possession.' Sir Simonds D'Ewes argued 'that we were not now to enter into the body of the cause, to examine the right; for admitting, which I did conceive, that these undertakers had no colour of title, yet now we were to preserve the corn and the peace of the kingdom, which I desired might be done anyways, so as they who reaped the corn might give security to the other side to answer the value of it'.

Clearly the undertakers were not popular in the House of Commons, where some members were in sympathy with the peasants, but the House had no intention of countenancing riots and the destruction of property. It ordered the sheriff and JPs of Lincolnshire to suppress all tumults and to preserve the corn and rapeseed that was growing on the disputed grounds. At the same time it referred to the committee of privileges the question whether the undertakers had infringed the privileges of the House by obeying the Lords' order. A few days later the House added that it did not intend to prejudice the rights of either side in the dispute, and that the committee of privileges was to hear all the parties.[67] The undertakers, however, looked to a more sympathetic hearing from the House of Lords. Sir William Killigrew, who was an associate of the earl of Lindsey and a leading undertaker in the drainage projects, introduced a private bill into the Lords for preventing riots and destruction of gates, sluices, drains, corn and rapeseed, on the improved grounds between South Kyme and Morton. It was read a first time on 2 August, but the commoners objected that they had exceptions to the decrees of sewers by which the 14,000 acres had been allotted to the earl of Lindsey; that they had been prevented by orders from the privy council from trying their right at law; that they feared the intention of Killigrew's bill was to prevent them seeking redress in the courts; that they had a petition depending in the House of Commons which had been put off until the Michaelmas term; and that they were now in the midst of the harvest and had no time to make their case. They asked the Lords to postpone consideration of the bill. The Lords read the bill a second time and then resolved to proceed no further until the Michaelmas term.[68]

The dispute between the earl of Manchester and the people of Somersham, Earith, Bluntisham and Colne also reached parliament and similarly caused a dispute between the two Houses. On 22 May 1641 Denzil Holles presented to the House of Commons a petition from lord Mandeville (representing his father, the earl of Manchester) and Sir Thomas Hatton (representing the queen) reporting the troubles at Somersham and asking that the enclosures be maintained until the dispute had been resolved. Oliver Cromwell, MP for Cambridge, rose and said 'that this much concerned the privilege of this House and of all the commons of England: for after the petition of the inhabitants of the said towns preferred here, and that it was in hearing before a committee of this House, the Lords made an order in the House of Peers to settle the possession, which made the people to commit this outrage, which he did not approve nor desire to justify; and that since, they had made another order to settle the possession again by the sheriff and by force of arms with the trained bands'. The House 'agreed that the breaking down of the hedges and fences in such a tumultuary manner was both against the law and of dangerous consequence; yet, because the Lords had broken the privileges of this House by sending down orders to settle possession after this House was possessed of this cause, it was thought fit for the present to forbear any order in it'.

Thus, while the Commons condemned the riot, they took no steps to punish it, nor to restore the queen and the earl of Manchester to possession of the disputed lands. The earl issued writs against sixty of the inhabitants of Somersham and the neighbouring villages. Cromwell reported this to the House on 9 June and presented another petition from the tenants. Lord Mandeville sent in a counter-petition on behalf of his father, and both petitions were referred to the committee for the queen's jointure. Cromwell was a member of this committee and Hyde the chairman. The committee heard lord Mandeville and the tenants of Somersham. According to Hyde, Cromwell 'appeared much concerned to countenance' the tenants; he instructed them and their witnesses 'in the method of the proceeding', 'and seconded, and enlarged upon what they said with great passion; and the witnesses, and persons concerned, who were a very rude kind of people, interrupted the counsel, and witnesses on the other side, with great clamour, when they said anything that did not please them; so that Mr Hyde (whose office it was to oblige men of all sorts to keep order) was compelled to use some sharp reproofs, and some threats, to reduce them to such a temper, that the business might be quietly heard. Cromwell in great fury reproached the chairman for being partial, and that he discountenanced the witnesses by threatening them; the other appealed to the committee, which justified him, and declared, that he behaved himself as he ought to do; which more inflamed him, who was already too much angry. When upon any mention of matter of fact, or the proceeding before, and at the enclosure, the lord Mandeville desired to be heard, and with great modesty related what had been done, or explained what had been said, Mr Cromwell did answer, and reply upon him, with so much indecency, and rudeness, and in language, so contrary, and offensive, that... in the end, his whole carriage was so tempestuous, and his behaviour so insolent, that the chairman found himself obliged to reprehend him; and to tell him, if he proceeded in the same manner, he would presently adjourn the committee; and the next morning complain to the House of him'.[69]

This story illuminates suddenly the real struggle taking place in England behind the political and religious controversies. Here was a direct confrontation between the aristocracy and the people, between lord Mandeville representing the great landowners and the tenants of Somersham representing the peasantry. This confrontation took place within the existing institutions, which were patently biased against the peasants. Lord Mandeville and the tenants were in theory equal parties to the dispute, but lord Mandeville was given a seat and allowed to keep his hat on his head as the mark of his superior rank, while the tenants stood bareheaded, huddled together at the back of the room. In the eyes of the chairman the tenants were merely 'a very rude kind of people' while the other party was a noble lord, and he revealed in every line his contempt for the former and his respect for the latter. No wonder lord Mandeville spoke so modestly; he had no difficulty in expressing himself and putting his case, he had no reason to become angry with frustration. But the ignorant and uneducated peasants, awkward in the presence of their social superiors, not understanding the proceedings, unable to express themselves, made nervous by the educated, smooth-spoken men arrayed against them, suspicious that their case had been prejudged—no wonder their feelings of frustration and sense of injustice broke out in angry cries. Hyde revealed his total inability to comprehend the social tragedy he inadvertently recorded, his lack of understanding and sympathy for the people whose grievances he was hearing: all which he shared with his class; but Cromwell not only sympathized with the grievances of the tenants, his understanding of the difficulties and disadvantages under which they laboured enabled him to transcend the prejudices of his class. It is easy to conceive how the gratitude and admiration he must have earned from such 'rude people' helped him to recruit the peasants of Cambridgeshire and Huntingdonshire into his regiment in 1642.

The struggle in the courts and in parliament was always loaded against the peasants; but the real battle was taking place in the villages and marshes of Lincolnshire, and here the outcome was different. The people obeyed the orders against destruction of the crops growing on the lands of the undertakers quite literally: they waited until they had been harvested by the undertakers' tenants, then they came and carted them off. Sixty or seventy people carried away forty roods of flax from the lands of Humphrey Walrond Esq. On 12 and 13 August the inhabitants of Donington took away some forty cart-loads of Sir William Killigrew's corn as soon as it had been cut. The Commons ordered the sheriff and JPs of Lincolnshire to suppress these tumults and riotous assemblies, adding 'that the House does not intend hereby to prejudice the parties interested, in point of title to the land; or to hinder the commoners in the legal pursuit of their interest'. In obedience to this order, two JPs went to the fens and found 'on August 27th on the fens of Mr Webster, great multitudes assembled, who committed great destruction there of wheat and other grain, and behaved furiously contrary to the peace, not regarding our commands in his majesty's name for keeping the peace, but utterly contemning the same, threatening further mischiefs by wounding those that opposed them; some of which were then committed to Lincoln gaol'.

On 30 August most of the JPs were at the assizes in Lincoln, and that day 'great numbers of people, both men and women, to the number of 200 or thereabouts, forcibly entered about 100 acres of land in Mr Walrond's possession, wounding his servants; and though Sir Thomas Bishop commanded them in his Majesty's name to keep the peace, and made proclamation for their departure, yet they did not wholly depart, but carried thence a great quantity of Mr Walrond's wheat'. Nicholas Gardner of Sibsey was alleged to have said, when asked whether certain shocks of wheat should be taken: 'Yes, yes; we will have it all, and what we cannot carry away we will burn, and the house too, before we sleep.' And later he said: 'If we do not take away all the corn... I would some of us might kill or be killed.' The next day men and women assembled again in great multitudes and by force took from the lands of George Kirke (one of the undertakers and a groom of the king's bed-chamber) great quantities of wheat and other grain belonging to his tenants, defying the orders of Sir Thomas Bishop to desist and depart. The two JPs who reported these events to the House of Commons on 6 September, concluded: 'We conceive unless some course be taken by this House for appeasing these riotous proceedings, there is just cause to fear greater mischiefs, to the disturbing his majesty's peace, the evil example of his subjects, and the endangering of a rebellion.' The earl of Lindsey and Sir William Killigrew complained to the House of Lords that the orders were disobeyed and that their tenants' corn was carried off and their cattle driven away, the drains and ditches filled in and the bridges destroyed. The messengers sent down by the Lords to apprehend the leaders of the riots were greeted with defiance. William Lockton Esq, a JP, was accused of freeing rioters and committing their accusers instead, and encouraging the commoners by saying that 'he did not care for the best undertaker in England'. He was sent for by the House of Lords and put out of the commission of the peace. Seven of the leaders of the riots were arrested and brought before the Lords, who sent them to the Fleet Prison. They expressed sorrow for their offence and were condemned to pay £30 compensation to Killigrew, to enter into bonds to keep the peace and to make public confession of their fault on market-day at Donington in the presence of a JP.[70] It was said that £2,000 worth of damage had been done to the king's tenants.

On 3 December the Lords ordered the sheriff of Lincolnshire to restore the king's tenants to their possessions, and to protect them while they repaired their fences. The sheriff was to publish in all the market towns within a radius of five miles of the fens that anyone who entered these disputed grounds, or threw down enclosures, or disquieted the king's tenants in their possessions, or encouraged or abetted anyone in doing these things, would be severely punished. Four more offenders were brought before the Lords: they refused to make submission and were kept in prison.[71] Following the example of their leaders, the commoners continued to defy the House of Lords throughout the winter of 1641-2 and remained in possession of the disputed grounds.

In March 1642 the sheriff of Lincolnshire, Sir Edward Heron, and three JPs—Humphrey Walrond, William Coney and Edward Heron, esquires—made strenuous efforts to expel the commoners and restore the undertakers, but as they were either undertakers themselves or closely related to undertakers, they brought discredit on the law they claimed to uphold. They turned out Christopher Quell 'and other

pretended commoners' and put Thomas Heron back in
possession; but as soon as the sheriff and JPs departed, Quell
and his companions forcibly re-entered the lands. The sheriff
and JPs went to Horbling and other places, ejecting the
commoners and restoring the undertakers, but each time the
people returned as soon as the sheriff and JPs had gone, threw
out the undertakers again and resumed possession. In April
John Pishey and a crowd of three hundred smashed dykes,
destroyed crops of cole and rapeseed, and pulled down houses
at Bolingbroke. They refused to obey the sheriff and JPs and
laughed at the orders of the House of Lords. The sheriff and
JPs finding that they were 'too many to be interfered with',
withdrew to Boston to draw up a record of the riot. 'Pishey and
other rioters came in a braving and daring manner near the
house, while the mayor of Boston refused in any way to
interfere; the sheriff however succeeded in arresting some of
the rioters, upon which a mob of more than a thousand persons
attacked the house where the sheriff and justices were, broke
in the windows, and having procured from the church the
instruments used to pull down houses in case of fire, threatened
to pull the house down unless the prisoners were released'. The
sheriff and JPs let their prisoners go and fled from Boston
amidst the jeers and insults of the crowd.

It was not possible to get juries to convict the rioters
because the jurymen sympathized with the accused. George
Banfield was turned out of possession of lands in Pinchbeck
Fen but when the evidence was given in court to prove the
indictment against the offenders some of the jury said 'that
whatever evidence might be given, they would not find a true
bill, for it was their own case'. On the other hand the sheriff,
JPs and their servants, who tried to restore the undertakers,
found themselves indicted in turn. On 9 May Sir William
Killigrew, Edward Heron, Richard Ligon and other
undertakers with the earl of Lindsey, complained to the House
of Lords that they had been turned off their lands by a riotous
multitude, who had destroyed the drainage works that cost
nearly £60,000, pulled down houses upon the heads of their
tenants, assaulted the sheriff and others who attempted to
interfere, and appointed 13 May as the day for completing the
destruction of the drainage works. The Lords ordered the

sheriff and JPs to muster the trained bands to suppress the riots. But they were powerless in the face of hundreds of people marching in troops and commanded by their own captains. They continued to destroy the drainage works, to burn and pull down the houses of the undertakers' tenants and throw the tenants themselves into the river. The people remained in possession of their ancient commons in all the fens drained by the earl of Lindsey and Sir Anthony Thomas.[72]

Disorder now spread to the fens in the north of Lincolnshire. The king, as lord of the manor of Epworth, in the Isle of Axholme, and of Hatfield Chase in the adjoining parts of Yorkshire, had made an agreement with Cornelius Vermuyden for draining the marshy and waste grounds: Vermuyden was to carry out the work and to be paid with the grant of one-third of the land he drained. The king was to have the other two-thirds, out of which he was to compensate the farmers, mostly small men, who claimed common rights in these grounds. Common rights went with the ownership of freehold land or any 'ancient' cottage, and were unstinted. In the summer the commoners pastured their cattle on these grounds, fattening them for the butcher; and they obtained hay, peat, wildfowl, fish and eels. Their whole economy depended on their common rights in these so-called waste grounds, which also supported poor cottagers who had little land of their own.

The commissioners who were appointed to compensate the commoners awarded them one-third of the land that was to be drained (whereas before it had all been theirs), which was accepted by the commoners of Hatfield Chase but not by the tenants of the manor of Epworth, and this 'gave great obstruction to the laudable and great undertaking'. An information was exhibited against 370 of them in the Court of Exchequer and they submitted to abide by such award as the attorney-general, Sir John Bankes, should make. He increased somewhat the share allotted to the commoners and they acquiesced, though protesting that they would be able to keep only half their usual numbers of cattle. Vermuyden carried out the draining of 70,000 acres—at a cost, it was claimed, of £55,825—and completed it in five years. He established a town called Sandtoft, where he settled two hundred French and Walloon protestant refugees, who built themselves houses and began to plough, till and plant the land.

But in June 1642 John Allen and sixteen others from Epworth broke down fences, destroyed crops and put their cattle back on their ancient commons: 'the inhabitants thereabouts, pretending they had right of common, said they were not bound by the before-specified decree: and therefore taking advantage of the present distractions... they arose in tumults, broke down the fences and enclosures of four thousand acres, destroyed all the corn growing, and demolished the houses built thereon'. 'No orders, no decrees of the commissioners of sewers, could now be put in execution, no officer of the court durst execute them for fear of their lives from the islanders, and several of the commissioners refused to act any more for fear of insults.' But as John Lilburne said, when he took up their cause later: 'as they had been put out of possession by force and could not through the tyranny of those times have any legal remedy; so by force they put themselves into possession again of above 3,000 acres'.[73] Considering the growing population in England and the shortage of land, it was asking for trouble to bring in foreigners and give them the precious pastures of the peasants.

The upper classes generally were shaken by the revolt of the peasantry against enclosures of commons and wastes. Sir John Coke the younger, MP for Derbyshire, warned his father as early as May 1641: 'This is no time to try titles of common'. 'This is no time to prosecute the enclosures of commons whilst the common people are at so much liberty'.[74] William Smith, a lawyer and MP for Winchelsea, probably a dependent of the duke of Richmond, warned the House of Commons on 28 October 1641: 'We must take care, that the common people may not carve themselves out justice by their multitudes. Of this we have too frequent experience, by their breaking down enclosures, and by raising other tumults, to as ill purposes. Which if they be not suddenly suppressed, to how desperate an issue, this may grow, I'll leave to your better judgements. My humble motion therefore is, that an intimation may go forth, unto the country, to wish those that are injured to resort to courts of law. And if there any fail of justice, in parliament they may be confident to receive it.'[75] The agrarian discontents and disorders were beginning to appear as a threat to the social order, and to the wealth and authority of the landlord class. They contributed, like the agitation against episcopacy, to the growth amongst the ruling class of a party of order; they generated, concurrently with the tumults and disorders of the London mob, a fear of popular disorder which was the main factor in bringing together the royalist party.[76]

The House of Lords issued, on 13 July 1641, a declaration against enclosure riots and a general order for the protection of existing enclosures: 'Whereas daily complaints are made unto this House, of violent breaking into possessions and enclosures, in riotous and tumultuous manner, in several parts of this kingdom, without any due proceeding by course of law to warrant the same, which have been observed to have been more frequently done since this parliament began than formerly', the Lords ordered 'that no enclosure or possession shall be violently, and in a tumultuous manner, disturbed or taken away from any man, which was in possession the first day of this parliament or before, but by due course and form of law; and that such possessions of all men shall continue and remain unto them as they were on the first day of this meeting of parliament'. They authorized any man who had such enclosures disturbed to obtain the assistance of any two justices of the peace and to go, with 'such others as he or they shall think fit to take with him or them', 'unto the place where such tumults happen to be, and appease and quiet the possession of the said lands and enclosures... and... see to, and cause that the possession be continued unto the present owners'.[77] The House of Commons condemned 'tumultuous and disorderly meetings' to pull down enclosures as 'altogether in themselves unlawful, and may, in these times prove of very dangerous consequence', and ordered sheriffs and JPs to use all means to suppress them, with the trained bands if necessary. 'Nevertheless this House doth further declare, that if any person or persons whatsoever be injured by any enclosure of late made... without just warrant of law, or consent of parties; upon their address to this House, by petition, or otherwise of their just complaint, this House will be careful to take speedy course for their relief as shall be agreeable to justice'.[78]

There was a distinct difference, however, between the attitudes of the two Houses: the Commons, or rather the dominant groups in the Commons, while condemning violence, disorder and breaking the law, adopted a softer and more conciliatory tone towards the rebellious peasants than the Lords. There was some sympathy in the Lower House with some of the grievances of the peasants, especially with those of the commoners in the fens, and the Grand Remonstrance enumerated amongst the evils of the regime of Charles I that 'large quantities of common and several grounds hath been taken from the subject by colour of the Statute of Improvement, and by abuse of the Commission of Sewers, without their consent, and against it'.[79] The House of Commons, in however limited a way, was a representative assembly and its members were elected. The gentry depended for election on the votes of yeomen and freeholders and were reluctant to offend these 'middle sort of people' in matters about which they felt strongly.[80] The interests of some local landowners, including MPs and JPs, were injured by the enclosures, which led them to sympathize with the rioters; but in any case JPs, with little force at their disposal, were reluctant to confront angry mobs. The JPs and sheriffs depended for the execution of their commands and for the maintenance of order on the richer peasants, and when the latter joined with the poorer peasants in the attacks on enclosures, as they often seem to have done in 1641-2, the authorities could not maintain order by ordinary means but only by full-scale military action, which was not as yet available to them.

Hopes and expectations were aroused amongst many of the peasants in the disturbed areas of the country that the popular party in the House of Commons would redress their grievances and right their wrongs. Some of the rioting peasants certainly expressed hostility towards the House of Lords while declaring respect for the House of Commons. The rioters who entered Sir William Killigrew's improved grounds in the Lincolnshire fens and carried away his corn 'spake unreverent and unbeseeming words of the orders of this House, saying, it was but an order of the Lords' House; and they would not obey it; but, if it had been an order of the House of Commons, they would have obeyed it'.[81] The king and the House of Lords were the foremost defenders of the enclosures of fens and other wastes and commons. In 1641-2 the majority in the House of

Commons was in conflict with the king and the majority in the House of Lords, and it was natural that the aggrieved peasants should have identified themselves with the Commons against crown and peers. Indeed, the most unpopular enclosures were those which had been made by the king, or under his countenance, by the royal family, courtiers, lords and bishops; in other words, by those very people who resisted the constitutional and religious demands of the Commons in 1641-2, and who were denounced by the leaders of the Commons as 'papists' and 'malignants'. But soon the Commons disappointed any such hopes and expectations; nevertheless the disturbances contributed to fear of disorder and insubordination.

THE CRAFTSMEN

Alongside these conflicts of the peasants with lords of manors and the crown, there were also conflicts of the craftsmen with merchants and the crown. In those cases where the craftsman did not sell his own products to the public directly but to a merchant, the livelihood of the craftsman depended on the price that the merchant would pay him and, in times of depressed trade, on whether the merchant would buy his goods at all. The basic conflicts in industry at this stage in history were between craftsmen and merchants, and these conflicts were concerned with the price and quality of the craftsman's products.

The largest industry in England was the manufacture of cloth, which dominated the export trade of the kingdom. The bulk of exports consisted of the traditional broadcloth, which was made in Wiltshire, Somerset and Gloucestershire, and exported to the Netherlands, Germany and eastern Europe. Despite booms and slumps the broadcloth industry remained basically prosperous until 1614. Thereafter it experienced a series of crises and catastrophic slumps, and from the 1630s onwards a persistent depression as the result of 'the long-term contraction in the traditional markets for English broadcloth'. Cheaper cloth manufactured on the continent priced English broadcloth out of its old markets.[82]

Most of the cloth was exported from London by a small number of big merchants who held a monopoly of the trade as the dominant group in the Company of Merchant Adventurers. These great merchants of London had always believed that regulations were necessary in order to ensure that the cloth was made uniformly, honestly and well, and they had been able to persuade the crown to accept their views. The London merchants provided the driving force behind the series of laws of the sixteenth century which fixed the length, breadth, weight and method of manufacture of various types of cloth, and set up searchers to see that the regulations were observed.[83] But periodic attempts by the central government to enforce the laws led to conflicts with the clothmakers. In the West Riding of Yorkshire in the reigns of Elizabeth I and James I the clothiers resisted the efforts to suppress tenters, which were used to stretch cloth into a uniformity of length and breadth after it had been fulled, and were successful in getting the ban relaxed in 1623.[84] In Gloucestershire in the reign of Charles I the clothiers resisted the efforts to suppress mozing mills, which were employed to raise the nap of the cloth after fulling, and at length persuaded the privy council to relent and to permit the existing mills to continue, while maintaining the ban on the erection of new ones.[85] But the reaction of the merchants was to blame the fall in exports on defects in the manufacture and decline in the quality of cloth, and to demand more efficient enforcement of the regulations.[86] The government of Charles I accepted the advice of the merchants and in the 1630s intensified the efforts to see that the laws were executed and the quality of cloth maintained.

'In the autumn of 1630 a weighty remonstrance of the Merchant Adventurers urged upon the council *inter alia* the appointment of some skilful person who should go to the west country broadcloth region with authority to see to the enforcement of the cloth laws; and eventually on October 29 there was issued a commission "for reformation of the abuses in clothmaking" to a certain Anthony Wither and Samuel Lively. By its terms these two individuals received general powers of investigating the observance of the clothing laws in Oxfordshire, Gloucestershire, Wiltshire and Somerset. They were authorized to inquire into the types of men appointed as searchers of cloth and the manner of their appointment, to have the unsuitable replaced, and to establish a watertight and detailed system of cloth inspection for the future. They were to report all obstinately delinquent or refractory persons to the privy council and were to be entitled to all possible assistance from the justices of the peace.'[87] In Gloucestershire Wither found that the clothiers, especially in Stroudwater, were openly defying the statutes, and that the searchers were ignorant and dishonest. In Wiltshire he was soon able to unearth corruption and negligence in the execution of the clothing laws by the searchers. He set about making the searchers more efficient and honest, and 'it would seem that the machinery of inspection was duly cranked up' to a new pitch of activity.[88] Wither's commission aroused widespread and persistent opposition in the west country clothmaking region, and on one occasion, while inspecting a consignment of cloths at a fulling mill, he was seized and flung into the river.[89] Many of the justices of the peace supported the clothiers: some of them were clothiers themselves or had 'social or economic ties with the cloth manufacturers'; some were producers of wool for the industry or had tenants who were clothmakers, and so were interested in the prosperity of the trade, and as local men in closer touch with the producers than the government, they were influenced by the belief of the clothiers that strict enforcement of the regulations would worsen rather than cure the depression; and they all resented governmental interference and the subjection of the industry to central rather than local control.[90]

In Gloucestershire Nathaniel Stephens, a well-to-do squire and a JP, and a puritan and an opponent of the Court, put himself at the head of the resistance to Wither and his commission. Wither reported to the privy council that Stephens encouraged the clothiers and searchers in their laxity, and opposed his commission; the Merchant Adventurers complained that Stephens interfered with the appointment of searchers and persuaded other JPs to obstruct Wither's work.[91] In Wiltshire resistance was led by Sir Edward Bayntun, a wealthy landowner and a JP, whose seat at Bromham became 'a centre of open opposition to Wither': he was accused of obstructing the work of the commissioner and of encouraging his tenants who were weavers to disobedience and violence. Both Bayntun and Stephens were prosecuted in the Court of Star Chamber for their conduct.[92] The reason for the violence of the clothiers' opposition to Wither's commission was that their reaction to the decline of sales abroad was the exact opposite to that of the Merchant Adventurers and the government. They sought to cut costs, and the only way open to them to do this was to reduce quality, which meant evading the statutory regulations. But the Merchant Adventurers and the privy council made persistent attempts to prevent the reduction of quality and to enforce the regulations, and had they been successful they would have driven many producers out of business, and probably did so in fact. But the strength of the opposition from the clothmakers, and especially because it was supported by the JPs, forced the government to modify its policy.[93] Nevertheless the Merchant Adventurers continued to press for action, and various schemes for regulating the cloth industry continued to be canvassed down to 1640.[94]

While the old broadcloth industry of the west country was declining, the 'new draperies' of East Anglia were expanding. These were lighter and cheaper cloths, which were exported to the warmer climates of southern Europe and the Mediterranean. Despite crises and slumps the new draperies continued to advance in the early seventeenth century and exports increased five-fold between 1600 and 1640. The main centres of production were at Colchester in Essex and the neighbouring villages of Bocking, Coggeshall and Braintree; all along the Essex-Suffolk border; at Sudbury and its neighbouring village of Long Melford in Suffolk; and in parts of Cambridgeshire and Norfolk.[95] This new manufacture grew up without the controls and regulations to which the older industry was subjected, and this freedom enabled it to be more competitive in prices and more flexible in meeting changes in fashion than the 'old draperies'.[96] But the new industry was persistently threatened by the merchants and the government with regulation, and no doubt the East Anglian producers of the new draperies feared under Charles I that they would have the same sort of regulation imposed on them as the west country producers of the old draperies were fighting against, and so have their costs raised and their products priced out of their markets.[97]

In a time of depression clothiers blamed the difficulties of the industry on high taxation and customs duties; and the smaller producers, especially of cheaper cloths, could scarcely continue to make a reasonable livelihood if taxes were increased.[98] In the West Riding of Yorkshire, which was an important region of cloth manufacture, the small clothmakers, who were very numerous there and produced a cheap cloth called a kersey, feared regulations and inspectors, and also increased taxation. All cloths had to bear the ulnager's seal before they could be sold: the clothier paid subsidy and ulnage, obtained his seals, and was then allowed to expose his cloth for sale. Under James I the ulnage became the property of the duke of Lennox, who farmed the Yorkshire ulnage to Sir Thomas Vavasour, Sir John Wattes and Sir John Middleton. They tried to increase the subsidy of a kersey from 1d to $1^1/_2$d. This caused a bitter conflict. The clothiers refused to pay the extra amount: they went to law and won their case in 1613. For twenty-four years the ulnage remained at 1d a kersey, but in 1636 the ulnager, now Thomas Metcalfe, tried again to raise it to $1^1/_2$d. Four clothiers of Halifax refused to pay: they went to law and won their case in 1638.[99] But the grievance of these worrying and expensive battles still rankled in 1642, when the clothiers of 'the parish of Leeds, the vicarage of Halifax and other parts adjoining' complained in a petition to the king of the various 'illegal pressures and impositions' from which they had suffered, and that they had been 'diversely vexed and grieved with sealings, searchings and the like devices most rigorously executed by promoters and other officers... by which means not only considerable sums of money have been screwed out of your petitioners' purses, but also divers of the meaner sort have been utterly disabled to manage their trades, their stock being exhausted by those crafty inventions'.[100]

The producers of cloth for export, both old and new draperies, in the West Country, East Anglia and the West Riding of Yorkshire blamed the slumps in trade on the monopolies of the Merchant Adventurers and other trading companies in London who had the sole rights to sell cloth in specified overseas markets. The bulk of the cloth for export had to be transported to London and it was argued that costs would be reduced by exporting the cloth from the provincial ports closer to the manufacturing centres. The aim of the great merchants of London was to buy cheap and sell dear: the *raison d'être* for the monopoly of the Merchant Adventurers was to restrict the number of buyers of cloth from the producers, for fear that too many buyers would inflate prices, and to fix amongst themselves the prices they would pay the clothmakers and the quantities they would buy; and to restrict the number of sellers of English cloth abroad, for fear that too many sellers would depress prices, and to fix amongst themselves the time and place of sale, the quantities they would offer and the prices they would ask. Their aim was to maintain the quality of English cloth and the prices it could command overseas, and they were more interested in the value than the volume of sales abroad.

But the cloth-producers believed that the channel for exports was too narrow and that if more merchants were allowed to trade there would be a greater volume of sales; and furthermore that if there was more competition amongst merchants the producers would get better prices for their goods. Typical of the feelings of manufacturers was the statement of the Suffolk clothiers: "the merchants being incorporated and settled into companies, do by constitutions among themselves so cross the ancient and accustomed course of their trade concerning the free selling and buying of their cloth (limiting it to certain times, persons, numbers and at what prices the members shall buy and sell again, as well here as beyond the seas) that they hold it to be one chief cause of [the depression]".' In 1619 the JPs of Suffolk attributed the depression of the industry to the lack of free trade in buying and selling of cloth, owing to the incorporation of merchants into monopoly companies. The Eastland Company was one of the main agencies for the export of Suffolk cloth, but some Ipswich clothiers themselves began to ship their cloths directly to the countries covered by the company's privileges, in a deliberate attempt to break its monopoly, because they blamed the difficulties of the Suffolk industry on the company, as a restrictive, inadequate and inefficient agency for the trade. So clothiers generally advocated that the solution for slumps and depressions in the cloth industry would be to end the monopolies of the Merchant Adventurers and other companies, and to throw open the trade to all willing and able to undertake it.[101]

In their hostility towards the Merchant Adventurers and other London companies the cloth-producers found powerful allies amongst the provincial merchants, who resented the drift of trade to the capital and the domination of rich London merchants over the biggest and most lucrative export trades. They could, of course, obtain membership of the companies, but the companies were controlled by Londoners, who fixed when exports would be shipped and where they would go, and the time and place of sale, which gave a decided advantage to the wealthier traders of London, 'who could afford to bear with the relatively longer turnover of capital', and a decided disadvantage to the provincial merchant with his smaller stock of capital and need for a more rapid turnover. Many of the gentry sympathized with the criticism of the companies: they resented the domination of London and wealthy London merchants, who, in their opinion, were draining wealth from their localities; they were predisposed to agree that the policies of the London companies were one cause of the depression in the cloth industry, and that an end to their monopolies would increase trade and revive the industry, whose difficulties presented them as JPs with immense problems of poor relief and maintenance of order, and whose prosperity was bound up with their own as woolgrowers and landlords of spinners and weavers.[102]

Under pressure from the House of Commons in 1621 and 1624 the privileges of the Merchant Adventurers were severely reduced: membership of the company was thrown open to all merchants who wished to join, and all merchants, whether they were members of the company or not, were permitted to export the new draperies and cheaper varieties of the old draperies to any place overseas. There followed 'a ten-year experiment in relative freedom'.[103] But with the establishment of the Personal Government of Charles I and the absence of a parliament, this policy was reversed. In the 1630s, as the government, at the instance of the Merchant Adventurers, intensified efforts to maintain quality in cloth-manufacture, so it also restored the monopoly of the Merchant Adventurers over the export of cloth. The company requested that its monopoly be extended again to 'all that trade in woollen draperies' to the Low Countries and Germany. In 1634 a royal proclamation gave the Merchant Adventurers 'the widest possible resumption of their original privileges: both old and new draperies were once again given over to the sole control of the company'; and the government made further attempts to strengthen the monopoly of the company in 1639.[104]

The government of Charles I thus identified itself with the monopolies of the Merchant Adventurers and other London companies, and with the great merchants of the capital, and disappointed the hopes of the clothmakers and the provincial merchants. The experience of the first two decades of the seventeenth century, however, aroused expectations that a parliament would favour the clothmakers and the provincial merchants, and would introduce a greater freedom of trade. It is true that the clothiers did not attack monopolies so long as the Merchant Adventurers bought their cloth and gave them reasonable prices, and that their demand for the abolition of monopolies and freedom of trade was the result of the depression which reduced the purchases made by the Adventurers and the prices they would pay.[105] But the main industrial problem of the two decades before the civil war was the depression in the cloth trade, and there had emerged two distinct and antagonistic solutions to this problem: the great merchants of London favoured the maintenance of monopoly in the export trade and of regulation in manufacture; the smaller merchants of the provinces and the clothiers advocated the freeing of the export trade from monopolies and the relaxation of regulations in manufacture. The crown was clearly identified with the former policy and parliament was thought to favour the latter. 'The agitation against the Merchant Adventurers was carried on in parliament with no less vigour than in the pamphlet literature of the time.' The Commons set up a committee in 1641 to consider the Merchant Adventurers' patents 'and to examine all complaints which were made touching the abuses practised by them in these respects'.[106] The Grand Remonstrance included the grievance of the provincial merchants that they were 'prohibited to unlade their goods in such ports as were for their own advantage, and forced to bring them to those places which were much for the advantage of the monopolisers and projectors'.[107]

There was a growing body of influential opinion that cloth must be cheaper in order to be more competitive in foreign markets, and this told against monopolies and regulations, which were thought to make cloth more expensive.[108] This body of opinion had greater hopes of influencing the Commons than the crown. At all events the crown was identified with slumps in trade and unsuccessful attempts to cure the depression in the cloth industry. It was believed that parliament would revive trade, and there was confidence in 1640 that 'if a parliament were called... that nothing must be denied for the advance of trade'.[109] 'In February 1642 the Commons appointed a committee to consider the "great and general decay of trade in this kingdom", and about this time a series of attempts were made to revive the clothing trade.'[110] The cloth-producers had 'a continual jealousy of the decay of trade' but believed that parliament, 'whose constant style was tenderness of commerce', would restore their prosperity.[111] For this reason they supported parliament rather than the king in the civil war.[112] They would have been influenced by the fact that men like Nathaniel Stephens and Sir Edward Bayntun sat in the House of Commons, who had backed the clothiers against the government and owed their seats in parliament very largely to the votes of the clothiers, and that these men supported the parliamentarian party in the civil war.

The disputes over the regulation of cloth manufacture and over monopolies in exportation were aspects of a wider and more fundamental conflict of interests between the industrial small producers in general and the merchant-capitalists in general. The merchants had established an economic and political domination over the craftsmen, and were constantly enforcing and reinforcing it, to the great resentment of the craftsmen. This domination was achieved and maintained by control of the government of the towns and with the help of the crown. 'The continuous growth of oligarchic magistracy is the most obvious theme in English urban history' in the sixteenth and early seventeenth centuries. 'The two hundred or so borough charters issued during the Tudor and early Stuart regimes reduced the democratic element in town government, and town magistrates orchestrated their own variations on the same theme'.[113] The trend was that all power in the town was concentrated in a small council, which was composed of men elected for life. Often the first set of councillors was nominated by the crown in the charter; sometimes they were empowered to fill by co-option vacancies that occurred subsequently as the result of death or resignation, and sometimes there was a complicated system of indirect elections that effectively gave to the existing councillors the power to choose their own future colleagues; either way there was established a virtually self-perpetuating oligarchy, composed of a tight ring of wealthy men closely related to each other by business interests and family ties.[114] This trend accelerated during the early seventeenth century and was probably intensified during the Personal Government of Charles I.[115] The expense of time and money involved in holding office in urban government tended to exclude all but the wealthiest townsmen. But the trend to oligarchy was actively encouraged by the monarchy, which believed that political order and social stability were most likely to be achieved through a form of government that excluded and subordinated the lower classes, and that the crown's power and influence were most likely to be supported and extended by giving control of the towns to small cliques of rich men, who would be able to look to the throne for political backing and economic privileges to bolster their position and increase their wealth. The trend to oligarchy was inspired by the fear of social and political disorder which wealthy townsmen shared with the king and the aristocracy. The recorder of Nottingham justified the extinction of democracy by arguing that 'if you shall suffer the commons to rule and follow their appetite and desire, farewell all good order', and quoting 'the inconveniences that have ensued upon the calling of the commons together in the City of London, and in other cities and boroughs'.[116]

But the primary drive towards oligarchy in the towns came from the desire of the leading merchants to monopolize the most lucrative trades of the town and its neighbourhood, and to control and exploit the lesser merchants, small shopkeepers and craftsmen, which could not be done without political power.[117] These urban oligarchies were in fact rings of merchants who sought to corner the most profitable trades, and needed the control of town government and the help of the monarch to do this. The Tudor and early Stuart rulers allied themselves with the greater merchants of the towns and assisted them in establishing their dominant position over trade, industry and municipal government. The Drapers of

Shrewsbury achieved a monopoly in buying cloth from the weavers of North Wales and selling it to the London merchants for export, reducing the weavers to economic dependence on themselves, making the shearmen of Shrewsbury, who finished the cloth, virtually their employees, and confining their rivals, the Mercers of Shrewsbury, to the retail trade only. They achieved this with the help of the privy council and control of the town's government.[118] The great merchants of Newcastle upon Tyne, organized in the Company of Hostmen, won and maintained a monopoly of the sale of coal shipped from the Tyne, and control of the coal mines, excluding the lesser merchants of the town and subordinating smaller mine-owners. They did this with the assistance of the crown and by means of their domination of the municipal government.[119] At Chester a small clique of merchants, led by the Gamull family, cornered the most lucrative trades of the city by means of grants of privileges from the crown (often secured by sharp practice) and through their leading role in the city's governing body.[120] In 1622-3 'the wealthier clothiers and merchants' of Leeds sought a charter from the king to incorporate the town as a borough. They sought this almost entirely for economic advantage, in order to increase their power over the 'multitude of small clothmakers' and reinforce their economic power with political control. Although 'many hundreds' of the inhabitants of Leeds protested that the request for the charter came only from some rich men, 'without the consent of the great number' of the inhabitants, and although the charter was opposed by 'a considerable body of the population of Leeds', probably mainly the small clothiers, Charles I granted the charter in 1626 and handed over the government of the town to an oligarchy of the richest traders in cloth and the largest employers in the cloth industry, who used their power 'for the increase of their own authority and for their own gain', to bring into subordination to themselves 'many thousands of poor clothiers'.[121]

The imposition of oligarchic government upon the towns and the steady erosion of democratic control was opposed and resisted by the general body of craftsmen.[122] In both Newcastle and London power had come to be concentrated in the aldermen, who were elected for life, and were virtually a self-perpetuating oligarchy of the richest financiers. In these cases the constitutional struggle took the form of seeking to reduce the power of the aldermen and to increase the power of the common council, which was elected annually and potentially more representative of the views of the middle ranks of the citizens. In 1633 some seven hundred or more burgesses of Newcastle protested that under the existing constitution the mayor and aldermen had so manipulated the elections to the common council that three-quarters of its members were relatives or special friends of the mayor and aldermen, and only one-quarter were truly representatives of the burgesses; and they demanded the abolition of the veto of the mayor and aldermen over the acts of the common council, which was 'the true cause wherefore the commons have no redress or reformation of their grievances'.[123] In London the central and most critical conflict before the civil war was over the powers of the aldermen, and in 1642 the influence of the aldermen over the elections to the Common Council, the right of the aldermen to prevent any business being discussed in the Common Council without their prior approval, and the power of the aldermen to veto decisions of the Common Council, were all challenged and overthrown for a time.[124]

The craftsmen found valuable allies in their struggle for more democratic government in the towns amongst individual merchants who were wealthy but excluded from the 'inner circle of power'; from business or trading interests that were not included in the 'inner ring'; from lesser merchants, younger merchants and newcomers to the town who, lacking influence and connections with the dominant clique, found their way barred by the entrenched oligarchy to a share in the more lucrative business and real political power.[125] Although such leaders commonly took their stand on general principles, they were usually more concerned to break into the inner ring themselves, or to broaden the oligarchy so far as to include themselves and their friends or interest group, or to establish a new oligarchy composed of themselves and their associates and interests; and having gained political power and access to the prized trade or business, they lost interest in changing the constitution of the town and making it more democratic. But the general body of the craftsmen, especially the more prosperous and educated, sought a form of government which would take more account of their interests, and give them a voice in the choice of the mayor and chief officers, the aldermen and councillors, and the representatives of the borough in parliament; though generally they did not think of extending democracy beyond their own sort to include journeymen, labourers and the poor.

The struggle of the lesser traders, craftsmen and middle sort of townsmen generally for a greater share in municipal government was gathering momentum in the 1620s and 1630s. It frequently found a focus on the question of the choice of representatives in parliament, which raised the issue of whether the franchise was restricted to the ruling oligarchy or opened to a wider body of townsmen, and challenges to a local oligarchy often led townsmen to become involved with national politics.[126] At Sandwich the privy council had ordered in 1604 that the commons should be excluded from elections and the franchise confined to the twenty-four members of the town council. The commons were anxious to recover their franchise and allied themselves with Sir Edwin Sandys, who 'uttered his affections to the place and people there with compassions, how they had lost some of their liberties, which would be recovered again'. He united the political demands of the townsmen with their economic grievances, for Sandwich had lost its trade to the great monopoly merchants of London and Sandys was regarded as an opponent of the London monopolies. Sandys was elected by the commons against the candidate of the oligarchy.[127] Whatever reservations wealthy MPs may have had, and did have, about such movements for the reform of town governments and for a greater measure of democracy, they found it expedient to support and lead such movements. Opponents of oligarchy in the towns inevitably looked to parliament rather than the crown for allies in their struggle.

The development of oligarchic government in the towns was contemporaneous with the development of oligarchic government in the companies and gilds in which most urban merchants and craftsmen were organized. In London the form of government of the Livery Company became 'strictly oligarchical'. Under Elizabeth I and James I power in the companies was concentrated in the Court of Assistants, just as in the municipalities it was in the Court of Aldermen. The

Assistants ceased to be elected by the general body; they were often restricted to those who had been Master or Warden of the company; and they held office for life and filled vacancies in their number as they occurred by co-option. The Master and Wardens were changed every year, but either they named their own successors or the choice was made by the Court of Assistants.[128] Often the rank and file of the company consisted of craftsmen and the governing body of merchants, and the growth of the oligarchic form of government represented the establishment of control over the craftsmen by the merchants.[129] Just as resistance to oligarchic government in the towns developed amongst the middle ranks of townsmen from Elizabeth's reign down to the eve of the civil war, so resistance to oligarchic government in companies and gilds developed amongst the commonalty of craftsmen over the same period.[130]

With the meeting of the Long Parliament the rank and file of several London companies demanded reforms of the governments of their companies. In 1640 there was unrest amongst the rank and file of the Carpenters' Company.[131] In May 1641 there was a revolt amongst the rank and file of the Watermen. The lord mayor ruled that in future the eight rulers of the company should be chosen by twenty persons nominated by fifty-five electors representing the towns and stairs between Windsor and Gravesend. But the overseers and rulers of the company complained to the House of Lords of the unseemly and even violent behaviour of some of their members. The leader of the revolt, on being told that he ought to be obedient to the law, order, and the lord mayor, answered 'that it was parliament time now, and that the lord mayor had nothing to do with them, and that the lord mayor was but their slave'. The rank and file demanded changes in the method of electing the Master and Overseers of the company, and that orders for its government should be made by the Masters, Overseers and the 'most able of the generality'.[132] In June 1641 certain members of the Woodmongers' Company complained to the House of Lords of oppressive laws being made by their Master and Wardens, contrary to their charter.[133] In September 1641 there was a 'difference' between the governors of the Pewterers' Company and their members. The generality claimed that according to their charter 'there is power given to the whole commonalty to rule and govern the brothers and members of this company as well as the Master, Wardens and Assistants', and demanded 'their privileges accordingly' to take part in the government of the company and the election of its officers. They threatened to take the dispute to parliament but the Master, Wardens and Assistants took the matter to the lord mayor and aldermen as the body more favourable to oligarchy.[134] In November and December 1641 the yeomanry of the Clothworkers' Company expressed dissatisfaction with the constitution of their company, because of the way in which the Court of Assistants was dealing with the grievances of the craftsmen.[135] The 'masters and workmen printers' of the Stationers' Company protested that the whole government of their company had been changed since it was incorporated by charter in 1555, 'by what power we know not': officers known as Assistants had been intruded upon them, who, together with the Master and Wardens, had usurped the entire government of the printing trade; and they demanded the right to regulate the trade themselves. This protest came from the small working printers who were in revolt against their subordination to the bigger printers and booksellers.[136]

The craftsmen saw the solution to their economic problems, and the means to escape from domination and exploitation by the merchants, in the establishment of more democratic forms of government in both towns and companies, which would give to the craftsmen a vote in the election of their political and economic rulers, and the means to ensure that their interests were not overlooked but promoted. The crafts- men were politicized by their struggles against the merchant oligarchies of town and company, and grew accustomed to organization, agitation and radical notions.[137] This fuelled and radicalized the agitations of the London mob in 1641-2. The attempts of the rank and file of some London companies to curb the power of their Courts of Assistants in 1641 were followed by the attempts to curb the power of the aldermen of the City of London in 1642. It was natural for the commonalty to identify the Master of the Company with the mayor and the Assistants with the aldermen, and the mayor with the king and the aldermen with the House of Lords. Indeed, just as the king and the Lords supported and encouraged oligarchic government in the towns, and the oligarchies of the towns supported the king and the Lords, so the mayor and aldermen supported and encouraged oligarchic government in the companies, and the oligarchies of the companies supported the mayor and aldermen.[138] Since the House of Commons was fighting against the vetoes of the king and the Lords, it was natural for the craftsmen to identify their own struggles against the mayor and aldermen, Masters, Wardens and Assistants, with the struggles of the House of Commons against crown, peers and bishops. The watermen played a prominent part in the London mobs of 1641-2, and the printers threw up a number of the radical leaders in the revolution.

The charters of the companies of merchants in London and provincial towns specifically excluded craftsmen from engaging in overseas trade, which was resented and resisted by the more prosperous craftsmen.[139] Town merchants sought to control the country industries that supplied goods for their trades; the bigger town manufacturers wanted to employ the small industrial producers in the countryside in order to increase their own output; the smaller urban craftsmen and retailers tried to control and regulate rural craftsmen and traders in order to eliminate their competition. Thus, for a variety of conflicting motives, the towns endeavoured to gain control over the industries in the countryside, which was resented and resisted by the independent small industrial producers in the rural areas.[140] But all small master-craftsmen in both town and country feared loss of their economic independence, which was menaced from two directions: on the one hand they were threatened with dependence on the middlemen-merchants who supplied them with their raw materials and advanced them credit, and on the merchants who bought their finished products and provided them with their profits and advances of capital; on the other hand they were threatened with dependence on men who rose from their own ranks, the more prosperous craftsmen and larger manufacturers, who gave them work and gradually drew them into the position of virtual employees working for wages.[141]

The craftsmen sought to escape from dependence on merchants by forming their own organizations of craftsmen.

This led to the movement in the early Stuart period to incorporate companies of craftsmen by royal charters. Frequently the result was not the protection of the small master but the domination of the new corporation by a few larger manufacturers, who used the organization to further their own interests against those of the smaller craftsmen; or the whole craft fell under the control of courtiers and projectors who had the influence to get the charter and the capital to finance the new company, and used the organization to make a quick, large profit at the expense of the craftsmen.[142] In 1638 Charles I decided to make the manufacture of beaver hats a separate trade and he granted a charter incorporating a Company of Beavermakers, at whose hall every beaver hat was to be stamped and pay a tax of 1s. The chief agent in procuring the charter was Francis Spatchurst, who represented the interests of the earl of Stirling, 'who had laid out considerable capital in promoting the beaver business and was to receive a rent out of the tax'. But when the Long Parliament met, the general body of beavermakers complained that only a few beavermakers, and those the larger manufacturers, had promoted the formation of the company. They had persuaded the others to accept it by threatening to exclude them from the industry, and by promising them that the making of mixed hats (only part beaver) would not be interfered with; for the demand for hats of pure beaver was too small, and the material too expensive, to employ many, and the smaller masters made chiefly mixed hats, while the eight large manufacturers who promoted the formation of the company made pure beavers. But in 1639 the king decreed that felt-making and beaver-making were separate trades and that mixed hats should not be made, thus depriving the smaller masters in the company of their principal means of employment. 'To the great majority, therefore, of those engaged in the manufacture, the abolition of the monopoly by the Long Parliament... must have come as an unmitigated relief.'[143]

The bigger manufacturers may often have seen opportunities to advance their own interests, to the detriment of the smaller producers, in alliance with the crown, courtiers, projectors and merchants, but all industrial producers in the 1630s were increasingly burdened and exploited by the efforts of the crown to tap new sources of revenue in industry, and of courtiers, aristocrats, merchants and City financiers to cream off the profits of old and new industrial enterprises. The Westminster Soap Company was set up by a group of courtiers to promote an invention for making soap from vegetable oils instead of fish oils. The king decreed that in future all soap must be made with vegetable oils, and the company was empowered to inspect and stamp all soap made by soap-boilers who were not members of the company. In return for its privileges the company was to pay the king £4 on every ton of soap. Soon the company was turned into a formal monopoly by a decree confining the manufacture of soap to members of the company and those licensed by it, and the king's share was increased to £6 a ton. Finally the invention proved a failure and the company was permitted to make soap with fish oil, and the original pretext for its privileges became inoperative.

Meantime the patent had been bitterly resisted by the soapboilers of London. In 1633 sixteen of them were summoned before the Court of Star Chamber for opposing the company, using fish oil, resisting the company's inspectors and selling unstamped soap: they were imprisoned and fined sums ranging from £500 to £1,500; and the pans, vats and utensils of these and forty other soap-boilers were destroyed. Thus 'many citizens of London were put out of an old trade, in which they had been bred all their time, and which was their only livelihood, by knights, esquires, and gentlemen, never bred up to the trade'. And for five years the soapmakers of London were kept from their trade, 'which was their only means of maintenance for them, their wives, children and families', and were 'brought into great want'. Then the London soapmakers were 'permitted' to buy out the Westminster Company for £43,000, plus £20,000 for their plant and materials, and in return for paying the king £8 a ton they were granted incorporation as the Society of Soapmakers of London.[144] The Long Parliament's condemnation of the Westminster Soap Company and other similar projects and monopolies won the sympathy of the industrial producers generally.

THE MIDDLE SORT OF PEOPLE

'The middle sort of people' were peasants and craftsmen. They were the independent small producers and the bulk of production in agriculture and industry was under their control. Typically the peasant was a small family farmer, who worked his land with his own labour and that of his family, did not employ outside wage-labour and produced for his own subsistence rather than for the market. Typically the craftsman was a small master, who purchased his own raw materials, worked in his own home, owned his own tools and instruments of production, sold his own goods either direct to the public or to a merchant for retail or export, and though he might have an apprentice or servant living in his household, he did not generally depend for his profits on the employment of wage-labour. These 'middle sort of people' were a distinct economic class: above them stood the class of rentiers (land-lords who lived chiefly off rents) and financiers (merchants who lived by the manipulation of money and credit); and below them lay the class of wage-earners (the servants and labourers who lived off wages in money or kind).[145] They were capable of an independence of opinion and action, which was rooted in their economic independence.[146]

But there was emerging from amongst 'the middle sort of people' a new class—a 'middle class' or capitalist class: the bigger farmers (or yeomen) who produced primarily for the market rather than for subsistence and employed wage-labourers; and the greater craftsmen who relied more on hired labour than on the labour of themselves and their families, put out work to smaller craftsmen, and were extending their operations towards the supervision of all the stages of production and towards the marketing of the finished product.[147] There were inherent conflicts of interests and open antagonisms between these bigger farmers and the mass of small peasants, and between the greater craftsmen and the mass of small craftsmen; but the government of Charles I and the existing political, social and religious regime antagonized these bigger farmers and larger craftsmen, and led them to feel more in common with the main body of peasants and craftsmen than with the governing order and ruling class. Some of them assumed the leadership of 'the middle sort of people' in opposition to king, lords and bishops.

'It would be an exaggeration to assert that the smaller men in the social structure had no political opinions. The yeomen or small freeholders... could undoubtedly think for themselves and resented anything that savoured of dictation.'[148] The development of the conflicts between the king and the House of Commons, and amongst the nobility and gentry, sharpened the political consciousness of the yeomen and their sense of their own distinct position. There is 'evidence that here and there the freeholders were showing some consciousness of their strength as a body'.[149] The same could also be said of the small traders, skilled craftsmen and apprentices of the towns and manufacturing areas. By the time of the Long Parliament the electorate 'reached down not only to the minor gentry and rich merchants, but to yeomen, craftsmen, shopkeepers in the majority of towns and all the counties'. Since Elizabethan times a new political nation had been born—'small, partially controlled, but no longer co-extensive with the will of the gentry'. 'It could not be called by the most fervent stretch of the imagination democratic, and yet the political system was no longer purely oligarchical.'[150] This was one of the most important factors in the English Revolution.

'No government during the seventeenth century was able to gain much feeling of loyalty from the English people'.[151] But the grievances of the 'middle sort of people' were not the same as the grievances of the nobility and gentry. Although yeomen and farmers, shopkeepers and craftsmen, joined with nobles and gentlemen in resisting shipmoney, it was not for quite the same reasons. In a tract, written in 1637 but not published until 1641, William Prynne claimed that the objection to shipmoney lay in 'the inequality of taxing of it', by which the burden fell more heavily on 'the middle and poor sort of people' than on the rich. 'In the first tax ordinary merchants charged to pay £10, £12, £15, yea, £25, or more; whenas divers of your great officers, earls and lords, who had forty times greater estates and annual revenues, paid but two, three, four or five pounds at the most. The last year's tax was rated accordingly in cities and corporations, where the middle and poor sort of people paid more than the richest; and in the country, where men are now rated by the acre, some farmers pay more than the richest knights or gentlemen, and many poor men who have scarce bread to put in their mouths, are fain to sell their pewter, bedding, sheep, and stock to pay it; the like inequality is in the present year, and how the poor who made such hard shift last year, can be able to discharge this, we are not able to conceive'.[152] The inhabitants of Mickleton in Gloucestershire complained of being overtaxed and 'of the favour and ear given to others of great estates and abilities'.[153] In the parish of Enfield in Middlesex a group of yeomen led the opposition to shipmoney in 1638, and their complaint was that the sheriff had altered the assessments 'so as to ease the burden on the wealthy landholders in the county, forcing it to fall more heavily on the yeomen and farmers'.[154] Thus the middle and poorer sort of people had grievances not just against the government of Charles I but also against the nobility, gentry and richer classes in general.

This complaint against shipmoney was part of a wider grievance of the middle sort of people against the system of taxation, whether imposed 'unconstitutionally' by the royal prerogative, like shipmoney, or 'constitutionally' with the consent of parliament, like the subsidy. 'There is reason to believe that in the century after 1523 there was a steady shift of the burden from the larger to the smaller taxpayers right down the social scale.'[155] The Bedfordshire subsidy roll of 1593 shows how much taxation fell upon the peasant farmers—250 knights, esquires and gentlemen paid a total of £206, and 1,177 yeomen and husbandmen paid a total of £531—and though the properties of the gentry were assessed at more than twice the value of those of the peasants, they paid less than twice the amount in taxation.'[156] In Wiltshire it appears that clothiers paid a disproportionate share of subsidies and were 'being immoderately fleeced for the ultimate benefit of the landed gentry'.[157] The nobility and gentry and the richer classes were not paying their fair proportion of taxation, and they were increasingly successful in passing on the burden to the rest of the population, and that meant specifically the middle sort of people, for the poor had nothing with which to pay. Indeed it was one of the aims of shipmoney to reverse this process and to make the rich pay more.[158] But it had little or no success in this because, as in all other national taxes, the gentry had too much influence in making the assessments and conducting the levies. So, when shipmoney was abolished by the Long Parliament, middle sort of people were little better off because they were now entirely at the mercy of parliamentary taxation, by way of the subsidy, which had long fallen more heavily on them than on the rich.

This grievance of middle sort of people found expression in a pamphlet of 1641, which urged the attention of parliament to 'the inequality, and unconscionable disproportion of rating of the subsidies'. 'The poorer sort cannot pay the king: the greater sort, as having the law in their own hands, will pay but what they please, but the middle sort, they must and shall pay; and in such a disproportion as is insufferable'. A yeoman of £100 a year was rated at £5 but, it was claimed, a landowner of £1,000 a year was rated at only £20, a mere four times more though his income was ten times greater; and a landowner of £10,000 a year was rated at only £100, a mere twenty times more though his income was a hundred times greater. This reduced the king's revenue and 'must necessarily beggar most of the poor inferior yeomanry of the kingdom' and ruin 'poor renters and farmers'. So the pamphlet demanded: 'let every man's estate...be made to pay proportionally. And as your... middle sort of people, are usually rated by the justices or their appointment, then shall you do right, both to the king and the middle sort of subjects: wherefore you can never do yourselves more right, than to redress this abuse'.[159] The gentry, who dominated the House of Commons, were aware that the subsidy fell more heavily on the middle ranks of the subjects than on the rich,[160] but a parliament of rich men was not ready to reform a system from which they benefited, and the grievance of middle sort of people against the tax system remained and contributed to their antagonism towards the ruling class. The state was the mechanism through which wealth was redistributed from the poorer and weaker to the richer and more powerful.

As in the state, so in the church, taxation fell more heavily on the middle and poorer sort of people than on the wealthy. 'There is great inequality of paying tithe in London, the rich men, for the most part paying very little; some that are worth many thousand, and dwell in houses of £40, £50, £60, £100 per annum, and some more, which pay for tithe 20s, 16s, yea 11s 9d per annum... so that the minister's maintenance ariseth, for the most part, from the meanest and poorest people'.[161] But the townsmen generally tended to get off lightly and the burden of tithes fell disproportionately on yeomen and farmers; and, to add insult to injury, many tithes had been impropriated and belonged now to lay landowners, and a tax intended for the support of the clergy and the poor became in many instances a tax for the support of the nobility and gentry.[162] Tithes were a grievance especially to the peasants—perhaps their greatest grievance at the time of the English Revolution.[163] 'The country people generally fancied that a parliament would free them from paying tithes'. But the nobility and gentry in the Long Parliament had no intention of taking away, or even reforming, a levy which was the property not only of the clergy but of many landlords, and this turned some peasants towards the ideas of the religious radicals, who had less scruples about the property of the rich. 'The secret thing which our common freeholders and grand-jurymen [usually yeomen] do so much aim at, if bishops and their courts were overthrown', was the abolition of tithes.[164]

In addition to these financial grievances against the existing regime, middle sort of people also had social grievances. They found their social advance increasingly blocked by the established élites in town and country. 'The accumulation of land by clothiers was certainly sufficiently large to arouse the fears of the country gentry, who procured the insertion into an act of 1576 of a clause by which their future acquisitions in Wiltshire, Somerset and Gloucestershire were to be so limited that each clothier should own no more than twenty acres. There is, however, no evidence to suggest that any serious attempt to enforce this curious piece of legislation was ever made, and its chief interest lies in the illustration it affords of the class jealousy subsisting between clothiers and country gentry in the west country textile area.' 'There are signs which suggest that social distinctions in Wiltshire were hardening during the reign of Elizabeth': in the heralds' visitation of 1565 'several indubitably clothing families were actually accepted as armigerous, but a number of clothiers were summoned before

Clarenceux king-of-arms where they "disclaimed the name of a gentleman", and a few, including so notable an industrialist as Henry Goldney... were even "disgraded" '.[165] But the fiercest reaction against social mobility came during the Personal Rule of Charles I in the 1630s. The king and his advisers set out 'to put the lid on the social mobility he found so distasteful', and made an intense effort to draw the lines between social ranks more sharply and to maintain them more rigidly.[166] But the inspiration came from the old-established noble and gentry families, who were resisting more bitterly the aspirations of well-to-do middle sort of people—yeomen farmers as well as clothiers—to be regarded as gentlemen.[167]

The achievement of the formal title of 'gentleman' could not ensure a man of acceptance as a gentleman by the leading county families, who ostracized or cold-shouldered the *nouveaux riches*. In Somerset 'there were a people of an inferior degree, who, by good husbandry, clothing, and other thriving arts, had gotten very great fortunes, and, by degrees getting themselves into the gentlemen's estates, were angry that they found not themselves in the same esteem and reputation with those whose estates they had', and they became political and religious radicals.[168] One such was John Ashe, reputed to be 'the greatest clothier in England', who owned large landed estates and several manors in Somerset and Wiltshire. He became the spokesman for the parliamentarian party in Somerset and expressed the resentment of the well-to-do clothiers and yeomen farmers against 'the gentlemen of ancient families and estates in that county' in a pamphlet attacking lord Poulett for recognizing as gentlemen only 'such whom he will allow to be so'.[169] Charles I sought to reinforce the social superiority and authority of the aristocracy: 'The privileges of generous blood are more to be cared for than heretofore', it was announced in 1634. 'Two draymen who ran down the coach of the earl of Exeter in 1637 were acquitted by a jury. The privy council promptly used prerogative powers to have the miscreants publicly flogged and then committed to hard labour in Bridewell.'[170] The attitude of the king and the privy council reflected the increasing arrogance of the aristocracy in the 1630s. The earl of Arundel regarded his function as Earl Marshal as being to support 'ancient nobility and gentry, and to interpose on their behalfs' and to keep the common people in their proper place. A waterman pressing a citizen of London for a fare, showed his badge, which was a swan, the crest of an earl whose servant he was, and the citizen, thinking the fare excessive, said 'Begone with thy goose', for which insult to an earl's crest he was imprisoned and fined by the Earl Marshal's court. A gentleman called a tailor a 'base fellow' for demanding payment of his bill, but when the tailor replied 'that he was as good a man as the other', he was forced by the Earl Marshal's court to pay damages to the gentleman. Hyde thought that the Earl Marshal's court was one of the greatest grievances of the people in 1640.[171] The social reaction of the 1630s contributed to the antagonism of middle sort of people towards Charles I and the aristocracy.

For some of the middle rank of the people the civil war came at the climax of a struggle for a greater measure of democracy: not a democracy extending so far as to include the mass of the poor (servants, labourers, paupers), but a democracy embracing the better-off farmers, traders and craftsmen. This struggle is well illustrated by a dispute which broke out in the parish of St Saviour in Southwark (an industrial suburb which supplied much of the support for the popular party in London during the revolution). In 1556 the parishioners at large had been excluded from electing the churchwardens and overseeing the expenditure of the parish's revenues, by a self-elected vestry of thirty, who chose the six churchwardens out of their own number and the four auditors of the accounts. In the reign of James I some of the parishioners petitioned parliament for the restoration of the right to elect the churchwardens and to oversee their accounts. 'In all ages and countries where civil offices are elective', they argued, 'the common people and handicraftsmen (though they were never admitted to exercise any public offices) yet they were never denied voices in elections of civil officers... mayors, sheriffs, bailiffs; and chief officers throughout the whole realm, are chosen by the inhabitants and commonalty assembled, except only in such places where there is power given by their charters to make laws to the contrary. The knights of the shire, and burgesses for parliament are chosen by the freeholders, which in most places consist of great multitudes.' But they did not advocate a 'popular election' by 'the ruder sort', but rather a restriction of the franchise to those parishioners who were rated £3 or more for the subsidy, who numbered about 200; and if parliament thought even this number too large or too 'popular', they would agree to raise the qualification to £5.[172]

The tradition of such a democracy was very much alive in 1642 amongst the middle rank of people, who tended to believe that ancient rights had been filched from them by the richer people and would be recovered in the coming struggle. The views of some of the middle sort of people were expressed by a pamphlet of 1642 which justified the Militia Ordinance of the two Houses of Parliament (the cause of the total breach with the king and the royalists) by claiming that according to 'the most ancient practice and custom of this kingdom... the lieutenants and supreme commanders of the militia in every county, were elected... by the common-counsel... through every province, country and county, in a full folkmoot or county court by the freeholders of the county': 'The freeholders in ancient times did thus in every county elect their lieutenants and captains of their militia, to train and order them; yea, and the high sheriffs too, who had the command of the whole power of the county, whom they then likewise elected'.[173] Another tract claimed that as the tithingman 'is chosen by the men of his own tithing', the constable 'is chosen by the inhabitants who are to be governed by him', and 'the great council of the king and kingdom namely the parliament, is chosen by the commons', so the coroner, sheriff, justices of the peace and lord lieutenant 'were anciently chosen by the freeholders in the county court', but that right had been taken away.[174] The reader of this tract could readily draw the conclusion that this right ought to be restored. The principle that the officers of local government ought to be elected was upheld by some of the middle sort of people.

Some of the middle sort of people claimed also a voice and a share in the conduct of the affairs of their local church, more especially a say in the choice of their minister.[175] This brought them into conflict not only with the bishops and the ecclesiastical hierarchy, who opposed attempts by congregations to elect their own ministers, but also with the nobility and gentry, for the local landlord frequently controlled the choice of parson and a large part of his income as well.[176] So, in order to increase their part in the running of their local church, men of the middle rank had to challenge not only the power of the bishops but also the power of the nobility and gentry; and this often attracted them towards some form of presbyterianism or congregationalism, in which lay elders elected by the congregation would participate in the government of the church, and who would be generally men of the middle sort. It was this that lay behind the warning that viscount Conway received from his chaplain in October 1641, that in Somerset 'our chiefest farmers have their loins girt with a divinity surcingle, and begin to bristle up for a lay eldership'.[177]

But the movement for more democratic government of the local congregation could make no headway until bishops were abolished, and bishops were in any case highly unpopular. William Lilly observed that the Londoners who went to Westminster to demonstrate against bishops 'were most of them men of mean or a middle quality themselves, no aldermen, merchants or Common Council-men...and yet most of them were either such as had public spirits, or lived a more religious life than the vulgar, and were usually called puritans, and had suffered under the tyranny of the bishops; in general they were... men in whose breasts the spirit of liberty had some place; and they were even glad to vent out their sighs and sufferings in this rather tumultuous than civil manner; being assured, if ever this parliament had been dissolved, they must have been wrackt, whipt and stript by the snotty clergy and other extravagant courses'.[178] 'The bishops and their courts', declared the Grand Remonstrance, had oppressed 'the meaner sort of tradesmen and artificers', impoverishing 'many thousand' of them and forcing 'great number' to flee during the 1630s, 'some into New England and other parts of America, others into Holland'.[179] It was not just the bishops that were unpopular but all the episcopalian clergy, even all the established clergy. 'A divine in his habit could not walk the streets of London without being reproached in every corner, by name of Baal's Priest, Popish Priest, Caesar's Friend, and the like scoffings'.[180]

The hostility of some of the middle sort of people to the bishops and many other of the clergy was compounded in large measure of anti-clericalism, which had its roots in resentment against clerical taxes and exactions, dislike of clerical interference in lay affairs, and the feeling of the more religious of the middle sort that they were as competent as the clergy, indeed more competent than most of the clergy, to decide theological and moral questions, to live godly lives and to teach the people.[181] 'The greater part of the nobility and gentry of England were inclined to look with contempt and loathing upon the claims of yeomen and handicraftsmen to throw off the yoke of authority, whilst the yeomen and handicraftsmen were well pleased to vindicate their independence against the upper classes on the ground of theology, in which they imagined themselves to be masters.'[182]

Puritanism inspired a concept of godliness that helped to create a self-consciousness amongst some of the middle sort of people. It distinguished them from the poor on the one hand and from the rich on the other. Francis Cheynell complained that in every parish there was 'a profane and ignorant multitude who are born with a pope in their belly, and are not yet redeemed from that gross superstition and vain conversation which they received by tradition from their fathers'.[183] They loved their Whitsun-ales and Lords-day sports,[184] and they would 'stand up and make much ado' to defend the 'ancient ceremonies, beloved customs and traditions of our fathers'.[185] 'Oh Beloved', cried Stephen Marshall, 'the generality of the people of England, is extremely wicked'.[186] 'The bulk of our people are wicked, and their hearts are not as yet prepared to the yoke of the Lord', lamented Edmund Calamy: 'They are unreformed themselves; and it is no wonder they are so opposite to a thorough reformation'.[187] 'The main bent and stream of nations runs downward to vice and profaneness: the general desires and endeavours of men are tending to looseness: nor unstained worship in the church, nor impartial justice in commonwealth, would they have'.[188]

On the other hand, asserted Stephen Marshall, 'many of the nobles, magistrates, knights, and persons of great quality' were 'patrons of alehouses and disorders'; and 'in many of their families (not to mention religion) there is not so much as a face of civility'.[189] The sins which the preachers of godliness most inveighed against were the sins of the nobility and gentry, whose bad examples had corrupted the mass of the people. Drunkenness was a sin that had spread from the upper classes to the lower;[190] swearing was another, being at one time 'the language only of great persons, who held it a matter of breeding... and an ornament of their speech', it had spread from 'graceless gentlemen' to the mass of the people, so that 'every base fellow thinks it is a graceful kind of speaking, to swear and to blaspheme, especially in such oaths as are in fashion at Court'.[191] Pride in dress had also spread from the upper classes to the lower.[192] Dress was the foremost symbol of status in this society and the puritan in his plain and sober attire was extending from the church to society at large his protest against a false regard for externals, and rejecting the standards of an aristocratic society. 'I more prize a poor, ragged, despised Christian in whom appears anything of Christ', wrote Oliver Heywood, 'than the most gaudy and glorious gallants in best attire and largest attendants; in my eyes a rich and revelling gentleman is but a vile person compared with a poor praying saint.'[193] Heywood, the son of a Lancashire yeoman, exhibited the influence of puritan preaching on the growth of middle-class consciousness: he was at school with 'many great men's sons' and he rejoiced that he was able to resist their bad examples, which 'too sadly verified that dreadful scripture of the paucity of rich men that are saved, and not many noble are called'.[194] 'It is more honour to be a gracious man than a rich man', wrote Adam Martindale, also the son of a Lancashire yeoman.[195]

The number of the saints was few and they were less likely to be found either amongst the great and rich or amongst the poor than amongst the middle rank of the people. 'Freeholders and tradesmen are the strength of religion and civility in the land: and gentlemen and beggars, and servile tenants, are the strength of iniquity; (though among these sorts there are some also that are good and just, as among the other there are many bad).' 'The freeholders... were not enslaved to their landlords as the tenants are', and 'the tradesmen have a correspondency with London, and so are grown to be a far more intelligent sort of men than ignorant peasants', their constant converse and traffic with London, promoting 'civility and piety' amongst them.[196] Richard Heywood of Bolton in Lancashire was a yeoman by rank and a clothier by trade, and he went once or twice a year to London, where he went to hear sermons by the chief puritan preachers, such as Edmund Calamy and Thomas Case, and where he purchased 'the best books, the most plain, practical experimental treatises in divinity such as Calvin, Luther in English, Mr Perkins, Dr Preston, Dr Sibbs, wherein he took much pleasure in reading'.[197] The strength of puritanism at Kidderminster in Worcestershire lay in the master-weavers, who were not rich and had to work hard for their living, but they had some leisure and some education and 'were of such a trade as allowed them time enough to read or talk of holy things: ...and as they stand in their loom they can set a book before them, or edify one another'.[198]

Puritanism taught some of the middle sort of people to think for themselves and to assert their independence against king, lords and bishops.[199] Godliness gave them status and the ability to express their identity as a separate class; and it enabled them to formulate and dignify their hostility towards the ruling class.

7

THE PEOPLE AND THE OUTBREAK OF THE CIVIL WAR

POPULAR RESISTANCE TO THE ROYALISTS

In the summer of 1642, with the king and parliament appealing to arms against each other, and the governing classes deeply divided in their allegiances or uncertain what to do or what lead to give, the people had a unique opportunity to express their own views. In most cases this took the form of 'a plague on both your houses'. But popular opinions, or prejudices, were also expressed on the religious and political issues, and often in the only form in which people who could not write pamphlets or make speeches, or organize petitions and marches, or raise and command armies, could express themselves, and that was by shouting slogans and abuse, and by physical violence against the persons or properties of those whom they hated. One deeply felt popular attitude that expressed itself in the summer of 1642 was fear and hatred of 'papists', which aroused popular opposition to the king and his party, who were identified in popular eyes with the papists.

The 'papists' were a minority and they were 'different': they kept to themselves and practised a secret religion and owed allegiance to a foreign power. The people had been brought up on stories of their cruelty and bloodthirstiness, and their plots and conspiracies to convert the nation by force to their false religion. All this seemed to be confirmed and given immediacy by the massacre of the protestants in Ireland; and refugees spread the stories of their own sufferings through the country and gave personal testimony to the truth of all that had ever been said against the papists. In Lancashire, which was both near to Ireland and inhabited by many papists, the protestants felt themselves 'seated in the mouth of danger, and having fresh and daily spectacles of the Irish cruelties presented to their eyes, cannot but choose but apprehend fear... lest... the war (or rather the massacre) should be transported hither'.[1] Manchester took to arms because of the 'multitude of papists near unto it, and being reputed a religious and rich town, hath been much envied and often threatened by the popish and malignant party'.[2] The protestants in Manchester felt themselves to be 'beset with papists';[3] and when lord Strange, the eldest son of the earl of Derby, took up arms for the king, he was thought to have put himself at the head of a 'popish faction and malignant party'.[4] The cloth-manufacturing districts of the West Riding of Yorkshire were swept with a panic fear of papists. John Hodgson, who lived near Halifax, recorded that 'the parliament had declared their fears and jealousies, that there was a popish party about the king, carrying on a design to alter religion; that the war with Scotland was procured for to make way for it; that the rebellion in Ireland was framed in England, and should have been acted here'.[5] 'And I well remember what sad discourses I heard about this time', recalled Joseph Lister of Bradford, 'the papists being desperate, bloody men'; seeing 'hundreds of protestants were daily murdered in Ireland, and fearing the same tragedy would be acted in England', the protestants of the West Riding armed to defend themselves against the 'great swarm of gentry, clergy, jesuits, and wicked papists' that gathered round the king.[6] They rose for parliament, Jonathan Priestley remembered, because they heard that 'hundreds of Protestants were daily massacred in Ireland', and they feared 'the same tragedy would be acted in England'.[7] In Somerset the efforts of the marquis of Hertford to raise forces for the king were defeated, and he and the royalist gentry put to flight by thousands of 'fighting men, and women, some bringing pitchforks, dungpicks, and such like weapons, not knowing (poor souls) whom to fight against, but afraid they were of the papists'.[8] The violence of the opposition of the people of South Molton in Devon to the attempt of the earl of Bath and royalist gentry to proclaim the king's commission of array, was probably connected with fear of papists, for they had a tradition of violence against papists, the men raised there to fight the Scots in 1640 having murdered their officer because they suspected him of being a papist.[9] But the main outbreak of violence against papists occurred in Essex and Suffolk. Mobs attacked and plundered the houses of eminent papists, notably the houses of the countess of Rivers at St Osyth in Essex and Long Melford in Suffolk, 'for no other ground than that she was a papist', and the house of Sir Francis Mannock, another Roman Catholic, at Stoke-by-Nayland, in Suffolk.[10]

Parliamentarian propaganda identified royalists with papists, and enlisted anti- popery on parliament's side; but mob violence could get out of control, and puritan-parliamentarian gentry and clergy endeavoured to put down the disorders.[11] Arthur Wilson, a puritan gentleman and steward to the parliamentarian earl of Warwick, thought that fear of papists was a mere pretence of the rioters: 'spoil and plunder was their aim'. He attributed these attacks on papists to the breakdown of authority, 'thereby a loose rein being put into the mouth of the unruly multitude', rather than to religion or politics.[12] But Sir Thomas Barrington and Harbottle Grimston, the MPs for Colchester, who were employed by parliament to restore order, found that the economic depression was blamed on the political distractions, which in turn were blamed on the papists, who were thus the cause 'they, their wives and children were brought into great want and extremity, (by the great decay of trading)'.[13] The intensity of the feeling against papists in the cloth-manufacturing districts of Essex, Suffolk, the West Riding of Yorkshire, the Manchester area and Somerset is obviously related to the strength of puritanism in those parts, but it also arose from the severe depression in the cloth industry.

As the royalists took all puritans for rebels against the king, so the parliamentarians took all Roman Catholics for enemies of the parliament, and the conflict in popular terms took on the character of a religious war. Just as the royalist soldiers attacked and plundered the houses of puritans, so the parliamentarian soldiers attacked and plundered the houses of papists. The earl of Essex's soldiers esteemed 'all those papists, or favourers of papists', that did not assist them.[14] A company of soldiers billeted at Radcliffe, near London, rifled the house of a gentleman who was believed to be a papist, and sold his goods 'to such persons as would buy them at any rate, and this at noonday and in the sight of 1,000 people; one featherbed I saw sold for four shillings, and one flockbed for one shilling, and many other things... The headborough of that place endeavoured to rescue some of the goods, which were afterwards violently taken again out of his house.'[15] As parliament's army marched out of London, the soldiers plundered the house of a gentleman at Acton, who was thought to be a papist; sold his beds, bedsteads, tables, doors, glass windows, chests, trunks 'for very small prices before his servants' faces'; tore up 'his bills, bonds, letters, and other writings', and destroyed his garden where he had planted 'the choicest flowers and outlandish trees which he could procure'.[16] 'Every day', wrote one of parliament's soldiers, 'our men by stealth do visit papists' houses, and constrain from them both meat and money. They give them whole great loaves and cheeses, which they triumphantly carry away upon the points of their swords.'[17] But some of the parliament's commanders did try to prevent their men from attacking all papists indiscriminately, whether supporters of the king or not. 'The horse troops behave themselves with great moderation, but the foot are something violent upon the papists, several of whose houses they have endeavoured to plunder, but the commanders use all diligence to prevent them, as too uncivil and not agreeable to the sense of parliament.'[18] In April 1643 soldiers who were quartered at St Albans threatened the countess of Sussex at Gorhambury because they thought she was a papist, 'but the gentleman they spoke it to assure them I was no papist nor malignant', and they let her alone.[19]

In the extreme north of England and the extreme south-west, in Wales and the border counties, the ruling classes were mostly royalists and in these areas the king's authority remained intact. But in other parts of the country the king's cause collapsed when the royalist leaders were attacked by hostile crowds. The marquis of Hertford was sent to secure the west for the king because 'his interest and reputation' was believed to be 'greater than any man's' in those parts,[20] but its collapse was almost instantaneous. He went first to Marlborough, which was on his own land, nearby lay his seat and main estate, and in the town itself his brother's house: 'which town... to express their affections as well to their lord, as to their prince, prepared to entertain him with a tumult, rising, just as the marquis was within view of the town, and in a rebellious manner breaking open the church-doors, and possessing themselves of the county-magazine that was kept there; but as soon as the marquis was come to town and alighted at the lord Seymour's house, the corporation attended their lordships with a dissembling submission, but made no restitution of the magazine, and the lords having no considerable strength, about them, did wisely pass it over, hoping by gentle means to reduce them to their duties'.[21] Here the local urban rulers seized the opportunity to shake off the yoke of their aristocratic overlords, but in a characteristically devious manner. Nevertheless the power of the Seymours could be restored only by overwhelming force, as it was a few months later by the king's army.[22] But this incident was an ill omen for the marquis's mission to Somerset. There, it is true, he had the support of 'gentlemen of the prime quality and interest' who were expected 'to be followed by as many men, as any such number of gentlemen in England could be'.[23] But they were not. They were hemmed in at Wells by a vast crowd of country people that gathered on the Mendip hills, said to number 40,000 men and women, many of them armed only with pitchforks and dungpicks, but supplied with all sorts of provisions, which the country from six, eight, or ten miles round about, sent on horses, carts and wagons. Deserted by the few men they had been able to raise, the royalist gentry fled to Sherborne castle, the seat of the earl of Bristol, in Dorset.[24] This popular uprising, for it was no less, was evoked and led throughout by the parliamentarian gentry in Somerset. It involved rejection of the political leadership of royalist landlords, repudiation of most of the old-established heads of the community and a decision to follow the minority party in the ruling class. It achieved the immediate objective of the parliamentarian gentry and went no further.

In Lancashire, the parliamentarian gentry gave a less

decisive lead. When lord Strange declared for the king and took
possession of the magazines at Liverpool and Preston, he was
prevented from taking the magazine from Manchester by the
parliament's deputy lieutenants of the militia. But both sides
were unwilling to resort at once to force, and the
parliamentarian gentry persuaded lord Strange to withdraw
for a time 'for prevention of effusion of blood'.[25] Lord Strange
came again towards Manchester on 15 July and was met at
Bury by 'near twenty of the chief men and officers' of
Manchester, who reached a compromise agreement with him
about the magazine and invited him into the town. At about
five o'clock in the evening he entered Manchester in his coach,
escorted by the sheriff, lord Molyneux and other 'gentlemen of
the best rank', in all about 120 horsemen. He was greeted with
cheers by the crowds lining the streets (glad probably that the
prospect of civil war had receded) and was taken to a banquet
in his honour provided by the chief men of the town. But some
of the townsmen disapproved of the agreement with lord
Strange and three of parliament's deputy lieutenants began to
assemble their companies of the militia. Lord Strange and his
companions came out to investigate; there was some scuffling;
shots were fired on both sides, and Richard Parcivall of
Kirkmanshulme, a linen-weaver, was killed, the first death in
the civil war. Lord Strange and his company hastily left the
town; but the next day 'the chief of the townsmen' went to
apologize to him for the incident.[26] Clearly the riot was led by
some of the parliamentarian gentry, and it was directed as
much against the town authorities as against lord Strange. As
a result the anti-Strange faction got the upper hand in
Manchester. The limits of lord Strange's power were revealed:
there were some people in Lancashire 'that durst affront' him,
and he had to resort to force in an attempt to re-establish his
authority over Manchester.

At Nottingham, lord Newark, the eldest son of the earl of
Kingston, and Sir John Digby, the sheriff, sought to 'borrow'
the magazine of powder for the king. The town council agreed
to lend him its powder. Of the seven aldermen, only one
supported parliament wholeheartedly, but he happened to be
mayor at the time, and he tried to prevent lord Newark taking
the county's as well as the town's powder. He went to get help

from the country; and John and George Hutchinson, the chief parliamentarians amongst the neighbouring gentry, tried to persuade lord Newark to leave the powder, but he refused. By this time 'a good company of the country was gathered together' outside the town hall. John Hutchinson spoke to them 'and they told him that if he would please to stand by them, they would part with their blood before he should have a corn of it; and... they would go up and tumble my lord and the sheriff out of the windows'. At a signal from Hutchinson 'the countrymen... came very fast up the stairs' and lord Newark and his companions made a hurried exit without the powder.[27] The town authorities had been willing to co-operate with lord Newark, and a parliamentarian gentleman played the leading role in defying him. But Hutchinson's intervention would have been fruitless without the backing of a mob (which, it should be noted, consisted of peasants, not townsmen) and he was willing to achieve his objective with the threat of mob violence.

At South Molton in Devonshire the royalist leaders were admitted to the town by the mayor, but here the poorer townsmen rose in protest, without apparently being incited or seconded by any paraliamentarian gentlemen. The earl of Bath was endeavouring to execute the king's commission of array in Devon, where he was 'thought then to be of notable power and interest'.[28] He sent one of his servants to the mayor of South Molton 'to know whether he should have a peaceable entrance' into the town, and 'the mayor answered the messenger, that if his intent were for peace, he should come'. The earl entered the town, accompanied by viscount Chichester, Sir Hugh Pollard, Sir Popham Southcot, Sir Ralph Sydenham, and several other gentry, 'with their followers', and went to the inn for a dinner of venison, prepared by the earl's own cook. 'The common sort of the town fell in a great rage with the mayor and his company, for giving licence that they should enter, and swore that if they did attempt anything there, or read their commission of array, they would beat them all down and kill them, if they were all hanged for it; and thereupon betook themselves to arms, both men, women, and children, about the cross in the market place. I do verily believe they were in number at least 1,000, some with muskets loaden, some with halberds and black bills, some with clubs, some with pikes, some with dunge evells, some with great poles; one I saw which had heat the calk of a sieve, and beat him out right, and set him in a long staff; the women had filled the steps of the cross with great stones and got up and sat on them, swearing if they did come there they would brain them. One thing which is worth the noting, a woman which is a butcher's wife, came running with her lap full of ramshorns for to throw at them... Amongst this crew there were both men and women with clubs and staves, which do daily beg from door to door'. When some of the gentry approached the cross 'the people gave a shout, and did cry, "They be come!" '. The gentry and their servants at once took cover, and the earl and his company left the town to the accompaniment of a hail of stones.[29] This rebuff seems to have demoralized the earl, who retired to his seat at Tawstock and made no further attempt to execute the commission of array. There he was arrested by a troop of parliament's horse and taken prisoner to London.[30]

A similarly rapid collapse of power and interest befell lord Montagu of Boughton in Northamptonshire. He was 'a person of great reverence, being above four-score years of age, and of unblemished reputation'. He had never been associated with the king's Court, but had lived in the country 'amongst his neighbours with great hospitality, and no man was more knowing in the county-affairs; (whether it was in relation to the king's service, or the common administration of justice, as at the assizes, and such other meetings) than he was'. Although he was loyal to the liturgy of the Church of England he was 'so severe and regular in his life, that he was by the most reckoned amongst the puritans'. 'He was a great benefactor unto the town of Northampton, and bore such sway there, that he turned everything at his beck, and the multitude of vulgars flocked about him, when he came to town, as if he had been their topical deity.'[31] None of this would avail any unless he followed the dominant trend in Northamptonshire and declared for parliament, but very reluctantly he agreed to execute the king's commission of array.[32] Few followed him now and he was arrested and sent prisoner to London. As he was driven in his coach through the town of Northampton, where he had been so much revered, 'the fanatic populacy even in that town followed his coach, reviling him as a malignant, and declaiming against him'. Such is, commented Sir Philip Warwick, 'the baseness of vulgar spirits, and the madness of a multitude'. He had 'an old maid' with him in the coach, who served him as a nurse, and the mob shouted at her 'in the usual phrases, which fill such mouths on such occasions'.[33] The earl of Berkshire also was arrested in Oxfordshire and similarly sent prisoner to London. When the three peers—Berkshire, Montagu and Bath—and other royalist gentlemen were led through the streets of the capital, they were 'exposed to the rudeness and reproach of the common people, who called them "traitors and rebels to the parliament", and pursued them with such usage as they use to the most infamous malefactors'.[34]

Lord Chandos attempted to execute the king's commission of array in Gloucestershire but his attempt 'was stifled in the birth, and crushed by the rude hand of the multitude before it saw the light'. He had called the gentry of the county to a meeting at Cirencester. But Cirencester was a centre of textile manufacture and close to the cloth-making area of south-west Gloucestershire, where puritanism and parliamentarianism were strong amongst the common people. The townsmen suspected that he intended to proclaim the commission of array and they put posts and chains across the streets to keep him out, and a thousand people came in from the surrounding countryside to assist them. When lord Chandos appeared on Rendcomb Down he was accompanied by no more than thirty men, armed only with swords, and the gentlemen who came out to meet him extracted a promise from him that he would not execute the commission of array. The parliamentarian gentry and the chief townsmen on this basis secured his peaceful entry into the town. He went to dinner with the justices of the peace and other gentry. But a large and angry crowd gathered outside the house where he was, demanding to know why he had come. He came out and told them 'that it was only to confer with the gentlemen for the peace of the county'. The crowd called to him to give them his commission of array or they would take him to parliament. They became increasingly menacing and the gentry and chief townsmen intervened and succeeded in pacifying a large part of the crowd by persuading lord Chandos to promise in writing that he would never execute the commission of array, which, 'being in extreme fear, he condescended unto'. Yet this did not satisfy all the people, and many continued to call for lord Chandos to be taken to London. There seemed to be real danger that he 'might have been torn in pieces by some of the enraged country people', and, it being now late at night, some of the gentry and townsmen smuggled him out of the town on foot through a back way. When the country people found that he had escaped them, they 'were extremely enraged, and had like to have pulled down the house' where he had been, but finding his coach, which he had been forced to leave behind him in his flight, they pulled it into the market-place, and 'cut it and tore it all in pieces', 'delighting in a contumelious revenge and rustic triumph'.[35] Again it is notable that the main part in this tumult was played by people from the country rather than from the town. But not many months later Cirencester was punished, for its insulting treatment of a peer of the realm, when it was stormed and taken by the king's army under the command of Prince Rupert.

The local parliamentarian leaders who observed such incidents were left feeling deeply uneasy. The parliamentarian gentleman who witnessed the riot at South Molton, while he approved of its outcome in preventing the execution of the commission of array, did not conceal his distaste for the instruments, consoling himself with the pious reflection that 'God is able with his smallest creatures to daunt the hearts of kings, as with lice and frogs and such like'.[36] A puritan-parliamentarian minister in Gloucester suspected that the 'fury that took hold of the ignoble multitude' at Cirencester sprang as much from the opportunity 'to vent their humours' in protest at their 'usual restraint and subjection' as from love of the causes of god and parliament. And though he was glad that the commission of array was crushed, he gave a warning that 'prudent men' should 'promote and maintain' such popular movements 'yet no further than themselves can overrule and moderate'.[37] He suspected that the people and himself were not really on the same side at all.

The people were taking the bit between their teeth. In the early part of August 1642 people from Staines, armed with swords and guns, came to the house of the king's ex-minister, lord Cottington, at Hanworth in Middlesex. They said they had come to search for arms, claiming the authority of the order of the two Houses of Parliament for disarming 'papists and delinquents'. Lord Cottington was not at home, but his servants had difficulty in preventing the searchers from ransacking and pillaging the house, and from pulling down the fences in the park. The House of Lords sent a messenger to arrest these 'rioters', but the sympathies of the constable of Staines lay with the rioters rather than with lord Cottington and the peers: he warned them that a messenger had come to arrest them and they disappeared.[38]

In August 1642 rioting against malignants and papists began in Colchester and spread through many parts of Essex and Suffolk. On Saturday 20 August 'a treacherous servant' informed the magistrates and others of Colchester that Sir John Lucas intended to set off the following Monday with twelve horses and arms to join the king. Sir John lived near Colchester and he was 'one of the best gentlemen of that county, and of the most eminent affection to the king'; he was rich and 'there were few peers who had much greater estates, or lived more noble therewith'. On Sunday alderman John Langley, a grocer and captain of the town militia, and alderman Henry Barrington, a brewer and religious radical, rode out of Colchester to the cloth-manufacturing districts to the west and north, where puritanism and economic depression agitated the people, visiting Coggeshall, Bocking, Braintree, Halstead and other villages and urging them to set guards with muskets to intercept Sir John on his way to York. On their return they persuaded the mayor, Thomas Wade, to set a watch on Sir John's house. After midnight the watch saw some horses coming out of a back gate and fired a shot to warn the town. 'Word was brought into the town', wrote the mayor, 'that there were a hundred men in arms in Sir John's. The drums thereupon beat up, the town got into an uproar'. The trained band assembled, and the 400-500 men who had volunteered for service in parliament's army; by order of alderman Dan Cole, 'the Fowke of Colchester', the beacon was fired and horsemen sent out 'to call in the country against the cavaliers in Sir John Lucas's house'. The house was beset with at least 2,000 people. The mayor put the number much higher: 'There are gathered together, besides the bands, 5,000 men, women, and children, which I feared might do some hurt. I therefore, being accompanied by some other justices and aldermen, made proclamation in several places where the tumults were, at one o'clock in the night and several times since, charging the people to depart. They however regarded us no more than they do a child, and then we charged the bands to keep careful watch about the house. This they did until daylight'.

When daylight came 'the rude sort of people' smashed their way into the house. The first person they came upon was Thomas Newcomen, the unpopular parson of Trinity Church in Colchester, who intended to go to the king with Sir John: 'they tear his clothes off his back, beat him with their cudgels and halberds, and with infinite exclamations, carry him in triumph through the chief streets of the town', debating whether to beat out his brains, or to drown him, or to stone him to death, until he was rescued by alderman Cole, who took him to the common gaol for his safety. Meanwhile twenty of the mob burst into lady Lucas' room and demanded to know where the arms and cavaliers were. The crowd swarmed through the house and outbuildings, seizing 'much armour and many new pistols and carbines ready charged, new great saddles and other warlike furniture', and a dozen horses, all of which they carried to the town hall. Then they laid hands on Sir John himself, his sister, and finally his mother, and carried them through the streets. The mayor rescued them and took them to his house, but 'nothing would satisfy these tumultuous people but that Sir John Lucas, his mother, and his servants should be committed... When the people knew that they were not committed', continued the mayor, 'they came in great numbers and told me to my face that they would pull down my house upon my head. Sir John, his lady mother and sister' were then taken to the common gaol, and so were all his servants that the crowds could lay their hands on.

By now the mob had been swollen by people from the surrounding country and they began to plunder the house, carrying away money, plate, jewels, brass, pewter, books, boxes, writings, linen, woollens and household-stuff. 'A few hours disrobe the house of that rich furniture that had adorned it many years. The mayor and aldermen standing by all this while, but either not able or not willing to conjure down the devil which themselves had raised up.' 'They are come to such a head', exclaimed the mayor, 'being a mixed company of town and country, that we know not how to quiet them. Believe we could not repress them if we had five trained bands, unless they be killed.' Then a new alarm was raised, 'that 200 armed horsemen are discovered in a vault at Sir John Lucas's, that they had killed nine men already and were issuing forth to destroy the town, the shops are shut up in an instant, and the multitude throng down thither to take or kill these cavaliers. And because they find none there, they now spend their rage upon the house, they batter down the doors and walls, beat down the windows, tear his evidences, deface his walks and gardens... From thence they go to his park, pull down his pales, kill his deer, drive away his cattle; and to show that their rage will know no bounds... they break into St Giles his church, open the vault where his ancestors were buried, and with pistols, swords, and halberds, transfix the coffins of the dead. And now the mayor's care begins to show itself, he sets a guard upon the house... yet that guard suffered £100 worth of corn (which at first was neglected as contemptible luggage) to be carried out, and the most of it, to their own houses. Another guard he sets upon the prison, lest the prisoners should be assaulted by the people who were so much incensed against them'.[39]

'The people yet are in great fear and amazement, and continue together in great multitudes, and will not return to their habitations until they have further satisfaction concerning' Sir John Lucas. 'The mayor not knowing what course to take with the people, nor how to pacify them', and hearing them say that they would go to the countess of Rivers' house at St Osyth, and to the houses of other papists and malignants near Colchester, he 'sent with all speed to know the pleasure of the parliament concerning the same'.[40] 'The tumult thus raised and made confident by success, they go on in triumph, and like a violent torrent swelling above its channel, carry all before them'. An elderly clergyman living in Colchester was abused in the streets by 'a multitude of boys and rude people' who threw 'stones and dirt at him' until he was taken to the common gaol for his own safety; and the mob rifled his house 'of all its furniture' and took away 'his bonds, bills, and evidences'. 'Fearing no opposition they divide themselves into several companies' and spread out over the country, attacking the houses of several ministers and taking away their goods, clothes, money, books and cattle. Some went to Sir Henry Audley's house which 'they plundered of its furniture, and his grounds and pastures of his cattle'. The next day a large crowd from Colchester went to the house of the countess of Rivers, a papist, at St Osyth but the countess, warned of their coming, fled to her house at Long Melford in Suffolk. 'They enter the house, and... they pull down, cut in pieces, and carry away her costly hangings, beds, couches, chairs, and the whole furniture of her house, rob her of her plate and moneys: they tear down her wainscot, leads, and windows, they leave not a door, nor so much as a bar of a window behind them', and they spoil her park.[41] Back in Colchester the people began to talk of going to the earl of Suffolk's house at Audley End, near Saffron Walden.[42]

When the mayor of Colchester's report reached London, the Commons, after some debate, decided to consult the Lords. The Houses were worried by the news but trod warily. They instructed Sir Thomas Barrington and Harbottle Grimston, the two MPs for Colchester (the latter also its recorder), to go down there with all speed and to endeavour to appease the people. They were to thank them for their forwardness to assist parliament, and to tell them that they had done an acceptable service in seizing Sir John Lucas' horses and arms; but now they should send Sir John and Thomas Newcomen to London as delinquents, and the horses, arms, ammunition, money and plate they had taken; and 'lest the gathering together of so many persons might seem to give some occasion to persons ill-affected of misconstruing their peaceable intentions, they are further to signify unto them, that it is thought fit they should, for the present, disperse themselves, and repair every man to his own home', in confidence that they may rely on parliament to protect them by disarming papists and all other persons disaffected to the public peace and the freedom of the subject.[43]

Barrington and Grimston arrived in Colchester on 25 August, where they found huge crowds still very much incensed against papists and other ill-affected persons, and heard of the attack on the countess of Rivers' house at St Osyth and that the people had also risen in Suffolk. Barrington addressed the townsmen in the market-place at Colchester, read them the orders of parliament 'and very lovingly besought the people to do no more'. He secured the release of Sir John Lucas' mother and sister and prepared to send Sir John himself and Thomas Newcomen prisoners to London. 'Many thousands of people were gathered together (both of town and country) a drum being struck up to give them warning.' As Lucas and Newcomen 'were brought out of the gaol, the crowd showed much greater hostility towards the parson than towards the squire and would have torn him in pieces if Grimston had not placed guards on both sides of the prison door, and hustled him quickly into Barrington's coach, 'the people then not daring to strike or stone him, lest the mischief intended him should light on Sir Thomas Barrington'. The coach was guarded a mile out of town but met with 'bitter curses and revilings' all the way to London, especially at Chelmsford and Romford.[44]

Meanwhile Sir Robert Crane, MP for Sudbury, reported to parliament that there were also tumults arising in Suffolk: 'The people in these parts begin to take example by the insurrection at Colchester'.[45] The heart of the disturbances lay in the cloth-manufacturing villages on the Essex-Suffolk border; and the countess of Rivers found that she had jumped out of the frying-pan into the fire, for her house at Long Melford near Sudbury became the main target on 24 or 25 August. 'Many thousands swarmed to the pulling down of Long Melford House, a gallant seat belonging to the Countess of Rivers'. The countess sent her steward to get help from the earl of Warwick (a leading parliamentarian), but he was at sea, lord Rich was at Oxford, and Charles Rich was out hunting, so Arthur Wilson, the earl's steward, set out with a coach and some men to go to the aid of the countess (as he was a puritan and parliamentarian going to the help of a papist and royalist, it was a good example of class solidarity). He gave a vivid account of the state of insurrection in the clothmaking villages of Essex and Suffolk through which he had to pass to get to Long Melford. 'With difficulty I passed through the little villages of Essex, where their black bills and coarse examinations put us to divers demurs. And, but that they had some knowledge of me and the coach, I had not passed with safety... When I came to Sudbury in Suffolk, within three miles of Long Melford, not a man appeared till we were within the chain. And then they began to run to their weapons, and, before we could get to the market-place, the streets swarmed with people. I came out of the coach, as soon as they took the horses by the heads, and desired, that I might speak with the mayor, or some of the magistrates; to know the cause of this tumult: for we had offended nobody. The Mouth cried out, this coach belongs to the lady Rivers; and they are going to her', for he had recognized her steward in the coach: 'And some, who pretended to be more wise and knowing than the rest, said, that I was the lord Rivers. And they swarmed about me, and were so kind as to lay hold on me. But I calmly entreated those many hundreds which encircled me, to hear me speak; which before they had not patience to do, the confusion and noise was so great. I told them, I was steward to the earl of Warwick, a lover of his country, and now in the parliament's employment. That I was going to Bury, about business of his. And that I had letters in my pockets (if they would let any of the magistrates see them) which would make me appear to be a friend and an honest man. This said, the Mouth cried out, Letters, Letters! The tops of the trees, and all the windows, were thronged with people, who cried the same. At last the mayor came crowding in with his officers; and I showed him my letters... The mayor's Wisdom said, he knew not my lord's hand; it might be, and it might not. And away he went, not knowing what to do with me, nor I to say to them'. But the town clerk, whose father was a servant to the earl of Warwick, 'told the mayor and the people, I was the earl of Warwick's steward: and his assurance got some credit with them. And so the great cloud vanished. But I could go no further to succour the lady Rivers. For I heard, from all hands, there was so great confusion at Melford, that no man appeared like a gentleman, but was made a prey to that ravenous crew.' So he left the coach at Sudbury 'and went a byeway to Sir Robert Crane's, a little nearer Melford, to listen after the countess'.[46]

The sheriff of Suffolk called out the trained bands 'for suppressing of a rebellious company of about 2,000', but they were reluctant to go: in Downham they mustered but 'refused to go with the sheriff, or lay down their arms for others', until at length 'Mr North their captain came, with whom they went, and on Friday apprehended some few of the company'.[47] By this time the sack of Melford Hall was complete. The windows were all broken, all iron pulled out, the ceilings torn down, 'all likely places digged where money might be hidden', 'beer and wine consumed, and let out (to knee deep in the cellar)', and all the goods in the house carried off in carts: 'in a few hours' the mob 'disfurnished' the house 'of all the goods which had been many years with great curiosity providing'. They destroyed the gardens, dug up the corn, drove away the cattle, and chased and killed the deer. The countess herself barely escaped with her life, 'after great insolence had been used to her person'; with the help of Sir Robert Crane, she made her way to Bury St Edmunds. But there 'the gates were shut against her an hour at least: at length she was suffered to lodge there that night, and next day with a strong guard she was conveyed out of town, and so keeping herself as private as she could, made an escape to London'. She put her losses at Long Melford and St Osyth at £50,000.[48] Although Sir Robert Crane was an MP and a parliamentarian, he was threatened by the mob for assisting her escape and 'was forced to retain a trained band in his house... to secure himself from the fury of that rabble'.[49] Gifford Hall at Stoke-by-Nayland in Suffolk, the house of another Roman Catholic, Sir Francis Mannock, 'was pillaged of all goods; (and, as is said, not his writings spared, which he craved, but were torn, nor his dogs). Also one Mr Martin's house pillaged. Doctor Warren's house was rifled for his "Gods", and a great many set about the market cross, termed young ministers. Him they huffed and shuffed about, but (as is said) hurt not otherwise, though he say they took money from him.'[50] The mobs did not confine themselves to attacking the houses of papists only, but 'they do plunder divers gentlemen's houses, as well protestants as papists, and have made great spoil', 'alleging them to be persons disaffected to the parliament'. The only security against attack was to 'speak well of the parliament', which many gentlemen did, whose hearts nevertheless were with the king.[51] Clergymen were also prime targets of the popular fury and all this points to the mobs being inspired to a large extent by parliamentarianism and puritanism.

It appears that the violence was directed basically against royalists, or suspected royalists. The crowd at Colchester would listen to the parliamentarian Sir Thomas Barrington and respect his authority. Association with the parliamentarian earl of Warwick carried Arthur Wilson safely through the turbulent villages of Essex and got him out of his difficulties at Sudbury. Sir Nathaniel Barnardiston, the leading parliamentarian in Suffolk, and William Heveningham came down to the county from parliament.[52] Parliamentarian gentry and ministers were busily engaged in persuading the crowds in Essex and Suffolk to disperse, and they were successful in restoring order to both counties.[53] But in any case the tumults had released tensions and would have subsided automatically after a few days: rioters given a more or less free rein became satiated in a short time.

The two Houses ordered that no one was to search houses without an order from parliament, or the Committee of Safety, or the Lord General, and then only under the supervision of the deputy lieutenants of the militia or the justices of the peace; and that anyone who broke into and robbed houses should be punished according to the law.[54] They followed this with a declaration condemning the violence in Essex and Suffolk and ordering that money, plate and goods which had been taken without authorisation from parliament must be restored: no person was to break into any house under pretence of disarming recusants or enemies of the peace of the kingdom, without particular command from the deputy lieutenants, on pain of exemplary punishment.[55] The House of Lords issued its own order to sheriffs, JPs and mayors to assist the countess of Rivers in recovering her goods.[56] Sir Thomas Barrington reported that when the people were told that parliament did not want them to search houses for arms and ammunition, and that they must not take goods from houses without order from parliament, they obeyed and restored the plate, money and goods that they had seized from those they called papists or malignants, expressing their zeal to serve parliament. Harbottle Grimston returned to London on 8 September, declaring that Essex was now calm, and bringing with him 150 volunteers to serve in the earl of Essex's army and six horse-loads of money and plate, worth £6,000, subscribed by the two Hundreds about Colchester for the service of parliament.[57] Colchester and the clothmaking region of Essex and Suffolk strongly supported parliament in the civil war.[58]

The tumults had served their purpose. The royalists in the eastern counties were crushed, never to rise again. 'This insurrection scareth all the malignant party', recorded John Rous.[59] In these counties 'many of the chief gentry... were for paying obedience to his majesty's commission of array, yet the freeholders and yeomen being generally of the other side, as oft as they attempted to show themselves, they were crushed, and their endeavours defeated'.[60] Boston in Lincolnshire was, like Colchester in Essex, a core of puritanism and parliamentarianism:[61] 'Boston men ride out and fetch in such as speak against the parliament, causing some to be sent to the parliament, some be to be bailed for appearance, etc, as their fault deserves—some imprisonment.'[62] The more deeply committed, or the more frightened, fled to the king;[63] the more moderate or circumspect kept their opinions to themselves and acquiesced in a nominal parliamentarianism.[64] But in this period of popular insurrections against royalists it was dangerous to set out to join the king, as the fate of Sir John Lucas dramatically demonstrated to all those who might have been thinking of following his example; and those who did set out were not always successful in reaching their goal safely. Sir William Boteler of Kent 'resolved to fly for protection to the king' but 'in his way thither... in Northamptonshire he was seized on by the country people' and sent prisoner to London.[65] On 10 September Sir John Byron with a troop of horse set out from Oxford, accompanied by three doctors of the university and 'divers scholars volunteers', to join the king's forces, but at Stow-on-the-Wold in Gloucestershire 'they were set upon by the country and lost ten of their men', and one of the doctors ended up in Northampton gaol.[66]

These popular insurrections in many different parts of the country, varying as they did in their character and intensity from place to place, all seem to have been inspired by a panic fear of imminent attack from some sort of enemies. The enemies were labelled 'papists', 'delinquents', 'malignants', 'cavaliers', 'enemies of the people's peace and freedom', and so the risings took place in the name of parliament and in support of parliament. There was an acute fear of soldiers, who, it was assumed, with some justification, would rob and plunder the civilian population wherever they came; and with bands of armed gentlemen and their followers moving about the country on their way to join the king or some royalist leader,

parliamentarian propaganda had little difficulty in arousing
dread of cavaliers. Sir Dudley North, parliamentarian MP for
Cambridgeshire, recalled that about this time 'the House of
Commons ordered me to go into the county for which I served,
where I found all full of terror, the common people generally
apprehending, that the cavaliers... were coming to plunder
them. This fear was artificially put into them... for the county
was full of strange fictions of their inhuman carriage in other
counties'.[67] 'They are all about us here in such grievous fears'
of being plundered, wrote the countess of Sussex from
Hertfordshire in November 1642, 'that if they see but a gentleman riding they think it 'tis to rob them.'[68] Such fears, however, were not invented by the parliamentarians, but exploited
by them, and the risings and riots against royalist nobles,
gentry and clergy were fundamentally spontaneous popular
movements, which were up to a point provoked or condoned by
some parliamentarian gentry and urban magistrates. At
Colchester some of the chief men of the town actively provoked
the uprising, but here and at Sudbury the local authorities for
a time lost control, witness the picture of panic-stricken
helplessness that the mayors of both towns presented.

The parliamentarian leaders reaped the benefit of the
uprisings but in a mood of deep distaste for the mobs who rose
in their interest, suspicion of the real intentions of the people
and apprehension of the consequences of popular movements.
Arthur Wilson considered that the disturbances in Essex and
Suffolk were good examples of what happened when 'a loose
rein' was 'put into the mouth of the unruly multitude': 'So
monstrous is the beast when it holds the bridle in the teeth.'[69]
'The rude multitude in divers counties', wrote Sir Simonds
D'Ewes, 'took advantage of those civil and intestine broils to
plunder and pillage the houses of the nobility, gentry, and
others, who were either known papists, or being protestants,
had sent or provided horses, money or plate to send to the king;
or such as being rich they would make malignants.'[70] These
parliamentarian gentlemen did not believe that the people,
whatever they professed, were really on their side.
Nevertheless these popular movements brought to a temporary
halt the growth of the royalist party and the raising of forces
for the king in south-east Lancashire, the West Riding of

Yorkshire, parts of the Midlands, Gloucestershire, Somerset and, above all, in Essex, Suffolk and the eastern counties. Vast tracts of the country thus fell under the sway of parliament rather than the king. This was not generally due to any actions by the local parliamentarian gentry, or to the intervention of parliament's army, but was the result of popular risings against the royalists. The popular movement of resistance to the royalists was decisive in gaining parliament time in which to gather forces and mobilise resources to encounter the king's army, and territory in which to manoeuvre.

At first sight these popular risings do not appear to have been directed against the ruling class as such, because the ruling class was divided, and the attacks on the royalist nobility and gentry were led or condoned by parliamentarian nobility and gentry. But what was happening was that the people were choosing between one set of rulers and another—in Somerset they opted for Alexander Popham and Sir John Horner rather than Sir Ralph Hopton and Sir John Stowell—and this meant that power lay with the people, rather than with Popham and Horner, at least for the moment. In the West Riding of Yorkshire the Saviles had identified themselves with the clothiers, whose support had been the base for their struggle for power in the county;[71] but when lord Savile declared for the king in 1642 his power collapsed, for the clothiers sided with parliament and found new leaders in the Fairfaxes.[72] In Gloucestershire Nathaniel Stephens, a wealthy landowner, associated himself with the interests of the clothiers, and probably owed his seat for the county in the Long Parliament to this: he took the side of parliament, as did the clothiers, and his influence in his county remained intact.[73] In Suffolk there was a powerful popular movement that declared support for parliament, and the principal county families, led by Sir Nathaniel Barnardiston, continued in power because they also opted for parliament in the civil war.[74] But popular attacks on the royalist nobility and gentry veered out of control of the parliamentarian nobility and gentry, and revealed an underlying rebelliousness against the ruling order. This somewhat incoherent feeling could at first find expression in attacks on the great men who were labelled by parliament the enemies of the people—papists and malignants. But change in the ruling order could be effected only by overthrowing the king and his party, and this could be achieved only through parliament and with the help of the parliamentarian nobility and gentry.

The question arises whether the royalists were regarded as 'the enemy' in the same way and for the same reasons by both the parliamentarian gentry and the people. The hatred that the country people of Gloucestershire exhibited towards lord Chandos was explained as reflecting how 'much they abhorred to be betrayed to slavery by one of their own country'.[75] The earl of Bath attributed the hostility that he encountered in trying to execute the commission of array in Devonshire to the popular belief that it was intended to set up an 'arbitrary and tyrannical government' and to tax poor men; and he found it necessary to swear an oath on the sacrament that this was not so, 'neither will I take the value of sixpence from any man'.[76] The marquis of Hertford explained the rising against himself in Somerset by the fact 'that great multitudes of people were poisoned and enraged against that service by false and scandalous suggestions, as if the intent of the commission were to enthrall the people and to take away great part of their estates'.[77] The people believed 'that the marquis was come down to put the commission of array in execution, by which commission a great part of the estate of every farmer or substantial yeoman should be taken from them; ...and so, taking advantage of the commission's being in Latin, translated it into what English they pleased; persuading the substantial yeomen and freeholders that at least two parts of their estates would by that commission be taken from them, and the meaner and poorer sort of people that they were to pay a tax for one day's labour in the week to the king... It is not easily believed how these gross infusions generally prevailed.'[78] The king accused the parliamentarians of 'infusing into' the people 'that there was an intention by the commission of array to take away a part of their estates from them'.[79]

This opened the way for a crucial shift, by which the commission of array appeared as an instrument of class as well as of royal tyranny, and distrust and dislike of the king's actions merged into fear and hatred of the aristocracy's intentions. It was alleged that the reason why 'a great part of the estate of every farmer or substantial yeoman' was to be taken away was because, as 'some lords had said', '£20 by the year was enough for any peasant to live by'.[80] This story was widely publicised by the Somerset parliamentarians, whose chief publicist, John Ashe, MP for Westbury, was a very wealthy clothier and may have been more sensitive to the outlook of the 'middle sort of people' than of the dangers to the established gentry. 'It is really reported by the mouths of those who were eye and ear witnesses, that my lord Poulett in opposition to the militia at a combustion in Wells, with many imprecations, oaths and execrations (in the height of fury) declared, that it was not fit for any yeoman to have allowed him from his own labours, any more than the poor moiety of ten pounds a year, and withal manifested to this purpose, though not perhaps in these words, that when the power should be totally on their side, they shall be compelled to live at that low allowance, notwithstanding their estates are gotten with a great deal of labour and industry'.[81] Clearly this story did play a large part in rousing the country people of Somerset against the royalists. 'The people murmured much at him'.[82] 'My lord Poulett is hated of all men.'[83] 'The people hearing such inhuman propositions (that have no precedent, neither warranted by law, old custom, nor religion, the lives of them and their families depending on their estates) attempted to lay violent hands on him'. 'The people did not take his speech as only directed to the yeoman, but to all men under the degree of a gentleman, or such whom he will allow to be so, for it was reasoned on this manner, if the yeoman's estate was his offence, therefore for that crime he must be limited a petty proportion of ten pounds a year, the tradesmen and merchants were rich, and by this consequence being guilty of the same crime receive the same punishment, and have such a limitation or less (as the yeoman)'. It was said that when the people of Somerset rose in arms for parliament it was in order to combat the Poulett doctrine.[84] 'The people have resolved rather to lose their lives than to be slaves';[85] believing that if the royalists triumphed 'all should be, upon the matter, no better than slaves to the lords, and that there was no way to free and preserve themselves from this insupportable tyranny than by adhering to the parliament, and submitting to the ordinance for the militia, which was puposely prepared to enable them to resist these horrid invasions of their liberties'.[86]

The royalists in Gloucestershire were described as 'powerful gentry' who desired 'vast dominion, dignity, revenge, or rapine', and cared not 'to render themselves slaves to princes, that they also might rule over their neighbours as vassals'.[87] The nobles and gentlemen were sufficiently numerous and prominent on the king's side to give the impression that the royalist party was the party of the nobility and gentry (a view which the king's own propaganda spread and confirmed), and in popular eyes the ruling class was identified with the king's party. The fact that some of the nobility and gentry were well disposed towards the people and offered through parliament to defend them against the aggression of the royalists, did not alter the belief, but rather confirmed it, that the triumph of the king's party would result in intensification of the oppression of the people by the nobility and gentry. Therefore the struggle against the royalists, to this way of thinking, was a struggle against the 'tyranny' of the ruling class, or the tyrannical intentions of the ruling class. The fact that some of the ruling class took the side of the people rather than of their own class was welcome and gratifying, if somewhat suspect. Inevitably a wealthy parliamentarian squire and a poor parliamentarian peasant or craftsman would not see the conflict in the same terms: the former took up arms against other squires for political or religious reasons; the latter took up arms against royalist squires because they were squires as well as for political or religious reasons. The spontaneity of the uprisings against the commissioners of array is an indication that the breach between the king and parliament was the occasion more than the cause of the popular revolt, and that the people and the parliamentarian gentry found themselves, for the moment, on the same side by coincidence, arising from different rather than the same causes.

On 4 August 1642 the king warned the Yorkshire gentry that the scandals which parliament had cast on his followers would 'by degrees involve all gentlemen'.[88] After the battle of Edgehill he deplored the 'implacable malice and hatred' which the commonalty showed towards the gentry, and that 'all persons of honour, courage, and reputation' were odious to them, 'insomuch as the highways and villages have not been safe for gentlemen to pass through without violence or affronts'.[89] Clarendon complained of 'the fury and license of the common people' and their 'barbarity and rage against the nobility and gentry'.[90] 'I believe such times were never before seen in England', lamented Sir John Oglander, 'when the gentry were made slaves to the commonalty and in their power, not only to abuse but plunder any gentleman.'[91] Parliamentarian gentry were also conscious that the popular attacks on 'royalists' represented a measure of popular hostility towards the ruling class. In part this hostility arose from fear—'if they see but a gentleman riding they think 'tis to rob them',[92] in part from social antagonism—'no man appeared like a gentleman, but was made a prey to that ravenous crew', recorded Arthur Wilson from his personal experience of the mobs in Essex and Suffolk;[93] and in part from hatred of the rich—'such as being rich they would make malignants'.[94]

PEASANT REVOLTS

The king relied chiefly, and far more than parliament did, upon the support of the wealth, power and influence of the greater landlords, both noble and gentry. His armies were recruited by aristocrats and squires from amongst their relatives, friends and neighbours, their servants, tenants and dependents. The royalist leaders relied on the traditional ties of loyalty and habits of deference that had bound the peasants to their lords. They were successful in those parts of the country where these ties and habits still remained intact,[95] or where the peasants had been cowed into submission by the resurgence of the landlords in the 1620s and 1630s. But the most decisive influence that the agrarian situation and peasant discontent had upon the civil war and its outcome was that in many parts of the countryside the landlords, including the king, had forfeited much of the loyalty and respect they had once elicited from their tenantry. The imposition of big increases in rents and fines caused resentments and disputes, and 'undermined the old relationship of dependence and loyalty between landlord and tenants', and put their relationship at best on a purely economic and interest basis, eliminating sentiment and trust. The enclosures of forests and wastes, marshes and fens, provoked violent conflicts between lords and tenants and left the peasants involved with little feeling of respect, deference or loyalty for the king, peers and most landlords.[96] Thus the unpopularity of some landlords and the decline of loyalty to some landlords affected the king in the civil war more adversely than parliament, because he depended far more than parliament on the loyalty of peasants to their lords; and the erosion or disappearance of that loyalty in parts of the countryside restricted the amount of support and resources the king and the royalist nobility and gentry could command. This probably explains the defeat of the royalists in the civil war. It was in the first place a negative factor—though no less important for that—and it did not mean that the aggrieved peasants necessarily supported parliament; far from it, in many cases. But it did mean in many districts a lack of enthusiasm for the cause of the king and royalist landlords and often a refusal to assist them further than compelled by power and force.

Some tenants of royalist landlords, however, actively supported parliament, and often this seems to have been caused by agrarian discontent. In the West Riding of Yorkshire many tenants supported parliament even when their landlords were royalists. The royalist lord Savile wrote that it was 'well known to all Yorkshire that many of his tenants and of other men's are favourers of that cause, and do pay his rents to the enemies [of the king]... but, to say the truth, there are few in the West Riding (my lord of Cumberland's tenants not excepted [the royalist commander in Yorkshire]) who do not in this case play the knaves'.[97] The royalist lord Capel ordered his tenants in Somerset to pay their rents to the marquis of Hertford for support of the king's cause, but they, and the tenants of other royalist landlords, petitioned parliament: 'We that are tenants to some that serve and assist the king against the parliament (though our hearts go not with our landlords, in those ways they go) would be glad the parliament would make an order that we should bring in our rents into Guildhall in London, we would more readily do it, than go one mile to pay it to any that shall employ it against parliament... But we expect to have an order of parliament to save us harmless from our landlords hereafter.'[98] This pressure provoked parliament to take the first steps towards sequestrating the estates of royalist landlords.[99] Although most of 'the gentlemen of eminent quality and fortune' in Somerset supported the king and expected to raise five thousand men amongst their neighbours and tenants, they were able to raise only a few hundred, and this could only have been because their tenants rejected their leadership.[100] Instead thousands of country people in Somerset flocked to the support of the parliamentarian gentry, who claimed that 'there came unto us every one' of the tenants of Thomas Smith of Long Ashton—a wealthy landowner, MP for Bridgwater, and brother-in-law of lord Poulett—including 'forty yeomen well armed'. Although Sir Ralph Hopton was 'a gentleman very well beloved in the whole county', when he took up arms for the king it was said that 'all the inhabitants of that quarter where [he] liveth unto his very gates' rose for parliament, and 'from Evercreech his own tenants and servants came against him and cry him down now'.[101] This resistance of the peasants in Somerset to the marquis of Hertford and the royalist landlords may not have been unconnected with their discontent at enclosures of forests and marshes there by the king, the marquis himself and other royalist landlords.

Some tenants in Cheshire refused to be enlisted in the king's forces by their royalist landlords.[102] On 17 September 1642 the royalist squire William Davenport of Bramhall in Cheshire was at dinner when a letter was brought to him from twenty-four of his tenants: 'Much Honored Sir,—We your Worships tenants here present, haveing these manie dayes with sadd spirites weighed not onelie the woffull distractions off our kingdome, but also the present standinge that is betwixt your woorshippe and ourselves, have thought it our dutie, as well for the workeing up off a sweete union, as for the takinge away off all jealousies amoungste us, to present youre woorshippe with these few lynnes off our humble request. Wherein wee doe most humbly intreat your woorshippe, That ethir you would be please to bend your intencions that waye which wee maye with upright hartes and saffe consciences cleave to you both in lyffe and death: (which in so doinge wee shalbe willinge to doe;) or else that your worshippe will not repute us ill affected or false-harted tenants in refusinge to venture our lyves in causses that our harts and consciences doe perswade us are not good or lawffull, nor such as wee dare safelye and with good consciences maintayne and deffend you in. For, howsoever wee would not for the world harbour a disloyall thought against his Majestie, yet wee dare not lifte upp our handes against that honorable assembly off Parl-ament, whom wee are conffidently assured doe labour both for the happiness off his Majestie and all his kingdome.' Davenport said that he would reply to this letter in a couple of days, but 'the verie next day (and it beinge the Saboth daye too), not stainge or belyke caringe much ffor me or my answer, they with some others off my tenants enrowled their names and listed themselves with Captain Hyde off Norburie to become soul-diers ffor the Parlement under his commaund'. This shows that it was not only landlords who tried to influence their tenants, but also tenants tried to persuade their landlords to their own way of thinking. But Davenport's reaction well illustrates the class bitterness that such acts of defiance injected into the civil war. He kept a careful record of 'how perfideously and treach-erously' his tenants had treated him, as 'a perpetuall rem-brance to my heires', so that when 'the Almightie great God shal inable you reward', ' and, as occation is... offerd... remem-ber theire passages in them or their posteritie to right me wherein I cannot right myself'.[103] It is not without significance that there is evidence Davenport was unpopular with his ten-ants over the demands he made for heriots (the payment to the lord of the manor of the best beast or good on the death of a ten-ant), and on the eve of the civil war heriots seem to have been a major grievance of Cheshire tenants against their lords.[104]

In Lancashire the king's cause was led by the greatest landlord and most powerful man in the county—the earl of Derby, whose wife complained of their neighbours at Lathom House that 'some of them were as bad tenants as subjects'.[105] Colonel John Moore, who commanded the parliamentarian forces at Liverpool, testified that the tenants of the earl's manors of West Derby and Wavertree 'ever faithfully adhered to the parliament, and some of them have lost their lives in the service, most of them their personal estate, by showing themselves for the parliament. They live within two miles of Liverpool and upon all occasions have been ready to assist that garrison.'[106] After the civil war a petition from Buckingham-shire claimed that copyholders, who are 'the body of the kingdom', 'have for the most part been very cordial and faithful to the parliament', while the generality of their lords 'have been very malignant, and much disaffected to parliamentary or thorough reformation'.[107]

The rioting against royalists in Essex and Suffolk at the outbreak of the civil war in 1642 exhibited undertones of peasant revolt. The violence of the attack on Sir John Lucas and his house at Colchester was not unconnected with the fact that he was an unpopular landlord. In June 1641 'some people of Colchester' had committed 'a riot and disorder... about his house and grounds' and pulled up and burnt his rails and fences.[108] When the mobs plundered his house in 1642, they took not only his money, plate, jewels, linen, but also his 'writings' and destroyed his 'evidences'—estate documents relating to his property, leases, and rents and dues owed by his tenants—and 'from thence they go to his park, pull down his pales, kill his deer, drive away his cattle'.[109] The mobs that attacked the houses of 'papists and malignants' paid off old scores against unpopular gentlemen: they destroyed the 'writings' of Sir Francis Mannock at Gifford Hall, Stoke-by-Nayland in Suffolk; and the 'bill, bonds, letters, and other writings' of a gentleman at Acton in Middlesex, who was probably an unpopular money-lender.[110]

The peasant rebellion which had burst out in the fens of Lincolnshire, Cambridgeshire and Huntingdonshire in 1641-2 continued after the outbreak of the civil war. The conflict between the tenants of the manor of Epworth, in the Isle of Axholme, and the king spread to the commoners of Hatfield Chase, who had also been deprived of two-thirds of their commons by the draining and enclosing of the land. In February 1643 'they pulled up the floodgates of Snow Sewer, which by letting in the tides from the river of Trent, soon drowned a great part of Hatfield Chase; divers persons standing there with muskets; and crying, that there they would stay till the whole level was drowned, and the inhabitants forced to swim away like ducks: and so continued guarding the said sluice for the space of seven weeks together, letting in the tides at every full water, and keeping the sluices shut at an ebb. And about that time, likewise, some of the inhabitants of Misterton, pulled down another sluice, near that town; which occasioned the river of Trent to break down the banks and overflow the whole level, so that the barns and stacks of corn were drowned a yard high, at the least.' The inhabitants of Epworth threw down the banks, filled in ditches, destroyed crops and put their cattle back on the whole of their old commons, driving off the settlers, demolishing their houses and burning their ploughs. This struggle carried the peasants into the parliamentarian party. 'The people of Epworth manor and Misterton did at the breaking out of the civil wars take up arms against his majesty', and two companies of foot (a total of 495 men) were raised for parliament in the Isle of Axholme. It was said that the commoners had 'the assistance of some of the parliament soldiers' in recovering their commons. 'The commoners of the Isle supported the parliamentary forces because these forces were in conflict with the state power which had expropriated them. The "law and order" of the monarchy no longer prevailing they simply took back much of what they considered to be theirs.'[111] Cromwell recruited the regiment that contributed so much to parliament's victory in the civil war from the peasant farmers of Huntingdonshire and Cambridgeshire, and he was helped no doubt by the fierce support that he had given to the fen commoners in their struggles against the drainage undertakers.[112]

Concurrently with both the enclosure riots and the attacks on the royalist nobility and gentry, peasant hostility towards the king and the great landlords broke out in 1642 in attacks on the most hated symbol of the aristocrat, his deer-park. Hunting was one of the privileges of the ruling class, and the game laws, intensified by James I and Charles I, reserved the sport for gentlemen and excluded the common people. The enclosure of vast areas to make parks for deer was the most hated sort of enclosure. Peasants were deeply affronted by the sight of parks made purely for purposes of pleasure and by 'the withdrawal from production of good farmland merely to provide landowners and aristocrats with "houses built alone like ravens' nests, no birds building near them".' In the face of the pressure of an increased population on the land and of the demand of the poorer people for smallholdings, the reservation of vast acreages merely for game and the sport of the rich, was an even more cynical affront and an even more bitter grievance. But on top of all, the parks were overstocked and the deer destroyed the crops of neighbouring farmers.[113]

The king's deer, like the king's enclosures, had been the first to come under attack. There was a dispute about the boundaries of the king's Great Forest at Windsor. The Long Parliament had appointed commissioners to restore the bounds as they had been in the twentieth year of the reign of king James. But the people of Surrey who lived in the neighbourhood of the forest became impatient with delays in setting out the new bounds. On 8 September 1641 the House of Commons ordered the sheriffs and JPs of the counties in and adjoining the forest 'to take care, that the deer in his majesty's forests be not destroyed; and to repress all tumults, that may arise thereupon; in regard there is a law provided, and that this House will take care, for the vindication of the right of the subject in that particular'. This order was published by the commission which met at Egham to ascertain the bounds of the forest, and read out at the Courts of Swanimote and in all the churches. But from the beginning of September the people of Egham were raiding the forest, in large numbers, and killing the deer. This continued regularly and on 14 October some men from Egham killed a brace of great stags and threatened to stab and shoot the keepers. The House of Lords sent for these men and their messenger apprehended them, but they 'were rescued out of his hands, by the violence of some of their companions'. The unlawful hunting of the king's deer went on, and in January 1642 the House of Lords ordered that, until it was determined whether the bounds of the forest in Surrey were properly set out, the sheriff and JPs of the county were to prevent this destruction of the king's game, and to assist the earl of Holland, Chief Justice in Eyre of the King's Forests south of Trent, and the keepers to apprehend the offenders and send them to be dealt with by the peers.[114]

Behind these disorders lay an agrarian grievance. The inhabitants of the parish of Egham claimed an ancient custom of pasturing their cattle in the Great Park at Windsor from 10 May until 1 August, and from 1 November until 25 December, 'at very easy rates, in consideration of divers services performed by them, as carrying in hay and sending in treaders and the like'. But a large part of the park had been taken out of the commons belonging to the parish and this custom had been taken from them. The richer farmers were willing to co-exist with the king's deer, providing that their ancient privilege was restored to them, and providing that no cattle 'from foreign parishes or counties' got the same privilege, 'so that there may be sufficient pasture left for his majesty's deer, and likewise for the cattle of the said parishioners'. They were ready to pay for this privilege, offering 4d a week for each cow and 6d a week for each horse or mare and colt, instead of the customary $1^1/_2$d a week. They expressed disapproval of the unlawful destruction of the king's deer, but were willing to utilise the disorders of their poorer neighbours to intimidate the authorities. In May 1642 they pointed out that 'the rude multitude' was still destroying the king's red deer, despite 'the best means that either the messengers of the parliament or the magistrates of the county could use to prevent it', and that they were now threatening 'to pull down the pales of the park and lay it all to common', but that if the ancient custom of pasturing in the Great Park were restored the attacks would cease.[115]

The disorders spread to the Berkshire side of the forest. In New Lodge the country people killed a hundred of the king's fallow deer, besides red deer, and threatened to pull down the pales about the lodge. The earl of Holland ordered the arrest of the ringleaders but his warrants were ignored, and the sheriff of Berkshire was summoned to the House of Lords to explain why he had not prevented the riots. He was ordered to arrest the ringleaders and bring them before the House. Two of them were apprehended and kept in custody for a time by the Lords, who then sent them to hard labour in the House of Correction in Berkshire. But the people of Berkshire in the neighbourhood of the forest continued to hunt the deer and to threaten to pull down the fences and make the land common. The earl of Holland, as Constable of Windsor Castle, came down to prevent this, and the sheriff and JPs of the county were ordered to help. In May 1642 the constable of Windlesham was ordered to apprehend certain persons who had shot a stag in Swinley Walk, in Berkshire, and threatened to shoot a keeper who interfered. Taking a party of men, the constable set off and met the offenders on the highway: they refused to surrender to his warrant and made off towards Chertsey. The constable pursued them but they shot his horse from under him and escaped.[116]

The trouble spread to other royal forests. In April 1642 a

crowd armed with guns, bills, pitchforks and clubs invaded the king's forest of Waltham in Essex, and killed and wounded many of the deer. They said that 'they came for venison and venison they would have, for there was no law settled at this time'. They laughed at the warrant of the earl of Carlisle, the Chief Keeper of the Forest, and told the underkeepers that 'if they complained of offenders, to complain of good store of them, that if they went to prison they might be merry together'. They were said to be led by the parson of Chingford, who, with twenty other 'principal actors', was sent for by the House of Lords, and their lordships ordered the sheriff and JPs of Essex to suppress the riot.[117] The Lords and Commons made an order on 12 May 1642:[118] 'Whereas information hath been given to the Lords and Commons in this present parliament assembled, that divers lewd and disordered persons since the sitting of this parliament, have in great assemblies, and in riotous manner, unlawfully chased, killed and destroyed many of his majesty's deer within his forests of Windsor, and Waltham, according to the known bounds, as now they are limited and set out by virtue of the late Act of Parliament. And that they together with divers other the like persons do threaten and give out, that they intend to commit the like outrages in other his majesty's forests, chases, and parks, presuming with their numbers, multitudes and menaces, to terrify and disable his majesty's officers of his forests, chases, and parks from doing their respective duties by apprehending their bodies, or otherwise bringing them to condign punishment for such their misdoing, according to the laws of the forests; which offences committed with force and violence (as scandalous to the public justice of the kingdom if not punished, and dangerous for the future) unless they be timely prevented, are at no time, (much less sitting the parliament) to be suffered.' The sheriffs and JPs were ordered to see that the offenders were arrested and punished according to the laws.[119] But this did not make much difference. In June the earl of Holland directed the keepers to search the parishes of Winkfield, Warfield, Easthampstead and Sunninghill, on the Berkshire side of Windsor forest, and to seize all dogs, greyhounds, hand-guns, cross-bows, sets, traps and other engines used to kill deer, and to report to him the names of the owners.[120] In July the House of Lords ordered the sheriff of

Berkshire to raise the power of the county to apprehend the persons named by the earl as invaders of the king's forest at Windsor.[121] The people, however, continued to course the king's deer with greyhounds and to shoot them in the forests of Windsor and Waltham through 1642 and 1643.[122]

The attack on deer, just like the attack on enclosures, spread from the parks of the king to those of other great landowners, and merged into the assaults on 'papists' and 'delinquents'. On 22 August 1642, after Sir John Lucas had been seized by the mob and his house near Colchester ransacked, the pales round his park were pulled down and his deer killed.[123] A few days later when the mob stormed the countess of Rivers' house at Long Melford, near Sudbury in Suffolk, they chased and destroyed her deer.[124] About the same time lord Capel's deer-park was 'spoiled by the rabble-rout and... there was the like attempt against the lord Monmouth's deer'.[125] On 21 September the earl of Carlisle informed the House of Lords that the people were attacking his house and park in Essex. He had been accused of being a royalist, but had recently cleared himself before the Lords, denying that he had raised a troop of horse for the king or put the commission of array in execution, and accepting the judgement of the two Houses that the commission was illegal. He went down to Essex and found that his house and park had suffered some violence, and that many of his deer had been destroyed. He managed to arrest some of the offenders, and the House of Lords ordered Colonel Essex's regiment to protect his house and park. But there were further attacks and more of his deer were slain. The House of Lords sent for the ringleaders, who mostly came from Epping: they were three yeomen, a draper; a shoemaker and a carpenter.[126] At Farnham in Surrey 'the country people... gathered together in a great multitude, and... killed and destroyed great store' of the bishop of Winchester's deer in the Great Park, 'killing above twenty at a time'. On Sunday 25 September a hundred people invaded the park with dogs and guns and hunted and killed 200 deer, which they carried off. They pulled down the fences and killed or chased off the cattle (indicating that this was probably another case of a claim to ancient common pastures). They threatened to kill the keeper when he told them that they ought to be in church. Also at

Farnham the people destroyed all the deer in the marquis of Hertford's park; and they threatened to destroy a cony-warren which a Westminster poulterer had recently constructed at a cost of £500.[127]

The House of Lords made an order to protect the earl of Dover's house in Surrey from being pillaged and the deer and cattle in his park from being killed; and instructed the deputy lieutenants, sheriff, JPs and constables of Surrey to prevent unlawful meetings and disorders there.[128] The earl of Middlesex, the financier who had become lord treasurer and an earl in James I's reign, declared for neither king nor parliament in the civil war, but his deer in his park at Forthampton in Gloucestershire were 'delinquents' in the eyes of the local people. 'He had always taken stern measures to protect his deer forest' and much of the time of the Tewksbury attorney who supervised his estate there had been taken up with bringing deer-stealers to justice. But in October 1642 old scores were settled and a 'rebellious, riotous, devilish' uprising destroyed about 600 deer, leaving only about 100 surviving. 'Middlesex's brother-in-law, Henry Osborne, hurriedly took refuge in Gloucester, since in the alehouses the deer-slayers were boasting that "they would not only destroy the remainder of deer but rifle your lordship's house at Forthampton and pull it down to the ground and not let... a tree or bush stand in all the chase".' Mrs Prestwich, the biographer of Middlesex, describes this uprising as a *'jacquerie'* and comments that 'the savage attack on Forthampton suggests that Middlesex was a harsh and unpopular landlord'.[129] This may stand as a general comment on the attacks on deer-parks in 1642. Many of the country people entered on the hard winter of 1642-3 with their bellies full of good venison: perhaps this took some of the edge off their appetite for revolution.

The hunting of lords and deer in the late summer and autumn of 1642 was only loosely connected with the challenge of parliament to the king: the rioters often had little sympathy with parliament or interest in the disputes between the king and the two Houses. Nevertheless the suggestion that hostility towards the ruling class gave the parliamentarian cause its momentum gains some confirmation from the way in which the attacks on lords and deer were continued by parliament's army as it marched out of London and through the midlands. 'At Chiswick they intended to pillage the earl of Portland's house', wrote one of the soldiers, Nehemiah Wharton, who described life in the army in a series of letters between 16 August and 7 October, 'but by our commanders they were prevented'.[130] Portland was at this time a parliamentarian. But his house did not long escape the attentions of the soldiers of his own party, and soon after it was broken open and robbed.[131]

Marching towards Buckingham, continued Wharton, 'early in the morning, I...gathered a complete file of my own men about the country, and marched to Sir Alexander Denton's park, who is a malignant fellow, and killed a fat buck, fastened his head upon my halberd, and commanded two of my pikes to bring the body after me to Buckingham with a guard of musketeers coming thither. With part of it I feasted my captain, captain Parker, captain Beacon, and colonel Hampden's son, and with the rest several lieutenants, ensigns, and serjeants, and had much thanks for my pains.'[132] At Coventry on 27 August 'several of our soldiers, both horse and foot, sallied out of the city to lord Dunsmore's park, and brought from thence great store of venison, which is as good as ever I tasted; and ever since they make it their daily practice, so that venison is almost as common with us as beef with you'. They took three asses out of lord Dunsmore's park, 'which they loaded with their knapsacks, and dignified them with the name of lord Dunsmore'.[133] Marching by the earl of Northampton's house in Northamptonshire 'we could not restrain our soldiers from entering his park and killing his deer, and had not the lord Grey and our sergeant-major general withstood them they had pillaged his house'.[134] 'Our soldiers brought in much venison and other pillage from the malignants about the country'; and 'all the venison belonging to malignants in the county are destroyed'.[135]

Finally, the peasants struck back at their landlords by a rent strike. They claimed, of course, that with the money they had to find for ever-increasing taxes to pay for the war, and with the losses they suffered from plundering by the armies and the disruption of markets, they had little left with which to pay their rents; and there was much truth in this. Nevertheless they took advantage of the times and the weakening of the authority of landlords to end the rise in rents and secure reductions; and at the same time to settle scores with unpopular landlords.

As the breach between king and parliament widened in 1642 and civil war approached, landlords were becoming worried about the difficulties they encountered in collecting their rents. On 5 April the countess of Sussex wrote: 'My Essex rents I am sure will be well paid, for they have good pennyworth and forfeit their leases if they pay not; but I doubt Buckinghamshire rents will not be paid well'.[136] But in May she complained 'rents are paid nowhere'.[137] In June Margaret Eure wrote from Yorkshire: 'I have still about half my rents behind'.[138] The earl of Middlesex's rents were not being paid on his Gloucestershire estate in the autumn of 1642, and his agent reported that 'to ask the question is a considerable discourtesy'.[139] Thomas Denne wrote from London to Henry Oxinden in Kent on 15 November 1642: 'I have received your letter dated November 1, and am sorry to [understand] that all my tenants except Mr Gibbs and Thomas Andrew[s] are so backward in paying their rents'.[140] 'I must expect little or no rent this our lady-day', complained the countess of Sussex in 1643: 'My bailiff came out of Essex...but brought not a penny of money'.[141] 'There are not any rents received nor are you to expect any—as I fear—this long time', Brian Middleton told Sir William Sheffield.[142] In Derbyshire Sir John Coke noted in 1643: 'I receive not half my revenue in one place' and very little from Leicestershire.[143] 'I never yet felt want, which now I suddenly fear', lamented Sir Thomas Roe: 'For my rents are either taken up, or upon such pretences not paid.'[144] 'The fortune I have is all in the rebels' hands', said Sir John Mennes in 1644, 'or in such tenants as have forgot to pay.'[145] Thomas Warde complained on 4 March 1644: 'I have not received any rent this three quarters of this year'.[146]

Landlords had to reduce rents by making allowances for the taxes and other payments that their tenants had to make, and for the losses that they suffered at the hands of plundering soldiers. Taxed heavily and plundered cruelly, many tenants, it was true, could not keep up the payment of their rents.[147] Henry Oxinden reported from Kent that 'most men' were 'compelled to abate one part of three'.[148] But it is just as clear that tenants took advantage of the times to secure a general reduction of rents. The steward of the Legh family reported of the tenants at Hoole in Lancashire that 'these times of liberty and distraction rendered them of that place incredibly forgetful and many would deny to pay any rent'.[149] The earl of Middlesex was informed by the bailiff of his Warwickshire estate: 'This devilish device that tenants need not pay more rent to their landlords than the times will afford and the great abatements some landlords make in these necessitous times hath (as more and more I find) so possessed the most part of your honour's tenants that they neither care for covenant nor fear hereafter. I know not what to do, but to entreat and take what they will pay'.[150] The earl's agent in Gloucestershire wrote: 'if my life lay at stake, I know not how... to mollify the hearts of the tenants so as that they will permit their landlords but to live, for between the great abatement of rents and the allowances they will have, the rent arising to the lord will hardly I declare come to one fourth part'. He complained of the 'hellish wickedness in most men's hearts': 'such kind of people as the tenants are, do now take no small liberty over their betters. They that see it not cannot believe it.'[151]

Thomas Knyvett wrote about his tenants to his wife, who was managing his estate in Norfolk during his absence: 'I am sorry thou hast so troublesome a game to play amongst those clowns... they will make a prey of my necessities, thinking to have what conditions they please rather than be turned out. And to tell thee true, I do not know what to advise in this case, only use them kindly and make thy bargain with them for the present as well as thou canst, and get this half year's rent as fast as you can persuade... 'Tis better to yield to a small inconvenience than to admit of a greater mischief, better abate something than lose all. But I suppose these abatements are desired but for future times, and therefore make no new agreements but from Michaelmas next, this year to go as they are.'[152] His bitterness must have been shared by the many other landlords who found that their tenants were in a stronger bargaining position than themselves. 'I have not patience yet to consider what course to run with that rascal Cooke. It seems I was no whit mistaken in his base condition. I know not what to advise; thou art amongst a company of bloodsucking knaves, whose religion is nothing but dissimulation and hypocrisy. Discretion and patience must act thy part to our best advantage for the present. I much wonder at Richard Turner's carriage, of whom I have had a better opinion. I thought he had been of a better nature, but I see a sow's ear ne'er made silken purse, though he may new cover his dame Alice in silk if he carves so largely out of my rent.'[153]

The tenants were in a strong position: if they did not get substantial reductions in their rents, they simply threw up their leases, and the landlords found that they could get no tenants to replace them. 'One proprietor complained that a fourth part of his leases in Suffolk had been returned on his hands, and that from some parts of his estate he received less than half of the income which he had enjoyed before the war'.[154] Thomas Warde reduced his rents by half but still his tenants left him, 'and now my land is thrown up into my own hand, and nobody will take it of me'.[155] The earl of Middlesex's tenants told him that other landlords 'offer their lands for half the usual rent, paying all charges and cannot have tenants'. His bailiff in Warwickshire warned him that tenants were turning in their leases and he could not let the vacant holdings: 'men that are able may now have choice of grounds and make their prices also' and he could not let any of the empty farms unless he reduced the rents by a quarter or a third. One large farm that was let before the war for £328 a year was vacated in 1645 and the only offer for it was £60 a year.[156] 'In Wirral Hundred, Cheshire, the rental of thirty-one estates dropped between 1642 and 1647, from £4,142 to £2,047; and in Gloucestershire the rental of twenty-seven estates was similarly reduced from £6,542 to £3,241, the fall to about half the amount being the same in both cases.'[157]

There were many ways open to tenants at this time of resisting their landlords: one defaulting tenant avoided eviction by reporting his landlord as a royalist and getting his estate sequestered.[158] Sometimes the refusal of tenants to pay their rents was an open act of revolt against an unpopular landlord. The *jacquerie* in Essex and Suffolk which sacked the countess of Rivers' houses was a more dramatic act of revolt, but the refusal to pay her any rents was more effective.[159] The Middletons of Leighton in Lancashire were unpopular landlords because they imposed greatly increased entry fines on their tenants. 'During the civil war some Middleton tenants apparently took advantage of the chaos to throw off the yoke of landlord oppression. In a bill of complaint to the duchy court on 11 February 1649 George Middleton stated that since the death of his father (in 1640) many of his tenants in Yealand, Silverdale and Lindeth had refused to pay their fines.'[160]

RESISTANCE OF THE INDUSTRIAL DISTRICTS

London, according to the royalist Clarendon, was 'the sink of all the ill humours of the kingdom';[161] and Sir Edward Walker described it as 'the head and fountain of this detested rebellion'.[162] 'The leading members in both Houses might have made a riot; they never had been able to have formed an army', observed a royalist pamphleteer, 'had not the treasure which first raised, and afterwards maintained that rebellious army been collected there'.[163] 'How forward and active the Londoners were to promote this rebellion, can hardly be imagined; people of all sorts pouring out their treasure'. 'The plate and moneys of the citizens came tumbling into Guildhall upon the public faith'; they came 'thronging in with their plate and rings; not sparing their very thimbles and bodkins. Neither were they backward in the adventure of their lives'.[164] The rank and file of parliament's army under the command of the earl of Essex was supplied largely by Londoners in 1642. 'In this summer the citizens listed themselves plentifully for soldiers... The youth of the City of London made up the major part of Essex his infantry'.[165] Five thousand listed themselves under the earl on 26 July in Moor Fields, 'which, with the other volunteers, then in readiness, amounted to near ten thousand men'; and on 1 August they were distributed into regiments and assigned to officers and 'ordered to be daily exercised, and to have constant pay'.[166] It was claimed that 8,000 apprentices of London joined the army in the summer of 1642.[167] The royalist aristocrats viewed this citizen army with contempt, which bred in them an overconfidence and underestimation of their enemy. But when prince Rupert and the royalist cavalry dashed on London in November 1642, it was the trained bands and citizens of London, massed on Turnham Green, that barred his way and frustrated his hopes of a quick victory for the king. It was the

trained bands of London that marched with Essex in the face
of the king's army to relieve the siege of Gloucester in 1643, and
fought their way back to London in the campaign that
Clarendon 'reckoned amongst the most soldierly actions of this
unhappy war'. The royalist historian was forced into this eulogy
of the citizen army: 'The London train-bands, and auxiliary
regiments, (of whose inexperience of danger, or any kind of
service beyond the easy practice of their postures in the
Artillery Garden, men had till then too cheap an estimation,)
behaved themselves to wonder, and were in truth the
preservation of that army that day; for they stood as a bulwark
and rampire to defend the rest, and, when their wings of horse
were scattered and dispersed, kept their ground so steadily
that, though prince Rupert himself led up the choice horse to
charge, and endured their storm of small shot, he could make
no impression upon their stand of pikes, but was forced to wheel
about.'[168] As the result of lack of support from the gentry,
parliament was short of good horsemen and sufficient
cavalry:[169] without them it could not win the war, but London's
infantry saved it from losing the war in 1642 and 1643. The
royalists were right in thinking that their most formidable
opponent was the ordinary citizen of London.

Although many of the wealthiest Londoners supported the
king, and most of the poorest citizens did not support
parliament, the extent of the popular resistance to the cavaliers
is well illustrated by the construction of extensive and massive
fortifications about the capital. The work began before the
battle of Edgehill and 'a prodigious number of persons of all
ranks, ages and sex' including 'the women and little children',
dug trenches and carried earth to build earthworks at the
approaches to London.[170] Then, in the spring and summer of
1643 a vast scheme of fortification was undertaken, encircling
the whole of the capital and its suburbs, both north and south
of the Thames. 'They have gone through the City with drums
beating and flags flying, to enlist men and women for the work.'
The ministers from their pulpits urged the people, with their
servants and children, to take part. 'Although they only give
them their bare food, without any pay, there has been an
enormous rush of people even of some rank'. Some 20,000 were
soon labouring every day, including women and children,

digging and carrying earth: 'they do not even cease work on Sundays'.

This mass movement was organized by neighbourhoods and occupations: each day a different group of parishes and a different group of trades went and worked on the fortifications. 'The greatest company which I observed to march out, according to their turns', wrote a wandering Scottish tailor who reached London in May 1643, 'were the tailors, carrying 46 colours, and seconded with 8,000 lusty men. The next in greatness of number were the watermen, amounting to 7,000 tuggers, carrying 37 colours: the shoemakers were 5,000 and odds, carrying 29 colours... Neither in this catalogue dare I forget the porters, that marched forth one day towards Tyburn Fields, carrying 23 colours, being 3,000 white shirts: and upon that same day, a thousand oyster-wives advanced from Billingsgate, through Cheapside, to Crabtree Field, all alone, with drums and flying colours, and in a civil manner... The next day following, May 17th, the feltmakers, fishmongers, and coopers marched three several ways to three sundry fields, carrying 24 colours, had their number amounted to 3,000 and odds.' 'On Tuesday last there went about 5,000 feltmakers and cappers, near 3,000 porters, besides other great companies of men, women and children.' On 24 May 'the whole company of gentlemen vintners went out with their wives, servants and wine porters. On Thursday the shoemakers of London took four to five thousand and all the inhabitants of St Clement Danes. On Friday at least 5,000 men, women and children of St Giles-in-the-Fields, Queen Street and other parts thereabouts.' 'Yesterday about 5,000 cordwainers, another day as many out of St Giles, St Martins and thereabouts went out to work in the fields.' On 29 May the 'inhabitants and trained bands of St Martins-in-the-Fields and Covent Garden', and the day after, 'the trained bands and all the well-affected inhabitants of the City of Westminster and the greatest part of the auxiliary forces of London went out to dig in the trenches about London'.[171]

Twenty-four elaborate forts were built of earth and timber, surrounded with ditches and stakes, and mounted with cannon. These were linked by a continuous line of ditch and rampart round the whole area of the metropolis, the rampart being nine feet thick and eighteen feet high, and extending for eighteen miles.[172] The Venetian ambassador commented on the 'incredible cost and effort' involved.[173] 'The gigantic work was made possible by unprecedented popular support, ably marshalled'.[174] The motive that inspired and united the citizens was self-defence. They were frightened of the king's army, especially after prince Rupert's cavalry had pillaged Brentford in November 1642; and, whatever their politics, they had no wish for their streets and houses to become a battleground, and for their homes, shops and warehouses to be plundered and burned. But the parliamentarians succeeded in mobilizing such fears into constructive activity because they had a strong core of popular support in London. The metropolis, however, could not win the war on its own, and the popular support for the parliamentarian party in the provinces was as important, probably decisive: 'while London with its trade and industries was the central stronghold of the revolution... it was from the provinces that a large part of the mass support for the revolution was drawn'.[175]

One of the first towns to defy the king in person was Coventry. Charles, having resolved to set up his standard at Nottingham in August 1642, heard that some of the earl of Essex's forces were marching towards Coventry, and he decided to get possession of the city before them and to give support to the earl of Northampton who was raising forces for him in Warwickshire. He thought this 'no hard matter', for though the city was 'encompassed with an old wall' it had 'no garrison in it' as yet. But this showed over-confidence or poor intelligence. Coventry, under the leadership of John Barker, a prosperous draper, alderman and MP for the city, despite the royalism of the mayor, had already defied the earl of Northampton and declared enthusiastically for parliament. 'They hung out the bloody flag, and stood upon their guard' with between one and two thousand men in arms raised from amongst the citizens and the surrounding towns and villages.[176] So when the king 'came thither, he found the gates shut against him, and the wall manned with armed men... and when some of his servants and attendants (for he had only horse with him) rode nearer the gate and walls than they within thought fit, they discharged some iron cannon they had planted, and thereby killed two or three horses, and hurt very dangerously a gentleman or two of note. Whereupon the king, being in no posture to force his way, was compelled, with this new indignity, to retire'. The parliamentarian forces from the earl of Essex's army then marched past the king's cavalry and 'went with incredible triumph into Coventry, where they were received with equal acclamation'.[177] This defiance by Coventry reduced the support that the king received when shortly after he raised his standard at Nottingham, and influenced his councillors to press him to open negotiations for peace with parliament, which with extreme reluctance he did, only to be rebuffed by the two Houses.[178]

This act was not Coventry's alone. Before the arrival of the king at its gates three hundred men had come from Birmingham 'to defend it against the king's forces' and it was said that they 'first stirred up those of Coventry to resist the king'.[179] 'So bravely have the Birmingham men (volunteers that came to assist the citizens) behaved themselves' that they were responsible for Coventry's resistance; and when the earl of Essex's men entered the city they were 'saluted with divers vollies of shot from the Birmingham men, who stood stoutly for our defence'.[180] With this crucial help from Birmingham, Coventry became a parliamentarian centre. But the parliamentarian party of the civil war will not be properly described, nor the nature of the conflict fully understood, if the stand of towns like Coventry is seen in isolation from the region in which they stood, and the parliamentarian party represented as being confined to certain towns and wholly urban in character. The parliamentarians from over a wide area, ten to twenty even thirty miles about the city, took refuge there. About thirty puritan ministers fled to Coventry, and its garrison 'consisted half of citizens, and half of country-men: the country-men were such as had been forced from their own dwellings... especially from Birmingham, Sutton Coldfield, Tamworth, Nuneaton, Hinckley, Rugby, etc.' Richard Baxter was one of the ministers who fled to Coventry, and he was joined there by his parliamentarian neighbours from Kidderminster: they were small master-weavers and 'some of them that had any estate of their own, lived there on their own charge; and the rest were fain to take up arms, and be garrison soldiers to get them bread'. Later some thirty or forty of them went with an expedition to settle a parliamentarian garrison at Wem in Shropshire.[181] Coventry was chosen as a refuge because, unlike Birmingham, it was a defensible place, and it stood out for parliament throughout the civil war.

Birmingham was a growing town, with a population of perhaps over 4,000, but it had no walls or defences. Its people and those of the surrounding villages were engaged in the manufacture of metal goods.[182] It did not follow the lead of its powerful neighbour, Sir Thomas Holte of Aston Hall, the chief of the local gentry and a JP, who became a royalist.[183] In the eyes of the royalists Birmingham was 'a pestilent and seditious town', 'than whom his majesty hath not found more malicious people in the whole course of this rebellion', and had 'as great fame for hearty, wilful disloyalty to the king, as any place in England'.[184] As well as assisting Coventry, they also defended Warwick Castle: 'a hundred brave men went from Birmingham unto Warwick Castle... with their arms of muskets and swords.[185] 'They sent 15,000 swords for the earl of Essex his forces and the aid of that party, and not only refused to supply the king's forces with swords for their money, but imprisoned divers who bought swords, upon suspicion that they intended to supply the king's forces with them.'[186] 'Mr Porter's blade-mill in the town', which cost £100 to erect, made sword-blades 'only for the service of the parliament'.[187]

When the king and his army marched from Bridgnorth, through Wolverhampton, Birmingham, and Kenilworth in October 1642 on the way to Edgehill, they were passing through hostile territory. 'The people were so disaffected to the king's party that they had carried away or hid all their provisions, insomuch as there was neither meat for man or horse; and the very smiths hid themselves, that they might not be compelled to shoe the horses, of which in those stony ways there was great need.' So that when they met the parliament's army at Edgehill 'there were very many companies of the common soldiers who had scarce eaten bread in eight and forty hours before'.[188] After the battle 'the country was so disaffected, that it not only not sent in provisions but many soldiers who straggled into the villages for relief were knocked in the head by the common people.'[189] On the other hand the country was 'so devoted' to the parliamentarians 'that they had all provisions brought to them without trouble'.[190] The king ordered the execution of two of his soldiers who stole 'some trifle of no value out of a house' in Birmingham, 'whose owner was at that time in the rebels' army'; but in return for this 'the next day after his remove thence the inhabitants of that place seized on his carriages, wherein were his own plate and furniture, and conveyed them to Warwick Castle'. The town was 'so generally wicked' that it rose upon small parties straggling from the king's army, killed some and sent others prisoners to Coventry, 'declaring a more peremptory malice to his majesty than any other place'.[191] They 'apprehended all messengers who were employed, or suspected to be so, in the king's service; and though it was never made a garrison by direction of the parliament, being built in such a form as was indeed hardly capable of being fortified, yet they had 'so great a desire to distinguish themselves from the king's good subjects that they cast up little slight works at both ends of the town, and barricaded the rest, and voluntarily engaged themselves not to admit any intercourse with the king's forces'.[192] 'And they have still continued upon all occasions violently to oppose the king, and to aid those who have taken up arms against him... and sent out parties to plunder the king's friends.'[193]

In some measure the hostility shown towards the king's army by the people of the Midlands sprang from fear of soldiers: there was no fear more deeply felt nor more generally experienced in early seventeenth-century England than the fear that soldiers would rob and burn, rape and murder wherever they came. Clarendon was no doubt right that the people were influenced by the 'belief, that the cavaliers were of a fierce, bloody, and licentious disposition, and that they committed all manner of cruelty upon the inhabitants of those places where they came, of which robbery was the least'.[194] But Clarendon also observed that the same fear was not felt of parliament's soldiers, which indicates that the hostility towards the king's soldiers did arise in large measure from popular support for parliament; though there are signs that parliament's soldiers were not always as welcome as Clarendon asserted.[195] Yet there were other places as fearful of soldiers and as concerned to defend themselves against plunderers or potential plunderers, but which did not show anything like the resoluteness and activity of Birmingham in defending itself, and sought refuge in neutrality, whereas Birmingham emphatically aligned itself with parliament. There was evidently strong popular support for parliament in this midland region ranging from Gloucestershire and the northern parts of Oxfordshire in the south, Northamptonshire in the east, through Warwickshire to parts of Worcestershire and Staffordshire: it included the area of the influence of the puritan and parliamentarian peers, viscount Saye and lord Brooke; the sword, scythe and nail makers of the Birmingham area, and the textile manufacturers of Coventry. Aside from the influence of Saye and Brooke over the peasants (not dissimilar from that of landlords on the other side), this leads to an identification of parliamentarianism with manufacturing areas. It was not Saye and Brooke who influenced Birmingham but Robert Porter, the owner of the mill that supplied swords to parliament's army, who employed a number of bladesmiths, and was also a big farmer.[196] But this should not be allowed to mask the extent to which the people who supported parliament were peasants: the sword, scythe and nail makers of Birmingham and the surrounding district were also generally farmers: some of them were farmers who engaged in metalworking as a secondary occupation, some of them were metalworkers who engaged in farming as a subsidiary occupation, but all were embedded in a rural and agricultural community.[197] They differed from many other peasants in that their manufacturing employment made them more independent of landlords and less deferential towards the gentry.

In 1643 'the town of Birmingham, as right as any to... parliament, having for a long time been without trade' hoped for relief when lord Brooke advanced across the Midlands with forces from the earl of Essex's army, and, drawing reinforcements from Coventry and Warwick, entered Lichfield. But Birmingham became fearful again when lord Brooke was killed at Lichfield on 2 March 1643 and the parliamentarian forces under Sir John Gell were defeated by the earl of Northampton at the battle of Hopton Heath, near Stafford, on 19 March. The death of Northampton in the battle, however, and the arrival of Sir William Brereton with fresh

parliamentarian forces from Cheshire, restored Birmingham's
hopes, though the control of the Midlands was still very much
in the balance. Three considerations seem to have influenced
Birmingham at this moment: they were troubled by robbers
and plunderers that infested their neighbourhood; they
expected to be attacked by the royalists, because they knew
that they had made themselves conspicuous in their loyalty to
parliament; and they wanted to participate in the effort to expel
the royalist forces from the Midlands, if only to recover their
trade. So they resolved to arm themselves: they had between
100 and 200 muskets, they formed a body of musketeers and
hired two captains to train and discipline them. They began to
fortify the town with some mounds and breastworks, and they
sent for help to Lichfield, from which came some of the
Coventry forces, notably a troop of horse commanded by
Captain Greaves and a troop of dragoons under Captain
Castledown.[198]

But at this moment, at the beginning of April, prince
Rupert set out from Oxford with 1,200 horse, 600-700 foot, and
some cannon, to take up where Northampton had left off and
recover Lichfield. When it became clear that he was going to
pass through Birmingham 'the minister of Birmingham
entreated the captains and chief of the town, by no means to
think of such an impossible defence of themselves against
2,000, themselves having scarce six-score musketeers in all the
town, but rather to march away with all their arms, and so
secure their arms and persons, though their goods were
hazarded, as a thing far more safe and rational; which motion
the captains and chief of the town readily embraced'. The
'better sort' of the town 'were sensible, that if the cavaliers
came, we were not likely to withstand them'. 'But the middle
and inferior sort of people, (especially those that bore arms)
would by no means be drawn to leave the town', and 'the general
desire of the town... would have them stand it out, and not
march away with their arms'. So 'the chief of the town and the
captains' acquiesced: they agreed 'to stay and try the issue'
rather than be stigmatised as cowards. But the Coventry forces
withdrew, for fear of being cut off, though Captain Greaves
halted a little distance from the town. The townsmen placed a
hundred musketeers in their little half-built defences, and hid

another sixty in the town.[199] Prince Rupert, 'hardly believing it possible that when they should discover his power they would offer to make resistance... sent his quarter-master thither to take up his lodging... but they... absolutely refused to let him quarter in the town'. 'From their little works' they shouted 'cursed dogs', 'devilish cavaliers', 'papist traitors', and 'with mettle equal to their malice, they discharged their shot upon him'.[200] They kept Rupert at bay for about an hour until they were overrun by his cavalry, which rode through the town and charged Captain Greaves' troop. Greaves retired and then turned and drove back the royalists, making time for his own retreat to Lichfield, and for the Birmingham musketeers to escape in twos and threes, hiding their weapons in ditches and pits as they went. 'All the considerable men escaped out of their snare', the minister Roberts having fled shortly before the attack.[201]

In the skirmish with Captain Greaves the royalist earl of Denbigh was mortally wounded. The lordly royalist historian thunders: 'And but for that accident, (and to remember the dismal inequality of this contention, in which always some earl, or person of great honour or fortune, fell, when, after the most signal victory over the other side, there was seldom lost a man of any known family, or of other reputation than of passion for the cause in which he fell,) I should not have wasted so much paper in mentioning an action of so little moment as was this of Birmingham'.[202] What price an earl? It is no more than justice to set down the names of the fourteen men and women of Birmingham who were killed, most or all of them cut down in the streets by the royalists after they had overrun the defences:

Samuel Elsmore, cutler
William Turton, cutler
William Ward, cutler
William Knight, glasier
Richard Hunt, cobbler
Richard Adams, cobbler
Henry Benton, labourer
Joseph Rastell
John Carter junior
William Billingsley junior

Widow Collins
'Lucas his wife'.

The royalists also killed a minister, thinking that he was the minister of the town, claiming that he died insulting the king and that they found 'some very obscene papers' in his pockets; but this was a mad old clergyman named Whitehall who had spent many years in Bedlam. 'Thomas the Ostler' seems to have been unaware that there was a revolution going on. He died obeying the dictates of the servility in which he had been born and trained. Hearing horses in the streets he went out to lead them to his inn and was pistolled down by the class he had lived to serve.[203] Three of the fourteen killed were described by Robert Porter, owner of the blademill that made swords for parliament's army, as 'my honest workmen, whose lives I would I had redeemed with mine estate'.[204] The casualty list reflects the importance of metal-working in Birmingham, but is a reminder that all the inhabitants were not sword, scythe or nail makers. The royalists plundered the town and took some thousands of pounds worth of money and goods, and pulled down Porter's blademill. The next day as they marched out they fired the town and eighty-seven houses were destroyed, besides barns, stables and outbuildings, 340 people being made homeless. Prince Rupert expressed regret and said that it was not done on his orders.[205]

It was 'the middle and inferior sort of people' who were responsible for Birmingham's defiance of prince Rupert, while the 'better sort' and 'the chief of the town' would have surrendered. The population of Birmingham was divided into three classes and in the middle of the sixteenth century the distribution was as follows: (1) Sixty to seventy 'subsidy men' (larger manufacturers, bigger farmers, merchants and the more prosperous shopkeepers); these were assessed for taxation on their property, and they included a dozen or more well-to-do families who formed a local plutocracy; (2) One hundred and twenty small craftsmen and lesser farmers, who were exempt from taxes on property but paid poll taxes; (3) Three hundred labourers, journeymen and apprentices.[206] In proportion to the growth of population the 'better sort' would have numbered about 180-210 in the middle of the seventeenth century; the 'middle sort' 360, and the poor or 'inferior sort' 900;

but more likely the last group had become larger than that, and the first group not so large. The 'middle sort' formed about a quarter of the population.

In the differing responses of the 'better sort' and 'chief of the town', and of 'the middle and inferior sort', to the approach of the royalist army, it may not be fanciful to see reflected social and economic antagonisms. The small handicraftsmen made only a little at a time and had to sell at once in order to be able to buy more iron or steel to continue at work, and they could afford to buy only a little at a time. They often had to sell when prices were low and buy when prices were high. The bigger manufacturers could afford to buy the raw material in large quantities when prices were low, and hold their finished products back from the market until prices rose. The small handicraftsmen often were forced to sell their products for payment part in cash and part in iron; and the merchants and bigger manufacturers who sold iron to the smaller men and bought their products from them, increasingly dominated them and drew them into a wage-earning relationship. 'Most of the working smiths were either wage-earners or so dependent on those who supplied the raw materials or dealt in the finished products that they could scarcely be described as their own masters.' The poor return that they received from their labour generated much bitterness against the larger manufacturer or merchant who paid them for their products. 'The nailer was a small industrialist employing workers for wages, and in his business dealings both giving and receiving credit. The scythe-smith, or bladesmith, was as a rule a larger employer... and probably... a farmer as well as a manufacturer.' [207] A few of the 'middle sort' rose to be larger manufacturers or bigger farmers, others declined into wage-earners. The 'middle sort' were those small men who retained their independence in a hard struggle against the big men and the economic pressures threatening their position; and it was probably they who formed the hard core of resistance to the royalists at Birmingham.

Manchester, with a population of about 5,000, was the commercial capital of south-east Lancashire and the 'very London of those parts'. [208] Between 16 July and early September 1642 it fell, somewhat precariously, under the control of the anti-Stanley faction (it would probably be wrong to say 'parliamentarian faction'), and this had a great deal to do with the fear of papists and the alleged association of lord Strange (the effective head of the house of Stanley since the retirement of his father, the earl of Derby) with the papists.[209] 'The town of Manchester having some malignants in it, and multitudes of papists near unto it, and being reputed a religious and rich town, hath been much envied and often threatened by the popish and malignant party, and therefore the townsmen being encouraged first by some justices of the peace, afterwards by the ordinance for the militia, did in a peaceable manner exercise and train up their youth in feats of arms'.[210]

Lord Strange was collecting forces and it was clear that he would make another attempt to gain Manchester before he took his regiments to the king.[211] Although many of the chief men of Manchester and most of the poorer sort would have come to terms with lord Strange (or earl of Derby as he was about to become), and John Rosworm thought that 'four for one in that town, if not more, favoured my lord of Derby';[212] the neighbouring gentlemen, Richard Holland esquire of Heaton, in Prestwich, Peter Egerton esquire of Shaw, in Flixton, and Robert Hyde esquire of Denton, as deputy lieutenants for the militia by the ordinance of parliament, 'did advise and consult with the town what was fittest to be done for the safety of the town and country adjacent'. They persuaded the town to hire a German engineer and professional soldier, John Rosworm, to fortify the place. He encountered much opposition from the townsmen when he set up posts and chains to keep out horses; but a report that royalist soldiers from Cheshire were plundering near Manchester, and taking arms from 'his majesty's loyal protestant subjects, even... such arms as they had provided for the necessary defence of their own houses', caused alarm in Manchester and the surrounding countryside: the bells were rung backwards, and soon 'many hundred men were suddenly up in arms in the town of Manchester' and many others came in from the country.[213] The alarm heightened 'the spirits of the well-affected in the town, above the opposition of the malcontents' and gave Rosworm the opportunity to complete the fortifying of the town with posts and chains and mud walls.[214]

This was the decisive moment at which the uneasy balance in Manchester was tipped against the royalists. The townsmen did not want soldiers—coming from they knew not where and probably papists—in their town to disarm them, and probably rob and plunder them as well, if they did no worse. They were not taking a conscious decision to oppose the king, nor expressing any views about the king's cause: they were merely agreeing to defend their town against marauding soldiers. But there was a core of parliamentarians in the town, and a group of parliamentarian gentry in the country nearby, and since they were anxious to defend the town, the average townsman let them get on with it once he was convinced that there was a need. Ralph Ashton esquire of Middleton, MP for the county, put 'about an hundred and fifty' of his tenants 'in complete arms' into the town under the command of Henry Bradshaw esquire of Marple.[215] Many of the chief men left the town as a clash with the earl of Derby became more inevitable, thus weakening the merchant oligarchy which governed the town and leaving the anti-Stanley faction more firmly in control.[216]

On Saturday night, 23 September 1642, news came that the earl was advancing from Warrington with a large force— said to be 2,000-3,000 horse and foot with six or seven cannon. 'The bells were rung, and posts immediately sent into the country to give them notice'; thereupon Richard Holland esquire of Prestwich; John Booth, a younger son of Sir George Booth of Dunham; Peter Egerton esquire of Flixton; Robert Hyde esquire of Denton; Robert Dukinfield esquire of Dukinfield; Hanmet Hyde esquire of Hyde; John Arderne esquire; Edward Butterworth esquire; Thomas Chetham of Nuthurst and other gentlemen 'came with their tenants and well-affected neighbours, to assist the town'. All Sunday and Monday the country came 'in abundantly with muskets, pikes, halberds, staves, and such like', so that there were between one and two thousand men in arms in Manchester.[217] Eighty of Henry Bradshaw's neighbours were late and had to fight their way to Manchester through the royalist lines, losing eleven killed.[218]

The earl of Derby began to assault the town on 26 September. When his cannon fired, half of Captain Rosworm's men at Salford-bridge took to their heels, and he only kept the rest at their stations with his drawn sword.[219] But the defenders generally stood firm and the following evening the earl asked for a parley, and there was a truce until 7am on the

28th. He asked them to surrender their arms but they replied that their arms were 'under God, one means of our lawful defence against malignant enemies and multitudes of bloody papists, which do abound in our county, and had not God by his infinite mercy prevented, had ere this day made the like rebellion in our county, and committed the like barbarous outrage against us and other of the true protestant religion, as their brethren have done in Ireland, seeing they are acted by the like hellish principles as they'. The earl would have been content with a token surrender of a small number of arms, for he was under pressure to march to the king in time for the impending battle with the earl of Essex's army.[220]

The defenders were also suffering great pressures: they did not have much powder or match left; the gentry and the country people feared that in their absence from home the royalist soldiers were plundering their houses and ill-treating their wives and children; and the farmers were anxious to get back to their fields, for it was 'now harvest time, our corn, the livelihood and subsistence of our family, is in the field ripe and groaning for the sickle' (though this last anxiety was mitigated by the fact that throughout the siege of Manchester—inevitably—it rained steadily).[221] The gentlemen were 'inclinable to condescend' to the earl's terms. Edward Butterworth having set off towards London to get help, Richard Holland, who favoured surrender, drew Peter Egerton and John Booth to his side, leaving Henry Bradshaw and Robert Hyde in a minority on the committee in favour of continued resistance. But the issue was decided by the rank and file of the defenders. The aged but unbending puritan minister, William Bourne, senior fellow of the collegiate church of Manchester, was 'lifted up from the gates of death, and raised in spirit' to go round the guards and urge the men to fight on. Encouraged by Hyde, Bradshaw and Rosworm, the men declared that they would not give the earl of Derby 'a yard of match, but would maintain their cause and arms to the last drop of blood'. Captain Bradshaw's men at Deansgate shouted 'that they would part with their arms and their lives together' and Captain Rosworm's men at Salford-bridge told him that they would 'never yield to my lord of Derby, so long as I would stand out, and they had an inch of match, or a shot of powder'.[222] The men 'spoke openly, that if all the gentlemen deserted the cause, yet would they cleave unto it', and 'gave out words, that if the head gentlemen did still persist in destroying them, they would commit them'.[223] Manchester did not surrender. The attack persisted for a time, but on 30 September the earl gave up and withdrew.

This was a serious setback for the royalists and a major success for the parliamentarians. 'And had not that town stood firmly for the king and parliament, in all probability the whole county had been brought into subjection to the oppression and violence of the cavaliers'.[224] 'And surely if the actions of Manchester had not sufficiently balanced the earl of Derby's forces, or had that town yielded either to his assaults or proposals', Lancashire and the whole of the north-west had fallen to the royalists. But Manchester not only prevented this, it became 'a strength, help, and magazine to all the adjacent counties, as they stood engaged for the parliament's service', and the means in time for gaining Lancashire and the whole of the north-west for parliament.[225] It was seen as a victory over the earl of Derby and his faction amongst the nobility and gentry; indeed it was represented as a victory over the ruling class: 'For encouragement rested only in the breasts of a company of poor despised Christians, who with our town, our poor Manchester, engaged themselves against the great mighty ones of our county; for ought I can learn, there was not one gentleman of eminency, knight or lord, throughout our shire, nor any eminent man of note, but either in person or best assistance he was against us.' [226] This was an exaggeration: the defence of Manchester had depended heavily on the local gentry and their influence over their tenants and neighbours; but they were less numerous and less eminent than the gentry that came to besiege Manchester.[227] The chief men of the town's ruling oligarchy fled before the siege, and the leading parliamentarian gentry urged surrender at the crisis of the attack. If, as seems to be the case, the tract in which this comment appears was written by William Bourne,[228] it probably reflects the speeches he made to the defenders at the barricades, when he urged them to fight on against the advice of the prime gentry. A note of class bitterness and class hostility was injected into the conflict. The struggle of Manchester against the earl of Derby and 'the great mighty ones' was represented as a fight in which the peasants had a prime interest: 'O England's yeomen and husbandmen look to yourselves, for if you stand not to it, as we of Manchester do, but be overcome, look for ever to be slaves, for you see how this bloody tyrant the earl of Derby rages'.[229]

It is significant that only a small minority of the townsmen took part in the fight: the main part of the resistance came from the country people nearby. The villages around Manchester were engaged in linen-weaving, but the weavers were also farmers, smallholders of 15 to 30 acres, or less. 'Agrarian politics in the seventeenth century came home as closely to the Lancashire cloth producer as the affairs of industry; questions of tenure, of grazing rights and the use of waste, were of almost as much concern to him as the price of wool or yarn, or the closing of a foreign market for cloth.'[230] The smallholder-weaver suffered the grievances of both peasants and artisans and was the most discontented and rebellious person in seventeenth-century society. But he was also more independent than the landless artisan or the mere farmer. The possession of land rendered him less dependent on the merchants and the larger manufacturers than the landless artisans, and able to resist being reduced from an independent small producer to a wage-earning employee.[231] Participation in industry made him less dependent on landlords and bigger farmers than small agriculturalists who had no industrial employment. Up to a point the smallholding linen-weavers of south-east Lancashire followed the lead of the local gentry who were parliamentarians. But they were as likely to take their religion and their politics from Manchester as from the gentry; for they depended on Manchester as the market for their cloth, and they were all the more ready to follow the lead of Manchester because there were few serious conflicts of interests between themselves and the townsmen. Unlike the old corporate towns, which tried to prevent the growth of industry in the countryside, Manchester, Bolton, Rochdale, Bury, Blackburn—the chief market towns of the cloth-manufacturing region of Lancashire—imposed no restrictions 'other than market regulations, concerning weights and measures, conditions of sale and the like'. 'The interests of the towns were so bound up with those of the surrounding countryside that there was no protection for urban as against country craftsmen... Urban and rural interests were thus to a large extent identical.'[232] This was reflected in the readiness of the country craftsmen to flock to the defence of Manchester, and the townsmen to go to the aid of the clothmaking region.

The West Riding of Yorkshire was another clothmaking region: in the early seventeenth century there were said to be 20,000 men, women and children engaged in textile manufacture in the parishes of Halifax, Bradford, Bingley and Keighley, and in 1638 the figure was put at 12,000 in the parish of Halifax and 10,000 in the parishes of Bradford, Bingley and Shipley.[233] The chief parliamentarians in the West Riding were lord Fairfax and his son, Sir Thomas Fairfax, but it was said by Clarendon that they 'were governed by two or three of inferior quality, more conversant with the people'.[234] The clothing towns were strongly parliamentarian, but their voices were muffled as long as the king remained in the county. When he decided to leave and raise his standard at Nottingham, he considered arresting the Fairfaxes. Fearing this, lord Fairfax remained on his guard at his house at Denton, near Leeds, and 'all the country about him for 15 or 16 miles stands by him, and will protect him against any violence... and especially the great towns thereabouts, as Wakefield, Leeds, Halifax, Bradford, and Otley'. The king gave up the idea of arresting the Fairfaxes.[235] But the Fairfaxes did not seem in a hurry to take any more positive action. And it was as a result of the importunity of the people in the surrounding area, who feared attacks from papists and cavaliers, that about the middle of September lord Fairfax went to Leeds, where 'the commonalty of the town' was 'wholly at his command', and had a meeting with the gentry and freeholders who sympathized with parliament, and they resolved to raise forces.[236] The earl of Cumberland, the king's commander in Yorkshire, tried to raise the trained bands of Halifax, 'but they refused, crying with loud acclamations, "a Fairfax! a Fairfax!" they would live and die with a Fairfax'.[237] 'Bradford was deeply engaged; the generality of the town and parish, and the towns about, stood up for the parliament, and it was made a little garrison, and though it was not easy to keep, yet they threw up bulwarks about it; and the inhabitants were firm to the cause, and to one another'; and 'many good men in the town and parish took up arms for the defence of the parliament'. [238] But then a bombshell fell upon the ordinary parliamentarians of the West Riding. On 29 September the Fairfaxes and the parliamentarian gentry entered into a peace treaty with the royalist gentry and agreed to hold the county neutral in the civil war. [239] Parliament condemned the treaty, and the Hothams and Hull (the chief parliamentarian stronghold in Yorkshire at that time) were not parties to the agreement. [240]

The peace broke down and hostilities recommenced towards the end of October. Royalist forces entered Leeds and Bradford, but were beaten back by Sir Thomas Fairfax, who advanced to Tadcaster. [241] His men were raised in the clothing towns of the West Riding, from which they were also supplied. [242] They included all the trained band soldiers and a number of volunteers from Bradford. [243] Jonathan Priestley was a member of a family of West Riding clothiers and he recalled: 'all trade and business was interrupted and laid aside, lord Fairfax and Sir Thomas his son, came to Leeds and those parts to list soldiers; my brother Samuel went amongst the rest, but he came over to Goodgreave to take his leave of my mother, uncles, and friends. What entreaty and persuasions there was to keep him at home, but could not prevail. My mother went along with him a quarter of a mile...she besought him with tears not to go... "Mother", saith he, "Pray be content; if I stay at home I can follow no employment, but be forced to hide myself in one hole or another, which I cannot endure; I had rather venture my life in the field, and, if I die, it is in a good cause"; and so most honest men thought in those times, when hundreds of protestants were daily murdered in Ireland, fearing the same tragedy would be acted in England; so he went, and was with my lord Fairfax, about Selby and Tadcaster'. [244] But the earl of Newcastle with his powerful army entered Yorkshire from the north and drove the parliamentarians from Tadcaster to Selby, opening the way for advance into the West Riding and cutting off the Fairfaxes' army from its base. [245] Lord Fairfax wrote to the Committee of Safety on 10 December: 'I have hitherto supported this army by the loans and contributions, for the most part, of the parishes of Leeds,

Halifax, and Bradford, and some other small clothing towns adjacent, being the only well-affected people of the county'.[246] He sent Sir Thomas with a force to break through to Leeds, Bradford and the other clothing towns, but without success. Leeds, though 'the great mass of the people were parliamentarians', 'the wealthy merchants, who comprised the municipal government, were royalists', and 'the malignant humour being predominant', surrendered to Newcastle.[247] If Bradford had not resolved to resist, the whole of the West Riding would immediately have fallen to the royalists.

Some in Bradford and its neighbourhood thought resistance hopeless: 'Our malignant spirits being charmed, now appeared breathing forth nothing but threatenings against those who had been most active for the parliament: and their apparition was so terrible, as it affrighted many of the best affected persons out of the town'. But 'some religious persons in the parish, considering what danger might result both to their consciences and country from such cowardice and treachery... resolved to stand upon their guard, invited all the well-affected in the parish to assist them and entered the town'. The neighbours 'judging our attempt desperate (as in the eye of reason it was) and fearing the issue would be our ruin, refused to help us, lest they should perish with us'. They could expect no help from the Fairfaxes. 'All our trained soldiers with their arms, were with the lord Fairfax, and the most of those who were fitted for service as volunteers. Nor could it be expected, that the well affected of our poor parish' could afford to hire soldiers for 'any long time, and none would tarry one day without pay'. We had 'neither wisdom nor strength sufficient to manage' a defence: 'there wanted both the head, body, and sinews of war, we had never a gentleman in the parish to command us, nor would any stranger be persuaded to undertake the charge'.[248]

The royalist forces approached the town on Sunday morning, 18 December 1642, and Bradford sent horsemen 'to Halifax, Bingley, and the small towns about' for help.[249] There were forty men with 'muskets and calivers' in Bradford, thirty with 'fowling, birding, and smaller pieces', and 'well nigh twice as many club-men'. 'I should now show how our men were marshalled, but tis a hard matter to marshal those who had neither commanders, colours, nor distinct companies.' But 'we had borrowed a commander of Halifax' and he stationed the men in several parts of the town and 'ten or twelve of our best marksmen upon the steeple, and some in the church'. The royalists, 'who expected a surrender, rather than resistance', were 'something daunted' when fired on from the church.[250] Meanwhile Bradford men were visiting the chapels of Halifax and appealing for help for 'their poor besieged neighbours, who were threatened with nothing less than destruction, *viz* burning, disarming, imprisoning, killing, and what not'. John Hodgson, a radical gentleman of Coley Hall, was at Sunday morning service in Coley chapel in Halifax parish, when 'a good man, one Isaac Baume... comes in haste... and there acquaints the minister, one Mr Latham, what their condition was at Bradford; and he enlargeth upon it to the congregation, with a great deal of tenderness and affection, so that many of us did put our hands to the plough with much resolution, being well appointed with necessary weapons'.[251] Some of the Halifax men had muskets, but most of them were armed only with clubs or 'scythes laid in poles'. It was about noon when they arrived at Bradford, together with another party of club-men from Bingley, and the royalists were preparing to assault the church.[252] They fell upon the royalists and drove them back. Although the royalist officers 'manifested great courage', their men hung back, and so attacks were concentrated on the officers. 'A stout, gallant officer, commanding a company of foot' got ahead of his reluctant soldiers and was separated from them: 'two of the townsmen met, and struck him down: he cried for quarter, and they poor men not knowing the meaning of it, said—"aye, they would quarter him" ', and cut him into four pieces. Our men 'would neither give nor take quarter; (nor was this their cruelty, as the enemy complains, but their ignorance)'.[253] 'And thus the terror of the Lord, and of us, falling upon them, sending their foot and artillery foremost, away they went, (using their feet better than they used their hands) and about fifty of our clubs and muskets after them; which courage in ours, did most of all astonish the enemy; who say, no fifty men in the world, except they were mad or drunk, would have pursued a thousand. Our men, indeed, shot as they were mad, and the enemy fell as they were drunk'. They pursued for a mile, but were kept at bay by the royalist horse, and, lacking any horse of their own, could do no more.[254] 'The night after, we spent our time upon the guards, in telling what exploits had been done, and blessing God for his deliverance.'[255]

The clothiers of the West Riding, like the linen-weavers of south-east Lancashire and the metal-workers of Birmingham, were smallholding farmers as well as manufacturers. 'As elsewhere, cloth-making was carried on in conjunction with farming, and about half the people whose wills have survived were engaged in both activities.'[256] 'Even the busiest clothier had his plot of land, and some part of his sustenance was drawn from that source. The word "yeoman" was often only an alias for "clothier", and it was by the joint produce of the land and the loom that the Yorkshireman found his livelihood secure.' In the Yorkshire textile industry small clothiers predominated, especially in the Halifax area, 'where they seem to have constituted the greater part of the population'. They owned their own looms, spinning-wheels, 'walker-sheres', and often a dye-vat or 'lead'. Each week they made one kersey and had to sell it at the end of the week in order to be able to buy wool for the next week's work. They bought wool in small quantities from wool-dealers, and sold the kersey to a merchant or his agent for finishing, or sometimes they sold it to a bigger clothier who took it along with his own cloths to York, Hull or London. They had to have cash each week for their kersey, but the bigger clothiers could afford to give credit to the merchants. 'They leased or owned a cottage, with a toft of ground adjoining, on which they fed a little livestock.' It was a hand-to-mouth existence: 'profits were small, but the men were independent, and that was probably worth a great deal... They... were able to jog along more or less contentedly, provided no new burden was imposed on them in the way of a levy for shipmoney or an increase in the subsidy on their kerseys.'[257] The bigger clothiers were concentrated in the Leeds area. They employed women spinners and journeymen weavers, took on apprentices, and the biggest employed twenty, even forty, persons. They carried out the finishing processes in their own establishments and sold their cloths directly to the merchants. They owned or rented some land and kept cows, pigs, poultry and a horse or ass. They engaged in farming as a by-occupation but their 'chief interest lay in the production of cloth in larger quantities'.[258]

The conflicts of interests between the small clothiers of the Halifax and Bradford area and the big clothiers of the Leeds area, and between the clothiers in general and the merchants of Leeds, explain the divergence in the civil war between the fiercer parliamentarianism of the Halifax-Bradford area and the tendency towards royalism in the Leeds area. The small clothiers needed the wool-dealers to bring wool to them in small quantities and at frequent intervals; the big clothiers could afford to go directly to the wool-growers and buy wool in large quantities and were hostile to the wool-dealers, accusing them of pushing up prices, but it was the wool-dealers who kept the small clothiers in business. The small clothiers needed to sell one cloth a week for ready cash; the big clothiers could afford to deal in many cloths on credit; thus the merchants preferred to deal with the big clothiers, and the small clothiers were forced to sell to the big clothiers, and fell in danger of being reduced to their employees. The merchants were concerned about the quality of cloth and supported the regulation of quality either by the government or, preferably, by themselves through a company incorporating the clothiers and run by the merchants. The incorporation of Leeds as a borough in 1626 had secured for the merchant oligarchy of that town the power to regulate and control many of the small clothiers of the West Riding, which the latter strongly resented.[259]

In the West Riding of Yorkshire, south-east Lancashire, the Birmingham area and elsewhere the smallholding handicraftsmen were the firmest and most radical supporters of parliament. They were part-farmers and part-manufacturers, not wholly dependent on the gentry, nor wholly dependent on the merchants or larger manufacturers; men not rich, nor yet impoverished, independent in their economic life and in their opinions. The clothiers of Halifax and Bradford, the weavers of the Manchester area, the metal-workers of the Birmingham district, exhibited a close resemblance in their attitudes and actions during the civil war. Their motives were many: fear of attacks by papists, royalists, and plundering soldiers; distress at the disruption of their livelihoods by economic depression and war; hope that parliament would redress their grievances and give them a more secure future;

they were yet sustained by ideals of religious reformation and political democracy as cures for all their problems and ills, and they were fearful and suspicious of the intentions of all superiors, whether royalists or parliamentarians or what.

RAISING THE PEOPLE IN ARMS

The resistance of Bradford, without formal leadership and without the help of the gentry, temporarily turned the tide of the earl of Newcastle's advance, and provided the starting-point and the spur for the reconquest of the West Riding by the parliamentarians. Some forces under the command of Sir Thomas Fairfax managed to get from Selby to Bradford, under cover of darkness, and there they fortified themselves. The royalists continued to hold Leeds and Wakefield. On 9 January 1643 Sir Thomas wrote to his father: 'These parts grow very impatient of our delay in beating them out of Leeds and Wakefield, for by them all trade and provisions are stopped, so that the people in these clothing towns are not able to subsist, and, indeed, so pressing are these wants, as some have told me, if I would not stir with them, they must rise of necessity of themselves in a thing of so great importance. I thought it fit to acquaint you with it, to desire your lordship's advice, before I would undertake it; therefore humbly desire your lordship not to defer this business, but if no aid can come to us, then to give us advice, and order what to do, for long this country cannot subsist; and to raise the country to assault the enemy, I would not do it, without your lordship's consent, being only commanded to defend the parts from them... I am sure I shall have above 600 muskets, if I summon the country to come in, besides 3,000 and more with other weapons, that would rise with us. If your lordship please to give me the power to join with the readiness of the people, I doubt not but, by God's assistance, to give your lordship a good account of what we do.' [260] 'To join with the readiness of the people'—this was the crucial decision for the Fairfaxes, and Sir Thomas's letter well expresses the gravity of the situation facing the gentry. The choice was simple: there was no alternative to either rising with the people or making peace with the king. Sir Thomas clearly thought that it was better for the gentry to lead the people than for the people to rise of their own accord; but the dangers to his own class of arming the people and permitting them to know their own strength were manifest.

Over in Hull the Hothams, who until now had been the focal point of resistance to the king in Yorkshire, were watching the situation in the West Riding with growing forebodings. They opted for peace, and when peace did not come speedily, they prepared to change their allegiance from parliament to the king, judging now that the royalists offered the better security for their class.[261] Captain John Hotham entered into correspondence with the earl of Newcastle, and on 9 January 1643, the very same day that Sir Thomas Fairfax asked his father for permission to raise the people of the West Riding, he wrote to Newcastle: 'I fear much, that if the honourable endeavours of such powerful men as yourself do not take place for a happy peace the necessitous people of the whole kingdom will presently rise in mighty numbers and whosoever they pretend for at first, within a while they will set up for themselves, to the utter ruin of all the nobility and gentry of the kingdom. I speak not this merely at random, the west part of this county affords mighty numbers of them, which I am very confident you will see necessitied and urged to rise in far greater bodies than these... If this unruly rout have once cast the rider, it will run like wildfire in the example through all the counties of England.'[262] The risings of the people of the West Riding propelled the Fairfaxes into positive action against the royalists, and the Hothams into royalism. Sir Thomas received permission to summon the country and thousands of men, most of them armed with clubs 'and such other country weapons as they can get', flocked to him from Bradford, Halifax and their neighbourhoods.[263] With 1,000 musketeers, 2,000 club-men, six troops of horse and three companies of dragoons, he marched on Leeds. Led by Jonathan Scholefield, minister of Croston chapel in Halifax parish, and singing the 68th psalm—'Let God arise, and then his enemies shall be scattered and those that hate him flee before him'—they drove the royalists out of Leeds and Wakefield.[264]

In Lancashire a few of the gentry—Ralph Ashton of Middleton, Richard Holland, Richard Shuttleworth—were willing, like the Fairfaxes in Yorkshire, to put themselves at the head of the popular movement. At Manchester, after the earl of Derby had been repulsed, the question was whether the townsmen should remain on the defensive or take the lead to drive the royalists from the rest of the county. 'God made a comfortable appearance that he had not saved Manchester to the intent they should sit still, nor had he placed a garrison there, to make their mountain to stand strong, but that they might be ready for action at the beat of His drum, which struck up after a reconciliation sought with Him by fasting and prayer.' [265] 'Nor were they satisfied with their own enlargement, but considering that God had not lent them power and ability to free and enlarge themselves, but that there was some other end in it, which consideration produced a public consultation, that consultation converted to resolution, resolution prompted them to action, and such actions as were full of honour, religion and love, they made their freedom the instrument to preserve those that were in danger of surprisal, and to redeem those that already were surprised... First they endeavoured to disarm all papists and evil affected persons... Second they endeavoured to their utmost endeavours to expulse the said earl and his forces out of the said county, and to take from him all such towns or places of any strength, which he had taken and to preserve all other places, as at present he had not taken'. [266]

There was a growing revolt in the country districts of Lancashire against the earl of Derby and his party of nobility and gentry: the earl complained that 'those ill affected in Lancashire grew proud, and the baser sort thought it a fine thing to set against the great ones'. [267] This revolt was provoked by the pressures of the royalists—their conscripting of men by force to fight for them, their demands for money and supplies, and the plunderings of their soldiers. [268] The earl gathered his forces at Warrington and Leigh and came towards Chowbent in December 1642: 'whereupon the country presently rose, and before one of the clock on that day we were gathered together about 3,000 horse and foot, encountering them at Chowbent aforesaid, and beat them back to Leigh... where you might wonder to have seen the forwardness of the young youths, farmers' sons, who indeed were too forward, having had little experience of the like times before this' and rode too far in front of the foot. 'I think they will trouble us no more out of that part of the county, but if they do, we shall be better provided for them than before, for we are all upon our guard, and the nailers of Chowbent instead of making nails, have busied themselves in making bills and battle-axes. And also this week the other part of the county meet, and intend not only to stand upon their guard, but to disarm all the papists and malignants within their precincts, which we are resolved upon in our precincts, and also by God's assistance to take the greatest papists and most dangerous malignants prisoners, and to carry them to Manchester... For now the men of Blackburn, Padiham, Burnley, Clitheroe, and Colne, with those sturdy churls in the two forests of Pendle and Rossendale have raised their spirits, and have resolved to fight it out rather than their beef and fat bacon shall be taken from them.' [269] In February three companies from Manchester 'and as many from Bolton', four or five companies from Blackburn Hundred and 'two thousand club-men' took Preston from the royalists.[270] The earl countered with an attack on Bolton and 'the country people', many armed only with pitchforks, 'in great numbers' 'come shouting' to its defence: 'There came to have aided us all the club-men in Middleton, Oldham, and Rochdale, and old Captain Radcliffe with two hundred fresh soldiers from Manchester, besides the country thereabouts to the number of one thousand five hundred men'.[271]

The stand of Bolton for parliament reflected not only the views of the townsmen merchants, shopkeepers, urban craftsmen—but also the views of the peasantry. 'Many yeomen's sons' who were unwilling to be conscripted into the earl of Derby's forces 'went to shelter themselves in Bolton, and took up arms there' for parliament.[272] Other countrymen carried on with their livelihoods as best they could and did not become garrison soldiers, but joined in the fighting on parliament's side as occasion offered, like William Critchlaw of Longworth near Bolton, who, 'when he heard of a fight near at hand, or a town to be taken by the parliament's army he used to take his musket, and run to the army and be the foremost in any hazardous expedition' and died of wounds received in an attack on Wigan.[273] But for many, employment as a soldier was the only livelihood left, as for the Martindales: 'The great trade that my father and two of my brethren had long driven, was quite dead; for who would either build or repair an house when he could not sleep a night in it with quiet and safety?' [274] At the root of the popular revolt against the royalists in Lancashire, however, lay agrarian discontent. There were many peasants in the county with grievances against royalist landlords, and especially against the king. 'The men of Blackburn, Padiham, Burnley, Clitheroe, and Colne, with those sturdy churls in the two forests of Pendle and Rossendale', who now rose against the king's party, were the peasants who had been engaged in a long struggle with James I and Charles I to obtain security of tenure as copyholders and fixed entry fines. They had been made to pay dear for their rights, but their titles were still not completely secure at the time of the civil war, and they owed the crown money.[275] They were medium-sized peasants, few were well-to-do and few were poor, and they were peasant-artisans, who combined dairy-farming with spinning and weaving.[276]

There was some reluctance amongst the gentry leaders at Manchester to conduct an offensive war, because this meant raising the country and joining with the mutinous peasants. At the end of March 1643 there was a crisis in Manchester, where they were 'in such torturing perplexity, that they knew not what course to follow, that is, whether they should any longer prosecute the defence of the whole county, or else to stand upon their own guard'. The fact that some of the leading gentry and the 'prime commanders' favoured the defensive strategy and declined to press attacks upon the royalists, led to accusations of cowardice or treachery from the more militant rank and file, and 'bred such exceeding diffidence of them, that they cannot trust them, either with the managing of their affairs, or conduct of their armies'. The issue was resolved by stirring up the religious party with a fast in the church from seven in the morning until eight at night, 'many of them not stirring out of the church, until all their sacred exercises of prayer and preaching were duly finished'. This resulted in the decision to summon the country and march on the royalist stronghold of Wigan.[277] The tide then turned decisively in favour of the parliamentarians in Lancashire. Unlike Yorkshire, where the royalists recovered from the assaults of the Bradford and Halifax men, Lancashire was lost to the royalists for good, as a result of the combination of Manchester with the linen-weavers of the south-east, the nailers of Chowbent and the discontented copy-holders of the north-east and north-west.

The resistance of Bradford and the risings in Lancashire were received with enthusiasm by the more radical parliamentarians, and 'Bradford Club-law' became the slogan for popular movements against the royalists.[278] Similarly in Devonshire it was reported that the country was rising against Sir Ralph Hopton and his army of Cornish royalists, and that thousands of club-men had joined with the parliamentarian forces: 'it is verily believed, Hopton will have club-law very suddenly'.[279] At Modbury the parliamentarian forces, with their club-men allies, defeated the royalists. 'The manner of the weapons which these club-men had with them (wherein they imitate the Bradfordians in the north) are some sad heavy clubs, some thick quarter-staves with iron and steel pikes at the end, some long poles with scythes at the end, others with a pike and a sickle, others with gardener's rakes with iron teeth, some with very long kelved pick-axes, some with hammers, some with saws instead of swords'.[280] But the parliamentarian gentry did not pursue this victory; perhaps influenced by the same considerations that led the Hothams in the north to embark on a desperate pursuit of peace, and frightened of the allies the parliamentarian cause had evoked, they agreed to a cessation of hostilities with the royalists and entered into prolonged negotiations with them for the pacification and neutralization of the south-western counties.[281] This appalled the more militant parliamentarians: 'The West hath produced the worst news this week: an indiscreet treaty, to the ruin and destruction of the Devonshire men, if not prevented.'[282] It was condemned by some of the Devonshire leaders, who declared that the trained bands and club-men having come in such numbers and 'so well charging and scattering the enemy at Modbury that our greatest and worthiest gentry there acknowledged their valour and resolution such as they might hereafter well trust as of men willing to fight and spirited to the work. Yet when the enemy fled in a small number from thence and from about Plymouth unto Tavistock in a very weak and undone condition, where without effusion of more blood... the work might have been finished for these parts... there fell in—God knows how—a treaty of cessation first for six or seven days and then renewed for twenty or twenty-one more.' [283] Parliament condemned the treaty and sent down two MPs to stop it, which at length they succeeded in doing, although negotiations continued between the two parties for some time and the cessation of hostilities did not end until 22 April. [284] The radicals blamed the failure to exploit the victory at Modbury, and the treaty with the royalists, on the lukewarmness and treachery of some of the parliament's commanders and chief gentry. 'This county stands firm to the parliament, and had made an end of the war before this time, had it not been for the treachery and instability of the commanders sent us'. Some of these were now removed and divers captains who 'seemed rather to stand as neuters than assist the war' were cashiered; and they were replaced by others of 'approved fidelity', 'to pursue the rebels, the treaty being at a period'. [285]

The north part of Staffordshire rises up to moors and low hills known as the Moorlands, 'so hard, so comfortless, bare, and cold, that it keepeth snow lying upon it a long while', and it was said of the village of Wootton below Weaver Hill:

Wotton under Wever

Where God never came...

'Yet in so hard a soil it breedeth and feedeth beasts of large bulk and fair spread'; [286] as well as a 'hardy breed of inhabitants' called the Moorlanders: [287] 'A rebellious place', commented a royalist gentleman. [288] While the gentry of the county hesitated the Moorlanders rose for parliament. They 'banded together with little help from the gentry, and were led by "a person of low quality" sometimes referred to as "the Grand-Juryman" '. [289] Early in February some thousands of them marched on Stafford and besieged the royalists: 'There is a great rabble of all sorts of people convened together, being neither disciplined nor armed', wrote the royalist sheriff; 'some with birding guns, others only with clubs, others with pieces of scythes, very few with muskets, and I believe as slenderly provided with ammunition'. [290] They attacked the town for a couple of days but lacked the resources to take it. They appealed for help to Sir William Brereton, the parliamentarian commander in Cheshire, and to Sir John Gell, the parliamentarian commander in Derbyshire, and hoped for cannon and some experienced soldiers from the latter. But they received no help and retired again to their moors without taking Stafford, but they continued loyal to parliament.[291] Ineffective as it was, this insurrection of the poorer peasants signified once again that popular support for parliament was not confined to the urban classes but extended deeply into the peasantry.

The club-men of the West Riding, Lancashire and Devon, the smiths of Birmingham and the Moorlanders of Staffordshire, were all seen by radical parliamentarians as showing the way to win the war, and as portents of a popular triumph over the royalists. 'The club-men, the true lovers of our liberties... at last must be the men that will do the deed'.[292] The same newspaper, in another issue, reporting that the earl of Derby's forces at Wigan were 'soundly beaten by the honest hearted club-men', commented that 'if the nobility and gentry of the kingdom still go on to make the commons of England, gentle slaves in their religion and liberty, they themselves (that is, so many of them as run these courses) may happen to be taken before they die, at least in esteem inferior to commons'; thus indicating that the encouragement of popular risings against the royalists was closely akin to regarding the civil war as a class conflict.[293] This same journal proposed that the whole kingdom be invited to rise and execute 'Bradford Club-law' on the cavaliers: young men of every county to come with clubs, scythes, forks and flails and fall upon the enemy.[294]

The influential and notorious radical pamphlet of 12 January 1643, **Plaine English**, declared: 'Hear, O people, consider that you are considerable or might be, if good counsel would be taken. Do you see how you are courted by the king, what care the parliament take for your satisfaction? Sure you are not so contemptible a thing as some would make you; your might is much, and your power no less, if you would know the one and use the other.' The author was well aware how this sort of talk disturbed the parliamentarian gentry: 'I am sensible how offensive this discourse is like to be, but it never was my intention (had it been possible) to please all men.' They feared the people and popular intervention in the war, and would discourage rather than encourage the people to rise. Some parliamentarians, the pamphleteer went on, suspected the forwardness of the people and 'say they doubt the people aim at some great *infandum*, something too big for their mouths though not for their hearts, which they are so horribly afraid of being serviceable to, that they many times doubt whether themselves should do their own duty, because they suspect other men forget theirs'. He correctly discerned that the lukewarmness and defeatism of many of the parliament-arian nobility and gentry, their anxiety to fight only a limited and defensive war and get out of it as quickly as possible by a compromise, negotiated peace, and the passing of more and more of them into neutrality or royalism, sprang from fear of the consequences for their class of the popular movements that parliament's conflict with the royalists had occasioned. But, the pamphlet argued, the unwillingness of the parliamentarian leaders to go along with or to encourage popular movements against the king's party, and their distrust of the people, caused the people to distrust them. 'But let me not be mistaken, I am far from the Monster of a Democracy, that which I call to the people for, is but a quick and regular motion in their own sphere, to do that which the parliament hath sometimes called them for, to contribute their best helps to two great works, of mercy and justice; mercy to the kingdom in its preservation, and justice to its enemies in their destruction. Suppose they hit not upon the same means, but... be constrained to out-run a command, their faithful prosecution of the end designed them, which is the safety and preservation of the kingdom, and in it their own, may justly excuse them, if not commend them'. He was willing to run the risks in order to win the war.[295]

In May 1643 the lord mayor and 'divers citizens' of London proposed to the House of Commons that every inhabitant of the City should be enrolled for active offensive against the royalists, either by serving in person or contributing money, under the leadership of members of parliament, aldermen and Common Council-men of London.[296] A meeting was called by the London radicals at Merchant-Tailors Hall on 19 July 1643: 'All sorts of well-affected persons, who desire a speedy end of this destructive war, are entreated to meet at Merchant-Tailors Hall tomorrow...there to hear, and subscribe a petition to the parliament, (to which thousands have already subscribed) for raising the whole people of the land as one man, against those popish-bloodthirsty forces raised to enslave, and destroy us, and our posterity.'[297] Many thousand citizens petitioned parliament the next day for raising a new army of volunteers in London, and for the kingdom to be invited to rise with them as one body.[298] A 'Committee for the General Rising' was set up. Pym wrote to Barrington on 2 August: 'The common people seem very hasty and earnest to rise in a body and to shut up all their shops.' Parliament paid lip-service to the idea but the chief leaders in the Houses and the City were intent upon sabotaging and killing it.[299]

Popular support for parliament was dissipated by lack of weapons and by discouragements from the parliamentarian leaders. The Moorlanders of Staffordshire had to abandon their siege of Stafford because they had no ordnance and received little or no support from the parliamentarian gentry and commanders.[300] A newspaper was referring specifically to Staffordshire and Warwickshire when it commented: 'The country people whose forwardness appears everywhere, had they any to encourage and direct them.'[301] At Lewes in Sussex the townsmen and 300-400 men from the country rose for parliament, 'but they want a head and leaders, and not one gentleman of that county offereth himself to do them service in that kind'.[302] After prince Rupert had taken Cirencester in Gloucestershire 'thousands of men armed and unarmed flocked together, and resolved to undertake the enemy under the conduct of a grave and well-minded patriot' (this was probably Nathaniel Stephens, the leading parliamentarian gentleman in the county) 'but the desired leader... refused to engage himself and them upon a certain destruction; nevertheless the people bitterly railed against him, and cursed him as a traitor to his country; neither could the experience of these times dispossess them of that absurd conceit'.[303] The response of this 'patriot' illustrates how unusual was the behaviour of Sir Thomas Fairfax in the almost precisely similar situation in Yorkshire.

In September 1642 volunteers that came to London from Essex and Suffolk went home again because they were not employed.[304] In November 1642 the Essex trained bands came to London but were sent back again because the lord general had no use for them.[305] The London radicals, led by Sir David Watkins, Richard Shute, and three ministers—John Goodwin,

Jeremiah Burroughes and Hugh Peter—petitioning the House of Commons against peace negotiations and for 'a more speedy and effectual prosecution of the wars', also complained of the people of Essex and Hertfordshire being sent back home after they had come up to serve parliament, and demanded that they be instantly recalled and employed.[306] In March 1643 multitudes came to Cambridge to serve parliament but they were thanked and sent away again, 'all but a thousand': 'Thus we see the hearts of the people if the parliament please to command them.'[307] The radicals protested at the 'hurrying the poor willing country people to and fro, as if they had been so many puppets for our Grandees to play withal. Summoning them to appear one month with horse, arms, and money of their own, and dismissing them the next, tiring them out with continual expectation of action, till they were unfit for action; as if their only design had been by these mock proceedings to render them either unable or unwilling to help the state in time of real necessity; to the infinite prejudice and dishonour of the parliament, who have by this means lost many thousand hands, if not hearts.'[308] It was one of the sources of the disillusionment of the radicals with parliament, and one of the roots of the Leveller movement after the civil war, that 'ye have never made that use of the people of this nation, in your war, as you might have done, but have chosen rather to hazard their coming in, than to arm your own native undoubted friends... Whereas ye might have ended the war long ere this'.[309]

The people who rose more or less spontaneously against the royalists were to a large extent more inspired and motivated by the cause than the soldiers who served only for pay and plunder in parliament's main armies. But they were less disciplined, less experienced and less well equipped. When the country people had driven the royalists from Somerset in August 1642, the earl of Bedford and Denzil Holles came down from London with a small force and, gathering some two or more thousand of the country people of Somerset and some hundreds from Devon and Dorset, they went to besiege the marquis of Hertford and royalist gentry in Sherborne castle. The castle proved stronger than expected; the parliamentarians' cannon made little impression and the prospect seemed to be a long siege. But the harvest was at hand and the peasants were anxious to return to their fields. 'Our countrymen with this long and tedious march grew very weary'. After two days and nights in the open 'our country fellows that were wont to have their bellies full of good beef, and then to their beds, would not long endure hunger and cold on a bleak hill', and 'abundance of them stole away from the camp, some of them throwing their arms away into the cornfields, the better to escape home'.[310] The peasants had no previous experience of war, and little or no military training. 'If a bullet comes over their heads, they fall flat upon their bellies, and some four or five being slain hath made about half of them run away', reported their commanders, 'and we are confident half of those that are left will follow... The deputy lieutenants and prime gentlemen of this country which are with us are willing to do anything they can, but... they presumed upon the country people who have deceived them. The short of all is we have no army, nor can possibly with these men do this work.'[311] The farmers were tenants for life and fearful that if they were killed their landlords, most of whom were royalists, would not renew their leases to their families. The earl of Bedford and Denzil Holles lifted the siege.[312] But there was some suspicion that the earl had not pressed the attack vigorously enough in the first place, because, as some of the country soldiers complained as they made their way home, he 'did favour the castle for his sister's sake', who lived there, being the wife of lord Digby.[313]

When prince Rupert fell upon Cirencester in February 1643 the parliamentarian common soldiers were 'quite off the hinges, either cowardly or mutinous'; and 'as for the country-men... it so fell out that in the midst of the service they were at their wits end, and stood like men amazed, fear bereft them of understanding and memory, begat confusion in the mind within, and the thronging thoughts did oppress and stop the course of action, that they were busied in everything, but could bring forth nothing'. But there were many other reasons for this disaster: Cirencester was 'a straggling and open town, neither well fortified nor capable of defence'; the country round about was open and advantageous for horse, of which the royalists had many and the parliamentarians none; the parliament's soldiers had not been paid, and they had only one experienced officer and no cannoneers. And in addition to 'weakness of spirit' amongst the peasants there was 'error in the chief manage of the business' by the gentry.[314] Nevertheless the conclusion drawn by one of the chief of the parliamentarian gentry was the impossibility of popular levies withstanding the royalist gentry and their all-powerful cavalry. When 'thousands of men armed and unarmed flocked together' in Gloucestershire and asked him to lead them in an attempt to reverse the defeat, he declined, being 'conscious of the people's madness, and knew well that they made a loud cry afar off, but if once brought up to the face of the army they would never abide the fury of the first onset. Wherefore he refused to engage himself and them upon a certain destruction'.[315]

Cromwell shared the prejudice of his class and after seeing the royalist cavalry at the battle of Edgehill, which was composed of 'gentlemen's sons, younger sons and persons of quality', concluded that 'base and mean fellows' would never be able 'to encounter gentlemen that have honour and courage and resolution in them'.[316] The earl of Bedford and Denzil Holles commented on their experience at Sherborne: 'We for our parts will gladly lay down our lives... but truly we would die like men and with men and not like fools in the company of heartless beasts, with whom we had no more wit than to engage our honour and lives.'[317] This led them to conclude that parliament could not win the war, for it had to rely on the common people, while the king depended on the nobility and gentry. So they became leaders of the Peace Party, advocating negotiations with the king and peace at almost any price. Experiences with untrained and cowardly, disorderly and mutinous soldiers persuaded many parliamentarian leaders that they would be beaten, and defeatism led them to seek peace with the king on any terms he would accept.

Nevertheless parliamentarian leaders also testified to the courage and good conduct of inexperienced, untrained and ill-equipped peasants and artisans in the West Riding, Lancashire and Devon. They fought well when it was in defence of their homes and their own neighbourhood against an invasion from outside, but when the immediate threat was removed, they expected to be able to return to their farms and workshops (how else could they support their families?), and would not pursue the war into distant parts. The countrymen, said Sir William

Brereton, the parliamentarian commander in Cheshire, 'were glad to take any occasion to make haste home to their crows'.[318] Sir George Chudleigh explained why he and the chief parliamentarian gentry in Devonshire had agreed to a cessation of arms with the royalists after the victory at Modbury: 'The great blessing of God upon our late endeavours, hath rendered the undisciplined forces of this county manageable to defend it against a small invasion. But consisting chiefly of trained bands altogether incapable to follow our victory into Cornwall'. Their 'affections to their families and husbandry carry them from us daily in very great numbers with their arms'. 'Therefore we have thought fit to accept of our enemy's importunity for a treaty, hoping to increase our volunteers, and to get supplies for our trained soldiers'.[319] There was a great deal in this but it loses some of its plausibility when soon afterwards, Sir George and his son, who was one of the chief commanders of the parliament's army in Devon, joined the royalists.[320] Still, there were some good reasons, apart from class interests, why the parliamentarian gentry were unwilling to trust popular forces and to urge a general rising of the people. The enthusiasm of the radicals for the club-men of Yorkshire, Lancashire and Devon, ignored genuine doubts whether such ill-armed, untrained, part-time soldiers could do more than, perhaps, win local successes, but never be able to pursue and defeat the king's main army with its powerful cavalry. It 'must not be the gathering of multitudes together' that will win the war, 'but the setting up of good armies of right, valiant and well-disciplined men: and these to be well paid, and to be in perpetual motion till all be ended'.[321] The idea of a general rising of the people was criticized on the grounds that it would bring all trade and husbandry to a standstill; that the royalists were so strong and so expert in arms that they would soon defeat such a rabble; and that as the weaker party the parliamentarians should remain on the defensive for a time and not risk all at one blow until they were stronger.[322] In any case large numbers of the people supported the king, and over a great deal of the kingdom masses of them were indifferent or opposed to both sides and wanted only to live their lives in peace and maintain their livelihoods.

The sterner puritans did not despair, and Cromwell did

not follow Bedford and Holles into defeatism and the pursuit of peace at almost any price. The demand for a general rising of the people against the royalists was translated into a demand for the raising an army of the godly. They were the firmest supporters of parliament; they did not fight for pay and plunder but for religion and reformation; they were disciplined and orderly and could be trained into soldiers able to withstand the cavaliers.[323] In July 1643 a petition was being circulated by the London radicals 'for the raising of an army of ten thousand volunteer soldiers... who are godly, or men of honest life or conversation, that will for the present either maintain themselves, or take the public faith for their pay, or shall be maintained by others, who will go in person and see them paid weekly, or send their money for doing thereof by some of the contributors, who shall go in person to see them paid, and that the Command-in-Chief may be some godly nobleman, or other godly man of worth, and that the colonels, captains, and all other commanders and officers may be godly, or men of honest life and conversation, who out of love to the maintenance of the true reformed protestant religion, the good laws of our land, the precious liberty of the subject, and just privileges of parliament, and of all well-affected protestants, which will go voluntarily upon this service, and ask no present pay; or if greater commanders or officers, a fourth part of their pay at most; or if inferior officers and common soldiers part, and will take the public faith for the residue'.[324] This petition was adopted at a meeting at Merchant-Tailors Hall on 19 July and presented to parliament the next day.[325] It led to the formation of a committee for volunteers, consisting of the leading radicals in London, but made no headway.[326] The aim was to by-pass the earl of Essex, who was fighting the war with a defensive rather than an offensive strategy, and to create an army that would fight the war more vigorously and offensively, be more valiant and less disorderly. This was not achieved by the agitation of 1643, but in the end it was the godly who took control of the parliamentarian party.

8

THE NOBILITY AND
THE PEOPLE

THE KING APPEALS TO THE RULING CLASS

The king and parliament had appealed against each other to the people for support. When Charles had fled to York in 1642 he was a king in name only. He had no force at his disposal, nor machinery of government; he could not compel anybody to serve him, nor punish anybody for opposing him; and the only material inducements he could offer had to be post-dated to an uncertain future, when he might recover his power and the means to reward his followers. The monarchy was reduced to its bare essence—the sentiment of loyalty to the person of the king.

Charles called a meeting of 'the freeholders, copyholders, and substantial farmers' of Yorkshire at Heworth Moor on 3 June. They came in such numbers that the parliamentarian Sir Mathew Boynton thought it 'the greatest appearance of people that ever I saw in this county', and the king's secretary of state, Edward Nicholas, estimated them at 'between three or four score thousand'. There was such tumultuous cheering for the king and his speech that Nicholas reported that 'his majesty's confidence is now most firmly settled upon the loyalty and affections of this his people'.[1] The king now toured the counties. At Newark and Lincoln he was 'attended with such an appearance of the gentlemen and men of quality, and so full a concourse of the people, as one might reasonably have guessed the affections of both those counties would have seconded any just and regular service for the king'.[2] In Leicester he was 'gladsomely received by above 10,000 of the gentry and better sort of inhabitants of that county, all cheerfully submitted to his obedience'.[3] In September the king went through Derbyshire, Staffordshire and Shropshire: 'And a more general and passionate expression of affection cannot be imagined than he received by the people of those counties... as he passed, or a better reception than he found at Shrewsbury', where 'multitudes came to him daily' and 'a very great conflux of the gentry of that and the [neighbouring counties]'.[4] He went on to Chester, where he was 'received and entertained with all demonstrations of duty by the city of Chester... and the nobility and gentry, and indeed the common people, flocked to him, the former in very good equipage, and the latter with great expressions of devotion'.[5] 'The king's custom was, in all counties through which he passed, to cause the high sheriff to draw all the gentlemen and the most substantial inhabitants of those parts together, to whom... he always spake something publicly, (which was afterwards printed,)... His majesty always took notice of any particular reports, which, either with reference to the public or their private [concerns], might make impression upon that people, and gave clear answers to them. So that, with this gracious and princely demeanour, it is hardly credible how much he won upon the people'.[6] But there was probably some truth in the parliamentarian claim that 'some when they see his royal person, cries, "For King Charles, For King Charles", but presently when his royal majesty is gone, then they stand for the parliament'.[7] It is doubtful if the people were much influenced by such gatherings as that on Heworth Moor, from which 'many thousands went away, saying they could give no account of the cause of their being called together'.[8] And Clarendon had to admit that the acclamations of the people were not generally translated into positive assistance for the king's cause.[9]

Stripped of the trappings of government, the monarchy was seen to rest, not upon the love of the people, but upon the interests of a class. For positive assistance the king had to turn to the nobility and greater gentry. As in the crisis of 1640, so in the crisis of 1642, he threw himself upon the mercy of the peers, summoning them to York and announcing his intention of taking no important decisions without their agreement.[10] He appealed first to the gentry of Yorkshire and only as a result of protests from the yeomen agreed to call the meeting of 'the freeholders, copyholders, and substantial farmers'.[11] In his recruiting tours through the counties, as well as speaking publicly to 'the gentlemen and the most substantial inhabitants', the king spoke privately to 'the principal gentlemen severally, familiarly, and very obligingly'.[12] He directed his appeals for help chiefly to the nobility and gentry, and based his case on the threat that, he maintained, the parliamentarians posed to the ruling class. He endeavoured to establish an identity of interests between monarchical government in the state and aristocratic order in society, and he argued that any reduction in the power of the crown, such as the two Houses demanded, would be bound to lead to weakening of the aristocracy. 'Is the constitution of the kingdom to be preserved, and monarchy itself upheld? ...Are not several books and papers... published by their direction, at least under their countenance, against monarchy itself? Is it possible for us to be made vile, and contemptible, and shall our good subjects continue as they are?' And he asserted that the destruction of the monarchy would result in the introduction of 'a parity and confusion of all degrees and conditions'.[13]

The earl of Southampton supported the king because he believed 'that a monarch cannot be deprived of a fundamental right, without a lasting wound to monarchy itself, that they who have most shelter from it and stand nearest to it, the nobility, could not continue long in their native strength, if the crown received a maim'.[14] The earl of Newcastle took up arms for the king 'to keep up his majesty's rights and prerogatives, for which he was resolved to venture both his life, posterity and estate; for certainly, said he, the nobility cannot fall if the king be victorious, nor can they keep up their dignities if the king be overcome'.[15] 'The security of the nobility and gentry depends upon the strength of the crown', declared a royalist pamphleteer, 'otherwise popular government would rush in like a torrent upon them.'[16] Lord Savile wrote to lady Temple to explain that he had joined the king because he feared that parliament would lessen the power of the king 'so much as to make a way for the people to rule us all'.[17] 'The lords are a part, and have a kindred and influence in the monarchy: the people have none', observed Sir Thomas Roe from the sidelines: 'all governments to them are hateful, but such of which they partake, which will soon resolve into anarchy, and confusion'.[18]

The king relied upon the power, influence and wealth of the greater landowners. Between February and July 1642 the earl of Worcester and his son lord Herbert secretly financed the king, supplying thousands of pounds to enable him to go to York, defy parliament and begin to raise forces.[19] The earl of Newcastle went to Northumberland, where 'in the first place he sent for all his tenants and friends in those parts, and presently raised a troop of horse consisting of 120, and a regiment of foot'.[20] The first to respond to his lead was his relative and friend Sir William Widdrington, 'a gentleman of the best and most ancient extraction of the county of Northumberland, and of very fair fortune', who was MP for the county and owned at least five manors there: he sent in his tenants to serve the earl.[21] Newcastle was the greatest man in Nottinghamshire and 'through his great estates, his liberal hospitality, and constant residence in his county' so endeared himself to the gentry 'that no man was a greater prince in all that northern quarter'; and 'most of the most ancient families in Northumberland, and other the northern parts' being related to him, accepted his leadership, out of respect to their kinsman and the feeling that 'by deserting my lord, they deserted themselves'; and they brought in their tenants, kinsmen and friends to form the king's northern army.[22] The earls of Derby had 'a greater influence' and 'a more absolute command over the people' in Lancashire and Cheshire 'than any subject in England had in any other quarter of the kingdom', being 'esteemed by most about them with little less respect than kings': they 'kept great hospitality which brought them much love and more applause', and 'were honoured and had in respect generally with all; the king could not be more... insomuch that there was not any within the county how great soever or independent to them that would, nay that durst, affront them'. Lord Strange, eldest son of the earl of Derby but head of the house since his father's retirement and shortly to inherit the title, employed the power of his family over its own tenants, and then over the gentry, who in turn brought in their tenants, to raise regiments of horse and foot for the king; and his chief agent was Thomas Tildesley, 'a gentleman of a good family and a good fortune' that had long served the earls, who 'raised men at his own charge', and 'having many well affected to him to follow him, besides many of the freeholders' band whom he allured or commanded to march with him', brought in many men to lord Strange.[23]

The earl of Lindsey 'was a man of a very noble extraction, and inherited a good fortune from his ancestors', and by his 'very good reputation with all men, and a very great interest in his county', he raised a regiment of near 1,000 foot for the king in Lincolnshire, and his son, lord Willoughby of Eresby, 'another excellent regiment, near the same number': 'The principal knights and gentlemen of Lincolnshire, who engaged themselves in the service principally out of their personal affection to him', brought in their tenants; and amongst them, Sir Gervase Scroope, 'an old gentleman of great fortune in Lincolnshire', 'raised a foot company amongst his tenants, and brought them into the earl of Lindsey's regiment, out of devotion and respect to his lordship as well as duty to the king'.[24] Lord Paget raised a regiment of foot for the king in Staffordshire, 'where his best interest was'.[25] Henry Hastings, a younger son of the earl of Huntingdon, raised a troop of horse in Leicestershire 'by the interest and relation of his family': 'And being master of certain coal mines he caused all his horses belonging to the engines, to be in readiness, and there raised about one hundred colliers out of Derbyshire, whom he armed with pikes, muskets and calivers', and so came to Leicester with 100 horse, 120 musketeers, and 80 pikemen.[26] In Monmouthshire 'the stream of the people...were at the devotion of the earl of Worcester, almost an universal landlord in that county'. The earl's eldest son, lord Herbert, claimed that 'in eight days' time, I raised six regiments, fortified Monmouth, Chepstow, and Raglan; fetching away the magazine from the earl of Pembroke's town, Caerleon, and placed it in Raglan castle, leaving a garrison in lieu thereof. Garrisoned likewise Cardiff, Brecon, Hereford, Goodrich castle, and the Forest of Dean, after I had taken them from the enemy'. He raised a troop of lifeguards 'consisting of six score noblemen and gentlemen, whose estates amounted to above £60,000 a year land of inherit-ance', furnishing them with 34 horses from his own stables worth £100 each, and 40 others worth £50 each, as well as arms, and keeping 'a constant table for them', at an allowance of £20 a meal, 'whereat they never wanted wine' and beer.[27]

The marquis of Hertford went to secure the west for the king, 'where his interest and reputation was greater than any man's... and with him went the lord Seymour, his brother, the lord Poulett, Hopton, Stowell, Coventry, Berkeley, Windham, and some other gentlemen of the prime quality and interest in the western parts, and who were like to give as good examples in their persons, and to be followed by as many men, as any such number of gentlemen in England could be'. The marquis made his headquarters at Wells in Somerset and lord Poulett came in with twenty-eight gentlemen 'of the prime quality', 'with their servants and retinue', and John Digby (a son of the earl of Bristol), Sir Ralph Hopton and Sir Francis Hawley each raised a troop of horse.[28] In Cornwall Sir Bevil Greenville, Sir Nicholas Slanning, John Arundell and John Trevanion, with 'many young gentlemen of the most considerable families of the county assisting them as inferior officers', raised 'amongst their neighbours and tenants who depended on them', near 1,500 foot, the nucleus of the king's western army.[29] Sir Edward Walker attributed their success to the fact that 'the gentry of this county retain their old possessions, their old tenants, and expect from them their ancient reverence and obedience'.[30] Thus the king's army 'was maintained and paid by the nobility and gentry, who served likewise in their own persons'.[31] At the battle of Edgehill 'most of the persons of honour and quality, (except those whose attendance was near the king's own per-son) put themselves into the king's troop of guards, commanded by the lord Bernard Stuart, and made indeed so gallant a body, that upon a very modest computation the estate and revenue of that single troop might justly be valued at least equal to all theirs who then voted in both Houses under the name of the Lords and Commons of parliament... Their servants, under the command of Sir William Killigrew, made another full troop, and always marched with their lords and masters.'[32]

Traditional ties of loyalty and habits of deference were sufficient to account for such success of the royalist nobility and gentry in gathering forces for the king; but these ties and habits were rooted in the self-interest of tenants whose landlords could do them so much good or so much harm. In the south-west the peasants held their leases for the term of their lives and were reluctant to oppose their landlords who might in revenge refuse to renew leases to the descendants of tenants who had been disloyal. Many of the country people who besieged the marquis of Hertford and royalist gentry in Sherborne castle in Dorset 'being tenants for life to the marquis, Sir Ralph Hopton, and many others that are in the said castle; when they saw their landlords express their fury out of the mouth of a cannon, they began to think that if they stood to it, they should not renew their lives, and so retreated back'.[33] Fear and force lay in the background, if loyalty and deference failed. In Somerset it was pointed out that Sir John Stowell 'hath great lordships and manors about the west part of the shire and that his tenants, most of them holdeth their lands by rack-rent; so that if they would not obey his command, he might out with them'.[34] Sir Bevil Greenville was accused of threatening his tenants 'to thrust them out of house and home, if they will not assist him and his confederates'.[35] In Lancashire it was said that the earl of Derby's officers had to resort to force to compel the peasants to fight for the king;[36] and Clarendon admitted that it soon appeared that the earl's 'ancient power there depended more upon the fear than love of the people'.[37]

PARLIAMENT APPEALS TO THE MIDDLE SORT OF PEOPLE

The parliamentarians recognized in 1642 that they could not, like the king, rely on the feudal power of the greatest landowners to raise forces, nor could they work through the existing holders of power in most counties and towns, but that they must look rather to the lesser gentry, greater yeomanry, middling merchants and larger manufacturers. 'By most circumstances it seems to be apprehended that those men below the justices of peace, enured to travel and business, will carry all the multitude below them, and make it too dangerous for their superiors that should sever from them, and no remedy against the worst consequences thereby except the king and parliament were thoroughly united.'[38] While the king directed his appeals to the nobility and gentry, the two Houses directed theirs to the yeomen and the middle sort of people. When the king went to York in 1642 the two Houses sent a committee to observe what he did and to hinder him 'from gaining the people of that county to his party: so that when his Majesty was courting the gentlemen there, the committee was instigating the yeomanry against him'.[39] A moderate pamphleteer, who urged speedy negotiations for peace and a compromise settlement, noted: 'It hath been observed, the parliament hath made little difference, (or not the right) between the gentry and yeomanry, rather complying and winning upon the latter, than regarding or applying themselves at all to the former.'[40]

As the war went on parliamentarians increasingly came to see the conflict, not so much a struggle against the king, as a struggle against the aristocracy. The cause of this struggle was the ambition of the nobles and greater gentry to increase their power over the people, and the issue of the war was freedom from the oppression of the aristocracy as well as from the tyranny of the king. More particularly, the nobility and greater gentry were jealous of the growing economic strength of some of the yeomanry and middle sort of people, and resentful of their claims for social esteem and political rights— a voice in the affairs of the community, both in state and church matters. Corbet said that the nobles and gentlemen who sided with the king did so from 'a desire of vast dominion, dignity, revenge, or rapine' and out of 'an hatred of the commons, and a strong disposition to the ends of tryanny', caring not 'to render themselves the slaves of princes, that they also might rule over their neighbours as vassals'.[41] Ludlow argued that 'many of the nobility and gentry were contented to serve' the king's 'arbitrary designs, if they might have leave to insult over such as were of a lower order'.[42] Jeremiah Burroughes, a leading puritan preacher, set out to explain in a sermon 'why so many of the gentry in most counties throughout the kingdom' supported the king: it was because 'many of them had rather enslave themselves and their posterities to those above them, than not to have their wills upon those that are under them: they would fain bring it to be with us as it is in France, that the gentry should be under the nobility and courtiers, and all the country people, the peasants, be under them as slaves, they live in miserable bondage under the gentry there, who generally are cavaliers. There is no country in the world, where country men, such as we call the yeomanry, yea, and their farmers and workmen under them, do live in that fashion and freedom as they do in England, in all other places they are slaves in comparison, their lives are so miserable as they are not worth the enjoying, they have no influence at all into the government they are under, nothing to do in the making of laws, or any way consenting to them, but must receive them from others, according to their pleasure; but in England every freeholder hath an influence into the making and consenting every law he is under, and enjoys his own with as true a title as the nobleman enjoys whatsoever is his. This freedom many of the proud gentry are vexed at, and hence it is their hearts rise so against those that are chosen by them, and against their ordinances. But the commons begin to discern this more than they have done, and to be so wise as to hold their own faster than they have.'[43] Another parliamentarian pamphleteer alleged that the royalists 'intend in England a government at discretion, and all made in all probability, after the French fashion'; but, the author claimed, 'the middle sort of people of England, and yeomanry' 'will especially oppose the change as whereby they from being in the happiest condition of any of their rank perhaps in Europe, nay in the world (who here live like men, and are wont to fight, or die like men in honour or defence of their country) might well be reduced to the terms of the peasants of France, of villeinage, and slavery'.[44] When the earl of Derby was repulsed from Manchester, the defenders appealed: 'O England's yeomen and husbandmen look to yourselves, for if you stand not to it, as we of Manchester do, but be overcome, look for ever to be slaves, for you see how this bloody tyrant [the earl of Derby] rages'.[45] 'If the nobility and gentry of the kingdom still go on to make the commons of England, gentle slaves in their religion and liberty, they themselves... may happen to be taken before they die, at least in esteem inferior to commons.'[46]

The parliamentarians played upon the fears of the middle rank of the people that, if the royalists won the civil war, not only would their desires for greater shares in the affairs of the community be frustrated, but their existing shares would be taken away; and they represented the royalist cause as being directed specifically against the middle sort of people. They exploited any evidence of royalist disregard for the yeomanry and the middle ranks. When the king 'borrowed' the arms of the trained bands the two Houses of Parliament accused him of practising one of 'the most mischievous principles of tyranny... that ever were invented, that is to disarm the middle sort of people, who are the body of the kingdom'.[47] A parliamentarian pamphleteer claimed that this was proof that the royalists intended a government after the French fashion in England, for 'the middle sort of people of England, and yeomanry' were the chief obstacle to such a change, and since they composed the main part of the trained bands, 'then by policy, or even plain force' the trained bands must be disarmed as the first step towards overcoming their opposition.[48] 'The cavaliers in Somersetshire have used violence on the yeomanry, and have turned them out of doors, and take their arms from them, the people seeing it could not suffer it, for if they prevail now they think they shall be slaves for ever.'[49]

The fears of the yeomen were increased when, in the summer of 1642, royalist gentry tried, often successfully, to exclude them from the grand juries, 'the representative bodies of the counties', on which they had long been accustomed to sit.[50] On 12 May 1642 the king summoned the gentry of Yorkshire to meet him at York, but 'thousands of freeholders' came to the city, 'though none but the gentry were summoned', and protested to the king at being barred from the meeting: 'conceiving ourselves according to the proportions of our estates, equally interested in the common good of the county', 'in our absence a referee of knights and gentlemen chosen without our knowledge or consent... We the freeholders... conceiving ourselves abundantly injured in the election (not knowing any warrant by writ or otherwise for the same) of the said referee, and that we ought not however to be concluded by any resolution of theirs without our assent in their election; do absolutely protest and declare against the said election: and as far as concerns us disavow whatsoever shall be the result of their consultation thereupon, and do desire, a new and fair election of a referee may be made, we admitted to our free votes in the same, and some one or more to be nominated by us, allowed to deliver our sense for us at another meeting'.[51] Mildred Campbell comments that this petition 'displays the spirit of the men from whom Cromwell was soon to choose his "russet-coated captains" '.[52]

Some royalists wanted to restrict the franchise in parliamentary elections and deprive the middle sort of people of their votes. Dudley Digges, in one of the most comprehensive and influential statements of the royalist case, pointed out that the property qualification for a vote in parliamentary elections was low enough for the electorate to consist of a majority of 'poor countrymen and beggarly tradesmen', and he urged that the 40s freehold qualification be raised 'to such a proportion as that estate was valuable at, in the first constitution, when the scarcity of money made it a competent fortune'. He feared that the existing electorate might return 'very mean men' to the House of Commons 'to make more profitable laws for the poorer sort, and to keep the gentry under, by laying subsidies and all burdens of the commonwealth upon them, not without a specious pretence, that they spend more in superfluities than would discharge all public expenses, and exempting themselves from all payments, as being such, who take great pains, and work very hard, even for necessaries'.[53] This was a shrewd account of the outlook of the middle sort of people, and an acute recognition that one of their main grievances was an inequitable tax system, under which they were overtaxed and the nobility and gentry undertaxed. Clearly Digges assumed that royalists preferred a system under which the poor rather than the rich paid the taxes.

The parliamentarians believed that the royalist nobility and gentry resented the wealth and status that some of the middle sort of people had acquired by diligence and thrift, and wished to thrust them back into the mass of the common people from which they had, somewhat precariously, distinguished themselves. The yeomen, farmers and clothiers of Gloucestershire were 'a generation of men truly laborious, jealous of their properties, whose principal aim is liberty and plenty, and whilst in an equal rank with their neighbours they desire only not to be oppressed, and account themselves extremely bound to the world, if they may keep their own'; and they became parliamentarians because they felt threatened by the nobility and gentry, 'who detesting a close, hardy, and industrious way of living, do eat their bread in the sweat of other men'.[54] Sir Edward Walker, the king's secretary at war, discerned the cause of the civil war in the unsubmissiveness and insubordination of the peasantry, and he dreamed of the reimposition of villeinage: 'And give me leave to say, if many of the nobility and gentry of this unhappy kingdom had not fallen from the lustre, virtue, and honour of their ancestors, and by their luxury been necessitated to manumize their villeins, but had paid that awful reverence to the majesty and greatness of their sovereign as they ought, they might have expected the same proportionably from their inferiors and tenants; and instead of having them their companions or rather masters, (as now they are) they might have had them their servants; and then I believe this war... in probability had not been.'[55]

MIDDLE SORT OF PEOPLE SUPPORT PARLIAMENT

August and September 1642, as the two sides were raising their armies and moving towards the first great battle of the civil war, were months of tumult and rioting. This might have been, and to some extent was, a passing phase, after which the people were crushed beneath the tramp of passing armies, bled by their incessant demands for men, money and supplies, and left with only a sullen resentment against the war and all connected with it. But there was one significant element in the popular disorders of the late summer and autumn of 1642 that made them of a rather different character from other mutinies of the common people. 'This fury', wrote Arthur Wilson of the riots in Essex and Suffolk, 'was not only in the rabble, but many of the better sort behaved themselves as if there had been a dissolution of all government'.[56] 'This *jacquerie*' (the attack on the earl of Middlesex's deer at Forthampton in Gloucestershire) 'in the opinion of Richard Dowdeswell, now Middlesex's main agent, was not only the work of the lower classes but of "very rich and able men" ': 'the countenances of men are so altered, especially of the mean and middle rank of men that the turning of a straw would set a whole county in a flame and occasion the plundering of any man's house or goods although much against the hearts and endeavours of all in authority'.[57] The readiness of the 'middle rank of men' to join with the 'rabble' gave to the riots a greater social and political significance. The 'rabble' was expected to be disorderly whenever it got the chance, and was as likely to favour the king as parliament, or neither, but the rebelliousness of the middle sort of men was far more a political act and orientated towards support of parliament: it converted riot into revolution.'

'Almost all the yeomanry (which is the most considerable rank of any nation)...at this time side against the king and the papists,' claimed Henry Parker in 1643.[58] But this was a great exaggeration. The yeomen were thought of as the richer peasants and the parliamentarians did believe that they had much support amongst them. The parliamentarians in Northamptonshire collected money, plate and horse for parliament, and there came in 'about two or three hundred horse, many yeoman men coming in with £10 and a horse, and £20 and a horse'.[59] From Warwickshire a parliamentarian reported that 'the yeomen of our county stands out very well':[60] on 14 November 1642 drums were beaten at Warwick for volunteers and many 'able yeomen's sons' came to serve parliament.[61] In the southern parts of Herefordshire, about Ross, Colonel Massey, the parliamentarian commander at Gloucester, in May 1644 'summons the country to come in, and to take the Covenant, and to pay contribution unto him; where he found willing obedience by the greatest part of the yeomanry'.[62] The royalists found 'the yeomanry' of Gloucestershire, who were 'very wealthy', 'most forward and seditious';[63] and Corbet claimed that the 'yeomen, farmers, petty-freeholders' of that county supported parliament.[64] The gentry carried the people of Wales into the king's camp, but support for parliament emerged amongst some of the yeomen of Wrexham, and some of 'the smaller gentry, yeomen and peasants' of Radnorshire.[65] 'Yeomen well armed' came prominently to the aid of parliament in Somerset in the summer of 1642.[66] In Lancashire 'many yeomen's sons' went to form the parliament's garrison at Bolton.[67] Freeholders, in the tenurial sense, were not necessarily wealthy, and many of them were small farmers or had very little land,[68] but the term was used loosely in the seventeenth century to indicate the more independent of the peasantry. In Nottinghamshire, according to Mrs Hutchinson, 'most of the middle sort, the able substantial freeholders, and the other commons, who had not their dependence upon the malignant nobility and gentry, adhered to the parliament'.[69] In Derbyshire Sir John Gell, 'with his brother, and some of his kindred, by the help of those freeholders and yeomen that inclined that way, made a party to resist those great ones' that declared for the king.[70] In Shropshire, it was said, 'the gentlemen and poor' supported the king, 'yet notwithstanding our freeholders are firm to... parliament'.[71] The freeholders of Yorkshire were expected to adhere to parliament in 1642.[72] In the eastern counties 'the freeholders and yeomen in general adhered to the parliament';[73] and 'though many of the chief gentry in those counties were for paying obedience to his majesty's commission of array, yet the freeholders and yeomen being generally of the other side, as oft as they attempted to show themselves, they were crushed, and their endeavours defeated'.[74]

But parliament also got support from middling and smaller peasant farmers. Two hundred volunteers that came from Essex and Suffolk to serve in the earl of Essex's army were 'men's sons of twenty, thirty, forty pounds a year'.[75] The freeholders and small farmers of the Isle of Axholme in Lincolnshire formed two companies of foot, totalling 495 men, for parliament in the civil war.[76] Cromwell's regiment of horse, recruited in Huntingdonshire and Cambridgeshire, and the cavalry of the Eastern Association, was composed of small peasants as well as tradesmen and apprentices.[77] In Lancashire, around Chowbent, 'the young youths, farmers' sons' were in the forefront of the resistance to the earl of Derby's forces, and some copyholders ('sturdy churls in the two forests of Pendle and Rossendale') rose for parliament.[78] After the civil war Colonel Moore, the parliamentarian governor of Liverpool, testified that the copyholders of West Derby and Wavertree 'have ever faithfully adhered to the parliament, and some of them have lost their lives in the service, most of them their personal estate, by showing themselves for the parliament. They live within two miles of Liverpool and upon all occasions have been ready to assist that garrison.'[79] In 1647 a petition from Buckinghamshire claimed that copyholders, who were 'the body of the kingdom', 'have for the most part been very cordial and faithful to the parliament'.[80] On the whole it would seem to have been from amongst the more independent sections of the peasantry that parliament got support: some of the richer farmers, commonly called yeomen, and some of the smaller farmers who gained independence by combining manufacture with agriculture.[81] Gloucestershire was a county in which independent small producers predominated,[82] and on them its parliamentarianism rested: smaller as well as the larger farmers there sided with parliament because, in Corbet's view, 'the countryman had of his own, and did not live by the breath of his great landlord'.[83]

'On the parliament's side were... the greatest part of the tradesmen, and freeholders, and the middle sort of men, especially in those corporations and counties which depend on clothing and such manufactures.'[84] In Gloucestershire, besides some few of the gentry, the only active supporters of parliament were 'yeomen, farmers, clothiers, and the whole middle rank of the people'.[85] Sir Arthur Aston wrote to prince Rupert from Painswick in Gloucestershire on 7 August 1643: 'indeed there is scarcely one of all these clothiers but have both lent money, and do maintain soldiers upon their own charges against... his majesty'.[86] Clarendon did not doubt that clothiers were parliamentarians: 'the common people, especially in the clothing parts of Somersetshire, were generally too much inclined to them';[87] and 'Leeds, Halifax, and Bradford, three very populous and rich towns (which depending wholly upon clothiers...) were wholly at their disposition'.[88] 'I have hitherto supported this army', confirmed lord Fairfax on 10 December 1642, 'by the loans and contributions, for the most part, of the parishes of Leeds, Halifax, and Bradford, and some other small clothing towns adjacent, being the only well-affected of the county'.[89] Parliamentarianism was strong in the cloth-manufacturing towns and villages of Essex and Suffolk, especially where the new draperies were made. Here small independent master-craftsmen predominated, as in the West Riding of Yorkshire,[90] and a stronger and more radical parliamentarianism developed than in Wiltshire, where larger manufacturers predominated and wage-earners were more numerous.[91] But some small masters employed labour. At Kidderminster in Worcestershire the parliamentarians of the town were small master-weavers: they were none of them rich, 'seeing their trade was poor, that would but find them food and raiment'; few of them earned as much as £40 a year, 'and most not half so much'; the richest of them might accumulate £500 or £600 in twenty years; and most of them 'lived but a little better than their journeymen, (from hand to mouth) but only that they laboured not altogether so hard'; but they were independent and they were employers of labour.[92] If in Kidderminster the 'poor journeymen and servants' rejected the lead of their employers and followed the royalist gentry and clergy,[93] elsewhere they took the part of their masters, as in Gloucestershire, where 'neither were the poor and needy at the will of the gentry, but observed those men by whom those manufactures were maintained that kept them alive'.[94] And in Essex and Suffolk the employers in clothmaking passed on their parliamentarianism 'to their workmen', observed a royalist, 'so that the clothiers through the whole kingdom were rebels by their trade'.[95]

At Portsmouth the royalists were supported by 'poor mechanic persons' but opposed by 'almost half the town and of the better sort'.[96] In Bristol 'the king's cause and party were favoured by the two extremes in that city; the one the wealthy and powerful men, the other of the basest and lowest sort, but disgusted by the middle rank, the true and best citizens'.[97] 'The chief men' at Manchester favoured the earl of Derby, and so did the 'rascality'.[98] The minister, the 'chief of the town and better sort' at Birmingham would have admitted prince Rupert in April 1643, but 'the middle and inferior sort of people' resolved to oppose his entry.[99] In Worcester the supporters of parliament 'were but of the middle rank of people, and none of any great power or eminence there to take their parts';[100] and from Chichester a parliamentarian reported that 'the strength of our parts consist mainly in honest tradesmen, the gentry are nought... and the country people are for the most part blinded and misled by their malevolent hedge-priests'.[101] The supporters of parliament were said to be a minority in Gloucester; less than a quarter of the population in Nottingham, and less than one-fifth in Manchester.[102]

The tradesmen of London gave mass support to parliament. The demonstrators who flocked to the defence of the House of Commons in 1641 and 1642 were described by

William Lilly as 'most of them men of mean or a middle quality';[103] and Sir Edward Walker thought that these demonstrators were the first to volunteer to serve in parliament's army.[104] Certainly the handicraftsmen of the capital provided the bulk of the earl of Essex's infantry, and the first to enlist were 71 dyers, 88 butchers, 186 weavers, 157 tailors, 124 shoemakers, 88 brokers and 49 sadlers.[105] After the civil war the commonalty of the Weavers' Company of London claimed 'that at the beginning of the war many of us and our servants engaged for the parliament'; and the working sadlers said that 'some of them, have served the parliament from the beginning in wars and otherwise'.[106] It was said that 8,000 apprentices of London enlisted in the earl of Essex's army: 'Neither are they of the base and mechanic scum of the people, who to support themselves in a riotous fashion, and to pillage the country under the name of being soldiers, do without fear of any conscionable respect, take pay and enter into service, but the greater part of those magnanimous 'prentices, are servants to honest and sufficient men, and by their own laborious endeavours can be both serviceable and profitable to their masters, and be very beneficial to them, in working at their trades', but their masters, preferring the public good to their private profit, gave them leave to serve in the army. 'Neither are they loose idle fellows that are fain to make war their profession, for want of other maintenance, for all these 'prentices as was aforesaid, have trades and callings, and most of them young men of good parentage; whose friends live honestly and thriftily in the country, and yet as if they all descended of generous blood' nothing could prevent them from putting their resolution into execution 'to live and die with the earl of Essex'.[107] By origins and vocation the apprentices belonged to the 'middle sort of people'. They were always anxious to have it known that they were 'men's sons of good rank'. It was expensive to put a boy to an apprenticeship in London: in James I's reign it cost £20, £40, £60, even £100 to bind a youth as an apprentice in the capital, and the cost had risen since then. A good number of the London apprentices were 'gentlemen's younger sons of good families', others were sons of the clergy, and a great many were sons of the richer peasant farmers. When they completed their training they expected to enter the middle ranks of the population.[108]

The Londoners, however, did not stand alone, and the raising of an army at London did not rest solely upon the support of the citizens. £6,000 in plate and money were sent up from the two Hundreds about Colchester in Essex and 150 volunteers.[109] Two hundred volunteers came up from Essex and Suffolk to join the army: 'men's sons of twenty, thirty, forty pounds a year'.[110] Sixty men came from Sussex to serve parliament: 'able and lusty men, and fit for service, and willing to lose their lives in service of the parliament and state'.[111] Henry Ireton brought in a troop of horse from Nottinghamshire;[112] and Northamptonshire sent in £1,000 worth of plate, and twice as much in money, 'and about two or three hundred horse, many yeoman men coming in with £10 and a horse, and £20 and a horse'.[113] Dartmouth in Devon contributed £1,700 to raising the army.[114] Nevertheless it was essentially with London's army that the earl of Essex set out to give battle to the king in the autumn of 1642. After the first skirmish of the civil war, near Worcester, lord Falkland reported that the royalists had taken fifty to sixty prisoners: 'most of them were men of mean quality, and so raw soldiers that they understood not the word quarter, but cried for mercy; being demanded of what condition they were: some said, they were tailors, some embroiderers, and the like'.[115]

There were, however, 'numerous royalists among the trading and industrial classes'. In a list of 300 Gloucestershire royalists drawn up in 1655-6 'in addition to the knights, esquires, gentlemen, and members of the professions, who constituted about one-fourth of the total, about one-fourth were merchants, shopkeepers, and tradesmen; about one-sixth were engaged in. the textile industry; and one-seventh were yeomen and husbandmen'.[116] Statistics from this source undoubtedly underestimate the numbers of royalists below the level of the gentry. But taking them at their face value, and in relation to the total population of the county, in which workers in the textile industry outnumbered the gentry by at least six to one, and yeomen and husbandmen were at least eleven times as numerous as gentry, if only 50 out of 2,545 workers in textiles and 43 out of 4,703 yeomen and husbandmen supported the king, this confirms rather than contradicts the evidence for the weakness of royalism among these social groups.[117] The adherence of the common people to the royalists was not always voluntary, but it is true that there were many yeomen and handicraftsmen in the king's ranks, as the parliament's records of delinquents amply demonstrate. But the king's party was essentially the party of gentlemen, who dominated its whole ethos. It was the more deferential and the less independent of the middle and poorer sort that followed the king, accepting the lead of their social superiors and contributing little to the royalist cause except perhaps a more virulent hostility towards puritans and puritanism. But the parliamentarian party derived crucial support from the middle rank of the people, which sustained and stiffened it, gave the direction to the cause, and effective leadership below the level of the gentry to the mass of the people. The middle sort of people who supported parliament did not generally do so merely out of respect for their social superiors or at the behest of the parliamentarian gentry and clergy, but for their own political and religious ideals, and they. injected into the parliamentarian cause an emphasis on godly reformation and a growing note of social rebellion.

A GODLY WAR

In both town and country the more deeply committed parliamentarians generally came from the 'godly people'. 'Yet was it principally the differences about religious matters that filled up the parliament's armies, and put the resolution and valour into their soldiers, which carried them on in another manner than mercenary soldiers are carried on. Not that the matter of bishops or no bishops was the main thing, (for thousands that wished for good bishops were on the parliament's side)... But the generality of the people through the land (I say not all, or every one) who were then called Puritans, Precisians, Religious Persons, that used to talk of God, and Heaven, and Scripture, and Holiness, and to follow sermons, and read books of devotion, and pray in their families, and spend the Lord's Day in religious exercises, and plead for mortification, and serious devotion, and strict obedience to God, and speak against swearing, cursing, drunkenness, profaneness, etc, I say, the main body of this sort of men, both preachers and people, adhered to the parliament.'[118] A great number of those persons that were accounted most religious fell in with the parliament, and 'the generality of the stricter diligent sort of preachers joined with them'. 'And abundance of the ignorant sort of the country, who were civil, did flock in to the parliament, and filled up their armies afterward, merely because they heard men swear for the Common Prayer and bishops, and heard others pray that were against them; and because they heard the king's soldiers with horrid oaths abuse the name of God, and saw them live in debauchery, and the parliament's soldiers flock to sermons, and talking of religion, and praying and singing psalms together on their guards.'[119] But Baxter was well aware that some 'religious men' supported the king and that many more were neutral;[120] and the fact that the royalists took all 'puritans' for their enemies, without inquiring whether they supported parliament or not, drove many of them to seek refuge in parliament's garrisons and armies and to take up arms in self-defence.[121] Nevertheless parliament was pledged to the reform of the church and to the reformation of men's lives; it was supported by leading reforming preachers; and so those who looked for reform of the church in a more protestant direction and for vigorous efforts to suppress vice and promote godliness, inevitably gravitated towards the parliamentarian side.

In the popular resistance to the royalists in certain parts of the country in the summer and autumn of 1642, the 'godly people' played a key part. When lord Strange and the royalist gentry entered Manchester on 15 July 1642 the riot that drove him out again was organized by 'some truly pious in the town'.[122] The great crowd that gathered on the Mendip hills in Somerset in August 1642, in response to the appeals of the parliamentarian gentry to drive the marquis of Hertford and the royalists from Wells, passed the night in the open, 'fasting and in the cold, and spent the time in prayers and singing of psalms'.[123] Colchester, in the view of the royalists, 'had been long possessed with the spirit of disobedience to the doctrine and discipline of the church, and heresy is always the forerunner of rebellion';[124] and the riot against Sir John Lucas was provoked by religious radicals, and the mob reserved its most violent expressions of hatred for the anti-puritan minister of Trinity church.[125] Boston, Lincolnshire, which propped up the resistance of Hull, was a 'factious and schismatical' town that declared enthusiastically for parliament from the beginning.[126] 'Religious feeling in Birmingham among a large part of the inhabitants was moving in the direction of puritanism... Dislike of the king's religious policy might well be increased by the "rayling sermons" of Orton, the curate';[127] and it was Birmingham men that precipitated Coventry's defiance of the king. Opposition to the earl of Newcastle at Newcastle upon Tyne did not come from the chief men of the town but from 'the labourers in the coal trade', who were 'the most puritanically inclined part of the population' and the 'largest single group' associated with the puritan movement in the town.[128]

The parts that rose in arms for parliament in 1642-3 were frequently those in which puritanism was strong, or there was a core of militant puritans. The small clothiers of the West Riding of Yorkshire were generally puritans. The people of the huge parish of Halifax claimed that by means of the cloth trade 'and of godly and true religion there professed and embraced, many thousands of his majesty's subjects are nourished and exercised in godly labour, many poor people and their families honestly maintained and virtuously brought up, a great number of impotent and aged persons relieved'. They recorded that the inhabitants of the parish 'out of zeal to God's holy religion, do freely and voluntarily, at their own charges, maintain and give wages to ten preachers, over and above the payment of all tithes and oblations... and by the special grace of God there is not one popish recusant inhabiting in the said great and populous parish'.[129] 'There were some places, some whole corporations', Clarendon wrote of the West Riding, 'so notoriously disaffected, especially in matters relating to the church, that they wanted only conductors to carry them into rebellion.'[130] When the earl of Newcastle's army advanced on Bradford in December 1642, 'many of the best affected' to the parliament fled from the town, but it was 'some religious persons in the parish' who resolved to stand it out and organized the successful resistance.[131] When the Fairfaxes summoned the West Riding to rise against the royalists in January 1643, one of the many puritans who responded to their call recorded the spirit in which the decision was taken: 'When I put my hand to the Lord's work... I did it not rashly, but had many an hour and night to seek God, to know my way'.[132] They stormed into Leeds, led by Jonathan Scholefield, minister of Croston chapel in Halifax parish, singing the 68th psalm, 'Let God arise, and then his enemies shall be scattered and those that hate him flee before him.'[133]

In south-east Lancashire the economic ties between the countryside and Manchester were reinforced by the puritanism that they shared. 'The more forward in raising companies into arms was Salford Hundred especially Manchester. And it is very observant what willingness and alacrity of spirit God put into the hands of the men of that Hundred there being no compulsion but all freely put themselves under such captains as they judged most convenient for them. And of those that first put themselves into arms were men of the best affection to religion'.[134] The countrymen who came to the defence of Manchester from the surrounding villages on 24 and 25 September 1642, when the earl of Derby and the royalists advanced from Warrington to attack the town, were 'religious honest men, of a civil and inoffensive conversation, which came out of conscience of their oath and protestation'. Throughout the siege the defenders 'from first to last had prayers and singing of psalms daily at the street ends', and in the town 'a spirit of piety and devotion in prayers and singing of psalms rested generally upon persons and families, yea taverns and inns where it might not put in the head formerly'. 'God kept up the soldiering spirit' of the defenders and the townsmen, 'by prayers and psalms, mutual encouragement, and the blast of the silver trumpets (the ministers of God)'. They were sustained by the belief 'that God had not mustered his precious servants, from all adjacent parts in Manchester, to shut them up into the hands of the enemy, but rather to show them his salvation'. When some of the leading gentry wanted to accept the earl of Derby's terms for the surrender of the town, it was William Bourne, the aged puritan minister and senior fellow of the collegiate church of Manchester, who played a crucial role in securing the rejection of the terms by the common soldiers. When the earl abandoned the siege 'the saints sung the Song of Moses' in the church, and outside in the streets the soldiers joined in, 'with a loud voice and one consent, clapping their hands apace they reported God fearful in praises, working wonders'.[135]

After this success the question was whether Manchester should remain on the defensive or launch attacks on the royalists throughout Lancashire. It was the religious party in Manchester that favoured an offensive war. 'God made a comfortable appearance that he had not saved Manchester to the intent they should sit still, nor had he placed a garrison there, to make their mountain to stand strong, but that they might be ready for action at the beat of his drum'. 'Nor were they satisfied with their own enlargement, but considering that God had not lent them power and ability to free and enlarge themselves, but that there was some other end in it, which consideration produced a public consultation'. Many of the gentry leaders favoured a defensive war but the religious party referred the question to god for decision: they proclaimed a fast and prayer-meeting in the church from seven in the morning until eight at night, 'many of them not stirring out of the church, until all their sacred exercises of prayer and preaching were duly finished'. God struck up his drum and instructed them to make their freedom the instrument of other men's freedom; and the town resolved to summon the country and to assault the royalists.[136] The puritans of Manchester and its neighbouring villages led the conquest of Lancashire by the parliamentarians. 'The honest-hearted and most courageous Manchesterians... are the principal men in the kingdom, next to the most famous and renowned city of London, that fight most prosperously for God and true religion'.[137] But not the 'Manchesterians' alone, for they were joined by the godly people of other towns and of some of the rural areas of the county: William Critchlaw of Longworth in the parish of Bolton belonged to a family that had long been accustomed to hold meetings in their house with 'some other Christians' 'for conference and prayer' (the bishops and Charles I's government called such meetings illegal conventicles and tried to put them down); he 'was an affectionate, solid and zealous Christian... In the wartime, though he was not a soldier, yet when he heard of a fight near at hand, or a town to be taken by the parliament's army he used to take his musket, and run to the army and be foremost in any hazardous expedition, which cost him his life, for when Colonel Holland, and Colonel Ashton with their regiments went to Wigan, though the town was taken yet this zealous champion got shot in the shoulder, and another bullet in the thigh, he was brought to his daughter's in Bolton, and there about a fortnight after died of those wounds'.[138]

At Nottingham when the royalist sheriff threatened to come to the town with a troop of horse: 'All the devout people of the town were very vigorous and ready to offer their lives and families' for parliament, 'but there was not half the half of the town that consisted of these; the ordinary civil sort of people coldly adhered to the better'. The town could not be held without help from the country, so they 'sent notice to all the towns about Nottingham, desiring the well-affected to come in to their assistance; which the ministers pressing them to do, upon Christmas-day, 1642, many came to them', 'very honest, godly men'.[139] 'The garrison of Coventry consisted half of citizens, and half of countrymen: the countrymen were such as had been forced from their own dwellings, the most religious men of the parts round about, especially from Birmingham, Sutton Coldfield, Tamworth, Nuneaton, Hinkley, Rugby, etc. These were men of great sobriety and soundness of understanding as any garrison heard of in England.' Thirty puritan ministers also took refuge in Coventry, including Richard Baxter, who was joined by 'the religious part of my neighbours at Kidderminster'.[140] When Gloucester held out against siege by the king's main field army, with apparently no prospect of relief, 'those stuck most to the business, who were held up by the deep sense of religion'.[141] The godly... generally were the parliament's friends', concluded Mrs Hutchinson.[142] They organized, led and stiffened resistance to the royalists, and they had a motivation that sustained them when popular support subsided or defeatism paralysed others, and they fought to win. 'Those who are most religious, have stuck most to the parliament', declared Jeremiah Burroughes.[143]

In Nottinghamshire the first forces for parliament were raised amongst puritan farmers by two members of the minor gentry. One was Henry Ireton: 'a very grave, serious, religious person', who had an upbringing 'in the strictest way of godliness', 'the chief promoter' of 'the parliament, and the godly interest in the county'. He recruited a troop of horse in the summer of 1642 'of those godly people which the cavaliers drove' from their homes.[144] The other was Charles White, who raised a troop of dragoons about the same time amongst his neighbours, 'who armed and mounted themselves out of devotion to the parliament's cause'. It is not necessary to take seriously Mrs Hutchinson's very prejudiced account of White, for at her hands his character suffered the fate of all those who opposed her husband, but it does bring out that it was 'godliness', whether real or assumed, that gave to minor gentry the influence and authority to raise and command forces of the godly. He 'was of mean birth and low fortunes, yet had kept company with the underling gentry of his neighbourhood... Knowing himself to be inferior to all gentlemen, he put on a vizard of godliness and humility, and courted the common people with all the plausibility and flattery that could be practised... To keep up a fame of godliness, he gave large contributions to puritan preachers, who had the art to stop the people's mouths from speaking ill of their benefactors. By a thousand arts this fellow became popular, and so insinuated himself into all the gentlemen that owned the parliament's party'.[145] Mrs Hutchinson's husband belonged to a well-established and influential county family, and though not yet head of the house, he could command the deferential support of tenants and dependents that Ireton and White lacked. He raised a company of foot 'out of the country' that came 'for love of him', but even they were 'very honest, godly men' that also came for love of 'the cause'.[146] Adam Martindale, a Lancashire puritan, became clerk to the regiment of foot raised by Colonel John Moore in and about Liverpool, and he 'enjoyed sweet communion with the religious officers of the company, which used to meet every night at one another's quarters, by turns, to read scripture, to confer of good things, and to pray together'.[147]

In Huntingdonshire and Cambridgeshire Oliver Cromwell raised a troop of horse, and 'he had a special care to get religious men into his troop: these men were of greater understanding than common soldiers, and therefore were more apprehensive of the importance and consequence of the war; and making not money, but that which they took for the public felicity, to be their end, they were the more engaged to be valiant; for he that maketh money his end, doth esteem his life above his pay, and therefore is like enough to save it by flight when danger comes, if possibly he can: but he that maketh the felicity of church and state his end, esteemeth it above his life, and therefore will the sooner lay down his life for it. And men of parts and understanding know how to manage their business, and know that flying is the surest way to death, and that standing to it is the likeliest way to escape; there being many usually that fall in flight, for one that falls in valiant fight. These things it's probable Cromwell understood; and that none would be such engaged valiant men as the religious'; and, besides, they would avoid 'those disorders, mutinies, plunderings, and grievances of the country, which debauched men in armies are commonly guilty of'.[148] He attracted to his regiment of horse religious radicals, not only from his own locality but from other parts of England as well, 'who upon matter of conscience engaged in this quarrel, and under Cromwell, And thus being well armed within, by the satisfaction of their own consciences, and without, by good iron arms, they would as one man stand firmly and charge desperately.'[149] He chose 'godly, precious men' for his officers; and a critic exclaimed: 'If you look upon his own regiment of horse, see what a swarm there is of those that call themselves the godly; some of them profess to have seen visions and had revelations.'[150]

There was a strongly puritan element in the earl of Essex's army. Nehemiah Wharton, a godly apprentice of London, volunteered for the army in order to fight 'the Lord's battle'.[151] His letters to his master described the appetite of the soldiers for sermons by puritan preachers, which 'wrought wonderfully upon many of us, and doubtless has fitted many of us for death, which we all shortly expect'.[152] Richard Baxter visited the army 'and there was such excellent preaching among them at Worcester, that I stayed there among them a few days'.[153] Wharton continued by describing how, when they had to spend the night in the open and in the rain, the soldiers sang psalms until morning.[154] They plundered the papists; they destroyed the rails around communion tables, smashed stained-glass windows, tore the books of common prayer, and ripped up surplices for handkerchiefs.[155] In Northamptonshire 'our soldiers sallied out about the country and returned in state, clothed in surplice, hood, and cap, representing the Bishop of Canterbury'.[156] At Coventry they seized 'an old base priest...

and led him ridiculously about the city'.[157] Arriving in Hereford on a Sunday, 'about the time of morning prayer, we went to the Minster, where the pipes played and the puppets sang so sweetly that some of our soldiers could not forbear dancing in the holy choir, whereat the Baalists were sore displeased. The anthem ended, they fell to prayer, and prayed so devoutly for the king, the bishops, etc; and one of our soldiers with a loud voice said, "What! never a bit for the parliament" which offended them much more. Not satisfied with this human service we went to divine; and, passing by, found shops open, and men at work, to whom we gave some plain dehortations, and went to hear Mr Sedgwick, who gave us two famous sermons'.[158] At Coventry 'a whore which had followed our camp from London was taken up by the soldiers, and first led about the city, then set in the pillory, after in the cage, then ducked in a river, and at last banished from the city'.[159] Thus Wharton gives a picture of the raw, popular puritanism in the earl of Essex's army; a picture which embraces the main features of the puritan movement—anti-papist and anti-clerical, seeking to enforce sabbatarianism and a stricter moral discipline, and to remove from the church all relics of popery, such as communion tables railed in like altars, ministers in surplices, images in stained-glass windows, and to bring in more preaching and less ceremony.

Robert Kyrle, the son of a Herefordshire gentleman, returned from service in the wars on the continent to become captain of a troop of horse in the earl of Stamford's regiment, and subsequently serjeant-major of the regiment. His reaction to the religious enthusiasm that he found in the army differed from Wharton's: 'Those few regiments then with us, were a perfect model of the whole army; and most certain I am, that all the officers of no one company were all of the same opinion what religion they fought for: some loved the book of common prayer and bishops, others were zealous for extemporary prayers and elders; another thought bishops so many elders, and elders so many bishops; and therefore they fought to set Jesus Christ in his throne, (meaning Independency): some liked the chaplain of the regiment, another thought his corporal preached better... and one would think, that every company had been raised out of the several congregations of

Amsterdam'.[160] He deserted to the king. Some of the soldiers viewed the conflict as a war between Christ and Antichrist which preluded the Second Coming of Christ to establish his kingdom in this world. A royalist clergyman 'asked parliamentary prisoners at Shrewsbury why they had taken up arms against their sovereign and was told: " 'tis prophesised in the Revelation, that the Whore of Babylon shall be destroyed with fire and sword, and what do you know, but this is the time of her ruin, and that we are the men that must help to pull her down" '.[161] Military service gave religious radicals of all sorts the opportunity to propagate their opinions amongst their fellow-soldiers, but also to carry their ideas to the civilian population up and down the country, in big cities and small towns, in villages and remote hamlets.[162]

Of course the large majority of parliament's soldiers were not 'godly men'. But service in the armies and garrisons was a formative circumstance, bringing them new experiences, shaking their old assumptions and exposing them to new influences. There was a puritan leaven in the parliament's forces, especially amongst the junior officers, serjeants and corporals, and concentrated in the horse regiments; and no doubt some of the common soldiers were influenced by the ideas they heard preached and discussed, learning for the first time about the religious and political issues at stake in the war. Nehemiah Wharton thought that the sermons of the puritan preachers had a great effect in disciplining the earl of Essex's soldiers and that they 'subdued and satisfied more malignant spirits amongst us than a thousand armed men could have done'.[163] The godly were more prominent amongst the commanders and senior officers in the New Model than in the earl of Essex's army, but still a minority amongst the rank and file. Hugh Peter declared that there were 5,000 'saints' in the New Model, but this was less than a quarter of the army;[164] and Baxter estimated the really radical at not much more than a thousand, or one in twenty of the soldiers.[165]

At first it had been assumed by the leaders and the pamphleteers that the conflict was primarily a constitutional and political one, but as puritans and, more especially, the religious extremists, the separatists, came to the support of parliament, playing key roles and gaining influential positions, religious issues were increasingly stressed and the war assumed more of a religious character. Gentry who were not puritans, but had supported parliament on constitutional and political grounds, became uneasy as the parliamentarian cause became more religious, and they relapsed into inactivity, neutrality or shifted to the king's side. One such was Sir John Hotham, who 'was a man that loved liberty, which was an occasion to make him join with the puritan party', though 'in more than concerned the civil liberty he did not approve their ways'.[166] 'He was manly for the defence of the liberty of the subject and privilege of parliament, but was not at all for their new opinion in church government';[167] and he 'was as well affected to the government of the Church of England... as any man that had concurred with them'.[168] Early in 1643 he was anxious for a speedy peace, and when that did not materialize he contemplated joining the king.[169]

The puritans challenged the view that the issues were primarily or only secular. Baxter dated the change in the character of the parliamentarian cause from a political to a religious one, to the beginning of 1643, with the publication of a tract entitled **Plaine English**.[170] Its author insisted that the only peace settlement that would be acceptable to parliament's supporters would be 'such an one as may extirpate popery and superstition, lay the grounds of a pious painful ministry, and to that end cast out those scandalous seditious persons, who have now showed themselves as ill affected to the state as formerly to the church... Such an one as may purge our doctrine... reform our discipline and make it more conducible to the end of all discipline, the preservation of a church from corruption in doctrine and manners. And let it be weighed whether that can be done without the supplanting... the bishops'.[171] This was not especially radical, but since the war had broken out over such questions as the control of the militia, the command of forts and garrisons, such as Hull, and the powers of the two Houses of Parliament, the religious supporters of parliament were suspicious that peace negotiations would be concerned with such questions and ignore religious issues; and that in a compromise peace the two Houses would make concessions to the king in ecclesiastical matters in return for concessions from him in constitutional matters, abandon the reformation of the church, and throw overboard their radical religious supporters. For this reason the religious radicals tended to oppose peace negotiations and to urge the vigorous prosecution of the war.

Seen in religious terms, as a conflict between god and the devil, the difference was irreconcilable and could not be resolved by negotiation or compromise, but only by the total defeat of the devil's party. 'Why, but though the house of the church is beset round with these Children of Belial, and they have forced the Spouse of Christ before their Lord's face, yet may there not be some way taken for an accommodation?' But this is an impossible work 'to accommodate a peace for Christ, whose House is beset round now, and His Spouse forced before His face, and His servants all have vowed, that they will not lay down arms till these horrid rebels be given up to the justice of the court... Believe then, that it is as impossible to accommodate a peace here, as it is to accord most contrary things, which stand in an eternal opposition, as the two Poles, or Christ and Belial. It is as possible to set those stars South and North together one by the other, to bring up Hell to Heaven, as to bring this business to a fair accommodation.'[172] 'To what end should we waste time about a discourse of Hull, and the militia? Come speak to the point. If a king of the protestant profession should give his strength and power to his queen a papist, and she give it to the jesuits, to the Beast, it is neither rebellion nor treason to fight for the king, to recover his power out of the hand of the Beast; I say, for the king, that the power regained may be settled upon the king's royal person, and posterity; and then it is to be hoped that the king and they will take warning and beware how they trust out their power another time. We are engaged to fight against the Anti-Christian faction by our very baptism', but must 'fight from Scripture motives, not from politique considerations'.[173] 'More affection should be for Christ's fundamental laws, for religion, than for the fundamental laws of a kingdom, or for the power and privileges of parliament... If prelates, papists and malignants be hated only as hurtful to your state, to the gain and external peace of the Commonwealth, and not as God's enemies, as idolaters, as they are under the King of the Bottomless Pit, the Antichrist... and not as servants of our king;

the war is shedding of innocent blood'.[174]

Prynne was one of the publicists for the parliamentarian party who reappraised the position in 1643. 'He claimed that parliament had not originally thought of resistance: the rescue of the king from his evil counsellors was the limit of its aims. But, by 1643, Prynne contended that the royalist army was papist-ridden, and that, therefore, the issue had changed. There was a grand conspiracy against the protestant religion, "the very embryo and primitive cause of this deplorable war": a conspiracy on a scale extensive enough to justify resistance.' [175] The redefinition of the cause was officially proclaimed by the puritan establishment in a sermon preached by Stephen Marshall on 18 January 1644 to the two Houses of Parliament, the earl of Essex, the lord mayor, aldermen and Common Council of London, the members of the Assembly of Divines and the Scots Commissioners: 'Noble and resolute commanders, go on and fight the battles of the Lord Jesus Christ, for so I will not now fear to call them, for although indeed at the first, the enemy did so disguise their enterprises, that nothing clearly appeared, but only that you were compelled to take up arms for the defence of your liberties, and to bring rebels and traitors to condign punishment, but now they have engaged all the Antichristian world so far, that all Christendom... do now see, that the question in England is, whether Christ or Antichrist shall be Lord or King, all in the world... see it; the Protestants owning the one, and the papists and popish-affected the other, as their cause.'[176]

The question was no longer 'whether the town of Hull shall be the king's: but whether this kingdom shall be the Lord's'.[177] 'We should likewise be encouraged to lay out ourselves freely now when the Almighty stands up, nay, when the Lord of Hosts is pleased to become the God of our armies, and to fight for us against our enemies: Oh! that we could now join hearts and hands, and stand up as one man in the common cause of the Church and State; now, I say, that God hath displayed a banner for them that fear him, and for the truth; now that God hath given out a Commission of Deliverance for Jacob; now that deliverance begins to come, we might pull it home to us by our wrestlings with God in prayer, and by going out into battle, to help the Lord against the mighty.' [178]

The conversion of the parliamentarian cause from a constitutional to a religious struggle took place during 1643. It was deplored by non-puritan parliamentarians, by moderates, and by all who hoped for a speedy, negotiated, compromise peace. 'I must confess', wrote John Greene in his diary at the beginning of 1643, 'I see little hopes of any accommodation, least of a final victory on either side yet... God grant I never see it made a war merely for religion'. But at the beginning of 1644 he wrote: 'Our trouble still menaces, the war being fiercer than ever and may probably hold a long time, for now 'tis made a war almost merely for religion, which I feared.'[179]

THE REVOLT AGAINST ARISTOCRATIC LEADERSHIP

There was a democratic undercurrent amongst the rank and file of the parliamentarian party, and a hostility towards the nobility and gentry, from which parliamentarian nobles and gentlemen were only partially and for a time exempt. Parliamentarian soldiers would follow only officers of whom they approved: soldiers in the earl of Essex's army objected to being commanded by 'profane wretches' and 'ungodly' officers, or by a 'God-damn blade... doubtless hatched in hell', and secured their removal.[180] Parliamentarian officers concluded that their men had to be governed with the iron hand in a velvet glove and persuaded by kindness and affability to obey.[181] But parliamentarian soldiers would obey only orders of which they approved: 'Although the horse would not obey Sir Thomas Fairfax, it was not out of cowardice, for the men were very stout and cheerful in the service, but only had the general fault of all the parliamentarian party, that they were not very obedient to commands, except they knew and approved their employment.'[182] Richard Baxter described how Sir William Brereton tried to persuade his men to march from Nantwich to Wem, 'but the soldiers were all commanders, and... they all resolved that they would not go'; but at three or four o'clock in the morning, 'when we thought they had been asleep, their minds all changed, and to Wem they would then go'.[183] In part this sprang from the 'godly' element, who, as a puritan minister explained, had been trained by 'a practical ministry' to believe that God would hold each one of them individually responsible for his actions, and not permit them to plead obedience to orders or the judgements and examples of other men. This made them 'apt to contradict and question.'[184] 'The most religious and the best people were so pragmatical', confessed Mrs Hutchinson, herself a puritan but also a gentlewoman, 'that no act, nor scarcely word, could pass without being strictly arraigned and judged at the bar of every common soldier's discretion, and thereafter censured and exclaimed at.'[185]

The parliamentarian gentry had no easy time in maintaining their authority over their party. Colonel Hutchinson, as governor of Nottingham for parliament, found 'the townsmen, being such as had lived free and plentifully themselves, could not subject themselves to government; but were so saucy, so negligent, and so mutinous, that the most honourable person in the world, could expect nothing but scandal, reproach, and ingratitude, for the payment of his greatest merit'.[186] The parliamentarian nobility and gentry were followed, not because of the rank they held but because of the cause they adopted; they were judged by their faithfulness to the cause and, more especially, by their godliness. The fact that in 1643 a large number of prominent parliamentarian nobles and gentlemen deserted to the king aroused in the rank and file of the party a deep suspicion of their commanders and leaders, and the belief that all noblemen and gentry were royalists at heart. They watched them closely for evidence of treachery. Colonel Hutchinson was godly but he had 'experience not only of the ungodly and ill-affected, but even of the godly themselves, who thought it scarcely possible for any one to continue a gentleman, and firm to a godly interest, and therefore repaid all his vigilancy and labours for them with a very unjust jealousy'.[187] Some parliamentarian gentlemen felt that behind this lay a hostility towards all noblemen and gentlemen. Robert Kyrle, a Herefordshire gentleman and serjeant-major of the earl of Stamford's regiment of horse, complained that parliament's soldiers 'wanted not Scripture for every mutiny, who plunder and call it God's providence, who if they cannot prove any of quality to be a papist, yet as he is a gentleman he shall want grace; and that is title enough to possess the estates of all that are more richer than themselves'.[188] He, like other gentlemen, found this a sufficient reason for deserting to the king's party.

The fact that so many of the nobility supported the king, and that the few who adhered to the parliament became increasingly unenthusiastic and unreliable, led the parliamentarians into attacks on the nobility in such general terms that the exceptions they made for the loyal parliamentarian peers were easily overlooked. On 15 June 1643, following the discovery of Waller's Plot, which implicated a number of the parliamentarian peers in a conspiracy with the royalists, Edmund Calamy preached in 'plain language' to the House of Lords: 'Let me speak my mind freely to you that are gentlemen and noblemen here assembled this day... Consider further the text, *1 Cor 1 26*. "You see your calling brethren, how that not many wise men after the flesh, not many mighty, nor many noble are called"... There are some noblemen called, but not many. There are but few that are great and rich here, and great and rich hereafter... This is the reason why so few of the noblemen and gentlemen of the kingdom appear on the parliament's side in this great time of necessity. "Not many mighty, not many noble are called". Thus it was in Christ's time. The great men and the great scholars crucified Christ, and the poor received the Gospel. The followers of Christ were a company of poor people and silly women... Thus it was in Christ's time, and thus it is in ours. "Poor Lazarus goeth to Heaven, when rich Dives is carried to Hell...".' Turning to the small number of lords remaining at Westminster, he reproached them: 'Let me persuade you to appear more and more publicly in this Cause... Let me exhort you to go on more and more resolutely in this great Cause... I am to beseech you that you would endeavour to approve yourselves more and more faithful to the Cause. It is with us as it was with Nehemiah when he undertook the great work of rebuilding the Temple, he was opposed by the great men especially. The "Nobles of Tekoah" "refused to put their necks to the yoke of the Lord". This is an eternal brand upon them, *Neh 3 5*. Many of the "Nobles of Judah", did seem to help Nehemiah, but they kept secret correspondency with Tobiah, and tarried with Nehemiah only to give private intelligence to the enemy, and to weaken his hands from going on in the work, *Neh 6 17*. Thus it was in Nehemiah's days. And this is one of the miseries of civil war above all other kinds of war: for there are always false brethren, some Judases in civil war. But I believe better things of you. The Lord make you more and more faithful to his cause. Remember what became of Judas for his treachery'.[189]

Richard Vines told the nobility that they must stoop 'to the reproofs of the Word of God, brought unto you by the ministers thereof... Let not your own iniquities take Sanctuary in your greatness': 'The highest hills are the barrenest ground, and I would, that saying did not so truly square to great ones'.[190] 'We all know', wrote Henry Parker, 'that the Apostle saith, *1 Cor 1 26*: "Not many wise men after the flesh, not many mighty men, not many noble, but God hath chosen the poor of this world"; and our blessed Saviour, *Matth 11 25*: "Thou hast hid these things from the wise, and prudent, and revealed them to babes", poor mechanical men. *John 7 48 49*: "Do any of the rulers, or of the Pharisees, believe on him?" The Scribes and Pharisees, great rabbis and doctors of the law, who of all others, should have been the greatest furtherers of the Gospel, and friends to Christ, were the greatest enemies, and most bitter opponents of both... The great men and worldly wisemen, generally in all ages have been most corrupt, and no friends to Christ and Reformation, *Neh 5 7*. "I rebuked the nobles and the rulers and I set a great assembly against them," *Chap 13 11*. "I contended with the rulers", *Vers 17*. I contended with the nobles; the commons generally stood right for the Reformation, and were freest from the sins of the times, but the nobles, and great ones were so faulty and corrupt, that good Nehemiah was constrained to make a great party of the commons to oppose them, and, as I remember, there is such a Scripture as this, "But the nobles put not their hands to the work".'[191] To what a sad condition our state is brought, when we may complain of our nobles and rulers set over us, as once the Prophet complained of Judah's forlorn estate. Thy princes are rebellious, and companions of thieves. *Isa 1 23*. And again with the same prophet, "As for my people, children are their oppressors, and women rule over them: O my people, they which lead thee cause thee to err, and destroy the way of thy paths. The Lord will enter into judgement with the ancients of his people, and the princes thereof, for ye have eaten up the vineyard: the spoil of the poor is in your houses", *Isa 3 12 14*.'[192]

By 1644, wrote Edmund Ludlow, 'it was clearly manifest

that the nobility had no further quarrel with the king, than till
they could make their terms with him, having, for the most
part, grounded their dissatisfactions upon some particular
affront, or the prevalency of a faction about him'.[193] The nobles
who adhered to parliament were most of them constantly
urging peace negotiations with the king and a settlement of the
war on almost any terms. To the militant parliamentarians this
seemed an admission of secret royalism, and to the religious
radicals it looked like treachery to the cause: it led to fierce
attacks on the House of Lords. 'If we will believe hearsay... the
nobles are upon it at this very hour, how to accomodate a
peace... it is reported, they have drawn up propositions, tending
that way, and even concluded... These men, (they are but men,
and they know it, I purposely forbear titles now of nobles and
worthies, now that the honour and glory of Christ is so
trampled upon in the world) these men are better employed
now, in making their peace with God, in thinking on a way, that
will make themselves noble and honourable indeed: whereas,
to consult about a way to accommodate the cause and quarrel
of Christ, and not in his own way, is to consult shame to their
own House, and rebuke to the Church of Christ'.[194]

It was realized, quite correctly, that the leading
Parliamentarians, including the chief generals of the armies,
did not intend to prosecute the war to an outright victory, but
to fight defensively until peace could be negotiated. They did
not, in fact, want to see either side completely victorious, but
to have the war ended in a compromise. 'It was too much
apparent how much the whole parliament cause had been often
hazarded, how many opportunities of finishing the war had
been overslipped by the earl of Essex his army; and it was
believed that he himself, with his commanders, rather
endeavoured to become arbiters of war and peace, than
conquerors for the parliament; for it was known that he had
given out such expressions.'[195] Cromwell accused the earl of
Manchester of 'backwardness to all action' and alleged that this
sprang not so much from 'dullness or indisposedness to
engagement', as from 'some principle of unwillingness in his
lordship to have this war prosecuted unto a full victory, and a
design or desire to have it ended by accommodation, and that
on some such terms to which it might be disadvantageous to

bring the king too low'.[196] 'The war I abhorred', wrote Sir William Waller, for a time the most successful of parliament's generals, 'though I acted in it, as upon the defensive (which I thought justifiable), but it was ever with a wish, that the sword... might be dipped in oil, rather than in blood; that the difference might end, rather in a peace than a conquest; that... the one party might not have the worse, nor the other the better; but such an accommodation might take effect as might be saving of honour to king and parliament, whereby both might have the best. And from this consideration... led me even in the time of my engagement, and upon all occasions afterward, to the last minute of my service in the House of Commons, to vote for propositions, and to endeavour a fair closure with his majesty'.[197] This made sense to political moderates, but to religious radicals it appeared like betrayal. As a policy it alienated even a number of moderates because it prolonged the war.

The reinterpretation of the cause of parliament in religious terms was associated with its reinterpretation in social terms as well: birth and rank were not sufficient qualifications for command without the addition of godliness, and godliness was a sufficient qualification without the addition of birth and rank. 'According to style of honour with us', preached Richard Vines, with greater moderation than others, 'a man may be noble by birth, descent, or blood. And though I be none of the new Switzers, that could wish princes cantoned into the common level; yet I may put you in mind that antiquity of race is but a moss of time growing upon the back of worth or virtue: and if a man carry not the primogenial virtue with him, which first made his race noble, he is but a flower by change of soil degenerated into a weed, as having nothing in him but the wax or matter, without the form and stamp of nobleness. And you know also that nobility is oftentimes the creature of a prince his fancy; which when there is no intrinsical worth to be the supporter of it, is... but nobility by parchment.'[198] 'A king may cause a man to be called "noble", but he cannot make a man "truly noble" ' for the true nobility are the saints of God.[199] 'Whenever Christ comes to the souls of any person, family or nation as their desire', preached Jeremiah Whittaker, 'then and not before, those persons, families and nations, are most desirable of all others... Why doth God prefer his people above all the world? It is not for their birth, their parts, their breeding, but because Christ is formed in them, therefore... God counts nothing too dear for them... For your sakes, "I sent to Babylon, and brought down their nobles".[200] 'In Christ there is neither male nor female, no respect of persons', declared Thomas Coleman: 'The people of God, they walk aright, and all men great and small, must follow them alike... No largeness of parts, greatness of place, eminency in gifts, of wisdom, learning, wit, not amplitude of rule, nor any high thoughts can exempt, but he must subject himself to the condition and courses of the lowest sort, heaven regards not the goodliness of the person, looks not as man looks, for God regards the heart.'[201]

On 29 August 1643 Cromwell wrote to the Suffolk county committee: 'I beseech you be careful what captains of horse you choose, what men be mounted; a few honest men are better than numbers... If you choose godly honest men to be captains of horse, honest men will follow them, and they will be careful to mount such... I had rather have a plain russet-coated captain that knows what he fights for, and loves what he knows, than that which you call a gentleman and is nothing else.'[202] He urged the committee to support Ralph Margery, who 'hath honest men will follow him', and help him to raise a troop: 'It much concerns your good to have conscientious men.' But the committee objected that Margery was not a gentleman. Cromwell replied on 28 September 1643: 'Gentlemen, it may be it provokes some spirits to see such plain men made captains of horse. It had been well that men of honour and birth had entered into these employments, but why do they not appear? Who would have hindered them? But seeing it was necessary the work must go on, better plain men than none, but best to have men patient of wants, faithful and conscientious in the employment'.[203] This cemented the association between the 'godly people' and the 'middle sort of people'. The 'godly people' were probably mostly drawn from the middle ranks of society in any case;[204] but for the middle sort of people who were not counted, or did not count themselves, amongst the godly, their cause and that of the godly were almost identical.

'His expressions were sometimes against the nobility', it was alleged against Cromwell, and that he said that 'he hoped to live to see never a nobleman in England, and that he loved such better than others because they did not love lords'.[205] The earl of Manchester came under attack not only for his unwillingness to press the war to victory, but also he was 'much condemned for his favour and courtesy to gentlemen in matters of sequestration'; and a royalist gentleman believed that in the eastern counties they would be much more harshly treated 'if his power be eclipsed'.[206] Thomas Pury, an alderman of Gloucester and a clothier, represented the town in the Long Parliament, where 'during the war he became increasingly prominent', and of him it was said that he 'bears no goodwill to gentlemen'.[207] 'Many worthy gentlemen', wrote Mrs Hutchinson, 'were wearied out of their commands and oppressed by a certain mean sort of people in the House, whom to distinguish from the more honourable gentlemen, they called "worsted-stocking men".'[208] With aristocratic power crumbling, power in the House of Commons was shifting towards a group of men who were not typical of the squires who composed the bulk of the membership of parliament, they were men of urban origins, of 'provincial and bourgeois background', who had been prominent in the affairs of the smaller towns.[209] It was said that a chief man at Chelmsford 'finds the case there to be far worse than he expected, for while they hoped that the power being wrested out of the king's hand, they should have shared it amongst themselves, they find that either the power is fallen into their hands that are far beneath them, or else hath raised these up far above them, for as he writes, "the town is governed by a tailor, two cobblers, two pedlars, etc".[210] Sir John Oglander of the Isle of Wight wrote: 'We had a thing called a committee, which overruled deputy lieutenants and also justices of the peace, and of this we had brave men: Ringwood of Newport, the pedlar: Maynard, the apothecary: Matthews, the baker: Wavell and Legge, farmers, and poor Baxter of Hurst Castle. These ruled the whole island and did whatsoever they thought good in their own eyes.'[211]

These statements greatly debased the status and substance of the men who were taking power in the parliamentarian party, but they reflected the bitterness of the older ruling families and the wealthy urban oligarchs at being removed from power by men of somewhat inferior rank.[212] In

June 1644 the parliamentarian peer lord Willoughby of Parham wrote to the earl of Denbigh: 'Here we are all hasting to an early ruin, for I cannot see that anything else can satisfy, self-ends so much. For peace I cannot so much as ever expect it nor see a thought by those that sit at the healm tending that ways: Nobility and gentry are going down apace... You are the only white boy I know, for I must confess till I saw this day the noble expressions of you so unanimously given by both Houses... I thought it a crime to be a nobleman'.[213] The earl of Essex was reported to have exclaimed in the House of Lords: 'Is this the liberty which we claim to vindicate by shedding our blood? This will be the reward of all our labours and our posterity will say that to deliver them from the yoke of the king we have subjected them to that of the common people. If we do this the finger of scorn will be pointed at us, and so I am determined to devote my life to repressing the audacity of the people.'[214] During the peace negotiations at Uxbridge in February 1645 the earl of Denbigh told Clarendon that he saw the 'full prospects of the vile condition himself and all the nobility should be reduced to; yet thought it impossible to prevent it by any activity of their own'.[215] Early in 1645, with the parliamentarians in revolt against their aristocratic leaders, the two Houses were forced to pass the Self-Denying Ordinance, which swept the peers out of military commands. A New Model Army was formed, under Fairfax and Cromwell, in which a more democratic spirit exhibited itself, and radical ideas in religion and politics found expression and a platform.[216]

Those of the nobility and gentry who supported the king, or veered towards his side, did so because they feared that the social order was menaced by the middle sort of people. Parliament was supported by those of the middle rank of society who felt that their political, social and economic advance was threatened and blocked by the nobility, greater gentry and wealthy merchants. The issues in this conflict were now crystallised and expressed by the Levellers. They articulated a secular political programme. With their emergence the popular movement finally became wholly revolutionary, because it then achieved full political consciousness, coherent political objectives of its own and the means to express itself in secular terms.

9

THE ENEMIES OF
THE PEOPLE

WHEN the civil war began the parliamentarians identified their enemies as the king's evil advisers, bishops and 'papists'; but by the time the civil war had ended, many more enemies had been added to the list, so that it came to embrace virtually the whole of the ruling class.

The claim by parliament that it was fighting for the king against his evil advisers, had never been very persuasive, even to parliament's own supporters. When Richard Baxter visited the New Model Army in 1645, after its victory over the king at Naseby, he found that many of the soldiers 'took the king for a tyrant and an enemy, and really intended absolutely to master him, or to ruin him; and that they thought if they might fight against him, they might kill or conquer him; and if they might conquer, they were never more to trust him further than he was in their power'.[1] When one of the elected representatives of the common soldiers was asked 'what they meant to do with the king', he replied 'What a deal ado you make with the king; you make the king your God! What is the king more than you, or I, or any other?'[2] In 1646 'many thousand citizens, and other free-born people of England' called upon the House of Commons to 'set forth King Charles his wickedness openly before the world... and so to declare King Charles an enemy'.[3] With the war ended, the supporters of parliament were bound to seek to establish responsibility for all the suffering it had caused, and the renewal of fighting in 1648 redoubled the need to seek out and remove the cause for ever. 'Divers well-affected persons inhabiting the City of London, Westminster, the Borough of Southwark, Hamlets, and places adjacent', who supported the Levellers, asked the Commons to lay 'to heart all the abundance of innocent blood that hath been spilt, and the infinite spoil and havoc that hath been made of peaceable harmless people, by express commission from the king'; and demanded that he be brought to justice.[4]

More significant, however, was the fact that hostility towards the king developed into opposition towards the institution of monarchy itself. This was expressed in terms of Anti-Normanism: the English were a conquered people who had been deprived of their rights and liberties by the Norman Conquest, but by defeating the king and his party in the civil war they had broken the Norman yoke.[5] 'The history of our forefathers since they were conquered by the Normans, doth manifest that this nation hath been held in bondage all along ever since by the policies and force of the officers of trust in the Commonwealth, amongst whom, we always esteemed kings the chiefest'. They have been 'the continual oppressors of the nation', and the Levellers called upon the Commons to recognize the historic significance of their victory in the war and to abolish 'kingly government' and 'to acquit us of so great a charge and trouble for ever, and to convert the great revenue of the crown to the public treasure, to make good the injuries. and injustices done heretofore, and of late by those that have possessed the' same'.[6]

But the monarchy was closely linked with the nobility: they had been the core of his party in the civil war, and his chief support. It was true that some of the nobility were parliamentarians, but they were few, and proved lukewarm and untrustworthy. So for the militant parliamentarians, the fight against 'malignant' nobles expanded into a fight against all nobles, including those who were nominally in their own party. This was expressed also in terms of Anti-Normanism. The nobility originated from the Norman Conquest. Their ancestors were the companions of William the Conqueror and helped him to conquer the people and destroy their freedoms. 'What were the lords of England?' asked soldiers in the New Model Army, 'but William the Conqueror's colonels? Or the barons but his majors? Or the knights but his captains?' [7] The titles, lands and powers of the nobility were derived from the rewards that the Conqueror had given to his fellow 'robbers, rogues, and thieves' for 'helping him to enslave and envassalize the people'. William stole the land from the people to give to his companions 'to maintain the grandeur of their tyranny, and prerogative peerage'. 'And the poor Englishmen having all their livelihoods taken from them, became slaves and vassals unto those lords to whom the possessions were given. And if by their diligence afterwards, they could obtain any portion of ground; they held it but only so long as it pleased their lords, without having any estates for themselves, or their children, and were oftentimes violently cast out upon any small displeasure, contrary to all right.' [8] Thus the Conquest explained how it was that the lords had vast estates, and a few men owned much of the land, and most of the people were tenants under them. Landlords and the whole system of land tenure, with its entry fines, rents and other obligations, were the result of the Conquest: 'Hence come landlord, tenant, holds, tenures, etc, which are slavish ties and badges upon men, grounded originally on conquest and power.' [9]

This myth was invoked to express the recognition that monarchy was embedded in a particular social order—a ruling hierarchy of nobles—which in turn was embedded in a particular economic order, of landlords and tenants, and extremes of wealth and poverty. The landlords upheld the king, 'protecting him from being questioned and his power thrown down', permitting him to be a tyrant so long as they were allowed to be 'petty tyrants' under him, and grow rich by making the people poor; and in return 'he doth defend, uphold, maintain and allow them to rend, tear, devour, rob, spoil, extort and tyrannize over the poor people, etc, and to this end doth invest them with strange names and titles... as Dukes, Princes, Earls, Marquesses, Viscounts, Lords, Barons, Sirs, Esquires, Gentlemen'. [10] Royal tyranny was the power which upheld the oppressions of nobles and landlords: the power of nobles and landlords was the foundation on which royal tyranny rested. Their privileges as peers, their legislative and judicial powers in the House of Lords, were the outer defences and instruments of monarchical despotism. The peers were 'thrust upon us by kings, to make good their interests, which to this day have been to bring us into a slavish subjection to their wills'.[11] 'The present House of Peers' are 'the lineal issue, and progeny' of William the Conqueror's 'fellow robbers, rogues, and thieves', 'having no better right nor title, to their present pretended judicature, than mere and absolute usurpation, and the will and pleasure of the potent and enslaving tyrants, alias kings, of this kingdom'.[12]

It was not only that the peerage had gained its position and power originally by conquest, but also that the peers continued to earn and hold their wealth, honours and authority by oppressing and exploiting the people, in alliance with the king. 'What means some of you came by your titles', a pamphleteer addressed the House of Lords, 'is very uncertain, but this is certain, that most of you gained no part of it yourselves: and the common ways your ancestors gained it for you, was generally by adhering to kings, in subduing and oppressing the commons, or by pleasing their lusts, malice, revenge, or covetousness; for so histories manifest, and those that have been made lords in our times, have been advanced by the same occasions': Cranfield 'for betraying the secrets of the City, and devising ways to shark the people'; Coventry 'for his great abilities in deceivings, and various ways to oppress the people, heaping up masses of wealth by extremity of bribery, extortion, and cruelty... for which virtues, his son, and son's son forsooth, must be lords for ever?'; Montagu 'by the most palpable corruption that ever was; and his son must now remain an earl, and Speaker in the House of Peers'.[13] The people had been enslaved, not just to kings but also to lords. 'For my part', declared a radical spokesman during the debate on the Levellers' proposals in the General Council of the Army at Putney in 1647, 'I cannot but think that both the power of King and Lords was ever a branch of tyranny'.[14] 'The House of Lords... have been and are... ever carrying on both the king and courtiers' designs': 'the Lords and Kings indeed are both one'.[15] 'Our case is to be considered thus, that we have been under slavery': 'the commons of England were overpowered by the Lords', who 'made us their vassals': 'we are now engaged for our freedom'.[16] 'And if ever a people shall free themselves from tyranny, certainly it is after seven years' war and fighting for their liberty.'[17] The putting down of the lords 'will be the restitution of our rights again'.[18] Although the radicals appealed to the past, they were talking about the present, for when challenged on their history, they replied that the history books were written by men who were under the power of the lords, and wrote only what pleased their masters.[19] The radicals' hatred of the nobility was the result of their own experiences.

How was it, though, that some of the lords had not been aware, apparently, that the nobility's interests were identical with the king's, and had supported parliament in the civil war? The answer to this question led the radicals to a profound reappraisal of the causes of the civil war, and to very significant conclusions about the role of the aristocracy. One theory was that those lords who stayed at Westminster had done so with the deliberate intention of sabotaging the parliamentarian cause, and their success explained why so little good had so far redounded to the people from their victory in the civil war. 'Now we not only see, but begin to feel, that the ground of all our wars... have been and is, to erect the power of the king and lords, above that of the people, in the House of Commons... When many of the lords went with the king... many of them also were left here, and sent back to corrupt the House of Commons, to devise plots and stifle discoveries... to pervert the City, to divide the people, to preserve traitors and delinquents from due punishment... to favour rich men and monopolising companies, to crush mean men, impose burthens, and destroy the parliament's armies'.[20]

Another theory was more profound. 'Time hath revealed hidden things unto us, things covered over thick and threefold'. The lords were divided before the civil war because the king had advanced some and not others to the management of state affairs and to profitable offices: those who were disappointed in their ambitions became 'malcontents, and vexed that the king had advanced others, and not themselves to the managing of state-affairs', and they took advantage of the discontents of the people to force the king to summon a parliament, by means of which they aimed to drive out those whom the king had advanced, 'to bring the king to their bow and regulation', and to install themselves in the management of state-affairs and in 'those high and mighty places of honour and profit that is now too much apparent they then aspired unto'. But they were unable to carry through their plan without provoking a war; they could not fight a war without the help of the people; and they could not get the help of the people without pretending to fight for religion and liberty. Their real aims, however, were always inconsistent with the people's aims, for they aspired to establish an 'aristocratical government' and 'to make themselves tyrannical lords and masters' over the people.[21] This interpretation was derived from royalist propaganda during the civil war, but it was placed now in the wholly different context of an attack on the aristocracy as a whole. It showed that lords could, and did, have interests distinct from, and opposed to, the king; but fundamentally all the nobles, both royalist and parliamentarian, had the same aim, and that was power over the people, and they differed only about how best to achieve that aim. The royalist peers sought to get more power with the help of the king, and the parliamentarian peers sought to get more power with the help of parliament. The royalist lords did not object to the king being a tyrant, so long as this ensured their own power over the people; the parliamentarian peers, in contradiction, did object to a royal tyranny which frustrated their ambitions and lessened their power, and so they sought to establish their own tyranny through a parliament which they dominated and controlled, and through a presbyterian church, which was aristocratic in its system of government, on the model of Scotland, where 'the lords and great men overrule all, as they please; the people are scarce free in anything'.[22]

By continuous struggle since the Norman Conquest the people had wrested some rights and liberties from the king and nobility, but the lords sought, in these different ways, to extinguish these gains and bring them back to slavery. Both parliamentarian and royalist lords aimed to make 'their power... answerable to their wills' and to reduce 'all the freemen of England' to 'as great slaves as the peasants in France are (who enjoy property neither in life, liberty, nor estate) if they did not make us as absolute vassals as the poor Turks are to the Grand Seignior, whose lives and liberties he takes away... when he pleaseth'.[23] Thus it was forced upon the Levellers, and other radicals, that the real enemy was not so much the king as the nobility (or the king only in so far as he was a supporter or instrument of the ambitions of the nobility) and this led them to be slightly less dogmatic in their republicanism, and not altogether without sympathy towards a limited or 'popular' monarchy.[24]

Obviously the leading country gentry, who filled most of the seats in the House of Commons, were a sort of 'lesser nobility', with interests, as wealthy landlords and as the rulers of the counties, identical with those of the peers. The more radical supporters of the Levellers drew the conclusion that the gentry were imposed on the people by the Norman Conquest, just like the peers, and upheld the monarchy and the aristocracy in return for a share in oppressing and exploiting the people.[25] The House of Commons, supposedly the representative of the people, was unsympathetic towards the Levellers' demands for the abolition of the monarchy and the House of Lords: it supported a system of mixed government, in which supremacy was shared between king, Lords and Commons, and it defended the rights of both king and Lords to have a veto on legislation. This led the radicals and the Levellers to question how far in fact the Commons did represent the people and act in their interests. In the counties, where the franchise was held by the owners of freehold land worth 40s a year or more, the radicals observed that the electors were generally tenants or neighbours of the person chosen or of his friends, and would not 'hazard his frown, or the lords and ladies displeasure who solicited for him', and commonly were 'more swayed by favour than reason in their choice'.[26] But the representatives of the boroughs far outnumbered the representatives of the counties. These boroughs had been incorporated by royal charters, which granted them the right to seats in parliament, and the mayor and aldermen often controlled or strongly influenced the choice of the borough's MPs. The Levellers observed that these mayors and aldermen upheld the interests of the king, lords and gentry, in order to secure favour in defence of their power over the general body of townsmen, and to obtain more privileges; so they chose as their representatives in parliament such 'as will be for the king, as Caterpillar Lawyers, Coliers [cheats] or lords of the manor, impropriators [laymen who owned tithes], or such like; and it is from those Patent Towns that the House of Commons is filled with so many kingified prerogative self-interest, proud and cheating varlets as now it is'.[27] Some of the boroughs were so small that their 'interest in the kingdom would in many not exceed, or in others not equal ordinary villages', and their electors were so few, or so poor, or so ignorant that they chose 'only those, that either some lord, or great man writes for, and recommends; or else one who bribes them for their votes'.[28]

The result of this electoral system was that the House of Commons was composed mostly of gentry, with some lawyers, and a few wealthy merchants. A great lord could secure the election of as many as twenty of his kinsmen and friends to parliament, and a wealthy squire could secure two, complained Colonel Rainsborough, the most radical of the senior officers of the army, but none of the common people was elected to parliament.[29] This 'hath been one main reason that the lost liberties of the kingdom have been from time to time no better vindicated and preserved',[30] and why 'we can expect never any hope of freedom by a parliament'.[31] Parliaments had thus been perverted into instruments of the tyranny of king, lords and gentry,[32] and become the means of oppressing the people and keeping them in their place: 'For though Magna Carta be so little, as less could not be granted with any pretence of freedom, yet as if our kings had repented them of that little, they always strove to make it less, wherein very many times they had the unnatural assistance of parliaments to help them: For Sir, if we should read over all the huge volume of our statutes, we might easily observe how miserably parliaments assembled, have spent most of their time, and we shall not find one statute made to the enlargement of that strait bounds, deceitfully and improperly called Magna Carta, (indeed so called to blind the people) but if you shall observe and mark with your pen, every particular statute made to the abridgement of Magna Carta, you would make a very blotted book, if you left any part unblotted. Sometimes you shall find them very seriously employed, about letting loose the king's prerogatives, then denominating what should be treason against him... sometimes enlarging the power of the church, and then again abridging the same, sometimes devising punishments for heresy, and as zealous in the old grossest superstitions, as in the more refined and new, but ever to the vexation of the people. See how busy they have been about regulating of petty inferior trades and exercises, about the ordering of hunting, who should keep deer and who should not, who should keep a greyhound, and who a pigeonhouse, what punishment for deer stealing, what for every pigeon killed, contrary to law, who should wear cloth of such a price, who velvet, gold, and silver, what wages poor labourers should have, and the like precious and rare business, being most of them put on of purpose to divert them from the very thoughts of freedom'.[33] Radicals had admired Magna Carta, and their condemnation of it now marked a sharpening of their hostility towards the aristocracy (whose ancestors had forced the charter on the king), and their recognition that parliament was an instrument of class tyranny rather than a bulwark of freedom. Magna Carta was 'but a beggarly thing, containing many marks of intolerable bondage, and the laws that have been made since by parliaments, have in very many particulars made our government much more oppressive and intolerable'.[34]

Nevertheless the majority of the House of Commons had opposed the king in the Long Parliament: but the explanation of this had already been hinted at, for the malcontent lords manipulated the Commons to serve their designs. 'The multitude of burgesses for decayed or inconsiderable towns' gave 'too much and too evident opportunity for men of power to frame parties in parliament to serve particular interests';[35] and through their influence over elections, the ambitious lords obtained a parliament which they could dominate through their dependents, relatives and allies who sat in the Lower House.[36] 'We see clearly it is from the House of Lords, that the House of Commons have been corrupted... the Lords have packed so many of their sons, servants and tenants therein, and countenance all lawyers there'.[37] Thus the so-called House of Commons was really no more than a second House of Lords: 'For we must deal plainly with you, ye have long time acted more like the House of Peers than the House of Commons'.[38] Just as there was little economic and social difference between the greater gentry and the nobility, so their politics were similar: the royalist nobility and gentry sought to strengthen and increase their power over the people through an absolute monarchy; the parliamentarian nobility and gentry aspired to assert their power through parliament and an aristocratic form of government. The latter needed the support of the people and so had to take up their grievances, but they never really intended to do anything substantial for the people, but only by extending the privileges of parliament to increase their own power. 'In all ages public pretences have been made use of, for the advantaging and securing of particular interests... And now O ye free commons of England, remember, at the beginning of this parliament, what public pretences were made use of to unite your affections in the management of their then designed undertakings?... At the beginning of this parliament the whole Representative declared against those illegal practices of the king and his council, touching patents, monopolies, illegal taxes... to the end they might the better catch the affections of the people'. But when the king resisted, and got a party to support him, and war broke out, the parliamentarian lords and gentry beguiled the people into supporting them by pretending that they fought for 'the public safety' and 'freedom'.[39]

Kings, Lords and Commons were enemies to the people's liberties; and so were lawyers, priests and merchants. Lawyers were undoubtedly the most unpopular men in England at the time of the civil war: 'lawyers... who are the manifest perverters of justice, and corrupters of all places', 'lawyers who are the vilest of men, and greatest abusers of mankind'.[40] For those who saw the cause of parliament as the cause of reform, reform of the law and lawyers was the touchstone of the sincerity of parliament's intentions. 'It seemeth a riddle, not only to me', wrote James Frese, 'but also to many thousand in the kingdom, that the greatest contest between king and parliament, being for the liberty of the subject', that 'the commonalty' are 'still enslaved (as formerly) into the arbitrary will and power of a few mercenary lawyers'.[41] The radical barrister, John Cooke, warned his own profession: 'the kingdom is drawing up an impeachment against us, for the errors and corruptions that are in the law and lawyers... He that knows anything in politics, may easily foresee that there is a great storm arising in this kingdom against us'.[42]

The law was slow and expensive. 'Men must travel term

after term, from all quarters of the land to London, tiring their persons and spirits, wasting their estates, and beggaring their families; tending to nothing but the vexation of the people, and enriching of lawyers'.[43] Lawyers charged excessive fees for their services, and fees also had to be paid to the judges and officers of the courts. James Frese asked 'whether it be according to God's law... that justice should not be executed nor administered unto the poor of the land in particular, nor to all in general, without the price and reward of iniquity, I mean without paying to judges, lawyers, attorneys, clerks, jailors, their deputies and servants, their several great (unjust) exacting fees... and New Year's gifts (besides bribes) for expedition and setting down a cause for hearing, or else it may be staved off by many juggling tricks and devices of our lawyers from being heard'.[44] 'Every man complains of the horrible delays in matters of justice', Cooke warned his profession, 'that we have an action to our clients purses, and spin out causes to an unreasonable length... that there is so much expense of coin, and time, that the remedy is worse than the disease, that a man had better lose his right, than go to law for it, and that delays in courts of justice are the greatest nuisance, and grievance to this kingdom: they think it the greatest mystery in the world that a man cannot get a cause ended in two or three years... that a man must spend above £10 to recover £5'.[45] The lawyers were suspected of deliberately prolonging suits by all the tricks and devices open to them in a cumbersome and inefficient legal system, which was riddled with overlapping jurisdictions and uncertainties as to what the law was on any particular matter, just so long as they could go on extracting fees from their clients. They were also suspected of encouraging 'men in unlawful and quarrelous suits, pleading wicked causes for large fees', advising a man that his cause was good, when they knew it was not, and inciting him to go to law, and though in the end he lost his case, the lawyer got his fees.[46] It was believed that the executioners of the law were 'unjust and corrupt, from the highest that sits in the throne, to the lowest, in the most inferior court of justice': 'The lawyers, which are termed the learned in the law, show their tricks of Hocus Pocus to all their clients, by the law, telling them all, their cause is just... and then, which side bribes the judge best carries the cause from the other; and thus the poor slavish people are cheated... and all the pride and vanity of the king, parliament, lawyers, etc, maintained, and these common cheats of England cannot be contested herewith, but argue, none ought to plead in courts of justice, but such as are called to the bar in some of their nurseries of cheating (the Inns of Court)'.[47] The laws and legal processes being in 'the Latin tongue, and Pedlar's French', 'a plain man cannot understand so much as a writ without the help of Counsel', and so complicated that people were compelled to employ lawyers to conduct their legal business and suits for them and '(like slaves) to walk by their light'.[48]

It was not merely that the lawyers exploited the law for their own private profit, the whole system was biased in favour of the rich and powerful against the poor and weak. The rich could afford to pay lawyers and bribe judges, but 'the price of right is too high for a poor man'.[49] There was 'no justice without money' and cases were decided 'according to the purse':[50] if a rich man threatened to take a poor man to law, the poor man was likely to surrender the point because he could not afford to pay the costs of defending a legal action; but if the poor man did go to law, his purse was certain to be exhausted long before that of the rich man, in combating the devices and delaying tactics of his opponent's lawyers, and so have to give up his suit. Juries were no guarantee of justice to the poor, for they were intimidated by judges and lawyers, and bribed by rich men, 'so that it is vain for any plain honest mean man to expect any reason, equity or justice against any sort of you rich and wealthy men'.[51]

The explanation of this situation was clear enough within the Levellers' system of thought: the law and the lawyers had been imposed on the people by the Norman Conquest. 'The Conqueror... introduced the Norman laws' and 'the Norman way for ending controversies' and for dealing with malefactors: 'He erected a trade of judges and lawyers, to sell justice and injustice at his own unconscionable rate, and in what time he pleased; the corruption whereof is yet remaining upon us, to our continual impoverishing and molestation'.[52] He transferred the courts from the Hundreds and Counties to London and made the people 'to come from all places of the kingdom, to seek for justice at Westminster'; he established the terms, officers and forms of pleas, of the courts, and introduced all the ambiguities and uncertainties into the law, with all 'the tedious, unknown, and impossible to be understood, common law practices in Westminster Hall'; he ordered the laws and legal processes to be in French and Latin, 'which is not our own tongue', 'that so the poor miserable people might be gulled, and cheated, and undone and destroyed'; and he forced them 'to plead by lawyers... not permitting themselves to plead their own causes'. All this 'is such an iron Norman Yoke... that if we were free in every particular else, that our hearts can think of, yet were we slaves by this alone'.[53]

The monarchy upheld the lawyers, and in return the lawyers defended the monarchy: 'all lawyers having dependence on the king, plead his interest', and are his 'hackneys, that with their quirks and deceits do deceive the poor people, and keep them in bondage' to the king.[54] 'And amongst those, see their preferment (as it's called) to suck the people; as Attorney, Counsellor, Barrister, Sergeant, and accordingly fees to rob, and they take oaths; and out of this rubbish stuff are all our creatures called judges, and they likewise all to be sworn. And then places of preferment (so called) to tyrannize, and to be the head Tyrants, Sycophants, Wolves, Lions, Leopards, etc, as Duchy General, Attorney-General, Lord-lubber Keeper, Lord Privy-Seal, Lord Treasurer, Lord Barons of the Exchequer, and I know not what great Catchpoles besides these; all to be sworn to their dread Sovereign Tyrant Beast... Then their dread tyrant... doth... all-to-bedaggle them... with hairy skinned robes, resembling the subtle nasty fox with his dirty tail. And because the Lord Keeper, Privy Seal, and Treasurer's long tails should not daggle in the dirt, they must have another sycophant slave apiece to carry up for them, with their hats off doing homage to their breech. Oh height of all baseness! What, will they creep in one another's arses for honour? Why, oh, his majesty's breath of honour it may be blows out there, and therefore he holds up his gown that it might blow him that holds it up, and make him to be called Sir. Likewise those men thus honoured must have a gewgaw silver mace carried before them, with a cross a top of it, to show they have their title from the Defender of the Popish Faith; the Lord Keeper having a fools-bable like a purse carried before him:

now all these lawyers, liars and twelve judges besides with their cowtred caps; and serjeants with their womanish coifs and petticoats on their shoulders, with their barristers, attorneys, etc. Howbeit, they rob and devour the people, striving who shall most play the knave and cozen; so that he may climb up into high places of profit: for all those upholding their king's pre-rogative, their tyranny is unquestionable, that is the reason that they maintain the king can do no wrong; that he is a God on earth, as God is God in Heaven, and that he is the life of the law; all writs, warrants, commissions, etc, his name gives the being to them: that he is the fountain of our honour and magistracy: yea and that he is supreme head ecclesiastical and civil; also that he is accountable to none but God, and all this the better to hide their tyranny'.[55]

The lawyers were amongst the main pillars of Charles I's tyranny, and so amongst the chief causers of the civil war. 'Was ever so desperate a wound given to the laws, liberties and properties, as the predetermined judgement of Shipmoney. Who gave that blow? Judges. What were they? Thieves *cum privilegio Rege majestatis*, who bought justice by wholesale, and sold it by retail. Who assisted them? Lawyers, who undertaking to plead for their clients against it, (pretending one thing and doing another thing for the most part); and betrayed the cause, all to get favour and preferment'.[56] There were a number of lawyers in the House of Commons, many of them being recorders of the boroughs for which they sat, and their task was to defend the interests of the privileged clique of aldermen and rich merchants who chose them. They had an influence in the House of Commons out of all proportion to their numbers, because, 'being a bold and talkative kind of men', they got the chairmanships of committees, and they used their power to prevent reforms of the legal system.[57] As a profession the lawyers were closely linked with the nobility and gentry, as well as with the crown, and the laws and the legal system had been perverted to serve the interests of these 'great men'. 'The pure and genuine intent of laws was to bridle princes, not the people, and to keep rulers within the bounds of just and righteous government', but 'such hath been the interest of princes in the world, that the sting of the law hath been plucked out as to them, and the weight of it fallen upon the people...

Thus the law becomes anything or nothing, at the courtesy of great men, and bended by them like a twig: yea, how easy is it for such men to break those customs which will not bow, and to erect traditions, of a more complying temper, to the wills of those whose end they serve. So that law comes to be lost in will and lust; yea, lust by the adoption of greatness is enacted law. Hence it comes to pass, that laws upon laws do bridle the people' and not their rulers, and 'the web of the law entangles the small flies, and dismisseth the great'.[58]

Such a protest reflected the plight of copyholders who appealed unsuccessfully to custom to defend themselves against lords who were trying to change their tenures, taking from them the right to pass their holdings to their heirs, increasing their entry fines and rents, enclosing their common pastures, denying them security of tenure. It became explicit in the manifesto of the Buckinghamshire Levellers: 'we, the lower sort of people, are made slaves to the wills of tyrants' because the law and lawyers defend the 'merciless privileges' of 'great men, as Lords, Gentlemen, and extorting lords of manors', and 'all wicked customs' as 'slavish and base tenures', entry fines, heriots (payments on death of a tenant), quit-rents, and also tithes, impropriations, and corporations; and 'will stand to justify and maintain any unjust, and wicked, and tyrannical custom, or illegal persecutions of any tyrant whatsoever, although to the utter deprivation and undoing of the poor widows, fatherless, etc, and advancing the wills of merciless tyrants'.[59] The actions of lawyers in supporting the king, declaring shipmoney and other prerogative exactions legal, opposing the reform of the legal system, serving as the agents of landlords and rich men, all amounted to identifying them as the allies and instruments of the ruling class, and the legal system as an institution of class rule.

No longer were the bishops and episcopalian clergy alone the enemies, the smouldering anti-clericalism of the radicals burst out against all the clergy, including puritans. An established church and a professional clergy, it was said, were introduced by the Norman Conqueror, who set up 'a public ministry to preach up the authority divine, and to be accountable to God only'.[60] He and his successors 'dressed up a company of dissembling hypocrites in a formal habit, of purpose to deceive you, telling you, these are the men that will give you a right understanding in all things'.[61] 'Thy priests have gulled, bewitched, cheated, and betrayed thee into these tyrants hands with their sorceries... preaching up the king to be the Supreme Head, Defender of the Faith, God's Anointed; and that if thou doest resist his power thou resisteth the ordinances of God: now all this is but as bridles in thy jaws, and blinds over thy eyes, that thou must be ruled by the Church, and they are thy enemies, and thou must believe them; and keep thyself a good subject to thy Prince, the condition is good: and by all these and a thousand tricks more they do but mould thee to slavery this five hundred years and more, and by this means the king and his creatures ride thee in thy estates and persons and labours. And the priests rule over thy conscience and soul, and keeps thee in all ignorance and malice; and for their so doing thy priests are thy princes and bear rule'.[62] In return for these services to the kings they were given their 'fat benefits', and the worst of all monopolies—'the patent of engrossing the preaching of the Word only to such men as wear black and rough garments to deceive... and have had a canonical ordination from the bishops, and so from the Pope, and consequently from the Devil'.[63]

The people were forced to depend on the clergy for spiritual advice, as on the lawyers for legal advice. The clergy pretended that a man did not become a minister 'as another man comes to be a merchant, bookseller, tailor, etc, either by disposal of him by his friends in his education, or by his own making choice to be of such a trade: no, there must be something spiritual in the business, a *Jure Divino* must be brought in, and a succession from the Apostles... their interest is to make of themselves a peculiar tribe, of a nearer relation to God than other men'. This was to awe the people and to make them to 'take things upon trust from the minister, as if whatsoever they spake, God spake in them'. It was their interest to make the people to distrust their own judgements and understandings, and to make them to believe that they could not fathom the Scriptures without the help of ministers who had studied at the university and had a knowledge of arts, languages, and theology. And, just as the lawyers deliberately made the law obscure and complicated in order to maintain their monopoly of pleading, so the divines deliberately made religion obscure and complicated in order to maintain their monopoly of preaching.[64] They were accused of confounding 'the clear streams of the Scripture', of perverting 'the true Gospel of Jesus Christ', and of scorning 'the simplicity and meanness of the Apostles', so that they could engross 'great livings, lordships, territories and dominions', and introduce 'another gospel suitable to the covetous, ambitious, and persecuting spirit of the clergy'.

The clergy fell into factions and in their efforts 'to supplant one another and divert the people from the prosecution of their own interest', they embroiled states and peoples in wars to maintain their quarrels.[65] They bore a great share of the responsibility for the civil war in England, and were 'the chief causers and still are the grand incendiaries of our present miseries'.[66] It was the division of the clergy into two factions that split the country and it was the divines that incited on both sides the people to fight, 'with their preaching and noises, thumping and bumping the pulpit cushions' and crying 'Oh rise, help your King, help your Parliament: Oh your lives, liberties and religion lyeth at stake: thus were the poor men made murder each other'.[67] Then the clergy on the parliament's side split into two factions, Presbyterians and Independents, and divided the parliamentarian party: the aim of 'the blackcoats' was 'to breed faction and division amongst the well-affected to the parliament, promoting thereby their own interest, which is laziness, pride, covetousness and domination'.[68] They cared nothing for religion or liberty or the good of the people, for their only concern was to advance the profits and power of their own faction of the clergy, and to keep 'their livings and preferments' by establishing their dominion over men's minds and consciences.[69] 'The clergy are such greedy dogs...that they can never have enough... they will be of any religion where riches or profit is to be had, and will be sure to avoid and hate that religion that brings in no profit to fill and cram their fat guts'.[70] That being so, they would support king or parliament according as to which was likely to give them the more power and wealth; 'and it is for those fat benefits that makes them turn changelings, either to king or parliament, which will best furnish their kitchen'.[71] Thus the clergy had their own distinct and separate interest that divided them from all laymen, whether king or parliament or common people; but that interest being to dominate the minds and exploit the pockets of the laity, aligned them with other dominators and exploiters of the people, the rich and the powerful, in a mutual league of common interest and defence. This was evidenced by the observation that the clergy deferred to the rich and powerful and ignored poor men.[72]

Alongside the king and the existing parliament, lawyers and divines, there were the oligarchies of wealthy merchants who controlled town governments and dominated trade and industry through monopoly companies. The governing corporations of the towns were given their powers by royal charters, which made them self-perpetuating oligarchies, composed of the richest men in the towns. They used their position to increase their own dominance over the town's trade and industry and were accused of exploiting their places to line their own pockets. In return they upheld the king's prerogative, from which they derived their powers and privileges. 'All Charters, Patents, and Corporations was devised only to uphold the king's tyranny, greatness, and interest'. They have 'a thing called a Mayor, and she all to be sworn to the king: then she shall be a Just-asse of Peace and Coram, and have a silver Hartichoak or toy called a Mace, carried before her; and she and her twelve aldermen following after in their coney-skin gowns, as so many fools in a Mid-summer Ale: and those petty-tyrants shall domineer over the inhabitants by virtue of their patent, and enclose all, letting and setting of the poor's lands to, and moneys, stocks of moneys to their own use: and claim a privilege from their Charters and Patents that they scorn to be accountable to others, but to their prerogative masters; so that you see all tyranny shelters itself under the king's wings...: these Patents and Charters is the main wheel and prop that upholds the king's tyranny; for by this means the prerogative people, strives to uphold the King and Lords interests, to get favours of them, to hold up their own knavery and deceit'. They gave seats in parliament to gentry and lawyers, who in return helped to defend and extend their powers and privileges.[73]

The lord mayor, aldermen, Common Council, and the livery companies of London had usurped from the commonalty 'the sole power and government of the city, changing and altering your laws and customs at their pleasure, and choosing of mayors and sheriffs, such, and whom they pleased'. The 'prerogative men' of London have 'enslaved not only this City, but been strong instruments from time to time to do the same to the whole land'. They had brought in and countenanced 'arbitrary laws, and unlimited power and government', and enforced shipmoney 'and many other illegal taxes and impositions' 'with rigour and force', and executed the decrees of the Privy Council, Star Chamber and High Commission. 'When before this parliament, the whole land was overburdened with unlawful taxes and patents, then the Magistrates, Aldermen, Common-Council and other rich citizens, joined therein with the king and courtiers, vexing, reproaching and imprisoning all that would not submit to anything imposed, though never so unjust; many of you becoming projectors yourselves, and so betrayed the liberties of the nation, and caused the evils of the Commonwealth to arise unto that height, which have occasioned and increased the troubles ever since.' Thus they 'have been main and principal instruments of all England's woe and misery'. Also, they secured and defended the monopolies of the great trading companies, which were the means of concentrating trade into the hands of the richer merchants, at the expense of the smaller traders, 'to the ruining of thousands'.

The companies of London, which controlled and regulated trade and industry, were governed by a Master, Wardens and a Court of Assistants, who formed a small self-perpetuating oligarchy of the biggest traders or largest manufacturers, and excluded the ordinary members and rank and file of lesser traders and small master-craftsmen from a voice in the affairs of the company, and were suspected of using their power to get more trade into their own hands and to embezzle the company's funds. 'In all the companies the commons and commonalty are all cheated and abused by their wealthy members'.[74] A pamphlet of 1648 complained that whereas 'by the Charters of the companies the Master, Wardens, and Liverymen are to be chosen by the commonalty of the said company; contrary thereunto of late years twelve and fifteen men of the said company have made orders and ordinances in the name of the commonalty'.[75] When the working sadlers of London demanded a voice in the election of the wardens of their company, they asserted that the company was 'set up and ordained originally by the late tyrannical king and his progenitors ever since King William I invaded and subdued this nation', and they demanded to be freed from the Norman Yoke of the tyrannical government of a Master and Wardens who had taken all the power into their own hands.[76] The oligarchies of the companies and the oligarchy of the City government mutually supported each other, and the king. Lilburne accused the companies of being always ready to execute the king's most arbitrary commands and to supply him with money;[77] though in fact the oligarchies of the companies were prepared to support whoever would maintain their powers and privileges.[78] The Levellers linked the monopolies of the great commercial companies in the export trades with the monopolies of the law by the corporations of lawyers and of religion by the ordained clergy.[79] Lilburne, observing the support for the Presbyterians of the rich and middling merchants of London, claimed 'that the temporal and other trade-monopolizers and other prerogative men in London' were the clergy's 'stalking horses, by which they act their designs the more strongly, the one helping the other to enslave the people'.[80]

Thus the radicals, on the basis of their own political experiences, and with the help of the theory of the Norman Yoke, linked together grievances against wealthy and monopolizing merchants, intolerant and tithe-collecting clergy, rich and rapacious lawyers, powerful and oppressive landlords, with the whole system of monarchical and oligarchic government in the state by king and parliament, in local government by mayor and aldermen, in trading and industrial companies by Master, Wardens and Assistants, and in the church by bishop and hierarchy, or minister and elders.[81] It was an attack upon the whole of the governing class: never before had there been an indictment so comprehensive, detailed and coherent.[82]

The guiding thread and linking theme through all the propaganda of the radicals and Levellers was an onslaught on the rich: the rich were the men with power and privileges, which they employed to oppress all those poorer and less powerful than themselves. There was 'a confederacy amongst the rich and mighty, to impoverish and so enslave all the plain and mean people throughout the land'.[83] 'Look about you... see how pale and wan' the poor look: 'how coldly, raggedly, and unwholesomely they are clothed; live one week with them in their poor houses, lodge as they lodge, eat as they eat, and no oftener, and be at the same pass to get that wretched food for a sickly wife, and hunger-starved children; (if you dare do this for fear of death or diseases) then walk abroad, and observe the general plenty of all necessaries, observe the gallant bravery of multitudes of men and women abounding in all things that can be imagined: observe the innumerable numbers of those that have more than sufficeth. Neither will I admit you to observe the inconsiderate people of the world, but the whole body of religious people themselves, and in the very churches and upon solemn days: view them well, and see whether they have not this world's goods; their silks, their beavers, their rings, and other devices will testify they have; aye, and the wants and distresses of the poor will testify that the love of God they have not.'[84] 'Ye are rich', the Levellers addressed the members of parliament, 'and abound in goods, and have need of nothing; but the afflictions of the poor; your hunger-starved brethren, ye have no compassion of... Nay, ye suffer poor Christians, for whom Christ died to kneel before you in the streets, aged, sick and crippled, begging your halfpenny charities, and ye rustle by them in your coaches and silks daily, without regard... it moves not you nor your clergy.'[85] 'O you Members of Parliament, and rich men in the City, that are at ease, and drink wine in bowls, and stretch yourselves upon beds of down, you that grind our faces, and flay off our skins, will no man amongst you regard, will no man behold our faces black with sorrow and famine? Is there none to pity?'[86] 'Ye are so rich, fat and swollen with wealth, that ye esteem far less of plain men than you do of your horses or dogs, which ye feed and pamper, whilst by your means such as we are enforced to starve or beg.'[87] The Levellers condemned the rich for lack of charity towards the poor, and accused them of stealing common lands and purloining 'ancient charitable donations' and hospitals that were meant for the relief of the poor. The diversion of 'lands, goods and stocks of money' from hospitals and the charitable uses to which they had been bequeathed was a widespread and bitter grievance: Sir William Strickland declared that 'there is not a greater grievance in England than the abuse of hospitals'.[88]

In the eyes of the Levellers the basic conflict in society was between 'rich' and 'poor'.[89] But they gave a great deal more precision to this conflict by their fundamental principle that a man was entitled to the fruit of his own labour; that he had a right of property in it and that to take it away from him was theft. In this they were advocating the case of the independent small producers—craftsmen and farmers—rather than of labourers and wage-earners; and when they spoke of the 'poor' they meant artisans and peasants—the 'middle sort of people'. The Levellers condemned the excise because it was taken 'out of the sweat of poor people's brows'.[90] 'Though the poor hatmakers, who earn their living with heavy and hot labour, both early and late, do pay excise both for all the material, and fire which they use, for the bread they eat, for the liquor they drink, and clothes they wear, yet when they have made their hats, and done all they can with great trouble and toil, day and night, they are forced to pay excise over again out of their very labour'.[91] There is, complained Lilburne, 'scarce anything free from excise that belongs to' the trade of soap-boiling, 'or to the backs or bellies of the men that work at it, but the very water; and yet notwithstanding when it is boiled and all hazard run, as spoiling or breaking of vessels, falling of the price of soap, or none vending it, besides many other accidental casualties, yet out of the very sweat of his brows and the industry and labour of the very finger ends, there must excise be paid of so much a barrel'.[92] The Levellers condemned tithes because they robbed the poor, especially 'the poor country people' of 'the tenth part of their labours, stock, and increase', and thereby 'the husbandman cannot eat the fruit of his labour'.[93]

The Levellers condemned the merchants who did not give the handicraftsman a fair price for the articles that he manufactured with his own labour. 'It is very strange to my understanding that one man should do the work, and another man receive the wages; I mean, that the honest clothier who has toiled much in making of his cloth', should not be able to sell it direct to the customer, at home or abroad, for his own profit, but be forced to sell it to merchants, 'in whose power it is to give him what price they please, whereby he is cheated of the fruit of his labour'.[94] This was not a free bargain between two equals, because the clothier had to sell for ready money but the merchant did not have to buy and could compel the clothier to take less than his labour was worth, and so the clothier was placed 'in a condition of vassalage'.[95] The 'poor tradesmen' complained to the merchants: 'you of the City that buy our work...will give us but little or nothing for our work, even what you please, because you know we must sell for moneys to set our families on work, or else we famish'.[96] The handicraftsman had to sell for ready cash not only to buy food for himself and his family, but also to buy the raw materials in order to keep at work. 'When with extreme care, racked credit and hard labour, ourselves and servants have produced our manufactures, with what cruelty have ye wrought, and still work upon our necessities, and enrich yourselves upon our extremities, offering yea frequently buying our work for less than (you know) the stuff whereof it was made cost us; by which the like unconscionable means in grinding the faces of the poor, and advancing yourselves on our ruins, most of you rich citizens come to your wealth, without any kind of remorse or Christian compassion for your so undoing of poor families, and pitifully eating the bread out of the young crying infants mouths.'[97]

The rich lived off the fruits of the labour of the poor. 'I... do confess, that few of our great and mighty men do either work the clay, or make the bricks; but they lay either all, or most part of the burthen on the poor by heavy labour, and sweat of their brows in the heat of the day, not only in working the clay, and making of the bricks, but if they do complain... upon their cruel and tyrannous taskmasters... they are further ordained... to gather stubble too... So that in this life, the rich have the pleasure, but poor Lazarus pains.'[98] 'Oh ye great men of England, will not (think you) the righteous God behold our affliction, doth not he take notice that you devour us as if our flesh were bread? are not most of you either Parliament-men, Committee-men, Customers, Excise-men, Treasurers, Governors of Towns and Castles, or Commanders in the Army, Officers in those Dens of Robbery, the Courts of Law? And are not your kinsmen and allies, collectors of the king's revenue, or the Bishops' rents, or Sequestrators? What then are your rustling silks and velvets, and your glittering gold and silver laces? Are they not the sweat of our brows, and the wants of our backs and bellies?... And then you of the City that buy our work, must have your tables furnished, and your cups overflow... our flesh is that whereupon you rich men live, and wherewith you deck and adorn yourselves.'[99] 'You rich and wealthy men... have... engrossed all our substance into your claws, which we have dearly earned with the sweat of our brows'.[100] 'When a man hath got bread, *viz* necessaries by his labour, it is his bread; now the other that sweats not at all, yet makes this man to pay him tribute out of his labour, by rates, taxes, rents, etc, it is theft... Mark this you great Curmudgeons, you hang a man for stealing for his wants, when you yourselves have stole from your fellow brethren all lands, creatures, etc... So first go hang yourselves for your great thefts of incloseness and oppressness, and then afterwards that you can go hang your poor brethren for petty thefts, as for a sheep, corn, etc.' 'And therefore weep and howl, ye rich men... You live on other men's labours, and give them their bran to eat, extorting extreme rents and taxes on your fellow-creatures.'[101]

However, the rich were condemned mainly on moral grounds, for the use to which they put the wealth that they derived from the fruits of other men's labours, in superfluities, in debauchery, in idleness. Kings, lords and courtiers 'live always upon the abused fruit of your labours and sweat of your brows in an idle, luxurious and sinful condition'.[102] Lilburne objected to the large salaries of the officers of the commonwealth because they were paid out of taxes on the fruits of poor people's labour, which is 'the highest oppression, theft and murder in the world, thus to rob poor people... to maintain their pomp, superfluities, and debauchery'.[103] Walwyn condemned 'such men as use all means to augment their tithes and profits, who being rich and abundantly provided for, yet exact from poor people, even such whose very bellies can hardly spare it; whose necessities ought to be relieved by them, and not the fruit of their labours so unreasonably wrested from them, as oft it is, and the same so superfluously spent, or so covetously hoarded up, as for the most part is known to be'.[104] The merchants took more than they needed out of the fruits of the handicraftsmen's labours and so their 'cups overflow' and their 'plenty and abundance' begot 'pride and riot'.[105] The excise was taken 'out of the bowels of labourers and poor people' to enrich 'the usurers, and other caterpillars of the Commonwealth'.[106] Lords of manors, clergy and lawyers 'do live altogether out of God's way, and in rebellion to his laws: first, because they live without a calling, and so are idle, being vagabonds, and wasters of the creatures, by drunkenness, pride, gluttony and so but vermin in the Commonwealth, and by their own law ought to be put into a House of Correction, and to be made to work. They are rebels against God's command, for saith he, "In the sweat of thy face thou shalt eat bread": by "thou" is meant all mankind, none exempted... "those that will not work, let them not eat", saith the Scripture.'[107] The Levellers attacked the rich for using their power to take more than they needed for a comfortable livelihood, to which every man was entitled, and so depriving 'the middle and poorer sort of people' of their right to a reasonable subsistence. This was closely related to their condemnations of the rich for uncharitableness, and it was an attack on excessive wealth, the abuse of wealth, and the exploitation of the poor. It was not an attack on wealth as such, nor on differences of wealth; it was not an attack on property, nor on the ownership of different amounts of property; it was not a demand for the equalization of wealth, nor for the abolition of private property, nor for having all things in common.

Many of the rich, in so far as they were parasites, battening off the people and performing functions that the society did not need or the people could do for themselves, could be dispensed with, as overpaid officials, lawyers, professional clergy, usurers. And the conclusion was drawn that it was wrong to live off other men's labours: 'I could not with freeness of my own spirit live upon the sweat of poor people's brows', said Lilburne.[108] He condemned the clergy for taking tithes because they 'never labour for it with their hands, nor earn it with the sweat of their brows'.[109] Samuel Chidley, the joint-treasurer of the Leveller party, advocating the abolition of tithes, proposed that 'the clergy should learn to work with their hands... as both Paul and many better men than they did'.[110] Some radicals at Chelmsford were alleged to have declared that 'it is now fit that the nobility and gentry should... work for their own maintenance; and if they will not work, they ought not to eat'.[111] Though this conclusion was drawn by the Levellers,[112] the general tenor was no more than an assertion of the entitlement of the producers (farmers and craftsmen) to a better return for their labours, and of the rights of those who worked with their hands against those who did not. Since the basic social distinction between the gentlemen and the people was that the latter gained their livelihood by the work of their hands, while the former could 'live without manual labour',[113] the Levellers were attacking the foundation of the status system in their society. When they spoke of the rich, they meant those who lived without manual labour and upon the labours of others; and when they spoke of the poor, they meant those who lived by working with their hands, whether the farmer gathering his corn, the small merchant packing his own goods in his warehouse, the handicraftsman working at his craft. They condemned all who did not work, the idle poor as well as the idle rich. This was implicit in Lilburne's defence of private property: 'who will take pains for that which when he hath gotten is not his own, but must equally be shared in, by every lazy, simple, dronish sot'.[114] Indeed, in defending the rights of a man to the fruits of his labour, the Levellers were defending property, for a man had property in his own labour.[115] The basis of the Levellers' conception of property was that it was created by a man's own labour, which was an implicit criticism of the property of the rich, which the more radical Levellers made explicit.[116] A man who had property in his own labour was free and independent; but when the fruits of his labour were forced or stolen from him rather than freely given or sold at a just price, his property was taken and his freedom undermined and he was 'in a condition of vassalage'. The Levellers' conception of freedom was based on property in a man's own labour. Thus the Levellers saw the cleavage and conflict in society as being between those who worked with their hands and sold the fruits of their labours, and those who did not work with their hands but lived off the fruits of other men's labour.

The root cause of the problem, as the Levellers saw it, was the association of wealth with power and privilege, not the mere existence of wealth as such. The fact that rich men ruled the world allowed them to use their position to exploit other men and add to their wealth at the expense of men less rich and powerful than themselves. 'Ye have by corruption in government, by unjust and unequal laws, by fraud, cozenage, tyranny and oppression gotten most of the land of this distressed and enslaved nation into your ravenous claws, ye have by monopolies, usuries and combinations engrossed all the wealth, moneys and houses into your possessions, yea and enclosed our commons in most counties.'[117] Thus the rift in society was never merely between rich and poor, but always also between the powerful and the weak.

Now 'religion' and 'liberty' meant one thing for a rich and powerful man and another thing for a poorer and weaker man. For the former religion meant order and discipline, the establishment of 'truth' and the suppression of 'heresy'; for the latter religion meant the right to think for himself, to express his own views, and find his own way to heaven. For the former liberty meant freedom to exploit other men's labour; for the latter liberty meant freedom to enjoy the fruits of his own labour. The radicals, in so far as they were outside or on the fringes only of the ruling class, were men who were conscious of this difference. The oppressors of the poor and weak were the rich and powerful. If the civil war were a struggle against tyranny, for the common people it could not stop at the tyranny of the king and the bishops, but was bound to extend to the tyranny of the nobility and gentry, the clergy, the lawyers, the rich merchants, who oppressed the people more directly than the king or bishops. On the one side were 'your great ones, whether the king, lords, parliament-men, rich citizens etc', and on the other side were 'you and your poor friends that depend on farms, trades, and small pay, have many an aching heart when these live in all pleasure and deliciousness'.[118]

'The general conclusion was this: on the one side were all the oppressors who "buy large possessions in the earth and call their houses after their own names", and on the other side were the oppressed, "the lower sort of people", or "the meaner and poor people", "the laborious husbandman, handicraftsman, and all kind of honest tradesmen"... The Hertfordshire Levellers even asserted that this division corresponded to the split between the two parties in the civil war, which had been fought by men "whose interest was in the people's oppression" against those who "were oppressed by great men". It was something like a conspiracy of the rich, was another opinion, that made "a prey of the poor people". These Levellers (we may think of them as representing the radical wing of the party) felt very strongly that there was a cleavage between the rich and the poor, between the "great' men" and the "common people".[119] But it was not just the opinion of 'the radical wing' for it was the dynamic of the whole movement.

Thus, between 1646 and 1649, the revolution became an open class conflict, of which the Levellers were the spokesmen. It was a conflict between rich and poor, strong and weak, rulers and ruled, those who eat their bread in the sweat of other men's brows and those who laboured for their living with their own hands and sold the fruits of their labour. This was the only form which class conflict could take in this type of society at this period of time. It was always present but latent before 1640; it came close to the surface in 1641-2 and propelled parliament to challenge the king and the king to resist parliament; it drove parliament to victory, and became explicit in the aftermath of economic hardship and disillusionment with the result of victory. Thus the Levellers and other radicals did not create but gave expression to the existing social conflicts, and revealed fully to view the social issues in the English revolution.

10

THE FRIENDS OF
THE PEOPLE

THE wartime system of taxation fell more heavily on the poor than on the rich, complained the Levellers. The excise 'lays the burden heavily upon the poor, and men of middle quality or condition, without all discretion, and scarcely maketh the rich touch it with one of their fingers'.[1] It 'lies heavy only upon the poorer, and most ingenious industrious people, to their intolerable oppression; and... all persons of large revenues in lands, and vast estates at usury, bear not the least proportionable weight of that burden'.[2] The Levellers demanded the abolition of the excise,[3] and they wanted to include in the written constitution under which they proposed that future parliaments should be elected, a prohibition on the continuation of the excise or its revival in the future.[4]

In place of the excise, the radicals urged a return to the pre-war and traditional system of taxation by means of the subsidy, 'which is the most just, equitable, and reasonable way of all, for it sets every tub on its own bottom, it lays the burden upon the strong shoulders of the rich, who only are able to bear it, but spareth and freeth the weak shoulders of the poor, because they are scarcely able to subsist, pay rent, and maintain their families'.[5] This was enshrined in the Leveller programme by the Petition of 11 September 1648, which demanded the abolition of the excise 'and all kinds of taxes, except subsidies, the old and only just way of England'.[6] The subsidy was a tax of 4s in the £ of the annual value of a man's land, or 2s 8d in the £ of the value of his goods. He was not taxed on both lands and goods, but on the one or the other, whichever was the greater. It tended to fall more on lands than on goods, and merchants and tradesmen with a large part of their wealth in goods escaped very lightly. But the system of assessment being under the control of the wealthy landowners, they passed a disproportionate share of the burden to the smaller land-owners and farmers.[7] In advocating a return to the subsidy, the Leveller leaders were probably thinking in terms of a land tax and hoping that reform of the method of assessment, by means of commissioners elected in every Hundred by 'the freemen' instead of appointed by the crown, would place the burden squarely on the wealthier landowners.[8]

However, it was more characteristic of radical thinking to advocate a wholly new system of taxation on different principles. Hugh Peter proposed to replace all existing taxes by a single tax, for both national and local purposes, on all that were able to pay, 'each according to his rents, estate, trade, and handicraft', unmarried men with an income of less than £10-20 a year would be exempt, married men with an income of less than £30-40 a year would also pay no tax, and the exemption level would rise by £5-10 for each child he had to support.[9] The Levellers also aimed at a more equitable system, and replaced their demand for a return to the subsidy by a demand for an income tax. In January 1648 they urged that 'all moneys be raised by equal rates, according to the proportion of men's estates'.[10] They added to the second Agreement of the People a ban on future parliaments raising money 'by any other way, except by an equal rate proportionably to men's real or personal estates, wherein all persons not worth above thirty pounds, shall be exempted'[11] and they included this in the final version of the Agreement of the People, stressing the liability of 'every real and personal estate in the nation' but omitting the reference to exemption of poorer people.[12] Clearly the Levellers attached importance to a reform of the system of taxation to shift the burden from the poor and middle sort of people to the wealthy landowners and merchants, and to reduce the abuses by which the rich evaded their proportionable share.

The Levellers condemned monopolies in the most general terms in industry and commerce, demanding the abolition of 'all monopolies whatsoever', and that parliament free 'all trade and merchandising from all monopolizing and engrossing, by companies or otherwise'.[13] But they were thinking mainly of monopolies in the export trade.[14] They claimed that it was the 'birthright' of 'every English native' who 'hath propriety of goods, wares, and merchandise' 'to transport the same to any place beyond the seas, and there to convert them to his own profit', and thus receive the full fruits of his own labour and assert his freedom to exclude others from his own property.[15] They argued that it was contrary to the native rights of Englishmen and the fundamental laws of the land to prevent a man from trading to certain parts of the world if he did not belong to a company.[16] Their objection was mainly to the great export companies of London, for these companies almost monopolized the export trade of the whole country. They were convinced that the merchants of these companies inflated their profits by buying cheap from the producer and selling dear to the consumer, and restricted the volume of exports, because they preferred to sell less goods at a high price rather than more goods at a low price.[17] They were expressing the views of the manufacturers and handicraftsmen, who protested at the prices given them for their products by the merchants, and blamed the companies for the decline of exports.[18]

The Levellers singled out especially the Merchant Adventurers, who were attacked as prejudicial to the cloth industry.[19] The cloth producers blamed the depression of their industry on the greater merchants. But the Levellers' condemnation of monopolies went further than the immediate crisis. Monopolies were privileges by which some few men had advantages over all others to get rich, and the oligarchic governments of the companies allowed already wealthy men to grow wealthier at the expense of those less powerful and rich than themselves. Walwyn thought that the abolition of the monopolies in foreign trade would result in there being more merchants, without individual ones being as wealthy as at present, but that trade and profits would be spread more widely.[20] Thus it was believed that free trade would lessen inequalities, and at the same time bring greater prosperity to industry, especially the cloth industry, bringing higher returns for labour and creating more employment. The Levellers were particularly concerned about the cloth industry,[21] because the problems and grievances of the 'industrious people' engaged in it were central to the causes of the civil war and to the dynamic of the parliamentarian party. So they concentrated upon advocating the abolition of the monopolies of the exporters of cloth, the Merchant Adventurers and the Eastland company. But they seemed also to have believed that a wider freedom to trade, in which it would not be restricted in towns to freemen of the corporation, would benefit the small producers in industry. Lilburne took up the case of the silkweavers of Spitalfields when they were forbidden by the lord mayor and aldermen of London to sell their laces and ribbons directly to persons who were not freemen of the City, but only to shopkeepers 'who will give them but what they pleased for them':[22] the silk-weavers protested 'you have put in execution an illegal wicked decree of the Common Council, whereby you have taken our goods from us if we have gone to the inns to sell them to country men; and you have murdered some of our poor wives that have gone to inns to find country men to buy them'.[23] 'Although I am not only a native and free denizen of England', complained Lilburne, 'and served many years to learn a trade in London, yet in any considerable corporation in England can I not with industry be suffered to follow a trade or merchandising to get me bread, unless I be a free man thereof'.[24]

Debt was a critical problem for small traders and small producers: on the one hand they had to extend credit to their customers, and so were concerned about the machinery for the recovery of debts; and on the other hand they frequently fell into debt to those who supplied them with raw materials, goods or services, or lent them cash to tide them over a difficult period; and this was the route by which small producers lost their independence and declined into wage-earners. 'A man cannot well keep any considerable trade in a shop, but he must trust much; which a man many times hazard the loss of; especially in these impoverishing times, or else to law for it'; and though he had good security for the debt, if his debtor were a well-to-do man and had a good lawyer, 'he shall keep a man in the courts in Westminster Hall three or four years in suit, let him do the worst he could, before he could get his money; nay, nor never shall get it neither, unless he have a purse also able in some reasonable measure to hold pace with him: but in case in any of that time (by sickness, loss or other casualties) he happen to fall poor, and so not able in money to pay fees, etc, it's lost for ever'. Tradesmen often had to make use of Chancery, where, it was said, it could cost £500 to recover £100, and suits last ten, fifteen, even thirty years.[25] On the other hand debtors who had the means to pay their debts might prefer to go to prison rather than pay; for, as they had money they could afford to live comfortably enough in prison (quite differently from the poor debtors who had no money), and they would expect that their creditors would become tired of waiting, or become so impoverished and so desperate for something, that they would take much less than they were owed and forgive the rest. The Levellers protested that creditors were defrauded and 'many honest people are brought to ruin' by debtors who had the wherewithal to satisfy them but sheltered themselves in prison; and they demanded that 'a speedy course be taken' to enforce such persons to pay their debts.[26]

However, the radicals and Levellers were as much concerned about the plight of the prisoners for debt who had no money. They pointed out that imprisoning them was no advantage to the creditors,[27] because it deprived them of any means of earning the money to pay their debts. But much more horrifying was the fact that the imprisoned debtor without money had to live on the charity of passers-by who left scraps of food in the basket provided for that purpose outside the prison, and some occasional help from charitable trusts. The Leveller newspaper, **The Moderate**, printed a petition to parliament from many thousands of prisoners for debt in England and Wales: 'That your petitioners having remained some twenty some forty years, in a most miserable slavery (contrary to the Law of God, Nature and Nations, and to the fundamental laws of this land) wanting all that might make our lives comfortable, bereaved of wives and families, fed with the scraps of the basket, our lodging many times the cold earth, wrapped in rags, or straw, under the hellish tyranny of gaolers, and officers, by whom your petitioners are manacled in irons, robbed, wounded, poisoned, starved... the slavery of Turkey not comparable to it. But your petitioners are men, born free, Christians, for whom Christ died... This honourable House having mentioned England's liberty, occasions your petitioners to beg a share in that liberty'.[28] Protests about the conditions of the poor prisoners for debt were not confined to the Levellers, but were general amongst reformers. 'If there be so much barbarous cruelty used in all the world', exclaimed the radical barrister John Cooke, 'as there is in this kingdom concerning poor prisoners, I dare lose my life for it: the Turks and others beat their galley slaves for their pleasures, but they feed them that they may endure the blow, but we cast men into a dungeon, and suffer them to rot and famish', and the law in effect says that as he has no estate 'take his body for satisfaction'.[29] It was a 'cruel practice', 'unchristian', and 'a reproach and prejudice to the commonwealth'.[30] The Levellers complained to parliament that 'multitudes of poor distressed prisoners for debt, lie still unregarded, in a most miserable and woeful condition throughout the land' ; 'ye think not of these many thousand persons and families that are destroyed thereby, ye are rich, and abound in goods, and have need of nothing; but the afflictions of the poor, your hunger-starved brethren, ye have no compassion of; your zeal makes a noise as far as Algiers, to deliver those captived Christians at the charge of others, but those whom your own unjust laws hold captive in your own prisons; these are too near you to think of'.[31]

The Levellers demanded that parliament 'take some speedy and effectual course to relieve all such prisoners for debt, as are altogether unable to pay, that they may not perish in prison through the hard-heartedness of their creditors'.[32] This was a matter of concern to all reformers, especially as the number of poor debtors had increased in the aftermath of the civil war and with the onset of a severe economic depression; but mostly they visualized the retention of imprisonment in some circumstances, while seeking to reduce the numbers and improve the conditions of the prisoners, and they were more interested in making it easier to recover debts.[33] The Levellers, however, went on to insist in the Agreement of the People on the outright and total abolition of imprisonment for debt:[34] clearly their sympathies lay with poor debtors more than with creditors, with the small producers more than with the traders.

In their criticisms of the excise, of the costs of litigation, of the monopolies of the export companies, and of the law relating to debt, the Levellers expressed the views of the small shopkeepers and master-craftsmen. In condemning the economic consequences of tithes they were dealing with a grievance of the peasants rather than the townsmen. 'It is most certain that some men that live in towns and follow a trade, as drapers, grocers, chandlers, tanners, vintners, and many others, in one year, with less pains, cost, and care, do gain more than the farmer doth in all his lifetime... and yet these men pay no tithes or tenths at all, of all their great increase'. The farmer was charged upon his capital, without allowance for his costs, as well as on his profits.[35] A petition from Buckinghamshire described tithes as 'exceeding oppressive and vexatious to all sorts of people, especially the poor husbandman';[36] and the Levellers agreed that tithes were an intolerable burden on 'the poor country people' and 'a great oppression of the country's industry and hindrance of tillage', 'whereby the husbandman cannot eat the fruit of his labours'.[37] Thus one objection to tithes was that they fell more heavily upon farmers than upon merchants, shopkeepers, craftsmen, and townsmen in general.[38] A second objection was that the clergy appropriated too large a share of the nation's wealth: 'the payment of tithes is an unjust and unequal thing in a civil sense, for that the priests, who are not one for a thousand of the rest of the inhabitants in the kingdom should have the tenth part, yea, or rather the seventh part of all things a man hath (saving his children)... is the most unjust thing in the world, and so intolerable oppressing a burden, that the free people of England are not able to bear it'.[39] A third objection was that tithes gave the clergy very unequal incomes: while, it was said, some ministers had £300, £400, £500 or £600 a year, others had scarce enough to feed and clothe themselves, and not enough to educate their children or to provide for their families after their death.[40] Many ministers had such small maintenance that they were obliged to work as schoolmasters, or physicians, or at some trade, and so were only part-time ministers.[41]

Some radicals favoured the replacement of tithes by some new form of tax for the maintenance of the public ministry, which would distribute the burden more fairly over the taxpayers and the income more equally over the clergy.[42] The point of view of the poorer husbandman, who resented the burden of keeping some clergy in affluence, and of the poorer ministers, who had too little to live on, were both met by proposals for the redistribution of the income from tithes, from the richer to the poorer clergy, giving the same to all, and the diversion of the surplus to the poor or secular uses.[43] The Levellers wavered towards the reform rather than the abolition of tithes in the hope of reaching agreement with the chief officers of the army and the reforming gentry; but as separatists in religion they favoured abolition and urged 'that all ministers may be paid only by those who voluntarily contribute to them, or choose them, and contract with them for their labours'.[44] This would have given the people the power to elect their own ministers and to decide for themselves how much of their income they would give to the church, and to pay more or less, according to how well they were satisfied with the minister and his efforts. It would have been the foundation for democracy not only in the church but also in the state. The question of tithes was potentially the most revolutionary issue of the English civil war because it could unite the economic grievances of the mass of small farmers with the religious programme of the separatists.

But in many parishes the tithes had been impropriated, and were owned by laymen, providing rich incomes for some of the nobility and gentry, who paid miserable stipends to curates to perform the spiritual functions of the living, and simply to abolish all tithes would have meant not only extinguishing a property right but also confiscating some of the wealth of the nobility and gentry.[45] In order not to frighten the more radical of the gentry, whose support they needed if they were to push through reforms by peaceful means, the Levellers were obliged to compromise and, while continuing to demand the abolition of tithes, to promise compensation to the lay impropriators for their losses.[46] Even so the clergy would have lost their property, and the property of the nobility and gentry would have appeared less sacrosanct. This was the closest the Levellers came to attacking property, and it is significant that it arose from their religious beliefs as separatists.

The attack on tithes spilled over into an attack on landlords. The Hertfordshire and Buckinghamshire Levellers coupled their complaints against tithes with their grievances against 'griping landlords' who demanded 'extreme rents' and unreasonable entry fines;[47] and some members of parliament observed 'that tenants who wanted to be quit of tithes would soon want to be quit of rent: nine-tenths were due to the landlords on the same ground that one-tenth was due to the minister'.[48] But the main agrarian issue of the 1640s was the enclosure of commons and waste grounds. This struggle ran parallel to the struggle against tithes because in both cases the issue was the preservation or recovery by the community of communal wealth which had been, or was threatened with being, taken from it and appropriated to individuals.[49] The Levellers' leaders gave expression to agrarian grievances, and they opposed the enclosure of commons and wastes. They insisted that the communal use of commons and wastes was the inheritance of the poor, and 'that all grounds which anciently lay in common for the poor, and are now impropriate, enclosed, and fenced in, may forthwith (in whose hands soever they are) be cast out, and laid open again to the free and common use and benefit of the poor'.[50] This grievance found a place in the leaders' statement of their minimum demands and the party's most authoritative manifesto, the Petition of 11 September 1648:[51] 'That you would have laid open all late enclosures of fens, and other commons, or have enclosed them only or chiefly to the benefit of the poor.'[52]

The most acute conflict over the enclosures of commons was taking place at this time in the fens. Lilburne and Wildman defended the commoners of Epworth in Lincolnshire and supported their action in seizing by force the 7,000 acres of their commons which had been taken from them by the drainers of the fens.[53] Lieutenant-Colonel John Jubbes, an army radical who supported the Levellers in 1647 but thereafter was associated with a group of more moderate London radicals,[54] proposed 'that all the marsh lands, fens and common pastures' be enclosed and one-quarter be allotted to the tenants of the manor in which they were situated, one-quarter to the landless poor, and one-half to the soldiers of the New Model Army in lieu of their arrears of pay (a shrewd assessment of the aspirations of the soldiers).[55] Appropriately it was this issue that produced the most revolutionary outburst of the period. In April 1649 a few poor men occupied the common and waste ground on St George's Hill near Cobham in Surrey and began to dig and sow corn. They appealed to the poor all over England to take over 'all the commons and waste ground' in the country and to plough and plant them for their own relief. They were supported by the radical Levellers of the Chiltern Hundreds in Buckinghamshire, and imitated by some poor people of Wellingborough in Northamptonshire, who began to dig and sow the common and waste ground near that town. Under the influence of Gerrard Winstanley the aim was to establish communities without landlords, private property or wage labour.[56] They were crushed by the opposition not only of the gentry but also of the freeholders: the yeomen and the middling farmers did not want to lose their commons to the poor any more than to the landlord. Lilburne disavowed the actions of the Diggers and the ideas of Winstanley,[57] and this reflected the identification of the main body of the Levellers with the middle sort of people, and the irrelevance of their programme to the poorer peasants and landless labourers.

The other main agrarian grievance was the insecurity of copyhold tenure. A struggle was taking place in many parts of the country, in which landlords were claiming that copyholders did not have rights of inheritance in their holdings and that entry fines could be increased at will, and copyholders were defending their rights of inheritance and entry fines fixed by custom.[58] A petition to the army in 1647 from 1,200 inhabitants of Hertfordshire, which was delivered to Fairfax by a deputation of 200, asked 'that the body of the kingdom consisting of copyholders, who have for the most part been very cordial and faithful to the parliament, may not now be left fineable at the will of the lord, in regard the generality of them have been very malignant, and much disaffected to parliamentary or thorough reformation, and from whom they cannot but expect very severe dealing'.[59] A meeting at Aylesbury 'of the middle sort of men within the three Chiltern Hundreds of Disbrough, Burnum, and Stoke, and part of Alisbury Hundred', declaring their support for the Leveller leaders, 'our worthy friends... Mr Lilburn, Mr Walwin, Mr Prince, Mr Overton', protested against entry fines and other payments demanded by lords of manors from tenants by copyhold, which was a 'slavish and base' tenure.[60]

The most significant development was the emergence from the agitation for fixed and 'reasonable' entry fines of a demand for the abolition of copyhold tenure and its conversion into freehold. It found its inspiration in Anti-Normanism, because it was believed that copyhold tenure had been introduced by William the Conqueror and imposed on a conquered people who before had been freeholders.[61] A manifesto of 1648, claiming to speak for 'many thousands' in London and the counties round about, demanded 'that the ancient and almost antiquated badge of slavery, *viz* all base tenures by copies, oaths of fealty, homage, fines at the will of the lord, etc, (being the Conqueror's marks upon the people) may be taken away; and to that end a certain valuable rate be set, at which all possessors of lands so holden may purchase themselves freeholders, and in case any shall not be willing or able, that there be a prefixed period of time after which all services, fines, customs, etc, shall be changed into and become a certain rent'.[62] Colonel Jubbes proposed 'that all enslaving tenures upon record by oaths of fealty, villeinage, homage, and fines at will of the lords, may all be bought in at such rates as shall not exceed twenty years' purchase to the lord, upon a conscientious computation of profits made according to the reign of King James'.[63] Lilburne added to the second Agreement of the People a request for the abolition of 'all base tenures'.[64] But although the demand for the extinction of copyhold tenure and the conversion of customary tenants into freeholders continued to inspire the Levellers' followers,[65] the leaders did not include it in the final programme on which the party took its stand, the Petition of 11 September 1648 and the third Agreement of the People. The evidence of Buckinghamshire and Hertfordshire points to the conclusion that the Levellers' supporters in the country were more conscious on agrarian grievances and more radical on agrarian issues than the leaders in London and their followers amongst the urban craftsmen.

The name 'Leveller' was the slur commonly cast on reformers by the rulers of society. By spreading the notion that they intended to level the rich with the poor, it was easy to unite the nobility, gentry, lawyers and merchants against them; by implying that they would abolish private property and have all things in common, it was possible to incite farmers, shopkeepers, master-craftsmen against them, because they all owned property and aspired to acquire more. The slur could be used against any particular item in the reforming programme by creating the impression that however desirable it might appear on its own and innocent of communistic intent, it was part of a general design of 'levelling'. It was not only wealth or property that was said to be threatened, but also social ranks and the degrees and distinctions of men, and this frightened not only the nobility and gentry but also the middle sort of people, who prided themselves on their superiority over the rabble, and indeed everyone who had somebody below them in the hierarchy of social status. The slur would not have been so successful if there had not been genuine fears that some, or all, of what the Levellers were saying would lead to social revolution, or would stir up the poor, even if the leaders did not intend it, to attack the rich and seize their property.

The Levellers were anxious to counter this propaganda, for, whatever their opinions of the richer classes, their aim was to achieve specific reforms, as outlined in their manifestos, with the help of the more radical of the gentry and chief officers of the army. In their apologia, 'in which... is to be seen all our very hearts',[66] the Leveller leaders insisted 'that we never had it in our thoughts 'to level men's estates'.[67] In the petition of 23 November 1647 they had complained of being 'reproached and slandered with... strange endeavours to level all men's estates';[68] and in the most authoritative statement of their aims, the petition of 11 September 1648, they demanded that 'all future parliaments' be bound 'from abolishing propriety, levelling men's estates, or making all things common'.[69] They incorporated this into the final version of their proposed constitution, denying to the legislature any power to 'level men's estates, destroy propriety, or make all things common'.[70] Lilburne claimed that the Levellers were 'the truest and constantest assertors of liberty and propriety (which are quite opposite to community and levelling)'; and that there was nothing in their writings or declarations 'that doth in the least tend to the destruction of liberty and propriety or to the setting up of levelling by universal community or anything really and truly like it'.[71] He endeavoured to dissociate the movement from 'all the erronious tenets of the poor Diggers at George Hill in Surrey'.[72] But the statements of the Leveller leaders were not always without ambiguity: they explained the prohibition of the legislature from levelling on the grounds that in a matter of such importance there should be a referendum and 'an universal assent thereunto from all and everyone of the people'.[73] Although subscribed by the other leaders, this gloss was probably the work of Walwyn, who himself evaded a direct answer to the accusation that he was a communist; referring to the Agreement of the People, he said: 'so far as this is, am I for plucking up of all the pales and hedges in the nation; so far, for all things common'.[74] Clearly he was dissociating his own personal opinions from the collective policy of the leadership, and he seems to have regarded community of goods and living as an ideal form of social organization, which could be achieved only by consent or by small voluntary groups.

On the other hand Lilburne made a positive defence of social organization based on private property, which carried a note of sincere and deeply held principles rather than of political tactics or expediency: 'In my opinion and judgement, this conceit of levelling of property and magistracy is so ridiculous and foolish an opinion, as no man of brains, reason or ingenuity, can be imagined such a sot as to maintain such a principle, because it would, if practised, destroy not only any industry in the world, but raze the very foundation of generation, and of subsistence or being of one man by another. For as for industry and valour by which the societies of mankind are maintained and preserved, who will take pains for that which when he hath gotten is not his own, but must equally be shared in, by every lazy, simple, dronish sot? Or who will fight for that, wherein he hath no interest, but such as must be subject to the will and pleasure of another, yea of every coward and base low-spirited fellow, that in his sitting still must share in common with a valiant man in all his brave noble achievements? The ancient encouragement to men that were to defend their country was this: that they were to hazard their persons for that which was their own, to wit, their own wives, their own children, their own estates.'[75] This was consistent with the idea that all should work, otherwise they should not eat, and that by his labour a man created a right of property in the fruits of his labour, which he was not obliged to share with anyone else. The people, declared Overton, have 'propriety... in their goods to do with them as they list'.[76] Every man had a natural right to own property, which was protected by the law of nature, the law of god, and the law of the land.[77] Everyone who was not a 'lazy, simple, dronish sot' should have some property; without it he could not be free and independent,[78] or keep from being forced to work for others, or to beg, or to steal; without it the commonwealth and the economy could not function properly, for the individual would only work or fight for his own possessions. The 'propertyless classes found the Leveller programme inadequate and, to a considerable measure, irrelevant to their situation'.[79]

Unlike a religious radical like John Cooke,[80] with his very traditional social and economic philosophy, the Leveller leaders never specifically denounced unlimited acquisition,[81] but the whole trend of their denunciations of the rich and powerful and the underlying implications of their programme was opposition to the extreme concentration of wealth, which reduced the opportunities for the small man to acquire property, and a desire for ownership of property to be more widely spread and the opportunities for the acquisition of property to be made more general, by relieving the burdens on small property.[82] The Levellers cannot be judged solely by their party manifestos and the actual items on their 'official' programme, because these 'were arrived at by compromise and destined for a particular political situation', seeking the support of one particular group or angled to reassure another particular group: 'The elusive spirit behind the words and actions was actually or potentially more radical than the Agreement of the People.'[83] 'The spirit of Leveller teaching was more revolutionary than its content, and there was a spirit of equalitarianism in their doctrines which existed not merely in the apprehensive imagination of the army grandees.'[84]

The Levellers, in their definition of property, and in basing rights on property so defined, were defending the small man. There were two sorts of property in seventeenth-century England: there was the property of the rich—that was sacred and could not be touched—and there was the property of the poor, which was much less free from interference—by the rich.[85] The Levellers were defending the property in the fruits of their labour of the men who earned their livelihoods by working with their hands, the property of the peasants in their common rights, the property of the copyholders in their estates, the property of the poor in their hospitals, almshouses and common lands. They wanted as much regard paid to these types of property as to the property of the landlords in their rents and fines, the property of the clergy in their tithes, and the property of the nobility and gentry in their impropriated tithes. They wanted one rule for both rich and poor.

The rich used their power as rulers, whether in the king's court and council, in parliament and its committees, in the governing bodies of towns and commercial companies, or in the church and the law-courts, to take the property and extinguish the rights of those less powerful than themselves. 'Nay thus', exclaimed Colonel Rainsborough, the most radical of the senior officers in the army: 'a gentleman lives in a county and hath three or four lordships, as some men have (God knows how they got them); and when a parliament is called he must be a parliament-man; and it may be he sees some poor men, they live near this man, he can crush them—I have known an invasion to make sure he hath turned the poor men out of doors; and I would fain know whether the potency of rich men do not this, and so keep them under the greatest tyranny there was ever thought of in the world'.[86] It was no use the copyholders appealing to the courts because 'the Chancellor or Judges... are themselves lords of such copyholds, and biased with their own interest and concernment'.[87]

The social and economic reforms proposed by the Levellers were not in themselves very revolutionary. These reforms were advocated not by the Levellers alone, but by a wide range of radicals besides, who often propounded more comprehensive or more radical social and economic changes than the Levellers. But the Levellers saw the solution to economic and social problems in political and constitutional changes which would dissociate wealth from power. They were distinguished from other radicals by the range and sweep, comprehensiveness and detail of their proposals for democratizing the institutions of central and local government.

God created all men equal, each one having a soul and reason, so that they were 'by nature all equal and alike in power, dignity, authority, and majesty'.[88] 'For as God created every man free in Adam: so by nature are all alike freemen born'.[89] 'By natural birth, all men are equal and alike born to the like propriety and freedom'.[90] Thus, 'by nature' no one had 'any authority, dominion or magisterial power, one over or above another, neither have they, or can they exercise any, but merely by institution, or donation, that is to say, by mutual agreement or consent, given, derived, or assumed, by mutual consent and agreement'.[91] 'To every individual in nature, is given an individual propriety by nature, not to be invaded or usurped by any... For every one as he is himself hath a self-propriety, else could not be himself, and on this no second may presume without consent'.[92] For one man to assume power over another without the other's consent was tyranny.[93] 'And unnatural, irrational, sinful, wicked, unjust, devilish, and tyrannical it is, for any man whatsoever, spiritual or temporal, clergyman or layman, to appropriate and assume unto himself, a power, authority and jurisdiction, to rule, govern, or reign over any sort of men in the world, without their free consent, and whosoever doth it, whether clergyman, or any other whatsoever, do thereby as much as in them lies, endeavour to appropriate and assume unto themselves the office and sovereignty of God, (who alone doth, and is to rule by his will and pleasure)'.[94] Therefore 'it is a maxim in nature and reason, that no man can be concluded but by his own consent, and that it is absolute tyranny, for any what (or whom) soever, to impose a law upon people, that was never chosen nor betrusted by them to make them laws'.[95] 'All just human powers are but betrusted, conferred and conveyed by joint and common consent'.[96] 'I conceive that's the undeniable maxim of government: that all government is in the free consent of the people. If so, then upon that account there is no person that is under a just government, or hath justly his own, unless he by his own free consent be put under that government.'[97]

The only just authority that a ruler had was that which had been, and continued to be conferred on him by the consent of the people; and the only just law was one which was made by the people through their representatives. 'All power is originally and essentially in the whole body of the people of this nation' and 'their free choice or consent by their representors is the only original or foundation of all just government'.[98] 'The only and sole legislative law-making power, is originally inherent in the people, and derivatively in their commissions chosen by themselves, by common consent, and no other... And I say the people by themselves, or their legal commissions chosen by them for that end, may make a law or laws to govern themselves, and to rule, regulate, and guide all their magistrates (whatsoever), officers, ministers, or servants, and ought not in the least to receive a law from them, or any of them, whom they have set over themselves, for no other end in the world, but for their better being, and merely with justice, equity, and righteousness, to execute the laws that they made themselves, and betrusted them with, as the public executors and dispensors of.'[99] The people gave the power to their rulers and representatives 'for better being, discipline, government, property, and safety';[100] 'for the good, benefit and comfort each of other, and not for the mischief, hurt, or damage of any';[101] 'for their weal, safety, peace and prosperity, the end of government'.[102] The trust has been abused and betrayed by the people's rulers and representatives, and had been employed to their hurt rather than their good.

Such abstract considerations might have had little practical outcome if they had not been combined with the conviction that men were corrupted by power. This originated in the Levellers' belief as protestants in the depravity of human nature, but they translated it into politics as a result of their own political experiences. 'We confess indeed, that the experimental defections of so many men as have succeeded in authority, and the exceeding difference we have hitherto found in the same men in a low, and in an exalted condition' had led the Leveller leaders to propose 'such an establishment, as supposing men to be too flexible and yielding to worldly temptation, they should not yet have a means or opportunity either to injure particulars, or prejudice the public, without extreme hazard, and apparent danger to themselves'.[103] 'It hath been a maxim amongst the wisest legislators, that whosoever means to settle good laws, must proceed in them with a sinister, or evil opinion of all mankind; and suppose that whosoever is not wicked, it is for want of opportunity, and that no state can be wisely confident of any public minister continuing good longer than the rod is over him.'[104] Lilburne learned the lesson that men who remained too long in office or power became corrupt and used their position for their own rather than public ends: 'for standing waters though never so pure at first, in time putrifies'.[105] 'And above all things, avoid the perpetuation of command, trust, or office, in the hand of any person or persons, it having proved by the sad experience of all ages and countries, and of our own in particular, the means of corruption and tyranny in those that are trusted, and of bondage to the people'.[106] It was in the light of this principle that the Levellers devised a new constitution for the country.

The basic principle of the new constitution was that it was to be subscribed by the people, who were thus to set up the supreme authority in the nation and to determine its powers by a law that it itself could not change. This supreme authority was to be a parliament (they preferred the term 'representative' as more indicative of its function) elected by the people. The key to the success of this constitution was seen to lie in the representatives being supreme, in not being subject to the veto of a king or House of Lords, and responsible to the people, in being subject to regular and frequent elections. Before they conceived the idea of a new constitution, the Levellers had thought that they could make parliaments more democratic and responsible to the people by having a new parliament elected every year, so that the people could 'renew and inquire once a year after the behaviour and carriage of those they have chosen'.[107] 'Let us earnestly contest for the enjoyment of our just, national liberties, and the long and ancient, just laws of England to have every year a fresh and new parliament... If never such base men be chosen, if we have a fresh parliament every year... it will be as a rod kept over their heads to awe them, that they shall not dare to do the kingdom one thousand part of that injustice that this parliament hath done, for fear the next parliament they shall be questioned, and then lose their heads or estates.'[108]

Although the first Agreement of the People demanded a new parliament only every two years, the reason was still that 'forasmuch as the long continuance of the power of parliament men proveth very destructive to the liberty of the people, and occasioneth their falling into parties and factions, and giveth them great countenance in the exercising of an arbitrary power: that therefore they be continued but a short time, and that during that time they may remain accountable to those that chose and entrusted them'.[109] Hugh Peter suggested 'that burgesses of parliament... give monthly some account to the places entrusting them, and that some laws may be probationer for a month or two';[110] and Richard Overton proposed that each county elect commissioners 'to receive all and every impeachment, and impeachments, by any person or persons whatsoever, of the respective counties, against any of their own respective knights or burgesses in parliament, for falsifying and betraying his or their country's trust, or anywise endeavouring the introducing of an arbitrary power in this land. And that the said commissioners have power and be firmly bound to impeach and attach... their said member or members, and to bring him or them to a legal and public trial. That in case such be found guilty, justice may be executed, and others in their room, by the free choice of the people be sent.'[111]

The Levellers, however, did not develop the device of 'the recall', but reverted to the demand for annual parliaments in the Petition of 11 September 1648 and in the second and third versions of the Agreement of the People, 'for avoiding the many dangers and inconveniences apparently arising from the long continuance of the same persons in authority'.[112] The third and final version of the Agreement also laid down that a member of parliament could not be re-elected until a year had elapsed.[113] 'Having by woeful experience found the prevalence of corrupt interests powerfully inclining most men once entrusted with authority, to pervert the same to their own domination, and to the prejudice of our peace and liberties', and 'that generally men make little or nothing... to exceed their time and power in places of trust, to introduce an arbitrary and tyrannical power', the Agreement laid down what a parliament could and could not do.[114] The reservations, prohibiting the representative from legislating in certain important areas, such as banning it from imposing any compulsion in religion or restraint on any person 'from the profession of his faith, or exercise of religion according to his conscience', and preventing it from imposing compulsory military service by land or sea,[115] dominated the Agreements and formed the most characteristic device of Leveller constitution-making.

Perhaps the most striking thing about the Agreements is what they omit: the lack of reference to executive government. The central government is almost eliminated. The second Agreement provided for the election by the representative of a Council of State 'for the managing of public affairs', 'to act and proceed therein according to such instructions and limitations as the representatives shall give, and not otherwise', and to serve for one year until the next representative was chosen.[116] But the final version of the Agreement laid down that the Council of State should exist only while a parliament was sitting, and when parliament was adjourned 'the managing of affairs' was to be referred 'to a committee of their own members', with instructions that were to be made public.[117] Lilburne argued that if a Council of State sat longer than a parliament and so was in power when a parliament was not sitting, 'they will have great opportunities to make themselves absolute and unaccountable', and he seemed to visualize the only central executive being 'committees of short continuance', composed of members of parliament, 'limited and bounded with express instructions', and 'frequently and exactly accountable for the discharge of their trusts'.[118] With the Levellers the distrust of the centralization of power reached its extreme point. They aimed at a massive decentralization of power from the central government to the local communities. The nature of Leveller democracy is only fully revealed by a consideration of their proposals for local self-government.

In the seventeenth century judges and justices of the peace performed governmental and executive functions as well as legal and judicial, and so it is not possible to understand the Levellers' proposals for the decentralization of government and administration without first examining their proposals for reform of the legal system. The administration of justice and the execution of the law were, for the Levellers, the main part of government, and so if government were to be democratized, the starting place had to be the legal system. The laws and legal proceedings were 'locked up from common capacities in the Latin or French tongues', so 'that a plain man cannot understand so much as a writ without the help of Counsel'; and were so complex and obscure, and deliberately kept so by the lawyers, that the people could not handle their own legal affairs nor conduct their own cases, but had to employ lawyers, who 'by keeping the people in ignorance, enforce them (like slaves) to walk by their own light'. Nor could they participate in the administration of justice.[119] The radicals demanded that the laws be translated into English, and that all legal proceedings and processes be in their own native language: 'that all records, orders, processes, writs, and other proceedings whatsoever, may be all entered and issued forth in the English tongue, and that in the most plain and common character used in the land, commonly called Roman or Secretary, and that without all or any Latin or French phrases or terms, and also without all or any abbreviations or abridgements of words';[120] that so 'the meanest English commoner that can but read written hand in his own tongue, may fully understand his own proceedings in the law'.[121] This was to be coupled with the simplification of the law and legal proceedings: by removing 'perplexity or absurdity in proceedings'; by revising 'the many great and needless volumes of Statute Laws'; by reducing the law to a few 'express and plain rules in English', which were to be written down and 'comprised in one volume'; and by precisely defining and limiting the jurisdiction of every court and judge, so ending the overlapping and conflicting of jurisdictions which allowed cases to be moved back and forth between courts and even started in two courts simultaneously.[122] The ultimate aim of all these reforms was to rid the kingdom 'of those vermin and caterpillars, the lawyers, the chief bane of this poor nation'.[123] A further step towards this would be to allow the people to plead their own cases in court, or to make 'use of whom they pleased to plead for them'.[124]

The final step would have been the abolition of the central courts altogether and the transfer of all criminal and civil jurisdiction to courts in every Hundred, meeting monthly, and consisting of a jury of twelve men 'annually chosen by freemen in that Hundred', with a president who was merely a chairman, for the jury was to decide matters of law as well as of fact: 'and then farewell jangling lawyers, the wild-fire destroyers and bane of all just, rational, and right governed commonwealths'.[125] This was how it had been before the Norman Conquest, when 'controversies of all natures' had 'a quick and final dispatch in every Hundred'; and 'every man could mind and attend his own cause, without such journeying to and fro, and such chargeable attendance, as at Westminster Hall. For, first, in the country, the law was plain, and controversies decided by neighbours of the Hundred, who could be soon informed in the state of the matter, and were ready to administer justice, as making it their own case'.[126] 'Oh, therefore that our honourable parliament... would for ever annihilate this Norman innovation, and reduce us back to that part of the ancient frame of government in this kingdom before the Conqueror's days, that we may have all cases and differences decided in the county or Hundred where they are committed, or do arise'.[127]

Nevertheless this final step was not incorporated by the leaders in the final 'official' programme of the party, being one of the more revolutionary proposals that they omitted in the hope of gaining the support of the army chiefs. They were prepared to settle for a limitation on the length of legal proceedings to six months, the translation of the laws and legal processes into English, permission to people to plead their own cases, the election by the people of all 'public officers that are in any kind to administer the law' in the localities (counties, hundreds, cities, towns and boroughs), and the provision that all trials involving 'life, limb, liberty, or estate', without exception, be 'by twelve sworn men of the neighbourhood; to be chosen in some free way by the people... not picked and imposed, as hitherto in many places they have been.' 'Fundamental to the Leveller programme was increased power to the jury': the wealthier people, and also the poorest people, for different reasons, distrusted the jury system, but 'the middle sort', who composed the juries, favoured it, and the Levellers wanted to reform its abuses and extend its use.[128] The central courts were to remain, but the demand for their abolition continued to inspire the Levellers' more radical supporters.[129]

For the mass of the people the small village or town, or the parish, in which they lived was the real community, rather than the county or hundred, and there they had long been accustomed to participate in the conduct of affairs, or at least some of them had, and for them democracy meant making that community more democratic and important. Ideas became more radical as the size of the community on which they focused became smaller. The Buckinghamshire Levellers were more inclined to want 'all controversies' ended 'in every town and hamlet' by 'two, three, or twelve men of our own neighbourhood', 'to be chosen, by the people', 'without any other or further trouble or charge', as it was 'before the Norman Conquest'.[130] But they also believed that in disputes between individuals there was little need for courts at all, because these could be settled by the arbitration of a neighbour or neighbours, acceptable to both parties: 'why may not all controversies be ended by arbitration of our own neighbourhood, by the rule of equity at home, than to be thus abused by the lawyer?'[131]

Alongside the official, elaborate and expensive machinery of the law-courts, there existed in the local communities an unofficial and traditional communal machinery for the settlement of disputes—arbitration by neighbours or by a respected and trusted member of the community—and one reason for the bitter hostility of the people towards the lawyers and the law-courts was that this free, quick, harmonious system was under attack and being undermined by the rich and powerful men who preferred to take disputes to the official law-courts, which they alone could afford to do.[132] The mere threat of this was enough to force many a poor man to surrender his point to a rich man, or if he did fight he was soon ruined by the expense and had to abandon the struggle, and in any case the judges and courts were thought to be biased in favour of the rich and powerful, whereas the poor had a better hope of justice from their own neighbours. A desire to reinvigorate and develop this system of arbitration, and reduce litigation, was shared by both moderate and extreme reformers. 'That justice may be near to all men', Hugh Peter proposed that in every county and hundred, or some small unit such as town, ward or parish, three men be chosen annually to serve for a year as 'Peace-makers, or friend-makers', to 'hear the differences between man and man, before any go to law, and if it be possible, let them end it: and fit men for such business, will end most controversies'. He was prepared to visualise it almost coming to replace the existing legal system, with the peace-makers hearing and determining 'all common controversies between man and man', and also all questions of debt, with lawyers being permitted to plead only when a large sum was involved, otherwise people to plead their own cases, or have friends or neighbours to plead for them, with a right of appeal in 'very weighty matters' from the three peace-makers to a panel of five or seven sitting once a month.[133]

The corollary of the decentralization of the legal system, and entrusting it to the local community, was the decentralization of government. The Levellers demanded that in all 'counties, hundreds, cities, towns, or boroughs', sheriffs, justices of the peace, mayors, deputy lieutenants and the officers of the militia, and all other public officers in the localities, be elected annually, to serve for one year only, by 'the people in their respective places', rather than imposed by the central government. Thus the people would be restored to 'their native, just and undoubted right, by common consent, from amongst themselves annually to choose' their officers, which had been unjustly taken from them.[134] Parsons were to be elected by the parishioners, and not imposed by lay patrons, bishops, king or parliament, 'the parishioners of every particular parish' choosing 'such as themselves shall approve; and upon such terms, and for such reward, as themselves shall be willing to contribute, or shall contract for'.[135] Assessments for taxation were to be made by persons elected by 'the freemen of every division or Hundred'.[136] If the legislature decided to raise an army, it was to be levied, furnished and paid by allocating 'to each particular county, city, town, and borough' a proportion of the men, arms and money to be provided; and only the commander-in-chief and general officers were to be appointed by the legislature, all other officers of regiments, troops and companies were to be elected by the people of the place where they were raised, and removed by them 'as they shall see cause'.[137]

These proposals, seen against the background of the Agreements of the People, which provided for annual parliaments, limited the powers of the legislature, and almost eliminated the central government, and taken in conjunction with the prohibition of compulsion in religion and in military service, amounted to a blueprint for a society of self-governing local communities, with a large degree of voluntaryism.

Overton even suggested 'that every county may have liberty to choose some certain number amongst themselves, to inquire and present to the parliament, what be the just laws, customs, and privileges of each county'.[138] It was indeed a logical corollary of the derivation of power and law from the people, that the local community and its customs were above parliament. Cromwell made a shrewd judgement when he suggested that the Levellers wanted to break up England into a federation of self-governing cantons like Switzerland;[139] and indeed, Switzerland may have been Walwyn's model.[140]

It is suggested that the Leveller 'notion of democratic self-government began... in the parish and the hundred'.[141] All mankind, wrote Lilburne, 'reigns and governs as much by God in their inferior orbs (of city, hundred, wapentakes, and families)... as kings in their kingdoms'; and it is argued that his proposals 'presuppose that the centre of gravity lies in the local communities whose members know each other'.[142] It is said that the Levellers' proposals for the decentralization of the legal system and for the democratization of local government might be regarded as 'the most important and original item in the whole Leveller programme'.[143] It was a protest against the erosion of the powers of the local communities by the growing centralization of government and economic power; against the conversion of the local communities from self-governing democracies into self-perpetuating oligarchies. It was, indeed, an attack on the ruling class whose power-base lay in the monopoly they held of the offices of local government, as deputy lieutenants of the militia, officers of the trained bands, sheriffs, justices of the peace, mayors and aldermen. The opening of these positions to annual election by the people, more than the right to elect members of parliament, was the only possible basis for popular participation in political power and government. If it did not result in the removal from power of the oligarchies of wealthy landowners in the counties and rich merchants in the towns, at least they would continue to exercise power only on the suffrage of peasants and artisans.[144]

But there was a faltering in the Levellers' stand: they gave way on the crucial question of local courts, and they were less emphatic than they might have been about local self-government. It was their more radical followers who laid the greater stress on these items, and who truly 'envisaged a federation of small communities of neighbours, fairly equal in ownership and status, ruling themselves without the interference of professional magistrates or lawyers according to simple and well-known rules'.[145] The Leveller leaders probably recognized in the traditional local communities, bulwarks against the tyrannical tendencies of centralized government, centralized church, centralized courts, centralized legislature; and against the oppressiveness of the ruling class. They were sympathetic towards strengthening and re-establishing local, communal democracy. But there was an ambiguity in their position. It was not they, but their more radical supporters, who pushed really hard for local courts; it was not they, but other radicals who showed interest in the system of local arbitration; it was not they, but other radicals who campaigned most strongly for communal rights in common lands and for the customs of the local communities in regard to tenures, fines, rents, inheritance. There remains an uncertainty about where the Levellers stood fundamentally in regard to the great issues dividing their society. A crucial test of their position may be their attitude towards the franchise: they made parliament the supreme body in the state, and upon obtaining a sympathetic parliament depended the achievement of the reforms on which they had set their hearts. The electorate for the officers of local government, commanders of the militia, assessors of taxes, parsons of parishes, was to be the same as that for parliament; so the degree of their democracy hung upon the franchise.

The aim of the Levellers was to reduce the political power, and end the political monopoly, of the rich. They had to wean the existing electorate from the habits of centuries; from the attitudes of deference towards their social superiors in which they were brought up; from the fears of the harm that powerful and influential men could do them, if their wishes were slighted; and from the urge, and indeed need, to curry favour with those who could do them many kindnesses, when their authority was respected. George Wither urged the electorate to end the folly of choosing men for parliament because of their wealth and rank rather than their wisdom and integrity, and elect rather men 'eminent for their virtues and abilities, than for their wealth, birth or titles'.[146] His advice was commended to the people by Lilburne.[147] 'It's only honest, discreet and plain men that are for your turn, and can be best contented with a competent subsistence, and are most sensible both of your oppressions, necessities and liberties. Why then do ye not choose such and no other?'[148] 'It is naturally inbred in the major part of the nobility and gentry... to judge the poor but fools and themselves wise, and therefore when you the commonalty calleth a parliament, they are confident such must be chosen, that are noblest and richest... but... reason affirmeth... these are not your equals, neither are these sensible of the burthen that lieth upon you; for indeed... your slavery is their liberty, your poverty is their prosperity'. 'For who are the oppressors, but the nobility and gentry; and who are oppressed, if not the yeoman, the farmer, the tradesman, and the labourer? Then consider, have you not chosen oppressors to redeem you from oppression?'[149] 'O foolish brethren and friends, why are you thus bewitched with an opinion of art and sophistry? What need you care so much for the tongue, estate or outside?': 'ye are monstrous ignorant, superstitious and foolish' to regard men because they are landlords, lawyers, clergymen, and have been to the university and Inns of Court, and 'dare neither trust your own judgements, nor dear bought experience'.[150] The Hertfordshire Levellers announced that they would not vote for 'lords of manors, impropriators, and lawyers, whose interest is in our oppression and at this day keep us in bondage like Egyptian taskmasters'.[151]

The existing electorate did not seem to the reformers to be well qualified to show this independence. Radicals complained that the voters were often 'more swayed by favour than reason in their choice, being tenants either to the persons chosen, or their friends'.[152] In the mass of small boroughs the qualifications for the franchise varied enormously and Lilburne protested that in some the electors of the members of parliament were 'alehouse-keepers, and ignorant sots, who want principles to choose any man, but only those that either some lord, or great man writes for, and recommends; or else one who bribes them for their voices'.[153] Many of the existing holders of the franchise were too ignorant, or too poor, or too dependent to cast their votes against their landlords, their employers, and the rich and powerful men who sought, or bought, their suffrages. At the same time there were men of more substance and greater independence, amongst the 'middle sort of people', who had been demanding, and often obtaining, the right to vote. The Levellers seem to have been unaware, or to have underestimated the extent to which such men were achieving their aims before the civil war,[154] but this had occurred piecemeal and haphazardly, and these gains were threatened by the conservative and royalist backlash in the 1640s. The Leveller leaders spoke for such men and what essentially they were seeking to express was a demand for a shift of power away from 'the rich and powerful' towards 'the middle sort'. Lilburne complained that there were men who had 'money and stock' but no votes.[155] In the debates in the general council of the army at Putney in 1647 on the franchise, supporters of the Levellers claimed that there well-to-do farmers without votes,[156] and, more interestingly: 'there are men of substance in the country with no voice in elections: there is a tanner in Staines worth £3,000, and another in Reading worth three horseskins', and the latter had a vote but not the former.[157]

The implication was that the process by which piecemeal and haphazardly the franchise was being extended gradually to many, but not all, of the 'middle sort', should be continued, completed, and confirmed, and, perhaps even more important, anomalies should be removed and the franchise made uniform throughout the land. The electorate was very unevenly distributed. The multitude of small boroughs resulted in the over-representation of some parts of the country, and the under-representation of other parts. 'Unrighteous it is, that Cornwall should choose almost fifty parliament-men; and Yorkshire twice as big, and three times as populous, and rich, not half so many', protested Lilburne; 'and my poor country the Bishopric of Durham, none at all; and so indeed, and in truth, are mere vassals and slaves, being in a great measure like the French peasants, and the vassals in Turkey.'[158] The conclusion to be drawn from these protests was the need for a more uniform franchise, the enfranchisement of substantial men who had no votes, the disfranchisement of very small boroughs, and the redistribution of seats from the south and south-west to the eastern, midland and northern counties. Cromwell and the army leaders were sympathetic and when they came to power carried out reforms on these lines.[159] This came close to satisfying the demands of the middle sort of people.

The first clause of the first Agreement of the People (1647) put the stress on the redistribution of seats: 'the people of England being at this day very unequally distributed by counties, cities, and boroughs, for the election of their deputies in parliament, ought to be more indifferently proportioned, according to the number of the inhabitants'.[160] But the sting lay in the tail—'according to the number of the inhabitants'— this could imply universal manhood suffrage, and was suspected of that by the chief officers of the army. Obviously there did lie behind this first clause of the Agreement a demand for a wider franchise. John Harris, a printer, who was an associate of Lilburne and printed manifestos for the army radicals in whose name the Agreement was published,[161] expounded the main points of the Agreement in a pamphlet. He stressed the first clause, showing that it was regarded as very important by the radicals, and maintained that it meant that 'from henceforth there might be persons chosen for representatives for every county, proportionable to the number of inhabitants in each county, and that not by freeholders only, but by the voluntary assent of all men that are not servants or beggars, it being pure equity, that as all persons are bound to yield obedience to the decrees of the Representative or Parliament, so they should have a voice in the electing of their representatives, or members of parliament'.[162] Major White, an army radical, called for 'a free parliament equally chosen, with every free man of age having voice';[163] and **The Case of the Armie truly stated** demanded votes for 'all the freeborn at the age of 21 years and upwards'.[164]

Now **The Case**, 'like the Agreement, was issued in the name of the representatives of the troopers of five regiments of horse, who said that the Agreement was based on **The Case**.[165] But **The Case** was drafted with the help of the London Levellers, and John Wildman was probably the chief penman. When the Agreement was laid before the general council of the army at Putney in 1647, it was Wildman who was the chief spokesman for the London Levellers and he defended the first clause of the Agreement as meaning that 'every person in

England hath as clear a right to elect his representative as the greatest person in England. I conceive that's the undeniable maxim of government: that all government is in the free consent of the people. If so, then upon that account there is no person that is under a just government, or hath justly his own, unless he by his own free consent be put under that government. This he cannot be unless he be consenting to it, and therefore, according to this maxim, there is never a person in England but ought to have a voice in elections'; and no person 'can justly be bound by law, who doth not give his consent that such persons shall make laws for him'.[166] However, when the Agreement said 'the people of England' and 'the inhabitants', and **The Case** said 'all the freeborn', and Harris said 'all persons' and Wildman said 'every person', they assumed important exceptions: they certainly did not intend to give votes to women and children;[167] nor, according to Harris, did they intend to give votes to 'servants or beggars'. The latter point was confirmed by another Leveller spokesman at Putney, Petty, who agreed to the exclusion from the franchise of 'servants and apprentices... and those that receive alms from door to door'.[168]

The Levellers did not intend to exclude any man from the franchise merely on the grounds of poverty: 'the poorest that lives', said Lilburne, 'hath as true a right to give a vote, as well as the richest and greatest'.[169] 'For really I think', declared Colonel Rainsborough during the debates at Putney, 'that the poorest he that is in England hath a life to live, as the greatest he; and therefore truly, Sir, I think it's clear, that every man that is to live under a government ought first by his own consent to put himself under that government; and I do think that the poorest man in England is not at all bound in a strict sense to that government that he hath not had a voice to put himself under'.[170] But these were not demands for universal suffrage, since there were unstated exceptions, for men so poor as to have to beg were excluded; rather they were assertions that poverty as such was no ground for exclusion from the franchise, no more than wealth as such ought to be a ground for having the vote; if the latter were the principle, protested Rainsborough, 'men of riches, men of estates' would make 'hewers of wood and drawers of water' and slaves of 'the greatest part of the nation'.[171] And Petty saw the dispute as being whether poor men should have the vote as well as rich men.[172] Nor ought the franchise to be regarded as a piece of property, which some men possessed and others did not: 'I desire to know how this comes to be a property in some men, and not in others', asked Rainsborough;[173] and a property qualification like the 40s freehold implied that ownership of the land carried with it the right to vote: 'men's titles to land and to a power of government are, or ought to be, of a different nature'.[174]

The radicals wanted to end the monopoly of political power by the rich. Lieutenant-Colonel Jubbes, who was active in the radical agitation in the army and a supporter of the Agreement of the People in 1647, maintained that the object of the reform of the franchise was to take power from the lords of manors and lawyers.[175] If the aim were to do this, then the crucial question was the capacity of the electors to cast independent votes. Lilburne had complained of the 'alehouse-keepers, and ignorant sots' who voted as 'some lord, or great man' told them, or took bribes for their votes;[176] and Harris thought the main reason for reform of the franchise was that the existing electors 'are commonly more swayed by favour than reason in their choice, being tenants either to the persons chosen, or their friends; which hath been one main reason that the lost liberties of the kingdom have been from time to time no better vindicated and preserved'.[177] Petty explained the exclusion of apprentices and servants and 'those that take alms' on the ground that 'they depend upon the will of other men and should be afraid to displease them'.[178] Jubbes produced his own version of the Agreement of the People in which he extended the franchise to copyholders worth 40s per annum and to all other persons worth £50 in personal estate.[179] But he was not a Leveller and was associated with a more moderate group of radicals in London.

Independence, however, could not have been the sole criterion in the minds of the Levellers. The ground for the exclusion of apprentices and servants from the franchise was the same as that for the exclusion of women and children: 'For servants and apprentices, they are included in their masters'.[180] The Levellers did not attempt to question the assumptions of the patriarchal society in which they lived: voting was to be by household, in which the male head cast the vote for his servants and apprentices as well as for his wife and children.[181] But this was not unconnected with independence, for given the existing structure of power in the family, wives and servants could not be expected to vote any other way than their master required them. Therefore the Levellers were advocating a household franchise, and in the Petition of 19 January 1648 they declared: 'Whereas it hath been the ancient liberty of this nation, that all the free-born people have freely elected their representers in parliament, and their sheriffs and justices of the peace, etc... that therefore, that birthright of all Englishmen, be forthwith restored to all which are not... under 21 years of age, or servants, or beggars'.[182] 'Beggar' was a vague term, but if it meant able-bodied vagrants who refused to work, they were excluded from the franchise because they had no households and had put themselves outside society.[183]

But the Levellers were prepared to compromise on the franchise issue, and in order to win the support of the army leaders in the second version of the Agreement of the People they restricted the vote to 'men of one and twenty years old, or upwards, and housekeepers, dwelling within the division, for which the election is', 'not persons receiving alms, but such as are assessed ordinarily towards the relief of the poor; not servants to, or receiving wages from any particular person';[184] and they were able to persuade the officers to stomach this.[185] This was a drastic restriction, excluding not only 'beggars' but all persons who through old age or sickness were unable to work or though able-bodied and willing to work were unable to find employment, and lived on poor-relief, and excluding not only apprentices and servants, who dwelt in their master's household, but all labourers who worked for wages, though they had houses and families of their own. But it was still a wide franchise, including the tenant-farmers and the small master-craftsmen, and a victory over the views expressed by Cromwell and Ireton during the debates at Putney. Up to a point the criterion was independence: it was not a property franchise but a ratepayer franchise, and in keeping with the common association of taxation with representation, which

Lilburne expressed in his protest that if he lived in Durham he would pay no taxes until the county had representation in parliament.[186]

But the Levellers reverted to their earlier position in the final version of the Agreement of the People, in which they declared that the electors should be '(according to natural right) all men of the age of one and twenty years and upwards (not being servants, or receiving alms...)'.[187] The restriction to householders and ratepayers was dropped, and wage-earners who were householders may now have been included.[188] By those 'receiving alms' may have been meant only sturdy beggars,[189] but it is more likely to have embraced all those who were in regular receipt of poor-relief—the old and sick who were unable to work, and the unemployed who were unable to find work. The Levellers derived rights from labour: those who did not work had no rights, whether this was voluntary, as in the case of sturdy beggars, or involuntary, as in the case of the old, the sick, and the unemployed. The latter, the deserving poor, were the responsibility of the community, which fed and housed them, and had them in the same relationship of dependence as wives, children, and servants in the family; so that it could be conceived that the community cast the votes on their behalf just as the father voted on behalf of his family.[190]

The franchise issue precipitated a serious crisis for radicals in general and for the Levellers in particular. The Levellers had stood for the poor and the weak against the rich and the powerful, and had expressed the conflict in terms of the division between those who earned their livelihood by working with their hands and those who could live idly without manual labour, but this had masked the further cleavage in society between the middle sort of people who worked with their hands, sold their produce or products—the fruits of their labour—and the poorer sort of people who sold their labour itself and worked for wages. The Levellers had really stood for the middle sort of people against the old ruling order; but the more substantial and educated of the middle sort became uneasy when the radicals seemed ready to extend democracy to the mass of poor peasants and artisans, even to wage-labourers; and the Leveller leaders found themselves pulled in different directions.

The Levellers regularly coupled together 'the middle sort of people' and 'the poor', showing their belief that the line that separated 'the middle sort' from 'the poor' was less important than the line which separated 'the middle sort' from the rich.[191] By 'men of middle quality or condition',[192] they seem to have meant shopkeepers;[193] 'men of inferior trading';[194] clothiers, hatmakers, soap-boilers and all such 'ingenious industrious people';[195] farmers and husbandmen.[196] Generally speaking they seem to have meant the small merchants, small master-craftsmen, and farmers (freeholders and copyholders). By the poor, therefore, they would have meant servants and journey-men in industry, labourers in agriculture, the general body of wage-earners in town and country, as distinct from the poor in the sense of paupers who lived on poor-relief and alms. The middle sort of people owned property and often employed labour, but the gulf between them and their servants was not great, as Baxter wrote of the small master-weavers of Kidderminster: 'The generality of the master workmen, lived but a little better than their journeymen, (from hand to mouth) but only that they laboured not altogether so hard.'[197] The Levellers probably hoped to unite the middle and poorer sorts and with this mass support to carry the revolution further and to achieve the reforms that they conceived to be the purpose of the revolution.

The leaders were men of some substance and status. William Walwyn was the second son of a gentleman of £300-400 a year in Worcestershire, and the grandson of a bishop; he was apprenticed to a silkman in London and became a member of the Merchant Adventurers Company, and 'from the profits of his trade, maintained his family in a middle and moderate but contentful condition'.[198] John Lilburne was the younger son of a gentry family with 500 acres in Durham: he was apprenticed to a dealer in woollen cloth in London, but spent most of his life as a religious and political agitator or in prison, with periods as a lieutenant-colonel in parliament's army, a brewer, and a soap-boiler.[199] Thomas Prince was a wholesale dealer in cheese and butter, and his fellow-treasurer of the party, Samuel Chidley, was a stocking-seller and haberdasher of London.[200] Richard Overton, who may have been the son of a Warwickshire parson, was a printer (there were several printers prominent in the Leveller movement); and John Wildman was a solicitor or attorney.[201] They were not rich, but neither were they poor. They were typical of the sort of men to whom the revolutionary period brought opportunities to gain positions of some influence and power and to participate in affairs. They did not intend to turn the world upside down.

They were not against 'distinctions of orders and dignities' amongst men, and they were in favour of 'government and against popular confusion'.[202] Walwyn replied to the accusations of John Price: 'He upbraids me, that I find fault, that riches, and estates, and the things of this world, should prefer men to offices, and places of trust: but say that virtue, though in poor men, should be more regarded, as in butchers, or cobblers: and truly I know some butchers, though not many, as fit as some in your congregations; and I think you do not exclude for that trade: and as for cobblers, there are trades more in credit, hardly so useful... But by the way, I am not so strong as to talk usually after this rule, I know the generality of our times cannot bear it; I indulge exceedingly towards the weakness of men for peace sake: who ever heard me speak either in behalf of butchers or cobblers, as to places of government? I profess, I know not where, nor when; though for their callings, I make no difference between them and myself, for the callings are honest, and mine can but be so.'[203] Although Walwyn seems to be saying that, whatever he might ideally have wished, he did not expect butchers and cobblers to take over the government; what he is really saying is that it is not the trade but the man that matters, and the core of his egalitarianism lies in the statement 'that virtue, though in poor men, should be more regarded', not because they are poor but because they are virtuous, and if not very many of them were virtuous it was not a very egalitarian doctrine. Lilburne spoke contemptuously of 'alehouse-keepers, and ignorant sots';[204] and Wildman, admittedly to score a debating point, could say: 'I have a reverent respect to all kind of trades. But if I should speak of all the several Companies, the bricklayers, bowyers, fletchers, turners, coopers, tallow-chandlers; etc, if I should speak of the education of most of the liverymen of forty companies of the City... will any man suppose that the education of all the handicraftsmen of the Liveries render them so able and discreet that they are fit for government?'[205]

The egalitarianism of the Leveller leaders was limited by their puritan backgrounds and preconceptions. 'Distinctions or orders and dignities', they said in their apologia, were desirable as 'animosities of virtue' and needful 'for the maintenance of the magistracy and government' and the preservation 'of the due respect and obedience in the people which is necessary for the better execution of the laws'; but they were undesirable if employed 'for the nourishment of ambition, or subjugation of the people'.[206] Lilburne's objection to the peers was that they were an aristocracy of wealth and power rather than of virtue: 'titles of honour, without honesty and justice, are not excellenter than a gold ring in a swine's snout'.[207] God 'regards neither fine clothes, nor gold rings, nor stately houses, nor abundance of wealth, nor dignities, and titles of honour, nor any man's birth or calling, indeed he regards nothing among his children but love', wrote Walwyn: 'Love will be as a new light in your understandings by which you will judge quite otherwise of all things, than formerly you have done... you will no longer mind high things, but make yourselves equal to men of low degree: you will no longer value men and women according to their wealth, or outward shows, but according to their virtue, and as the love of God appeareth in them.'[208] 'God judgeth not as man judgeth: the poor tradesman, and the rich; the noble and ignoble, are all one in his sight'.[209]

This was the doctrine that formed the spearhead of the attack on the claims of wealth and rank to rule, but it replaced an aristocracy of birth and riches by an aristocracy of virtue. This was the characteristic doctrine of men of an intermediate status in society. They hated the rich and feared the poor. Opposed to the abuse of power by the rich, which harmed the middle sort of people; sympathetic towards the plight of the poor, into whose ranks they could so easily fall; anxious to end poverty, they did not mean to take power from the rich in order to give it to the poor. They did not propose to underpin political democracy with economic and social equality: that is why the Levellers concentrated upon political and constitutional rather than economic and social reforms. The middle sort of people wanted changes, but only in so far as their own status was maintained and improved. Therefore the most convenient doctrine for them was not the democracy towards which the more radical were tending but the rule of the saints. They would take power from the rich, not to give it to the masses but to men of virtue; they would preserve government and distinctions of men, but based on virtue, in order to keep the unvirtuous masses in order. This was the doctrine for men who wished to challenge and change the ruling order without placing the masses in power. The Leveller leaders were pulled in this direction, which accounted for the ambiguities, uncertaintities, shifts and compromises in their proposals for greater democracy.

Many of the godly and middle sort of people were turning away from political democracy and political action. Richard Jackson, writing specifically on behalf of 'the middle sort', expressed the fear that the people, through 'ignorance, weakness and irresolution' were 'unfit for the stronger nutriment of refined reason, and framed only to common ways, received by authority of law and reverence of ancient custom'; on the other hand, their 'ignorance, cruelty, envy and injustice' were such that they might overthrow all order, reduce the state to 'a shapeless mass' without distinctions between its members, and crush 'all ability of brain and spirit'.[210] The more prosperous, more godly, more educated people increasingly put the stress on the rule of talent and virtue. Instead of seeking to obtain reforms through the ignorant and ungodly majority, they looked to a more authoritarian regime of virtuous and talented men, who would assert the rights of the godly and the talented rather than the rights of the people.

In any case the poorer people tended to be stirred by sectional economic grievances, and then to fall back into acceptance of the traditional order of things, and they failed to back the schemes of general reform propounded by the radicals. At the same time they were often hostile towards the more prosperous middle sort of people, against whom they often had economic grievances, and whose pretensions to superior godliness, virtue, and status they disliked and despised. The Leveller movement, under pressure from the separatist congregations and the army officers to moderate its demands, and from the small master-craftsmen of London and the small peasants of the nearby counties to make more revolutionary demands; deserted both by many of the godly and middle sort of people and by its more radical supporters, and undermined by the opportunism and careerism of many of its leaders, the Leveller movement collapsed.

The Leveller and allied radical agitations were inspired by the belief that if the small man had a vote and a share in the conduct of affairs his social and economic grievances would be redressed and his aspirations would be satisfied. This was the central issue and the dynamic of the English Revolution, and in this sense it was a democratic revolution. But it did not achieve a democratic transformation of England because the democratic movement was divided and uncertain over the extent and depth of the transformation it wanted to bring about. The ruling class was overthrown. Its obituary notice —prematurely as it turned out—was written by one of the Five Members that Charles I had tried to seize on 4 January 1642 in an effort to prevent the very revolution that had now taken place: 'The meanest of men, the basest and vilest of the nation, the lowest of the people have got the power into their hands; trampled upon the crown; baffled and misused the parliament; violated the laws; destroyed or suppressed the nobility and gentry of the kingdom...; broke in sunder all bonds and ties of religion, conscience, duty, loyalty, faith, common honesty, and good manners'.[211] But they had not got the power into their hands: the richer farmers and the larger manufacturers—the emerging capitalist class—were not strong enough to take power on their own, and the mass of peasants and craftsmen were too dispersed in small local communities, too impoverished, too involved in a struggle merely to subsist. In a society such as England was in the seventeenth century—an agricultural society on the eve of industrialization, a society of independent small producers governed by a landed aristocracy —the ruling order could be overthrown, but it could be replaced only by military rule. The generals took power, but not in the name of democracy but of the rule of the saints: once in power they could not be overthrown by the people.

NOTES AND
ABBREVIATIONS

ABBREVIATIONS

BL : British Library. (The British Library references are given to tracts consulted in the Thomason Collection: all other tracts were consulted in the John Rylands Library, Manchester.)

Civil War Tracts: Lancashire : 'Tracts Relating to Military Proceedings in Lancashire during the Great Civil War', in **Chetham Society**, volume 2 (1844).

CJ : **Journals of the House of Commons**

Clarendon, **History** : Edward, Earl of Clarendon, **The History of the Rebellion and Civil Wars in England**, edited by W D Macray (six volumes, Oxford 1888).

Clarendon, **Life** : **The Life of Edward Earl of Clarendon** (Oxford 1759)

CSPD : **Calendar of State Papers Domestic**

CSP Venetian : **Calendar of State Papers Venetian**

Gardiner, **Documents** : S R Gardiner, **The Constitutional Documents of the Puritan Revolution 1625-1660** (third edition, Oxford 1906).

Gardiner, **History** : S R Gardiner, **History of England from the Accession of James I to the Outbreak of the Civil War 1603-1642** (ten volumes, London 1883-4)

HMC : Historical Manuscripts Commission

LJ : **Journals of the House of Lords**

State Papers Clarendon : **State Papers Collected by Edward, Earl of Clarendon** (two volumes, Oxford 1767-73)

Verney, **Memoirs** : F P Verney, **Memoirs of the Verney Family during the Civil War** (two volumes, London 1892)

Verney, **Notes** : 'Verney Papers. Notes of Proceedings in the Long Parliament by Sir Ralph Verney', in **Camden Society**, first series, volume 31 (1845)

Introduction

I am grateful for the advice of Dr Keith Lindley on this new introduction.

1. **The English People and the English Revolution** (Heinemann Educational Books, London 1976; reprinted by Penguin Books, Harmondsworth 1978) is located in the historiography of the revolution by R C Richardson, **The Debate on the English Revolution** (London 1977) and **The Debate on the English Revolution revisited** (London 1988); Alfonso Prandi's introduction to the Italian edition, *Popolo e rivoluzione in Inghilterra* (Bologna 1977) pages 9-33; and in Russian in I I Sharifzhanov, **Contemporary English Historiography of the Bourgeois Revolution in the Seventeenth Century** (Moscow 1982).

2. David Underdown, 'Community and class: Theories of local politics', in Barbara C Malament (editor) **After the Reformation** (Manchester 1980) page 158.

3. John Morrill (editor) **Reactions to the English Civil War 1642-49** (London 1982) pages 10-11.

4. Derek Hirst, **Authority and Conflict: England 1603-58** (London 1986) page 230.

5. Keith Wrightson, **English Society 1580-1680** (London 1982) page 225.

6. See above, pages 230-1. Also J M Neeson, 'The opposition to enclosure in eighteenth-century Northamptonshire', in **Past and Present**, number 105 (1984) pages 132-3.

7. Barry Reay (editor) **Popular Culture in Seventeenth-century England** (London 1985) page 1.

8. Tim Harris, **London Crowds in the Reign of Charles II: Propaganda and Politics from the Restoration to the Exclusion Crisis** (London 1987) pages 17-18.

9. Reay, page 1.

10. F D Dow, **Radicalism in the English Revolution 1640-60** (Oxford 1985) chapter 1. For an attempt to sum up the 'conservative interpretation', see J C D Clark, **Revolution and Rebellion:**

State and Society in England in the Seventeenth and Eighteenth Centuries (Cambridge 1986).

11. Morrill (editor) Reactions to the English civil war, pages 10-11; John Morrill, 'Provincial squires and "middling sorts" in the Great Rebellion', in The Historical Journal, volume 20 (1977) page 231.

12. A J Fletcher, 'Parliament and people in seventeenth-century England', in Past and Present, number 98 (1983) page 154.

13. Dow, page 6.

14. Derek Hirst, The Representative of the People? Voters and Voting in England under the Early Stuarts (Cambridge 1975) pages 150-1; A J Fletcher, A County Community in Peace and War: Sussex 1600-60 (London 1975) pages 205-9 and 212; John Morrill, The Revolt of the Provinces: Conservatives and Radicals in the English Civil War 1630-50 (London 1976) pages 24-8.

15. Christopher Hill, 'Parliament and people in seventeenth-century England', in Past and Present, number 92 (1981) pages 111-12; Christopher Hill, 'The poor and the people in seventeenth-century England', in Frederick Krantz (editor) History from Below: Studies in Popular Protest and Popular Ideology (Oxford 1985) page 44.

16. Margaret Spufford, Contrasting Communities: English Villagers in the Sixteenth and Seventeenth Centuries (Cambridge 1974) pages 230-41; Jim Sharpe, 'Scandalous and malignant priests in Essex: The impact of grassroots Puritanism', in Colin Jones, Malyn Newitt and Stephen Roberts (editors) Politics and People in Revolutionary England (Oxford 1986) pages 260-1 and 271.

17. Hirst, The Representative of the People?, pages 147-53, 157, 187 and 192.

18. Hirst, The Representative of the People?, pages 145-50.

19. Peter Lake, 'Anti-popery: The structure of a prejudice', in Richard Cust and Ann Hughes (editors) Conflict in early Stuart England: Studies in Religion and Politics 1603-42 (London 1989) pages 73-4 and 94-7.

20. Robin Clifton, 'Fear of popery', in Conrad Russell (editor) The Origins of the English Civil War (London 1973) pages 158-62.

21. K J Lindley, 'Riot prevention and control in early Stuart London', in Transactions of the Royal Historical Society, fifth series, volume 33 (1983).

22. K J Lindley, 'London and popular freedom in the 1640s', in R C Richardson and G M Ridden (editors) Freedom and the English Revolution (Manchester 1986) pages 121-2.

23. Robert Ashton, The English Civil War: Conservatism and Revolution 1603-49 (London 1978); A J Fletcher, The Outbreak of the English Civil War (London 1981).

24. Ashton, pages 146-52 and 303.

25. Lindley, 'London and popular freedom', pages 122-4.

26. William Hunt, **The Puritan Movement: The Coming of Revolution in an English County** (Cambridge, Massachusetts 1982) page 289.

27. Lindley, 'London and popular freedom', page 124.

28. Fletcher, **Outbreak of the English Civil War**, pages 171-6.

29. Fletcher, 'Parliament and people', page 154.

30. Morrill, **Revolt of the Provinces**, pages 34-5; Andrew Charlesworth (editor) **An Atlas of Rural Protest in Britain 1548-1900** (London 1983) page 41 notes 'five incidents in which property titles and records of leases, rents and dues were destroyed' in this period.

31. Fletcher, **Outbreak of the English Civil War**, pages 375-9.

32. Morrill, **Revolt of the Provinces**, pages 34-5.

33. Fletcher, **Outbreak of the English Civil War**, pages 375-9; 'The coming of the war', in Morrill (editor) **Reactions to the English Civil War**, page 42.

34. Morrill, **Revolt of the provinces**, pages 34-5.

35. Morrill, **Revolt of the provinces**, page 13.

36. Hunt, page 289.

37. Ashton, pages 148-52.

38. Ann Hughes, 'Local history and the origins of the civil war', in Cust and Hughes, page 240.

39. Barry Reay, 'Radicalism and religion in the English revolution: An introduction', in J F McGregor and Barry Reay (editors) **Radical Religion in the English Revolution** (Oxford 1984) page 6.

40. Cust and Hughes, page 37.

41. K J Lindley, **Fenland Riots and the English Revolution** (London 1982) page 108.

42. Hughes, 'Local history and the origins of the civil war', pages 242-3 and 247.

43. Morrill, **Revolt of the Provinces**, page 113.

44. Clive Holmes, **The Eastern Association in the English Civil War** (Cambridge 1974) pages 45, 51-2, 56-61 and 68; Clive Holmes, **Seventeenth-century Lincolnshire** (Lincoln 1980) pages 155-7.

45. Hunt, pages 305-6; Reay, 'Radicalism and religion', page 6.

46. See above, pages 261, 262, 265 and 266.

47. David Underdown, **Revel, Riot and Rebellion: Popular Politics and Culture in England 1603-60** (Oxford 1985) page 169.

48. Clifton, pages 152-3.

49. Ann Hughes, **Politics, Society and Civil War in Warwickshire 1620-60** (Cambridge 1987) pages 155-6.

50. Hunt, pages 309-10.

51. Fletcher, **Outbreak of the English Civil War**, page 378; Fletcher, 'Parliament and people', pages 154-5; Underdown, **Revel, Riot**

and Rebellion, page 169; see also above, pages 251-7.

52. Hughes, **Warwickshire**, pages 155-6.
53. See above, page 265.
54. Hunt, pages 272, 290, 301-2 and 308-9; see also above, pages 252-6 and 270.
55. See above, page 246.
56. Morrill, 'Provincial squires', page 232; see also above, page 262.
57. David Underdown, **Somerset in the Civil War and the Interregnum** (Newton Abbot 1973) pages 31-41.
58. Underdown, **Revel, Riot and Rebellion**, page 173.
59. Hunt, page 307.
60. Holmes, **Eastern Association**, pages 38-40.
61. Underdown, **Revel, Riot and Rebellion**, page 173.
62. See above, pages 188-212 and 270-86.
63. Buchanan Sharp, **In Contempt of all Authority: Rural Artisans and Riot in the West of England 1586-1660** (Berkeley 1980) pages 220-1, 247-52 and 263-4; Lindley, **Fenland Riots**, pages 64-5, 108, 139, 140-5, 160 and 257-8.
64. See above, pages 181, 267 and 271-7; George Rudé, **Ideology and Popular Protest** (London 1980) page 88.
65. See above, page 267.
66. Buchanan Sharp, page 264, note 9; Holmes, **Eastern Association**, pages 44-5.
67. Buchanan Sharp, pages 7-8, 36-42 and 264.
68. See above, pages 281-304, 331, 333, 337 and 350-9; Rudé, pages 88-9.
69. Morrill, **Revolt of the Provinces**, pages 50-1, 70 and 77-8; Morrill, 'Provincial squires', page 231; John Morrill, 'The Northern gentry and the Great Rebellion', in **Northern History**, volume 15 (1979) pages 83-4; Morrill, **Reactions to the English Civil War**, pages 10-11; Morrill, 'Christopher Hill's revolution', in **History**, volume 74, number 241 (1989) pages 250-1.
70. See above, page 336.
71. B G Blackwood, 'Parties and issues in the civil war in Lancashire', in **Transactions of the Historic Society of Lancashire and Cheshire**, volume 132 (1983) page 112.
72. See above, page 337.
73. Morrill, 'Northern gentry', pages 79-83; J T Cliffe, **The Yorkshire Gentry from the Reformation to the Civil War** (London 1979) chapter 15; B G Blackwood, **The Lancashire Gentry and the Great Rebellion 1640-60** (Manchester 1978) chapter 2.
74. Hughes, **Warwickshire**, pages 137-8 and 161-2.
75. Fletcher, **Outbreak of the English Civil War**, pages 329-33, 346 and 356-8; see above, pages 322-4.
76. Underdown, **Revel, Riot and Rebellion**, page 171.
77. See above, page 324-5.

78. Underdown, **Revel, Riot and Rebellion**, pages 172 and 192-207.
79. Dow, page 6.
80. Lindley, 'London and popular freedom', pages 131-2.
81. John Morrill, 'The Church in England 1642-9', in Morrill (editor) **Reactions to the English Civil War**.
82. E J Hobsbawm, **Primitive Rebels** (Manchester 1959; new edition 1971) chapter 7: 'The city mob'; George Rudé, **The Crowd in History: A Study of Popular Disturbances in France and England 1730-1848** (New York 1964) chapter 9: 'Church and King riots'; Ashton, pages 302-3.
83. Morrill, **Revolt of the Provinces**, pages 110-11.
84. See above, pages 242, 267, 277, 316-17 and 330.
85. Underdown, 'Community and class', pages 156-8.
86. Brian Manning, 'Neutrals and neutralism in the English civil war' (unpublished D Phil thesis, Oxford 1959); Morrill, **Revolt of the Provinces**, pages 98-111; David Underdown, 'The chalk and the cheese: Contrasts among the English Clubmen', in **Past and Present**, number 85 (1979); Garry Lynch, 'The risings of the Clubmen in 1644-5', in Charlesworth, pages 122-4; Ronald Hutton, 'The Worcestershire Clubmen in the English civil war', in **Midland History**, volume 5 (1980); Ronald Hutton, 'The Royalist war effort', in Morrill (editor) **Reactions to the English Civil War**, pages 61-4; Ian Roy, 'The English civil war and English society', in Brian Bond and Ian Roy (editors) **War and Society** (London 1975) pages 39-42.
87. Mark Gould, **Revolution in the Development of Capitalism: The Coming of the English Revolution** (Berkeley 1987) page 414, note 30.
88. Fletcher, 'Parliament and people', page 154; Fletcher, **Outbreak of the English Civil War**, page 417.
89. Hunt, page 313.
90. Hirst, **Authority and Conflict**, page 230.
91. Dow, page 8.
92. Underdown, **Revel, Riot and Rebellion**, page 276.
93. Roger Howell, 'Resistance to change: The political élites of provincial towns during the English revolution', in A L Beier, David Cannadine and James M Rosenheim (editors) **The First Modern Society** (Cambridge 1989) pages 435-6.
94. Lindley, **Fenland Riots**, pages 140-5; see above, pages 270-1.
95. Clive Holmes, 'Drainers and fenmen: The problem of popular political consciousness in the seventeenth century', in A J Fletcher and J Stevenson (editors) **Order and Disorder in Early Modern England** (Cambridge 1985) pages 183-6.
96. Roy, pages 35-6.
97. Underdown, **Somerset**, pages 31-41.
98. Hughes, **Warwickshire**, pages 137-62.

99. See above, pages 285-92.

100. Hughes, **Warwickshire**, pages 8-9.

101. Hirst, **Authority and Conflict**, page 239.

102. Underdown, **Revel, Riot and Rebellion**, pages 168-71 and 192-207.

103. Hirst, **Authority and Conflict**, page 239.

104. Hunt, pages 19-23; Buchanan Sharp, page 7.

105. Jill R Dias, 'Lead, society and politics in Derbyshire before the civil war', in **Midland History**, volume 6 (1981).

106. Underdown, **Revel, Riot and Rebellion**, page 204.

107. See above, pages 83-101 and 337-50.

108. Morrill, 'Provincial squires', page 231; Morrill, 'Northern gentry', pages 83-4; Morrill, **Reactions to the English Civil War**, pages 10-11.

109. Underdown, **Revel, Riot and Rebellion**, page 169; Keith Wrightson and David Levine, **Poverty and Piety in an English Village: Terling 1525-1700** (New York 1979) pages 161-2 and 166-7.

110. Blackwood, 'Parties and issues', pages 117 and 119-20.

111. Murray Tolmie, **The Triumph of the Saints: The Separate Churches of London 1616-49** (Cambridge 1977) pages 39-41 and 80.

112. J F McGregor, 'The Baptists: Fount of all heresy', in McGregor and Reay, pages 35-9.

113. B S Capp, **The Fifth Monarchy Men: A Study in Seventeenth-century English Millenarianism** (London 1972) pages 76-89 and 231.

114. Barry Reay, **The Quakers and the English Revolution** (New York 1985) pages 20-6.

115. Reay, 'Radicalism and religion', in McGregor and Reay, pages 18-19.

116. See above, page 241.

117. John Miller, 'Two types of historical method', in **The Times Higher Education Supplement** (28 May 1976) page 16; J P Cooper, 'The people's war', in **The Times Literary Supplement** (3 September 1976) page 1072; Morrill, 'Provincial squires'.

118. See above, pages 337, 350 and 386.

119. Hirst, **Authority and Conflict**, page 12; see also Alex Callinicos, 'Bourgeois revolutions', in **International Socialism**, second series, number 43 (1989) page 161.

120. Wrightson, pages 64-5.

121. Underdown, **Revel, Riot and Rebellion**, page 168.

122. Wrightson, pages 64-5.

123. Robin Briggs, **Communities of Belief: Cultural and Social Tensions in Early Modern France** (Oxford 1989) pages 161, 168 and 174.

124. Roger Howell, 'Neutralism, conservatism and political alignment in the English revolution: The case of the towns 1642-9', in Morrill (editor) **Reactions to the English Civil War**, page 76; John T Evans, **Seventeenth-century Norwich: Politics, Religion and Government 1620-90** (Oxford 1979) pages 107 and 139-43.

125. Blackwood, 'Parties and issues', page 113.

126. Hirst, **Authority and Conflict**, pages 258-9.

127. Lindley, **Fenland Riots**, pages 142-3 and 256.

128. Hughes, **Warwickshire**, pages 155-6; see also Charlesworth, pages 56-60: 'deer parks were singled out for attack... partly because they were symbols of aristocratic power.'

129. Dias, in **Midland History**, volume 6.

130. Hirst, **Authority and Conflict**, page 230.

131. Underdown, 'Community and class', pages 155-6; Underdown, **Revel, Riot and Rebellion**, pages 168-71.

132. Hughes, **Warwickshire**, page 342; Hughes, 'Local history', page 240.

133. See above, pages 305, 343, 351 and 356.

134. Hunt, pages 309-10 and 313.

135. Hughes, 'Local history', pages 243-7.

136. Hughes, **Warwickshire**, pages 155-6.

137. J H Elliott, 'Revolts in the Spanish monarchy', in Robert Forster and Jack P Greene (editors) **Preconditions of Revolution in Early Modern Europe** (Baltimore 1970) page 112.

138. Underdown, **Somerset**, pages 47, 124-5, 157-8 and 167-9; Hughes, **Warwickshire**, pages 169, 179-80 and 272-3; David Underdown, **Pride's Purge: Politics in the Puritan Revolution** (Oxford 1971) pages 34-6 and 306-9; G E Aylmer, 'Crisis and regrouping in the political élites: England from the 1630s to the 1660s', in J G A Pocock (editor) **Three British Revolutions: 1641, 1688 and 1776** (Princeton 1980) pages 149-52.

139. Underdown, **Revel, Riot and Rebellion**, pages 25-8; Morrill and Walter, 'Order and disorder in the English revolution', in Fletcher and Stevenson, pages 151-4 and 156-7; Wrightson and Levine, pages 103-9, 117, 140, 156-62 and 176-9; J A Sharpe, 'Crime and delinquency in an Essex parish 1600-40', in J S Cockburn (editor) **Crime in England 1550-1800** (London 1977) pages 94-5.

140. Hill, 'Parliament and people', pages 121-2; Hill, 'The poor and the people', page 44.

141. Morrill and Walter, pages 151-4.

142. Norah Carlin, 'Marxism and the English civil war', in **International Socialism**, second series, number 10 (1980-1).

143. Wrightson, pages 223-4 and 226-8.

144. Alan Everitt, 'Farm labourers', in Joan Thirsk (editor) **The Agrarian History of England and Wales**, volume 4 (Cambridge 1967) pages 462-5.

Chapter 1: THE PEOPLE AND THE LONG PARLIAMENT

1. **CSPD 1640-1641**, pages 112 and 139; HMC, 12th Report (1888) 'Rutland Manuscripts', volume 1, page 523; *Persecutio Undecima* (1648) page 6.

2. M F Keeler, **The Long Parliament 1640-1641** (Philadelphia 1954) pages 7-8.

3. J H Plumb, 'The growth of the electorate in England from 1600 to 1715', in **Past and Present**, number 45 (1969) pages 93-107; Hirst, **Representative of the People?** pages 29-43 and 90-105.

4. M R Frear, 'The Election at Great Marlow in 1640', in **Journal of Modern History**, volume 14 (1942).

5. R N Kershaw, 'The Elections for the Long Parliament, 1640', in **English Historical Review**, volume 38 (1923) pages 447-8.

6. Keeler, page 72.

7. **The Diurnall Occurrences or Dayly Proceedings** (3 November 1640-3 November 1641) (London 1641) BL E523, page 8; HMC, 9th Report (1884) 'Pyne and Woodforde Manuscripts', page 499; HMC, 12th Report (1890) 'Le Fleming Manuscripts', page 18; HMC (1926) 'Buccleuch Manuscripts', volume 3, page 395; HMC (1966) 'De L'Isle and Dudley Manuscripts', volume 6, page 346; **The Letters and Journals of Robert Baillie**, edited by David Laing (three volumes, Edinburgh 1841) volume 1, page 277; Clarendon, **History**, volume 1, pages 264-70; Thomas May, **The History of the Parliament of England** (London 1647) book 1, pages 79-80; P Heylyn, *Cyprianus Anglicus* (London 1668) page 465; 'Letters of the Lady Brilliana Harley', in **Camden Society**, first series, volume 58 (1854) page 104; Thomas Hobbes, 'Behemoth: the History of the Causes of the Civil Wars of England', in **The English Works of Thomas Hobbes of Malmesbury**, edited by Sir William Molesworth (London, 1840) volume 6, page 245.

8. Baillie, volume 1, page 283; Clarendon, **History**, volume 1, page 269; **CSPD 1640-1641**, page 323; Nehemiah Wallington, **Historical Notices of Events Occurring Chiefly in the Reign of Charles I**, edited by R Webb (two volumes, London 1869) volume 1, page 137.

9. Clarendon, **History**, volume 1, page 137.

10. Heylyn, *Cyprianus Anglicus*, page 465.

11. Clarendon, **History**, volume 1, page 269.

12. Wallington, volume 1, page 137.

13. HMC, 9th Report (1884) 'Pyne and Woodforde Manuscripts', page 499.

14. Baillie, volume 1, page 283.

15. Clarendon, **History**, volume 1, page 269.

16. Heylyn, *Cyprianus Anglicus*, page 465.

17. **The Diurnall Occurrences or Dayly Proceedings** BL E523, page 8.

18. May, book 1, page 79.
19. Clarendon, **History**, volume 1, page 269.
20. May, book 1, page 79; John Nalson, **An Impartial Collection** (London 1682-3) volume 1, page 570.
21. May, book 1, page 79; **Diary of Henry Townshend of Elmley Lovett 1640-1663**, edited by J W Willis-Bund (two volumes, London 1920) volume 1, page 10.
22. Heylyn, *Cyprianus Anglicus*, page 465.
23. Clarendon, **History**, volume 1, pages 265 note and 270.
24. May, book 1, pages 79-80; HMC (1966) 'De L'isle and Dudley Manuscripts', volume 6, page 346; **CSPD 1640-1641**, page 312.
25. Clarendon, **History**, volume 1, page 270; Nalson, volume 1, page 570.
26. Baillie, volume 1, pages 273, 275 and 280.
27. **The Journal of Sir Simonds D'Ewes**, edited by W Notestein (New Haven 1923) pages 138-41; Baillie, volume 1, page 280; John Rushworth, **Historical Collections** (eight volumes, London 1721) volume 4, page 175; Valerie Pearl, **London and the outbreak of the Puritan revolution** (Oxford 1961) page 214 note 62; Wallington, volume 1, page 146.
28. Pearl, pages 176-84.
29. Rushworth, volume 4, page 175; D'Ewes, edited by Notestein, page 339.
30. D'Ewes, edited by Notestein, pages 138-41.
31. Gardiner, **History**, volume 9, page 247; Clarendon, **History**, volume 1, page 271.
32. Gardiner, **History**, volume 9, pages 248-9 and 275.
33. Clarendon, **History**, volume 1, page 271; D'Ewes, edited by Notestein, pages 335-8; *Persecutio Undecima*, page 59.
34. Clarendon, **History**, volume 1, pages 282 and 308-9; HMC (1966) 'De L'Isle and Dudley Manuscripts', volume 6, pages 367-8; HMC, 12th Report (1888) 'Cowper Manuscripts', volume 2, page 272; Gardiner, **History**, volume 9, page 281.
35. Baillie, volume 1, page 307.
36. **The Third Speech of Lord George Digby, to the House of Commons** (1641) BL E196 (30); Rushworth, volume 4, pages 170-4.
37. **A Speech by the Honourable Nathaniel Fiennes** (1641) BL E196 (32); Rushworth, volume 4, pages 174-83.
38. D'Ewes, edited by Notestein, page 339; Pearl, pages 214-15.
39. Baillie, volume 1, page 302; Gardiner, **History**, volume 9, page 287.
40. **CJ**, volume 2, pages 100-2; D'Ewes, edited Notestein, pages 458-60 and 466-70; Baillie, volume 1, pages 308-9; Gardiner, **History**, volume 9, page 299.
41. Baillie, volume 1, page 314.
42. G Bankes, **The Story of Corfe Castle** (London 1853) pages 84-5.
43. **The Works of Archbishop Laud** (Oxford 1853) volume 3, pages

240 and 436-7; Heylyn, *Cyprianus Anglicus*, page 466; Daniel Neal, **The History of the Puritans** (four volumes, London 1732-8) volume 2, page 384.

44. **CSP Venetian 1640-1642**, pages 128-9.
45. HMC, 12th Report (1888) 'Cowper Manuscripts', volume 2, page 278.
46. **CSPD 1640-1641**, pages 534-5.
47. **CSPD 1640-1641**, page 538.
48. HMC, 12th Report (1888) 'Cowper Manuscripts', volume 2, page 278.
49. Pearl, page 216; **CJ**, volume 2, page 125; **CSPD 1640-1641**, pages 524-5; HMC, 12th Report (1888) 'Cowper Manuscripts', volume 2, page 280.
50. **The Lord Digby His Last Speech against the Earl of Strafford** (1641) BL E198 (1); Rushworth, volume 4, pages 225-8.
51. HMC, 12th Report (1888) 'Cowper Manuscripts', volume 2, pages 278, 279, 280, 281 and 283-4; Sir Philip Warwick, **Memoires of the reigne of King Charles I** (London 1701) page 160.
52. Arthur, Lord Capel, **Excellent Contemplations, Divine and Moral** (London 1683) pages 4, 138-9 and 197.
53. Nalson, volume 2, pages 188 and 259; Bulstrode Whitelock, **Memorials of the English Affairs** (four volumes, Oxford 1853) volume 1, page 130; May, book 1, page 96; Warwick, page 161; **CSPD 1640-1641**, page 560; **Diurnall Occurrences or Dayly Proceedings**, BL E523, page 115; **A Brief and Perfect Relation** (1647) BL T809, page 85; *Reliquiae Baxterianae*, edited by Matthew Sylvester (London 1696) page 19.
54. J L Sanford, **Studies and Illustrations of the Great Rebellion** (London 1858) page 346.
55. HMC, 12th Report (1888) 'Cowper Manuscripts', volume 2, pages 280-1.
56. Nalson, volume 2, pages 186-8; **A Brief and Perfect Relation**, BL T809, page 84.
57. Whitelock, volume 1, page 130.
58. HMC, 12th Report (1888) 'Cowper Manuscripts', volume 2, pages 280-1.
59. Gardiner, **History**, volume 9, pages 348-9; HMC, 4th Report (1874) 'De la Warr Manuscripts', page 295; May, book 1, page 94; Baillie, volume 1, page 351.
60. **Diurnall Occurrences or Dayly Proceedings**, BL E523, page 93; Whitelock, volume 1, page 130; **The Autobiography and Correspondence of Sir Simonds D'Ewes**, edited by J O Halliwell (two volumes, London 1845) volume 2, page 268; Nalson, volume 2, page 188.
61. **CSPD 1640-1641**, page 569.
62. Wallington, volume 1, page 242.

63. **Diurnall Occurrences or Dayly Proceedings**, BL E523, page 90; **A Briefe and Perfect Relation**, BL T809, page 84; Baillie, volume 1, page 352; Wallington, volume 1, page 242; Whitelock, volume 1, page 130; May, book 1, page 94; **CSP Venetian 1640-1642**, pages 147-8; Nalson, volume 2, page 188.

64. **A Briefe and Perfect Relation**, BL T809, pages 84-5; Nalson, volume 2, page 188.

65. LJ, volume 4, pages 232-3; HMC, 4th Report (1874) 'House of Lords Manuscripts', page 61; **Diurnall Occurrences or Dayly Proceedings**, BL E523, page 90.

66. Nalson, volume 2, page 188.

67. **Diurnall Occurrences or Dayly Proceedings**, BL E523, page 90; May, book 1, page 94.

68. Whitelock, volume 1, page 130; **CSPD 1641-1643**, page 62; HMC, 12th Report (1888) 'Cowper Manuscripts', volume 2, page 281.

69. **A Briefe and Perfect Relation**, BL T809, page 87; LJ, volume 4, page 233; HMC, 10th Report (1887) 'Braye Manuscripts', pages 140-1.

70. **CSPD 1640-1641**, page 569; **A Briefe and Perfect Relation**, BL T809, page 87.

71. Whitelock, volume 1, page 130; **A Briefe and Perfect Relation**, BL T809, page 84.

72. Nalson, volume 2, page 188.

73. Baillie, volume 1, page 352.

74. **Diurnall Occurrences or Dayly Proceedings**, BL E523, page 90; D'Ewes, edited Halliwell, volume 2, page 268; **CSPD 1640-1641**, page 569; **CSP Venetian 1640-1642**, pages 147-8.

75. Clarendon, **History**, volume 1, page 455; Pearl, pages 187-8.

76. Pauline Gregg, **Free-born John: A Biography of John Lilburne** (London 1961).

77. LJ, volume 4, page 233; HMC, 10th Report (1887) 'Braye Manuscripts', pages 140-1.

78. Wallington, volume 1, page 242; **A Briefe and Perfect Relation**, BL T809, page 89; HMC, 4th Report (1874) 'De La Warr Manuscripts', page 295; Pearl, page 217.

79. **Works of Archbishop Laud**, volume 3, page 441.

80. Clarendon, **History**, volume 1, page 337.

81. LJ, volume 4, page 233.

82. **Diurnall Occurrences or Dayly Proceedings**, BL E523, page 92; HMC, (1900) 'Montagu of Beaulieu Manuscripts', page 129.

83. **CSP Venetian 1640-1642**, page 148; D'Ewes, edited Halliwell, volume 2, page 269.

84. **CSPD 1640-1641**, page 569.

85. **Diurnall Occurrences or Dayly Proceedings**, BL E523, pages 93-4; HMC, 12th Report (1888) 'Cowper Manuscripts', volume 2, pages 282-3; Gardiner, **History**, volume 9, pages 356-9.

86. Sanford, pages 373-5; Wallington, volume 1, page 244; Baillie, volume 1, page 352; Rushworth, volume 8, pages 744-5; Nalson, volume 2, pages 191-2; **Diurnall Occurrences or Dayly Proceedings,** BL E523, pages 93-4; HMC (1900) 'Lord Montagu of Beaulieu Manuscripts', pages 129-30.

87. HMC, 12th Report (1888) 'Cowper Manuscripts', volume 2, page 280.

88. **CSPD 1640-1641**, page 571; **A Briefe and Perfect Relation,** BL T809, page 89; **The Copy of a Letter of Father Philips** (1641) BL E160 (28).

89. [Dudley North], **A Narrative of Some Passages in or relating to the Long Parliament** (London 1670) page 14; Heylyn, *Cyprianus Anglicus*, page 479; Griffith Williams, **The Discovery of Mysteries** (1643) page 8; King Charles I, *Eikon Basilike*, edited by E Almack (London 1904) page 10; John Hacket, *Scrinia Reserata* (London 1693) part 2, page 149; Nalson, volume 2, pages 188 and 192.

90. **CSP Venetian 1640-1642**, page 150.

91. Clarendon, **History,** volume 1, page 337.

92. C H Firth, **The House of Lords during the Civil War** (London 1910) page 91.

93. Gardiner, **History,** volume 9, pages 359 and 361.

94. Firth, **House of Lords,** page 91.

95. Gardiner, **History,** volume 9, page 361.

96. **Copy of a Letter of Father Philips,** BL E160 (28).

97. Clarendon, **History,** volume 1, pages 339-40.

98. Edward Husbands, **An Exact Collection** (London 1642) pages 220-4 and 227; **CSPD 1640-1641,** pages 531-2, 535 and 565.

99. Sanford, pages 573-5.

100. Hacket, page 149.

101. CSP Venetian 1640-1642, pages 150-1; Wallington, volume 1, pages 244-5; **Copy of a Letter of Father Philips,** BL E160 (28).

102. Whitelock, volume 1, page 130.

103. **A Briefe and Perfect Relation,** BL T 809, page 93.

104. **Works of Archbishop Laud,** volume 3, page 441.

105. Wallington, volume 1, pages 244-5; Pearl, page 217.

106. Gardiner, **History,** volume 9, pages 366-7.

107. John Forster, **Eminent British Statesmen** (London 1838) volume 6, page 71.

108. **CSP Venetian 1640-1642**, page 151.

109. Warwick, pages 163-4.

110. *Reliquiae Baxterianae*, page 19; **A Speech Made by Master Waller Esquire in the Honourable House of Commons, concerning Episcopacy** (1641) BL E198 (30).

111. Husbands, pages 107, 228, 523-4 and 563-4.

112. *Reliquiae Baxterianae*, pages 19 and 24-5.

Chapter 2: FEAR OF POPISH PLOTS
AND THE RISE OF RELIGIOUS RADICALISM

1. **A Briefe and Perfect Relation**, BL T809, pages 83-4; Nalson, volume 2, pages 187-8.

2. LJ, volume 4, pages 244, 252 and 253; CJ, volume 2, pages 143 and 149; Nalson, volume 2, pages 237-8 and 246-7.

3. LJ, volume 4, pages 382, 389 and 390; 'Nicholas Papers', in **Camden Society**, second series, volume 40 (1886) page 37; Nalson, volume 2, page 468.

4. LJ, volume 4, page 389; HMC, 4th Report (1874) 'House of Lords Manuscripts', page 100.

5. CJ, volume 2, page 290; LJ, volume 4, pages 398-9; **The Journal of Sir Simonds D'Ewes**, edited by W H Coates (New Haven 1942) pages 9-10, 14-15, 21 note 13, and 58-9.

6. Neal, volume 2, page 501.

7. CJ, volume 2, page 300; LJ, volume 4, page 446; D'Ewes, edited Coates, pages 58-9, 63-4, 68, 73-4, 108 and 119-20.

8. D'Ewes, edited Coates, pages 119-20.

9. D'Ewes, edited Coates, page 125.

10. **A Great Discovery of a Damnable Plot at Ragland Castle** (London 1641) BL E176 (13).

11. **A Discovery of a horrible and Bloody Treason and Conspiracie** (London 1641) BL E176 (12); **England's Deliverance, Or, A Great Discovery** (London 1641) BL E176 (11); D'Ewes, edited Coates, pages 144-5; LJ, volume 4, pages 439-40; **Diary and Correspondence of John Evelyn**, edited by W Bray (four volumes, London 1857) volume 4, page 126.

12. D'Ewes, edited Coates, pages 145-6, 171-3 and 174-5.

13. D'Ewes, edited Coates, pages 147-8, 149, 150 and 152; CJ, volume 2, page 317; LJ, volume 4, pages 440 and 442.

14. LJ, volume 4, page 442; D'Ewes, edited Coates, pages 153-4.

15. D'Ewes, edited Coates, page 146.

16. D'Ewes, edited Coates, page 149 note 8.

17. D'Ewes, edited Coates, page 120 note 9.

18. **Bloody Newes from Norwich** (London 1641) BL E179 (10).

19. D'Ewes, edited Coates, pages 201-2.

20. CJ, volume 2, page 319; LJ, volume 4, page 440; D'Ewes, edited Coates, page 163.

21. Wallington, volume 1, page 275.

22. **CSPD 1641-1643**, pages 264-5.

23. Evelyn, volume 4, pages 98-9.

24. *Reliquiae Baxterianae*, pages 28-9.

25. HMC, 14th Report (1894) 'Portland Manuscripts', volume 3, pages 81-2; HMC, 11th Report (1888) 'Bridgewater Manuscripts', page 147; HMC, 10th Report (1885) 'Corporation of Bridgnorth Manuscripts', pages 433-4; Penry Williams, 'Government and

Politics in Ludlow, 1590-1642', in **Transactions of the Shropshire Archaeological Society**, volume 56, number 3 (1960) pages 290-1.

26. **The Autobiography of Joseph Lister**, edited by T Wright (London 1842) pages 6-8.

27. Evelyn, volume 4, page 126; 'Sir Roger Twysden's Journal', in *Archaeologia Cantiana*, volume 1 (1858) pages 199-200.

28. D'Ewes, edited Coates, page 153.

29. HMC, 14th Report (1894) 'Portland Manuscripts', volume 3, pages 81- 2.

30. Evelyn, volume 4, pages 98-9.

31. **Table Talk of John Selden**, edited by Sir Frederick Pollock, Selden Society (London 1927) page 99.

32. Evelyn, volume 4, pages 71-3 and 98-9.

33. Lister, pages 8 and 10; Robin Clifton, 'The Popular Fear of Catholics during the English Revolution', in **Past and Present**, number 52 (1971).

34. Verney, **Memoirs**, volume 2, page 88.

35. D'Ewes, edited Coates, pages 14-15.

36. Wallington, volume 1, pages 138-9.

37. Baillie, volume 1, page 291.

38. Wallington, volume 1, pages 138-9.

39. 'Letters of the Lady Brilliana Harley', page 111.

40. Lister, pages 5-6.

41. **The Autobiography and Diaries of Oliver Heywood**, edited by J H Turner (Brighouse 1882) volume 1, pages 77, 83 and 97-8.

42. Clarendon, **History**, volume 1, page 308.

43. Heylyn, *Cyprianus Anglicus*, pages 468-9.

44. Baillie, volume 1, page 293.

45. *Persecutio Undecima*, page 20.

46. HMC, 12th Report (1888) 'Cowper Manuscripts', volume 2, page 291.

47. LJ, volume 4, pages 100-1, 107 and 113; HMC (1926) 'Buccleuch Manuscripts', volume 3, pages 395 and 401.

48. [Bruno Ryves], *Mercurius Rusticus*, number 3.

49. **The Anatomy of the Separatists** (London 1642) BL E238 (14).

50. LJ, volume 4, page 142.

51. **The Speech of Master Plydell Esquire: Concerning the Church** (London 1641) BL E196 (29).

52. LJ, volume 4, page 134.

53. LJ, volume 4, pages 225 and 262; HMC, 4th Report (1874) 'House of Lords Manuscripts', page 55; **CSPD 1641-1643**, page 77; Sir Thomas Aston, **A Remonstrance against Presbytery** (1641) BL E163 (1); **The Brownists Conventicle** (1641) BL E164 (13).

54. Baillie, volume 1, page 293.

55. LJ, volume 4, page 174.

56. **LJ**, volume 4, pages 270, 271, 277-8 and 318; HMC, 4th Report (1874) 'House of Lords Manuscripts', pages 73, 75, 77 and 89.

57. **LJ**, volume 4, pages 270, 271, 277-8 and 323-4; HMC, 4th Report (1874) 'House of Lords Manuscripts', pages 73, 74 and 90.

58. **LJ**, volume 4, pages 295 and 312; **CJ**, volume 2, page 194; HMC, 4th Report (1874) 'House of Lords Manuscripts', pages 80 and 81.

59. **CJ**, volume 2, pages 246, 278, 283 and 287.

60. **CJ**, volume 2, pages 286-7; **LJ**, volume 4, pages 392 and 395.

61. D'Ewes, edited Coates, pages 3, 5, 7 and 17.

62. HMC, 14th Report (1894) 'Portland Manuscripts', volume 3, page 81.

63. Lucy Hutchinson, **Memoirs of the Life of Colonel Hutchinson**, edited by J Hutchinson and revised by C H Firth (London 1906) page 80.

64. *Reliquiae Baxterianae*, page 40.

65. **CSPD 1641-1643**, page 134.

66. Wallington, volume 1, page 259.

67. D'Ewes, edited Coates, pages 6-7.

68. [Ryves] *Mercurius Rusticus*, number 3.

69. Wallington, volume 1, page 259.

70. *Reliquiae Baxterianae*, page 39; *Persecutio Undecima*, page 59.

71. *Reliquiae Baxterianae*, pages 26 and 39.

72. [Henry Burton], **The Protestation Protested** (1641).

73. [Burton] **The Protestation Protested; The Brownists Synagogue** (1641) BL E172 (32).

74. John Latimer, **The Annals of Bristol in the Seventeenth Century** (Bristol 1900) pages 150-1.

75. **The Knyvett Letters (1620-1644)**, edited by B Schofield (London 1949) page 98.

76. [Ryves] *Mercurius Rusticus*, number 3.

77. HMC, 14th Report (1894) 'Portland Manuscripts', volume 3, page 73.

78. HMC, 14th Report (1894) 'Portland Manuscripts', volume 3, page 74.

79. **LJ**, volume 4, pages 133-4; **CSPD 1640-1641**, page 418; HMC, (1926) 'Buccleuch Manuscripts', volume 3, pages 408-9; Baillie, volume 1, page 293; Neal, volume 2, pages 391-4; Champlin Burrage, **The Early English Dissenters** (two volumes, Cambridge 1912) volume 1, page 201, and volume 2, pages 305-8.

80. **The Brothers of the Separation** (London 1641) BL E172 (11); **The Brownists Synagogue**, BL E172 (32); Burrage, volume 2, page 301.

81. **The Discovery of a Swarme of Separatists** (London 1641) BL E180 (25); **The Preachers New** (1641) BL E180 (26); **Diurnal Occurrences, or, the Heads of Several Proceedings** (13-20

December 1641) BL E201 (3); Burrage, volume 1, page 325.

82. **The Brownists Synagogue**, BL E172.

83. **The Parliamentary or Constitutional History of England** (London 1762) volume 10, pages 132-3.

84. **The Brownists Synagogue**, BL E172 (32).

85. **Anatomy of the Separatists**, BL E238 (14).

86. **Parliamentary or Constitutional History of England**, volume 10, pages 132-3.

87. **CJ**, volume 2, pages 168 and 170; Gardiner, **History**, volume 9, pages 394-5.

88. **The Brownists Synagogue**, BL E172 (32); **The Brothers of the Separation**, BL E172 (11); **The Preachers New**, BL E180 (26).

89. **The Preachers New**, BL E180 (26).

90. **A Discoverie of Six Women Preachers** (London 1641) BL E166 (1).

91. **Lucifers Lacky** (London 1641) BL E180 (3).

92. Burrage, volume 2, pages 305-8.

93. **The Brownists Synagogue**, BL E172 (32).

94. **His Majesty's Special Command under the great Seal of England to the Lord Mayor of the Honourable City of London** (London 1641) BL E179 (19).

95. [Thomas Aston], **A Collection of Sundry Petitions** (1642) pages 11-12.

96. **The Brownists Conventicle**, BL E164 (13); **The Brownists Synagogue**, BL E172 (32).

97. **CSPD 1641-1643**, page 143.

98. *Reliquiae Baxterianae*, page 26; **Lucifers Lacky**, BL E180 (3).

99. **CSPD 1641-1643**, pages 25, 158 and 163.

100. **The Brownists Synagogue**, BL E172 (32).

101. **A Collection of Speeches Made by Sir Edward Dering Knight and Baronet in matter of Religion** (London 1642) BL E197 (1) pages 98-9 and 105.

102. [Aston] **A Collection of Sundry Petitions**, pages 33-4.

103. HMC, 14th Report (1894) 'Portland Manuscripts', volume 3, pages 79-80.

104. Cornelius Burgess, **Another Sermon Preached to the Honorable House of Commons** (London 1641) page 60.

105. **Parliamentary or Constitutional History of England**, volume 10, pages 132-3.

106. **A Short History of the Anabaptists of High and Low Germany** (London 1642) BL E148 (5); **A Warning for England Especially for London in the Famous History of the Frantic Anabaptists their wild preachings and practices in Germany** (1642) BL E136 (33).

107. Aston, **A Remonstrance against Presbytery**, BL E163 (1).

108. Gardiner, **History**, volume 10, page 13.

109. **A Survay of that Foolish, Seditious, Scandalous, Prophane Libell, the Protestation Protested** (London 1641).
110. May, book 1, pages 113-18.

Chapter 3:
THE POPULAR PARTY AND THE PARTY OF ORDER

1.   **LJ**, volume 4, pages 430-2 and 435; **CJ**, volume 2, page 307; D'Ewes, edited Coates, pages 94-5, 99-101 and 104-5.
2.   **Speeches by Sir Edward Dering**, BL E197 (1) pages 3 and 5-6 (I owe this reference to Mr W M Lamont); **CJ**, volume 2, page 159.
3.   Neal, volume 2, pages 459-69, 471-2 and 478.
4.   **CSPD 1641-1643**, page 7.
5.   **CSPD 1641-1643**, pages 15-16.
6.   **CSPD 1641-1643**, page 140; Evelyn, volume 4, page 83.
7.   D'Ewes, edited Coates, pages 51-4.
8.   D'Ewes, edited Coates, page 133; **LJ**, volume 4, page 314.
9.   Gardiner, **Documents**, pages 202-32.
10. HMC, 12th Report (1888) 'Cowper Manuscripts', page 295; D'Ewes, edited by Coates, pages 183-6; Verney, **Notes**, pages 121-5; Clarendon, **History**, volume 1, pages 427-9 note; **Speeches by Sir Edward Dering**, BL E197 (1) pages 109 and 118-19.
11. D'Ewes, edited Coates, pages 186-7; Warwick, pages 201-2; Clarendon, **History**, volume 1, pages 417-20.
12. D'Ewes, edited Coates, pages 192-6.
13. D'Ewes, edited Coates, pages 214-15 and 216; Verney, **Notes**, page 129.
14. For example Richard Gough, **Antiquityes and Memoyres of the Parish of Myddle** (Fontwell, Sussex, 1968) pages 122-5 and 182-6. I am grateful to Mr M R D Wanklyn for this reference.
15. *Ovatio Carolina* (London 1641) in **The Harleian Miscellany** (twelve volumes, London 1810-11) volume 5, pages 86-103.
16. **LJ**, volume 4, pages 452, 453 and 455.
17. **CSPD 1641-1643**, page 188.
18. **The Heads of Several Proceedings in both Houses of Parliament** (29 November-6 December 1641) BL E201 (2); **His Majesties Speciall Command to the Lord Mayor**, BL E179 (19); **CSPD 1641-1643**, pages 186 and 188; D'Ewes, edited Coates, page 213 note 6; Warwick, page 186; HMC (1926) 'Buccleuch Manuscripts', volume 3, page 287.
19. D'Ewes, edited Coates, pages 211, 213 and 222; Clarendon, **History**, volume 1, page 451; HMC (1926) 'Buccleuch Manuscripts', volume 3, page 287.
20. **CSPD 1641-1643**, page 202.
21. *Ovatio Carolina*, in **Harleian Miscellany**, volume 5, page 101.
22. **CSPD 1641-1643**, page 192; **His Majesties Speciall Command to the Lord Mayor**, BL E179 (19).

23. **The Heads of Several Proceedings in both Houses,** BL E201 (2).

24. D'Ewes, edited Coates, page 222.

25. D'Ewes, edited Coates, page 230.

26. D'Ewes, edited Coates, page 211 note 17.

27. **The Heads of Several Proceedings in both Houses,** BL E201 (2); **His Majesties Speciall Command to the Lord Mayor,** BL E179 (19).

28. D'Ewes, edited Coates, pages 218 and 222; **CJ,** volume 2, pages 327 and 329.

29. *Ovatio Carolina,* in **Harleian Miscellany,** volume 5, pages 99-101.

30. HMC, 15th Report (1899) 'Buccleuch Manuscripts', volume 1, page 287.

31. D'Ewes, edited Coates, pages 213-14, 218 note 16, 225 and 230.

32. Thomas Warmstry, **A Convocation Speech... Against Images, Altars, Crosses, the New Canons, and the Oath, etc** (London 1641).

33. Thomas Warmstry, *Pax Vobis* **or A Charm for Tumultuous Spirits (London 1641)** BL E180 (24).

34. William Thomason, **Regulated Zeal** (London 1641) BL E160 (29).

35. Warmstry, *Pax Vobis,* BL E180 (24).

36. **A Remonstrance of Londons Occurrences** (1642) BL E153 (5).

37. **Speech Made by Master Waller Esquire,** BL E198 (30).

38. [Ryves] *Mercurius Rusticus,* number 3.

39. **Speech Made by Master Waller Esquire,** BL E198 (30).

40. D'Ewes, edited Coates, pages 214-16; Verney, **Notes,** page 129.

41. D'Ewes, edited Coates, pages 212, 221 and 232-3.

42. D'Ewes, edited Coates, page 215.

43. D'Ewes, edited Coates, pages 232-4.

44. D'Ewes, edited Coates, page 216 note 11; Clarendon, **History,** volume 1, page 455.

45. D'Ewes, edited Coates, pages 213, 217-18 and 219.

46. D'Ewes, edited Coates, pages 225-6 and 229-31.

47. **The Citizens of London's Humble Petition** (11 December 1641) BL E180 (16).

48. Pearl, pages 316-20.

49. *Persecutio Undecima,* pages 58-60.

50. **CSPD 1641-1643,** pages 193 and 197.

51. D'Ewes, edited Coates, page 319 note 6.

52. **CJ,** volume 2, page 350; D'Ewes, edited Coates, page 319.

53. Verney, **Memoirs,** volume 2, page 69.

54. D'Ewes, edited Coates, page 319 note 6.

55. **LJ,** volume 4, pages 458 and 460; D'Ewes, edited Coates, page 222 note 12.

56. **His Majesties Speciall Command to the Lord Mayor,** BL E179

(19).

57. **CSPD 1641-1643**, page 202.

58. D'Ewes, edited Coates, pages 263-9; **CJ**, volume 2, pages 338-9; HMC, 4th Report (1874) 'House of Lords Manuscripts', page 108.

59. D'Ewes, edited Coates, pages 264-6 and 268-9.

60. **The Citizens of London's Humble Petition**, BL E180 (16); **CSPD 1641-1643**, pages 195-6 and 202; D'Ewes, edited Coates, pages 270- 73; **Orders Voted by the High Court of Parliament** (1641) BL E179 (20).

61. **The Apprentices of Londons Petition** (London 1641) BL E180 (18).

62. Nalson, volume 2, pages 775-6.

63. **CSPD 1641-1643**, page 212.

64. Nalson, volume 2, page 735.

65. Clarendon, **History**, volume 1, pages 453-4.

66. **His Majesties Speciall Command to the Lord Mayor**, BL E179 (19); Clarendon, **History**, volume 1, pages 453-4; Nalson, volume 2, page 735; D'Ewes, edited Coates, page 283.

67. Rushworth, volume 4, page 462; Nalson, volume 2, pages 775-6; Clarendon, **History**, volume 1, pages 449-50.

68. D'Ewes, edited Coates, page 337 note 16.

69. D'Ewes, edited Coates, pages 337-8.

Chapter 4: THE DECEMBER DAYS

1. Peter Laslett, **The World We Have Lost** (London 1965) pages 55-6; Lawrence Stone, **The Causes of the English Revolution 1529-1642** (London 1972) pages 70-1; E A Wrigley, 'London's Importance 1650-1750', in **Past and Present**, number 37 (1967).

2. Peter Clark and Paul Slack (editors) **Crisis and Order in English Towns 1500-1700** (London 1972) page 38.

3. Neal, volume 2, pages 496-7.

4. HMC, 12th Report (1888) 'Cowper Manuscripts', volume 2, pages 283, 289, 291, 292, 293 and 294; 'Letters of Lady Brilliana Harley', pages 126 and 129-30; 'The Nicholas Papers', volume 1, pages 14 and 26; Evelyn, volume 4, pages 60, 71 and 87-8. My attention was drawn to this factor by Professor Vernon F Snow.

5. Wallington, volume 1, pages 279 and 280; Neal, volume 2, pages 496-7.

6. D'Ewes, edited by Coates, page 172; **LJ**, volume 4, page 447.

7. **CJ**, volume 2, pages 321 and 329.

8. D'Ewes, edited Coates, pages 243, 257 and 267-8.

9. D'Ewes, edited Coates, page 314.

10. D'Ewes, edited Coates, page 330; **CJ**, volume 2, page 352; **CSPD 1641-1643**, page 209.

11. D'Ewes, edited Coates, pages 294-5.

12. Gardiner, **History**, volume 10, pages 107-8; Pearl, pages 132-9.

13. Wallington, volume 1, page 274.
14. A Letter from *Mercurius Civicus* to *Mercurius Rusticus* (1643) in Somers's Tracts, volume 4, pages 588-9.
15. Clarendon, History, volume 1, page 501.
16. Pearl, page 134.
17. Clarendon, History, volume 1, pages 477-8.
18. CJ, volume 2, page 354; LJ, volume 4, page 487; HMC, 4th Report (1874) 'House of Lords Manuscripts', page 109; Rushworth, volume 4, page 459; Nalson, volume 2, pages 773-4; D'Ewes, edited Coates, page 340.
19. D'Ewes, edited Coates, pages 340, 342-3 and 344-5; CJ, volume 2, pages 354-5 and 356; LJ, volume 4, page 487.
20. LJ, volume 4, pages 489-90; D'Ewes, edited Coates, pages 346-7.
21. D'Ewes, edited Coates, page 347.
22. Wallington, volume 1, pages 276-7.
23. Diurnall Occurrences: or the Heads of Several Proceedings in both Houses of Parliament (27 December 1641-3 January 1642) BL E201 (5); Diurnall Occurrences, Touching the daily Proceedings in Parliament (27 December 1641-3 January 1642) BL Burney 8a (5); CSPD 1641-1643, page 216; CSP Venetian 1640-1642, page 271.
24. 'The Autobiography of Sir John Bramston', in Camden Society, first series, volume 32 (1845) page 82; HMC (1930) 'Hastings Manuscripts', volume 2, page 83; Diurnall Occurrences in Parliament (27 December 1641-2 January 1642) BL Burney 8a (4); Griffith Williams, The Discovery of Mysteries (1643) pages 21-3.
25. Diurnall Occurrences, Touching the daily Proceedings in Parliament, BL Burney 8a (5); Diurnall Occurrences: or the Heads of Several Proceedings in both Houses of Parliament, BL E201 (5); CSPD 1641-1643, page 217.
26. HMC (1900) 'Lord Montagu of Beaulieu Manuscripts', pages 137-8.
27. Rushworth, volume 4, page 463.
28. Wallington, volume 1, page 277; CSPD 1641-1643, page 217; Diurnall Occurrences in Parliament, BL Burney 8a (4).
29. Wallington, volume 1, page 277; A Bloody Massacre Plotted by the Papists (London 1641) BL E181 (9).
30. LJ, volume 4, pages 491-3.
31. D'Ewes, edited Coates, pages 352-3.
32. HMC (1900) 'Lord Montagu of Beaulieu Manuscripts', pages 137-8; A Bloody Massacre, BL E181 (9); Wallington, volume 1, page 277; Diurnall Occurrences in Parliament, BL Burney 8a (4); The Scots Loyaltie (1641) BL E181 (16); William Haller and Godfrey Davies (editors) The Leveller Tracts (New York 1944, reprinted Gloucester, Massachusetts 1964) page 406.
33. Diurnall Occurrences in Parliament, BL Burney 8a (4).

34. HMC, 5th Report (1876) 'House of Lords Manuscripts', page 4.

35. **LJ**, volume 4, pages 491-3.

36. BL 669f3 (26); **Diurnall Occurrences, Touching the daily Proceedings in Parliament**, BL Burney 8a (5); **Diurnall Occurrences: or the Heads of Several Proceedings in both Houses of Parliament**, BL E201 (5).

37. **Diurnall Occurrences in Parliament**, BL Burney 8a (4).

38. **CSPD 1641-1643**, page 214.

39. Joseph Hall, **Works** (three volumes in two, London 1647-62) volume 3, page 21.

40. HMC (1930) 'Hastings Manuscripts', volume 2, page 83.

41. **Diurnall Occurrences, Touching the daily Proceedings in Parliament**, BL Burney 8a (5).

42. Griffith Williams, pages 21-3.

43. Hall, volume 3, page 21.

44. **LJ**, volume 4, page 598.

45. HMC (1900) 'Lord Montagu of Beaulieu Manuscripts', page 138.

46. **LJ**, volume 4, page 598; D'Ewes, edited Coates, page 365 note 6.

47. **Diurnall Occurrences, Touching the daily Proceedings in Parliament**, BL Burney 8a (5); **Diurnall Occurrences, or, the Heads of Several Proceedings in both Houses of Parliament**, BL Burney 8a (6); Hacket, part 2, pages 177-8; HMC (1930) 'Hastings Manuscripts', volume 2, page 83.

48. Hacket, part 2, pages 177-8; Griffith Williams, pages 21-3.

49. **Diurnall Occurrences in Parliament**, BL Burney 8a (4); **A Bloody Massacre**, BL E181 (9); **Diurnall Occurrences, or, the Heads of Several Proceedings in both Houses of Parliament**, BL Burney 8a (6); *Persecutio Undecima*, pages 64-5.

50. **Diurnall Occurrences, or, the Heads of Several Proceedings in both Houses of Parliament**, BL Burney 8a (6); **Diurnall Occurrences, Touching the daily Proceedings in Parliament**, BL Burney 8a (5); Griffith Williams, pages 21-3.

51. **CSPD 1641-1643**, pages 216 and 217.

52. HMC, 12th Report (1888) 'Cowper Manuscripts', volume 2, page 302.

53. **CSPD 1641-1643**, pages 216, 217 and 241; HMC (1900) 'Lord Montagu of Beaulieu Manuscripts', page 138; **Diurnall Occurrences, Touching the daily Proceedings in Parliament**, BL Burney 8a (5); **Diurnall Occurrences in Parliament**, BL Burney 8a (4); **Diurnall Occurrences, or, the Heads of Several Proceedings in both Houses of Parliament**, BL Burney 8a (6).

54. **LJ**, volume 4, page 494; **Diurnall Occurrences in Parliament**, BL Burney 8a (4); D'Ewes, edited Coates, page 361; Gardiner, **History**, volume 10, pages 119-20.

55. **CSPD 1641-1643**, pages 216-17.

56. **CJ**, volume 2, page 359; D'Ewes, edited Coates, page 356; Gardiner, **History**, volume 10, page 118.

57. Whitelock, volume 1, page 156.

58. HMC, 12th Report (1888) 'Cowper Manuscripts', volume 2, page 302.

59. **Mr Smith's Speech in Parliament, made in the House of Commons on Wednesday the 29 of December 1641**, BL E199 (46); Keeler, page 344.

60. Hacket, page 177.

61. **A Common Councell, held at Guildhall, in the City of London, the 31 of December 1641** (London 1641) BL E131 (12).

62. **CSP Venetian 1640-1642**, pages 271-2.

63. HMC, 5th Report (1876) 'House of Lords Manuscripts', page 4.

64. William Lilly, **Monarchy or No Monarchy in England** (London 1651) pages 105-7.

65. **Diurnall Occurrences, Touching the daily Proceedings in Parliament**, BL Burney 8a (5); **Diurnall Occurrences, or, the Heads of Several Proceedings in both Houses of Parliament**, BL Burney 8a (6); **CSPD 1641-1643**, page 215.

66. **LJ**, volume 4, pages 494-6.

67. **Diurnall Occurrences, Touching the daily Proceedings in Parliament**, BL Burney 8a (5); **Diurnall Occurrences, or the Heads of Several Proceedings in both Houses of Parliament**, BL Burney 8a (6).

68. **CSPD 1641-1643**, page 215; Hacket, page 177; P Heylyn, **Aerius Redivivus** (Oxford 1670) pages 442-3; Husbands, page 533; Nalson, volume 2, pages 788-9.

69. **Diurnall Occurrences, Touching the daily Proceedings in Parliament**, BL Burney 8a (5); **A True Relation of the Most Wise and Worthy Speech Made by Captain Ven** (1641) BL E181 (21); **CSPD 1641-1643**, pages 215 and 216; Gardiner, **History**, volume 10, page 121.

70. **CSPD 1641-1643**, page 217.

71. **CSP Venetian 1640-1642**, page 272.

72. **Diurnall Occurrences in Parliament**, BL Burney 8a (4); **Diurnall Occurrences, Touching the daily Proceedings in Parliament**, BL Burney 8a (5); HMC, 12th Report (1888) 'Cowper Manuscripts', volume 2, page 302; **CSPD 1641-1643**, pages 216 and 217.

73. Lilly, page 106.

74. **A Bloody Massacre**, BL E181 (9); **CJ**, volume 2, page 361; Nalson, volume 2, pages 792-3.

75. **LJ**, volume 4, page 496.

76. **CJ**, volume 2, page 361; **A Bloody Massacre**, BL E181 (9).

77. **LJ**, volume 4, page 496.

78. **CJ**, volume 2, page 362.

79. **Speech Made by Captain Ven**, BL E181 (21).

80. **CJ**, volume 2, pages 362-3.

81. **Diurnall Occurrences, or, the Heads of Several Proceedings in both Houses of Parliament**, BL Burney 8a (6).

82. **CSPD 1641-1643**, pages 241-2.

83. Lilly, page 106.

84. **CSPD 1641-1643**, page 216; **Diurnall Occurrences, Touching the daily Proceedings in Parliament**, BL Burney 8a (5).

85. **CSPD 1641-1643**, page 217; HMC, 12th Report (1888) 'Cowper Manuscripts', volume 2, page 302; HMC (1900) 'Lord Montagu of Beaulieu Manuscripts', page 139; D'Ewes, edited Coates, page 380; **Diurnall Occurrences in Parliament**, BL Burney 8a (4).

86. **CSPD 1641-1643**, pages 241-2.

87. **A Common Councell, held at Guildhall**, BL E131 (12).

88. **Letter from *Mercurius Civicus***, page 589.

89. **CSPD 1641-1643**, page 238.

90. **CSPD 1641-1643**, page 235.

91. Sir Edward Walker, **Historical Discourses** (London 1705) page 274.

92. HMC (1900) 'Lord Montagu of Beaulieu Manuscripts', pages 137-8.

93. **CSPD 1641-1643**, page 216.

94. HMC, 12th Report (1888) 'Cowper Manuscripts', volume 2, page 302.

95. **CSPD 1641-1643**, page 217.

96. Griffith Williams, page 20.

97. BL 669f5 (89).

98. **CSPD 1641-1643**, page 215.

99. Griffith Williams, page 22.

100. **A Common Councell, held at Guildhall**, BL E131 (12); **The Humble Petition of the Mayor, Aldermen, and Commons of the City of London** (1643) BL E84 (14).

101. **CSPD 1641-1643**, page 218; HMC (1900) 'Lord Montagu of Beaulieu Manuscripts', page 139.

102. **A Complaint to the House of Commons** (Oxford 1643) BL E244 (31).

103. Husbands, pages 532-3; Hacket, page 177.

104. **Speech Made by Captain Ven**, BL E181 (21).

105. Lilly, pages 106-7; **A Common Councell, held at Guildhall**, BL E131 (12).

106. John Stow, **A Survey of the Cities of London and Westminster**, edited by John Strype (London 1720) volume 2, book 5, pages 285-6, 413-24, and appendix 1, pages 4-5; F J Fisher, 'The Growth of London', in E W Ives (editor) **The English Revolution 1600-1660** (London 1968) page 78.

107. **CSP Venetian 1640-1642**, pages 271-2; Nalson, volume 2, pages 775-6.

108. Husbands, page 691.
109. A Declaration of The Valiant Resolutions of the Famous Prentices of London (1642) BL E109 (5); An Humble Declaration of the Apprentices and other Young Men of the City of London (London 1643) BL E245 (2); The Protestation and Declaration of the Well-affected young men and Prentices, in and about the City of London (1643) BL E89 (12); Louis B Wright, Middle-class Culture in Elizabethan England (1935, reprinted New York 1958) pages 23-30.
110. George Unwin, The Gilds and Companies of London (fourth edition, London 1963) pages 91-2 and 265-6; George Unwin, Industrial Organiaztion in the Sixteenth and Seventeenth Centuries (Oxford 1904; new edition, London 1957) page 48; The Apprentices of Londons Petition (London 1641) BL E180 (18).
111. Lilly, pages 106-7.
112. Some Few Observations upon His Majesties Late Answer to the Declaration, or Remonstrance of the Lords and Commons of the 19 May 1642 (1642) page 12.
113. Lilly, pages 106-7.
114. CSP Venetian 1640-1642, pages 271-2.
115. [Dudley Digges], An Answer to a Printed Book (Oxford 1642) page 25.
116. Works of Archbishop Laud, volume 3, page 452.
117. LJ, volume 4, page 501; Husbands, page 534.
118. Husbands, pages 522-3; HMC (1900) 'Lord Montagu of Beaulieu Manuscripts', page 138; Nalson, volume 2, pages 784-5, 788-9 and 792-3.
119. Husbands, page 557; Griffith Williams, page 91; A Complaint to the House of Commons, BL E244 (31).
120. Sir Edward Walker, pages 271-2; The Humble Petition of the Mayor, Aldermen, and Commons of the City of London, BL E84 (14); Griffith Williams, pages 21-3.
121. Sir Edward Walker, pages 271-2; Griffith Williams, pages 21-3; Persecutio Undecima, pages 62 and 64.
122. Cornelius Burgess, A Sermon Preached to the Honourable House of Commons (London 1641) page 70; Edmund Calamy, Englands Looking-Glasse (London 1642) pages 48-9, and Gods Free Mercy to England (London 1642) page 7.
123. Herbert Palmer, The Glasse of Gods Providence (London 1644) page 61.
124. Herbert Palmer, Scripture and Reason Pleaded for Defensive Armes (London 1643) pages 54-5.
125. [Charles Herle], A Fuller Answer to A Treatise Written by Doctor Ferne (London 1642) page 4.
126. Husbands, page 691; 'J M', A Reply to the Answer (London 1642) page 24; Some Few Observations, page 12.

127. Nalson, volume 2, pages 792-3; Eliot Warburton, **Memoirs of Prince Rupert and the Cavaliers** (three volumes, London 1849) volume 1, page 210; **Dictionary of National Biography.**

128. **CSPD 1641-1643**, pages 216 and 217; **Diurnall Occurrences in Parliament**, BL Burney 8a (4); **Diurnall Occurrences, or the Heads of Several Proceedings in both Houses of Parliament**, BL Burney 8a (6); **A Bloody Massacre**, BL E181 (9); HMC (1930) 'Hastings Manuscripts', volume 2, page 83; Heylyn, *Cyprianus Anglicus*, page 490; C V Wedgwood, **The King's War 1641-1647** (London 1958) page 52; Pearl, page 224.

129. **Diurnall Occurrences in Parliament**, BL Burney 8a (4); **A Bloody Massacre**, BL E181 (9).

130. *Mercurius Aulicus* (12 March 1643) BL E92 (25).

131. **Mr Smith's Speech in Parliament**, BL E199 (46).

132. **The King's Majesties Demand of the House of Commons** (London 1641) BL E131 (19).

133. Lilly, pages 106-7.

134. HMC (1900) 'Lord Montagu of Beaulieu Manuscripts', page 139.

135. **Speech Made by Captain Ven**, BL E181 (21).

136. **CSPD 1641-1643**, page 218.

137. Lilly, pages 106-7; Clarendon, **History**, volume 2, page 522.

138. Husbands, page 533.

139. Wallington, volume 1, page 279.

140. **CSPD 1641-1643**, page 218; **The Oxinden Letters, 1607-1642**, edited by Dorothy Gardiner (London 1933) page 272.

141. HMC (1900) 'Lord Montagu of Beaulieu Manuscripts', page 139.

142. **CSPD 1641-1643**, page 237.

143. **CSPD 1641-1643**, page 215.

144. **CSPD 1641-1643**, page 218.

145. **CSPD 1641-1643**, page 218.

146. D'Ewes, edited Coates, pages 378-80; **CJ**, volume 2, pages 367-8.

147. Wallington, volume 1, page 280.

148. **CSPD 1641-1643**, page 237.

149. Wallington, volume 1, page 280.

150. **CJ**, volume 2, pages 368-9; D'Ewes, edited Coates, pages 381-4 and 393-5.

151. **CSPD 1641-1643**, pages 241-2 and 244; **Diurnall Occurrences, or the Heads of Several Proceedings in both Houses of Parliament** (3-10 January 1642) BL E201 (7); **CSP Venetian 1640-1642**, page 277.

152. Clarendon, **History**, volume 1, page 505.

153. **CSPD 1641-1643**, page 239.

154. **CSPD 1641-1643**, page 240.

155. HMC, 12th Report (1888) 'Cowper Manuscripts', volume 2, page 303.

156. **Letter from *Mercurius Civicus***, pages 589-90.

157. **CSPD 1641-1643**, pages 242-3.

158. HMC (1900) 'Lord Montagu of Beaulieu Manuscripts', page 141.

159. **Letter from** *Mercurius Civicus*, page 590.

160. **CSPD 1641-1643**, page 241.

161. **Letter from** *Mercurius Civicus*, page 590.

162. **CSP Venetian 1640-1642**, page 277.

163. HMC (1900) 'Lord Montagu of Beaulieu Manuscripts', page 141.

164. **CSPD 1641-1643**, page 241.

165. **Letter from** *Mercurius Civicus*, page 590; HMC (1900) 'Lord Montagu of Beaulieu Manuscripts', page 141; **Diurnall Occurrences, or the Heads of Several Proceedings in both Houses of Parliament** (3-10 January 1642) BL E201 (7).

166. Wallington, volume 1, pages 289-90; **Letter from** *Mercurius Civicus*, pages 587-8; D'Ewes, edited Coates, pages 392-3; **CSPD 1641-1643**, pages 245-6 and 249; **Diurnall Occurrences, or the Heads of Several Proceedings in both Houses of Parliament** (3-10 January 1642) BL E201 (7).

167. D'Ewes, edited Coates, pages 398, 400 and 401; **The Passages in Parliament** (3-10 January 1642) BL Burney 12; Clarendon, **History**, volume 1, page 509 note 1.

168. D'Ewes, edited Coates, page 401; Wallington, volume 2, pages 1-2; **A True Diurnall of the last Weeks Passages in Parliament** (10-17 January 1642) BL Burney 12.

169. D'Ewes, edited Coates, pages 398 and 400-1.

170. Husbands, pages 533 and 564; King Charles I, *Eikon Basilike*, pages 22-3, 30 and 35; **The State of the Whole Kingdom** (London 1642) BL E148 (24); [Digges] **An Answer to a Printed Book**, page 25; John Bramhall, **Works** (1844) volume 3, page 402; **State Papers Clarendon**, volume 2, page 160.

171. Clarendon, **History**, volume 1, page 508.

172. Clarendon, **History**, volume 1, page 508; **CSPD 1641-1643**, pages 252, and 254; **A Deep Sigh Breathd Through the Lodgings at White-Hall** (London 1642).

Chapter 5: ECONOMIC CRISIS AND POPULAR TRIUMPH

1. Baillie, volume 1, page 313.

2. B E Supple, **Commercial Crisis and Change in England 1600-1642** (Cambridge 1959) pages 120 and 124.

3. Supple, page 128; Margaret James, **Social Problems and Policy during the Puritan Revolution 1640-1660** (London 1930) pages 44-9, 57-60 and 243-4.

4. LJ, volume 4, page 237; HMC, 4th Report (1874) 'House of Lords Manuscripts', page 62.

5. Supple, pages 128-9.

6. **CSPD 1640-1641**, pages 524-5.

7. **The Diurnall Occurrences or Dayly Proceedings** (3 November

1640-3 November 1641) BL E523, pages 90 and 91-2; Whitelock, volume 1, page 130; May, book 1, page 93.

8. CJ, volume 2, page 143; LJ, volume 4, page 244; Nalson, volume 2, pages 237-8.

9. *Ovatio Carolina*, in Harleian Miscellany, volume 5, pages 93-4.

10. *Ovatio Carolina*, in Harleian Miscellany, volume 5, pages 101-2.

11. The Citizens of London's Humble Petition (11 December 1641) BL E180 (16).

12. Rushworth, volume 4, page 462; Clarendon, History, volume 1, pages 449-50; Nalson, volume 2, pages 775-6.

13. The Apprentices of Londons Petition, BL E180 (18).

14. CSPD 1641-1643, pages 264-5.

15. D'Ewes, edited Coates, page 340; LJ, volume 4, pages 489- 90.

16. Mr Smith's Speech in Parliament, BL E199 (46).

17. The King's Majesties Demand, BL E131 (19).

18. Wallington, volume 2, pages 1-2; A True Diurnall of the Last Weeks Passages in Parliament (10-17 January 1642) BL Burney 12; Clarendon, History, volume 1, pages 510-12; The Two Petitions of the County of Buckingham (1642) BL E181 (29); The Parliament's Answer to the two Petitions of the County of Buckingham (1642) BL E181 (36).

19. Clarendon, History, volume 1, page 512.

20. The Diurnall Occurrences in Parliament (17-24 January 1642) BL E201 (11); A Perfect Diurnall of the Passages in Parliament (24-31 January 1642) BL E201 (12); A True Diurnal Occurrences or Proceedings in the Parliament this last week (24-31 January 1642) BL Burney 12.

21. Wallington, volume 2, page 9.

22. HMC, 15th Report (1890) 'Buccleuch Manuscripts', volume 1, page 290.

23. Wallington, volume 2, pages 11, 12 and 15; A Perfect Diurnal of the Passages in Parliament (14-21 February 1642) BL Burney 12.

24. CJ, volume 2, pages 412 and 423; LJ, volume 4, page 573; Diurnal Occurrences. Or, The Heads of the Proceedings in both Houses of Parliament (7-14 February 1642) BL E201 (16); A Continuation of the True Diurnall of Passages in Parliament (7-14 February 1642) BL Burney 12; Wallington, volume 2, page 9.

25. Three Petitions. The One, Of the Inhabitants of the Towne of Colchester: The other Two, Of the County of Essex (1642) BL E134 (13).

26. The Clothiers Petition to His Majesty (1642) BL 669f3 (48).

27. LJ, volume 4, page 573.

28. Supple, page 130.

29. LJ, volume 4, pages 536-7.

30. **A Continuation of the True Diurnall of Passages in Parliament** (17-24 January 1642) BL Burney 12; **A Continuation of the True Diurnall Occurrences and passages in both Houses of Parliament** (21-28 March 1642) BL E201 (38).

31. **Memoirs of the Reign of Charles I: The Fairfax Correspondence**, edited by G W Johnson (two volumes, London 1848) volume 2, pages 367-72; **The Humble Petition of the Clothiers, inhabiting in the Parish of Leeds, Vicarage of Halifax and other parts adjoining** (14 April 1642) BL E144 (6).

32. **Two Petitions of the Knights, Gentlemen, Freeholders, and other of the inhabitants of the County of Hertford** (1642) BL E146 (16); **LJ**, volume 4, page 575.

33. Supple, page 131.

34. **CSP Venetian 1640-1642**, pages 284 and 291; **CSP Venetian 1642-1643**, page 7.

35. **CSPD 1641-1643**, pages 281-2.

36. **The Oxinden Letters**, pages 272, 285, 286 and 300.

37. **CSP Venetian 1640-1642**, pages 281-2.

38. **A True Copy of the Masterpiece of all those Petitions which have formerly been presented by the Mayor, Aldermen, and the rest of the Common Council of the City of London** (1642) BL E134 (7); **LJ**, volume 4, pages 534-5 and 537-9.

39. **LJ**, volume 4, pages 523-4, 527, 530, 531 and 532-3; HMC, 12th Report (1888) 'Cowper Manuscripts', volume 2, page 304.

40. **LJ**, volume 4, pages 540-3; **A Speech Delivered at a Conference with the Lords, January 25, 1641, By John Pym Esq** (1642) BL E200 (21).

41. **LJ**, volume 4, page 544.

42. **The humble Petition of many thousand poor people, in and about the City of London** (31 January 1642) BL 669f4 (54); **The True Diurnal Occurrences or, The Heads of the Proceedings of Both Houses in Parliament** (31 January-7 February 1642) BL E201 (13); Clarendon, **History**, volume 1, pages 549-51.

43. HMC, 12th Report (1888) 'Cowper Manuscripts', volume 2, page 306.

44. Clarendon, **History**, volume 1, page 550.

45. Husbands, page 364.

46. **CSPD 1641-1643**, page 274.

47. **LJ**, volume 4, page 559; **Mr Hollis His Speech in Parliament on Monday the 31st of January** (1642) BL E200 (25).

48. **CJ**, volume 2, page 407; **The True Diurnal Occurrences or, The Heads of the Proceedings of Both Houses in Parliament** (31 January-7 February 1642) BL E201 (13); **CSPD 1641-1643**, page 274; Patricia Higgins, 'The Reactions of Women, with Special Reference to Women Petitioners', in Brian Manning (editor) **Politics, Religion and the English Civil War** (London 1973)

pages 185-8.

49. **To the Honourable the Knights, Citizens and Burgesses, in the Commons House of Parliament now assembled,** BL 669f4 (55).

50. **CJ**, volume 2, page 408.

51. **LJ**, volume 4, pages 558-60.

52. **LJ**, volume 4, pages 562, 564 and 565.

53. Gardiner, **History**, volume 10, page 162.

54. Husbands, pages 364 and 557.

55. Clarendon, **History**, volume 1, page 552.

56. **CSP Venetian 1640-1642**, page 290.

57. **CSP Venetian 1640-1642**, page 291; Husbands, page 365.

58. **CSPD 1641-1643**, pages 272-3, 277-8 and 282; HMC, 12th Report (1888) 'Cowper Manuscripts', volume 2, page 306.

59. **CSP Venetian 1640-1642**, page 294.

60. **CSPD 1641-1643**, page 278.

61. **CSPD 1641-1643**, page 276.

62. **LJ**, volume 4, page 317.

63. **LJ**, volume 4, page 363.

64. **A Letter** (1642) BL 669f6 (43).

65. Clarendon, **History**, volume 1, page 552.

66. Husbands, pages 364, 365 and 557; **State Papers Clarendon**, volume 2, pages 160 and 162; *Persecutio Undecima*, page 65.

67. [Sir John Spelman], **The Case of Our Affaires** (Oxford 1643) page 21.

Chapter 6: THE MIDDLE AND POORER SORT OF PEOPLE

1. Laslett, pages 54-5.

2. S I Archangelsky, **Agrarian Legislation and the Agrarian Movement in England during the Revolution of the Seventeenth Century** (Moscow 1955) pages 74-9.

3. Peter Bowden, 'Agricultural prices, farm profits, and rents', in Joan Thirsk (editor) **The Agrarian History of England and Wales**, volume 4 (Cambridge 1967) pages 594 and 608-9; Eric Kerridge, 'The movement of rent, 1540-1640', in **Economic History Review**, second series, volume 6 (1953-4) pages 28-9.

3. R H Tawney, **The Agrarian Problem in the Sixteenth Century** (London 1912; reprinted New York 1967, with an introduction by Lawrence Stone) pages 115-21; W G Hoskins, 'The Leicestershire Farmer in the Sixteenth Century', in **Essays in Leicestershire History** (Liverpool 1950) page 179; W G Hoskins, **The Midland Peasant: The Economic and Social History of a Leicestershire Village** (London 1957) pages 176-9 and 186-9; W G Hoskins, 'The Rebuilding of Rural England, 1570-1640', in **Past and Present**, number 4 (1953) pages 49-52; G H Tupling, **The Economic History of Rossendale** (Manchester 1927) pages 90-2,

98, 105, 109, 113, 115 and 127; V H T Skipp, 'Economic and Social Change in the Forest of Arden 1530-1649', in **Agricultural History Review**, volume 18 (1970) supplement: 'Land, Church, and People: Essays Presented to Professor H P R Finberg', pages 101-4.

5. Bowden, page 608.

6. Hoskins, **Leicestershire History**, pages 127-30, 132-6, 154-9 and 178; Hoskins, **Midland Peasant**, pages 112-17, 141-4 and 175-8; Margaret Spufford, **A Cambridgeshire Community: Chippenham from Settlement to Enclosure**, Department of English Local History, University of Leicester, Occasional Papers, number 20 (Leicester 1965) pages 37-41; Tawney, **Agrarian problem**, pages 55-97 and 200-30; Mildred Campbell, **The English Yeoman under Elizabeth and the Early Stuarts** (New Haven 1942).

7. Bowden, pages 598-600; Everitt, 'Farm labourers', pages 397-9 and 435-7; Skipp, pages 107-9; Spufford, pages 39-41.

8. Hoskins, **Midland Peasant**, page 208; Campbell, pages 314-60; Plumb, in **Past and Present**, number 45, pages 90-109.

9. Eric Kerridge, **Agrarian Problems in the Sixteenth Century and After** (London 1969) pages 54-8; Tupling, page 144; Tawney, **Agrarian problem**, pages 292-3 and 296-7.

10. Tupling, pages 150-9; 'The causes of the Civil War in Lancashire', in **Transactions of the Lancashire and Cheshire Antiquarian Society**, volume 65 (1955) pages 17-20.

11. Tawney, **Agrarian problem**, pages 285-7; Tupling, pages 147- 8; Kerridge, **Agrarian Problems**, pages 45 and 86-7.

12. Tupling, pages 70-5 and 147-50.

13. Kerridge, **Agrarian Problems**, pages 45 and 86-90.

14. Tawney, **Agrarian problem**, pages 301-3; Spufford, pages 45 and 51; Skipp, page 106; Lawrence Stone, **The Crisis of the Aristocracy 1558-1641** (Oxford 1965) pages 308-9.

15. S J Watts, 'Tenant Right in Early Seventeenth-Century Northumberland', in **Northern History**, volume 6 (1971) pages 84-5.

16. C M L Bouch and G P Jones, **A Short Economic and Social History of The Lake Counties 1500-1830** (Manchester 1961) pages 25, 65-9, 71-4 and 75-6; Watts, pages 64-86; Tupling, pages 142-4; Campbell, pages 147-53.

17. B G Blackwood, 'The Lancashire Cavaliers and their Tenants', in **Transactions of the Historic Society of Lancashire and Cheshire**, volume 117 (1965) pages 24 and 31.

18. Stone, **Crisis of the Aristocracy**, pages 312-21.

19. Stone, **Crisis of the Aristocracy**, page 322; Blackwood, 'Lancashire Cavaliers', page 27.

20. Bowden, pages 690-1 and 695; Stone, **Crisis of the Aristocracy**,

pages 324-8; Kerridge, 'The movement of rent'.

21. Bowden, pages 597-8; Hoskins, **Midland Peasant**, page 171; Hoskins, in **Past and Present**, number 4, pages 55-7; Skipp, page 107; W G Howson, 'Plague, Poverty and Population in Parts of North-West England, 1580-1720', in **Transactions of the Historic Society of Lancashire and Cheshire**, volume 112 (1961).

22. Hoskins, **Leicestershire History**, pages 144-5; Hoskins, **Midland Peasant**, pages 238-40; Skipp, pages 92-9; Joan Thirsk, **English Peasant Farming: The Agrarian History of Lincolnshire from Tudor to Recent Times** (London 1957) pages 36-8, 97 and 112-17; Philip A J Pettit, **The Royal Forests of Northamptonshire: A Study of their Economy 1558-1741**, Northamptonshire Record Society, volume 23 (1968) pages 177-9.

23. Stone, **Crisis of the Aristocracy**, page 329; Pettit, pages 175-6.

24. Tupling, pages 47-9, 57-70, 127 and 161-70; Pettit, pages 141-7, 170-1 and 174; Cyril E Hart, **Royal Forest** (Oxford 1966) pages 92, 96, 113, 115, 138 and 151; Everitt, 'Farm labourers', pages 409-12; Thirsk, **English Peasant Farming**, pages 28-47 and 54-76.

25. Bowden, pages 621, 625-6, 629, 631-3 and 641; Kerridge, pages 71-2; W G Hoskins, 'Harvest Fluctuations and English Economic History, 1620-1759', in **Agricultural History Review**, volume 16 (1968); Joan Thirsk, 'Seventeenth Century Agriculture and Social Change', in **Agricultural History Review**, volume 18 (1970) supplement: 'Land, Church, and People: Essays Presented to Professor H P R Finberg', page 168; Howson, pages 40 and 50; Supple, chapters 3-7; G D Ramsay, **The Wiltshire Woollen Industry in the Sixteenth and Seventeenth Centuries** (Oxford 1943; second edition, London 1965) pages 76-84 and 101; E Lipson, **The Economic History of England**, volume 3 (fifth edition, London 1948) pages 255, 258-9 and 305-12.

26. Stone, **Crisis of the Aristocracy**, pages 495-9; J P Cooper, 'Differences between English and Continental Governments in the Early Seventeenth Century', in J S Bromley and E H Kossmann (editors) **Britain and the Netherlands** (London 1960) page 89; Campbell, pages 137, 358-60 and 368; W B Willcox, **Gloucestershire: A Study in Local Government 1590-1640** (New Haven 1940) page 130; [William Prynne], **An Humble Remonstrance to His Majesty Against the Tax of Ship-Money** (1641) page 23; **Considerations Touching Trade** (1641) pages 11-14.

27. Thirsk, **English Peasant Farming**, page 109.

28. Maurice Dobb, **Studies in the Development of Capitalism** (London 1946) page 226.

29. Pettit, pages 149, 153, 158, 162-3 and 177.

30. Hart, pages 93-4, 111-12, 130 and 155-6.
31. D G C Allan, 'The Rising in the West, 1628-1631', in **Economic History Review**, second series, volume 5 (1952-3); Eric Kerridge, 'The Revolts in Wiltshire against Charles I', in **The Wiltshire Archaeological and Natural History Magazine**, volume 57 (1957-8); **Victoria County History: Wiltshire**, volume 4, pages 405-7, 413-14 and 417; T G Barnes, **Somerset 1625-1640: A County's Government during the 'Personal Rule'** (Oxford 1961) pages 157-9; Pettit, pages 51-2 and 65-7.
32. LJ, volume 4, page 219; HMC, 4th Report (1874) 'House of Lords Manuscripts', page 70; Hart, pages 123-30; Willcox, pages 194-202.
33. Thirsk, **English Peasant Farming**, pages 19-20, 54-76, 180-9, 129-33 and 147-56.
34. Thirsk, **English Peasant Farming**, page 147.
35. HMC, 4th Report (1874) 'House of Lords Manuscripts', pages 44, 53 and 59-60; HMC, 5th Report (1876) 'House of Lords Manuscripts', pages 20 and 22; LJ, volume 5, pages 39, 45, 61-2 and 83.
36. Tawney, **Agrarian problem**, pages 248, 250 and 252-3; Tupling, pages 47-9, 54 and 68; Kerridge, **Agrarian Problems**, pages 94-6.
37. Thirsk, **English Peasant Farming**, pages 26-30, 37, 108-12 and 119-21.
38. Barnes, pages 150-5.
39. Thirsk, **English Peasant Farming**, pages 117-29; 'The Farming Regions of England', in **Agrarian History**, volume 4 (Cambridge 1967) pages 38-40; Archangelsky, pages 75-7; H C Darby, **The Draining of the Fens** (Cambridge 1940) pages 40-64.
40. Thirsk, 'Seventeenth-century agriculture', pages 167-8; Tawney, **Agrarian problem**, pages 394-5.
41. Tawney, **Agrarian problem**, pages 316-17 and 331-40.
42. Kerridge, 'The revolts in Wiltshire', page 72.
43. Thirsk, **English Peasant Farming**, pages 123-4.
44. LJ, volume 4, pages 257 and 263.
45. LJ, volume 4, page 326, and volume 5, page 42; HMC, 4th Report (1874) 'House of Lords Manuscripts', page 90; HMC, 5th Report (1876) 'House of Lords Manuscripts', page 21.
46. LJ, volume 4, pages 187, 204 and 209; HMC, 4th Report (1874) 'House of Lords Manuscripts', page 52; HMC, 5th Report (1876) 'House of Lords Manuscripts', page 25.
47. LJ, volume 4, pages 274, 439 and 544; HMC, 4th Report (1874) 'House of Lords Manuscripts', page 74; HMC, 5th Report (1876) 'House of Lords Manuscripts', page 5.
48. LJ, volume 4, page 483; HMC, 4th Report (1874) 'House of Lords Manuscripts', page 109.
49. LJ, volume 4, page 704, and volume 5, pages 101 and 130; HMC, 4th Report (1874) 'House of Lords Manuscripts', page 111; HMC,

5th Report (1876) 'House of Lords Manuscripts', page 28.

50. Hart, pages 125-30.

51. **LJ**, volume 4, pages 281, 289 and 304; HMC, 4th Report (1874) 'House of Lords Manuscripts', pages 76 and 85.

52. **CJ**, volume 2, pages 469 and 471; **A Declaration of the Great and Weighty Affairs and Matters of Consequence concerning this Kingdom** (London 1642) BL E140 (28).

53. **LJ**, volume 4, page 262; HMC, 4th Report (1874) 'House of Lords Manuscripts', page 69.

54. **LJ**, volume 4, page 483; HMC, 4th Report (1874) 'House of Lords Manuscripts', page 109.

55. **LJ**, volume 4, page 699, and volume 5, pages 32, 43, 66, 70 and 83; HMC, 5th Report (1876) 'House of Lords Manuscripts', pages 16, 19, 21, 23 and 29; Verney, **Memoirs**, volume 1, pages 264 and 270.

56. **Victoria County History: Huntingdon**, volume 2, pages 176 and 224; Sanford, pages 367-72; W C Abbott (editor) **The Writings and Speeches of Oliver Cromwell** (four volumes, Cambridge, Massachusetts 1937-47) volume 1, page 130; Darby, page 64.

57. **LJ**, volume 4, pages 204, 219, 227, 236 and 252; HMC, 4th Report (1874) 'House of Lords Manuscripts', page 62.

58. **LJ**, volume 4, page 343; HMC, 4th Report (1874) 'House of Lords Manuscripts', page 94.

59. HMC, 4th Report (1874) 'House of Lords Manuscripts', page 106; HMC, 5th Report (1876) 'House of Lords Manuscripts', page 93; **LJ**, volume 4, pages 224, 269, 312, 336, 453 and 524, and volume 5, pages 80, 138 and 485.

60. William Dugdale, **The History of Imbanking and Drayning of Divers Fenns** (London 1662) pages 418-19.

61. Dugdale, pages 420-3; **CSPD 1640-1641**, pages 308-10.

62. HMC, 4th Report (1874) 'House of Lords Manuscripts', pages 29, 32, 39 and 95.

63. **CSPD 1640-1641**, pages 308-10 and 592-3; **CSPD 1641-1643**, pages 227-8; HMC, 4th Report (1874) 'House of Lords Manuscripts', page 36.

64. **LJ**, volume 4, pages 220, 269 and 299; HMC, 4th Report (1874) 'House of Lords Manuscripts', pages 71 and 72.

65. **LJ**, volume 4, pages 208, 221, 243, 247, 248, 251, 264, 271, 282 and 297; HMC, 4th Report (1874) 'House of Lords Manuscripts', pages 77, 82 and 85.

66. **LJ**, volume 4, page 299; HMC, 4th Report (1874) 'House of Lords Manuscripts', page 83.

67. **LJ**, volume 4, page 247; **CJ**, volume 2, pages 164, 191- 2, 205 and 211-12; HMC, 4th Report (1874) 'House of Lords Manuscripts', pages 63 and 70; Sanford, pages 367-73.

68. **LJ**, volume 4, pages 332, 337, 343, 371 and 376; HMC, 4th Report (1874) 'House of Lords Manuscripts', page 94.

69. Sanford, pages 367-73; Clarendon, **Life**, pages 40-1; HMC, 12th Report (1888) 'Cowper Manuscripts', volume 2, page 284; CJ, volume 2, pages 155 and 172.

70. LJ, volume 4, pages 375-6, 390, 393, 403, 410, 428, 439 and 447; CJ, volume 2, pages 254, 261 and 263; HMC, 4th Report (1874) 'House of Lords Manuscripts', pages 100 and 105; CSPD **1641-1643**, pages 116-17.

71. LJ, volume 4, pages 461, 462, 524 and 559; HMC, 5th Report (1876) 'House of Lords Manuscripts', page 6.

72. LJ, volume 5, pages 55-6, 79, 115 and 137; HMC, 5th Report (1876) 'House of Lords Manuscripts', pages 22, 24-5 and 29; Dugdale, page 419.

73. G Stavin, 'A Brief Account of the Drainage of the Levels of Hatfield Chase and parts adjacent' (1752) in **The Yorkshire Archaeological and Topographical Journal**, volume 27 (1948-51) pages 385-7; Dugdale, pages 144-6; J D Hughes, 'The Drainage Disputes in the Isle of Axholme', in **The Lincolnshire Historian**, volume 2, number 1 (1954).

74. HMC, 12th Report (1888) 'Cowper Manuscripts', volume 2, pages 282 and 284.

75. **An Honourable and Worthy Speech: Spoken in the High Court of Parliament, By Mr Smith of the Middle-Temple** (1641) BL E199 (8); Keeler, page 344.

76. **A Speech Made by Master Waller Esquire in the Honourable House of Commons** (1641) BL E198 (30); HMC, 4th Report (1874) 'House of Lords Manuscripts', page 55; Aston, **A Remonstrance against Presbytery**, BL E163 (1).

77. LJ, volume 4, page 312.

78. CJ, volume 2, pages 469 and 471; **A Declaration of the Great and Weighty Affairs**, BL E140 (28).

79. Gardiner, **Documents**, page 212.

80. Barnes, page 154; Plumb, pages 104-6.

81. LJ, volume 4, page 428.

82. Supple, pages 135-40.

83. George Unwin, **Studies in Economic History** (London 1927) pages 186-7; Ramsay, pages 53-8.

84. Herbert Heaton, **The Yorkshire Woollen and Worsted Industries** (second edition, Oxford 1965) pages 138-44.

85. Willcox, pages 167-9.

86. Ramsay, pages 75-6; Supple, pages 59 and 143.

87. Ramsay, page 87.

88. Ramsay, pages 93-4; Willcox, pages 162-9.

89. Ramsay, page 92.

90. Ramsay, page 92; Willcox, pages 162-9.

91. Willcox, pages 162-9; Keeler, pages 350-1.

92. Ramsay, page 92; Keeler, pages 101-2.

93. Supple, pages 59-60, 120 and 143-7.

94. Ramsay, page 98.

95. Unwin, **Studies in Economic History**, pages 291-2; Supple, pages 102, 153 and 155.

96. Supple, pages 155-7.

97. Supple, pages 123, 156-7 and 248-9; Unwin, **Studies in Economic History**, pages 291-3.

98. Heaton, pages 93-5 and 203-5.

99. Heaton, pages 177-84 and 197-203.

100. Heaton, page 207.

101. Unwin, **Studies in Economic History**, pages 133-220, 287-90; Supple, pages 62-72 and 242.

102. Supple, pages 30 and 241-2; Heaton, pages 165-7.

103. Supple, pages 62-72 and 241-3.

104. Supple, pages 121-2, 124-5 and 241-3.

105. James, **Social Problems**, pages 148-9; Supple, page 242.

106. James, **Social Problems**, pages 148-9.

107. Gardiner, **Documents**, page 212.

108. Supple, pages 222-3 and 242.

109. *Persecutio Undecima*, pages 7-8.

110. James, **Social Problems**, page 29.

111. HMC, 12th Report (1891) 'Beaufort Manuscripts', page 23.

112. Clarendon, **History**, volume 2, page 464, and volume 3, page 80; *Reliquiae Baxterianae*, page 30; John Corbet, 'An Historical Relation of the Military Government of Gloucester' (London 1645) in *Bibliotheca Gloucestrensis*, edited by J Washbourn (Gloucester 1823) volume 1, pages 9 and 16.

113. Clark and Slack, pages 20-5.

114. Unwin, **Industrial Organization**, pages 73-4; J E Neale, **The Elizabethan House of Commons** (London 1949) pages 250-1; Wallace T MacCaffrey, **Exeter 1540-1640** (Cambridge, Massachusetts, 1958) pages 16-7, 21-2, 246 and 251-4; Penry Williams, 'Government and politics in Ludlow'; Roger Howell, **Newcastle upon Tyne and the Puritan Revolution** (Oxford 1967) pages 34-53; A M Johnson, 'Politics in Chester during the Civil Wars and the Interregnum 1640-62', in Clark and Slack, pages 204-12; Alfred Wadsworth and Julia de Lacy Mann, **The Cotton Trade and Industrial Lancashire 1600-1780** (Manchester 1931) page 29; Pearl, pages 45-68 and 91-4; Willcox, pages 205-8.

115. J H Sacret, 'The Restoration Government and Municipal Corporations', in **English Historical Review**, volume 45 (1930) pages 235-6; Heaton, pages 220-24; Pearl, page 67; T C Mendenhall, **The Shrewsbury Drapers and the Welsh Wool Trade in the Sixteenth and Seventeenth Centuries** (Oxford 1953) pages 37, 131 and 223-4; Sanford, pages 232-7; Abbott **The Writings and Speeches of Oliver Cromwell**, volume 1, pages 66-9; Hirst, **The**

Representative of the People?, pages 47- 50.

116. Clark and Slack, pages 20-5; Neale, pages 250-1 and 268.

117. Dobb, pages 89-100, 103-7 and 121.

118. Mendenhall, pages 38-9, 41-5, 97-100, 112, 117, 122-31, 145, 160, 162, 199-200, 216-18 and 223-4.

119. J U Nef, The Rise of the British Coal Industry (two volumes, London 1932) volume 1, page 405, and volume 2, pages 18-23, 120-33, 268-9 and 279-80.

120. Johnson, 'Politics in Chester', pages 204-10.

121. Heaton, pages 220-7.

122. Penry Williams, pages 283-8, 291; Howell, pages 39-42, 53-61 and 163; Mendenhall, pages 30-1; Heaton, pages 220-27; D M Palliser, 'The trade gilds of Tudor York', in Clark and Slack, pages 107-9.

123. Howell, pages 53-62.

124. Pearl, pages 137-9, 146-55, 248, 249 and 274.

125. Dobb, pages 104-9 and 219-20; Penry Williams, pages 286-7; Nef, volume 2, pages 122-31; Howell, pages 40, 55, 61 and 163; Pearl, pages 241 and 243; Heaton, pages 225-6; Palliser, page 109; Johnson, 'Politics in Chester', pages 204-10; Peter Clark, 'The migrant in Kentish towns 1580-1640', in Clark and Slack, page 151.

126. Clark, page 162 note 98; MacCaffrey, pages 222-4; Richard L Bushman, 'English Franchise Reform in the Seventeenth Century', in The Journal of British Studies, volume 3, number 1 (1963) pages 37-47; Plumb, pages 100-7; Neale, pages 247-8, 251-2, 254-5 and 262-81; Hirst, The Representative of the People?, pages 51-9, 90-6, 135-44; Fletcher, County Community, pages 245-6 and 249-50.

127. Bushman, pages 43-4.

128. Unwin, Gilds and Companies of London, pages 217-21; Unwin, Industrial Organization, pages 42-3 and 73; Mendenhall, pages 94-7; G I H Lloyd, The Cutlery Trades (London 1913) pages 113-21.

129. Unwin, Gilds and Companies, pages 227-8, 231 and 251-4; Unwin, Industrial Organization, pages 20-5, 37 and 107; Nef, volume 1, pages 405-10.

130. Unwin, Gilds and Companies, pages 223-4; Palliser, pages 104-5.

131. James, Social Problems, page 213.

132. James, Social Problems, page 375 note 106; Unwin, Gilds and Companies, page 353.

133. James, Social Problems, page 375 note 106; Nef, volume 1, pages 405-10.

134. James, Social Problems, pages 221-3; Unwin, Gilds and Companies, pages 335-6.

135. James, Social Problems, pages 200-1.

136. James, Social Problems, page 212; Unwin, Gilds and Companies, pages 259-60.

137. Unwin, **Industrial Organization**, page 204.

138. Unwin, **Gilds and Companies**, pages 231-2, 236-7 and 335-6.

139. Unwin, **Industrial Organization**, pages 75-7, 98-100; Unwin, **Studies in Economic History**, pages 173-4, 181-2, 196-7 and 288-9; MacCaffrey, pages 136-48 and 151; Johnson, 'Politics in Chester', page 206.

140. Unwin, **Studies in Economic History**, pages 281-6; Heaton, pages 217-34; Wadsworth and Mann, pages 54-69.

141. Dobb, pages 85-6 and 89.

142. Unwin, **Industrial Organization**, pages 145, 146-7, 170-1 and 204; Dobb, pages 134-8 and 162-8.

143. Unwin, **Industrial Organization**, page 320; Unwin, **Gilds and Companies**, pages 145-7.

144. **A Short and True Relation** concerning the Soap-business (London 1641); Unwin, **Gilds and Companies**, pages 321-3; Lipson, volume 3, pages 362-5.

145. R H Tawney, **Religion and the Rise of Capitalism** (Penguin edition, London 1938) page 207; Christopher Hill, **Economic Problems of the Church from Archbishop Whitgift to the Long Parliament** (Oxford 1956) pages 11-12; Christopher Hill, **Society and Puritanism in Pre-Revolutionary England** (London 1964) chapter 4.

146. Corbet, pages 8-10.

147. Dobb, pages 123-38; Tawney, **Agrarian Problem**, pages 55-97, 137 and 200-30.

148. A C Wood, **Nottinghamshire in the Civil War** (Oxford 1937) pages 8-9; Barnes, page 13.

149. Campbell, pages 352-3 and 356-7.

150. Plumb, pages 103 and 107.

151. E Trotter, **Seventeenth Century Life in the Country Parish** (Cambridge 1919) page 219.

152. [Prynne] **An Humble Remonstrance to His Majesty Against the Tax of Ship-Money** (1641) page 23; Fletcher, pages 205-6.

153. Willcox, page 130.

154. Campbell, page 368; Morrill, **Revolt of the Provinces** pages 25 and 27.

155. Stone, **Crisis of the Aristocracy**, pages 495-9; Cooper, page 89; Tawney, **Agrarian Problem**, pages 345-6; Fletcher, **A County Community in Peace and War**, pages 203-4.

156. Campbell, pages 137 and 358-60.

157. Ramsay, page 48.

158. M D Gordon, 'The Collection of Ship-Money in the Reign of Charles I', in **Transactions of the Royal Historical Society**, third series, volume 4 (1910).

159. **Considerations Touching Trade** (1641) pages 11-14.

160. D'Ewes, edited Coates, page 121.

161. **Good Workes** (London 1641) BL E179 (1).

162. **The Countrey's Plea Against Tythes** (London 1647); Hill, **Economic Problems of the Church**, chapters 5 and 6.

163. Margaret James, 'The Political Importance of the Tithes Controversy in the English Revolution, 1640-60', in **History**, volume 26 (1941-2) pages 9-10.

164. *Persecutio Undecima*, page 7; **A Certificate from Northamptonshire** (London 1641) page 14; 'Stanley Papers', part 3, volume 3, in **Chetham Society**, volume 70 (1867) 'The History and Antiquities of the Isle of Man', page 9.

165. Ramsay, pages 45-9.

166. Stone, **Causes of the English Revolution**, pages 125-6; Stone, **Crisis of the Aristocracy**, pages 34, 498 and 750-2; Cliffe, page 9.

167. Barnes, page 13.

168. Clarendon, **History**, volume 2, page 296.

169. Keeler, pages 91-2; F T R Edgar, **Sir Ralph Hopton** (Oxford 1968) pages 35-8; **A Memento for Yeomen, Merchants, Citizens, and all the Commons in England** (1642) BL E113 (13).

170. Stone, **Crisis of the Aristocracy**, pages 34 and 751.

171. Clarendon, **Life**, pages 37 and 39; Sir Edward Walker, pages 222-3.

172. Stowe, volume 2, book 4, pages 9-10.

173. [?William Prynne], **A Soveraign Antidote to Prevent, Appease, Determine our unnaturall and destructive Civill Warres and dissentions** (London 1642) page 9.

174. **Militia Old and New** (London 1642). (The late Professor John Western very kindly supplied me with this tract.)

175. Heywood, volume 1, pages 83-4; 'Some Memoirs Concerning the Family of the Priestleys', in **Surtees Society**, volume 87 (1883) page 17; Johnson (editor) **Fairfax Correspondence**, volume 2, pages 381-2; Campbell, pages 296-7.

176. Hill, **Economic Problems of the Church**, chapter 4 and 13.

177. **CSPD 1641-1643**, pages 144-5.

178. Lilly, pages 106-7.

179. Gardiner, **Documents**, pages 214-15.

180. *Persecutio Undecima*, page 21.

181. Hill, **Society and Puritanism**, chapters 8-10.

182. Gardiner, **History**, volume 10, page 13.

183. Francis Cheynell, **Sions Memento, and Gods Alarum** (London 1643) page 38.

184. William Mewe, **The Robbing and Spoiling of Jacob and Israel** (London 1643) pages 26-7.

185. Humphrey Hardwick, **The Difficulty of Sions Deliverance and Reformation** (London 1644) pages 9-12.

186. Stephen Marshall, **Reformation and Desolation** (London 1642) pages 45-6.

187. Calamy, **Englands Looking-Glasse**, pages 56-7.
188. Hardwick, pages 9-12.
189. Marshall, pages 45-6.
190. Samuel Fairecloth, **The Troublers Troubled** (London 1641) page 31; 'The Life of Master John Shaw', in **Surtees Society**, volume 65 (1875) pages 396-7 and 411.
191. Peter Smith, **A Sermon Preached before the Honorable House of Commons** (London 1644) page 36.
192. Smith, pages 34-5; 'The Life of Adam Martindale', in **Chetham Society**, volume 4 (1845) pages 6-7 and 9.
193. Heywood, volume 1, page 141.
194. Heywood, volume 1, page 159; *Reliquiae Baxterianae*, page 94.
195. Martindale, page 102.
196. *Reliquiae Baxterianae*, pages 30-2, 40, 42, 85, 89 and 94.
197. Heywood, volume 1, page 84.
198. *Reliquiae Baxterianae*, pages 89 and 94.
199. Corbet, pages 9-10 and 17-18.

Chapter 7:
THE PEOPLE AND THE OUTBREAK OF THE CIVIL WAR

1. Keith J Lindley, 'The Impact of the 1641 Rebellion upon England and Wales, 1641-5', in **Irish Historical Studies**, volume 18 (1970); **Civil War Tracts: Lancashire**, pages 3-4.
2. **Civil War Tracts: Lancashire**, pages 49-50.
3. **Civil War Tracts: Lancashire**, pages 20-4.
4. **Civil War Tracts: Lancashire**, pages 64 and 110.
5. 'Memoirs of Captain John Hodgson', in **Original Memoirs, written during the Great Civil War** (Edinburgh 1806) pages 95-6.
6. Lister, pages 6-14.
7. Priestley, pages 26-7.
8. **A True and Exact Relation** (19 August 1642) BL E112 (33).
9. **CSPD 1640**, pages 476, 490, 494-5, 496-7, 509, 579, 583 and 613; R W Cotton, **Barnstaple and the Northern Part of Devonshire during the Great Civil War, 1642-1646** (London 1889) pages 58-69.
10. Clarendon, **History** volume 2, page 319; Francis Peck, *Desiderata Curiosa* (London 1735) volume 2, book 12, pages 23-5; 'Diary of John Rous', in **Camden Society**, first series, volume 66 (1856) pages 121-2; **A Message Sent to the Parliament from the Members of the House of Commons at Colchester** (27 August 1642) BL E114 (30); **Special Passages** (23-30 August 1642) BL E114 (36); **A Perfect Diurnall of the Passages in Parliament** (12-19 August 1642) BL E240 (5).
11. **A Message Sent to the Parliament**, BL E114 (30); Peck, volume 2, book 12, page 24; 'The Diary of the Reverend Ralph Josselin

1616-1683', in **Camden Society**, third series, volume 15 (1908) page 13.

12. Peck, volume 2, book 12, page 23.

13. **A Message Sent to the Parliament**, BL E114 (30); HMC, 12th Report (1891) 'Beaufort Manuscripts', page 23.

14. **Exceeding Joyfull Newes from his Excellence the Earle of Essex** (London 1642) BL E121 (28); Clarendon, **History**, volume 2, page 318.

15. **A Relation of the rare exployts of the London Souldiers, and Gentlemen Prentizes** (London 1642) BL E114 (13).

16. **A Relation of the rare exploytes**, BL E114 (13); **CSPD 1641-1643**, page 372.

17. **CSPD 1641-1643**, page 373.

18. HMC, 13th Report (1891) 'Portland Manuscripts', volume 1, page 64.

19. Verney, **Memoirs**, volume 1, page 266.

20. Clarendon, **History**, volume 2, pages 283-4.

21. Ralph Hopton, *'Bellum Civile'*, in **Somerset Record Society**, volume 17 (1902) pages 1-2.

22. Clarendon, **History**, volume 2, pages 403-5.

23. Clarendon, **History**, volume 2, pages 283-4.

24. **A True and Sad Relation of divers passages in Somersetshire** (London 1642) BL E109 (34); **A True and Exact Relation**, BL E112 (33); Hopton, pages 9-10.

25. **Civil War Tracts: Lancashire**, pages 16-17; **LJ**, volume 5, page 174.

26. **Civil War Tracts: Lancashire**, pages 30-4, 36 and 112-13.

27. Hutchinson, pages 81-8 and appendix 5, pages 392-5; **CSPD 1641-1643**, page 368.

28. Clarendon, **History**, volume 2, page 227.

29. **A Declaration Made by the right Honourable the Earle of Bath** (London 1642) BL E119 (11); **The Latest Remarkable Truths from Worcester, Chester, Salop, Norwich, Stafford, Somerset, Devon, York and Lincoln Counties** (1642) BL E119 (5); Cotton, pages 58-69.

30. **Some Late Occurrences in Shropshire and Devonshire** (1642) BL E121 (4); Clarendon, **History**, volume 2, page 318; Cotton, pages 69-71.

31. Warwick, pages 221-3; Clarendon, **History**, volume 2, page 317.

32. HMC (1926) 'Buccleuch Manuscripts', volume 3, pages 414 and 416-17; HMC (1900) 'Lord Montagu of Beaulieu Manuscripts', pages 157-8.

33. Warwick, page 225.

34. Clarendon, **History**, volume 2, pages 317-18.

35. **A Letter Sent to a worthy Member of the House of Commons, Concerning the Lord Shandois** (22 August 1642) BL E113 (6);

Corbet, pages 7-8; 'A Relation of the Taking of Cicester' (London 1642) in *Bibliotheca Gloucestrensis*, volume 2, pages 177-8; John Vicars, *Magnalia Dei Anglicana*, Or, Englands Parliamentary-Chronicle (London 1646) page 137; A J and R H Tawney, 'An Occupational Census of the Seventeenth Century', Economic History Review, volume 5 (1934).

36. **A Declaration Made by the right Honourable the Earle of Bath** (London 1642) BL E119 (11).

37. Corbet, page 8.

38. LJ, volume 5, pages 289, 303 and 315; HMC, 5th Report (1876) 'House of Lords Manuscripts', page 43.

39. HMC, 10th Report (1887) 'Braye Manuscripts', pages 146-7; [Ryves] *Mercurius Rusticus* (1646) number 1, pages 1-6; **A Message Sent to the Parliament** (27 August 1642) BL E114 (30); **Special Passages** (23-30 August 1642) BL E114 (36); Clarendon, **History**, volume 2, pages 318-19; Margaret, Duchess of Newcastle, **The Life of William Cavendish Duke of Newcastle**, edited by C H Firth (London 1886) pages 275, 290 and note 1; J H Round, 'Colchester during the Commonwealth', in **English Historical Review**, volume 15 (1900) page 642.

40. **A Message Sent to the Parliament** (27 August 1642) BL E114 (30); HMC, 10th Report (1887) 'Braye Manuscripts', pages 146-7.

41. [Ryves] *Mercurius Rusticus*, number 2, pages 11-15, and number 3, page 28; HMC, 5th Report (1876) 'House of Lords Manuscripts', page 45.

42. CSPD 1641-1643, page 377.

43. **A Message Sent to the Parliament** (27 August 1642) BL E114 (30); **CJ**, volume 2, pages 736, 737 and 738; **LJ**, volume 5, page 319.

44. [Ryves] *Mercurius Rusticus* (1646) number 1, pages 1-6.

45. **CJ**, volume 2, page 740; **Special Passages** (23-30 August 1642) BL E114 (36).

46. Peck, volume 2, book 12, pages 23-5.

47. Rous, page 121.

48. Rous, pages 121-2; **LJ**, volume 5, page 331; HMC, 5th Report (1876) 'House of Lords Manuscripts', page 45; Clarendon, **History**, volume 2, page 319; *Mercurius Rusticus*, number 2, pages 13-14.

49. Peck, volume 2, book 12, page 24.

50. Rous, page 122.

51. **A Perfect Diurnall of the Passages in Parliament** (12-19 September 1642) BL E240 (5); **Special Passages** (23-30 August 1642) BL E114 (36); Josselin, page 13.

52. **A Perfect Diurnall of the Passages in Parliament** (12-19 September 1642) BL E240 (5).

53. **CJ**, volume 2, pages 745 and 762; **LJ**, volume 5, page 337; **A Continuation of Certain Special and Remarkable Passages from both Houses of Parliament** (5-9 September 1642) BL E116

(26); Josselin, page 13.

54. **LJ**, volume 5, page 327.

55. **A Declaration of the Lords and Commons Assembled in Parliament, For the appeasing and quietting of all unlawful tumults and insurrections in the several counties of England, and Dominion of Wales** (2 September 1642) BL E115 (15).

56. **LJ**, volume 5, page 33.

57. **CJ**, volume 2, pages 745 and 762; **LJ**, volume 5, page 337; A **Continuation of Certain Special and Remarkable Passages from both Houses of Parliament** (5-9 September 1642) BL E116 (26).

58. HMC, 12th Report (1891) 'Beaufort Manuscripts', page 23.

59. Rous, page 122.

60. Rushworth, volume 4, page 680; May, book 2, page 108, and book 3, page 78.

61. **LJ**, volume 5, pages 131-2; Clarendon, **History**, volume 2, pages 261 note and 267.

62. Rous, page 130.

63. Warwick, pages 215-16; Clarendon, **History**, volume 2, page 318.

64. **Special Passages** (23-30 August 1642) BL E114 (36).

65. *Mercurius Rusticus*, number 1, pages 6-11.

66. **The Life and Times of Anthony Wood**, edited by Andrew Clark (Oxford 1891) volume 1, page 59.

67. [Dudley North], **A Narrative of Some Passages in or relating to the Long Parliament** (London 1670) pages 36-8; Clarendon, **History**, volume 2, pages 358-9.

68. Verney, **Memoirs**, volume 2, page 151.

69. Peck, volume 2, book 12, pages 23-5.

70. Quoted by A Kingston, **Hertfordshire During the Great Civil War** (London 1894) page 36.

71. R R Reid, **The King's Council in the North** (London 1921) pages 394-403.

72. **The Last true news from York, Nottingham, Coventry and Warwick** (24 August-4 September 1642) BL E116 (9); **Special Passages** (27 September-4 October 1642) BL E119 (24); 'Short Memorials of Thomas, Lord Fairfax', in **Somers's Tracts** (London 1811) volume 5, pages 376-7 and 390-1.

73. Willcox, pages 162-71; Keeler, pages 350-1.

74. Compare Alan Everitt, **Suffolk and the Great Rebellion 1640-1660**, Suffolk Records Society, volume 3 (1960) pages 11-28.

75. 'A Relation of the Taking of Cicester', page 178.

76. **A Declaration Made by the right Honourable the Earle of Bath**, BL E119 (11).

77. **A Declaration Made the Lord Marquis of Hertford** (1642) BL E118 (31).

78. Clarendon, **History**, volume 2, pages 295-6.

79. Husbands, page 649.

80. Clarendon, **History**, volume 2, pages 295-6.

81. **A Memento for Yeomen, Merchants, Citizens, and all the Commons in England** (23 August 1642) BL E113 (13).

82. **A True and Sad Relation of divers passages in Somersetshire** (London, 9 August 1642) BL E109 (34).

83. **Joyful News from Wells** (12 August 1642) BL E111 (4).

84. **A Memento for Yeomen** (23 August 1642) BL E113 (13).

85. **A True and Sad Relation of divers passages in Somersetshire**, BL E109 (34).

86. Clarendon, **History**, volume 2, pages 295-6.

87. Corbet, pages 8-9.

88. Husbands, page 489.

89. Husbands, page 649.

90. Clarendon, **History**, volume 2, page 318; Kingston, page 30.

91. **A Royalist's Notebook: The Commonplace Book of Sir John Oglander**, edited by Francis Bamford (London 1936) pages 103-6.

92. Verney, **Memoirs**, volume 2, page 151.

93. Peck, volume 2, book 12, page 24.

94. Kingston, page 36.

95. Sir Edward Walker, page 50.

96. Stone, **Crisis of the Aristocracy**, pages 164, 214-17 and 299-332.

97. 'Papers Relating to the Delinquency of Lord Savile', in **Camden Society**, second series, volume 31 (1883) pages 9-11 and 14.

98. **Special Passages** (20-27 September 1642) BL E118 (45).

99. **LJ**, volume 5, page 367; **CJ**, volume 2, page 789.

100. Clarendon, **History**, volume 2, pages 294-8; **Exceeding Joyfull Newes from the Earl of Bedford** (London 1642) BL E113 (17).

101. **A Perfect Relation** (12 August 1642) BL E111 (5); **Joyful News from Wells** (12 August 1642) BL E111 (4).

102. **The Unfaithfulness of the Cavaliers** (1643) BL E84 (37); **Civil War Tracts: Lancashire**, pages 75 and 121.

103. HMC, 12th Report (1891) 'Manuscripts of Southwell Cathedral', pages 550-1.

104. Aston, **Remonstrance against Presbytery**, BL E163 (1); HMC, 4th Report (1874) 'House of Lords Manuscripts', page 55.

105. **Civil War Tracts: Lancashire**, page 162.

106. HMC, 10th Report (1885) 'Captain Stewart Manuscripts', pages 81-2.

107. **Four Petitions to His Excellency Sir Thomas Fairfax** (London 1647) BL E393 (7) page 15.

108. **LJ**, volume 4, pages 272, 285, 293, 307, 313 and 322; HMC, 4th Report (1874) 'House of Lords Manuscripts', pages 86, 93 and 94.

109. HMC, 10th Report (1887) 'Braye Manuscripts', pages 146-7; **Mercurius Rusticus**, number 1, pages 1-5.

110. Rous, pages 121-2; **A Relation of the rare explo3ts**, BL E114 (13).

111. Dugdale, pages 144-6; Stavin, pages 385-7; Hughes, 'Drainage disputes in the Isle of Axholme'.

112. Whitelock, volume 1, page 209.

113. Chester and Ethyn Kirby, 'The Stuart Game Prerogative', in **English Historical Review**, volume 46 (1931); Penry Williams, 'The Activity of the Council in the Marches under the early Stuarts', in **The Welsh History Review**, volume 1, number 2 (1961) page 141; Campbell, page 311; Kerridge, **Agrarian Problems**, page 102.

114. **LJ**, volume 4, pages 406, 434 and 547; HMC, 4th Report (1874) 'House of Lords Manuscripts', page 103; **CJ**, volume 2, page 282.

115. **CSPD 1641-1643**, pages 318-19.

116. **LJ**, volume 4, pages 595, 602 and 653, and volume 5, pages 25, 33 and 35; HMC, 5th Report (1876) 'House of Lords Manuscripts', page 24.

117. **LJ**, volume 5, pages 37 and 38; HMC, 5th Report (1876) 'House of Lords Manuscripts', page 20.

118. **LJ**, volume 5, page 61; **CJ**, volume 2, pages 561, 566 and 567.

119. **An Order of the Lords and Commons** (12 May 1642) BL 669f5 (19).

120. **CSPD 1641-1643**, page 346.

121. **LJ**, volume 5, page 199.

122. **LJ**, volume 6, pages 21, 39 and 78; HMC, 5th Report (1876) 'House of Lords Manuscripts', pages 82, 84 and 89.

123. *Mercurius Rusticus*, number 1, page 3.

124. Rous, page 122.

125. **A Continuation of certain Special and Remarkable passages from both Houses of Parliament** (30 August-6 September 1642) BL E116 (8).

126. **LJ**, volume 5, pages 362, 366, 373 and 526.

127. **LJ**, volume 5, pages 380 and 387; HMC, 5th Report (1876) 'House of Lords Manuscripts', pages 51 and 52; **A Perfect Diurnall of the Passages in Parliament** (3-10 October 1642) BL E240 (34).

128. **LJ**, volume 5, page 365.

129. Menna Prestwich, **Cranfield: Politics and Profits under the Early Stuarts** (Oxford 1966) pages 568-9.

130. **CSPD 1641-1643**, page 372.

131. HMC, 5th Report (1876) 'House of Lords Manuscripts', page 47.

132. **CSPD 1641-1643**, page 379.

133. **CSPD 1641-1643**, pages 382 and 384.

134. **CSPD 1641-1643**, page 384.

135. **CSPD 1641-1643**, pages 385 and 388.

136. Verney, **Memoirs**, volume 2, pages 82 and 83-4.

137. Verney, **Memoirs**, volume 2, page 85.

138. Verney, **Memoirs**, volume 2, pages 86 and 90.
139. HMC, 4th Report (1874) 'De La Warr Manuscripts', page 296; Prestwich, page 569.
140. **The Oxinden and Peyton Letters 1642-1670**, edited by Dorothy Gardiner (London 1937) pages 9-10.
141. Verney, **Memoirs**, volume 2, pages 154 and 156.
142. HMC, 13th Report (1891) 'Portland Manuscripts', volume 1, page 84.
143. HMC, 12th Report (1888) 'Cowper Manuscripts', volume 2, pages 338 and 341.
144. Sir Thomas Roe, **Letter-Book 1642-1644**, BL Harley Manuscript 1901, page 185.
145. Warburton, volume 2, pages 371-2.
146. HMC, 4th Report (1874) 'Denbigh Manuscripts', page 266.
147. Verney, **Memoirs**, volume 1, pages 267-8, and volume 2, page 156; HMC, 4th Report (1874) 'Denbigh Manuscripts', page 266; HMC, 11th Report (1888) 'Reading Corporation Manuscripts', page 217; HMC, 13th Report (1891) 'Portland Manuscripts', volume 1, page 84.
148. **Oxinden and Peyton Letters**, pages 67-8.
149. 'A Discourse of the War in Lancashire', in **Chetham Society**, volume 62 (1864) page 131; **The Parliament Scout** (22-29 August 1644) BL E7 (24).
150. Prestwich, pages 574-5.
151. Prestwich, pages 569-70.
152. **The Knyvett Letters**, page 134.
153. **The Knyvett Letters**, page 137.
154. S R Gardiner, **History of the Great Civil War 1642-1649** (four volumes, London 1893) volume 3, page 196.
155. HMC, 4th Report (1874) 'Denbigh Manuscripts', page 266.
156. Prestwich, pages 568-77.
157. Gardiner, **Civil War**, page 196.
158. HMC, 13th Report (1891) 'Portland Manuscripts', volume 1, page 165.
159. HMC, 5th Report (1876) 'House of Lords Manuscripts', page 82.
160. Blackwood, 'Lancashire Cavaliers', page 26.
161. Clarendon, **History**, volume 1, page 264.
162. Sir Edward Walker, pages 28 and 239.
163. **A Plaine Discovery** (Oxford 1643) BL E75 (5).
164. **A Short View of the Late Troubles in England** (Oxford 1681) page 99; Lilly, pages 111-12.
165. Lilly, pages 111-12; **A Plaine Discovery**, BL E75 (5).
166. **A Short View of the Late Troubles in England**, page 99.
167. **A Declaration of the Valiant Resolutions of the Famous Prentices of London** (1642) BL E109 (5); [North], **A Narrative of Some Passages in or relating to the Long Parliament,**

pages 31-2.

168. Clarendon, History, volume 3, pages 169-77.

169. Lilly, page 112.

170. N G Brett-James, The Growth of Stuart London (London 1935) pages 269-70.

171. William Lithgow, 'The present Surveigh of London and England's state' (London 1643) in Somers's Tracts (London 1811) volume 4, pages 534-45; Brett-James, pages 274-6; Pearl, pages 262-5.

172. Lithgow, pages 534-45.

173. CSP Venetian 1642-1643, pages 256, 273 and 274.

174. Pearl, page 263.

175. Dobb, pages 169-70.

176. LJ, volume 5, pages 164-5, 195-6; A True and Exact Relation (London 1642) BL E113 (1); The True Proceedings of the Severall Counties of Yorke Coventry Portsmouth Cornewall (London 1642) BL E114 (6); Newes from the Citie of Norwich (1642) BL E114 (15); Clarendon, History, volume 2, pages 288-90; Keeler, page 96.

177. Clarendon, History, volume 2, pages 288-9; CSPD 1641-1643, page 382.

178. Clarendon, History, volume 2, pages 299-305.

179. A letter Writen from Walshall (1643) BL E96 (22).

180. Special Passages (23-30 August 1642) BL E114 (36).

181. Reliquiae Baxterianae, pages 44-5 and 94.

182. W H B Court, The Rise of the Midland Industries (Oxford 1938) pages 33-46; Conrad Gill, History of Birmingham, volume 1 (Oxford 1952) pages 45-7 and 48-9; The Kingdomes Weekly Intelligencer (4-11 April 1643) BL E96 (4).

183. Gill, page 50,

184. Mercurius Aulicus (2-9 April 1643) BL E97 (10); Clarendon, History, volume 3, page 19.

185. Some Speciall Passages from Warwickshire (London 1642) BL E109 (3).

186. A Letter Writen from Walshall, BL E96 (22).

187. Court, page 46.

188. Clarendon, History, volume 2, pages 358-9.

189. Clarendon, History, volume 2, page 364.

190. Clarendon, History, volume 2, pages 358 and 363.

191. Clarendon, History, volume 2, page 359, and volume 3, page 19; A Letter writen from Walshall, BL E96 (22).

192. Clarendon, History, volume 3, pages 19-20.

193. A Letter writen from Walshall, BL E96 (22).

194. Clarendon, History, volume 2, page 359.

195. Exceeding joyfull Newes From his Excellence the Earle of Essex (London, 10 October 1642) BL E121 (28).

196. Gill, page 64; A True Relation of Prince Ruperts Barbarous

Cruelty against the Towne of Brumingham (London 1643) BL E96 (9).

197. Court, pages 37, 43, and 73-4.

198. **Special Passages** (4-11 April 1643) BL E96 (2); **Prince Ruperts Burning love to England Discovered in Birminghams Flames** (London 1643) BL E100 (8) page 2; **Prince Ruperts Barbarous Cruelty**, BL E96 (9); Clarendon, **History**, volume 2, pages 473-7.

199. **Prince Ruperts Burning love to England**, BL E100 (8) page 3; **Prince Ruperts Barbarous Cruelty**, BL E96 (9).

200. Clarendon, **History**, volume 3, page 20; **A Letter Writen from Walshall**, BL E96 (22).

201. **Prince Ruperts Burning love**, BL E100 (8) pages 3-5; **Prince Ruperts Barbarous Cruelty**, BL E96 (9).

202. Clarendon, **History**, volume 3, pages 20-21.

203. **Prince Ruperts Burning love**, BL E1OO (8) page 4; **A Letter Written from Walshall**, BL E96 (22).

204. **Prince Ruperts Barbarous Cruelty**, BL E96 (9).

205. **Prince Ruperts Burning love**, BL E100 (8) pages 6-7; **A Letter Written from Walshall**, BL E96 (22); *Mercurius Aulicus* (2-9 April 1643) BL E97 (10); **Speciall Passages** (4-11 April 1643) BL E96 (2).

206. Gill, pages 42-3.

207. Court, pages 61-5; Gill, pages 46-7.

208. Ernest Broxap, **The Great Civil War in Lancashire (1642-1651)** (Manchester 1910) pages 37-8.

209. **Civil War Tracts: Lancashire**, pages 20-4, 64 and 110.

210. **Civil War Tracts: Lancashire**, pages 49-50.

211. **Civil War Tracts: Lancashire**, page 50.

212. **Civil War Tracts: Lancashire**, pages 30-5, 112-13 and 220.

213. **Civil War Tracts: Lancashire**, pages 50-1, 114 and 220-1.

214. **Civil War Tracts: Lancashire**, pages 51, 114 and 221.

215. **Civil War Tracts: Lancashire**, pages 45 and 51.

216. **A true and exact Relation of the several passages at the Siege of Manchester** (London 1642) BL E121 (45) page 9.

217. **Civil War Tracts: Lancashire**, pages 45 and 52.

218. **Several passages at the Siege of Manchester**, BL E121 (45) page 6.

219. **Civil War Tracts: Lancashire**, page 222.

220. **Civil War Tracts: Lancashire**, pages 48-9 and 53-5.

221. **Civil War Tracts: Lancashire**, pages 117-18 and 222.

222. **Civil War Tracts: Lancashire**, pages 55, 120, 222 and 223; **Several passages at the Siege of Manchester**, BL E121 (45) pages 7-8.

223. **Several passages at the Siege of Manchester**, BL E121 (45) pages 8 and 10.

224. **Civil War Tracts: Lancashire**, page 103.

225. **Civil War Tracts: Lancashire**, pages 223-4.

226. **Several passages at the Siege of Manchester**, BL E121 (45) page 9.

227. **Civil War Tracts: Lancashire**, pages 51-2.

228. The author describes himself as 'one risen from the grave'.

229. **Weekly Intelligence**, BL E121 (34).

230. Wadsworth and Mann, pages 25 and 27-8; Norman Lowe, 'The Lancashire Textile Industry in the Sixteenth Century', in **Chetham Society**, third series, volume 20 (1972) chapters 3 and 4.

231. Dobb, pages 149-51.

232. Wadsworth and Mann, pages 55-6; compare H W Clemsha, **A History of Preston in Amounderness** (Manchester 1912) pages 123-30.

233. Heaton, pages 183 and 197.

234. Clarendon, **History**, volume 2, page 287.

235. Clarendon, **History**, volume 2, pages 285, 287 and 464; 'Short Memorials of Thomas, Lord Fairfax', pages 390-1; **The last true news from York, Nottingham, Coventry and Warwick** (24 August-4 September 1642) BL E116 (9).

236. Clarendon, **History**, volume 2, page 287; 'Short Memorials of Thomas, Lord Fairfax', pages 376-7 and 390-1; **A Continuation of Certain Special and Remarkable Passages from both Houses of Parliament** (16-21 September 1642) BL E240 (8); **A Perfect Diurnall of the Passages in Parliament** (19-26 September 1642) BL E240 (11); **Certain Intelligence from York** (30 September 1642) BL E119 (27).

237. **Special Passages** (27 September-4 October 1642) BL E119 (24).

238. Lister, pages 10 and 14.

239. **Certain Intelligence from York** (30 September 1642) BL E119 (27); **Fourteen Articles of Peace. Propounded to the King and Parliament by the Gentry and Commonalty of the County of York** (London 1642) BL E119 (29).

240. **Reasons Why Sir John Hotham Cannot in Honour agree to the Treaty of Pacification** (1642) BL E240 (30); **The Declaration of Captain Hotham** (1642) BL E121 (32); **The Declaration and Votes of the Lords and Commons Assembled in Parliament: Concerning the late Treaty of Peace in Yorkshire** (1642) BL E121 (2).

241. **Englands Memorable Accidents** (31 October-7 November 1642) BL E242 (6); 'Short Memorials of Thomas, Lord Fairfax', pages 376-7.

242. Robert Bell (editor) **Memorials of the Civil War: Comprising the Correspondence of the Fairfax Family** (two volumes, London 1849) volume 1, pages 28-9.

243. 'The Rider of the White Horse' (London 1643) in Lister, page 64.

244. Priestley, pages 26-7.

245. 'Short Memorials of Thomas, Lord Fairfax', pages 377-8.

246. Bell (editor) **Correspondence of the Fairfax Family**, volume 1, pages 25-30.

247. Heaton, page 227; 'The Rider of the White Horse', in Lister, page 63.

248. 'The Rider of the White Horse', in Lister, pages 63-4.

249. Lister, page 14.

250. 'The Rider of the White Horse', in Lister, page 65; **LJ**, volume 5, page 527.

251. Hodgson, pages 93-4.

252. 'The Rider of the White Horse', in Lister, page 66.

253. 'The Rider of the White Horse', in Lister, page 67; Lister, page 17.

254. 'The Rider of the White Horse', in Lister, page 68; Hodgson, pages 94-5; **LJ**, volume 5, page 527.

255. Hodgson, page 95.

256. Thirsk, **Agrarian History**, volume 4, page 29.

257. Heaton, pages 93-5 and 203-5.

258. Heaton, pages 96-9 and 203-5.

259. Heaton, pages 118-23, 203-5 and 221-8.

260. Bell (editor) **Correspondence of the Fairfax Family**, volume 1, pages 33-4.

261. HMC, 13th Report (1891) 'Portland Manuscripts', volume 1, pages 80, 81-2, 83-4, 87, 89-90, 90-91, 99, 105, 109, 699, 701, 702-3, 704 and 707.

262. HMC, 13th Report (1891) 'Portland Manuscripts', volume 1, page 87.

263. **The Kingdomes Weekly Intelligencer** (3-10 January 1643) BL E84 (29); **Englands Memorable Accidents** (2-9 January 1643) BL E244 (46).

264. 'A True Relation of the Passages at Leeds, on Munday, the 23 of January, 1642' in Lister, pages 76-7.

265. **Civil War Tracts: Lancashire**, page 125.

266. **Civil War Tracts: Lancashire**, page 92.

267. 'Stanley Papers', part 3, volume 3, in **Chetham Society**, volume 70 (1867) page 8.

268. 'The Life of Adam Martindale', in **Chetham Society**, volume 4 (1845) pages 31-2.

269. **Civil War Tracts: Lancashire**, pages 64-5.

270. **Civil War Tracts: Lancashire**, pages 71, 74 and 79.

271. **Civil War Tracts: Lancashire**, pages 77, 78 and 83-4.

272. 'The life of Adam Martindale', pages 31-2.

273. Heywood, volume 1, pages 96-7.

274. 'The life of Adam Martindale', page 31.

275. Tupling, pages 70-5 and 145-59; 'The causes of the Civil War in

Lancashire', in **Transactions of the Lancashire and Cheshire Antiquarian Society**, volume 65 (1955) pages 17-20.

276. Mary Brigg, 'The Forest of Pendle in the Seventeenth Century', part 1, in **Transactions of the Historic Society of Lancashire and Cheshire**, volume 113 (1961) pages 73-5, 83-4 and 88-91, and part 2, in volume 115 (1964) pages 77-8, 78-9 and 85.

277. **Certain Informations from Several Parts of the Kingdom** (3-10 April 1643) BL C21 b1 (12); **The Kingdomes Weekly Intelligencer** (4-11 April 1643) BL E96 (4); **Civil War Tracts: Lancashire**, pages 225-7; 'A Discourse of the War in Lancashire', in Chetham Society, volume 62 (1864) page 32.

278. **Englands Memorable Accidents** (2-9 January 1643) BL E244 (46); **The Kingdomes Weekly Intelligencer** (17-24 January 1643) BL E86 (5) and (21-28 February 1643) BL E91 (8).

279. **A Perfect Diurnall of the Passages in Parliament** (13-20 February 1643) BL E246 (20); **A Continuation of Certain Special and Remarkable Passages from both Houses of Parliament** (23 February-2 March 1643) BL E246 (33); **A Perfect Diurnall of the Passages in Parliament** (27 February-6 March 1643) BL E246 (37); *Mercurius Aulicus* (19-25 February 1643) BL E246 (41).

280. **The Kingdomes Weekly Intelligencer** (21-28 February 1643) BL E91 (8); **A Continuation of certain special and remarkable Passages informed to both Houses of Parliament** (2-9 March 1643) BL E92 (20); **Certain Informations from several parts of the kingdom** (6-13 March 1643) BL E93 (4).

281. **The Protestation Taken by the Commissioners of Cornwall and Devon** (5 March 1643) BL E94 (21); Clarendon, **History**, volume 2, pages 459-60.

282. **The Kingdomes Weekly Intelligencer** (7-14 March 1643) BL E93 (6).

283. HMC, 13th Report (1891) 'Portland Manuscripts', volume 1, pages 101-2.

284. CJ, volume 2, pages 1002-4, and volume 3, pages 7-8 and 11-12; LJ, volume 5, pages 657-8.

285. **Special Passages and Certain Informations from Several Places** (18-25 April 1643) BL E99 (21); **A Perfect Diurnall of the Passages in Parliament** (24 April-1 May 1643) BL E247 (32).

286. William Camden, **Britain, Or a Chorographicall Description of the Most Flourishing Kingdomes, England, Scotland, and Ireland** (London 1610) pages 586-7.

287. Daniel Defoe, **A Tour Thro' the whole Island of Great Britain** (three volumes, London 1724-7) volume 2, part 4, pages 119-20.

288. Richard Symonds, 'Diary of the Marches of the Royal Army', in **Camden Society**, first series, volume 74 (1859) pages 175-6.

289. D H Pennington and I A Roots (editors) **The Committee at**

Stafford 1641-1645 (Manchester 1957) page lxii.

290. HMC (1930) 'Hastings Manuscripts', volume 2, pages 89 and 91; **Special Passages and Certain Informations from several places** (7-14 February 1643) BL E89 (17); **Certain Informations from several parts of the Kingdom** (13-20 February 1643) BL E90 (3) and (20 February-6 March 1643) BL E92 (3).

291. Pennington and Roots, pages lxii-lxv.

292. **The Kingdomes Weekly Intelligencer** (21-28 February 1643) BL E91 (8).

293. **The Kingdomes Weekly Intelligencer** (4-11 April 1643) BL E96 (4).

294. **The Kingdomes Weekly Intelligencer** (17-24 January 1643) BL E86 (5).

295. [Edward Bowles], **Plaine English: or, A Discourse Concerning the Accommodation...** Printed (**unless men be the more careful and God the more merciful) the last of Liberty. 1643,** BL E84 (42).

296. Pearl, page 269.

297. BL E61 (3).

298. Pearl, pages 269-71; *Mercurius Civicus* (13-20 July 1643) BL E61 (11); **The Special Passages Continued** (18-22 July 1643) BL E61 (15); **The Parliament Scout** (13-20 July 1643) BL E61 (13); **The Kingdomes Weekly Intelligencer** (18-25 July 1643) BL E61 (22).

299. Pearl, pages 269-73; Lotte Glow, 'Pym and Parliament: the Methods of Moderation', in **Journal of Modern History**, volume 36 (1964) pages 375-84; **A Continuation of Certain Special and Remarkable Passages** (10-18 August 1643) BL E65 (21) and (17-25 August 1643) BL E65 (33).

300. Pennington and Roots, page lxii; **Certain Informations from several parts of the Kingdom** (20 February-6 March 1643) BL E92 (3).

301. **Special Passages and Certain Informations from several places** (7-14 February 1643) BL E89 (17).

302. **Englands Memorable Accidents** (28 November-5 December 1642) BL E242 (37).

303. Corbet, pages 21-2.

304. **A Perfect Diurnall of the Passages in Parliament** (12-19 September 1643) BL E239 (16).

305. **Englands Memorable Accidents** (21-28 November 1642) BL E242 (28).

306. **The True and Original Copy of the first Petition** (15 December 1642) BL E130 (26); **A True Copy of the Remonstrance and Petition** (13 December 1642) BL E130 (7); Pearl, pages 253-4.

307. **Special Passages and Certain Informations from several places** (7-14 March 1647) BL E93 (7).

308. **The City Alarum** (London 1645) page 17.

309. **A Remonstrance of Many Thousand Citizens** (1646) in Don M Wolfe, **Leveller Manifestoes of the Puritan Revolution** (London 1944, reprinted 1967) pages 123-4; Joseph Frank, **The Levellers** (Cambridge, Massachusetts, 1955) page 55.

310. **Special Passages** (6-13 September 1642) BL E116 (41); **A Diurnall, of True Proceedings of our armies at Sherbourne** (10 September 1642) BL E116 (48).

311. HMC, 10th Report (1887) 'Braye Manuscripts', pages 147-8.

312. **The Newest and Truest, and most Unpartial Relation of all the late occurrence which hath happened at Sherbourne-Castle** (14 September 1642) BL E117 (4); **Happy News from Sherborn** (13 September 1642) BL E116 (39); **Special Passages** (6-13 September 1642) BL E239 (22).

313. **Special Passages** (6-13 September 1642) BL E116 (41).

314. Corbet, pages 20-1; 'A Relation of the taking of Ciceter', page 185.

315. Corbet, pages 20-21.

316. Abbott (editor) **Writings and Speeches of Oliver Cromwell**, volume 1, page 204.

317. HMC, 10th Report (1887) 'Braye Manuscripts', pages 147-8.

318. J Webb, **Memorials of the Civil War between King Charles I and the Parliament of England as it affected Herefordshire and the adjacent counties**, edited by T W Webb (two volumes, London 1879) volume 2, page 208.

319. HMC, 13th Report (1891) 'Portland Manuscripts', volume 1, page 100.

320. Rushworth, volume 4, page 272; Clarendon, **History**, volume 3, pages 73-4.

321. **Special Passages** (4-11 April 1643) BL E96 (2).

322. **The Parliament Scout** (17-20 July 1643) BL E61 (13).

323. Abbott (editor) **Writings and Speeches of Oliver Cromwell**, volume 1, pages 204-5; **A worthy speech made by the Right Honourable the Lord Brooke** (1643) BL E90 (27).

324. **Instructions and Propositions** (7 July 1643) BL E59 (15).

325. *Mercurius Civicus* (13-20 July 1643) BL E61 (11); **The Parliament Scout** (13-20 July 1643) BL E61 (13); **The Special Passages Continued** (18-22 July 1643) BL E61 (5); **The Kingdomes Weekly Intelligencer** (18-22 July 1643) BL E61 (22).

326. Pearl, pages 267-73.

Chapter 8: THE NOBILITY AND THE PEOPLE

1. **CSPD 1641-1643**, pages 330, 334 and 336.

2. Clarendon, **History**, volume 2, pages 228-9; **CSPD 1641-1643**, page 359.

3. **CSPD 1641-1643**, page 362; Clarendon, **History**, volume 2, page 241.

4. Clarendon, **History**, volume 2, pages 313 and 337; Gough, page 39.

5. Clarendon, **History**, volume 2, page 343.

6. Clarendon, **History**, volume 2, pages 343-4.

7. **His Majesties Proceedings in Northamptonshire, Gloucestershire, Wiltshire, and Warwickshire** (1642) BL E113 (14).

8. **LJ**, volume 5, page 107; **A Letter Sent by a Yorkshire Gentleman, to a friend in London** (London 1642) BL E150 (5).

9. Clarendon, **History**, volume 2, page 472.

10. Clarendon, **History**, volume 2, pages 74, 181 and 183-4.

11. **CSPD 1641-1643**, pages 317, 322-3, 323-4, 325 and 330; **A Letter from the Right Honourable Ferdinando Lord Fairfax** (1642) BL E148 (4); **His Majesty's Declaration to the Ministers, freeholders, farmers, and substantial copyholders of the County of York** (1642) BL E149 (27).

12. Clarendon, **History**, volume 2, pages 343-4.

13. Husbands, pages 557-8.

14. Clarendon, **Life**, page 412.

15. Newcastle, page 175.

16. **The True Informer** (Oxford 1643) BL E96 (10) page 39.

17. 'Papers Relating to the Delinquency of Lord Savile', pages 6-7.

18. Roe, pages 134-5.

19. Henry Dircks, **The Life, Times, and Scientific Labours of the Second Marquis of Worcester** (London 1865) pages 33, 34, 35-6, 41-2, 44-6 and 58-9.

20. Newcastle, page 20.

21. Clarendon, **History**, volume 5, pages 185-6; **LJ**, volume 5, page 170; Keeler, page 394.

22. Clarendon, **History**, volume 2, page 227; Newcastle, page 156; **A True Relation of a Great Victory** (1643) BL E84 (23); Hutchinson, page 92.

23. Clarendon, **History**, volume 2, pages 335 note, 342 and 469, and volume 5, page 186; 'A Discourse of the War in Lancashire', pages 19-20, 63 and 77; **Good News out of Cheshire** (1642) BL E127 (44); F Walker, 'Historical Geography of Southwest Lancashire', in **Chetham Society**, new series, volume 103 (1939) pages 50-1.

24. Clarendon, **History**, volume 2, pages 335 note, 367 and 372.

25. Clarendon, **History**, volume 2, page 335 note.

26. Clarendon, **History**, volume 2, pages 241 and 473-4; **A True Relation of the Transaction of the Commands of both Houses of Parliament in the execution of the Militia in the County of Leicester** (1642) BL E154 (4).

27. Warburton, volume 3, pages 523-30; Corbet, pages 31-2; Clarendon, **History**, volume 2, page 481 note.

28. Clarendon, **History**, volume 2, pages 283-4 and 297.

29. Clarendon, **History**, volume 2, page 452; Mary Coate, **Cornwall in the Great Civil War and Interregnum 1642-1660** (1933)

pages 31-2, 33, 35 and 37-8.

30. Sir Edward Walker, page 50.

31. Clarendon, **History**, volume 2, pages 313, 343-4 and 346-7.

32. Clarendon, **History**, volume 2, page 348.

33. **Special Passages** (6-13 September 1642) BL E239 (22); **The Newest and Truest, and most Unpartial Relation of all the late occurrence which hath happened at Sherbourne-Castle** (1642) BL E117 (4); **Happy News from Sherborn** (1642) BL E116 (39).

34. **Exceeding Joyfull Newes from the Earl of Bedford** (London 1642) BL E113 (17).

35. **A Remonstrance or Declaration** (1642) BL E123 (29); Coate, page 9.

36. 'The Life of Adam Martindale', pages 31-2; 'The Farington Papers', pages 88-90; Tupling, in **Transactions of the Lancashire and Cheshire Antiquarian Society**, volume 65 (1955) page 31 note 91.

37. Clarendon, **History**, volume 2, page 471.

38. **CSPD 1641-1643**, page 368.

39. Hobbes, 'Behemoth', in **The English Works of Thomas Hobbes**, volume 6, page 291.

40. **The Moderator Expecting Sudden Peace or Certain Ruin** (1643) BL E89 (21).

41. Corbet, pages 8-9 and 16-17.

42. **The Memoirs of Edmund Ludlow**, edited by C H Firth (two volumes, Oxford 1894) volume 1, page 96.

43. Jeremiah Burroughes, **The glorious Name of God** (London 1643) pages 50-1.

44. **A Soveraigne Salve to Cure the Blind** (1643) BL E99 (23).

45. **Weekly Intelligence**, BL E121 (34).

46. **The Kingdomes Weekly Intelligencer** (4-11 April 1643) BL E86 (5).

47. Husbands, page 575; *Mercurius Britanicus*, number 55, BL E14 (13).

48. **A Soveraigne Salve** (1643) BL E99 (23).

49. **A True and Sad Relation of divers Passages in Somerset-shire** (London 1642) BL E109 (34).

50. 'Sir Roger Twysden's Journal', in *Archaeologia Cantiana*, volume 1 (1858) pages 200-3; Alan Everitt, **The Community of Kent and the Great Rebellion 1640-60** (Leicester 1966) pages 95-6; **Advertisements from York and Beverly** (1642) BL E107 (30); Johnson (editor) **Fairfax Correspondence**, volume 2, page 413; **Diary of Henry Townshend of Elmley Lovett 1640-1663**, volume 2, pages 65 and 68; HMC, 15th Report (1899) 'Buccleuch Manuscripts', volume 1, page 295; **Speciall Passages and Certain Informations from Severall Places** (23-30 August

1642) BL E114 (36).

51. **A Letter from the right honourable Ferdinando Lord Fairfax**, BL E184 (4).

52. Campbell, pages 356-7.

53. Dudley Digges, **The Unlawfulness of Subjects Takeing Up Armes Against Their Soveraigne** (1643) pages 142-5.

54. Corbet, page 9.

55. Sir Edward Walker, pages 50-1.

56. Peck, volume 2, book 12, page 23.

57. Prestwich, page 569.

58. Henry Parker, **The Contra-Replicant** (1643) BL E87 (5).

59. **Newes from the Citie of Norwich** (26 August 1642) BL E114 (15).

60. **The Proceedings at Banbury** (1642) BL E111 (11).

61. **The English Intelligencer** (12-18 November 1642) BL E127 (26).

62. 'Eben-Ezer. A Full and Exact Relation of The Several Remarkable and Victorious Proceedings of the ever-renowned Colonell Massy' (London 1644) in *Bibliotheca Gloucestrensis*, volume 2 (1823) page 330.

63. Clarendon, **History**, volume 3, page 130; Warburton, volume 2, pages 276-7.

64. Corbet, pages 9 and 16.

65. A H Dodd, **Studies in Stuart Wales** (Cardiff 1952) pages 111-14.

66. **A Perfect Relation** (12 August 1642) BL E111 (5); HMC, 5th Report (1876) 'Sutherland Manuscripts', page 161; Clarendon, **History**, volume 2, pages 295-6.

67. 'The life of Adam Martindale', page 32.

68. Hirst, **The Representative of the People?**, pages 29-34.

69. Hutchinson, page 80.

70. May, book 3, page 84.

71. **Special Passages** (23-30 August 1642) BL E114 (36); **Weekly Intelligence**, BL E121 (34).

72. **Advertisements from York and Beverly** (1642) BL E107 (30).

73. May, book 2, page 108, and book 3, page 78.

74. Rushworth, volume 4, page 680.

75. **A Perfect Diurnall of the Passages in Parliament** (5-12 September 1642) BL E239 (16).

76. Hughes, 'Drainage disputes in the Isle of Axholme', page 23.

77. Holmes, **Eastern Association**, pages 172-3; Whitelock, volume 1, page 209.

78. **Civil War Tracts: Lancashire**, pages 64-5.

79. HMC, 10th Report (1885) 'Captain Stewart Manuscripts', pages 81-2.

80. **Four Petitions to His Excellency Sir Thomas Fairfax** (London 1647) page 17.

81. See above pages 281-304.

82. A J and R H Tawney, 'An occupational census of the seventeenth century'.

83. Corbet, pages 8-9.

84. *Reliquiae Baxterianae*, page 30.

85. Corbet, pages 8-9 and 16-17.

86. Warburton, volume 2, pages 276-7.

87. Clarendon, History, volume 3, page 80; HMC, 5th Report (1876) 'Sutherland Manuscripts', page 161.

88. Clarendon, History, volume 2, page 464.

89. Bell (editor) The Fairfax Correspondence, volume 1, pages 25-30.

90. Supple, pages 157-8.

91. Ramsay, page 113.

92. *Reliquiae Baxterianae*, page 94.

93. *Reliquiae Baxterianae*, pages 30 and 89.

94. Corbet, page 9.

95. HMC, 12th Report (1891) 'Beaufort Manuscripts', page 23.

96. Exceeding Joyful News from Dover (12 August 1642) BL E110 (14).

97. Corbet, page 14; Latimer, Annals of Bristol in the Seventeenth Century, pages 165-6 and 170-5.

98. Civil War Tracts: Lancashire, pages 30-5 and 112-13.

99. Prince Ruperts Burning love, BL E100 (8); Prince Ruperts Barbarous Cruelty, BL E96 (9).

100. Special Passages (6-13 September 1642) BL E239 (22).

101. An Exact Relation of 14 days Passages from Portsmouth (1642) BL E112 (34).

102. Corbet, volume 1, page 42; Hutchinson, page 105; Civil War Tracts: Lancashire, pages 50-1 and 219-21.

103. Lilly, page 106.

104. Sir Edward Walker, page 272.

105. The Earl of Essex His Desires to the Parliament (1642) BL E112 (7); Lilly, pages 111-12; A Short View of the Late Troubles in England (Oxford 1681) page 99.

106. James, Social Problems, pages 208 and 217.

107. A Declaration of the Valiant Resolutions of the Famous Prentices of London (1642) BL E109 (5).

108. Stow, volume 2, book 5, pages 328-35; An Humble Declaration of the Apprentices and other Young Men of the City of London (London 1643) BL E245 (2); The Protestation and Declaration of the Well-affected young men and Prentices, in and about the City of London (1643) BL E89 (12); Campbell, pages 277-8; Louis B Wright, Middle-Class Culture in Elizabethan England, pages 23-30.

109. CJ, volume 2, page 762; A Continuation of Certain Special and Remarkable Passages from both Houses of Parliament (5-9

September 1642) BL E116 (26).

110. **A Perfect Diurnall of the Passages in Parliament** (5-12 September 1642) BL E239 (16).

111. **Certain Speciall and Remarkable Passages** (1-6 October 1642) BL E121 (14).

112. Hutchinson, page 94.

113. **Newes from the Citie of Norwich** (26 August 1642) BL E114 (15).

114. HMC, 13th Report (1891) 'Portland Manuscripts', volume 1, page 77.

115. **A Letter Sent from the Lord Falkland** (Shrewsbury, 27 September 1642) BL E121 (22).

116. Paul H Hardacre, **The Royalists during the Puritan Revolution** (The Hague 1956) pages 5-6.

117. A J and R H Tawney, 'An occupational census of the seventeenth century'.

118. *Reliquiae Baxterianae*, page 31.

119. *Reliquiae Baxterianae*, page 33.

120. *Reliquiae Baxterianae*, pages 33 and 34-5.

121. *Reliquiae Baxterianae*, pages 44-5.

122. **Civil War Tracts: Lancashire**, pages 32 and 112-13.

123. **A Perfect Relation** (12 August 1642) BL E111 (5).

124. HMC, 12th Report (1891) 'Beaufort Manuscripts', page 23. .

125. *Mercurius Rusticus*, number 1 (20 May 1643) BL E103 (3) pages 1 and 4; Round, 'Colchester during the Commonwealth', page 642.

126. Clarendon, History, volume 2, pages 216 note and 267; LJ, volume 5, pages 131-2.

127. Gill, volume 1, page 52.

128. Howell, **Newcastle upon Tyne and the Puritan Revolution**, pages 123-4 and 145-6.

129. Heaton, pages 183 and 201; Priestley; Lister.

130. Clarendon, History, volume 2, page 285.

131. 'The Rider of the White Horse', in Lister, pages 63-4,

132. Hodgson, pages 95-6.

133. **A True Relation of the Passages at Leeds** (1643) in Lister, page 76.

134. 'A Discourse of the War in Lancashire', page 10.

135. **Civil War Tracts: Lancashire**, pages 56, 120-2 and 223.

136. **Civil War Tracts: Lancashire**, pages 92 and 125; **Certain Informations from Several Parts of the Kingdom** (3-10 April 1643) BL C21 b1 (12).

137. Vicars, page 297.

138. Heywood, volume 1, pages 96-9.

139. Hutchinson, pages 105, 110-11 and 112.

140. *Reliquiae Baxterianae*, pages 44-5.

141. Corbet, page 42.

142. Hutchinson, page 91.

143. Burroughes, page 56.

144. Hutchinson, pages 79 and 94.

145. Hutchinson, pages 103-4.

146. Hutchinson, pages 110-11.

147. 'The life of Adam Martindale', page 37.

148. *Reliquiae Baxterianae*, page 98.

149. Holmes, **Eastern Association**, pages 171-2 and 177; Whitelock, volume 1, page 209.

150. 'The Quarrel between the Earl of Manchester and Oliver Cromwell', in **Camden Society**, second series, volume 12 (1875) page 72.

151. **CSPD 1641-1643**, pages 380 and 397.

152. **CSPD 1641-1643**, pages 372, 382-3, 388, 391, 397 and 400.

153. *Reliquiae Baxterianae*, page 43.

154. **CSPD 1641-1643**, page 393.

155. **CSPD 1641-1643**, pages 372-3; Verney, **Memoirs**, volume 2, page 155; HMC, 5th Report (1876) 'House of Lords Manuscripts', pages 45-6.

156. **CSPD 1641-1643**, page 384.

157. **CSPD 1641-1643**, page 382.

158. **CSPD 1641-1643**, pages 399-400.

159. **CSPD 1641-1643**, page 382.

160. **A Copy of a Letter Writ from Serjeant Major Kirle** (1643) BL E246 (35); **A Continuation of the True Narration of the Most Observable Passages in and about Plymouth** (London 1644) BL E247 (1).

161. William M Lamont, **Marginal Prynne, 1600-1669** (London 1963) page 61.

162. C H Firth, **Cromwell's Army** (third edition 1921, reprinted with introduction by P H Hardacre, London 1962) pages 331-4.

163. **CSPD 1641-1643**, page 388.

164. R P Stearns, **The Strenuous Puritan: Hugh Peter, 1598-1660** (Urbana 1954) page 322.

165. *Reliquiae Baxterianae*, pages 50-1.

166. **State Papers Clarendon**, volume 2, page 185.

167. **The Diary of Sir Henry Slingsby of Scriven, Bart**, edited by D Parsons (London 1836) page 92.

168. Clarendon, **History**, volume 2, page 259.

169. *Mercurius Aulicus* (8-14 January 1643) BL E86 (22); **CJ**, volume 2, page 924; Rushworth, volume 5, page 275; HMC, 13th Report (1891) 'Portland Manuscripts', volume 1, pages 87, 89-90, 105, 699 and 707.

170. *Reliquiae Baxterianae*, page 49.

171. [Bowles], **Plaine English** (1643) BL E84 (42); **An Answer to a Seditious Pamphlet Entitled, Plain English** (Oxford 1643) BL E89 (33); **A Plain Fault in Plain-English** (London 1643) BL E88

(30).

172. **The Late Covenant Asserted** (1643) pages 16-17.

173. Francis Cheynell, **Sions Memento, and Gods Alarum** (London 1643) pages 9-10.

174. Samuel Rutherford, **A Sermon Preached to the Honorable House of Commons** (31 January 1644) page 23.

175. Lamont, page 108.

176. Stephen Marshall, **A Sacred Panegyrick** (London 1644) page 21.

177. **A Sudden Answer to a Sudden Moderatour** (London 1643) BL E93 (16).

178. John Strickland, **A Discovery of Peace** (London 1644) page 32.

179. 'The Diary of John Greene 1635-59', edited by E M Symonds, in **English Historical Review**, volume 43 (1928) pages 391 and 598.

180. **CSPD 1641-1643**, pages 372-3, 379 and 392.

181. John Aubrey, **Brief Lives**, edited by Andrew Clark (two volumes, Oxford 1898) volume 1, page 157; Hutchinson, pages 27-8.

182. Hutchinson, page 164.

183. *Reliquiae Baxterianae*, page 45.

184. Corbet, page 10.

185. Hutchinson, page 156.

186. Hutchinson, page 156.

187. Hutchinson, pages 133-4.

188. **A Copy of a Letter Writ from Serjeant Major Kirle**, BL E246 (35).

189. Edmund Calamy, **The Noblemans Pattern of true and real Thankfulness** (1643) BL E56 (3).

190. Richard Vines, **The Hearse of the Renowned, the Right Honourable Robert Earle of Essex** (London 1646) pages 9-11 and 20-5.

191. [Henry Parker], **The Oath of Pacification** (1643) BL E70 (27).

192. **The Unfaithfulness of the Cavaliers** (11 January 1643) BL E84 (37).

193. 'Memoirs of Edmund Ludlow', volume 1, page 105.

194. **The Late Covenant Asserted**, pages 16-17.

195. Hutchinson, page 185.

196. 'The Quarrel between the Earl of Manchester and Oliver Cromwell', pages 78-80 and 99.

197. Sir William Waller, **Vindication** (London 1793) pages 7-9.

198. Vines, pages 9-11 and 20-5.

199. Calamy, **The Noblemans Pattern**, BL E56 (3).

200. Jeremiah Whittaker, **Christ the Settlement of Unsettled Times** (London 1643) page 53.

201. Thomas Coleman, **The Hearts Ingagement** (London 1643) pages 26-7.

202. Abbott (editor) **Writings and Speecges of Oliver Cromwell**, volume 1, page 356.

203. Abbott (editor) **Writings and Speecges of Oliver Cromwell**, volume 1, pages 256 and 262.

204. *Reliquiae Baxterianae*, pages 30 and 89.

205. 'A Letter from the Earl of Manchester on the Conduct of Cromwell', in **Camden Society**, second series, volume 31 (1883) pages 1-3.

206. **The Knyvett Letters**, pages 136 and 137; Holmes, **Eastern Association**, pages 193- 4.

207. HMC, 14th Report (1894) 'Portland Manuscripts', volume 3, pages 125-6; Keeler, pages 316-17.

208. Hutchinson, page 227.

209. Lotte Glow, 'The Committee-Men in the Long Parliament, August 1642-December 1643', in **The Historical Journal**, volume 8 (1965).

210. [Ryves] *Mercurius Rusticus* (1646) number 3, page 26.

211. **A Royalist's Notebook**, pages 110-11.

212. Pennington and Roots, pages xxii-xxiii; Everitt, **Community of Kent**, pages 143-55; Dodd, pages 120-1 and 135; Holmes, **Eastern Association**, pages 123-9 and 192; Underdown, **Pride's Purge**, pages 29-38.

213. HMC, 4th Report (1874) 'Denbigh Manuscripts', page 268.

214. **CSP Venetian 1643-1647**, page 162.

215. Clarendon, **History**, volume 3, page 496.

216. *Reliquiae Baxterianae*, pages 50-8; HMC, 14th Report (1894) 'Portland Manuscripts', volume 3, pages 155-6; Firth, **Cromwell's Army**, pages 346-62.

Chapter 9: THE ENEMIES OF THE PEOPLE

1. *Reliquiae Baxterianae*, page 51.

2. Peck, volume 2, book 9, page 38.

3. **A Remonstrance of Many Thousand Citizens** (1646) in Wolfe, page 116

4. **To the Right Honorable, the Commons of England in Parliament Assembled** (11 September 1648) in Wolfe, pages 289-90.

5. Christopher Hill, 'The Norman Yoke', **Puritanism and Revolution** (London 1958).

6. **A Remonstrance of Many Thousand Citizens**, in Wolfe, pages 113-16; **To the Right Honorable, the Commons of England in Parliament Assembled**, in Wolfe, page 285; [Ryves] *Mercurius Rusticus* (1646) number 3, page 27.

7. *Reliquiae Baxterianae*, page 51.

8. [?John Lilburne and Richard Overton], **Regall Tyrannie discovered** (London 1647) pages 45 and 90.

9. John Warr, **The Corruption and Deficiency of the Laws of England** (London 1649) in **The Harleian Miscellany** (London 1810) volume 6, page 219.

10. **More light shining in Buckingham-shire** (London 1649) in George H Sabine (editor) **The Works of Gerrard Winstanley** (New York 1941, reprinted 1965) page 628; **Light shining in Buckingham-shire** (1648) in Sabine, pages 616-17 and 618-19 (these two tracts are not by Winstanley but by a group of Levellers in Buckinghamshire).

11. **A Remonstrance of Many Thousand Citizens**, in Wolfe, page 117; **To the Right Honorable, the Commons in Parliament Assembled**, in Wolfe, pages 284-5.

12. [?Lilburne and Overton] **Regall Tyrannie discovered**, page 86.

13. [Richard Overton], **An Alarum to the House of Lords** (London 1646) page 4.

14. A S P Woodhouse, **Puritanism and Liberty: Being the Army Debates, 1647-9** (London 1938) page 89.

15. **Englands Troublers Troubled, Or the just Resolutions of the plaine-men of England, Against the Rich and Mightie** (1648) pages 2 and 3.

16. Woodhouse, pages 64 and 65-6.

17. Woodhouse, page 89.

18. **Light shining in Buckingham-shire**, in Sabine, pages 618-9.

19. Woodhouse, pages 65-6.

20. **Englands Troublers Troubled**, page 3.

21. **A Remonstrance of Many Thousand Citizens**, in Wolfe, pages 117-24; John Lilburne, **The Oppressed Mans Oppressions declared** (1647) page 34; John Lilburne, **The resolved mans Resolution** (1647) page 13.

22. **A Remonstrance of Many Thousand Citizens**, in Wolfe, page 123.

23. [?John Lilburne and Richard Overton], **Regall Tyrannie discovered**, page 65.

24. Gregg, chapters 17, 21 and 27.

25. *Reliquiae Baxterianae*, page 51; Major Francis White, **The Copy of a Letter Sent to his Excellencie Sir Thomas Fairfax** (1647) page 7; **More light shining in Buckinghamshire**, in Sabine, page 628.

26. Sirrahniho [John Harris], **The Grand Designe** ('Printed in the last yeare of Englands Slavery, 1647'); George Wither, **Letters of Advice Touching the Choice of Knights and Burgesses for the Parliament** (London 1645) pages 5, 8, 17-18 and 20.

27. **Light shining in Buckingham-shire**, in Sabine, pages 619-22.

28. **A Declaration, Or, Representation** (London 1647) in William Haller and Godfrey Davies (editors) **The Leveller Tracts 1647-1653** (New York 1944, reprinted Gloucester, Massachusetts, 1964) pages 60-1; John Lilburne, **Londons Liberty in Chains discovered** (1646).

29. Woodhouse, page 56.

30. Sirrahniho [Harris], **The Grand Designe** (1647).

31. **Light shining in Buckingham-shire**, in Sabine, page 620.

32. **Warr**, page 219.

33. [William Walwyn], **Englands Lamentable Slaverie** (London 1645) in William Haller (editor) **Tracts on Liberty in the Puritan Revolution 1638-1647** (three volumes, New York 1933-4) volume 3, pages 314-15.

34. **A Remonstrance of Many Thousand Citizens**, in Wolfe, page 124; [?Lilburne and Overton] **Regall Tyrannie discovered**, page 25; John Lilburne, **The Just Mans Justification** (1646).

35. **A Declaration, Or, Representation** (London 1647) in Haller and Davies, pages 60-1.

36. **A Remonstrance of Many Thousand Citizens**, in Wolfe, page 118.

37. **Englands Troublers Troubled**, page 2.

38. **A Remonstrance of Many Thousand Citizens**, in Wolfe, page 120.

39. Sirrahniho [Harris] **The Grand Designe** (1647).

40. **Englands Troublers Troubled**, pages 2 and 6.

41. James Frese, **Every mans Right** ('This year of Hope, 1646') pages 5-6.

42. John Cooke, *Unum Necessarium:* Or, The Poore Mans Case (London 1648) page 66. Cooke was the solicitor for the commonwealth in the trial of Charles I.

43. [William Walwyn], **A Helpe to the right understanding** (London 1645) in Haller, volume 3, page 195.

44. Frese, page 6; Warr, page 220.

45. Cooke, page 66.

46. [?John Lilburne], **Englands Birth-Right Justified** (1645) in Haller, volume 3, pages 266 and 293-5.

47. **The Moderate**, number 18 (7-14 November 1648).

48. [Walwyn] **A Helpe to the right understanding**, in Haller, volume 3, pages 194-5; Frese, page 7; [?Lilburne] **Englands Birth-Right Justified**, in Haller, volume 3, page 266.

49. Warr, page 220.

50. **A declaration of the wel-affected in the County of Buckinghamshire** (1649) in Sabine, pages 643-4.

51. **Englands Troublers Troubled**, page 6.

52. **A Remonstrance of Many Thousand Citizens** (1646) in Wolfe, pages 124-5; *Mercurius Populus* (1647); [Overton] **An Alarum to the House of Lords** (1646) page 8.

53. Lilburne, **The Just Mans Justification**; [?Lilburne and Overton] **Regall Tyrannie discovered**, pages 15 and 25.

54. White, page 7; **More light shining in Buckingham-shire**, in Sabine, page 637.

55. **Light shining in Buckingham-shire**, in Sabine, pages 613 and

617-18.

56. [?Lilburne] **Englands Birth-Right Justified**, in Haller, volume 3, page 294; **A declaration of the wel-affected**, in Sabine, page 643.

57. [?Lilburne] **Englands Birth-Right Justified** (1645) in Haller, volume 3, page 293.

58. Warr, pages 213-14.

59. **A declaration of the wel-affected**, in Sabine, pages 643-4.

60. White, page 7.

61. *Mercurius Populus* (1647).

62. **Light shining in Buckingham-shire**, in Sabine, page 619.

63. [?Lilburne] **Englands Birth-Right Justified**, in Haller, volume 3, pages 266-7.

64. [William Walwyn], **The Compassionate Samaritane** (London 1644) in Haller, volume 3, pages 75-80; **The Vanitie of the present Churches** (London 1649) in Haller and Davies, pages 262 and 269.

65. [Walwyn] **The Compassionate Samaritane**, in Haller, volume 3, page 81.

66. [Walwyn] **The Compassionate Samaritane**, in Haller, volume 3, page 82.

67. **More light shining in Buckingham-shire** (London 1649) in Sabine, pages 632-4.

68. John Lilburne, **A Copie of a Letter** (1645) in Haller, volume 3, page 182.

69. [Walwyn] **The Compassionate Samaritane**, in Haller, volume 3, pages 77, 82 and 83.

70. [?Lilburne] **Englands Birth-Right Justified**, in Haller, volume 3, page 271.

71. **Light shining in Buckinghamshire**, in Sabine, page 619.

72. [Walwyn] **The Compassionate Samaritane**, in Haller, volume 3, page 85; **A Prediction of Mr Edwards His Conversion** (London 1646) in Haller, volume 3, page 347.

73. **Light shining in Buckingham-shire**, in Sabine, pages 619-22; **More light shining in Buckingham-shire**, in Sabine, page 636.

74. John Lilburne, **Londons Liberty in Chaines discovered**, pages 5 and 54-5; John Lilburne, **The Charters of London** (1646) page 5; **Englands Troublers Troubled**, pages 1 and 6; James, **Social Problems**, page 225.

75. James, **Social Problems**, pages 193-6.

76. James, **Social Problems**, pages 207-9.

77. James, **Social Problems**, pages 145-6.

78. James, **Social Problems**, pages 149-58.

79. [?Lilburne] **Englands Birth-Right Justified**, in Haller, volume 3, pages 266-8.

80. James, **Social Problems**, pages 145-6.

81. Perez Zagorin, **A History of Political Thought in the English Revolution** (London 1954) page 35.

82. Eduard Bernstein, **Cromwell and Communism. Socialism and Democracy in the Great English Revolution** (London 1930) page 98.

83. **Englands Troublers Troubled**, page 2.

84. William Walwyn, **The Power of Love** (London 1643) in Haller, volume 2, pages 274-5.

85. **A Remonstrance of Many Thousand Citizens**, in Wolfe, page 125.

86. **The mournfull Cryes of many thousand poor Tradesmen** (1648) in Wolfe, page 275.

87. **Englands Troublers Troubled**, pages 9-10.

88. Richard Overton, **An Appeale** (London 1647) in Wolfe, page 194; **The Case of the Armie truly stated** (London 1647) in Wolfe, page 216; **To the Supream Authority of England, the Commons Assembled in Parliament** (19 January 1648) in Wolfe, page 270; James, **Social Problems**, pages 253-4.

89. H N Brailsford, **The Levellers and the English Revolution**, edited by Christopher Hill (London 1961) page 315.

90. [John Lilburne, Richard Overton and Thomas Prince], **The second Part of Englands New-Chaines Discovered** (1649) in Haller and Davies, page 185; John Lilburne, **The Legall Fundamentall Liberties of the People of England** (London 1649) in Haller and Davies, page 435; [?Lilburne] **Englands Birth-Right Justified**, in Haller, volume 3, pages 302-3.

91. [?Lilburne] **Englands Birth-Right Justified**, in Haller, volume 3, pages 302-3.

92. Lilburne, **The Legall Fundamentall Liberties**, in Haller and Davies, pages 438-9.

93. [Walwyn] **The Compassionate Samaritane**, in Haller, volume 3, page 83; John Lilburne, **The Juglers Discovered** (1647) pages 11-12; **The Case of the Armie truly stated** (London 1647) in Wolfe, page 216; **The Moderate**, number 32 (13-20 February 1649).

94. Francis Johnson, **Plea for Free-mens Liberties** (1646) in Lilburne, **The Charters of London** (1646) page 43.

95. Johnson, **Plea for Free-mens Liberties**, in Lilburne, **The Charters of London**, page 43.

96. **The mournfull Cryes**, in Wolfe, page 276.

97. **Englands Troublers Troubled**, pages 6-7.

98. [?Lilburne] **Englands Birth-Right Justified**, in Haller, volume 3, pages 302-3.

99. **The mournfull Cryes**, in Wolfe, pages 275-6.

100. **Englands Troublers Troubled**, page 6.

101. **More light shining in Buckingham-shire**, in Sabine, pages

633-4; **Light shining in Buckingham-shire**, in Sabine, page 616; W Schenk, **The Concern for Social Justice in the Puritan Revolution** (London 1948) page 71.

102. *Mercurius Populus* (1647).

103. Lilburne, **Legall Fundamentall Liberties**, in Haller and Davies, page 435.

104. [Walwyn] **The Compassionate Samaritane**, in Haller, volume 3, page 83.

105. **The mournfull Cryes**, in Wolfe, page 276.

106. [Lilburne, Overton and Prince] **The Second Part of Englands New-Chaines Discovered**, in Haller and Davies, page 185.

107. **More light shining in Buckingham-shire**, in Sabine, page 633.

108. Lilburne, **The Legall Fundamentall Liberties**, in Haller and Davies, page 435.

109. [?Lilburne] **Englands Birth-Right Justified**, in Haller, volume 3, page 271; Lilburne, **The Juglers Discovered**, pages 11-12.

110. Schenk, page 76.

111. [Ryves] *Mercurius Rusticus*, number 3, page 27.

112. **Light shining in Buckingham-shire**, in Sabine, pages 611-12 and 615-16; **More light shining in Buckingham-shire**, in Sabine, pages 627-8 and 633-4.

113. **Harrison's Description of England**, edited by F J Furnivall (London 1877) pages 128-9; Fynes Moryson, **An Itinerary** (Glasgow 1908) volume 4, pages 169-70; Ruth Kelso, **The Doctrine of the English Gentleman in the Sixteenth Century** (Urbana 1929) pages 42, 54 and 60-1; Stone, **Crisis of the Aristocracy**, page 50.

114. D B Robertson, **The Religious Foundations of Leveller Democracy** (New York 1951) page 87.

115. C B Macpherson, 'The Levellers: Franchise and Freedom', **The Political Theory of Possessive Individualism** (Oxford 1962) pages 137-9 and 143-51.

116. **Light shining in Buckingham-shire**, in Sabine, pages 611-12 and 615-16; **More light shining in Buckingham-shire**, in Sabine, pages 627-8 and 633-4.

117. **Englands Troublers Troubled**, page 5.

118. [William Walwyn], **The Bloody Project** (1648) in Haller and Davies, page 144.

119. Schenk, pages 66-7.

Chapter 10: THE FRIENDS OF THE PEOPLE

1. [?Lilburne] **Englands Birth-Right Justified**, in Haller, volume 3, page 303.

2. **To the Supream Authority of England**, in Wolfe, page 270.

3. **The Case of the Armie truly stated**, in Wolfe, page 213; **To the Supream Authority of England**, in Wolfe, page 270; **To the**

Right Honorable the Commons of England, in Wolfe, page 288.

4. **Foundations of Freedom** (London 1648) in Wolfe, page 302; **An Agreement of the Free People of England** (1649) in Wolfe, page 407.

5. [?Lilburne] **Englands Birth-Right Justified**, in Haller, volume 3, page 303; [Walwyn] **The Bloody Project**, in Haller and Davies, page 144; [John Jubbes], **Several Proposals for Peace and Freedom** (London 1648) in Wolfe, page 317; **Englands Troublers Troubled**, page 8.

6. **To the Right Honorable the Commons of England**, in Wolfe, page 288.

7. F C Dietz, **English Public Finance 1558-1641** (New York 1932, reprinted London 1964) pages 382-93.

8. **Foundations of Freedom**, in Wolfe, page 303.

9. [Hugh Peter], **Good Work for a Good Magistrate** (1651) pages 65-6 and 80.

10. **To the Supream Authority of England**, in Wolfe, page 270.

11. **Foundations of Freedom**, in Wolfe, page 302.

12. **An Agreement of the Free People of England**, in Wolfe, page 407.

13. **The Case of the Armie truly stated**, in Wolfe, pages 200 and 215; **To the Supream Authority of England**, in Wolfe, page 268.

14. Overton, **An Appeale**, in Wolfe, page 193; John Lilburne, **Englands New Chains Discovered** (1649) in Haller and Davies, page 159.

15. Overton, **An Appeale** (London 1647) in Wolfe, page 193; **To the Supream Authority of England**, in Wolfe, page 268; Johnson, **Plea for Free-mens Liberties**, page 43.

16. Lilburne, **The Juglers Discovered**, page 12; Lilburne, **The Oppressed Mans Oppression declared**, page 38.

17. [?Lilburne and Overton] **Regall Tyrannie discovered**, page 101; Lilburne, **The Charters of London**, pages 5-6 and 43-5; Lilburne, **Legall Fundamentall Liberties**, in Haller and Davies, page 441.

18. James, **Social Problems**, pages 144-58.

19. **A Remonstrance of Many Thousand Citizens**, in Wolfe, page 124; **To the right honourable and supreme Authority of this Nation, the Commons in Parliament assembled** (March 1647) in Wolfe, page 137; **To the Supream Authority of England**, in Wolfe, page 268.

20. James, **Social Problems**, pages 155-7.

21. Johnson, **Plea for Free-mens Liberties**, pages 43-5; **To the right honourable and supreme Authority of this Nation**, in Wolfe, page 137; Lilburne, **Englands New Chains Discovered**, in Haller and Davies, page 159; Lilburne, **Legall Fundamentall Liberties**, in Haller and Davies, page 441.

22. Brailsford, pages 104-5.

23. **The mournfull Cryes**, in Wolfe, page 276.

24. Lilburne, **Legall Fundamentall Liberties**, in Haller and Davies, page 436.

25. Lilburne, **Legall Fundamentall Liberties**, in Haller and Davies, pages 437-8; **The Moderate**, number 39 (3-10 April 1649); Frese, pages 6-7.

26. **To the right honourable and supreme Authority of this Nation**, in Wolfe, page 140; **The Moderate**, number 33 (20-27 February 1649).

27. **An Agreement of the Free People of England**, in Wolfe, page 407.

28. **The Moderate**, number 34 (27 February-6 March 1649).

29. Cooke, pages 42-3; Hugh Peter, **A Word for the Armie. And Two words to the Kingdome** (London 1647) page 12; **Imprisonment of Mens Bodyes for Debt** (1641).

30. Overton, **An Appeale**, in Wolfe, page 193; **An Agreement of the Free People of England**, in Wolfe, page 407.

31. **A Remonstrance of Many Thousand Citizens**, in Wolfe, page 125; **To the right honourable and supreme Authority of this Nation**, in Wolfe, page 137.

32. Overton, **An Appeale**, in Wolfe, page 193; **To the right honourable and supreme Authority of this Nation**, in Wolfe, page 140; **To the Right Honorable, the Commons of England in Parliament assembled**, in Wolfe, page 288.

33. [Peter] **Good Work for a Good Magistrate**, pages 23 and 47; James, **Social Problems**, pages 335-8.

34. **Foundations of Freedom**, in Wolfe, page 302; **An Agreement of the Free People of England**, in Wolfe, page 407.

35. **The Countrey's Plea Against Tythes** (London 1647) pages 8-9.

36. **The Moderate**, number 32 (13-20 February 1649).

37. Lilburne, **The Juglers Discovered**, pages 11-12; **The Case of the Armie truly stated**, in Wolfe, page 216; Lilburne, **Englands New Chains Discovered**, in Haller and Davies, page 159; Lilburne, **Legall Fundamentall Liberties**, in Haller and Davies, page 436.

38. Hill, **Economic Problems of the Church**, chapter 5.

39. [?Lilburne] **Englands Birth-Right Justified**, in Haller, volume 3, page 271; [Walwyn] **The Compassionate Samaritane**, in Haller, volume 3, page 83.

40. *Vox Militaris* (1647) pages 7-8.

41. **The Countrey's Plea Against Tythes**, page 6.

42. *Vox Militaris*, pages 7-8; **Several Proposals for Peace and Freedom**, in Wolfe, page 318; **An Agreement of the People** (London 1649) (the officers' Agreement) in Wolfe, page 353.

43. [?Lilburne] **Englands Birth-Right Justified**, in Haller, volume 3, page 271; Peter, **A Word for the Armie**, page 10.

44. Overton, **An Appeale**, in Wolfe, pages 193-4; **To the right**

honourable and supreme Authority of this Nation, in Wolfe, page 140; **More light shining in Buckingham-shire**, in Sabine, page 637.

45. Hill, **Economic Problems of the Church**, chapter 6.

46. **To the Right Honorable the Commons of England**, in Wolfe, page 288; **Foundations of Freedom**, in Wolfe, page 302; **An Agreement of the Free People of England**, in Wolfe, page 408 (clause 23 needs to be read in conjunction with clause 24).

47. **Four petitions to His Excellency Sir Thomas Fairfax**, page 15; **More light shining in Buckingham-shire**, in Sabine, page 628; **A declaration of the wel-affected**, in Sabine, pages 643-7; **The Moderate**, number 32 (13-20 February 1649); James, 'Tithes Controversy', in **History**, volume 26 (1941-2) pages 9-10.

48. Gardiner, **Civil War**, volume 3, page 124.

49. Christopher Hill, 'The Agrarian Legislation of the Revolution', **Puritanism and Revolution** (London 1958) page 193.

50. Overton, **An Appeale**, in Wolfe, page 194; **The Case of the Armie truly stated**, in Wolfe, page 216.

51. John Lilburne, William Walwyn, Thomas Prince, Richard Overton, **A Manifestation** (1649) in Haller and Davies, page 279; Lilburne, **Englands New Chains Discovered**, in Haller and Davies, pages 157, 168 and 169; [Lilburne, Overton and Prince] **The second Part of Englands New-Chaines**, in Haller and Davies, pages 172, 182 and 183; Lilburne, **Legall Fundamentall Liberties**, in Haller and Davies, page 415; **Walwyn's Just Defence** (London 1649) in Haller and Davies, page 388.

52. **To the Right Honorable, the Commons of England in Parliament Assembled** (11 September 1648) in Wolfe, page 288.

53. Brailsford, page 610; Hughes, 'Drainage disputes in the Isle of Axholme'.

54. Schenk, appendix B, pages 172-7.

55. **Several Proposals for Peace and Freedom**, in Wolfe, page 319.

56. Sabine, pages 11-21, 245-349, 641-7 and 649-51; Keith Thomas, 'Another Digger Broadside', in **Past and Present**, number 42 (1969).

57. Lilburne, **Legall Fundamentall Liberties**, in Haller and Davies, page 449.

58. James, **Social Problems**, pages 94-7, 102 and 125.

59. **Four Petitions to His excellency Sir Thomas Fairfax**, page 15.

60. **A declaration of the wel-affected**, in Sabine, pages 643-7; **The Moderate**, number 32 (13-20 February 1649).

61. Warr, page 219; **Light shining in Buckingham-shire**, in Sabine, pages 616-17; **More light shining in Buckingham-shire**, in Sabine, pages 631-2; Donald Veall, **The Popular Movement for Law Reform 1640-1660** (Oxford 1970) pages 212-16.

62. Brailsford, page 440.

63. **Several Proposals for Peace and Freedom**, in Wolfe, pages 318-19.

64. **Foundations of Freedom**, in Wolfe, page 303.

65. **The Moderate**, number 39 (3-10 April 1649); Brailsford, pages 449 and 454 note 33.

66. **Walwyns Just Defence**, in Haller and Davies, page 370.

67. Lilburne, Walwyn, Prince, Overton, **A Manifestation**, in Wolfe, pages 390-1.

68. **To the Supream Authority of England** (23 November 1647) in Wolfe, page 238.

69. **To the Right Honorable the Commons of England in Parliament Assembled**, in Wolfe, page 288.

70. **An Agreement of the Free People of England**, in Wolfe, page 409.

71. David W Petegorsky, **Left-Wing Democracy in the English Civil War** (London 1940) page 110.

72. Lilburne, **Legall Fundamentall Liberties**, in Haller and Davies, page 449.

73. Lilburne, Walwyn, Prince, Overton, **A Manifestation**, in Wolfe, page 390.

74. **Walwyn's Just Defence**, in Haller and Davies, page 384.

75. Robertson, page 87.

76. Overton, **An Appeale**, in Wolfe, page 176.

77. Woodhouse, pages 59, 75 and 80; [?Lilburne] **Englands Birth-Right Justified**, in Haller, volume 3, page 261; Lilburne, Walwyn, Prince, Overton, **A Manifestation**, in Wolfe, page 391.

78. Macpherson, page 149-51.

79. Petegorsky, page 109.

80. Cooke, pages 33-9.

81. Macpherson, page 154.

82. Macpherson, pages 154-6.

83. Schenk, page 78.

84. Gregg, page 353.

85. James, **Social Problems**, page 128.

86. Woodhouse, page 59.

87. James, **Social Problems**, pages 95-6.

88. John Lilburne, **The Free-mans Freedome Vindicated** (1646) page 11.

89. *Vox Plebis* (London 1646) page 4.

90. Overton, **An Appeale** (London 1647) in Wolfe, page 162.

91. Lilburne, **The Free-mans Freedome Vindicated**, page 11.

92. Overton, **An Appeale**, in Wolfe, page 162.

93. [?Lilburne and Overton] **Regall Tyrannie discovered**, page 11.

94. Lilburne, **The Free-mans Freedome Vindicated**, pages 11-12.

95. [?Lilburne and Overton] **Regall Tyrannie discovered**, page 46.

96. Overton, **An Appeale**, in Wolfe, page 162.

97. Woodhouse, page 66.

98. **The Case of the Armie truly stated,** in Wolfe, page 212.

99. Lilburne, **The Charters of London,** page 4.

100. Overton, **An Appeale,** in Wolfe, pages 162-3.

101. Lilburne, **The Free-Mans Freedome Vindicated,** page 11.

102. Lilburne, **The Free-Mans Freedome Vindicated,** page 9.

103. Lilburne, Walwyn, Prince, Overton, **A Manifestation,** in Wolfe, page 394.

104. **To the Supream Authority of England,** in Wolfe, page 270 note.

105. Lilburne, **The Juglers Discovered,** pages 10-11; Lilburne, **The Resolved mans Resolution,** page 22; Lilburne, **Englands New Chains Discovered,** in Haller and Davies, pages 166 and 167.

106. **The Moderate,** number 28 (16-23 January 1649).

107. [?Lilburne] **Englands Birth-Right Justified,** in Haller, volume 3, pages 290-1; **A Remonstrance of Many Thousand Citizens,** in Wolfe, page 129; White, page 13.

108. Lilburne, **The resolved mans Resolution,** page 22.

109. **An Agreement of the People,** in Wolfe, pages 226-7; Sirrahniho [Harris], **The Grand Designe** (1647).

110. Peter, **A Word for the Armie,** pages 12 and 13.

111. Overton, **An Appeale,** in Wolfe, pages 189-90.

112. **To the Right Honorable, the Commons of England in Parliament Assembled,** in Wolfe, page 287; **Foundations of Freedom,** in Wolfe, page 295; **An Agreement of the Free People of England,** in Wolfe, pages 403-4.

113. **An Agreement of the Free People of England,** in Wolfe, page 404.

114. **An Agreement of the Free People of England,** in Wolfe, pages 405 and 409.

115. **An Agreement of the People,** in Wolfe, page 227; **Foundations of Freedom,** in Wolfe, page 300; **An Agreement of the Free People of England,** in Wolfe, page 405.

116. **Foundations of Freedom,** in Wolfe, page 299.

117. **An Agreement of the Free People of England,** in Wolfe, pages 404-5.

118. Lilburne, **Englands New Chains Discovered,** in Haller and Davies, pages 158 and 167. Lilburne (?) once proposed that the offices of 'the civil state' should be performed by the 'freemen of England', serving in turn for not more than one year, without pay or not more than £50 or £60 a year. (**Englands Birth-Right Justified,** in Haller, volume 3, pages 306-7).

119. [Walwyn] **A Helpe to the right understanding,** in Haller, volume 3, pages 104-5; [?Lilburne] **Englands Birth-Right Justified,** in Haller, volume 3, page 266; Frese, page 7; Overton, **An Appeale,** in Wolfe, page 192; Warr, pages 222-3.

120. Overton, **An Appeale,** in Wolfe, page 192; **To the right**

honourable and supreme Authority of this Nation, in Wolfe, page 139; **To the Supream Authority of England**, in Wolfe, pages 266-7; **Foundations of Freedom**, in Wolfe, page 301; **An Agreement of the Free People of England**, in Wolfe, page 406; Cooke, page 68.

121. Overton, **An Appeale**, in Wolfe, page 192; **The Case of the Armie truly stated**, in Wolfe, page 216; **To the right honourable and supreme Authority of this Nation**, in Wolfe, page 139.

122. **The Case of the Armie truly stated**, in Wolfe, page 216; **To the Supream Authority of England**, in Wolfe, page 265; **The mournfull Cryes**, in Wolfe, pages 276-7; **Foundations of Freedom**, in Wolfe, page 303; Lilburne, **Englands New Chains Discovered**, in Haller and Davies, page 162; **The Moderate**, number 32 (13-20 February 1649).

123. **Foundations of Freedom**, in Wolfe, page 303.

124. **An Agreement of the Free People of England**, in Wolfe, page 406.

125. Lilburne, **The Just Mans Justification**; [?Lilburne and Overton] **Regall Tyrannie discovered**, page 25; Overton, **An Appeale**, in Wolfe, page 190; **The Case of the Armie truly stated**, in Wolfe, page 216; *Mercurius Populus* (1647) page 5; **Foundations of Freedom**, in Wolfe, page 303; Gregg, pages 299-300 and 332.

126. **A Remonstrance of Many Thousand Citizens**, in Wolfe, pages 124-5; Warr, page 223.

127. [?Lilburne and Overton] **Regall Tyrannie discovered**, page 25.

128. **An Agreement of the Free People of England**, in Wolfe, pages 406-8; **Foundations of Freedom**, in Wolfe, pages 301-2 and 303; Veall, pages 100 and 156-9.

129. **The Moderate**, number 32 (13-20 February 1649); **More light shining in Buckinghamshire**, in Sabine, page 638; **A Declaration of the wel-affected**, in Sabine, pages 643-4 and 646.

130. **Light shining in Buckingham-shire**, in Sabine, pages 615-16; **A declaration of the wel-affected**, in Sabine, page 646.

131. **More light shining in Buckingham-shire**, in Sabine, page 638.

132. Edward Chamberlayne, *Anglia Notitia: or, the Present State of England*, edited by John Chamberlayne (21st edition, London 1704) page 209; 'The Life of Master John Shaw', Yorkshire Diaries and Autobiographies, in **Surtees Society**, volume 65 (1875) page 399; Clarendon, Life, page 3; 'Some Memoirs Concerning the Family of the Priestleys', Yorkshire Diaries and Autobiographies of the Seventeenth and Eighteenth Centuries, volume 2, in **Surtees Society**, volume 77 (1883) page 7; Adam Eyre, 'A Dyurnall, or Catalogue', Yorkshire Diaries and Autobiographies, in **Surtees Society**, volume 65 (1875) pages 9, 32-3, 80, 84, 94 and 106; 'The Journal of Nicholas Assheton', in **Chetham Society**, volume 14 (1848) pages 39-40; W F Irvine (editor) **Liverpool in King**

Charles II's Time (Liverpool 1899) pages 53-4; Campbell, pages 384-8.

133. Peter, **A Word for the Armie**, page 11; [Peter] **Good Work for a Good Magistrate**; Cooke, page 68; Gerrard Winstanley, **The Law of Freedom** (London 1652) in Sabine, pages 545-8; Veall, pages 170-1.

134. Lilburne, **Londons Liberty in Chains discovered**, page 7; Overton, **An Appeale**, in Wolfe, pages 190-1; **To the Supream Authority of England**, in Wolfe, pages 269-70; **Foundations of Freedom**, in Wolfe, page 303; **An Agreement of the Free People of England**, in Wolfe, pages 480-9; **The Moderate**, number 16 (24-31 October 1648) and number 28 (16-23 January 1649); **More light shining in Buckingham-shire**, in Sabine, pages 638-9.

135. 'An Agreement of the Free People of England', in Wolfe, page 408.

136. **Foundations of Freedom**, in Wolfe, page 303.

137. 'An Agreement of the Free People of England', in Wolfe, page 409.

138. Overton, **An Appeale**, in Wolfe, pages 189-90.

139. Woodhouse, pages 7-8.

140. Brailsford, page 253 note 4.

141. Brailsford, page 10.

142. Schenk, pages 33-4.

143. Brailsford, pages 321-2.

144. Zagorin, page 39; Brailsford, pages 10 and 321-2.

145. Schenk, pages 78-9.

146. Wither, pages 5 and 8.

147. [?Lilburne] **Englands Birth-Right Justified**, in Haller, volume 3, pages 291-2.

148. *Mercurius Populus* (1647).

149. Laurence Clarkson quoted by Zagorin, page 31.

150. *Mercurius Populus* (1647).

151. Schenk, page 66.

152. Sirrahniho [Harris] **The Grand Designe** (1647).

153. Lilburne, **Londons Liberty in Chains discovered**, pages 53-4.

154. Bushman, 'English Franchise Reform', in **Journal of British Studies**, volume 3, number 1 (1963); Plumb, in **Past and Present**, number 45 (1969); Hirst, **The Representative of the People?**.

155. Lilburne, **Londons Liberty in Chains discovered**, pages 53-4.

156. Woodhouse, pages 61-2.

157. Woodhouse, page 64.

158. Lilburne, **Londons Liberty in Chains discovered**, pages 53-4.

159. Woodhouse, pages 62-3 and 73; Vernon F Snow, 'Parliamentary Reapportionment Proposals in the Puritan Revolution', in **English Historical Review**, volume 74 (1959).

160. 'An Agreement of the People', in Wolfe, page 226.

161. Brailsford, pages 410-12; Wolfe, pages 212-13.

162. Sirrahniho [Harris] **The Grand Designe** (1647).

163. White, pages 12-13.
164. **The Case of the Armie truly stated**, in Wolfe, pages 212-13.
165. Wolfe, page 231.
166. Woodhouse, page 66.
167. Macpherson, pages 126 and 296.
168. Woodhouse, page 83.
169. Lilburne, **The Charters of London**, page 4.
170. Woodhouse, page 53.
171. Woodhouse, pages 67 and 71.
172. Woodhouse, page 78.
173. Woodhouse, page 63.
174. **Londons Liberties** (1650) in Woodhouse, pages 371-2.
175. Schenk, appendix B, pages 172-7.
176. Lilburne, **Londons Liberties in Chains discovered**, pages 53-4.
177. Sirrahniho [Harris] **The Grand Designe** (1647).
178. Woodhouse, page 83.
179. **Several Proposals for Peace and Freedom**, in Wolfe, page 317.
180. Woodhouse, page 83.
181. Keith Thomas, 'The Levellers and the Franchise', in G E Aylmer (editor) **The Interregnum: The Quest for Settlement 1646-1660** (London 1972) pages 72-3; Gordon J Schochet, 'Patriarchalism, Politics and Mass Attitudes in Stuart England', in **The Historical Journal**, volume 12 (1969) pages 422-3; Peter Laslett, 'Market Society and Political Theory', in **The Historical Journal**, volume 7 (1964).
182. **To the Supream Authority of England**, in Wolfe, page 269.
183. Macpherson, page 147.
184. **Foundation of Freedom**, in Wolfe, page 297.
185. **A Petition from His Excellency Thomas Lord Fairfax** (London 1649) in Wolfe, page 342.
186. Lilburne, **Londons Liberty in Chains discovered**, pages 53-4; James, **Social Problems**, page 209.
187. 'An Agreement of the Free People of England', in Wolfe, pages 402-3.
188. Macpherson, pages 282-6; Thomas, 'The Levellers and the Franchise', pages 70-73.
189. Thomas, 'The Levellers and the Franchise', pages 69-70; Macpherson, pages 286-7.
190. Macpherson, page 147.
191. Schenk, pages 66-7.
192. [?Lilburne] **Englands Birth-Right Justified**, in Haller, volume 3, page 303; Lilburne, **Englands New Chains Discovered**, in Haller and Davies, page 159.
193. Lilburne, **Legall Fundamentall Liberties**, in Haller and Davies, pages 437-8.
194. **A Remonstrance of Many Thousand Citizens**, in Wolfe, page

159.

195. **To the right honourable and supreme Authority of this Nation**, in Wolfe, page 137; Lilburne, **Englands New Chains Discovered**, in Haller and Davies, page 159; Lilburne, **Legall Fundamentall Liberties**, in Haller and Davies, pages 438-9 and 441; Lilburne, **The Charters of London**, page 43; [?Lilburne] **Englands Birth-Right Justified**, in Haller, volume 3, pages 302-3; [Overton] **An Alarum to the House of Lords**, page 8.

196. Lilburne, **The Juglers Discovered**, pages 11-12; **The Case of the Armie truly stated**, in Wolfe, page 216; Lilburne, **Legall Fundamental Liberties**, in Haller and Davies, page 436; **The Moderate**, number 32 (13-20 February 1649).

197. *Reliquiae Baxterianae*, page 94.

198. [Humphrey Brooke], **The Charity of Church-Men** (London 1649) in Haller and Davies, page 344.

199. Gregg, **Free-born John**.

200. G E Aylmer, 'Gentlemen Levellers?', in **Past and Present**, number 49 (1970) pages 123-4; James, **Social Problems**, page 385.

201. Aylmer, 'Gentlemen Levellers?', pages 122-3; Gregg, pages 136 and 156.

202. Lilburne, Walwyn, Prince, Overton, **A Manifestation**, in Wolfe, page 391.

203. **Walwyns Just Defence**, in Haller and Davies, page 383.

204. Lilburne, **Londons Liberty in Chains discovered**.

205. **Londons Liberties** (1650) in Woodhouse, page 376.

206. Lilburne, Walwyn, Prince, Overton, **A Manifestation**, in Wolfe, page 391.

207. Lilburne, **The Oppressed Mans Oppression declared**, page 36.

208. [Walwyn] **The Power of Love**, in Haller, volume 2, pages 274 and 297.

209. [Overton] **An Alarum to the House of Lords**, page 7.

210. Richard Jackson, **Quaeries Proposed for the Agitators** (London 1647) pages 1-6 and 15-16.

211. **Memoirs of Denzil Lord Holles** (London 1699) page 1.

INDEX

Index 1: SUBJECTS

98-100
—women as: 96
Presbyterianism: 375
Privy Council: 69, 74, 137, 224, 235
Puritanism: 17, 31, 36-7, 51, 63, 83-8,
   90-2, 98, 101, 121, 127, 156, 239-41,
   244, 250, 258, 260, 337-50
Putney Debates: 414-18

Quakers: 38-9

Revolution, causes of: 45-7
'Root and Branch' Petition: 53-7
'Roundheads': 147, 157-8, 159
Royalist gentry and nobility:
   16-19, 21-2, 28, 33, 36, 41, 70,
   151-2, 178-80, 242-52, 259-60, 262,
   267, 271, 281, 306, 314, 319-25,
   328-9
   —popular action against: 242-59,
   275-7
Royalist party ('Party of order'): 16,
   70-1, 100-1, 111-18, 130, 209-10
   —formation of: 319-21
   —composition: 28-9, 33, 42, 266,
   320-1
   —leadership of: 28, 266
   —support for: 24, 27-9, 32, 36-7,
   41-2, 261-2, 266-7, 303, 324-5

Sabbath observance: 11, 88
Seamen: 163, 167, 175
Sects: 9, 35, 38-9, 85, 96, 100, 115, 154
Self-denying Ordinance: 358
Separatism: 35, 91-101, 127-8, 157,

346, 394
Sequestration of royalist lands: 267,
   280
Shipmoney: 10, 12, 19, 50, 231-3, 302,
   373
Strikes: 161-2, 174

Taxation, and the 'Subsidy': 10, 133,
   135, 167, 181, 188, 193, 215-16,
   231-4, 278, 387-8, 393-4
Tenancies, and struggles over: 181-7,
   396-7
Toleration, religious: 96-7, 100
Town oligarchies: 220-3, 365, 376-8
   —resistance to: 223-4, 226-7
Tradesmen: 10, 29, 33, 38-9, 173-4,
   283, 334-5, 388
Trained bands: 19, 73, 109, 135, 140,
   143, 145, 148, 153, 163-4, 167, 199,
   208, 252, 257-8, 281-3, 298-9, 313,
   328, 411

Unemployment: 24, 173, 176-8

Waller's Plot: 352
Weavers and other cloth workers: 20,
   27, 29, 33, 35, 37-8, 44, 172-5,
   213-17, 220, 232, 241, 262, 285,
   297, 302-3, 329, 333-7, 380-1

Yeomen and freeholders: 7-11, 24, 26,
   28, 31, 33, 36-9, 44-6, 50, 182, 195,
   226, 230, 232-5, 237, 239-40, 260,
   263-4, 325, 328-9, 331-3, 336-7,
   396

Index 2: NAMES AND PLACES

Accrington (Lancashire): 183, 184
Acton (Middlesex): 245, 270
Acton, Sir William: 76
Adams, Richard: 290
Allen, John: 209
Almond, lord: 73
Andrews, Thomas: 278
Arderne, John: 294
Argyle, earl of: 73, 74
Arundel, earl of (Earl Marshal): 61,
   235
Arundell, John: 324
Ashe, John: 235, 264
Ashton, Ralph: 294, 305, 341
Asser, George: 198
Astley, Sir Francis: 10
Aston, Sir Arthur: 333
Aston, John: 79
Audley, Sir Henry: 255
Audley End (Essex): 255
Axholme, Isle of (Lincolnshire): 32-3,
   208, 270, 271, 332
Aylesbury (Buckinghamshire): 78, 396

Baggstarre (the goldsmith): 75

Baillie, Robert: 51, 54, 63, 83, 85,
   86, 165
Baines, Jeremy: 111
Baker, Mary: 75
Balderton (Nottinghamshire): 195
Balfour, Sir William (Lieutenant of
   the Tower): 61, 63, 135
Banfield, George: 207
Bankes, Adam: 95
Bankes, Sir John: 208
Barebone, Praise-God: 94, 95
Barker, John: 284
Barking (Essex): 198
Barnardiston, Sir Nathaniel: 19, 157,
   158, 259, 262
Barnardiston, Samuel: 157
Barnet (Middlesex): 163
Barrington, Henry: 252
Barrington, Sir Thomas: 244, 255,
   256, 258, 259, 313
Bastwick, John: 51, 52, 64
Bath, earl of: 179, 244, 248, 249, 250,
   263
Batings, the (Lancashire): 80
Baume, Isaac: 301